ORIENTAL INSTITUTE COMMUNICATIONS • *No. 27*

THE ORIENTAL INSTITUTE OF THE UNIVERSITY OF CHICAGO

D1501552

The High Gate at Medinet Habu: Ramesses III Attended by a Princess (Chic. Or. Inst. 1985; Nelson Number MH D 281a)

THE REGISTRY
OF THE PHOTOGRAPHIC ARCHIVES
OF THE EPIGRAPHIC SURVEY

by

THE EPIGRAPHIC SURVEY

with plates from

KEY PLANS SHOWING LOCATIONS
OF THEBAN TEMPLE DECORATIONS
(*by* Harold H. Nelson)

Published with the assistance of the Getty Grant Program

THE ORIENTAL INSTITUTE OF THE UNIVERSITY OF CHICAGO
ORIENTAL INSTITUTE COMMUNICATIONS • *No. 27*
CHICAGO • ILLINOIS

Library of Congress Catalog Card Number: 94-69120
ISBN: 0-918986-98-2
ISSN: 0146-678X

The Oriental Institute, Chicago

Printed by McNaughton & Gunn

TABLE OF CONTENTS

PREFACE

In the seventy years since its founding in 1924, the Epigraphic Survey has devoted a significant amount of its field time and resources to the photographic documentation of pharaonic monuments in the Theban area. The corpus of prints and negatives that is presently housed at Chicago House in Luxor may be considered the most exhaustive single resource of its kind on the temples of ancient Thebes. This publication is intended as a convenient reference tool for scholars in their efforts to locate pertinent documentation on Egyptian monuments, in particular those in the Theban area, that are represented in the Survey's archives. Although a good many of the Chicago House negatives are listed by Porter and Moss throughout the pages of their important work (1972), an additional four thousand negatives have been taken in the twenty-two years since the second edition of that work appeared, so that a more complete listing is desirable.

Compiled as a geographical listing, the *Registry* is organized alphabetically by site. The major site headings employed in this volume are provided in a separate list immediately following the preface. The reader will note that, for Theban temples, the sequence of numbers devised by Harold H. Nelson, the first field director of the Epigraphic Survey, is employed wherever possible to designate specific locations ("Nelson numbers"),[1] in preference to the locus designations of Porter and Moss. While the latter are in more general use among scholars worldwide, the Nelson numbers are more specific as to location and serve as the basis for planning the Epigraphic Survey's own field work. Nelson's scheme was initially developed at the Survey's first concession at Medinet Habu, prior to the publication of any numbering system for decorated temple relief, with two purposes in mind: "first, to facilitate reference to any particular scene or inscription … ; second, as a necessary preliminary to a catalogue of the decorative material, both scenes and inscriptions, on the walls of Theban temples" (Nelson 1941, p. vii), a project of Nelson's own devising and one that he was never able to bring to completion.

In the following registry the Nelson numbers for Theban monuments are listed consecutively under each site name and are placed at the head of the listing for each site. The Nelson numbers usually begin with an abbreviated letter code that corresponds to the pertinent monument (see the *List of Site Headings Used in the* Registry), followed by an arabic numeral that identifies a specific relief or inscription. For reasons of space, the entries of the registry have been kept as concise as possible. The first column of the registry gives the locus description, which is then cross-referenced to a negative number[2] in the registry at Chicago House, followed by the size of the negative in inches (some negatives are 35 mm). It is well for the user to keep in mind that one negative can show several Nelson numbers, and that any one Nelson number can be shown on several negatives: there is not necessarily a direct correlation.

The salient guidelines for the use of Nelson's system may be summarized in the words of its inventor:

> Certain large units—the vast Karnak precinct of Amon, the Karnak precinct of Mut, the Luxor temple, and Medinet Habu—have for convenience been subdivided into sections. Each section is designated by a capital letter [for example, Karnak bears letter designations A through O], and its decorations are numbered in a separate series beginning with 1. Even when, as at Karnak, scenes and inscriptions by thousands cover the surviving walls, it has thus been possible to avoid use of four-place numbers and consequent increase in size and complexity of the plans. … Lowercase letters are added for differentiation when a single number applies to more than one decorative element. (Nelson 1941, p. vii)

> [On the plans] the numbers of the reliefs in any given register have, as far as possible, been kept on the same horizontal level. If a number refers to the lowest register, in cases where more than one register is preserved, a line has been placed above the number. If it refers to the middle of three registers a line appears both above and below the number, while if the relief is in the top register a line is drawn below the number. On any particular wall the numbers have been placed in the same relative position above or below one another as are the reliefs to which they

---

1. For full details of the classification system and its early history, see Nelson 1941, pp. vii–viii.

2. These negative numbers are the same as those designated as "Chic. Or. Inst. photos" by Porter and Moss (1972, p. xxxii).

refer. ... The registers are shown only by the positions of the numbers in relation to one another, above or below; whether a series reads down *from* or down *to* a wall line depends merely on the direction of the lettering, which determines how the plan is to be held when in use.

The presence of an inscription in large hieroglyphs, such as often extends along the top or bottom of a decorated area without forming an integral part of the main decoration, is generally indicated by a long line in the middle of which is placed the number assigned to the inscription. An arrow at one extremity of such a line marks the beginning of the inscription, the point from which it is to be read. ... Numbers applying to decorative elements on the lower faces of architraves and on ceilings are enclosed in ovals.

Round columns have usually been distinguished from square pillars by being numbered in separate series, each series independent of that used for wall decorations (Nelson 1941, p. viii).

It should be noted that even the Nelson numbers are not foolproof. While there is a substantial advantage over the Porter and Moss system in terms of precision, some Nelson numbers do not correspond exactly to the extant divisions and scenes on a wall. And like all established numbering systems, the Nelson scheme is not directly applicable to certain types of inscribed or painted decoration: for example, material that is not incorporated into standing architecture (such as loose blocks); sites outside the Theban area; recently uncovered monuments; or even, on occasion, informal but often important reliefs and inscriptions that are to be classified as graffiti.[3]

If a Nelson number cannot be assigned to a photographic image, a brief written description is provided instead, in an alphabetic listing that concludes each site heading. This is the case, for example, with general architectural overviews as well as inscriptions or objects that fall outside the specific Nelson categories. General views of temples or portions thereof are likely to be found in the alphabetic section, and the reader is encouraged to consult both listings. In a very few instances the entry in the first column will read "none," especially for monuments located outside of Luxor.

The thirty-eight plates from Nelson's *Key Plans*, which elucidate the numbering system thoroughly, have been reprinted in reduced format at the back of this volume to provide the user with an immediate reference in convenient format. Spelling conventions and cross-references in the plate captions have been reproduced exactly as they appear in the original; thus the reader will find the older spellings "Thutmose," "Ramses," and "Epet" used in the plates, while "Thutmosis," "Ramesses," and "Opet" are employed in the text of this volume. The plates also retain outdated references to certain kings: "Mentuhotep III" for "Mentuhotep II" and "Ptolemy IX Euergetes II" for "Ptolemy VIII Euergetes II."

Many of the negatives maintained at Chicago House also exist in the form of duplicate negatives or prints at the Oriental Institute. It should be noted at this point that requests for prints and for permission to publish should be directed to the Archivist, The Oriental Institute Museum, 1155 East 58th Street, Chicago, Illinois 60637.

The information presented in the individual entries is primarily derived from the typewritten registration books maintained at Chicago House by a long succession of photographers since 1924. During the last seven decades a good number of discrepancies and variant usages have appeared in regard to the maintenance of the registration books. The early entries in particular are exceedingly spare, consisting only of a negative number, Nelson number, and the size of the negative. Written locus descriptions, where provided in lieu of early Nelson numbers, are often brief and cryptic. With the passage of time, other information was routinely included, such as the site name, a description of the scene, the date the negative was taken, the photographer responsible, the medium, the existence of a duplicate at the Oriental Institute, and other comments, including pertinent conservation notes. Another irregularity of the early registration books is that the sequence of negatives is not entirely consecutive. At some time in the past, certain blocks of numbers were purposely skipped and reserved for a special purpose; then the sequence may not have been fully used.

For consistency and completeness, many of the earlier, abbreviated entries in the registry have been updated in the last three years on the basis of information gleaned from other documents or written on the outside of storage boxes in which older negatives were once housed, and these data have now been incorporated as part of the formal record. An effort has also been made to standardize spelling conventions throughout the registry. Other differences in registration method—for example, the numbering systems used for individual block fragments at different sites over many years—have been necessarily maintained as recorded in the registration books, lest inadvertent errors be introduced. The reader will consequently notice a certain variety in the way the alphabetic entries have been composed.

The present publication represents only the large-format archival registry of the Survey; smaller format film negatives are not included.[4] Two other significant corpora of photographic material have been omitted as well, since these have not yet

---

3. A good number of graffiti were in fact classified by Nelson himself. According to recent practice, undesignated graffiti are assigned the closest applicable Nelson number.

4. The large-format negatives generally include exposures measuring 4 × 5 inches and larger, although a few smaller negatives are listed. The small-format registries are maintained separately from the main listing and consist of negatives measuring 2.25 × 2.25 inches or smaller. For example, the sizable 35 mm registry is generally reserved for informal staff pictures, record photography, and development and administrative purposes.

been fully accessioned. The first is comprised of a large number of negatives, slides, and prints bequeathed to Chicago House by the late Labib Habachi in 1984 and reflects his prolific professional activities.[5] The second is a collection of 850 glass plate negatives purchased from a local vendor in Luxor in 1987 and consists of portraits, images of monuments, and landscapes taken in Egypt from approximately 1880 to 1935.[6]

Several other categories of negatives exist in the archival registry, but they are not included in this publication. One such category is "antiquity," a term that usually denotes portable objects obtained by excavation or by purchase, or in museum collections. Other negatives deleted from this publication include images of Harold H. Nelson's unpublished iconographic index; almost all copy prints of photographs, maps, and drawings that exist elsewhere in published form or are maintained in other archives; images of the old Chicago House on the west bank and the present Chicago House, as well as Survey staff photographs; and negatives of finished Survey drawings, which have been published.

Several other sections of the *Registry* deserve further explication.

> **Abydos:** Only a single identified negative is listed in this volume. Another group of forty-one images exist in the registry, but without any written description that would identify each negative.[7]

> **Beit el Wali Temple:** The scenes were originally designated with project numbers that have no relation to any otherwise established scheme. The project numbers have been converted in the present volume to Porter and Moss numbers, and are prefixed by "PM."

> **Temple of Khonsu at Karnak:** One instance of nonstandard terminology was employed during the Survey's field work in the Temple of Khonsu, when all Khonsu Nelson numbers were prefixed with "Kh" in preference to the canonical "Kar M."

> **Saqqara:** The numbers listed for the mastaba of Mereruka correspond to the room numbers published by the Sakkarah Expedition (1938), further distinguished by the cardinal directions of the walls.

> **Theban Tombs and Valley of the Kings:** Private and royal tombs are listed consecutively by tomb number.

The publication of this volume has been made possible through a grant awarded by the Getty Grant Program of the J. Paul Getty Trust, in November 1989, for the conservation of the Epigraphic Survey's photographic archives. The grant proposal itself was a culmination of preliminary conservation efforts initiated in the archives at Chicago House during the directorship of Lanny Bell, at which time the archival holdings were reviewed for signs of deterioration and several hundred negatives were duplicated. It was clear, however, that further efforts were urgently required to monitor and salvage the deteriorating images on early nitrate films and to provide proper storage facilities on a permanent basis. In addition to the major series of large-format negatives, several hundred rolls of 35 mm film needed registration, and the personal archives of Labib Habachi, which includes approximately 12,000 prints, negatives, and slides, had to be catalogued in order to make them accessible to visiting scholars. The assistance of the Getty Grant Program was solicited in 1989 for several purposes: the continuing duplication of deteriorating negatives; the printing and identification of unregistered negatives; the continued cleaning and accessioning of the special glass plate collection; the housing of all negatives and prints in archival conditions; the transfer of the typewritten registry to a computer database; and the publication of the registry information in an accessible form. Although the outbreak of hostilities in the Persian Gulf during the 1990–1991 field season resulted in the abrupt cancellation of duplication efforts for a full year, the subsequent extension of the grant period happily coincided with the completion of the renovation of Chicago House, which made provision for archival storage. The photographic archives of the Survey are presently maintained in a three-room suite in the library building, consisting of a registrar's office, a storage room for negatives, and a separate room for the reorganized print collection. All negatives are sleeved in archival envelopes and boxes, which are in turn housed in metal cabinets. This publication now serves as an index to the resources of the main registry.

I wish to acknowledge here the contribution of many individuals who have made possible the successful completion of the conservation effort, in particular Dr. Deborah Marrow and Dr. Charles J. Meyers of the Getty Grant Program, who recognized the importance of the project and remained its enthusiastic advocates. The day-to-day supervision of the work in Luxor, the

---

5. For an account of the bequest, see Bell 1985, p. 15. The cleaning, printing, identification, cataloguing, and housing of the Habachi materials remain an ongoing project.

6. The acquisition is described by Bell (1987, pp. 7–8). A selection of thirty prints made from these negatives has been published as a limited collectors' edition in three portfolio volumes, for which see the Epigraphic Survey 1993. The first efforts in cleaning and cataloguing the glass plate collection were made possible by generous funds given to the Epigraphic Survey by the Friends of Chicago House tour of November 1988.

7. Eventually, each negative can be pulled and identified according to the number codes assigned by Porter and Moss. A similar case exists with the blocks of Hatshepsut's quartzite bark sanctuary, which are here listed alphabetically under Karnak Temple, but without individual designations. These can ultimately be assigned block numbers corresponding to the publication of Lacau and Chevrier (1977/79).

off-season planning and logistics, and the tasks of on-site duplication and printing were placed in the talented hands of photographer Susan Lezon. The truly enormous labor of transferring the typewritten records to the computer database was indomitably undertaken by Elinor Smith, volunteer archivist, who also completed most of the rehousing of negatives and the endless numbering of sleeves and boxes as well. The database for the registry itself was devised by the Survey's administrator, Dr. Peter A. Piccione, and refined by his successor, Paul Bartko, who also assisted in determining the preliminary format of the entries.[8] The final appearance of the published *Registry* owes much to good advice offered by Professor Janet Johnson, John Larson, Professor William Sumner, Dr. Emily Teeter, and Professor Edward Wente.

Many other colleagues and friends must be acknowledged with grateful thanks, for their help in identifying images, in rehousing prints and negatives, in supplementary duplicating and printing, in fund-raising, and in proofing the manuscript for this volume: Sarah Bevington, Deborah and John Darnell, Christina Di Cerbo, Kathryn Dorman, Dr. Eberhard Dziobek, Diana Grodzins, James B. Heidel, Drs. Helen and Jean Jacquet, Dr. Richard Jasnow, Susan Johnson, Dr. W. Raymond Johnson, Cecile Keefe, Daniel Lanka, Carlotta Maher, Crennan Ray, Dr. Henri Riad, Charles Secchia, Thomas Van Eynde, and many others whom we collectively importuned for assistance. Dr. Thomas Holland and Thomas Urban of the Publication Office of the Oriental Institute shepherded the manuscript through the final stages of formatting and publication. For their great patience and unhesitating offers of assistance with logistical aspects of the conservation program, I am particularly grateful to Dr. Kenton Keith, Dr. Marjorie Ransom, and Dr. Frank Ward of the United States Embassy in Cairo.

A final note: the text portions of this first edition of the *Registry* will eventually be made available as an electronic database accessible over the Internet. An announcement of availability and directions for accessing and downloading the database will be made shortly. It is envisioned that future editions of this volume will incorporate more definitive entries and that the published *Registry* will expand along with its matchless resources.

PETER F. DORMAN

CHICAGO HOUSE, LUXOR
OCTOBER, 1994

---

8. The database was created on Double Helix software. The fields selected for this Registry were formatted and transferred to a Microsoft Excel file, which was then converted into Microsoft Word and finally to PageMaker for publication.

LIST OF SITE HEADINGS USED IN THE *REGISTRY*

The *Registry* entries are entered according to the following site headings. The prefixes for Nelson numbers are given in parentheses, where applicable.

LIST OF PLATES

(from *Key Plans Showing Locations of Theban Temple Decorations*, by Harold H. Nelson)

LIST OF ABBREVIATIONS

Col.	Column
coll.	collection
fig.	figure
neg.	negative
p(p).	page(s)
Pil.	Pillar
Tut.	Tutankhamun
var	variant

BIBLIOGRAPHY

Bell, Lanny

 1985 "The Epigraphic Survey, 1984–1985." In *The Oriental Institute Annual Report 1984/1985*, edited by Janet H. Johnson, pp. 7–19. Chicago: The Oriental Institute.

 1987 "The Epigraphic Survey, 1986–1987." In *The Oriental Institute Annual Report 1986–1987*, edited by Janet H. Johnson, pp. 4–17. Chicago: The Oriental Institute.

Epigraphic Survey

 1993 *Lost Egypt*, 3 volumes. Chicago: The Oriental Institute.

Lacau, Pierre and Chevrier, Henri

 1977/79 *Une Chapelle d'Hatshepsout à Karnak*, 2 volumes. Cairo: Service des antiquités de l'Égypte avec la collaboration de l'Institut français d'archéologie orientale.

Nelson, Harold H.

 1941 *Key Plans Showing Locations of Theban Temple Decorations*. Oriental Institute Publications, volume 56. Chicago: The Oriental Institute. (Second printing, 1965)

Porter, Bertha and Moss, Rosalind

 1972 *Topographical Bibliography of Ancient Egyptian Hieroglyphic Texts, Reliefs, and Paintings, Volume 2: Theban Temples*. 2nd edition, revised and augmented. Oxford: Clarendon Press.

Sakkarah Expedition

 1938 *The Mastaba of Mereruka*, Parts 1 and 2. Oriental Institute Publications, volumes 31 and 39. Chicago: The Oriental Institute.

REGISTRY OF THE PHOTOGRAPHIC ARCHIVES
OF THE EPIGRAPHIC SURVEY

Abydos

Nelson Number/Description	Negative, Format
Sety I Temple: east wall of first Osiris Hall	2702, 5 × 7

Armant Temple

Nelson Number/Description	Negative, Format
Pylon, south face, east wing	10261, 5 × 7

Aswan

Nelson Number/Description	Negative, Format
Exposition prints of Heqaib Sanctuary	13551, 8 × 10

Bahriya Oasis

Nelson Number/Description	Negative, Format
Tomb of Amenhotep-Huy	13175, 5 × 7
Tomb of Amenhotep-Huy	13176, 5 × 7
Tomb of Amenhotep-Huy	13177, 5 × 7
Tomb of Amenhotep-Huy	13178, 5 × 7
Tomb of Amenhotep-Huy	13179, 5 × 7
Tomb of Amenhotep-Huy	13180, 5 × 7
Tomb of Amenhotep-Huy	13181, 5 × 7
Tomb of Amenhotep-Huy	13182, 5 × 7
Tomb of Amenhotep-Huy	13183, 5 × 7

Beit el Wali Temple

Nelson Number/Description	Negative, Format
PM (1)-(2)	11326, 5 × 7
PM (3)	11327, 5 × 7
PM (3)	11328, 5 × 7
PM (3), montage	11401, 5 × 7
PM (4)	11329, 5 × 7
PM (4)	11330, 5 × 7
PM (4), montage	11402, 5 × 7
PM (6)	11331, 5 × 7
PM (6)	11332, 5 × 7
PM (6)	11333, 5 × 7
PM (6), detail	11412, 5 × 7
PM (6), detail	11413, 5 × 7
PM (6), detail	11414, 5 × 7
PM (6)-(7)	11334, 5 × 7
PM (6)-(7)	11335, 5 × 7
PM (6)-(7)	11336, 5 × 7
PM (6)-(7), detail	11415, 5 × 7

Beit el Wali Temple (*cont.*)

Nelson Number/Description	Negative, Format
PM (6)-(7), detail	11416, 5 × 7
PM (6)-(7), detail	11417, 5 × 7
PM (6)-(7), detail	11418, 5 × 7
PM (6)-(7), detail	11419, 5 × 7
PM (6)-(7), detail	11420, 5 × 7
PM (6)-(7), detail	11421, 5 × 7
PM (6)-(7), detail	11422, 5 × 7
PM (8)-(9)	11337, 5 × 7
PM (8)-(9)	11338, 5 × 7
PM (8)-(9)	11339, 5 × 7
PM (8)-(9)	11340, 5 × 7
PM (8)-(9), detail	11423, 5 × 7
PM (8)-(9), detail	11424, 5 × 7
PM (9)	11341, 5 × 7
PM (9), detail	11425, 5 × 7
PM (9), detail	11426, 5 × 7
PM (9), detail	11427, 5 × 7
PM (10), (18)	11344, 5 × 7
PM (11)	11347, 5 × 7
PM (13)	11352, 5 × 7
PM (13)	11353, 5 × 7
PM (13), montage	11403, 5 × 7
PM (14)	11346, 5 × 7
PM (14), (18)-(19)	11343, 5 × 7
PM (15)	11348, 5 × 7
PM (15)	11349, 5 × 7
PM (16)	11351, 5 × 7
PM (17)	11355, 5 × 7
PM (17)	11356, 5 × 7
PM (17), montage	11404, 5 × 7
PM (18)-(19)	11342, 5 × 7
PM (18)-(19)	11345, 5 × 7
PM (21)	11350, 5 × 7
PM (22)	11354, 5 × 7
PM (23)	11371, 5 × 7
PM (24)	11357, 5 × 7
PM (25)-(26)	11370, 5 × 7
PM (26)	11359, 5 × 7
PM (26)	11360, 5 × 7
PM (27)	11366, 5 × 7
PM (27)	11428, 5 × 7
PM (27)	11429, 5 × 7
PM (27)-(28)	11361, 5 × 7
PM (27)-(28)	11363, 5 × 7
PM (29)-(30)	11358, 5 × 7
PM (30)	11368, 5 × 7
PM (30)	11369, 5 × 7
PM (31)	11362, 5 × 7
PM (31)	11430, 5 × 7

Beit el Wali Temple (*cont.*)

Nelson Number/Description	Negative, Format
PM (31)-(32)	11365, 5 × 7
PM (31)-(32)	11367, 5 × 7
PM (33)-(34)	11364, 5 × 7
PM (35)	11389, 5 × 7
PM (36)	11390, 5 × 7
PM (37)	11391, 5 × 7
PM (38)	11392, 5 × 7
PM (38)	11393, 5 × 7
PM (39)	11394, 5 × 7
PM (40)	11398, 5 × 7
PM (41)	11396, 5 × 7
PM (41)	11397, 5 × 7
PM (42)	11395, 5 × 7
PM (43)	11433, 5 × 7
PM (43)	11434, 5 × 7
Ceiling between architraves	11380, 5 × 7
Ceiling between architraves	11431, 5 × 7
Ceiling between architraves	11432, 5 × 7
Court	11410, 5 × 7
Court	11411, 5 × 7
General view	11407, 5 × 7
General view	11408, 5 × 7
General view	11409, 5 × 7
Loose block	11399, 5 × 7
North column	11381, 5 × 7
North column	11382, 5 × 7
North column	11383, 5 × 7
North column	11384, 5 × 7
North column	11385, 5 × 7
North column	11406, 5 × 7
North column architrave, south side	11386, 5 × 7
North column architrave, underside	11387, 5 × 7
North column architrave, underside	11388, 5 × 7
Pillared hall	11400, 5 × 7
Rock drawing	11537, 5 × 7
South column	11372, 5 × 7
South column	11373, 5 × 7
South column	11374, 5 × 7
South column	11375, 5 × 7
South column	11376, 5 × 7
South column	11405, 5 × 7
South column architrave, north side	11377, 5 × 7
South column architrave, underside	11378, 5 × 7
South column architrave, underside	11379, 5 × 7

Deir el Bahri

Nelson Number/Description	Negative, Format
DB 051	13348, 5 × 7
DB 052	13348, 5 × 7
DB 060	9357, 5 × 7
DB 060	9364, 8 × 10
DB 060	9365, 8 × 10
DB 060	13355, 5 × 7

Deir el Bahri (*cont.*)

Nelson Number/Description	Negative, Format
DB 061	9366, 8 × 10
DB 061	9367, 8 × 10
DB 061	9368, 8 × 10
DB 061	13350, 5 × 7
DB 061	13441, 5 × 7
DB 061	13345, 5 × 7
DB 062	13351, 5 × 7
DB 062	13388, 5 × 7
DB 087	13348, 5 × 7
DB 133	13434, 5 × 7
DB 134	13434, 5 × 7
DB 135	13434, 5 × 7
DB 150	13358, 5 × 7
DB 150	13439, 5 × 7
DB 463	9358, 5 × 7
DB 465	9359, 5 × 7
DB 466	9360, 5 × 7
DB 469	9361, 5 × 7
DB 471	9362, 5 × 7
DB 471	9363, 5 × 7
DB 475	9369, 8 × 10
DB 525	3943, 8 × 10
None	2385, 5 × 7
None	7282, 8 × 10
None	7283, 8 × 10
None	7284, 8 × 10
None	7285, 8 × 10
None	7286, 8 × 10
None	7287, 8 × 10
None	7288, 8 × 10
None	7289, 8 × 10
None	7290, 8 × 10
None	7290-a, 8 × 10
None	8268, 5 × 7
None	8270, 5 × 7
None	11576, 5 × 7
None	11577, 5 × 7
None	11578, 5 × 7
None	13150, 5 × 7
None	13562, 5 × 7
None	13577, 5 × 7
None	13578, 5 × 7

Deir el Medina

Nelson Number/Description	Negative, Format
Antiquity	3142, 8 × 10
General view	8410, 8 × 10
Plan	8267, 5 × 7
View of temple	13614, 5 × 7

Deir el Medina Temple

Nelson Number/Description	Negative, Format
DM 001	8920, 8 × 10
DM 004	8921, 8 × 10
DM 005	8886, 5 × 7
DM 006	8887, 5 × 7
DM 007	8888, 5 × 7
DM 008	8888, 5 × 7
DM 008a	8889, 5 × 7
DM 009	8890, 5 × 7
DM 010	8891, 5 × 7
DM 011	8893, 5 × 7
DM 012	8893, 5 × 7
DM 013	8892, 5 × 7
DM 014	8892, 5 × 7
DM 015	8893, 5 × 7
DM 016	8893, 5 × 7
DM 017	8892, 5 × 7
DM 018	8892, 5 × 7
DM 019	8894, 5 × 7
DM 019	8895, 5 × 7
DM 020	8895, 5 × 7
DM 020	8896, 5 × 7
DM 021	8897, 5 × 7
DM 022	8897, 5 × 7
DM 023	8898, 5 × 7
DM 025	8899, 5 × 7
DM 026	8900, 5 × 7
DM 027	8886, 5 × 7
DM 028	8922, 8 × 10
DM 029	8922, 8 × 10
DM 035	8923, 8 × 10
DM 036	8924, 8 × 10
DM 037	8923, 8 × 10
DM 038	8923, 8 × 10
DM 038	8924, 8 × 10
DM 039	8901, 5 × 7
DM 040	8902, 5 × 7
DM 041	8925, 8 × 10
DM 042	8926, 8 × 10
DM 042	13448, 5 × 7
DM 044	8903, 5 × 7
DM 044	13448, 5 × 7
DM 045	8904, 5 × 7
DM 045	13448, 5 × 7
DM 046	8926, 8 × 10
DM 047	8926, 8 × 10
DM 047	8927, 8 × 10
DM 047	8928, 8 × 10
DM 048	8928, 8 × 10
DM 051	8905, 5 × 7
DM 052	8905, 5 × 7
DM 055	8906, 5 × 7
DM 057	8891, 5 × 7
DM 066	8907, 5 × 7
DM 067	8908, 5 × 7
DM 068	8909, 5 × 7

Deir el Medina Temple (*cont.*)

Nelson Number/Description	Negative, Format
DM 069	8910, 5 × 7
DM 070	8910, 5 × 7
DM 071	8929, 8 × 10
DM 072	8929, 8 × 10
DM 073	8929, 8 × 10
DM 074	8929, 8 × 10
DM 075	8929, 8 × 10
DM 076	8929, 8 × 10
DM 077	8929, 8 × 10
DM 078	8900, 5 × 7
DM 080	8898, 5 × 7
DM 091	8911, 5 × 7
DM 092	8911, 5 × 7
DM 095	8930, 8 × 10
DM 095	8931, 8 × 10
DM 096	8912, 5 × 7
DM 096	8932, 8 × 10
DM 096	8933, 8 × 10
DM 097	8913, 5 × 7
DM 097	8935, 8 × 10
DM 097	8936, 8 × 10
DM 098	8930, 8 × 10
DM 098	8937, 8 × 10
DM 099	8930, 8 × 10
DM 100	8931, 8 × 10
DM 101	8932, 8 × 10
DM 102	8933, 8 × 10
DM 103	8934, 8 × 10
DM 104	8932, 8 × 10
DM 105	8933, 8 × 10
DM 106	8912, 5 × 7
DM 107	8913, 5 × 7
DM 108	8914, 5 × 7
DM 109	8914, 5 × 7
DM 109	8915, 5 × 7
DM 110	8915, 5 × 7
DM 111	8935, 8 × 10
DM 112	8936, 8 × 10
DM 113	8937, 8 × 10
DM 114	8935, 8 × 10
DM 115	8936, 8 × 10
DM 116	8938, 8 × 10
DM 126	8916, 5 × 7
DM 127	8916, 5 × 7
DM 130	8939, 8 × 10
DM 130	8940, 8 × 10
DM 130	8941, 8 × 10
DM 131	8917, 5 × 7
DM 131	8942, 8 × 10
DM 131	8943, 8 × 10
DM 131	8944, 8 × 10
DM 132	8945, 8 × 10
DM 132a	8945, 8 × 10
DM 134	8939, 8 × 10
DM 134	8940, 8 × 10

Deir el Medina Temple (*cont.*)

Nelson Number/Description	Negative, Format
DM 134	8941, 8 × 10
DM 136	8946, 8 × 10
DM 136a	8946, 8 × 10
DM 137	8942, 8 × 10
DM 137	8943, 8 × 10
DM 137	8944, 8 × 10
DM 142	8918, 5 × 7
DM 143	8918, 5 × 7
DM 146	8919, 5 × 7
DM 147	8947, 8 × 10
DM 147a	8947, 8 × 10
DM 148	7204, 8 × 10
DM 148	8948, 8 × 10
DM 148	8949, 8 × 10
DM 149	7205, 8 × 10
DM 149	8949, 8 × 10
DM 149	8950, 8 × 10
DM 150	8951, 8 × 10
DM 150a	8951, 8 × 10
DM 151	8952, 8 × 10
DM 151	8953, 8 × 10
DM 151	8954, 8 × 10
DM 160	8955, 8 × 10
DM 160	8956, 8 × 10
DM 161	8955, 8 × 10
DM 162	8956, 8 × 10
DM 163	8957, 8 × 10
DM 164	8958, 8 × 10

Deir Shelwit

Nelson Number/Description	Negative, Format
Deir Shelwit 001	10469, 5 × 7
Deir Shelwit 002	10469, 5 × 7
Deir Shelwit 003	10469, 5 × 7
Deir Shelwit 004	10470, 5 × 7
Deir Shelwit 005	10471, 5 × 7
Deir Shelwit 006	10472, 5 × 7
Deir Shelwit 007	10472, 5 × 7
Deir Shelwit 008	10473, 5 × 7
Deir Shelwit 009	10474, 5 × 7
Deir Shelwit 010	10474, 5 × 7
Deir Shelwit 011	10474, 5 × 7
Deir Shelwit 012	10475, 5 × 7
Deir Shelwit 013	10476, 5 × 7
Deir Shelwit 014	10476, 5 × 7
Deir Shelwit 016	10477, 5 × 7
Deir Shelwit 017	10477, 5 × 7
Deir Shelwit 018	10477, 5 × 7
Deir Shelwit 019	10478, 5 × 7
Deir Shelwit 021	10479, 5 × 7
Deir Shelwit 022	10479, 5 × 7
Deir Shelwit 023	10479, 5 × 7
Deir Shelwit 024	10480, 5 × 7

Deir Shelwit (*cont.*)

Nelson Number/Description	Negative, Format
Deir Shelwit 026	10481, 5 × 7
Deir Shelwit 027	10481, 5 × 7
Deir Shelwit 028	10481, 5 × 7
Deir Shelwit 028	10482, 5 × 7
Deir Shelwit 029	10482, 5 × 7
Deir Shelwit 030	10483, 5 × 7
Deir Shelwit 031a	10484, 5 × 7
Deir Shelwit 031b	10484, 5 × 7
Deir Shelwit 031c	10484, 5 × 7
Deir Shelwit 031d	10484, 5 × 7
Deir Shelwit 031e	10484, 5 × 7
Deir Shelwit 031f	10484, 5 × 7
Deir Shelwit 031g	10484, 5 × 7
Deir Shelwit 031g	10485, 5 × 7
Deir Shelwit 031h	10485, 5 × 7
Deir Shelwit 031i	10485, 5 × 7
Deir Shelwit 031j	10484, 5 × 7
Deir Shelwit 031k	10484, 5 × 7
Deir Shelwit 031l	10485, 5 × 7
Deir Shelwit 031m	10485, 5 × 7
Deir Shelwit 031n	10485, 5 × 7
Deir Shelwit 033a	10486, 5 × 7
Deir Shelwit 033b	10486, 5 × 7
Deir Shelwit 034	10487, 5 × 7
Deir Shelwit 035	10487, 5 × 7
Deir Shelwit 035	10488, 5 × 7
Deir Shelwit 036	10488, 5 × 7
Deir Shelwit 037	10489, 5 × 7
Deir Shelwit 038	10490, 5 × 7
Deir Shelwit 039	10491, 5 × 7
Deir Shelwit 039	10492, 5 × 7
Deir Shelwit 040a	10491, 5 × 7
Deir Shelwit 040b	10491, 5 × 7
Deir Shelwit 040b	10492, 5 × 7
Deir Shelwit 040c	10492, 5 × 7
Deir Shelwit 040d	10492, 5 × 7
Deir Shelwit 041	10493, 5 × 7
Deir Shelwit 041	10494, 5 × 7
Deir Shelwit 042	10493, 5 × 7
Deir Shelwit 043	10494, 5 × 7
Deir Shelwit 044	10495, 5 × 7
Deir Shelwit 045	10496, 5 × 7
Deir Shelwit 046	10497, 5 × 7
Deir Shelwit 047	10498, 5 × 7
Deir Shelwit 048	10499, 5 × 7
Deir Shelwit 048	10500, 5 × 7
Deir Shelwit 049a	10499, 5 × 7
Deir Shelwit 049b	10499, 5 × 7
Deir Shelwit 049c	10499, 5 × 7
Deir Shelwit 049c	10500, 5 × 7
Deir Shelwit 049d	10500, 5 × 7
Deir Shelwit 049e	10500, 5 × 7
Deir Shelwit 050a	10501, 5 × 7
Deir Shelwit 050a	10502, 5 × 7
Deir Shelwit 050b	10501, 5 × 7

Deir Shelwit (*cont.*)

Nelson Number/Description	Negative, Format
Deir Shelwit 050b	10502, 5 × 7
Deir Shelwit 052	10503, 5 × 7
Deir Shelwit 054	10505, 5 × 7
Deir Shelwit 055	10506, 5 × 7
Deir Shelwit 056	10507, 5 × 7
Deir Shelwit 057	10508, 5 × 7
Deir Shelwit 058a	10509, 5 × 7
Deir Shelwit 058b	10509, 5 × 7
Deir Shelwit 059a	10510, 5 × 7
Deir Shelwit 059b	10510, 5 × 7
Deir Shelwit 060	10511, 5 × 7
Deir Shelwit 061	10511, 5 × 7
Deir Shelwit 062	10512, 5 × 7
Deir Shelwit 063	10513, 5 × 7
Deir Shelwit 064	10514, 5 × 7
Deir Shelwit 065	10515, 5 × 7
Deir Shelwit 066	10516, 5 × 7
Deir Shelwit 067	10517, 5 × 7
Deir Shelwit 068	10518, 5 × 7
Deir Shelwit 069	10519, 5 × 7
Deir Shelwit 070	10520, 5 × 7
Deir Shelwit 071	10521, 5 × 7
Deir Shelwit 072a	10522, 5 × 7
Deir Shelwit 072b	10522, 5 × 7
Deir Shelwit 072c	10522, 5 × 7
Deir Shelwit 072d	10523, 5 × 7
Deir Shelwit 072e	10523, 5 × 7
Deir Shelwit 072f	10523, 5 × 7
Deir Shelwit 072g	10524, 5 × 7
Deir Shelwit 072h	10524, 5 × 7
Deir Shelwit 072i	10524, 5 × 7
Deir Shelwit 073	10525, 5 × 7
Deir Shelwit 074	10526, 5 × 7
Deir Shelwit 075	10527, 5 × 7
Deir Shelwit 076	10528, 5 × 7
Deir Shelwit 077	10529, 5 × 7
Deir Shelwit 078	10530, 5 × 7
Deir Shelwit 079	10531, 5 × 7
Deir Shelwit 080	10532, 5 × 7
Deir Shelwit 081	10533, 5 × 7
Deir Shelwit 082	10534, 5 × 7
Deir Shelwit 083	10535, 5 × 7
Deir Shelwit 084	10536, 5 × 7
Deir Shelwit 085a	10537, 5 × 7
Deir Shelwit 085b	10537, 5 × 7
Deir Shelwit 085c	10537, 5 × 7
Deir Shelwit 085d	10538, 5 × 7
Deir Shelwit 085e	10538, 5 × 7
Deir Shelwit 085f	10538, 5 × 7
Deir Shelwit 085g	10539, 5 × 7
Deir Shelwit 085h	10539, 5 × 7
Deir Shelwit 085i	10539, 5 × 7
Deir Shelwit 086	10540, 5 × 7
Deir Shelwit 086	10542, 5 × 7
Deir Shelwit 087	10541, 5 × 7

Deir Shelwit (*cont.*)

Nelson Number/Description	Negative, Format
Deir Shelwit 087	10543, 5 × 7
Deir Shelwit 088	10540, 5 × 7
Deir Shelwit 089	10541, 5 × 7
Deir Shelwit 090	10542, 5 × 7
Deir Shelwit 091	10543, 5 × 7
Deir Shelwit 092	10504, 5 × 7
Deir Shelwit 092a	10540, 5 × 7
Deir Shelwit 092b	10525, 5 × 7
Deir Shelwit 092b	10526, 5 × 7
Deir Shelwit 092b	10527, 5 × 7
Deir Shelwit 092b	10528, 5 × 7
Deir Shelwit 092c	10504, 5 × 7
Deir Shelwit 093a	10541, 5 × 7
Deir Shelwit 093b	10511, 5 × 7
Deir Shelwit 093b	10512, 5 × 7
Deir Shelwit 093b	10513, 5 × 7
Deir Shelwit 093c	10503, 5 × 7
Deir Shelwit 094a	10544, 5 × 7
Deir Shelwit 094a	10545, 5 × 7
Deir Shelwit 094b	10537, 5 × 7
Deir Shelwit 094b	10538, 5 × 7
Deir Shelwit 094b	10539, 5 × 7
Deir Shelwit 094c	10510, 5 × 7
Deir Shelwit 095a	10544, 5 × 7
Deir Shelwit 095a	10546, 5 × 7
Deir Shelwit 095b	10522, 5 × 7
Deir Shelwit 095b	10523, 5 × 7
Deir Shelwit 095b	10524, 5 × 7
Deir Shelwit 095c	10509, 5 × 7
Deir Shelwit 096a	10544, 5 × 7
Deir Shelwit 096b	10545, 5 × 7
Deir Shelwit 096b	10546, 5 × 7
Deir Shelwit 096c	10545, 5 × 7
Deir Shelwit 096c	10546, 5 × 7
Deir Shelwit 096d	10545, 5 × 7
Deir Shelwit 096d	10546, 5 × 7
Deir Shelwit 097a	10544, 5 × 7
Deir Shelwit 101	10547, 5 × 7
Deir Shelwit 102	10548, 5 × 7
Deir Shelwit 104	10549, 5 × 7
Deir Shelwit 311	10484, 5 × 7
General view	10467, 5 × 7
General view	10468, 5 × 7

Dendera

Nelson Number/Description	Negative, Format
Exterior of back wall	13161, 4 × 5
Exterior of back wall	13162, 4 × 5
Hathor Temple: outer hall, ceiling, first strip from east, no. 1	11104, 5 × 7
Hathor Temple: outer hall, ceiling, first strip from east, no. 2	11105, 5 × 7
Hathor Temple: outer hall, ceiling, first strip from east, no. 3	11106, 5 × 7

Dendera (*cont.*)

Nelson Number/Description	Negative, Format
Hathor Temple: outer hall, ceiling, first strip from east, no. 4	11107, 5 × 7
Hathor Temple: outer hall, ceiling, first strip from west, no. 1	11124, 5 × 7
Hathor Temple: outer hall, ceiling, first strip from west, no. 2	11125, 5 × 7
Hathor Temple: outer hall, ceiling, first strip from west, no. 3	11126, 5 × 7
Hathor Temple: outer hall, ceiling, first strip from west, no. 4	11127, 5 × 7
Hathor Temple: outer hall, ceiling, second strip from east, no. 1	11108, 5 × 7
Hathor Temple: outer hall, ceiling, second strip from east, no. 2	11109, 5 × 7
Hathor Temple: outer hall, ceiling, second strip from east, no. 3	11110, 5 × 7
Hathor Temple: outer hall, ceiling, second strip from east, no. 4	11111, 5 × 7
Hathor Temple: outer hall, ceiling, second strip from west, no. 1	11120, 5 × 7
Hathor Temple: outer hall, ceiling, second strip from west, no. 2	11121, 5 × 7
Hathor Temple: outer hall, ceiling, second strip from west, no. 3	11122, 5 × 7
Hathor Temple: outer hall, ceiling, second strip from west, no. 4	11123, 5 × 7
Hathor Temple: outer hall, ceiling, third strip from east, no. 1	11112, 5 × 7
Hathor Temple: outer hall, ceiling, third strip from east, no. 2	11113, 5 × 7
Hathor Temple: outer hall, ceiling, third strip from east, no. 3	11114, 5 × 7
Hathor Temple: outer hall, ceiling, third strip from east, no. 4	11115, 5 × 7
Hathor Temple: outer hall, ceiling, third strip from west, no. 1	11116, 5 × 7
Hathor Temple: outer hall, ceiling, third strip from west, no. 2	11117, 5 × 7
Hathor Temple: outer hall, ceiling, third strip from west, no. 3	11118, 5 × 7
Hathor Temple: outer hall, ceiling, third strip from west, no. 4	11119, 5 × 7
Hathor Temple: roof, east central room, center	10108, 5 × 7
Hathor Temple: roof, east inner room, east half	10109, 5 × 7
Hathor Temple: roof, east inner room, east half	10110, 5 × 7
Hathor Temple: roof, east inner room, west half	10111, 5 × 7
Hathor Temple: roof, east inner room, west half	10112, 5 × 7
Hathor Temple: roof, west inner room, east half	10113, 5 × 7
Hathor Temple: roof, west inner room, east half	10114, 5 × 7

Edfu Temple

Nelson Number/Description	Negative, Format
Forecourt	9042, 7 × 9
Forecourt	9043, 7 × 9
Forecourt, northeast doorway	9044, 7 × 9
Forecourt, northwest doorway	9041, 7 × 9

El Kanais

Nelson Number/Description	Negative, Format
Sety I Temple	3791, 5 × 7
Sety I Temple: inner hall, east wall (center)	3786, 5 × 7
Sety I Temple: inner hall, east wall (left)	3783, 5 × 7
Sety I Temple: inner hall, north wall, east	3780, 5 × 7
Sety I Temple: inner hall, north wall, west	3781, 5 × 7
Sety I Temple: inner hall, pillar (d), east side	3777, 5 × 7
Sety I Temple: inner hall, pillar from northwest corner	3790, 5 × 7
Sety I Temple: inner hall, west wall (center)	3785, 5 × 7
Sety I Temple: inner hall, west wall (right)	3776, 5 × 7
Sety I Temple: outer hall door to inner hall	3779, 5 × 7
Sety I Temple: outer hall, east wall (left)	3778, 5 × 7
Sety I Temple: outer hall, east wall (right)	3788, 5 × 7
Sety I Temple: outer hall, south wall, east side	3782, 5 × 7
Sety I Temple: outer hall, south wall, west side	3787, 5 × 7
Sety I Temple: outer hall, west wall (left)	3789, 5 × 7
Sety I Temple: outer hall, west wall (right)	3784, 5 × 7

El Salamuni

Nelson Number/Description	Negative, Format
Tomb 03, inner room, ceiling	10204, 5 × 7
Tomb 03, inner room, ceiling	10205, 5 × 7
Tomb 03, inner room, ceiling	10206, 5 × 7
Tomb 03, inner room, ceiling	10207, 5 × 7
Tomb 03, inner room, ceiling	10208, 5 × 7
Tomb 03, outer room, ceiling	10199, 5 × 7
Tomb 03, inner room, ceiling	11286, 8 × 10
Tomb 03, outer room, ceiling	10200, 5 × 7
Tomb 03, outer room, ceiling	10201, 5 × 7
Tomb 03, outer room, ceiling	10202, 5 × 7
Tomb 03, outer room, ceiling	10203, 5 × 7
Tomb 06, ceiling	11287-a, 8 × 10
Tomb 06, ceiling	11287-b, 8 × 10
Tomb 06, inner room, ceiling	10209, 5 × 7
Tomb 06, inner room, ceiling	10210, 5 × 7
Tomb 07, outer room, ceiling	10211, 5 × 7
Tomb 08, inner room, ceiling	10214, 5 × 7
Tomb 08, inner room, ceiling	10215, 5 × 7
Tomb 08, inner room, ceiling	10216, 5 × 7
Tomb 08, inner room, ceiling	10217, 5 × 7
Tomb 08, inner room, ceiling	10218, 5 × 7
Tomb 08, inner room, ceiling	10219, 5 × 7
Tomb 08, inner room, ceiling	11288, 8 × 10
Tomb 08, outer room, ceiling	10212, 5 × 7
Tomb 08, outer room, ceiling	10213, 5 × 7
None	10103, 5 × 7
None	10104, 5 × 7
None	10105, 5 × 7
None	10106, 5 × 7
None	10107, 5 × 7

Elkab

Nelson Number/Description	Negative, Format
Amenhotep III Temple	3686, 5 × 7
Amenhotep III Temple	3687, 5 × 7
Amenhotep III Temple	3688, 5 × 7
Amenhotep III Temple	3689, 5 × 7
Amenhotep III Temple	3690, 5 × 7
Amenhotep III Temple	3691, 5 × 7
Amenhotep III Temple	3692, 5 × 7
Amenhotep III Temple	3693, 5 × 7
Amenhotep III Temple	3767, 5 × 7
Amenhotep III Temple	3768, 5 × 7
Tomb of Ahmose Pennekhbet	3775, 5 × 7
Tomb of Ahmose, son of Abana: east wall	3769, 5 × 7
Tomb of Ahmose, son of Abana: east wall	3772, 5 × 7
Tomb of Ahmose, son of Abana: north wall	3774, 5 × 7
Tomb of Ahmose, son of Abana: south wall, east	3773, 5 × 7
Tomb of Ahmose, son of Abana: south wall, west	3770, 5 × 7
Tomb of Ahmose, son of Abana: west wall	3771, 5 × 7
Tomb of Bebi: north wall	3800, 5 × 7
Tomb of Paheri	3677, 5 × 7
Tomb of Paheri	3678, 5 × 7
Tomb of Paheri	3679, 5 × 7
Tomb of Paheri	3680, 5 × 7
Tomb of Paheri	3681, 5 × 7
Tomb of Paheri	3802, 5 × 7
Tomb of Renni	3682, 5 × 7
Tomb of Renni	3683, 5 × 7
Tomb of Renni	3684, 5 × 7
Tomb of Renni	3685, 5 × 7
Tomb of Setau	3801, 5 × 7
Tomb of Setau: east wall	3823, 5 × 7
Tomb of Setau: east wall	3824, 5 × 7
Tomb of Sobeknakht	3676, 5 × 7

Esna Temple

Nelson Number/Description	Negative, Format
Calendar, north and south portions, inside	8996, 5 × 7
Calendar, north and south portions, outside	8995, 5 × 7
Ceiling, first strip north of center	9011, 5 × 7
Ceiling, first strip north of center	9012, 5 × 7
Ceiling, first strip north of center	9013, 5 × 7
Ceiling, first strip north of center	9014, 5 × 7
Ceiling, first strip north of center	9015, 5 × 7
Ceiling, first strip north of center	9016, 5 × 7
Ceiling, first strip north of center	9017, 5 × 7
Ceiling, first strip north of center	9018, 5 × 7
Ceiling, first strip south of center	9019, 5 × 7
Ceiling, first strip south of center	9020, 5 × 7
Ceiling, first strip south of center	9021, 5 × 7
Ceiling, first strip south of center	9022, 5 × 7
Ceiling, first strip south of center	9023, 5 × 7
Ceiling, first strip south of center	9024, 5 × 7
Ceiling, first strip south of center	9025, 5 × 7
Ceiling, first strip south of center	9026, 5 × 7

Esna Temple (*cont.*)

Nelson Number/Description	Negative, Format
Ceiling, second strip north of center	9002, 5 × 7
Ceiling, second strip north of center	9003, 5 × 7
Ceiling, second strip north of center	9004, 5 × 7
Ceiling, second strip north of center	9005, 5 × 7
Ceiling, second strip north of center	9006, 5 × 7
Ceiling, second strip north of center	9007, 5 × 7
Ceiling, second strip north of center	9008, 5 × 7
Ceiling, second strip north of center	9009, 5 × 7
Ceiling, second strip north of center	9010, 5 × 7
Ceiling, second strip south of center	9027, 5 × 7
Ceiling, second strip south of center	9028, 5 × 7
Ceiling, second strip south of center	9029, 5 × 7
Ceiling, second strip south of center	9030, 5 × 7
Ceiling, second strip south of center	9031, 5 × 7
Ceiling, second strip south of center	9032, 5 × 7
Ceiling, second strip south of center	9033, 5 × 7
Ceiling, second strip south of center	9034, 5 × 7
Ceiling, second strip south of center	9035, 5 × 7
Ceiling, third strip north of center	8997, 5 × 7
Ceiling, third strip north of center	8998, 5 × 7
Ceiling, third strip north of center	8999, 5 × 7
Ceiling, third strip north of center	9000, 5 × 7
Ceiling, third strip north of center	9001, 5 × 7
Ceiling, third strip south of center	9036, 5 × 7
Ceiling, third strip south of center	9037, 5 × 7
Ceiling, third strip south of center	9038, 5 × 7
Ceiling, third strip south of center	9039, 5 × 7
Ceiling, third strip south of center	9040, 5 × 7

Gurna Temple

Nelson Number/Description	Negative, Format
Sety I 001	8314, 5 × 7
Sety I 002	8314, 5 × 7
Sety I 003	8314, 5 × 7
Sety I 004	6250, 8 × 10
Sety I 005	6250, 8 × 10
Sety I 006	6250, 8 × 10
Sety I 007	6250, 8 × 10
Sety I 008	6250, 8 × 10
Sety I 009	6250, 8 × 10
Sety I 010	6250, 8 × 10
Sety I 011	6250, 8 × 10
Sety I 012	6251, 8 × 10
Sety I 013	6251, 8 × 10
Sety I 014	6252, 8 × 10
Sety I 014	8301, 5 × 7
Sety I 014	8308, 5 × 7
Sety I 015	6252, 8 × 10
Sety I 016	6252, 8 × 10
Sety I 017b	8256, 8 × 10
Sety I 018	6252, 8 × 10
Sety I 018	8299, 5 × 7
Sety I 018	8303, 5 × 7

Gurna Temple (*cont.*)

Nelson Number/Description	Negative, Format
Sety I 019	8299, 5 × 7
Sety I 019	8303, 5 × 7
Sety I 020	6252, 8 × 10
Sety I 020	8299, 5 × 7
Sety I 020	8303, 5 × 7
Sety I 021	9892, 5 × 7
Sety I 024	8262, 8 × 10
Sety I 025	8300, 5 × 7
Sety I 025	8305, 5 × 7
Sety I 025	8306, 5 × 7
Sety I 025	8307, 5 × 7
Sety I 026a	8257, 8 × 10
Sety I 026b	8255, 8 × 10
Sety I 027	8259, 8 × 10
Sety I 028	8258, 8 × 10
Sety I 030	8296, 5 × 7
Sety I 030	8298, 5 × 7
Sety I 030	8304, 5 × 7
Sety I 031	8254, 8 × 10
Sety I 031	8296, 5 × 7
Sety I 031	8298, 5 × 7
Sety I 031	8304, 5 × 7
Sety I 032	8254, 8 × 10
Sety I 032	8296, 5 × 7
Sety I 032	8298, 5 × 7
Sety I 032	8304, 5 × 7
Sety I 033	8254, 8 × 10
Sety I 033	8316, 5 × 7
Sety I 034	8261, 8 × 10
Sety I 035	8261, 8 × 10
Sety I 037	6319, 8 × 10
Sety I 038	6319, 8 × 10
Sety I 039	6319, 8 × 10
Sety I 041	8260, 8 × 10
Sety I 044	8260, 8 × 10
Sety I 045	8317, 5 × 7
Sety I 046	8317, 5 × 7
Sety I 047	8315, 5 × 7
Sety I 048	8315, 5 × 7
Sety I 050	6368, 8 × 10
Sety I 052	6368, 8 × 10
Sety I 053	6369, 8 × 10
Sety I 055	6369, 8 × 10
Sety I 056	6370, 8 × 10
Sety I 057	6370, 8 × 10
Sety I 060	6368, 8 × 10
Sety I 062	6368, 8 × 10
Sety I 063	6369, 8 × 10
Sety I 065	6369, 8 × 10
Sety I 066	6370, 8 × 10
Sety I 068	6370, 8 × 10
Sety I 069	6323, 8 × 10
Sety I 071	6323, 8 × 10
Sety I 072	6324, 8 × 10
Sety I 074	6324, 8 × 10

Gurna Temple (*cont.*)

Nelson Number/Description	Negative, Format
Sety I 075	6325, 8 × 10
Sety I 076	6325, 8 × 10
Sety I 081	6368, 8 × 10
Sety I 083	6368, 8 × 10
Sety I 084	6369, 8 × 10
Sety I 086	6369, 8 × 10
Sety I 087	6370, 8 × 10
Sety I 089	6370, 8 × 10
Sety I 090	6323, 8 × 10
Sety I 092	6323, 8 × 10
Sety I 093	6324, 8 × 10
Sety I 095	6324, 8 × 10
Sety I 096	6325, 8 × 10
Sety I 097	6325, 8 × 10
Sety I 098	6325, 8 × 10
Sety I 112	8186, 8 × 10
Sety I 113	8186, 8 × 10
Sety I 114	8193, 8 × 10
Sety I 115	8193, 8 × 10
Sety I 116	8209, 8 × 10
Sety I 117	8284, 8 × 10
Sety I 118	8209, 8 × 10
Sety I 119	8229, 8 × 10
Sety I 120	8202, 8 × 10
Sety I 121	8230, 8 × 10
Sety I 122	8182, 8 × 10
Sety I 123	6317, 8 × 10
Sety I 124a	8187, 8 × 10
Sety I 124b	8295, 8 × 10
Sety I 125	8183, 8 × 10
Sety I 126	8242, 8 × 10
Sety I 128	8290, 8 × 10
Sety I 129	8236, 8 × 10
Sety I 133	8294, 8 × 10
Sety I 134	8231, 8 × 10
Sety I 135a	8188, 8 × 10
Sety I 135b	8293, 8 × 10
Sety I 136	8242, 8 × 10
Sety I 137	6330, 8 × 10
Sety I 138	8225, 8 × 10
Sety I 139	8225, 8 × 10
Sety I 139	8243, 8 × 10
Sety I 140	8225, 8 × 10
Sety I 141	8244, 8 × 10
Sety I 142	8227, 8 × 10
Sety I 143	8227, 8 × 10
Sety I 143	8246, 8 × 10
Sety I 144	8227, 8 × 10
Sety I 145	8245, 8 × 10
Sety I 146	8185, 8 × 10
Sety I 147	8185, 8 × 10
Sety I 148	8191, 8 × 10
Sety I 163	7182, 8 × 10
Sety I 164	7211, 8 × 10
Sety I 165	7211, 8 × 10

Gurna Temple (*cont.*)

Nelson Number/Description	Negative, Format
Sety I 166	7184, 8 × 10
Sety I 167b	6386, 8 × 10
Sety I 168	6244, 8 × 10
Sety I 168	6245, 8 × 10
Sety I 169	6316, 8 × 10
Sety I 170	6328, 8 × 10
Sety I 170	6329, 8 × 10
Sety I 174	7185, 8 × 10
Sety I 175	7208, 8 × 10
Sety I 176	7183, 8 × 10
Sety I 180	8201, 8 × 10
Sety I 181	8211, 8 × 10
Sety I 183	8289, 8 × 10
Sety I 184	8289, 8 × 10
Sety I 185	8217, 8 × 10
Sety I 186	6246, 8 × 10
Sety I 188	8198, 8 × 10
Sety I 189	8288, 8 × 10
Sety I 190	8292, 8 × 10
Sety I 197	7190, 8 × 10
Sety I 198	7186, 8 × 10
Sety I 199	7192, 8 × 10
Sety I 202	7187, 8 × 10
Sety I 203	7189, 8 × 10
Sety I 204	7188, 8 × 10
Sety I 207	7206, 8 × 10
Sety I 213	8371, 5 × 7
Sety I 214	8373, 5 × 7
Sety I 216	8215, 8 × 10
Sety I 217	8222, 8 × 10
Sety I 219	6383, 8 × 10
Sety I 219	7261, 8 × 10
Sety I 219	8218, 8 × 10
Sety I 220	6383, 8 × 10
Sety I 220	7261, 8 × 10
Sety I 220	8218, 8 × 10
Sety I 221	6079, 8 × 10
Sety I 222	6079, 8 × 10
Sety I 223	6079, 8 × 10
Sety I 227	6382, 8 × 10
Sety I 228	6382, 8 × 10
Sety I 229	6382, 8 × 10
Sety I 230	8219, 8 × 10
Sety I 230	8220, 8 × 10
Sety I 231	8219, 8 × 10
Sety I 231	8220, 8 × 10
Sety I 232	8372, 5 × 7
Sety I 234	7260, 8 × 10
Sety I 235	6249, 8 × 10
Sety I 240	6384, 8 × 10
Sety I 241	6247, 8 × 10
Sety I 242	6241, 8 × 10
Sety I 245	8265, 8 × 10
Sety I 248	8287, 8 × 10
Sety I 249	8287, 8 × 10

Gurna Temple (*cont.*)

Nelson Number/Description	Negative, Format
Sety I 250	8287, 8 × 10
Sety I 251	7939, 8 × 10
Sety I 251	8287, 8 × 10
Sety I 252	8212, 8 × 10
Sety I 253	8212, 8 × 10
Sety I 254	6085, 8 × 10
Sety I 255	6085, 8 × 10
Sety I 256	6326, 8 × 10
Sety I 257	6326, 8 × 10
Sety I 259	6085, 8 × 10
Sety I 259	8287, 8 × 10
Sety I 263	7938, 8 × 10
Sety I 264	7938, 8 × 10
Sety I 265	7938, 8 × 10
Sety I 266	7938, 8 × 10
Sety I 280	8376, 5 × 7
Sety I 281	8376, 5 × 7
Sety I 283	6371, 8 × 10
Sety I 284	8210, 8 × 10
Sety I 285	8210, 8 × 10
Sety I 294	8184, 8 × 10
Sety I 295	8192, 8 × 10
Sety I 296	8203, 8 × 10
Sety I 297	8208, 8 × 10
Sety I 298	8208, 8 × 10
Sety I 299	8207, 8 × 10
Sety I 300	8194, 8 × 10
Sety I 301	6242, 8 × 10
Sety I 302	8180, 8 × 10
Sety I 303	8196, 8 × 10
Sety I 304	8199, 8 × 10
Sety I 305	8190, 8 × 10
Sety I 306	8195, 8 × 10
Sety I 307	8205, 8 × 10
Sety I 308a	8205, 8 × 10
Sety I 308b	8206, 8 × 10
Sety I 309	8206, 8 × 10
Sety I 310	7207, 8 × 10
Sety I 311	8200, 8 × 10
Sety I 312	8181, 8 × 10
Sety I 313	8204, 8 × 10
Sety I 332	8276, 8 × 10
Sety I 333	8247, 8 × 10
Sety I 334	8251, 8 × 10
Sety I 335	6332, 8 × 10
Sety I 336	8252, 8 × 10
Sety I 337	8250, 8 × 10
Sety I 338	8283, 8 × 10
Sety I 342a	8223, 8 × 10
Sety I 342b	8224, 8 × 10
Sety I 344a	8223, 8 × 10
Sety I 344b	8224, 8 × 10
Sety I 346	8233, 8 × 10
Sety I 347	6243, 8 × 10
Sety I 348	8253, 8 × 10

Gurna Temple (*cont.*)

Nelson Number/Description	Negative, Format
Sety I 349	8232, 8 × 10
Sety I 350	8234, 8 × 10
Sety I 350	8235, 8 × 10
Sety I 356	8275, 8 × 10
Sety I 357	8249, 8 × 10
Sety I 358	8277, 8 × 10
Sety I 359	7191, 8 × 10
Sety I 360	7191, 8 × 10
Sety I 361	8278, 8 × 10
Sety I 362	8248, 8 × 10
Sety I 363	8281, 8 × 10
Sety I 372	6248, 8 × 10
Sety I 373	6248, 8 × 10
Sety I 374	6248, 8 × 10
Sety I 375	6084, 8 × 10
Sety I 377	6084, 8 × 10
Sety I 378	6083, 8 × 10
Sety I 379	6084, 8 × 10
Sety I 381	6084, 8 × 10
Sety I 382	6083, 8 × 10
Sety I 383	6083, 8 × 10
Sety I 384	6083, 8 × 10
Sety I 391	7213, 8 × 10
Sety I 392	7212, 8 × 10
Sety I 393	7209, 8 × 10
Sety I 394	7210, 8 × 10
Sety I 395	8214, 8 × 10
Sety I 396	8216, 8 × 10
Sety I 397	8282, 8 × 10
Sety I 398	8279, 8 × 10
Sety I 405	8297, 5 × 7
Sety I 410	6080, 8 × 10
Sety I 411	6080, 8 × 10
Sety I 412	6080, 8 × 10
Sety I 413	6080, 8 × 10
Sety I 414	6080, 8 × 10
Sety I 420	8266, 8 × 10
Sety I 421	8266, 8 × 10
Sety I 422	8266, 8 × 10
Sety I 423	8197, 8 × 10
Sety I 424	8197, 8 × 10
Sety I 425	8221, 8 × 10
Sety I 426	8221, 8 × 10
Sety I 427	8221, 8 × 10
Sety I 428	6385, 8 × 10
Sety I 429	6385, 8 × 10
Sety I 430	8221, 8 × 10
Sety I 431	8221, 8 × 10
Sety I 432	6385, 8 × 10
Sety I 433	6385, 8 × 10
Sety I 441	6331, 8 × 10
Sety I 442	6331, 8 × 10
Sety I 449	8280, 8 × 10
Sety I 450	8280, 8 × 10
Sety I 451	8264, 8 × 10

Gurna Temple (*cont.*)

Nelson Number/Description	Negative, Format
Sety I 452	8263, 8 × 10
Sety I 453	8263, 8 × 10
Sety I 454	8378, 8 × 10
Sety I 455	8378, 8 × 10
Sety I 475	8370, 5 × 7
Sety I 476	8213, 8 × 10
Sety I 477	8213, 8 × 10
Sety I 478	8213, 8 × 10
Sety I 479	6333, 8 × 10
Sety I 480	6321, 8 × 10
Sety I 481	6321, 8 × 10
Sety I 482	6321, 8 × 10
Sety I 484	8228, 8 × 10
Sety I 485	8228, 8 × 10
Sety I 486	6322, 8 × 10
Sety I 487	6322, 8 × 10
Sety I 488	6082, 8 × 10
Sety I 489	6082, 8 × 10
Sety I 490	6082, 8 × 10
Sety I 491	6081, 8 × 10
Sety I 492	6081, 8 × 10
Sety I 493	6081, 8 × 10
Sety I 494	8228, 8 × 10
Sety I 495	8228, 8 × 10
Sety I 496	6322, 8 × 10
Sety I 497	6322, 8 × 10
Sety I 498	6082, 8 × 10
Sety I 499	6082, 8 × 10
Sety I 500	6082, 8 × 10
Sety I 501	6081, 8 × 10
Sety I 502	6081, 8 × 10
Sety I 503	6081, 8 × 10
Sety I 505	6254, 8 × 10
Sety I 506	6254, 8 × 10
Sety I 507	6253, 8 × 10
Sety I 508	6253, 8 × 10
Sety I 509	6254, 8 × 10
Sety I 510	6254, 8 × 10
Sety I 511	6253, 8 × 10
Sety I 512	6253, 8 × 10
Sety I 513	6253, 8 × 10
Sety I 514	8302, 5 × 7
Sety I 515	8377, 5 × 7
Sety I 516	8377, 5 × 7
Sety I Pil. 001	6320, 8 × 10
Sety I Pil. 002	6320, 8 × 10
Sety I Pil. 003	6318, 8 × 10
Sety I Pil. 004	6318, 8 × 10
Building north of Sety temple: block in situ	10192, 5 × 7
Plan	2386, 5 × 7
Sety I Temple: general view	6327, 8 × 10
Sety I Temple: general view	8226, 8 × 10
Sety I Temple: near pylon	6280, 8 × 10
Sety I Temple: near pylon	6281, 8 × 10

Karnak Temple

Nelson Number/Description	Negative, Format
Kar A 004	5249, 8 × 10
Kar A 004	5250, 8 × 10
Kar A 015	5247, 8 × 10
Kar A 016	6348, 8 × 10
Kar A 016	8035, 8 × 10
Kar A 024	5172, 8 × 10
Kar A 034	8014, 5 × 7
Kar A 035	8014, 5 × 7
Kar A 038	8070, 8 × 10
Kar A 039	8070, 8 × 10
Kar A 040	8037, 8 × 10
Kar A 041	8037, 8 × 10
Kar A 049	8040, 8 × 10
Kar A 050	5171, 8 × 10
Kar A 055	8028, 8 × 10
Kar A 056	8030, 8 × 10
Kar A 057	8029, 8 × 10
Kar A 058	8024, 8 × 10
Kar A 060	8032, 8 × 10
Kar A 061	8032, 8 × 10
Kar A 062	8032, 8 × 10
Kar A 063	8033, 8 × 10
Kar A 064	8033, 8 × 10
Kar A 065	8033, 8 × 10
Kar A 066	8032, 8 × 10
Kar A 067	8032, 8 × 10
Kar A 068	8032, 8 × 10
Kar A 069	8033, 8 × 10
Kar A 071	8033, 8 × 10
Kar A 075	8673, 8 × 10
Kar A 076	8673, 8 × 10
Kar A 077	8674, 8 × 10
Kar A 078	8674, 8 × 10
Kar A 079	8675, 8 × 10
Kar A 080	8675, 8 × 10
Kar A 081	8676, 8 × 10
Kar A 082	8676, 8 × 10
Kar A 082	8677, 8 × 10
Kar A 083a	8677, 8 × 10
Kar A 083b	8677, 8 × 10
Kar A 084	8673, 8 × 10
Kar A 085	8673, 8 × 10
Kar A 086	8674, 8 × 10
Kar A 087	8674, 8 × 10
Kar A 088	8675, 8 × 10
Kar A 089	8675, 8 × 10
Kar A 090	8676, 8 × 10
Kar A 091	8676, 8 × 10
Kar A 091	8677, 8 × 10
Kar A 101	6282, 8 × 10
Kar A 118	5256, 8 × 10
Kar A 142	8774, 8 × 10
Kar A 143	8774, 8 × 10
Kar A 144	8774, 8 × 10
Kar A 159	8775, 8 × 10

Karnak Temple (*cont.*)

Nelson Number/Description	Negative, Format
Kar A 160	5704, 8 × 10
Kar A 160	8775, 8 × 10
Kar A 161	5704, 8 × 10
Kar A 175	8773, 5 × 7
Kar A 176	8773, 5 × 7
Kar A 179	8776, 8 × 10
Kar A 179	8780, 8 × 10
Kar A 180	8776, 8 × 10
Kar A 180	8780, 8 × 10
Kar A 181	8776, 8 × 10
Kar A 181	8777, 8 × 10
Kar A 181	8780, 8 × 10
Kar A 181	8781, 8 × 10
Kar A 182	8776, 8 × 10
Kar A 182	8777, 8 × 10
Kar A 182	8780, 8 × 10
Kar A 182	8781, 8 × 10
Kar A 183	8776, 8 × 10
Kar A 183	8777, 8 × 10
Kar A 183	8780, 8 × 10
Kar A 183	8781, 8 × 10
Kar A 184	8776, 8 × 10
Kar A 184	8777, 8 × 10
Kar A 184	8780, 8 × 10
Kar A 184	8781, 8 × 10
Kar A 185	8776, 8 × 10
Kar A 185	8779, 8 × 10
Kar A 185	8780, 8 × 10
Kar A 185	8782, 8 × 10
Kar A 186	8776, 8 × 10
Kar A 186	8779, 8 × 10
Kar A 186	8780, 8 × 10
Kar A 186	8782, 8 × 10
Kar A 187	8778, 8 × 10
Kar A 187	8779, 8 × 10
Kar A 187	8782, 8 × 10
Kar A 187	8783, 8 × 10
Kar A 188	8778, 8 × 10
Kar A 188	8779, 8 × 10
Kar A 188	8782, 8 × 10
Kar A 188	8783, 8 × 10
Kar A 190	13335, 5 × 7
Kar A 190	13374, 5 × 7
Kar A 190	13391, 5 × 7
Kar A 191	8786, 8 × 10
Kar A 191	13335, 5 × 7
Kar A 191	13374, 5 × 7
Kar A 191	13391, 5 × 7
Kar A 192	8786, 8 × 10
Kar A 192	13335, 5 × 7
Kar A 192	13374, 5 × 7
Kar A 192	13391, 5 × 7
Kar A 193	8786, 8 × 10
Kar A 193	13335, 5 × 7
Kar A 193	13374, 5 × 7

Karnak Temple (*cont.*)

Nelson Number/Description	Negative, Format
Kar A 193	13391, 5 × 7
Kar A 194	8785, 8 × 10
Kar A 194	13335, 5 × 7
Kar A 194	13374, 5 × 7
Kar A 194	13391, 5 × 7
Kar A 195	8785, 8 × 10
Kar A 195	13335, 5 × 7
Kar A 195	13374, 5 × 7
Kar A 195	13391, 5 × 7
Kar A 196	8402, 8 × 10
Kar A 196	9622, 8 × 10
Kar A 196	13335, 5 × 7
Kar A 196	13374, 5 × 7
Kar A 196	13391, 5 × 7
Kar A 200	8787, 8 × 10
Kar A 201	8787, 8 × 10
Kar A 203	8784, 8 × 10
Kar A 204	8784, 8 × 10
Kar A 205	8784, 8 × 10
Kar A 218	13335, 5 × 7
Kar A 218	13374, 5 × 7
Kar A 218	13391, 5 × 7
Kar A 219	13335, 5 × 7
Kar A 219	13374, 5 × 7
Kar A 219	13391, 5 × 7
Kar A 220	13335, 5 × 7
Kar A 220	13374, 5 × 7
Kar A 220	13391, 5 × 7
Kar A 221	13335, 5 × 7
Kar A 221	13374, 5 × 7
Kar A 221	13391, 5 × 7
Kar A 222	8401, 8 × 10
Kar A 222	13335, 5 × 7
Kar A 222	13374, 5 × 7
Kar A 222	13391, 5 × 7
Kar A 223	8401, 8 × 10
Kar A 223	13335, 5 × 7
Kar A 223	13374, 5 × 7
Kar A 223	13391, 5 × 7
Kar A 224	8400, 8 × 10
Kar A 224	13335, 5 × 7
Kar A 224	13374, 5 × 7
Kar A 224	13391, 5 × 7
Kar A 228	8788, 8 × 10
Kar A 229	8788, 8 × 10
Kar B 001	8789, 8 × 10
Kar B 002	8789, 8 × 10
Kar B 003	8789, 8 × 10
Kar B 003	8790, 8 × 10
Kar B 004	8789, 8 × 10
Kar B 004	8790, 8 × 10
Kar B 005	8790, 8 × 10
Kar B 006	8790, 8 × 10
Kar B 009	5183, 8 × 10
Kar B 010	7558, 8 × 10

Karnak Temple (*cont.*)

Nelson Number/Description	Negative, Format
Kar B 011	7558, 8 × 10
Kar B 012	7558, 8 × 10
Kar B 013	7558, 8 × 10
Kar B 014	7558, 8 × 10
Kar B 015	7558, 8 × 10
Kar B 031	5998, 8 × 10
Kar B 032	6046, 8 × 10
Kar B 033	6046, 8 × 10
Kar B 034	6046, 8 × 10
Kar B 034	6047, 8 × 10
Kar B 035	6046, 8 × 10
Kar B 035	6047, 8 × 10
Kar B 036	9765, 5 × 7
Kar B 038	5989, 8 × 10
Kar B 038	5990, 8 × 10
Kar B 038	5998, 8 × 10
Kar B 041	3732, 8 × 10
Kar B 042	3732, 8 × 10
Kar B 043	3735, 8 × 10
Kar B 044	3735, 8 × 10
Kar B 045	3734, 8 × 10
Kar B 046	3734, 8 × 10
Kar B 047	3733, 8 × 10
Kar B 048	3733, 8 × 10
Kar B 049	3732, 8 × 10
Kar B 050	3732, 8 × 10
Kar B 051	3732, 8 × 10
Kar B 052	3735, 8 × 10
Kar B 053	3734, 8 × 10
Kar B 053	3735, 8 × 10
Kar B 054	3734, 8 × 10
Kar B 056	3706, 8 × 10
Kar B 056	3733, 8 × 10
Kar B 057	3706, 8 × 10
Kar B 057	3733, 8 × 10
Kar B 058	3705, 8 × 10
Kar B 059	3705, 8 × 10
Kar B 060	3698, 8 × 10
Kar B 060	3735, 8 × 10
Kar B 061	3698, 8 × 10
Kar B 061	3735, 8 × 10
Kar B 062	3719, 8 × 10
Kar B 062	7094, 8 × 10
Kar B 063	3719, 8 × 10
Kar B 064	3720, 8 × 10
Kar B 065	3740, 8 × 10
Kar B 066	9677, 8 × 10
Kar B 066	9766, 5 × 7
Kar B 066	9767, 5 × 7
Kar B 066	9768, 5 × 7
Kar B 067	3165, 8 × 10
Kar B 067	9677, 8 × 10
Kar B 067	9766, 5 × 7
Kar B 067	9767, 5 × 7
Kar B 067	9768, 5 × 7

Karnak Temple (*cont.*)

Nelson Number/Description	Negative, Format
Kar B 068	3165, 8 × 10
Kar B 069	3166, 8 × 10
Kar B 070	3131, 8 × 10
Kar B 070	5906, 8 × 10
Kar B 071	3153, 8 × 10
Kar B 071	5193, 8 × 10
Kar B 072	3152, 8 × 10
Kar B 072	5192, 8 × 10
Kar B 073	3718, 8 × 10
Kar B 074	3724, 8 × 10
Kar B 075	6045, 8 × 10
Kar B 086	6044, 8 × 10
Kar B 086	6212, 8 × 10
Kar B 087	5988, 8 × 10
Kar B 087	6044, 8 × 10
Kar B 087	6212, 8 × 10
Kar B 088	3727, 8 × 10
Kar B 088	5982, 8 × 10
Kar B 088	5988, 8 × 10
Kar B 089	5982, 8 × 10
Kar B 089	5983, 8 × 10
Kar B 090	3708, 8 × 10
Kar B 090	6044, 8 × 10
Kar B 090	6212, 8 × 10
Kar B 091	3707, 8 × 10
Kar B 091	5988, 8 × 10
Kar B 091	6212, 8 × 10
Kar B 092	3707, 8 × 10
Kar B 092	5988, 8 × 10
Kar B 093	3727, 8 × 10
Kar B 093	5982, 8 × 10
Kar B 093	5988, 8 × 10
Kar B 094	3727, 8 × 10
Kar B 094	5982, 8 × 10
Kar B 094	6931, 5 × 7
Kar B 095	5983, 8 × 10
Kar B 096	5983, 8 × 10
Kar B 097	3167, 8 × 10
Kar B 097	6044, 8 × 10
Kar B 098	3168, 8 × 10
Kar B 098	5181, 8 × 10
Kar B 099	5863, 8 × 10
Kar B 100	5179, 8 × 10
Kar B 100	5182, 8 × 10
Kar B 100	5861, 8 × 10
Kar B 100	5862, 8 × 10
Kar B 101	6209, 8 × 10
Kar B 101	6210, 8 × 10
Kar B 101	6211, 8 × 10
Kar B 101	6216, 8 × 10
Kar B 101	6217, 8 × 10
Kar B 101c	3739, 8 × 10
Kar B 101d	3739, 8 × 10
Kar B 102	5984, 8 × 10
Kar B 102	5985, 8 × 10

Karnak Temple (*cont.*)

Nelson Number/Description	Negative, Format
Kar B 103	5986, 8 × 10
Kar B 104	5986, 8 × 10
Kar B 104	5987, 8 × 10
Kar B 105	5987, 8 × 10
Kar B 107	5973, 8 × 10
Kar B 108	5973, 8 × 10
Kar B 109	5984, 8 × 10
Kar B 110	3728, 8 × 10
Kar B 110	5985, 8 × 10
Kar B 111	5985, 8 × 10
Kar B 112	5986, 8 × 10
Kar B 113	5986, 8 × 10
Kar B 113	5987, 8 × 10
Kar B 114	5987, 8 × 10
Kar B 115	5973, 8 × 10
Kar B 115	5975, 8 × 10
Kar B 116	5973, 8 × 10
Kar B 116	5974, 8 × 10
Kar B 117	5170, 8 × 10
Kar B 117	6217, 8 × 10
Kar B 117	6218, 8 × 10
Kar B 118	5168, 8 × 10
Kar B 118	6218, 8 × 10
Kar B 118	6219, 8 × 10
Kar B 119	6219, 8 × 10
Kar B 120	5860, 8 × 10
Kar B 121	5859, 8 × 10
Kar B 122	7061, 8 × 10
Kar B 125	8804, 8 × 10
Kar B 126	8804, 8 × 10
Kar B 131	3757, 8 × 10
Kar B 133	6604, 8 × 10
Kar B 134	3817, 8 × 10
Kar B 134	6604, 8 × 10
Kar B 135	3817, 8 × 10
Kar B 136	3817, 8 × 10
Kar B 137	3818, 8 × 10
Kar B 138	3757, 8 × 10
Kar B 139	3757, 8 × 10
Kar B 140	6604, 8 × 10
Kar B 141	6604, 8 × 10
Kar B 142	3817, 8 × 10
Kar B 143	3817, 8 × 10
Kar B 144	3817, 8 × 10
Kar B 145	3818, 8 × 10
Kar B 146	3757, 8 × 10
Kar B 147	6605, 8 × 10
Kar B 148	6605, 8 × 10
Kar B 151	3673, 8 × 10
Kar B 152	3673, 8 × 10
Kar B 153	3670, 8 × 10
Kar B 154	3670, 8 × 10
Kar B 155	3821, 8 × 10
Kar B 156	3821, 8 × 10
Kar B 157	6605, 8 × 10

Karnak Temple (*cont.*)

Nelson Number/Description	Negative, Format
Kar B 158	6605, 8 × 10
Kar B 160	6606, 8 × 10
Kar B 160	6607, 8 × 10
Kar B 170	7146, 8 × 10
Kar B 173	7011, 8 × 10
Kar B 174	7146, 8 × 10
Kar B 175	7146, 8 × 10
Kar B 176	6848, 8 × 10
Kar B 177	6075, 8 × 10
Kar B 178	7146, 8 × 10
Kar B 179	6848, 8 × 10
Kar B 179	7011, 8 × 10
Kar B 180	3671, 8 × 10
Kar B 181	5876, 8 × 10
Kar B 182	6075, 8 × 10
Kar B 182	7011, 8 × 10
Kar B 183	7145, 8 × 10
Kar B 183	7146, 8 × 10
Kar B 184	7145, 8 × 10
Kar B 184	7146, 8 × 10
Kar B 185	6848, 8 × 10
Kar B 186	3671, 8 × 10
Kar B 187	5876, 8 × 10
Kar B 188	5876, 8 × 10
Kar B 189	3672, 8 × 10
Kar B 189	6075, 8 × 10
Kar B 189	7011, 8 × 10
Kar B 189	7012, 8 × 10
Kar B 190	7145, 8 × 10
Kar B 190	7146, 8 × 10
Kar B 191	7145, 8 × 10
Kar B 191	7146, 8 × 10
Kar B 192	3657, 8 × 10
Kar B 193	3671, 8 × 10
Kar B 194	6608, 8 × 10
Kar B 195	5876, 8 × 10
Kar B 195	6608, 8 × 10
Kar B 196	3672, 8 × 10
Kar B 196	6075, 8 × 10
Kar B 196	7012, 8 × 10
Kar B 197	7144, 8 × 10
Kar B 198	7144, 8 × 10
Kar B 199	3657, 8 × 10
Kar B 201	6018, 8 × 10
Kar B 205	6018, 8 × 10
Kar B 206	6018, 8 × 10
Kar B 206	8477, 8 × 10
Kar B 207	8477, 8 × 10
Kar B 208	8477, 8 × 10
Kar B 209	6018, 8 × 10
Kar B 209	6048, 8 × 10
Kar B 209	8477, 8 × 10
Kar B 210	7132, 5 × 7
Kar B 211	6048, 8 × 10
Kar B 211	7132, 5 × 7

Karnak Temple (*cont.*)

Nelson Number/Description	Negative, Format
Kar B 212	6213, 8 × 10
Kar B 213	6213, 8 × 10
Kar B 216	6018, 8 × 10
Kar B 216	6048, 8 × 10
Kar B 216	6049, 8 × 10
Kar B 216	13381, 5 × 7
Kar B 217	6213, 8 × 10
Kar B 217	7170, 8 × 10
Kar B 218	7170, 8 × 10
Kar B 219	7169, 8 × 10
Kar B 219	8434, 8 × 10
Kar B 220	7169, 8 × 10
Kar B 220	8434, 8 × 10
Kar B 221	7008, 8 × 10
Kar B 221	8444, 8 × 10
Kar B 222	7167, 8 × 10
Kar B 223	7166, 8 × 10
Kar B 224	6213, 8 × 10
Kar B 225	6213, 8 × 10
Kar B 225	7170, 8 × 10
Kar B 226	7170, 8 × 10
Kar B 227	6934, 8 × 10
Kar B 227	7169, 8 × 10
Kar B 227	7170, 8 × 10
Kar B 228	7169, 8 × 10
Kar B 229	7008, 8 × 10
Kar B 230	7008, 8 × 10
Kar B 230	7167, 8 × 10
Kar B 231	7167, 8 × 10
Kar B 232	7166, 8 × 10
Kar B 232	7168, 8 × 10
Kar B 233	3661, 8 × 10
Kar B 233	6213, 8 × 10
Kar B 234	3489, 8 × 10
Kar B 234	3797, 5 × 7
Kar B 235	3214, 8 × 10
Kar B 235	3669, 8 × 10
Kar B 236	3127, 8 × 10
Kar B 236	3726, 8 × 10
Kar B 237	3726, 8 × 10
Kar B 238	8404, 8 × 10
Kar B 239	7168, 8 × 10
Kar B 240	3172, 8 × 10
Kar B 240	4003, 8 × 10
Kar B 240	6609, 8 × 10
Kar B 240	6942, 8 × 10
Kar B 240	7134, 8 × 10
Kar B 241	3171, 8 × 10
Kar B 241	3172, 8 × 10
Kar B 241	5316, 8 × 10
Kar B 241	6941, 8 × 10
Kar B 241	6942, 8 × 10
Kar B 241	7134, 8 × 10
Kar B 242	3171, 8 × 10
Kar B 242	5316, 8 × 10

Karnak Temple (*cont.*)

Nelson Number/Description	Negative, Format
Kar B 242	6941, 8 × 10
Kar B 242	7171, 8 × 10
Kar B 242	7173, 8 × 10
Kar B 243	7171, 8 × 10
Kar B 243	7332, 8 × 10
Kar B 244	7174, 8 × 10
Kar B 244	7332, 8 × 10
Kar B 245	3590, 8 × 10
Kar B 246	3590, 8 × 10
Kar B 246	3593, 8 × 10
Kar B 247	3593, 8 × 10
Kar B 248	3591, 8 × 10
Kar B 249	3591, 8 × 10
Kar B 250	3589, 8 × 10
Kar B 250	5931, 8 × 10
Kar B 251	3589, 8 × 10
Kar B 252	3594, 8 × 10
Kar B 253	3594, 8 × 10
Kar B 254	3592, 8 × 10
Kar B 255	3592, 8 × 10
Kar B 256	7172, 8 × 10
Kar B 266	3417, 8 × 10
Kar B 266	12323, 5 × 7
Kar B 267	3417, 8 × 10
Kar B 268	3416, 8 × 10
Kar B 269	3416, 8 × 10
Kar B 270	3415, 8 × 10
Kar B 271	3415, 8 × 10
Kar B 272	3414, 8 × 10
Kar B 273	3414, 8 × 10
Kar B 274	5248, 8 × 10
Kar B 275	5248, 8 × 10
Kar B 275	5251, 8 × 10
Kar B 276	5251, 8 × 10
Kar B 276	5252, 8 × 10
Kar B 277	5252, 8 × 10
Kar B 278	5254, 8 × 10
Kar B 279	5248, 8 × 10
Kar B 280	6215, 8 × 10
Kar B 280	9872, 8 × 10
Kar B 280	9884, 5 × 7
Kar B 280f	3170, 8 × 10
Kar B 280g	3170, 8 × 10
Kar B 280h	3170, 8 × 10
Kar B 280i	3170, 8 × 10
Kar B 281	3421, 8 × 10
Kar B 282	3413, 8 × 10
Kar B 283	3413, 8 × 10
Kar B 283	13415, 5 × 7
Kar B 284	3412, 8 × 10
Kar B 284	13415, 5 × 7
Kar B 285	3411, 8 × 10
Kar B 285	3412, 8 × 10
Kar B 285	13415, 5 × 7
Kar B 286	3411, 8 × 10

Karnak Temple (*cont.*)

Nelson Number/Description	Negative, Format
Kar B 286	13415, 5 × 7
Kar B 287	3410, 8 × 10
Kar B 287	13415, 5 × 7
Kar B 288	3410, 8 × 10
Kar B 289	3421, 8 × 10
Kar B 290	3421, 8 × 10
Kar B 291	5255, 8 × 10
Kar B 292	5255, 8 × 10
Kar B 293	3169, 8 × 10
Kar B 294	3169, 8 × 10
Kar B 295	6214, 8 × 10
Kar B 296	6036, 8 × 10
Kar B 297	6036, 8 × 10
Kar B 301	3290, 8 × 10
Kar B 302	5875, 8 × 10
Kar B 305	5893, 8 × 10
Kar B 306	5893, 8 × 10
Kar B 307	5893, 8 × 10
Kar B 308	3290, 8 × 10
Kar B 308	5898, 8 × 10
Kar B 309	5875, 8 × 10
Kar B 310	5893, 8 × 10
Kar B 311	5893, 8 × 10
Kar B 312	5893, 8 × 10
Kar B 313	5932, 8 × 10
Kar B 313	10434, 5 × 7
Kar B 314	3290, 8 × 10
Kar B 314	5898, 8 × 10
Kar B 315	5875, 8 × 10
Kar B 316	5893, 8 × 10
Kar B 317	5893, 8 × 10
Kar B 318	5893, 8 × 10
Kar B 319	3154, 8 × 10
Kar B 320	3154, 8 × 10
Kar B 321	3154, 8 × 10
Kar B 321	5932, 8 × 10
Kar B 322	3154, 8 × 10
Kar B 322	5932, 8 × 10
Kar B 323	3154, 8 × 10
Kar B 323	5907, 8 × 10
Kar B 324	3154, 8 × 10
Kar B 324	5907, 8 × 10
Kar B 325	3154, 8 × 10
Kar B 325	5907, 8 × 10
Kar B 326	3154, 8 × 10
Kar B 326	3290, 8 × 10
Kar B 326	5892, 8 × 10
Kar B 326	5898, 8 × 10
Kar B 327	3154, 8 × 10
Kar B 327	5892, 8 × 10
Kar B 328	3154, 8 × 10
Kar B 328	5893, 8 × 10
Kar B 328	8739, 8 × 10
Kar B 329	3154, 8 × 10
Kar B 329	5893, 8 × 10

Karnak Temple (*cont.*)

Nelson Number/Description	Negative, Format
Kar B 329	8739, 8 × 10
Kar B 330	3154, 8 × 10
Kar B 330	5893, 8 × 10
Kar B 330	8739, 8 × 10
Kar B 331	3154, 8 × 10
Kar B 332	3154, 8 × 10
Kar B 333	3154, 8 × 10
Kar B 334	5253, 8 × 10
Kar B 334	5932, 8 × 10
Kar B 335	5907, 8 × 10
Kar B 336	5907, 8 × 10
Kar B 337	5907, 8 × 10
Kar B 338	5892, 8 × 10
Kar B 338	8740, 8 × 10
Kar B 339	5892, 8 × 10
Kar B 340	5892, 8 × 10
Kar B 341	5893, 8 × 10
Kar B 341	8739, 8 × 10
Kar B 342	3419, 8 × 10
Kar B 342	5893, 8 × 10
Kar B 342	8739, 8 × 10
Kar B 352	6074, 8 × 10
Kar B 352	6984, 8 × 10
Kar B 353	6870, 8 × 10
Kar B 354	3244, 8 × 10
Kar B 354	13400, 5 × 7
Kar B 356	6849, 8 × 10
Kar B 357	6074, 8 × 10
Kar B 357	6986, 8 × 10
Kar B 358	6074, 8 × 10
Kar B 358	6984, 8 × 10
Kar B 358	6986, 8 × 10
Kar B 359	6870, 8 × 10
Kar B 361	3244, 8 × 10
Kar B 361	13400, 5 × 7
Kar B 362	3244, 8 × 10
Kar B 362	13400, 5 × 7
Kar B 363	6849, 8 × 10
Kar B 363	13400, 5 × 7
Kar B 364	6074, 8 × 10
Kar B 364	6985, 8 × 10
Kar B 364	6986, 8 × 10
Kar B 365	6074, 8 × 10
Kar B 365	6984, 8 × 10
Kar B 365	6985, 8 × 10
Kar B 365	6986, 8 × 10
Kar B 366	6870, 8 × 10
Kar B 366	13427, 5 × 7
Kar B 368	3244, 8 × 10
Kar B 368	13400, 5 × 7
Kar B 369	3244, 8 × 10
Kar B 369	13400, 5 × 7
Kar B 370	3244, 8 × 10
Kar B 370	13400, 5 × 7
Kar B 371	3244, 8 × 10

Karnak Temple (*cont.*)

Nelson Number/Description	Negative, Format
Kar B 371	13400, 5 × 7
Kar B 372	6849, 8 × 10
Kar B 372	13400, 5 × 7
Kar B 373	6074, 8 × 10
Kar B 373	6883, 8 × 10
Kar B 373	6985, 8 × 10
Kar B 374	6074, 8 × 10
Kar B 374	6883, 8 × 10
Kar B 374	6985, 8 × 10
Kar B 375	6870, 8 × 10
Kar B 375	13427, 5 × 7
Kar B 377	3244, 8 × 10
Kar B 378	3244, 8 × 10
Kar B 378	13400, 5 × 7
Kar B 379	3244, 8 × 10
Kar B 379	13400, 5 × 7
Kar B 380	3244, 8 × 10
Kar B 380	8544, 5 × 7
Kar B 380	13400, 5 × 7
Kar B 381	3656, 8 × 10
Kar B 381	8545, 5 × 7
Kar B 381	13400, 5 × 7
Kar B 382	3736, 8 × 10
Kar B 382	6074, 8 × 10
Kar B 382	6883, 8 × 10
Kar B 382	8544, 5 × 7
Kar B 383	3736, 8 × 10
Kar B 383	6074, 8 × 10
Kar B 383	6883, 8 × 10
Kar B 384	6870, 8 × 10
Kar B 384	6871, 8 × 10
Kar B 384	13427, 5 × 7
Kar B 385	3244, 8 × 10
Kar B 385	13400, 5 × 7
Kar B 386	3244, 8 × 10
Kar B 386	13400, 5 × 7
Kar B 387	3656, 8 × 10
Kar B 387	13400, 5 × 7
Kar B 388	3736, 8 × 10
Kar B 388	6074, 8 × 10
Kar B 388	6883, 8 × 10
Kar B 389	3736, 8 × 10
Kar B 389	6074, 8 × 10
Kar B 389	6883, 8 × 10
Kar B 390	6871, 8 × 10
Kar B 390	13427, 5 × 7
Kar B 400	6805, 8 × 10
Kar B 401	6805, 8 × 10
Kar B 402	6803, 8 × 10
Kar B 403	6803, 8 × 10
Kar B 404	6804, 8 × 10
Kar B 405	6804, 8 × 10
Kar B 418	8433, 8 × 10
Kar B 419	8433, 8 × 10
Kar B 420	8433, 8 × 10

Karnak Temple (*cont.*)

Nelson Number/Description	Negative, Format
Kar B 421	8433, 8 × 10
Kar B 422	8433, 8 × 10
Kar B 423	8433, 8 × 10
Kar B 436	13378, 5 × 7
Kar B 475	13378-a, 5 × 7
Kar B 478	13442, 5 × 7
Kar B 479	13442, 5 × 7
Kar B 496	13377, 5 × 7
Kar B Col. General view	7485, 8 × 10
Kar B Col. General view	7486, 8 × 10
Kar B Col. General view	7487, 8 × 10
Kar B Col. General view	7488, 8 × 10
Kar B Col. General view	7489, 8 × 10
Kar B Col. 001	3658, 8 × 10
Kar B Col. 001	13376, 5 × 7
Kar B Col. 002	3658, 8 × 10
Kar B Col. 002	13376, 5 × 7
Kar B Col. 003	3658, 8 × 10
Kar B Col. 003	13376, 5 × 7
Kar B Col. 003	13416, 5 × 7
Kar B Col. 004	3658, 8 × 10
Kar B Col. 004	13376, 5 × 7
Kar B Col. 004	13378, 5 × 7
Kar B Col. 004	13416, 5 × 7
Kar B Col. 005	3658, 8 × 10
Kar B Col. 005	13378, 5 × 7
Kar B Col. 005	13378-a, 5 × 7
Kar B Col. 006	3658, 8 × 10
Kar B Col. 007	7644, 5 × 7
Kar B Col. 007	13376, 5 × 7
Kar B Col. 008	3653, 8 × 10
Kar B Col. 008	7646, 5 × 7
Kar B Col. 008	7956, 8 × 10
Kar B Col. 008	13376, 5 × 7
Kar B Col. 009	7643, 5 × 7
Kar B Col. 009	13376, 5 × 7
Kar B Col. 009	13378, 5 × 7
Kar B Col. 009	13416, 5 × 7
Kar B Col. 010	7645, 5 × 7
Kar B Col. 010	13376, 5 × 7
Kar B Col. 010	13378, 5 × 7
Kar B Col. 010	13416, 5 × 7
Kar B Col. 011	7647, 5 × 7
Kar B Col. 011	7648, 5 × 7
Kar B Col. 011	7650, 5 × 7
Kar B Col. 011	13376, 5 × 7
Kar B Col. 011b	7907, 5 × 7
Kar B Col. 012	7649, 5 × 7
Kar B Col. 016	3655, 8 × 10
Kar B Col. 017a	7618, 5 × 7
Kar B Col. 017a	7904, 5 × 7
Kar B Col. 018a	7920, 5 × 7
Kar B Col. 018c	7918, 5 × 7
Kar B Col. 019	3655, 8 × 10
Kar B Col. 020c	7623, 5 × 7

Karnak Temple (*cont.*)

Nelson Number/Description	Negative, Format
Kar B Col. 022	7913, 5 × 7
Kar B Col. 025	3655, 8 × 10
Kar B Col. 027c	7699, 5 × 7
Kar B Col. 027c	7900, 5 × 7
Kar B Col. 028	4041, 8 × 10
Kar B Col. 028a	7917, 5 × 7
Kar B Col. 034	3655, 8 × 10
Kar B Col. 035b	7619, 5 × 7
Kar B Col. 035c	7620, 5 × 7
Kar B Col. 037c	7912, 5 × 7
Kar B Col. 038c	9236, 5 × 7
Kar B Col. 041	6982, 5 × 7
Kar B Col. 043	3655, 8 × 10
Kar B Col. 044a	7911, 5 × 7
Kar B Col. 044c	7919, 5 × 7
Kar B Col. 046	6983, 5 × 7
Kar B Col. 046b	7698, 5 × 7
Kar B Col. 046b	7915, 5 × 7
Kar B Col. 047a	7903, 5 × 7
Kar B Col. 050	3695, 8 × 10
Kar B Col. 052	3655, 8 × 10
Kar B Col. 055c	7908, 5 × 7
Kar B Col. 056b	7700, 5 × 7
Kar B Col. 058b	7906, 5 × 7
Kar B Col. 061	3655, 8 × 10
Kar B Col. 062b	7916, 5 × 7
Kar B Col. 062d	7910, 5 × 7
Kar B Col. 064c	7914, 5 × 7
Kar B Col. 067	7901, 5 × 7
Kar B Col. 070	3654, 8 × 10
Kar B Col. 070	3655, 8 × 10
Kar B Col. 070	13378, 5 × 7
Kar B Col. 071	13378, 5 × 7
Kar B Col. 074b	9237, 5 × 7
Kar B Col. 075b	9073, 5 × 7
Kar B Col. 076	13416, 5 × 7
Kar B Col. 076b	9073, 5 × 7
Kar B Col. 077	3660, 8 × 10
Kar B Col. 077	13378, 5 × 7
Kar B Col. 077	13416, 5 × 7
Kar B Col. 077	13442, 5 × 7
Kar B Col. 077b	9074, 5 × 7
Kar B Col. 077b	9075, 5 × 7
Kar B Col. 078	3660, 8 × 10
Kar B Col. 078	13378, 5 × 7
Kar B Col. 078	13442, 5 × 7
Kar B Col. 078b	7902, 5 × 7
Kar B Col. 078b	9074, 5 × 7
Kar B Col. 078b	9075, 5 × 7
Kar B Col. 079	3660, 8 × 10
Kar B Col. 079	13378-a, 5 × 7
Kar B Col. 079b	9076, 5 × 7
Kar B Col. 080	3660, 8 × 10
Kar B Col. 080	13427, 5 × 7
Kar B Col. 080b	9076, 5 × 7

Karnak Temple (*cont.*)

Nelson Number/Description	Negative, Format
Kar B Col. 082b	7617, 5 × 7
Kar B Col. 082c	7905, 5 × 7
Kar B Col. 083	7131, 5 × 7
Kar B Col. 083c	9077, 5 × 7
Kar B Col. 084	13378, 5 × 7
Kar B Col. 084	13416, 5 × 7
Kar B Col. 084c	7615, 5 × 7
Kar B Col. 085	8462, 5 × 7
Kar B Col. 085	8463, 5 × 7
Kar B Col. 085	3694, 8 × 10
Kar B Col. 085	13378, 5 × 7
Kar B Col. 085	13416, 5 × 7
Kar B Col. 090c	7909, 5 × 7
Kar B Col. 092a	9238, 5 × 7
Kar B Col. 093	13378, 5 × 7
Kar B Col. 093	13416, 5 × 7
Kar B Col. 094	13378, 5 × 7
Kar B Col. 094	13416, 5 × 7
Kar B Col. 099a	7614, 5 × 7
Kar B Col. 099c	9239, 5 × 7
Kar B Col. 102	13377, 5 × 7
Kar B Col. 102	13416, 5 × 7
Kar B Col. 103	13416, 5 × 7
Kar B Col. 105	6928, 5 × 7
Kar B Col. 107	6927, 5 × 7
Kar B Col. 108c	7613, 5 × 7
Kar B Col. 109c	7624, 5 × 7
Kar B Col. 110	13377, 5 × 7
Kar B Col. 111	6930, 5 × 7
Kar B Col. 111	13377, 5 × 7
Kar B Col. 111	13416, 5 × 7
Kar B Col. 112	13337, 5 × 7
Kar B Col. 112	13377, 5 × 7
Kar B Col. 112	13416, 5 × 7
Kar B Col. 112	13430, 5 × 7
Kar B Col. 114	6929, 5 × 7
Kar B Col. 114	7164, 5 × 7
Kar B Col. 116	3289, 8 × 10
Kar B Col. 117a	7601, 5 × 7
Kar B Col. 117c	7621, 5 × 7
Kar B Col. 118c	7622, 5 × 7
Kar B Col. 118c	9240, 5 × 7
Kar B Col. 121	13337, 5 × 7
Kar B Col. 126b	7616, 5 × 7
Kar B Col. 126c	7625, 5 × 7
Kar B Col. 129	13430, 5 × 7
Kar B Col. 132a	9241, 5 × 7
Kar B Col. 132c	9242, 5 × 7
Kar C 001	5991, 8 × 10
Kar C 002	5991, 8 × 10
Kar C 003	5991, 8 × 10
Kar C 004	5991, 8 × 10
Kar C 005	6990, 8 × 10
Kar C 005	6991, 8 × 10
Kar C 005	6994, 8 × 10

Karnak Temple (*cont.*)

Nelson Number/Description	Negative, Format
Kar C 005	6996, 8 × 10
Kar C 005	13379, 5 × 7
Kar C 005	13382, 5 × 7
Kar C 005	13385, 5 × 7
Kar C 005	13436, 5 × 7
Kar C 006	6990, 8 × 10
Kar C 006	6991, 8 × 10
Kar C 006	6994, 8 × 10
Kar C 006	6996, 8 × 10
Kar C 006	13379, 5 × 7
Kar C 006	13385, 5 × 7
Kar C 006	13436, 5 × 7
Kar C 007	5992, 8 × 10
Kar C 008	7175, 8 × 10
Kar C 009	7175, 8 × 10
Kar C 010	7259, 8 × 10
Kar C 013	8490, 8 × 10
Kar C 015c	8451, 5 × 7
Kar C 015d	8451, 5 × 7
Kar C 020	8461, 5 × 7
Kar C 021	8413, 5 × 7
Kar C 022	7075, 5 × 7
Kar C 024	8050, 8 × 10
Kar C 024s	8153, 8 × 10
Kar C 025j	7076, 5 × 7
Kar C 025k	7076, 5 × 7
Kar C 025l	7072, 5 × 7
Kar C 025m	7072, 5 × 7
Kar C 035a	6893, 5 × 7
Kar C 035b	6894, 5 × 7
Kar C 036b	10193, 5 × 7
Kar C 039	6768, 8 × 10
Kar C 039	7325, 8 × 10
Kar C 041E	5993, 8 × 10
Kar C 042	7152, 8 × 10
Kar C 044	5317, 8 × 10
Kar C 044	8043, 8 × 10
Kar C 048	6340, 8 × 10
Kar C 048c	13375, 5 × 7
Kar C 049	6020, 8 × 10
Kar C 050	6020, 8 × 10
Kar C 052	8022, 5 × 7
Kar C 055	6999, 8 × 10
Kar C 059	5222, 8 × 10
Kar C 060	7149, 8 × 10
Kar C 061	7149, 8 × 10
Kar C 068	3215, 8 × 10
Kar C 068	3216, 8 × 10
Kar C 069	3215, 8 × 10
Kar C 069	3216, 8 × 10
Kar C 071	3216, 8 × 10
Kar C 072	3216, 8 × 10
Kar C 073	3216, 8 × 10
Kar C 074	3215, 8 × 10
Kar C 075	3215, 8 × 10

Karnak Temple (*cont.*)

Nelson Number/Description	Negative, Format
Kar C 101	7659, 8 × 10
Kar C 102	7659, 8 × 10
Kar C 103	3326, 5 × 7
Kar C 103	3327, 5 × 7
Kar C 103	7981, 8 × 10
Kar C 103	8519, 8 × 10
Kar C 104	3173, 8 × 10
Kar C 104	3174, 8 × 10
Kar C 104	3175, 8 × 10
Kar C 104	3325, 5 × 7
Kar C 104	3328, 5 × 7
Kar C 104	7980, 8 × 10
Kar C 104	8519, 8 × 10
Kar C 105	8519, 8 × 10
Kar C 110	6285, 8 × 10
Kar C 114	3176, 8 × 10
Kar C 115	3176, 8 × 10
Kar C 116	8395, 5 × 7
Kar C 117	8395, 5 × 7
Kar C 118	8087, 5 × 7
Kar C 119	8087, 5 × 7
Kar C 124	7074, 5 × 7
Kar C 124	8414, 5 × 7
Kar C 129E	8578, 8 × 10
Kar C 129S	6033, 8 × 10
Kar C 131	8015, 5 × 7
Kar C 132	8042, 8 × 10
Kar C 136	7073, 5 × 7
Kar C 138	6952, 5 × 7
Kar C 147	6019, 8 × 10
Kar C 148	6019, 8 × 10
Kar C 149	8011, 5 × 7
Kar C 151	7006, 8 × 10
Kar C 152	6283, 8 × 10
Kar C 152	8579, 8 × 10
Kar C 152	8589, 8 × 10
Kar C 152	13414, 5 × 7
Kar C 156	8415, 5 × 7
Kar C 156	8416, 5 × 7
Kar C 157	5286, 8 × 10
Kar C 157	8421, 5 × 7
Kar C 158	5287, 8 × 10
Kar C 159	5287, 8 × 10
Kar C 159	8589, 8 × 10
Kar C 166N	8021, —
Kar D 002	5976, 8 × 10
Kar D 002	13444, 5 × 7
Kar D 003	5976, 8 × 10
Kar D 003	13444, 5 × 7
Kar D 008	8825, 5 × 7
Kar D 009	8456, 5 × 7
Kar D 013	6888, 8 × 10
Kar D 014	8456, 5 × 7
Kar D 015	8456, 5 × 7
Kar D 022	8165, 8 × 10

Karnak Temple (*cont.*)

Nelson Number/Description	Negative, Format
Kar D 026	6906, 8 × 10
Kar D 028	5894, 8 × 10
Kar D 030	5877, 8 × 10
Kar D 030	5878, 8 × 10
Kar D 032	6284, 8 × 10
Kar D 033	6284, 8 × 10
Kar D 034	5977, 8 × 10
Kar D 034	13444, 5 × 7
Kar D 035	5977, 8 × 10
Kar D 035	13444, 5 × 7
Kar D 036	8455, 5 × 7
Kar D 037	7933, 8 × 10
Kar D 038	3218, 8 × 10
Kar D 039a	3218, 8 × 10
Kar D 039b	3218, 8 × 10
Kar D 041	8826, 5 × 7
Kar D 042	8826, 5 × 7
Kar D 043	7933, 8 × 10
Kar D 049	8460, 5 × 7
Kar D 053	3218, 8 × 10
Kar D 056	3219, 8 × 10
Kar D 058	8458, 5 × 7
Kar D 066	7630, 8 × 10
Kar D 067	7630, 8 × 10
Kar D 068	7628, 8 × 10
Kar D 069	7629, 8 × 10
Kar D 070	7631, 8 × 10
Kar D 071	5849, 8 × 10
Kar D 072	5850, 8 × 10
Kar D 073	7655, 8 × 10
Kar D 074	7655, 8 × 10
Kar D 076	7611, 5 × 7
Kar D 077	7929, 8 × 10
Kar D 078	7626, 8 × 10
Kar D 079	7627, 8 × 10
Kar D 080	7635, 8 × 10
Kar D 081	7632, 8 × 10
Kar D 082	7633, 8 × 10
Kar D 083	7634, 8 × 10
Kar D 085	8453, 5 × 7
Kar D 088	8827, 5 × 7
Kar D 089	8827, 5 × 7
Kar D 090	3217, 8 × 10
Kar D 090	8499, 8 × 10
Kar D 091	3217, 8 × 10
Kar D 091	8499, 8 × 10
Kar D 094	6157, 8 × 10
Kar D 098	8397, 8 × 10
Kar D 099	7928, 8 × 10
Kar D 104	5169, 8 × 10
Kar D 104	8496, 8 × 10
Kar D 104	8497, 8 × 10
Kar D 105	5167, 8 × 10
Kar D 106	8498, 8 × 10
Kar D 150N	8565, 8 × 10

Karnak Temple (*cont.*)

Nelson Number/Description	Negative, Format
Kar D 151	8791, 8 × 10
Kar D 152	8791, 8 × 10
Kar D 152	8792, 8 × 10
Kar D 158a	8424, 5 × 7
Kar D 160a	8565, 8 × 10
Kar D 160b	6006, 8 × 10
Kar D 160b	8565, 8 × 10
Kar D 161	6006, 8 × 10
Kar D 161	8546, 5 × 7
Kar D 163	7937, 8 × 10
Kar D 164a	6850, 8 × 10
Kar D 164b	6850, 8 × 10
Kar D 164c	6850, 8 × 10
Kar D 167	7937, 8 × 10
Kar D 170E	8419, 5 × 7
Kar D 170W	8420, 5 × 7
Kar D 171	8019, 5 × 7
Kar D 171E	8417, 5 × 7
Kar D 171E	8418, 5 × 7
Kar D 179	8734, 8 × 10
Kar D 179	8746, 5 × 7
Kar D 180	6975, 5 × 7
Kar D 181	6975, 5 × 7
Kar D 182	6051, 8 × 10
Kar D 182	6953, 8 × 10
Kar D 182	7026, 8 × 10
Kar D 183	8735, 8 × 10
Kar D 184	8735, 8 × 10
Kar D 185	5981, 8 × 10
Kar D 185	6837, 8 × 10
Kar D 185	7026, 8 × 10
Kar D 186	6154, 8 × 10
Kar D 186	8559, 8 × 10
Kar D 187	6007, 8 × 10
Kar D 187	6009, 8 × 10
Kar D 187	8558, 5 × 7
Kar D 187	8559, 8 × 10
Kar D 187	8560, 8 × 10
Kar D 187	8561, 8 × 10
Kar D 187	8710, 5 × 7
Kar D 189	6851, 8 × 10
Kar D 191	8399, 8 × 10
Kar D 194a	8452, 5 × 7
Kar D 194a	8457, 5 × 7
Kar D 194b	8454, 5 × 7
Kar D 196	8459, 5 × 7
Kar D 197	3819, 8 × 10
Kar D 198	3822, 8 × 10
Kar D 199	5864, 8 × 10
Kar D 199	5866, 8 × 10
Kar D 199	5867, 8 × 10
Kar D 199	8562, 8 × 10
Kar D 199	8563, 8 × 10
Kar D 199	8564, 8 × 10
Kar D 200	8494, 8 × 10

Karnak Temple (*cont.*)

Nelson Number/Description	Negative, Format
Kar D 200	8495, 8 × 10
Kar D 201	8403, 8 × 10
Kar D 210	6851, 8 × 10
Kar D 211	6851, 8 × 10
Kar D 214	5184, 8 × 10
Kar D 217	5184, 8 × 10
Kar D 218	5184, 8 × 10
Kar D 218	10683, 8 × 10
Kar D 219	10683, 8 × 10
Kar D 219	10684, 8 × 10
Kar D 220	10683, 8 × 10
Kar D 220	10684, 8 × 10
Kar D 221	5184, 8 × 10
Kar D 222	5184, 8 × 10
Kar D 223	10683, 8 × 10
Kar D 223	10684, 8 × 10
Kar D 224	5184, 8 × 10
Kar D 224	10683, 8 × 10
Kar D 224	10684, 8 × 10
Kar D 225	5851, 8 × 10
Kar D 225a	8521, 8 × 10
Kar D 227	5852, 8 × 10
Kar D 228	5853, 8 × 10
Kar D 229	5854, 8 × 10
Kar D 230	5855, 8 × 10
Kar D 231	8423, 5 × 7
Kar D 232	8422, 5 × 7
Kar D 233	8425, 5 × 7
Kar D 234	8425, 5 × 7
Kar D 235	6165, 8 × 10
Kar D 236	6166, 8 × 10
Kar D 237	6167, 8 × 10
Kar D 238	5999, 8 × 10
Kar D 240	8023, 8 × 10
Kar D 241	6856, 8 × 10
Kar D 241	6857, 8 × 10
Kar D 241	8179, 8 × 10
Kar D 242	6856, 8 × 10
Kar D 242	6857, 8 × 10
Kar D 242	8179, 8 × 10
Kar D 243	6856, 8 × 10
Kar D 243	6857, 8 × 10
Kar D 243	8177, 8 × 10
Kar D 243	8179, 8 × 10
Kar D 244	6856, 8 × 10
Kar D 244	6857, 8 × 10
Kar D 244	8177, 8 × 10
Kar D 245	6856, 8 × 10
Kar D 245	6857, 8 × 10
Kar D 245	8177, 8 × 10
Kar D 246	6856, 8 × 10
Kar D 246	6857, 8 × 10
Kar D 247	6856, 8 × 10
Kar D 247	6857, 8 × 10
Kar D 247	8023, 8 × 10

Karnak Temple (*cont.*)

Nelson Number/Description	Negative, Format
Kar D 248	6856, 8 × 10
Kar D 248	6857, 8 × 10
Kar D 248	8179, 8 × 10
Kar D 249	6856, 8 × 10
Kar D 249	6857, 8 × 10
Kar D 249	8179, 8 × 10
Kar D 250	6856, 8 × 10
Kar D 250	6857, 8 × 10
Kar D 250	8179, 8 × 10
Kar D 251	6856, 8 × 10
Kar D 251	6857, 8 × 10
Kar D 251	8177, 8 × 10
Kar D 252	6856, 8 × 10
Kar D 252	6857, 8 × 10
Kar D 252	8177, 8 × 10
Kar D 253	6856, 8 × 10
Kar D 253	6857, 8 × 10
Kar D 253	8177, 8 × 10
Kar D 254	6856, 8 × 10
Kar D 254	6857, 8 × 10
Kar D 255	8023, 8 × 10
Kar D 255	6856, 8 × 10
Kar D 255	6857, 8 × 10
Kar D 255	8177, 8 × 10
Kar D 255	8179, 8 × 10
Kar D 260	6811, 8 × 10
Kar D 260	6858, 8 × 10
Kar D 261	6858, 8 × 10
Kar D 262	6858, 8 × 10
Kar D 262	8178, 8 × 10
Kar D 263	6858, 8 × 10
Kar D 263	8178, 8 × 10
Kar D 264	6858, 8 × 10
Kar D 265	6858, 8 × 10
Kar D 265	8023, 8 × 10
Kar D 266	6858, 8 × 10
Kar D 267	6858, 8 × 10
Kar D 268	6858, 8 × 10
Kar D 269	6858, 8 × 10
Kar D 270	6858, 8 × 10
Kar D 270	8178, 8 × 10
Kar D 271	6858, 8 × 10
Kar D 271	8178, 8 × 10
Kar D 272	6858, 8 × 10
Kar D 272	8178, 8 × 10
Kar D 273	6858, 8 × 10
Kar D 273	8023, 8 × 10
Kar D 274	6811, 8 × 10
Kar D 274	6858, 8 × 10
Kar D 274	8023, 8 × 10
Kar D 274	8178, 8 × 10
Kar D 277	6806, 8 × 10
Kar D 277	6807, 8 × 10
Kar D 282	10164, 5 × 7
Kar D 283	10164, 5 × 7

Karnak Temple (*cont.*)

Nelson Number/Description	Negative, Format
Kar D 284	10164, 5 × 7
Kar D 291	10164, 5 × 7
Kar D 292	10164, 5 × 7
Kar D 292	10165, 5 × 7
Kar D 300	10164, 5 × 7
Kar D 301	10164, 5 × 7
Kar D 301	10165, 5 × 7
Kar D 302	10164, 5 × 7
Kar D 302	10165, 5 × 7
Kar D 310	10164, 5 × 7
Kar D 311	10164, 5 × 7
Kar D 311	10165, 5 × 7
Kar D 312	10164, 5 × 7
Kar D 312	10165, 5 × 7
Kar D 316	6806, 8 × 10
Kar D 316	6807, 8 × 10
Kar D 318	6801, 8 × 10
Kar D 318	6802, 8 × 10
Kar D 348b	9081, 8 × 10
Kar D 363	6801, 8 × 10
Kar D 363	6802, 8 × 10
Kar D 401	5206, 8 × 10
Kar D 401	5209, 8 × 10
Kar D 401	6164, 8 × 10
Kar D 401	8741, 8 × 10
Kar D 401	8742, 8 × 10
Kar D 402	8016, 5 × 7
Kar D 402	8828, 5 × 7
Kar D 402	8829, 5 × 7
Kar D 402a	8829, 5 × 7
Kar D 403a	8830, 5 × 7
Kar D 404	5207, 8 × 10
Kar D 404a	5994, 8 × 10
Kar D 405	5207, 8 × 10
Kar D 406	5994, 8 × 10
Kar D 408	6947, 5 × 7
Kar D 410	8065, 5 × 7
Kar D 411	8017, 5 × 7
Kar D 411	8018, 5 × 7
Kar D 411	8065, 5 × 7
Kar D 411	8805, 8 × 10
Kar D 411	8813, 5 × 7
Kar D 412	8814, 5 × 7
Kar D 412a	8615, 5 × 7
Kar D 413	8805, 8 × 10
Kar D 415	8012, 5 × 7
Kar D 417	8815, 5 × 7
Kar D 418	8815, 5 × 7
Kar D 419	8816, 5 × 7
Kar D 419	8831, 5 × 7
Kar D 420	8678, 8 × 10
Kar D 421	8817, 5 × 7
Kar D 422	8832, 5 × 7
Kar D 423	8817, 5 × 7
Kar D 425	7063, 8 × 10

Karnak Temple (*cont.*)

Nelson Number/Description	Negative, Format
Kar D 426	7062, 8 × 10
Kar D 427	8833, 5 × 7
Kar D 429	8500, 8 × 10
Kar D 431	8501, 8 × 10
Kar D 434	8818, 5 × 7
Kar D 434	8834, 5 × 7
Kar D 436	8835, 5 × 7
Kar D 441	8020, 5 × 7
Kar D 442	8020, 5 × 7
Kar D 447	5912, 8 × 10
Kar D 448	5912, 8 × 10
Kar D 449	8398, 8 × 10
Kar D 451	5911, 8 × 10
Kar D 452	5910, 8 × 10
Kar D 452	5911, 8 × 10
Kar D 453	5910, 8 × 10
Kar D 454	5910, 8 × 10
Kar D 455	5909, 8 × 10
Kar D 456	5908, 8 × 10
Kar D 457	5908, 8 × 10
Kar D 458	3333, 8 × 10
Kar D 459	3334, 8 × 10
Kar D 463	8396, 8 × 10
Kar D 470	6188, 8 × 10
Kar D 471	8038, 8 × 10
Kar D 472	8038, 8 × 10
Kar D 475	6184, 8 × 10
Kar D 475	8502, 8 × 10
Kar D 476	6185, 8 × 10
Kar D 477	6186, 8 × 10
Kar D 477	6187, 8 × 10
Kar D 479	6948, 5 × 7
Kar D 489	6949, 5 × 7
Kar D 490	8844, 8 × 10
Kar D 491	8844, 8 × 10
Kar D 492	8654, 8 × 10
Kar D 493	8655, 8 × 10
Kar D 493a	8656, 8 × 10
Kar D 494	8657, 8 × 10
Kar D 495	8845, 8 × 10
Kar D 495b	8846, 8 × 10
Kar D 495c	8505, 8 × 10
Kar D 495c	8568, 8 × 10
Kar D 495d	8504, 8 × 10
Kar D 496	8566, 8 × 10
Kar D 496a	8567, 8 × 10
Kar D 497	8847, 8 × 10
Kar D 498	7024, 5 × 7
Kar D 501	8658, 8 × 10
Kar D 502	8659, 8 × 10
Kar D 502a	8659, 8 × 10
Kar D 502b	8660, 8 × 10
Kar D 503	8848, 8 × 10
Kar D 503a	8660, 8 × 10
Kar D 504	8507, 8 × 10

Karnak Temple (*cont.*)

Nelson Number/Description	Negative, Format
Kar D 504	8849, 8 × 10
Kar D 507	8506, 8 × 10
Kar D 507	8507, 8 × 10
Kar D 508	8506, 8 × 10
Kar D 508a	8506, 8 × 10
Kar D 508b	9616, 8 × 10
Kar D 509	8850, 8 × 10
Kar D 510	8850, 8 × 10
Kar D 511	8851, 8 × 10
Kar D 512	8852, 8 × 10
Kar D 513	6163, 8 × 10
Kar D 514	6160, 8 × 10
Kar D 515	6000, 8 × 10
Kar D 516	5868, 8 × 10
Kar D 516	6000, 8 × 10
Kar D 517	5869, 8 × 10
Kar D 518	8503, 8 × 10
Kar D 519	8503, 8 × 10
Kar D 520	6162, 8 × 10
Kar D 521	6162, 8 × 10
Kar D 522	8661, 8 × 10
Kar D 523	8661, 8 × 10
Kar D 524	3245, 8 × 10
Kar D 525	3245, 8 × 10
Kar D 526	3245, 8 × 10
Kar D 526	6161, 8 × 10
Kar D 527	6161, 8 × 10
Kar D 550	9615, 8 × 10
Kar D Pil. 170	13444, 5 × 7
Kar D Pil. 171	13444, 5 × 7
Kar E 470	3815, 8 × 10
Kar F 005	6189, 8 × 10
Kar F 007	6189, 8 × 10
Kar F 009	6155, 8 × 10
Kar F 013	6918, 5 × 7
Kar F 015	6917, 5 × 7
Kar F 017	6158, 8 × 10
Kar F 023	6944, 5 × 7
Kar F 024	6945, 5 × 7
Kar F 025	6902, 8 × 10
Kar F 025	8099, 5 × 7
Kar F 025	8102, 5 × 7
Kar F 025	8106, 5 × 7
Kar F 026	6903, 8 × 10
Kar F 026	8394, 5 × 7
Kar F 031	6899, 5 × 7
Kar F 032	6900, 5 × 7
Kar F 033	6900, 5 × 7
Kar F 034	6841, 8 × 10
Kar F 035	6841, 8 × 10
Kar F 038	6862, 8 × 10
Kar F 039	6864, 8 × 10
Kar F 039	6865, 8 × 10
Kar F 040	6905, 8 × 10
Kar F 041	6863, 8 × 10

Karnak Temple (*cont.*)

Nelson Number/Description	Negative, Format
Kar F 042	6860, 8 × 10
Kar F 042	6861, 8 × 10
Kar F 044	6840, 8 × 10
Kar F 045	6866, 8 × 10
Kar F 046	6904, 8 × 10
Kar F 047	6838, 8 × 10
Kar F 048	6855, 8 × 10
Kar F 049	6939, 8 × 10
Kar F 051	6845, 8 × 10
Kar F 052	6852, 8 × 10
Kar F 053	6867, 8 × 10
Kar F 054	6943, 5 × 7
Kar F 055	6853, 8 × 10
Kar F 056	6854, 8 × 10
Kar F 057	6938, 8 × 10
Kar F 059	6868, 8 × 10
Kar F 060	6869, 8 × 10
Kar F 061	6843, 8 × 10
Kar F 062	6847, 8 × 10
Kar F 064	6843, 8 × 10
Kar F 066	6846, 8 × 10
Kar F 067	6844, 8 × 10
Kar F 069	6842, 8 × 10
Kar F 070	6830, 8 × 10
Kar F 071	6831, 8 × 10
Kar F 072	6839, 8 × 10
Kar F 084	6004, 8 × 10
Kar F 090	6829, 8 × 10
Kar F 090a	6937, 8 × 10
Kar F 091	6828, 8 × 10
Kar F 091a	6940, 8 × 10
Kar F 092	6814, 8 × 10
Kar F 093	5865, 8 × 10
Kar F 093	6815, 8 × 10
Kar F 094	6812, 8 × 10
Kar F 095	6813, 8 × 10
Kar F 098	6834, 8 × 10
Kar F 099	6832, 8 × 10
Kar F 100	6818, 8 × 10
Kar F 101	6874, 5 × 7
Kar F 103	6876, 5 × 7
Kar F 104	8086, 5 × 7
Kar F 105	6820, 5 × 7
Kar F 107	8097, 5 × 7
Kar F 111	6875, 5 × 7
Kar F 113	6877, 5 × 7
Kar F 114	6821, 5 × 7
Kar F 115	6824, 5 × 7
Kar F 116	6822, 5 × 7
Kar F 117	6823, 5 × 7
Kar F 120	6827, 8 × 10
Kar F 121	6827, 8 × 10
Kar F 122	6826, 8 × 10
Kar F 123	6826, 8 × 10
Kar F 124b	6817, 8 × 10

Karnak Temple (*cont.*)

Nelson Number/Description	Negative, Format
Kar F 126	6833, 8 × 10
Kar F 127	6833, 8 × 10
Kar F 128	6836, 8 × 10
Kar F 129	6835, 8 × 10
Kar F 130	6529, 8 × 10
Kar F 130	8103, 5 × 7
Kar F 131	6946, 5 × 7
Kar F 132	6885, 8 × 10
Kar F 133	6911, 5 × 7
Kar F 133	7154, 5 × 7
Kar F 134	6911, 5 × 7
Kar F 135	6889, 5 × 7
Kar F 136	6890, 5 × 7
Kar F 136a	8104, 5 × 7
Kar F 137	6884, 8 × 10
Kar F 139	6528, 8 × 10
Kar F 140	6170, 8 × 10
Kar F 147	6898, 5 × 7
Kar F 148	6898, 5 × 7
Kar F 149	6910, 5 × 7
Kar F 150	6910, 5 × 7
Kar F 153	6910, 5 × 7
Kar F 156	8092, 5 × 7
Kar F 161	6926, 5 × 7
Kar F 163	8066, 5 × 7
Kar F 165	8821, 5 × 7
Kar F 167	8819, 5 × 7
Kar F 168	8820, 5 × 7
Kar F 169	6168, 8 × 10
Kar F 170a	6169, 8 × 10
Kar F 171	6001, 8 × 10
Kar F 181	6891, 5 × 7
Kar F 182	6891, 5 × 7
Kar F 184	7156, 5 × 7
Kar F 185	5648, 8 × 10
Kar F 185	5980, 8 × 10
Kar F 185	7325, 8 × 10
Kar F 186	7160, 5 × 7
Kar F 186a	7160, 5 × 7
Kar F 191	8853, 8 × 10
Kar F 192	7025, 5 × 7
Kar F 193	6913, 5 × 7
Kar F 194	6915, 5 × 7
Kar F 200	6923, 5 × 7
Kar F 201	6923, 5 × 7
Kar F 202	6923, 5 × 7
Kar F 203	6901, 5 × 7
Kar F 204	6901, 5 × 7
Kar F 206	6183, 8 × 10
Kar F 208	6183, 8 × 10
Kar F 210	6183, 8 × 10
Kar F 212	6183, 8 × 10
Kar F 214	8083, 8 × 10
Kar F 215	8083, 8 × 10
Kar F 216	6882, 8 × 10

Karnak Temple (*cont.*)

Nelson Number/Description	Negative, Format
Kar F 216	6951, 5 × 7
Kar F 216	8100, 5 × 7
Kar F 217	6882, 8 × 10
Kar F 217	6951, 5 × 7
Kar F 217	8100, 5 × 7
Kar F 218	7018, 5 × 7
Kar F 218	8082, 8 × 10
Kar F 219	8083, 8 × 10
Kar F 220	8083, 8 × 10
Kar F 221	8083, 8 × 10
Kar F 221	8101, 5 × 7
Kar F 222	8101, 5 × 7
Kar F 223	8082, 8 × 10
Kar F 225	6916, 5 × 7
Kar F 226	6908, 5 × 7
Kar F 227	6919, 5 × 7
Kar F 236	7660, 8 × 10
Kar F 237	7660, 8 × 10
Kar F 238	6002, 8 × 10
Kar F 239	6002, 8 × 10
Kar F 240	7660, 8 × 10
Kar F 241	7660, 8 × 10
Kar F 242	7660, 8 × 10
Kar F 243	6002, 8 × 10
Kar F 244	6002, 8 × 10
Kar F 245	7932, 8 × 10
Kar F 246	7932, 8 × 10
Kar F 247	3820, 8 × 10
Kar F 247	6950, 5 × 7
Kar F 248	3820, 8 × 10
Kar F 249	4037, 8 × 10
Kar F 249	7932, 8 × 10
Kar F 250	4037, 8 × 10
Kar F 250	7932, 8 × 10
Kar F 251	3820, 8 × 10
Kar F 251	6950, 5 × 7
Kar F 252	3820, 8 × 10
Kar F 253	7159, 5 × 7
Kar F 254	8854, 8 × 10
Kar F 255	6909, 5 × 7
Kar F 256	7165, 5 × 7
Kar F 257	7161, 5 × 7
Kar F 258	6892, 5 × 7
Kar F 259	6912, 5 × 7
Kar F 260	8854, 8 × 10
Kar F 271	3942, 8 × 10
Kar F 272	3942, 8 × 10
Kar F 273	7930, 8 × 10
Kar F 273	8170, 8 × 10
Kar F 274	3942, 8 × 10
Kar F 275	3942, 8 × 10
Kar F 276	7930, 8 × 10
Kar F 276	8170, 8 × 10
Kar F 277	7927, 5 × 7
Kar F 278	7927, 5 × 7

Karnak Temple (*cont.*)

Nelson Number/Description	Negative, Format
Kar F 280	6932, 5 × 7
Kar F 281	6932, 5 × 7
Kar F 281	8074, 5 × 7
Kar F 282	8074, 5 × 7
Kar F 283	6816, 8 × 10
Kar F 283	7931, 8 × 10
Kar F 284	6816, 8 × 10
Kar F 284	7931, 8 × 10
Kar F 285	6182, 8 × 10
Kar F 285	6816, 8 × 10
Kar F 285	7931, 8 × 10
Kar F 286	6182, 8 × 10
Kar F 286	7931, 8 × 10
Kar F 287	8081, 5 × 7
Kar F 288	6895, 5 × 7
Kar F 289	8109, 5 × 7
Kar F 290	8096, 5 × 7
Kar F 291	6005, 8 × 10
Kar F 292	6896, 5 × 7
Kar F 293	6003, 8 × 10
Kar F 301	7043, 5 × 7
Kar F 302	7043, 5 × 7
Kar F 303	7071, 5 × 7
Kar F 304	7071, 5 × 7
Kar F 305	6897, 5 × 7
Kar F 306	8807, 8 × 10
Kar F 307	8807, 8 × 10
Kar F 308	6914, 5 × 7
Kar F 310	7039, 5 × 7
Kar F 311	8836, 5 × 7
Kar F 312	3816, 8 × 10
Kar F 321	7153, 5 × 7
Kar F 322	7153, 5 × 7
Kar F 323	8836, 5 × 7
Kar F 324	6933, 5 × 7
Kar F 324	13384, 5 × 7
Kar F 325	6933, 5 × 7
Kar F 325	13384, 5 × 7
Kar F 326	8821, 5 × 7
Kar F 326	13384, 5 × 7
Kar F 327	8821, 5 × 7
Kar F 327	13384, 5 × 7
Kar F 328	13384, 5 × 7
Kar F 329	7088, 5 × 7
Kar F 329	13384, 5 × 7
Kar F 331	8837, 5 × 7
Kar F 332	8837, 5 × 7
Kar F 333	8837, 5 × 7
Kar F 336	6924, 5 × 7
Kar F 337	6924, 5 × 7
Kar F 338	6922, 5 × 7
Kar F 339	6922, 5 × 7
Kar F 342	8838, 5 × 7
Kar F 343	8838, 5 × 7
Kar F 344	8838, 5 × 7

Karnak Temple (*cont.*)

Nelson Number/Description	Negative, Format
Kar F 345	8838, 5 × 7
Kar F 346	8839, 5 × 7
Kar F 347	8839, 5 × 7
Kar F 348	8839, 5 × 7
Kar F 350	7019, 5 × 7
Kar F 351	7019, 5 × 7
Kar F 360	5649, 8 × 10
Kar F 362	5649, 8 × 10
Kar F 363	5649, 8 × 10
Kar F 364	8840, 5 × 7
Kar F 365	8840, 5 × 7
Kar F 366	6921, 5 × 7
Kar F 369	5651, 8 × 10
Kar F 370	5650, 8 × 10
Kar F 371	5651, 8 × 10
Kar F 372	5655, 8 × 10
Kar F 372	5656, 8 × 10
Kar F 373	5656, 8 × 10
Kar F 374	5652, 8 × 10
Kar F 375	5652, 8 × 10
Kar F 375	5653, 8 × 10
Kar F 376	5653, 8 × 10
Kar F 377	5657, 8 × 10
Kar F 378	5654, 8 × 10
Kar F 380	5654, 8 × 10
Kar F 381	5658, 8 × 10
Kar F 382	5658, 8 × 10
Kar F 382	5659, 8 × 10
Kar F 383	5659, 8 × 10
Kar F 384	5660, 8 × 10
Kar F 385	5660, 8 × 10
Kar F 386	5661, 8 × 10
Kar F 387	5661, 8 × 10
Kar F 388	5651, 8 × 10
Kar F 389	5650, 8 × 10
Kar F 395	6177, 8 × 10
Kar F 395	6178, 8 × 10
Kar F 397	6179, 8 × 10
Kar F 397	8841, 5 × 7
Kar F 398	6180, 8 × 10
Kar F 398	6181, 8 × 10
Kar F 399	6174, 8 × 10
Kar F 399	6175, 8 × 10
Kar F 399	6176, 8 × 10
Kar F 410	7155, 5 × 7
Kar F 411	7155, 5 × 7
Kar F 425	7180, 8 × 10
Kar F 426	7180, 8 × 10
Kar F 427	7180, 8 × 10
Kar F 428	7180, 8 × 10
Kar F 429	7180, 8 × 10
Kar F 430	6887, 8 × 10
Kar F 431	6887, 8 × 10
Kar F 432	6887, 8 × 10
Kar F 433	6887, 8 × 10

Karnak Temple (*cont.*)

Nelson Number/Description	Negative, Format
Kar F 434	6887, 8 × 10
Kar F 438	6173, 8 × 10
Kar F 438	7477, 8 × 10
Kar F 439	6172, 8 × 10
Kar F 439	7477, 8 × 10
Kar F 441	6171, 8 × 10
Kar F 442	7163, 5 × 7
Kar F 443	7017, 5 × 7
Kar F 444	7017, 5 × 7
Kar F 445	5371, 8 × 10
Kar F 446	5371, 8 × 10
Kar F 446	5856, 8 × 10
Kar F 447	5857, 8 × 10
Kar F 448	5370, 8 × 10
Kar F 448	5371, 8 × 10
Kar F 449	5370, 8 × 10
Kar F 450	5370, 8 × 10
Kar F 457	5370, 8 × 10
Kar F 458	5978, 8 × 10
Kar F 459	5978, 8 × 10
Kar F 461	5979, 8 × 10
Kar F 462	9617, 8 × 10
Kar F 463	9618, 8 × 10
Kar F 463a	9618, 8 × 10
Kar F 464	3246, 8 × 10
Kar F 464	8443, 8 × 10
Kar F 465	8442, 8 × 10
Kar F 466	6886, 8 × 10
Kar F 467	6886, 8 × 10
Kar F 468	6907, 8 × 10
Kar F 469	6907, 8 × 10
Kar F 471	7040, 5 × 7
Kar F 507	6925, 5 × 7
Kar F 525	8822, 5 × 7
Kar F 525	8823, 5 × 7
Kar F 525	8824, 5 × 7
Kar F 525	5273, 8 × 10
Kar F 525	5274, 8 × 10
Kar F 525	8540, 8 × 10
Kar F 525	8541, 8 × 10
Kar F 525	8542, 8 × 10
Kar F 525	8543, 8 × 10
Kar F 525	8553, 5 × 7
Kar F 525	8554, 5 × 7
Kar F 525	8555, 5 × 7
Kar F 525	8556, 5 × 7
Kar F 525	8557, 5 × 7
Kar F 525	8570, 8 × 10
Kar F 525	8571, 8 × 10
Kar F 525	8572, 8 × 10
Kar F 525	8573, 8 × 10
Kar F 525	8624, 5 × 7
Kar F 525	8625, 5 × 7
Kar F 525	8630, 8 × 10
Kar F 525	8631, 8 × 10

Karnak Temple (*cont.*)

Nelson Number/Description	Negative, Format
Kar F Col. 032	13384, 5 × 7
Kar F Col. 033	13384, 5 × 7
Kar F Col. 034	13384, 5 × 7
Kar F Col. 035	13384, 5 × 7
Kar F Col. 036	6925, 5 × 7
Kar F Col. 037	6925, 5 × 7
Kar F Pil. 011E	8088, 5 × 7
Kar F Pil. 012E	8093, 5 × 7
Kar F Pil. 013E	8094, 5 × 7
Kar F Pil. 014	8073, 5 × 7
Kar F Pil. 014E	8105, 5 × 7
Kar F Pil. 015	8073, 5 × 7
Kar F Pil. 015E	8092, 5 × 7
Kar F Pil. 015S	8111, 5 × 7
Kar F Pil. 016E	8105, 5 × 7
Kar F Pil. 016S	8111, 5 × 7
Kar F Pil. 020	8079, 5 × 7
Kar F Pil. 021	8077, 5 × 7
Kar F Pil. 024S	7086, 5 × 7
Kar F Pil. 027S	7087, 5 × 7
Kar F Pil. 031E	8095, 5 × 7
Kar F Pil. 031S	6960, 5 × 7
Kar F Pil. 031S	7016, 5 × 7
Kar F Pil. 032	6920, 5 × 7
Kar G 001	6993, 8 × 10
Kar G 002	3941, 8 × 10
Kar G 003	6193, 8 × 10
Kar G 004	6194, 8 × 10
Kar G 005	6194, 8 × 10
Kar G 006	6193, 8 × 10
Kar G 007	6194, 8 × 10
Kar G 008	6194, 8 × 10
Kar G 010	8026, 8 × 10
Kar G 011	8026, 8 × 10
Kar G 012	8026, 8 × 10
Kar G 013	6221, 8 × 10
Kar G 015	6220, 8 × 10
Kar G 016	6220, 8 × 10
Kar G 017	6221, 8 × 10
Kar G 018	6221, 8 × 10
Kar G 019	6220, 8 × 10
Kar G 020	6220, 8 × 10
Kar G 021	6220, 8 × 10
Kar G 021	6221, 8 × 10
Kar G 021	8026, 8 × 10
Kar G 026	6021, 8 × 10
Kar G 027	6021, 8 × 10
Kar G 028	8055, 5 × 7
Kar G 029	8055, 5 × 7
Kar G 030	8055, 5 × 7
Kar G 031	5173, 8 × 10
Kar G 032	5174, 8 × 10
Kar G 032	5219, 8 × 10
Kar G 033	8047, 8 × 10
Kar G 033	8048, 8 × 10

Karnak Temple (*cont.*)

Nelson Number/Description	Negative, Format
Kar G 033	8049, 8 × 10
Kar G 034	5242, 8 × 10
Kar G 035	8056, 5 × 7
Kar G 036	3615, 5 × 7
Kar G 036	8056, 5 × 7
Kar G 037	5242, 8 × 10
Kar G 037	8047, 8 × 10
Kar G 037	8048, 8 × 10
Kar G 037	8049, 8 × 10
Kar G 039	8069, 8 × 10
Kar G 040	8475, 8 × 10
Kar G 040	8743, 8 × 10
Kar G 043	8476, 8 × 10
Kar G 043	8488, 8 × 10
Kar G 052	8041, 8 × 10
Kar G 053	8041, 8 × 10
Kar G 054	8039, 8 × 10
Kar G 055	8039, 8 × 10
Kar G 056	8027, 8 × 10
Kar G 057	8027, 8 × 10
Kar G 058	8036, 8 × 10
Kar G 059	3545, 5 × 7
Kar G 059	8036, 8 × 10
Kar G 060	8041, 8 × 10
Kar G 061	8041, 8 × 10
Kar G 062	8039, 8 × 10
Kar G 063	8039, 8 × 10
Kar G 064	8027, 8 × 10
Kar G 065	8027, 8 × 10
Kar G 065	8036, 8 × 10
Kar G 065	8039, 8 × 10
Kar G 065	8041, 8 × 10
Kar G 066	7999, 8 × 10
Kar G 067	7999, 8 × 10
Kar G 070	8051, 8 × 10
Kar G 071	8051, 8 × 10
Kar G 072	8051, 8 × 10
Kar G 073	8051, 8 × 10
Kar G 074	8051, 8 × 10
Kar G 075	8051, 8 × 10
Kar G 079	6008, 8 × 10
Kar G 079	10160, 5 × 7
Kar G 080	6223, 8 × 10
Kar G 081	6222, 8 × 10
Kar G 082	6223, 8 × 10
Kar G 083	6222, 8 × 10
Kar G 083	6223, 8 × 10
Kar G 084	6222, 8 × 10
Kar G 085	6222, 8 × 10
Kar G 085	6223, 8 × 10
Kar G 088	6610, 8 × 10
Kar G 090	6196, 8 × 10
Kar G 092a	5221, 8 × 10
Kar G 092b	5221, 8 × 10
Kar G 093	5223, 8 × 10

Karnak Temple (*cont.*)

Nelson Number/Description	Negative, Format
Kar G 094	5223, 8 × 10
Kar G 095	5224, 8 × 10
Kar G 096	5224, 8 × 10
Kar G 097	5233, 8 × 10
Kar G 098	5223, 8 × 10
Kar G 098	5224, 8 × 10
Kar G 098	5233, 8 × 10
Kar G 099	5232, 8 × 10
Kar G 100	5232, 8 × 10
Kar G 101	5232, 8 × 10
Kar G 101	8007, 8 × 10
Kar G 102	8793, 8 × 10
Kar G 102	8794, 8 × 10
Kar G 103	8440, 8 × 10
Kar G 104	5277, 8 × 10
Kar G 104	8794, 8 × 10
Kar G 105	8441, 8 × 10
Kar G 107	5288, 7 × 9
Kar G 108	8795, 8 × 10
Kar G 108	8796, 8 × 10
Kar G 109	8795, 8 × 10
Kar G 109	8796, 8 × 10
Kar G 110	5284, 8 × 10
Kar G 111	5283, 8 × 10
Kar G 112	5285, 8 × 10
Kar G 113	5282, 8 × 10
Kar G 114	5281, 8 × 10
Kar G 115	5281, 8 × 10
Kar G 116	5279, 8 × 10
Kar G 117	5279, 8 × 10
Kar G 118	5278, 8 × 10
Kar G 119	5278, 8 × 10
Kar G 120	5280, 8 × 10
Kar G 121	5280, 8 × 10
Kar G 127e	5220, 8 × 10
Kar G 131	6022, 8 × 10
Kar G 135	6198, 8 × 10
Kar G 136	6197, 8 × 10
Kar G 139	7549, 8 × 10
Kar G 141	7549, 8 × 10
Kar G 143	6199, 8 × 10
Kar G 145	8583, 8 × 10
Kar G 149	7593, 5 × 7
Kar G 150	8797, 8 × 10
Kar G 152	7594, 5 × 7
Kar G 154	8006, 8 × 10
Kar G 155	6549, 8 × 10
Kar G 156	9616, 8 × 10
Kar G 157	9616, 8 × 10
Kar G 160	9619, 8 × 10
Kar G 161	9619, 8 × 10
Kar G 164	7577, 8 × 10
Kar G 165	7578, 8 × 10
Kar G 166	7577, 8 × 10
Kar G 166	7578, 8 × 10

Karnak Temple (*cont.*)

Nelson Number/Description	Negative, Format
Kar G 166	7579, 8 × 10
Kar G 166	7580, 8 × 10
Kar G 166	7584, 8 × 10
Kar G 167	7584, 8 × 10
Kar G 168	7584, 8 × 10
Kar G 169	7579, 8 × 10
Kar G 170	7580, 8 × 10
Kar G 171	7585, 8 × 10
Kar G 172	7583, 8 × 10
Kar G 173	7579, 8 × 10
Kar G 173	7580, 8 × 10
Kar G 173	7583, 8 × 10
Kar G 174	7540, 8 × 10
Kar G 174	7541, 8 × 10
Kar G 175	8798, 8 × 10
Kar G 176	8798, 8 × 10
Kar G 177	8798, 8 × 10
Kar G 177	8799, 8 × 10
Kar G 178	8799, 8 × 10
Kar G 179	7573, 8 × 10
Kar G 180	7574, 8 × 10
Kar G 181	7575, 8 × 10
Kar G 182	7582, 8 × 10
Kar G 183	7573, 8 × 10
Kar G 183	7574, 8 × 10
Kar G 183	7575, 8 × 10
Kar G 183	7582, 8 × 10
Kar G 184a	9370, 8 × 10
Kar G 184b	9371, 8 × 10
Kar G 184c	9371, 8 × 10
Kar G 184d	9371, 8 × 10
Kar G 184e	9372, 8 × 10
Kar G 184f	9372, 8 × 10
Kar G 184g	9373, 8 × 10
Kar G 185	8052, 5 × 7
Kar G 191	8053, 5 × 7
Kar G 193	7576, 8 × 10
Kar G 195	6207, 8 × 10
Kar G 196	6207, 8 × 10
Kar G 204	8584, 8 × 10
Kar G 205	8584, 8 × 10
Kar G 207	6201, 8 × 10
Kar G 208	6200, 8 × 10
Kar G 209	6200, 8 × 10
Kar G 211	8060, 5 × 7
Kar G 213	8057, 5 × 7
Kar G 214	8113, 5 × 7
Kar G 215	8113, 5 × 7
Kar G 217	8137, 5 × 7
Kar G 218	8136, 5 × 7
Kar G 220a	8085, 5 × 7
Kar G 220b	8084, 5 × 7
Kar G 223	8138, 5 × 7
Kar G 232	8054, 5 × 7
Kar G 235	11211, 5 × 7

Karnak Temple (*cont.*)

Nelson Number/Description	Negative, Format
Kar G 238	8004, 8 × 10
Kar G 239	8005, 8 × 10
Kar G 240	8138, 5 × 7
Kar G 260	5225, 8 × 10
Kar G 261	5225, 8 × 10
Kar G 262	5225, 8 × 10
Kar G 263S	8110, 5 × 7
Kar G 263W	8107, 5 × 7
Kar G 265	8080, 5 × 7
Kar G 266	8080, 5 × 7
Kar G 267W	8107, 5 × 7
Kar G 268	8078, 5 × 7
Kar G 269	8078, 5 × 7
Kar G 274	7595, 5 × 7
Kar G 275	7595, 5 × 7
Kar G 280	7597, 5 × 7
Kar G 281	7597, 5 × 7
Kar G 282	7597, 5 × 7
Kar G 283	7596, 5 × 7
Kar G 284	7596, 5 × 7
Kar G 291	6023, 8 × 10
Kar G 292	6023, 8 × 10
Kar G 294	6024, 8 × 10
Kar G 294	8800, 8 × 10
Kar G 295	6024, 8 × 10
Kar G 295	8800, 8 × 10
Kar G 296	8801, 8 × 10
Kar G 297	8801, 8 × 10
Kar G 298	8801, 8 × 10
Kar G 299	8802, 8 × 10
Kar G 299	13332, 5 × 7
Kar G 299	13411, 5 × 7
Kar G 299	13412, 5 × 7
Kar G 300	13332, 5 × 7
Kar G 300	13411, 5 × 7
Kar G 300	13412, 5 × 7
Kar G 301	7539, 8 × 10
Kar G 302	5732, 8 × 10
Kar G 302	5734, 8 × 10
Kar G 302	5737, 8 × 10
Kar G 302	13332, 5 × 7
Kar G 302	13411, 5 × 7
Kar G 302	13412, 5 × 7
Kar G 303	5739, 8 × 10
Kar G 303	9946, 8 × 10
Kar G 303	13332, 5 × 7
Kar G 303	13411, 5 × 7
Kar G 303	13412, 5 × 7
Kar G 304	13332, 5 × 7
Kar G 304	13411, 5 × 7
Kar G 304	13412, 5 × 7
Kar G 310	3420, 8 × 10
Kar G 310	6202, 8 × 10
Kar G 311	6203, 8 × 10
Kar G 311	6204, 8 × 10

Karnak Temple (*cont.*)

Nelson Number/Description	Negative, Format
Kar G 311	8523, 8 × 10
Kar G 311	8548, 5 × 7
Kar G 312	6205, 8 × 10
Kar G 313	8549, 5 × 7
Kar G 314	3420, 8 × 10
Kar G 314	6202, 8 × 10
Kar G 314	6203, 8 × 10
Kar G 314	6204, 8 × 10
Kar G 314	6205, 8 × 10
Kar G 314	8523, 8 × 10
Kar G 314	8549, 5 × 7
Kar G 315	8524, 8 × 10
Kar G 315	8549, 5 × 7
Kar G 316	8524, 8 × 10
Kar G 316	8525, 8 × 10
Kar G 317	8525, 8 × 10
Kar G 317	8526, 8 × 10
Kar G 318	8524, 8 × 10
Kar G 318	8525, 8 × 10
Kar G 318	8526, 8 × 10
Kar G 320	13332, 5 × 7
Kar G 320	13411, 5 × 7
Kar G 320	13412, 5 × 7
Kar G 320E	8552, 5 × 7
Kar G 320S	8551, 5 × 7
Kar G 320W	8550, 5 × 7
Kar G 321	13332, 5 × 7
Kar G 321	13411, 5 × 7
Kar G 321	13412, 5 × 7
Kar G 321E	8552, 5 × 7
Kar G 321S	8551, 5 × 7
Kar G 321W	8550, 5 × 7
Kar G 323	8003, 8 × 10
Kar G 326	8585, 8 × 10
Kar G 327	8585, 8 × 10
Kar G 328	8002, 8 × 10
Kar G 329	8002, 8 × 10
Kar G Pil. 014	8057, 5 × 7
Kar G Pil. 015	8059, 5 × 7
Kar G Pil. 016	8059, 5 × 7
Kar G Pil. 017	8058, 5 × 7
Kar G Pil. 018	8058, 5 × 7
Kar G Pil. 021	8062, 5 × 7
Kar G Pil. 022	8062, 5 × 7
Kar G Pil. 023	8064, 5 × 7
Kar G Pil. 024	8060, 5 × 7
Kar G Pil. 024	8064, 5 × 7
Kar G Pil. 026	7998, 8 × 10
Kar G Pil. 026	8075, 5 × 7
Kar G Pil. 027E	8131, 8 × 10
Kar G Pil. 027E	8133, 8 × 10
Kar G Pil. 028	8072, 5 × 7
Kar G Pil. 029	8072, 5 × 7
Kar G Pil. 030	8072, 5 × 7
Kar G Pil. 031	7998, 8 × 10

Karnak Temple (*cont.*)

Nelson Number/Description	Negative, Format
Kar G Pil. 031	8010, 5 × 7
Kar G Pil. 031	8072, 5 × 7
Kar G Pil. 031	8076, 5 × 7
Kar G Pil. 032	8009, 5 × 7
Kar G Pil. 032	8072, 5 × 7
Kar G Pil. 032E	8131, 8 × 10
Kar G Pil. 032E	8133, 8 × 10
Kar G Pil. 033	8072, 5 × 7
Kar G Pil. 033S	8272, 5 × 7
Kar G Pil. 034	8001, 8 × 10
Kar G Pil. 035	8001, 8 × 10
Kar G Pil. 036	8008, 8 × 10
Kar G Pil. 036E	8130, 8 × 10
Kar G Pil. 036W	8135, 5 × 7
Kar G Pil. 037	8008, 8 × 10
Kar G Pil. 037E	8132, 8 × 10
Kar G Pil. 038	8071, 5 × 7
Kar G Pil. 038E	8129, 8 × 10
Kar G Pil. 039	8000, 8 × 10
Kar G Pil. 039	8061, 5 × 7
Kar G Pil. 039	8071, 5 × 7
Kar G Pil. 039E	8134, 8 × 10
Kar G Pil. 040	8000, 8 × 10
Kar G Pil. 040	8063, 5 × 7
Kar G Pil. 040	8071, 5 × 7
Kar G Pil. 041	8063, 5 × 7
Kar G Pil. 041	8071, 5 × 7
Kar G Pil. 041E	8130, 8 × 10
Kar G Pil. 041S	8273, 5 × 7
Kar G Pil. 042	8031, 8 × 10
Kar G Pil. 042	8063, 5 × 7
Kar G Pil. 042	8071, 5 × 7
Kar G Pil. 042E	8132, 8 × 10
Kar G Pil. 043	8031, 8 × 10
Kar G Pil. 043	8063, 5 × 7
Kar G Pil. 043	8071, 5 × 7
Kar G Pil. 043E	8129, 8 × 10
Kar G Pil. 044	8044, 8 × 10
Kar G Pil. 044	8061, 5 × 7
Kar G Pil. 044	8063, 5 × 7
Kar G Pil. 044E	8134, 8 × 10
Kar G Pil. 045	8044, 8 × 10
Kar G Pil. 045	8063, 5 × 7
Kar G Pil. 068E	8274, 5 × 7
Kar H	12315, 5 × 7
Kar H	12316, 5 × 7
Kar H	12317, 5 × 7
Kar H	12318-a, 5 × 7
Kar H	12318-b, 5 × 7
Kar H	12319, 5 × 7
Kar H	12320, 5 × 7
Kar H	12321, 5 × 7
Kar H	12322, 5 × 7
Kar H	12324, 5 × 7
Kar H	12325, 5 × 7

Karnak Temple (*cont.*)

Nelson Number/Description	Negative, Format
Kar H	12423, 8 × 10
Kar H	15481, 5 × 7
Kar H	15482, 5 × 7
Kar H	15483, 5 × 7
Kar H	15484, 5 × 7
Kar H	15485, 5 × 7
Kar H	15486, 5 × 7
Kar H	15489, 5 × 7
Kar H	15490, 5 × 7
Kar H	15491, 5 × 7
Kar H	15492, 5 × 7
Kar H	15493, 5 × 7
Kar H	15494, 5 × 7
Kar H	15495, 5 × 7
Kar H	15496, 5 × 7
Kar H	15497, 5 × 7
Kar H	15498, 5 × 7
Kar H	15499, 5 × 7
Kar H	15500, 5 × 7
Kar H	15501, 5 × 7
Kar H	15502, 5 × 7
Kar H	15503, 5 × 7
Kar H	15504, 5 × 7
Kar H	15505, 5 × 7
Kar H	15506, 5 × 7
Kar H	15507, 5 × 7
Kar H	15508, 5 × 7
Kar H	15509, 5 × 7
Kar H	15510, 5 × 7
Kar H	15511, 5 × 7
Kar H	15512, 5 × 7
Kar H	15513, 5 × 7
Kar H	15514, 5 × 7
Kar H	15515, 5 × 7
Kar H	15516, 5 × 7
Kar H	15517, 5 × 7
Kar H	15518, 5 × 7
Kar H	15519, 5 × 7
Kar H	15520, 5 × 7
Kar H	15521, 5 × 7
Kar H	15522, 5 × 7
Kar H	15523, 5 × 7
Kar H	15524, 2.25 × 3.25
Kar H 001	8663, 8 × 10
Kar H 001	8664, 8 × 10
Kar H 001	12381, 8 × 10
Kar H 001a	12378, 8 × 10
Kar H 001a	12379, 8 × 10
Kar H 001b	12378, 8 × 10
Kar H 001b	12379, 8 × 10
Kar H 001c	12394, 8 × 10
Kar H 001c	12395, 8 × 10
Kar H 002	8665, 8 × 10
Kar H 002	9166, 8 × 10
Kar H 002	12142, 8 × 10

Karnak Temple (*cont.*)

Nelson Number/Description	Negative, Format
Kar H 002	12220, 5 × 7
Kar H 002	12221, 5 × 7
Kar H 002	12381, 8 × 10
Kar H 002	12394, 8 × 10
Kar H 002	14437, 5 × 7
Kar H 002	14438, 5 × 7
Kar H 002	14439, 5 × 7
Kar H 002a	12395, 8 × 10
Kar H 002b	12396, 8 × 10
Kar H 003	8665, 8 × 10
Kar H 003	12142, 8 × 10
Kar H 003	12381, 8 × 10
Kar H 003	12393, 8 × 10
Kar H 003	14437, 5 × 7
Kar H 003	14438, 5 × 7
Kar H 003	14439, 5 × 7
Kar H 003a	8665, 8 × 10
Kar H 003a	12384, 5 × 7
Kar H 003a	12392, 8 × 10
Kar H 003a	14437, 5 × 7
Kar H 003a	14438, 5 × 7
Kar H 003a	14439, 5 × 7
Kar H 003a	15525, 2.25 × 3.25
Kar H 004	8666, 8 × 10
Kar H 004	12142, 8 × 10
Kar H 004	12380, 8 × 10
Kar H 004	12381, 8 × 10
Kar H 004	14437, 5 × 7
Kar H 004	14438, 5 × 7
Kar H 004	14439, 5.× 7
Kar H 004a	12126, 8 × 10
Kar H 004a	12140, 8 × 10
Kar H 004a	12141, 8 × 10
Kar H 005	8663, 8 × 10
Kar H 005	8664, 8 × 10
Kar H 005	12381, 8 × 10
Kar H 005	12397, 8 × 10
Kar H 006	3309, 8 × 10
Kar H 006	12381, 8 × 10
Kar H 006	12425, 8 × 10
Kar H 006	15480, 5 × 7
Kar H 007	3313, 8 × 10
Kar H 007	8667, 8 × 10
Kar H 007	12142, 8 × 10
Kar H 007	12420, 8 × 10
Kar H 007	14438, 5 × 7
Kar H 007	14439, 5 × 7
Kar H 008	3546, 8 × 10
Kar H 008	12142, 8 × 10
Kar H 008	12427, 8 × 10
Kar H 008	14438, 5 × 7
Kar H 008	14439, 5 × 7
Kar H 008a	12222, 5 × 7
Kar H 008b	12222, 5 × 7
Kar H 008c	12222, 5 × 7

Karnak Temple (*cont.*)

Nelson Number/Description	Negative, Format
Kar H 008c	12223, 5 × 7
Kar H 009	8668, 8 × 10
Kar H 009	12224, 5 × 7
Kar H 009	12421, 8 × 10
Kar H 009	15488, 5 × 7
Kar H 010	8668, 8 × 10
Kar H 010	15488, 5 × 7
Kar H 011	7975, 5 × 7
Kar H 011	8669, 8 × 10
Kar H 011	13337, 5 × 7
Kar H 011a	12391, 8 × 10
Kar H 011b	12391, 8 × 10
Kar H 011c	12390, 8 × 10
Kar H 011d	12215, 8 × 10
Kar H 011e	12215, 8 × 10
Kar H 011f	12215, 8 × 10
Kar H 012	8806, 8 × 10
Kar H 012	12304, 8 × 10
Kar H 012a	12225, 5 × 7
Kar H 012a	12226, 5 × 7
Kar H 012b	12225, 5 × 7
Kar H 012b	12226, 5 × 7
Kar H 012c	12225, 5 × 7
Kar H 012c	12226, 5 × 7
Kar H 012d	12227, 5 × 7
Kar H 012d	12228, 5 × 7
Kar H 012d	12229, 5 × 7
Kar H 012e	12227, 5 × 7
Kar H 012e	12228, 5 × 7
Kar H 012e	12229, 5 × 7
Kar H 014	3310, 8 × 10
Kar H 014	12305, 8 × 10
Kar H 014	12398, 8 × 10
Kar H 014	13337, 5 × 7
Kar H 014c	12306, 8 × 10
Kar H 015	8670, 8 × 10
Kar H 015	12307, 8 × 10
Kar H 016	8671, 8 × 10
Kar H 016	12216, 8 × 10
Kar H 016b	12217, 8 × 10
Kar H 017	8672, 8 × 10
Kar H 018	8672, 8 × 10
Kar H 018	12230, 5 × 7
Kar H 018	12217, 8 × 10
Kar H 018	12231, 5 × 7
Kar H 018	15479, 5 × 7
Kar H 019	8670, 8 × 10
Kar H 019	12424, 8 × 10
Kar H 020	3312, 8 × 10
Kar H 020	8670, 8 × 10
Kar H 020	8671, 8 × 10
Kar H 020	12422, 8 × 10
Kar H 020	15477, 5 × 7
Kar H 020	15478, 5 × 7
Kar H 020	15538, 5 × 7

Karnak Temple (*cont.*)

Nelson Number/Description	Negative, Format
Kar H 020a	12232, 5 × 7
Kar H 020a	12233, 5 × 7
Kar H 020b	12232, 5 × 7
Kar H 020b	12233, 5 × 7
Kar H 020c	12418, 8 × 10
Kar H 021	8672, 8 × 10
Kar H 021	12234, 5 × 7
Kar H 021	12235, 5 × 7
Kar H 021	12308, 8 × 10
Kar H 021	12309, 8 × 10
Kar H 021	12387, 8 × 10
Kar H 022	8672, 8 × 10
Kar H 022	12230, 5 × 7
Kar H 022	12231, 5 × 7
Kar H 022	12310, 8 × 10
Kar H 022	15540, 5 × 7
Kar H 023	12419, 8 × 10
Kar H 023a	12389, 8 × 10
Kar H 023b	12388, 8 × 10
Kar H 024	3291, 8 × 10
Kar H 024	12143, 8 × 10
Kar H 024	12426, 8 × 10
Kar H 024	15540, 5 × 7
Kar H 051	6311, 8 × 10
Kar H 052	6311, 8 × 10
Kar H 054	7151, 8 × 10
Kar H 057	7151, 8 × 10
Kar H 058	9655, 8 × 10
Kar H 059	9655, 8 × 10
Kar H 060	6312, 8 × 10
Kar H 061	6312, 8 × 10
Kar H 064	7069, 5 × 7
Kar H 065	7069, 5 × 7
Kar H 071	7044, 5 × 7
Kar H 075	7068, 5 × 7
Kar H 080	6313, 8 × 10
Kar H 081	3311, 8 × 10
Kar H 081	6313, 8 × 10
Kar H 082	6313, 8 × 10
Kar H 088	9623, 5 × 7
Kar H 090	6345, 8 × 10
Kar H 091	6346, 8 × 10
Kar H 092	6346, 8 × 10
Kar H 093	6346, 8 × 10
Kar H 094	9656, 8 × 10
Kar H 094	9657, 8 × 10
Kar H 095	9656, 8 × 10
Kar H 096	9656, 8 × 10
Kar H 096	9657, 8 × 10
Kar H 097	9657, 8 × 10
Kar H 099	9658, 8 × 10
Kar H 100a	9659, 8 × 10
Kar H 100a	9660, 8 × 10
Kar H 100b	9659, 8 × 10
Kar H 101	9660, 8 × 10

Karnak Temple (*cont.*)

Nelson Number/Description	Negative, Format
Kar H 102	9660, 8 × 10
Kar H 103	7150, 8 × 10
Kar H 103	9661, 8 × 10
Kar H 104	7150, 8 × 10
Kar H 104	9661, 8 × 10
Kar H 105	7150, 8 × 10
Kar H 105	9661, 8 × 10
Kar H 106	6347, 8 × 10
Kar H 107	6347, 8 × 10
Kar H 108	7046, 8 × 10
Kar H 108	9662, 8 × 10
Kar H 109	7046, 8 × 10
Kar H 109	9662, 8 × 10
Kar H 110	7046, 8 × 10
Kar H 110	9662, 8 × 10
Kar H 113	9663, 8 × 10
Kar H 114	9664, 8 × 10
Kar H 115	9665, 8 × 10
Kar H 117	9624, 5 × 7
Kar H 118	9625, 5 × 7
Kar H 119	9626, 5 × 7
Kar H 120	9627, 5 × 7
Kar H 121	9628, 5 × 7
Kar H 121a	9629, 5 × 7
Kar H 122	9630, 5 × 7
Kar H 123	9631, 5 × 7
Kar H 124	9632, 5 × 7
Kar H 125	9633, 5 × 7
Kar H 126	9634, 5 × 7
Kar H 126a	9635, 5 × 7
Kar H 127	9636, 5 × 7
Kar H 128	9637, 5 × 7
Kar H 129	9638, 5 × 7
Kar H 130	9639, 5 × 7
Kar H 133	12326, 35 mm
Kar H 134	7070, 5 × 7
Kar H 136	6992, 8 × 10
Kar H 137	9666, 8 × 10
Kar H 138	9667, 8 × 10
Kar H 139	9667, 8 × 10
Kar H 139	9668, 8 × 10
Kar H 139	9669, 8 × 10
Kar H 140	9669, 8 × 10
Kar H 141	9670, 8 × 10
Kar H 142	9671, 8 × 10
Kar H 143	9669, 8 × 10
Kar H 144	7045, 8 × 10
Kar H 145	7049, 8 × 10
Kar H 146	7049, 8 × 10
Kar H 147	7067, 8 × 10
Kar H 148	7060, 8 × 10
Kar H 149	7048, 8 × 10
Kar H 150	7048, 8 × 10
Kar H 152	9672, 8 × 10
Kar H 153	9672, 8 × 10

Karnak Temple (*cont.*)

Nelson Number/Description	Negative, Format
Kar H 154	9673, 8 × 10
Kar H 155	9673, 8 × 10
Kar H 156	9674, 8 × 10
Kar H 157	9675, 8 × 10
Kar H 158	9676, 8 × 10
Kar H 159	9676, 8 × 10
Kar H 160	9640, 5 × 7
Kar H 161	9640, 5 × 7
Kar H 162	9641, 5 × 7
Kar H 162	9642, 5 × 7
Kar H 163	9643, 5 × 7
Kar H 163	9644, 5 × 7
Kar H 164	9645, 5 × 7
Kar H 164	9646, 5 × 7
Kar H 165	9647, 5 × 7
Kar H 165	9648, 5 × 7
Kar H 166	9649, 5 × 7
Kar H 167	9650, 5 × 7
Kar H 168	9651, 5 × 7
Kar H 168	9652, 5 × 7
Kar H 169	9653, 5 × 7
Kar H 170	9654, 5 × 7
Kar H 177	7078, 5 × 7
Kar H 190	8128, 8 × 10
Kar H 191	8128, 8 × 10
Kar H 195	6310, 8 × 10
Kar H 196	6310, 8 × 10
Kar H 197	6310, 8 × 10
Kar H 198	6310, 8 × 10
Kar H 200	8478, 8 × 10
Kar H 201	8124, 8 × 10
Kar H 202	8124, 8 × 10
Kar H 203	8124, 8 × 10
Kar H 204	8124, 8 × 10
Kar H 210	8127, 8 × 10
Kar H 211	8127, 8 × 10
Kar H 212	8127, 8 × 10
Kar H 213	8127, 8 × 10
Kar H 216a	8108, 5 × 7
Kar H 216b	8112, 5 × 7
Kar H 222	8125, 8 × 10
Kar H 223	8125, 8 × 10
Kar H 224	8125, 8 × 10
Kar H 225	8125, 8 × 10
Kar H 226	8125, 8 × 10
Kar H 227	8125, 8 × 10
Kar H 230	8126, 8 × 10
Kar H 230	8574, 8 × 10
Kar H 231	8168, 8 × 10
Kar H 232	8168, 8 × 10
Kar H 233	8168, 8 × 10
Kar H 234	8089, 5 × 7
Kar H 235	8089, 5 × 7
Kar H 236	8167, 8 × 10
Kar H 237	8167, 8 × 10

Karnak Temple (*cont.*)

Nelson Number/Description	Negative, Format
Kar H 238	8091, 5 × 7
Kar H 239	8582, 8 × 10
Kar H 239	8616, 5 × 7
Kar H 240	8090, 5 × 7
Kar H 241	8166, 8 × 10
Kar H 242	8166, 8 × 10
Kar H 250	7176, 8 × 10
Kar H 251	7176, 8 × 10
Kar H 252	7176, 8 × 10
Kar H 253	7147, 8 × 10
Kar H 254	7148, 8 × 10
Kar H 255	8617, 5 × 7
Kar H 257	8618, 5 × 7
Kar I 070	5441, 8 × 10
Kar I 072	7094, 8 × 10
Kar I 073	5441, 8 × 10
Kar I 074	5445, 8 × 10
Kar I 075	5445, 8 × 10
Kar I 076	5445, 8 × 10
Kar I 077	5444, 8 × 10
Kar I 079	5444, 8 × 10
Kar I 080	5443, 8 × 10
Kar I 082	5443, 8 × 10
Kar I 085	5442, 8 × 10
Kar I 086	5442, 8 × 10
Kar I 087	5440, 8 × 10
Kar I 089	5440, 8 × 10
Kar I 090a	9374, 8 × 10
Kar I 090b	9374, 8 × 10
Kar I 091a	9374, 8 × 10
Kar I 091b	9374, 8 × 10
Kar I 092a	9375, 8 × 10
Kar I 092b	9375, 8 × 10
Kar I 093a	9375, 8 × 10
Kar I 093b	9375, 8 × 10
Kar I 094a	9376, 8 × 10
Kar I 094b	9376, 8 × 10
Kar I 095a	9376, 8 × 10
Kar I 095b	9376, 8 × 10
Kar I 096a	9377, 8 × 10
Kar I 096b	9377, 8 × 10
Kar I 097a	9377, 8 × 10
Kar I 097b	9377, 8 × 10
Kar I 098	8681, 8 × 10
Kar I 098	8682, 8 × 10
Kar I 098	8683, 8 × 10
Kar I 098	8684, 8 × 10
Kar I 098	8685, 8 × 10
Kar I 098	9377, 8 × 10
Kar I 099	8681, 8 × 10
Kar I 099	8682, 8 × 10
Kar I 099	8683, 8 × 10
Kar I 099	8684, 8 × 10
Kar I 099	8685, 8 × 10
Kar I 106	6955, 5 × 7

Karnak Temple (*cont.*)

Nelson Number/Description	Negative, Format
Kar I 107	6962, 5 × 7
Kar I 108	6963, 5 × 7
Kar I 109	7162, 5 × 7
Kar I 110	6967, 5 × 7
Kar I 111	6967, 5 × 7
Kar I 112	6954, 5 × 7
Kar I 113	6954, 5 × 7
Kar I 113	6962, 5 × 7
Kar I 114	6962, 5 × 7
Kar I 114	6963, 5 × 7
Kar I 115	6963, 5 × 7
Kar I 117	6973, 5 × 7
Kar I 118	6959, 5 × 7
Kar I 119	7158, 5 × 7
Kar I 121	6965, 5 × 7
Kar I 122	6961, 5 × 7
Kar I 125	6974, 5 × 7
Kar I 126	7162, 5 × 7
Kar I 127	6958, 5 × 7
Kar I 128	6958, 5 × 7
Kar I 129	6957, 5 × 7
Kar I 130	6159, 8 × 10
Kar I 132	6956, 5 × 7
Kar I 134	6956, 5 × 7
Kar I 135	5858, 8 × 10
Kar I 135	6969, 5 × 7
Kar I 136	6980, 5 × 7
Kar I 137	6970, 5 × 7
Kar I 137a	7157, 5 × 7
Kar I 138	6156, 8 × 10
Kar I 139	6972, 5 × 7
Kar I 140	6971, 5 × 7
Kar I 141	6964, 5 × 7
Kar I 142	6966, 5 × 7
Kar I 143	6976, 5 × 7
Kar I 144	6978, 5 × 7
Kar I 145	6968, 5 × 7
Kar I 150	7036, 5 × 7
Kar I 151	7013, 5 × 7
Kar I 152	7015, 5 × 7
Kar I 153	6981, 5 × 7
Kar I 154	6997, 8 × 10
Kar I 154	7035, 5 × 7
Kar I 155	6977, 5 × 7
Kar I 155	7035, 5 × 7
Kar I 156	6977, 5 × 7
Kar I 157	7257, 8 × 10
Kar I 160	7009, 8 × 10
Kar I 161	6341, 8 × 10
Kar I 162	7010, 8 × 10
Kar I 163	7010, 8 × 10
Kar I 164	6342, 8 × 10
Kar I 165	6342, 8 × 10
Kar I 166	6314, 8 × 10
Kar I 167	6315, 8 × 10

Karnak Temple (*cont.*)

Nelson Number/Description	Negative, Format
Kar I 168	6314, 8 × 10
Kar I 169	6315, 8 × 10
Kar I 170	7064, 8 × 10
Kar I 171	7079, 5 × 7
Kar I 172	7003, 8 × 10
Kar I 173	7004, 8 × 10
Kar I 174	7003, 8 × 10
Kar I 175	7000, 8 × 10
Kar I 176	7000, 8 × 10
Kar I 177	6998, 8 × 10
Kar I 178	6190, 8 × 10
Kar I 179	7177, 8 × 10
Kar I 180	7177, 8 × 10
Kar I 181	7178, 8 × 10
Kar I 182	6979, 5 × 7
Kar I 183	6979, 5 × 7
Kar I 184	7179, 8 × 10
Kar I 185	7179, 8 × 10
Kar I 187	7255, 8 × 10
Kar I 188	7256, 8 × 10
Kar I 189	7258, 8 × 10
Kar I 195	7005, 8 × 10
Kar I 196	7005, 8 × 10
Kar I 197	7001, 8 × 10
Kar I 198	7001, 8 × 10
Kar I 206	7021, 5 × 7
Kar I 207	7021, 5 × 7
Kar I 208	7077, 5 × 7
Kar I 209	7077, 5 × 7
Kar I 210	7077, 5 × 7
Kar I 211	7083, 5 × 7
Kar I 212	7083, 5 × 7
Kar I 222	7080, 5 × 7
Kar I 223	7038, 5 × 7
Kar I 224	7022, 5 × 7
Kar I 228	7042, 5 × 7
Kar I 229	7042, 5 × 7
Kar I 231	7028, 8 × 10
Kar I 231a	7034, 5 × 7
Kar I 232	7028, 8 × 10
Kar I 233	7029, 8 × 10
Kar I 234	7029, 8 × 10
Kar I 235a	7027, 8 × 10
Kar I 235b	6995, 8 × 10
Kar I 236a	7085, 5 × 7
Kar I 236b	7934, 8 × 10
Kar I 237a	7084, 5 × 7
Kar I 237b	6995, 8 × 10
Kar I 238a	7027, 8 × 10
Kar I 238b	7934, 8 × 10
Kar I 250	6191, 8 × 10
Kar I 251	6192, 8 × 10
Kar I 252	7041, 5 × 7
Kar I 253	7020, 5 × 7
Kar I 254	7020, 5 × 7

Karnak Temple (*cont.*)

Nelson Number/Description	Negative, Format
Kar I 255	7014, 5 × 7
Kar I 256	7023, 5 × 7
Kar I 257	7023, 5 × 7
Kar I 258	7037, 5 × 7
Kar I 259	7037, 5 × 7
Kar I 260	7658, 5 × 7
Kar I 265	7002, 8 × 10
Kar I 266	7047, 8 × 10
Kar I 267	7007, 8 × 10
Kar I 268	7082, 5 × 7
Kar I 269	7081, 5 × 7
Kar I 270	7050, 8 × 10
Kar I 438	7934, 8 × 10
Kar K	3141, 8 × 10
Kar K	3253, 8 × 10
Kar K	3254, 8 × 10
Kar K	3316, 8 × 10
Kar K	5145, 11 × 14
Kar K	5146, 11 × 14
Kar K	5212, 11 × 14
Kar K	5213, 11 × 14
Kar K	5214, 11 × 14
Kar K	5612, 8 × 10
Kar K	5632, 8 × 10
Kar K	5635, 8 × 10
Kar K	5644, 8 × 10
Kar K	5647, 8 × 10
Kar K	5699, 7 × 9
Kar K	5708, 8 × 10
Kar K	5773, 8 × 10
Kar K	5777, 8 × 10
Kar K	5779, 8 × 10
Kar K	5792, 8 × 10
Kar K	5807, 8 × 10
Kar K	5814, 8 × 10
Kar K	5956, 8 × 10
Kar K	9620, 8 × 10
Kar K	10431, 8 × 10
Kar K	12198, 5 × 7
Kar K	12199, 5 × 7
Kar K	12218, 5 × 7
Kar K	12219, 5 × 7
Kar K	12385, 5 × 7
Kar K	12386, 5 × 7
Kar K 001	3081, 5 × 7
Kar K 001	3082, 5 × 7
Kar K 001	3083, 5 × 7
Kar K 001	3084, 5 × 7
Kar K 001	3085, 5 × 7
Kar K 001	3086, 5 × 7
Kar K 001	3087, 5 × 7
Kar K 001	5001, 8 × 10
Kar K 001	5260, 8 × 10
Kar K 001	5303, 8 × 10
Kar K 001	5315, 8 × 10

Karnak Temple (*cont.*)

Nelson Number/Description	Negative, Format
Kar K 001	5530, 5 × 7
Kar K 001	5531, 5 × 7
Kar K 001	5672, 5 × 7
Kar K 001	5710, 8 × 10
Kar K 001a	5569, 5 × 7
Kar K 001a	5571, 5 × 7
Kar K 001b	5564, 5 × 7
Kar K 001b	5574, 5 × 7
Kar K 002	5001, 8 × 10
Kar K 002	5534, 5 × 7
Kar K 002	5720, 8 × 10
Kar K 002	5700, 7 × 9
Kar K 002a	5572, 5 × 7
Kar K 002b	5576, 5 × 7
Kar K 003	5593, 8 × 10
Kar K 003a	5573, 5 × 7
Kar K 003b	5575, 5 × 7
Kar K 004	5633, 8 × 10
Kar K 005a	5578, 5 × 7
Kar K 005b	5568, 5 × 7
Kar K 006	5302, 8 × 10
Kar K 006	5303, 8 × 10
Kar K 006	5706, 7 × 9
Kar K 006a	5567, 5 × 7
Kar K 006b	5566, 5 × 7
Kar K 007	5667, 8 × 10
Kar K 007	5668, 8 × 10
Kar K 007	5669, 8 × 10
Kar K 007	5720, 8 × 10
Kar K 007	5511, 8 × 10
Kar K 007b	5570, 5 × 7
Kar K 008 8	5488, 8 × 10
Kar K 009	5235, 8 × 10
Kar K 009a	5589, 5 × 7
Kar K 010	5002, 8 × 10
Kar K 010	5238, 8 × 10
Kar K 010	5258, 8 × 10
Kar K 010	5259, 8 × 10
Kar K 010	5290, 8 × 10
Kar K 010	5302, 8 × 10
Kar K 010a	5582, 5 × 7
Kar K 010b	5584, 5 × 7
Kar K 011	5002, 8 × 10
Kar K 011	5237, 8 × 10
Kar K 011	5258, 8 × 10
Kar K 011	5259, 8 × 10
Kar K 011	5290, 8 × 10
Kar K 011a	5579, 5 × 7
Kar K 011b	5585, 5 × 7
Kar K 012	5002, 8 × 10
Kar K 012	5236, 8 × 10
Kar K 012	5512, 8 × 10
Kar K 012	5705, 8 × 10
Kar K 012b	5583, 5 × 7
Kar K 013	5298, 8 × 10

Karnak Temple (*cont.*)

Nelson Number/Description	Negative, Format
Kar K 013	5431, 8 × 10
Kar K 013	5432, 8 × 10
Kar K 013a	5590, 5 × 7
Kar K 014	5292, 8 × 10
Kar K 014	5429, 8 × 10
Kar K 014	5430, 8 × 10
Kar K 014	5636, 8 × 10
Kar K 014a	5588, 5 × 7
Kar K 014b	5581, 5 × 7
Kar K 015	5257, 8 × 10
Kar K 015	5264, 5 × 7
Kar K 015	5296, 8 × 10
Kar K 015	5429, 8 × 10
Kar K 015	5803, 8 × 10
Kar K 015a	5580, 5 × 7
Kar K 015b	5586, 5 × 7
Kar K 016	5291, 8 × 10
Kar K 016	5429, 8 × 10
Kar K 016a	5587, 5 × 7
Kar K 016b	5577, 5 × 7
Kar K 017	5513, 8 × 10
Kar K 017	5634, 8 × 10
Kar K 018	5634, 8 × 10
Kar K 020	5018, 8 × 10
Kar K 020	5261, 8 × 10
Kar K 020	5304, 8 × 10
Kar K 020	5320, 8 × 10
Kar K 020	5634, 8 × 10
Kar K 021	5016, 8 × 10
Kar K 021	5262, 8 × 10
Kar K 021	5306, 8 × 10
Kar K 022	5017, 8 × 10
Kar K 022	5306, 8 × 10
Kar K 023	5017, 8 × 10
Kar K 023	5306, 8 × 10
Kar K 024	5019, 8 × 10
Kar K 024	5305, 8 × 10
Kar K 024	5307, 8 × 10
Kar K 025	5020, 8 × 10
Kar K 025	5305, 8 × 10
Kar K 025	5307, 8 × 10
Kar K 026	5020, 8 × 10
Kar K 026	5305, 8 × 10
Kar K 026	5307, 8 × 10
Kar K 028	3314, 8 × 10
Kar K 028	5061, 8 × 10
Kar K 029	3314, 8 × 10
Kar K 029	5061, 8 × 10
Kar K 029	5072, 8 × 10
Kar K 030	5062, 8 × 10
Kar K 030	5063, 8 × 10
Kar K 030	5064, 8 × 10
Kar K 030	5065, 8 × 10
Kar K 031	5062, 8 × 10
Kar K 031	5072, 8 × 10

Nelson Number/Description	Negative, Format
Kar K 031	5073, 8 × 10
Kar K 031	5824, 5 × 7
Kar K 031	5827, 5 × 7
Kar K 032	5065, 8 × 10
Kar K 032	5073, 8 × 10
Kar K 033	5066, 8 × 10
Kar K 033	5067, 8 × 10
Kar K 033	5073, 8 × 10
Kar K 034	5068, 8 × 10
Kar K 034	5069, 8 × 10
Kar K 034	5070, 8 × 10
Kar K 034	5071, 8 × 10
Kar K 034	5073, 8 × 10
Kar K 034	5293, 8 × 10
Kar K 035	5073, 8 × 10
Kar K 035	5074, 8 × 10
Kar K 035	5294, 8 × 10
Kar K 036	5711, 8 × 10
Kar K 037	5719, 8 × 10
Kar K 037	5809, 8 × 10
Kar K 038	5410, 8 × 10
Kar K 039	5394, 8 × 10
Kar K 040	5021, 8 × 10
Kar K 041	5021, 8 × 10
Kar K 042	5003, 8 × 10
Kar K 042	5022, 8 × 10
Kar K 042	5023, 8 × 10
Kar K 042	5024, 8 × 10
Kar K 042	5025, 8 × 10
Kar K 042	5134, 8 × 10
Kar K 042	5135, 8 × 10
Kar K 042	5136, 8 × 10
Kar K 042	5139, 8 × 10
Kar K 042	5150, 8 × 10
Kar K 042	5707, 7 × 9
Kar K 042	5709, 8 × 10
Kar K 042	5712, 8 × 10
Kar K 042	5713, 8 × 10
Kar K 042	5718, 8 × 10
Kar K 043	5032, 8 × 10
Kar K 043	5033, 8 × 10
Kar K 043	5034, 8 × 10
Kar K 043	5563, 8 × 10
Kar K 044	5003, 8 × 10
Kar K 044	5004, 8 × 10
Kar K 044	5025, 8 × 10
Kar K 044	5026, 8 × 10
Kar K 044	5027, 8 × 10
Kar K 044	5484, 8 × 10
Kar K 044	5563, 8 × 10
Kar K 045	5004, 8 × 10
Kar K 045	5005, 8 × 10
Kar K 045	5026, 8 × 10
Kar K 045	5027, 8 × 10
Kar K 045	5100, 8 × 10

Karnak Temple (*cont.*)

Nelson Number/Description	Negative, Format
Kar K 045	5140, 8 × 10
Kar K 045	5141, 8 × 10
Kar K 045	5484, 8 × 10
Kar K 045	5563, 8 × 10
Kar K 046	5468, 8 × 10
Kar K 047	3156, 8 × 10
Kar K 047	5028, 8 × 10
Kar K 047	5029, 8 × 10
Kar K 047	5030, 8 × 10
Kar K 047	5468, 8 × 10
Kar K 048	5031, 8 × 10
Kar K 048	5032, 8 × 10
Kar K 048	5468, 8 × 10
Kar K 049	5468, 8 × 10
Kar K 050	5076, 8 × 10
Kar K 050	5468, 8 × 10
Kar K 051	5076, 8 × 10
Kar K 051	5468, 8 × 10
Kar K 052	5078, 8 × 10
Kar K 052	5468, 8 × 10
Kar K 052	5560, 8 × 10
Kar K 052	5561, 8 × 10
Kar K 053	5466, 8 × 10
Kar K 054	5077, 8 × 10
Kar K 054	5562, 8 × 10
Kar K 054	5613, 8 × 10
Kar K 055	5326, 8 × 10
Kar K 056	3252, 8 × 10
Kar K 057	5327, 8 × 10
Kar K 058	5613, 8 × 10
Kar K 058a	5514, 8 × 10
Kar K 059	5501, 8 × 10
Kar K 059	5609, 8 × 10
Kar K 059b	5515, 8 × 10
Kar K 059b	5516, 8 × 10
Kar K 060	5469, 8 × 10
Kar K 060b	5673, 5 × 7
Kar K 060c	5692, 5 × 7
Kar K 061	5469, 8 × 10
Kar K 062	5469, 8 × 10
Kar K 063	5469, 8 × 10
Kar K 064	5465, 8 × 10
Kar K 065	5465, 8 × 10
Kar K 066	5156, 8 × 10
Kar K 066	5465, 8 × 10
Kar K 066	5624, 8 × 10
Kar K 067	5147, 8 × 10
Kar K 067	5148, 8 × 10
Kar K 067	5156, 8 × 10
Kar K 067	5465, 8 × 10
Kar K 068	5510, 8 × 10
Kar K 069	5510, 8 × 10
Kar K 070	5510, 8 × 10
Kar K 071	5681, 8 × 10
Kar K 072	5681, 8 × 10

Karnak Temple (*cont.*)

Nelson Number/Description	Negative, Format
Kar K 073	5681, 8 × 10
Kar K 074	5466, 8 × 10
Kar K 075	5075, 8 × 10
Kar K 075	5502, 8 × 10
Kar K 075	5613, 8 × 10
Kar K 076	5079, 8 × 10
Kar K 076	5503, 8 × 10
Kar K 076	5613, 8 × 10
Kar K 077	5501, 8 × 10
Kar K 077	5609, 8 × 10
Kar K 077	5611, 8 × 10
Kar K 078	5048, 8 × 10
Kar K 078	5592, 8 × 10
Kar K 079	5048, 8 × 10
Kar K 079	5592, 8 × 10
Kar K 080	5008, 8 × 10
Kar K 080	5046, 8 × 10
Kar K 080	5592, 8 × 10
Kar K 081	5008, 8 × 10
Kar K 081	5046, 8 × 10
Kar K 081	5464, 8 × 10
Kar K 082	3161, 8 × 10
Kar K 082	5006, 8 × 10
Kar K 082	5007, 8 × 10
Kar K 082	5045, 8 × 10
Kar K 082	5126, 8 × 10
Kar K 082	5127, 8 × 10
Kar K 082	5464, 8 × 10
Kar K 083	5006, 8 × 10
Kar K 083	5007, 8 × 10
Kar K 083	5045, 8 × 10
Kar K 083	5126, 8 × 10
Kar K 083	5127, 8 × 10
Kar K 083	5464, 8 × 10
Kar K 084	5464, 8 × 10
Kar K 086	5153, 8 × 10
Kar K 086	5154, 8 × 10
Kar K 086	5610, 8 × 10
Kar K 087	5153, 8 × 10
Kar K 087	5154, 8 × 10
Kar K 088	5088, 8 × 10
Kar K 088	5089, 8 × 10
Kar K 088	5151, 8 × 10
Kar K 088	5152, 8 × 10
Kar K 088	5318, 8 × 10
Kar K 088	5319, 8 × 10
Kar K 088	5411, 8 × 10
Kar K 088	5412, 8 × 10
Kar K 088	5413, 8 × 10
Kar K 089	5088, 8 × 10
Kar K 089	5089, 8 × 10
Kar K 089	5151, 8 × 10
Kar K 089	5152, 8 × 10
Kar K 089	5318, 8 × 10
Kar K 089	5319, 8 × 10

Karnak Temple (*cont.*)		Karnak Temple (*cont.*)	
Nelson Number/Description	*Negative, Format*	*Nelson Number/Description*	*Negative, Format*
Kar K 089	5411, 8 × 10	Kar K 112	3317, 8 × 10
Kar K 089	5412, 8 × 10	Kar K 112	5042, 8 × 10
Kar K 089	5413, 8 × 10	Kar K 112	5234, 8 × 10
Kar K 089	5608, 8 × 10	Kar K 112	5375, 8 × 10
Kar K 090	5406, 8 × 10	Kar K 113	3317, 8 × 10
Kar K 090	5407, 8 × 10	Kar K 113	5234, 8 × 10
Kar K 090	5622, 8 × 10	Kar K 114	5050, 8 × 10
Kar K 091	5717, 8 × 10	Kar K 114	5244, 8 × 10
Kar K 093	5329, 8 × 10	Kar K 114	5418, 8 × 10
Kar K 095	5081, 8 × 10	Kar K 115	5050, 8 × 10
Kar K 096	5517, 8 × 10	Kar K 115	5243, 8 × 10
Kar K 096	5518, 8 × 10	Kar K 115	5300, 8 × 10
Kar K 096	5295, 8 × 10	Kar K 115	5420, 8 × 10
Kar K 097	5339, 8 × 10	Kar K 116	3329, 8 × 10
Kar K 097	5639, 8 × 10	Kar K 116	4028, 8 × 10
Kar K 098	5339, 8 × 10	Kar K 116	5044, 8 × 10
Kar K 098	5639, 8 × 10	Kar K 116	5246, 8 × 10
Kar K 099	5122, 8 × 10	Kar K 117	3329, 8 × 10
Kar K 099	5338, 8 × 10	Kar K 117	5245, 8 × 10
Kar K 100	5038, 8 × 10	Kar K 117	5301, 8 × 10
Kar K 100	5297, 8 × 10	Kar K 117	5414, 8 × 10
Kar K 100	5338, 8 × 10	Kar K 118	5301, 8 × 10
Kar K 101	5639, 8 × 10	Kar K 118	5325, 8 × 10
Kar K 101	5805, 8 × 10	Kar K 118	5414, 8 × 10
Kar K 102	5714, 8 × 10	Kar K 119	5084, 8 × 10
Kar K 103	5037, 8 × 10	Kar K 119	5415, 8 × 10
Kar K 103	5343, 8 × 10	Kar K 119	5832, 8 × 10
Kar K 103	5805, 8 × 10	Kar K 120	5059, 8 × 10
Kar K 104	5036, 8 × 10	Kar K 120	5416, 8 × 10
Kar K 104	5123, 8 × 10	Kar K 120	5832, 8 × 10
Kar K 104	5344, 8 × 10	Kar K 121	5340, 8 × 10
Kar K 104	5638, 8 × 10	Kar K 121	5832, 8 × 10
Kar K 104	5715, 8 × 10	Kar K 122	5341, 8 × 10
Kar K 105	5035, 8 × 10	Kar K 122	5832, 8 × 10
Kar K 105	5123, 8 × 10	Kar K 123	5060, 8 × 10
Kar K 105	5345, 8 × 10	Kar K 123	5342, 8 × 10
Kar K 105	5638, 8 × 10	Kar K 123	5830, 8 × 10
Kar K 106	5124, 8 × 10	Kar K 124	5058, 8 × 10
Kar K 106	5328, 8 × 10	Kar K 124	5830, 8 × 10
Kar K 107	5125, 8 × 10	Kar K 125	5058, 8 × 10
Kar K 107	5470, 8 × 10	Kar K 125	5831, 8 × 10
Kar K 107	5813, 8 × 10	Kar K 126	5057, 8 × 10
Kar K 108	5039, 8 × 10	Kar K 126	5831, 8 × 10
Kar K 108	5467, 8 × 10	Kar K 127	5057, 8 × 10
Kar K 108	5638, 8 × 10	Kar K 127	5831, 8 × 10
Kar K 109	3317, 8 × 10	Kar K 128	5056, 8 × 10
Kar K 109	5040, 8 × 10	Kar K 128	5831, 8 × 10
Kar K 109	5234, 8 × 10	Kar K 129	3164, 11 × 14
Kar K 110	3317, 8 × 10	Kar K 129	5056, 8 × 10
Kar K 110	5041, 8 × 10	Kar K 129	5330, 8 × 10
Kar K 110	5234, 8 × 10	Kar K 130	3322, 8 × 10
Kar K 111	3317, 8 × 10	Kar K 130	3932, 8 × 10
Kar K 111	5043, 8 × 10	Kar K 130	3973, 8 × 10
Kar K 111	5234, 8 × 10	Kar K 130	5055, 8 × 10
Kar K 111	5375, 8 × 10	Kar K 130	5299, 8 × 10

Karnak Temple (*cont.*)

Nelson Number/Description	Negative, Format
Kar K 130	5372, 8 × 10
Kar K 131	3240, 11 × 14
Kar K 131	3321, 8 × 10
Kar K 131	5054, 8 × 10
Kar K 131	5373, 8 × 10
Kar K 131	5643, 8 × 10
Kar K 132	3240, 11 × 14
Kar K 132	3321, 8 × 10
Kar K 132	5054, 8 × 10
Kar K 132	5373, 8 × 10
Kar K 132	5643, 8 × 10
Kar K 133	3240, 11 × 14
Kar K 133	3321, 8 × 10
Kar K 133	5053, 8 × 10
Kar K 133	5374, 8 × 10
Kar K 133	5643, 8 × 10
Kar K 134	3240, 11 × 14
Kar K 134	3321, 8 × 10
Kar K 134	5049, 8 × 10
Kar K 134	5337, 8 × 10
Kar K 134	5643, 8 × 10
Kar K 135	3240, 11 × 14
Kar K 135	3321, 8 × 10
Kar K 135	5049, 8 × 10
Kar K 135	5337, 8 × 10
Kar K 135	5643, 8 × 10
Kar K 136	3236, 11 × 14
Kar K 136	3320, 8 × 10
Kar K 136	5308, 8 × 10
Kar K 136	5899, 8 × 10
Kar K 137	3236, 11 × 14
Kar K 137	3320, 8 × 10
Kar K 137	5051, 8 × 10
Kar K 137	5309, 8 × 10
Kar K 137	5417, 8 × 10
Kar K 137	5637, 8 × 10
Kar K 137	5899, 8 × 10
Kar K 138	3236, 11 × 14
Kar K 138	3320, 8 × 10
Kar K 138	5051, 8 × 10
Kar K 138	5419, 8 × 10
Kar K 138	5899, 8 × 10
Kar K 139	3236, 11 × 14
Kar K 139	3320, 8 × 10
Kar K 139	5052, 8 × 10
Kar K 139	5899, 8 × 10
Kar K 140	3236, 11 × 14
Kar K 140	3320, 8 × 10
Kar K 140	5050, 8 × 10
Kar K 140	5051, 8 × 10
Kar K 140	5080, 8 × 10
Kar K 140	5899, 8 × 10
Kar K 141	3237, 11 × 14
Kar K 141	3319, 8 × 10
Kar K 142	3237, 11 × 14

Karnak Temple (*cont.*)

Nelson Number/Description	Negative, Format
Kar K 142	3319, 8 × 10
Kar K 143	3237, 11 × 14
Kar K 143	3319, 8 × 10
Kar K 144	3237, 11 × 14
Kar K 144	3319, 8 × 10
Kar K 145	3237, 11 × 14
Kar K 145	3319, 8 × 10
Kar K 146	3180, 8 × 10
Kar K 146	3240, 11 × 14
Kar K 146	3319, 8 × 10
Kar K 146	3321, 8 × 10
Kar K 146	5701, 7 × 9
Kar K 147	3240, 11 × 14
Kar K 147	3321, 8 × 10
Kar K 147	5701, 7 × 9
Kar K 148	3240, 11 × 14
Kar K 148	3321, 8 × 10
Kar K 148	5701, 7 × 9
Kar K 149	3240, 11 × 14
Kar K 149	3321, 8 × 10
Kar K 149	5701, 7 × 9
Kar K 150	3240, 11 × 14
Kar K 150	3321, 8 × 10
Kar K 150	5701, 7 × 9
Kar K 151	3236, 11 × 14
Kar K 151	3320, 8 × 10
Kar K 151	5702, 7 × 9
Kar K 152	3236, 11 × 14
Kar K 152	3320, 8 × 10
Kar K 152	5702, 7 × 9
Kar K 153	3236, 11 × 14
Kar K 153	3320, 8 × 10
Kar K 153	5702, 7 × 9
Kar K 153	5829, 5 × 7
Kar K 154	3236, 11 × 14
Kar K 154	3320, 8 × 10
Kar K 154	5702, 7 × 9
Kar K 155	3236, 11 × 14
Kar K 155	3320, 8 × 10
Kar K 155	5702, 7 × 9
Kar K 155	5828, 5 × 7
Kar K 156	3120, 8 × 10
Kar K 156	3237, 11 × 14
Kar K 156	3319, 8 × 10
Kar K 157	3120, 8 × 10
Kar K 157	3237, 11 × 14
Kar K 157	3319, 8 × 10
Kar K 158	3120, 8 × 10
Kar K 158	3237, 11 × 14
Kar K 158	3319, 8 × 10
Kar K 159	3120, 8 × 10
Kar K 159	3237, 11 × 14
Kar K 159	3319, 8 × 10
Kar K 160	3120, 8 × 10
Kar K 160	3237, 11 × 14

Karnak Temple (*cont.*)

Nelson Number/Description	Negative, Format
Kar K 160	3319, 8 × 10
Kar K 161	3318, 8 × 10
Kar K 161	5646, 8 × 10
Kar K 162	3318, 8 × 10
Kar K 162	5646, 8 × 10
Kar K 163	3318, 8 × 10
Kar K 163	5645, 8 × 10
Kar K 164	3318, 8 × 10
Kar K 164	5520, 8 × 10
Kar K 164	5645, 8 × 10
Kar K 165	5772, 8 × 10
Kar K 166	5697, 8 × 10
Kar K 167	5521, 8 × 10
Kar K 168	5521, 8 × 10
Kar K 168	5666, 5 × 7
Kar K 169	5159, 8 × 10
Kar K 169	5160, 8 × 10
Kar K 169	5161, 8 × 10
Kar K 169	5666, 5 × 7
Kar K 169	5696, 8 × 10
Kar K 170	3159, 8 × 10
Kar K 170	5159, 8 × 10
Kar K 170	5160, 8 × 10
Kar K 170	5161, 8 × 10
Kar K 171	5158, 8 × 10
Kar K 172	5090, 8 × 10
Kar K 172	5217, 8 × 10
Kar K 173	5091, 8 × 10
Kar K 173	5092, 8 × 10
Kar K 173	5093, 8 × 10
Kar K 173	5695, 8 × 10
Kar K 174	3160, 8 × 10
Kar K 174	5091, 8 × 10
Kar K 174	5093, 8 × 10
Kar K 174	5721, 8 × 10
Kar K 175	5523, 8 × 10
Kar K 175	5662, 5 × 7
Kar K 175	5785, 8 × 10
Kar K 175a	5380, 8 × 10
Kar K 175b	5381, 8 × 10
Kar K 175d	5535, 5 × 7
Kar K 175f	5471, 5 × 7
Kar K 176	5523, 8 × 10
Kar K 176	5662, 5 × 7
Kar K 176	5785, 8 × 10
Kar K 176	5826, 5 × 7
Kar K 176a	5382, 8 × 10
Kar K 176b	5383, 8 × 10
Kar K 176c	5473, 5 × 7
Kar K 176d	5472, 5 × 7
Kar K 177	5663, 5 × 7
Kar K 177	5785, 8 × 10
Kar K 177	5826, 5 × 7
Kar K 177a	5384, 8 × 10
Kar K 177b	5385, 8 × 10

Karnak Temple (*cont.*)

Nelson Number/Description	Negative, Format
Kar K 177c	5537, 5 × 7
Kar K 177d	5475, 5 × 7
Kar K 177f	5476, 5 × 7
Kar K 178	5528, 8 × 10
Kar K 178	5663, 5 × 7
Kar K 178	5785, 8 × 10
Kar K 178	5825, 5 × 7
Kar K 178a	5386, 8 × 10
Kar K 178b	5387, 8 × 10
Kar K 178c	5477, 5 × 7
Kar K 178d	5478, 5 × 7
Kar K 179	5092, 8 × 10
Kar K 179	5526, 8 × 10
Kar K 179	5527, 8 × 10
Kar K 179	5664, 5 × 7
Kar K 179	5793, 8 × 10
Kar K 179	5825, 5 × 7
Kar K 179a	5388, 8 × 10
Kar K 179b	5389, 8 × 10
Kar K 179c	5479, 5 × 7
Kar K 179d	5480, 5 × 7
Kar K 180	5524, 8 × 10
Kar K 180	5664, 5 × 7
Kar K 180	5691, 5 × 7
Kar K 180	5793, 8 × 10
Kar K 180a	5390, 8 × 10
Kar K 180b	5391, 8 × 10
Kar K 180c	5481, 5 × 7
Kar K 180d	5456, 5 × 7
Kar K 181	5525, 8 × 10
Kar K 181	5665, 5 × 7
Kar K 181	5691, 5 × 7
Kar K 181	5793, 8 × 10
Kar K 181a	5392, 8 × 10
Kar K 181b	5396, 8 × 10
Kar K 181c	5455, 5 × 7
Kar K 181c	5538, 5 × 7
Kar K 181d	5482, 5 × 7
Kar K 181g	5532, 5 × 7
Kar K 182	5601, 8 × 10
Kar K 182	5665, 5 × 7
Kar K 182	5692, 5 × 7
Kar K 182	5793, 8 × 10
Kar K 182a	5393, 8 × 10
Kar K 182b	5395, 8 × 10
Kar K 182c	5483, 5 × 7
Kar K 182d	5540, 5 × 7
Kar K 183	5603, 8 × 10
Kar K 183	5677, 5 × 7
Kar K 183	5690, 8 × 10
Kar K 183	5787, 8 × 10
Kar K 183a	5398, 8 × 10
Kar K 183a	5682, 5 × 7
Kar K 183b	5399, 8 × 10
Kar K 183b	5683, 5 × 7

Karnak Temple (*cont.*)

Nelson Number/Description	Negative, Format
Kar K 183d	5541, 5 × 7
Kar K 184	5604, 8 × 10
Kar K 184	5605, 8 × 10
Kar K 184	5674, 5 × 7
Kar K 184	5677, 5 × 7
Kar K 184	5787, 8 × 10
Kar K 184a	5400, 8 × 10
Kar K 184a	5684, 5 × 7
Kar K 184b	5401, 8 × 10
Kar K 184b	5685, 5 × 7
Kar K 184c	5454, 5 × 7
Kar K 184d	5542, 5 × 7
Kar K 185	5602, 8 × 10
Kar K 185	5674, 5 × 7
Kar K 185	5678, 5 × 7
Kar K 185	5787, 8 × 10
Kar K 185	5808, 8 × 10
Kar K 185a	5402, 8 × 10
Kar K 185a	5686, 5 × 7
Kar K 185b	5403, 8 × 10
Kar K 185b	5687, 5 × 7
Kar K 185c	5543, 5 × 7
Kar K 185d	5453, 5 × 7
Kar K 185d	5670, 8 × 10
Kar K 185d	5671, 8 × 10
Kar K 186	5602, 8 × 10
Kar K 186	5675, 5 × 7
Kar K 186	5678, 5 × 7
Kar K 186	5787, 8 × 10
Kar K 186	5808, 8 × 10
Kar K 186a	5404, 8 × 10
Kar K 186b	5405, 8 × 10
Kar K 186c	5452, 5 × 7
Kar K 186d	5451, 5 × 7
Kar K 187	5606, 8 × 10
Kar K 187	5607, 8 × 10
Kar K 187	5675, 5 × 7
Kar K 187	5679, 5 × 7
Kar K 187	5782, 8 × 10
Kar K 187a	5620, 8 × 10
Kar K 187b	5621, 8 × 10
Kar K 187c	5544, 5 × 7
Kar K 187d	5545, 5 × 7
Kar K 188	5676, 5 × 7
Kar K 188	5679, 5 × 7
Kar K 188	5782, 8 × 10
Kar K 188a	5618, 8 × 10
Kar K 188b	5619, 8 × 10
Kar K 188c	5546, 5 × 7
Kar K 188d	5547, 5 × 7
Kar K 189	5676, 5 × 7
Kar K 189	5680, 5 × 7
Kar K 189	5782, 8 × 10
Kar K 189a	5616, 8 × 10
Kar K 189b	5617, 8 × 10

Nelson Number/Description	Negative, Format
Kar K 189c	5548, 5 × 7
Kar K 189d	5549, 5 × 7
Kar K 190	5522, 8 × 10
Kar K 190	5673, 5 × 7
Kar K 190	5680, 5 × 7
Kar K 190	5782, 8 × 10
Kar K 190a	5614, 8 × 10
Kar K 190b	5615, 8 × 10
Kar K 190c	5550, 5 × 7
Kar K 190d	5551, 5 × 7
Kar K 191	3158, 8 × 10
Kar K 191	5267, 8 × 10
Kar K 191	5268, 8 × 10
Kar K 191	5269, 8 × 10
Kar K 192	5397, 8 × 10
Kar K 193	5397, 8 × 10
Kar K 193	5408, 8 × 10
Kar K 194	5263, 8 × 10
Kar K 194	5266, 8 × 10
Kar K 194	5409, 8 × 10
Kar K 195	5265, 8 × 10
Kar K 196	5265, 8 × 10
Kar K 196a	5439, 8 × 10
Kar K 196b	5438, 8 × 10
Kar K 197	5265, 8 × 10
Kar K 197a	5437, 8 × 10
Kar K 197b	5436, 8 × 10
Kar K 197c	5459, 8 × 10
Kar K 198	5529, 8 × 10
Kar K 198a	5435, 8 × 10
Kar K 198b	5457, 8 × 10
Kar K 198c	5458, 8 × 10
Kar K 199b	5433, 8 × 10
Kar K 199a	5434, 8 × 10
Kar K 200	5446, 8 × 10
Kar K 200	5447, 8 × 10
Kar K 200	5519, 8 × 10
Kar K 201	5289, 8 × 10
Kar K 202	5289, 8 × 10
Kar K 203	5289, 8 × 10
Kar K 204	3956, 8 × 10
Kar K 204	5275, 8 × 10
Kar K 204	5276, 8 × 10
Kar K 205	6611, 8 × 10
Kar K 207	5270, 8 × 10
Kar K 207	5271, 8 × 10
Kar K 207	5272, 8 × 10
Kar K 207	6612, 8 × 10
Kar K 208	5085, 8 × 10
Kar K 208	5376, 8 × 10
Kar K 209	5086, 8 × 10
Kar K 209	5087, 8 × 10
Kar K 209	5377, 8 × 10
Kar K 209	5378, 8 × 10
Kar K 210	5086, 8 × 10

Karnak Temple (*cont.*)

Nelson Number/Description	Negative, Format
Kar K 210	5087, 8 × 10
Kar K 210	5377, 8 × 10
Kar K 210	5378, 8 × 10
Kar K 211	5083, 8 × 10
Kar K 211	5177, 8 × 10
Kar K 212	5083, 8 × 10
Kar K 213	5083, 8 × 10
Kar K 214	3242, 8 × 10
Kar K 215	3242, 8 × 10
Kar K 215	5178, 8 × 10
Kar K 216	5082, 8 × 10
Kar K 217	5082, 8 × 10
Kar K 217	5552, 5 × 7
Kar K 217	5553, 5 × 7
Kar K 217	5554, 5 × 7
Kar K 224	5157, 8 × 10
Kar K 225	5157, 8 × 10
Kar K 226	3296, 8 × 10
Kar K 226	3330, 8 × 10
Kar K 226	5157, 8 × 10
Kar K 227	3262, 8 × 10
Kar K 227	3297, 8 × 10
Kar K 227	5157, 8 × 10
Kar K 227	5698, 8 × 10
Kar K 228	3298, 8 × 10
Kar K 228	5157, 8 × 10
Kar K 229	3299, 8 × 10
Kar K 229	5157, 8 × 10
Kar K 230	5157, 8 × 10
Kar K 234	3263, 8 × 10
Kar K 235	5103, 8 × 10
Kar K 235	5104, 8 × 10
Kar K 235	5105, 8 × 10
Kar K 235	5106, 8 × 10
Kar K 236	5106, 8 × 10
Kar K 237	5104, 8 × 10
Kar K 237	5105, 8 × 10
Kar K 238	3155, 8 × 10
Kar K 238	3157, 8 × 10
Kar K 238	3263, 8 × 10
Kar K 238	5102, 8 × 10
Kar K 238	5103, 8 × 10
Kar K 239	3140, 8 × 10
Kar K 239	5101, 8 × 10
Kar K 239	5137, 8 × 10
Kar K 239	5594, 8 × 10
Kar K 240	3263, 8 × 10
Kar K 240	5101, 8 × 10
Kar K 240	5102, 8 × 10
Kar K 240	5103, 8 × 10
Kar K 240	5104, 8 × 10
Kar K 240	5105, 8 × 10
Kar K 240	5106, 8 × 10
Kar K 240	5137, 8 × 10
Kar K 240	5594, 8 × 10

Karnak Temple (*cont.*)

Nelson Number/Description	Negative, Format
Kar K 245	5108, 8 × 10
Kar K 245	5113, 8 × 10
Kar K 245	5116, 8 × 10
Kar K 245	5332, 8 × 10
Kar K 245	5333, 8 × 10
Kar K 246	5107, 8 × 10
Kar K 246	5118, 8 × 10
Kar K 246	5120, 8 × 10
Kar K 247	5113, 8 × 10
Kar K 247	5332, 8 × 10
Kar K 248	5116, 8 × 10
Kar K 248	5333, 8 × 10
Kar K 249	5114, 8 × 10
Kar K 249	5115, 8 × 10
Kar K 249	5332, 8 × 10
Kar K 250	5117, 8 × 10
Kar K 250	5333, 8 × 10
Kar K 251	5108, 8 × 10
Kar K 252	5107, 8 × 10
Kar K 253	5118, 8 × 10
Kar K 253	5120, 8 × 10
Kar K 255	5119, 8 × 10
Kar K 256	5121, 8 × 10
Kar K 260	3243, 8 × 10
Kar K 260	5149, 8 × 10
Kar K 261	3243, 8 × 10
Kar K 261	5149, 8 × 10
Kar K 262	3243, 8 × 10
Kar K 262	5149, 8 × 10
Kar K 263	3243, 8 × 10
Kar K 263	5149, 8 × 10
Kar K 264	3243, 8 × 10
Kar K 264	5149, 8 × 10
Kar K 265	3243, 8 × 10
Kar K 265	5149, 8 × 10
Kar K 266	3243, 8 × 10
Kar K 266	5149, 8 × 10
Kar K 267	3243, 8 × 10
Kar K 267	5149, 8 × 10
Kar K 268	3243, 8 × 10
Kar K 268	5149, 8 × 10
Kar K 275	5155, 8 × 10
Kar K 275	5186, 8 × 10
Kar K 275	5187, 8 × 10
Kar K 275	5188, 8 × 10
Kar K 275	5189, 8 × 10
Kar K 275	5190, 8 × 10
Kar K 275	5191, 8 × 10
Kar K 275	5504, 8 × 10
Kar K 276	5155, 8 × 10
Kar K 277	5155, 8 × 10
Kar K 277	5191, 8 × 10
Kar K 278	5191, 8 × 10
Kar K 279	5187, 8 × 10
Kar K 280	5186, 8 × 10

Karnak Temple (*cont.*)

Nelson Number/Description	Negative, Format
Kar K 280	5187, 8 × 10
Kar K 281	5186, 8 × 10
Kar K 281	5187, 8 × 10
Kar K 281	5190, 8 × 10
Kar K 282	5186, 8 × 10
Kar K 282	5190, 8 × 10
Kar K 283	5189, 8 × 10
Kar K 283	5190, 8 × 10
Kar K 284	5189, 8 × 10
Kar K 284	5190, 8 × 10
Kar K 285	5189, 8 × 10
Kar K 285	5190, 8 × 10
Kar K 286	5190, 8 × 10
Kar K 286	5504, 8 × 10
Kar K 287	5504, 8 × 10
Kar K 288	5188, 8 × 10
Kar K 288	5504, 8 × 10
Kar K 289	5188, 8 × 10
Kar K 289	5504, 8 × 10
Kar K 290	5188, 8 × 10
Kar K 290	5504, 8 × 10
Kar K 292	5423, 8 × 10
Kar K 293	5138, 8 × 10
Kar K 293	5423, 8 × 10
Kar K 294	5138, 8 × 10
Kar K 294	5424, 8 × 10
Kar K 295	5132, 8 × 10
Kar K 295	5424, 8 × 10
Kar K 296	5132, 8 × 10
Kar K 296	5424, 8 × 10
Kar K 297	5130, 8 × 10
Kar K 297	5425, 8 × 10
Kar K 298	5130, 8 × 10
Kar K 298	5425, 8 × 10
Kar K 299	5129, 8 × 10
Kar K 299	5426, 8 × 10
Kar K 300	5129, 8 × 10
Kar K 300	5426, 8 × 10
Kar K 301	5128, 8 × 10
Kar K 301	5427, 8 × 10
Kar K 302	5128, 8 × 10
Kar K 302	5427, 8 × 10
Kar K 302	5504, 8 × 10
Kar K 303	5131, 8 × 10
Kar K 303	5428, 8 × 10
Kar K 303	5504, 8 × 10
Kar K 304	5131, 8 × 10
Kar K 304	5428, 8 × 10
Kar K 304	5504, 8 × 10
Kar K 305	5096, 8 × 10
Kar K 305	5504, 8 × 10
Kar K 306	5096, 8 × 10
Kar K 306	5504, 8 × 10
Kar K 307	5097, 8 × 10
Kar K 307	5098, 8 × 10

Karnak Temple (*cont.*)

Nelson Number/Description	Negative, Format
Kar K 308	5099, 8 × 10
Kar K 308	5594, 8 × 10
Kar K 311	5096, 8 × 10
Kar K 311	5097, 8 × 10
Kar K 311	5098, 8 × 10
Kar K 311	5099, 8 × 10
Kar K 311	5128, 8 × 10
Kar K 311	5129, 8 × 10
Kar K 311	5130, 8 × 10
Kar K 311	5131, 8 × 10
Kar K 311	5132, 8 × 10
Kar K 311	5138, 8 × 10
Kar K 311	5148, 8 × 10
Kar K 311	5423, 8 × 10
Kar K 311	5424, 8 × 10
Kar K 311	5425, 8 × 10
Kar K 311	5426, 8 × 10
Kar K 311	5427, 8 × 10
Kar K 311	5428, 8 × 10
Kar K 311	5504, 8 × 10
Kar K 311	5594, 8 × 10
Kar K 340	9455, 8 × 10
Kar K 341	5185, 8 × 10
Kar K 341	9084, 8 × 10
Kar K 342	5185, 8 × 10
Kar K 342	9136, 8 × 10
Kar K 343	5185, 8 × 10
Kar K 343	9136, 8 × 10
Kar K 344	5162, 8 × 10
Kar K 344	5202, 8 × 10
Kar K 344	5203, 8 × 10
Kar K 344	8662, 8 × 10
Kar K 344	9621, 8 × 10
Kar K 345	5202, 8 × 10
Kar K 345	9455, 8 × 10
Kar K 346	5202, 8 × 10
Kar K 346	9167, 8 × 10
Kar K 347	8698, 5 × 7
Kar K 347	9084, 8 × 10
Kar K 348a	8679, 8 × 10
Kar K 348a	9081, 8 × 10
Kar K 348b	8680, 8 × 10
Kar K 348c	8959, 8 × 10
Kar K 348c	9137, 8 × 10
Kar K 348d	8959, 8 × 10
Kar K 348d	9137, 8 × 10
Kar K 350	5111, 8 × 10
Kar K 350	9598, 8 × 10
Kar K 351	5111, 8 × 10
Kar K 351	9598, 8 × 10
Kar K 352	5013, 8 × 10
Kar K 352	5111, 8 × 10
Kar K 352	5175, 8 × 10
Kar K 352	10144, 8 × 10
Kar K 352	10145, 8 × 10

Karnak Temple (*cont.*)

Nelson Number/Description	Negative, Format
Kar K 353	5014, 8 × 10
Kar K 353	5015, 8 × 10
Kar K 353	5763, 8 × 10
Kar K 353	5764, 8 × 10
Kar K 353	10146, 8 × 10
Kar K 353	10147, 8 × 10
Kar K 354	5112, 8 × 10
Kar K 354	5165, 8 × 10
Kar K 354	5166, 8 × 10
Kar K 354	10148, 8 × 10
Kar K 355	5112, 8 × 10
Kar K 355	5165, 8 × 10
Kar K 355	5166, 8 × 10
Kar K 355	10148, 8 × 10
Kar K 356	5109, 8 × 10
Kar K 356	5110, 8 × 10
Kar K 356	5163, 8 × 10
Kar K 356	5164, 8 × 10
Kar K 356	5165, 8 × 10
Kar K 356	5166, 8 × 10
Kar K 356	10148, 8 × 10
Kar K 356	10149, 8 × 10
Kar K 360	5723, 8 × 10
Kar K 360	10185, 8 × 10
Kar K 360	10410, 8 × 10
Kar K 360	13450, 5 × 7
Kar K 360	15646, 5 × 7
Kar K 360	15647, 5 × 7
Kar K 361	5723, 8 × 10
Kar K 361	10183, 5 × 7
Kar K 361	10184, 8 × 10
Kar K 361	10185, 8 × 10
Kar K 361	10186, 8 × 10
Kar K 361	10187, 8 × 10
Kar K 361	10196, 5 × 7
Kar K 361	10197, 5 × 7
Kar K 361	10198, 5 × 7
Kar K 361	10259, 8 × 10
Kar K 361	10260, 8 × 10
Kar K 361	10410, 8 × 10
Kar K 361	10433, 5 × 7
Kar K 361	13450, 5 × 7
Kar K 361	15647, 5 × 7
Kar K 365	5421, 8 × 10
Kar K 366	5422, 8 × 10
Kar K 367	5508, 8 × 10
Kar K 368	5509, 8 × 10
Kar K 369	5505, 8 × 10
Kar K 369	5506, 8 × 10
Kar K 369	5507, 8 × 10
Kar K Col. A	5815, 8 × 10
Kar K Col. B	5815, 8 × 10
Kar K Col. C	5815, 8 × 10
Kar K Col. D	5815, 8 × 10
Kar K Pil. 002	5818, 8 × 10

Karnak Temple (*cont.*)

Nelson Number/Description	Negative, Format
Kar K Pil. 006	5819, 8 × 10
Kar K Pil. 008	5817, 8 × 10
Kar K Pil. 009	5821, 8 × 10
Kar K Pil. 010	5822, 8 × 10
Kar K Pil. 010b	5047, 8 × 10
Kar K Pil. 013	5820, 8 × 10
Kar K Pil. 022a	5076, 8 × 10
Kar K Pil. 025b	5047, 8 × 10
Kar L 001	5369, 8 × 10
Kar L 002	5369, 8 × 10
Kar L 003	5369, 8 × 10
Kar L 004	5368, 8 × 10
Kar L 006	5368, 8 × 10
Kar L 007	5367, 8 × 10
Kar L 009	5367, 8 × 10
Kar L 010	5366, 8 × 10
Kar L 011	5366, 8 × 10
Kar L 012	5366, 8 × 10
Kar L 013	5365, 8 × 10
Kar L 014	5365, 8 × 10
Kar L 015	5364, 8 × 10
Kar L 015	5365, 8 × 10
Kar L 018	5364, 8 × 10
Kar L 019	5363, 8 × 10
Kar L 021	5363, 8 × 10
Kar L 022	5362, 8 × 10
Kar L 023	5362, 8 × 10
Kar L 024	5362, 8 × 10
Kar L 025	5361, 8 × 10
Kar L 026	5361, 8 × 10
Kar L 027	5361, 8 × 10
Kar L 028	5360, 8 × 10
Kar L 029	5360, 8 × 10
Kar L 030	5360, 8 × 10
Kar L 031	5359, 8 × 10
Kar L 032	5359, 8 × 10
Kar L 033	5359, 8 × 10
Kar L 034	5358, 8 × 10
Kar L 035	5358, 8 × 10
Kar L 036	5358, 8 × 10
Kar L 037	5357, 8 × 10
Kar L 038	5357, 8 × 10
Kar L 039	5356, 8 × 10
Kar L 040	5356, 8 × 10
Kar L 041	5355, 8 × 10
Kar L 042	5355, 8 × 10
Kar L 043	5354, 8 × 10
Kar L 044	5354, 8 × 10
Kar L 045	5353, 8 × 10
Kar L 046	5353, 8 × 10
Kar L 047	5353, 8 × 10
Kar L 048	5352, 8 × 10
Kar L 049	5352, 8 × 10
Kar L 050	5352, 8 × 10
Kar L 051	5351, 8 × 10

Karnak Temple (*cont.*)

Nelson Number/Description	Negative, Format
Kar L 052	5351, 8 × 10
Kar L 053	5350, 8 × 10
Kar L 054	5350, 8 × 10
Kar L 055	5349, 8 × 10
Kar L 056	5349, 8 × 10
Kar L 057	5348, 8 × 10
Kar L 058	5348, 8 × 10
Kar L 059	5347, 8 × 10
Kar L 060	5347, 8 × 10
Kar L 061	5346, 8 × 10
Kar L 062	5346, 8 × 10
Kar L 063	5346, 8 × 10
Kar L 067	7030, 8 × 10
Kar L 067	7031, 8 × 10
Kar L 067	7032, 8 × 10
Kar L 067	7033, 8 × 10
Kar L 067	9378, 8 × 10
Kar L 067	9379, 8 × 10
Kar L 068	8586, 8 × 10
Kar L 069a	8619, 5 × 7
Kar L 069a	8620, 5 × 7
Kar L 070	8587, 8 × 10
Kar L 071	3699, 8 × 10
Kar L 073	3699, 8 × 10
Kar L 074	3699, 8 × 10
Kar L 075	3699, 8 × 10
Kar L 077	8588, 8 × 10
Kar L 080	3702, 8 × 10
Kar L 080	13567, 5 × 7
Kar L 081	3702, 8 × 10
Kar L 081	13567, 5 × 7
Kar L 084	3700, 8 × 10
Kar L 085	3701, 8 × 10
Kar L 086	5176, 8 × 10
Kar L 088	8569, 8 × 10
Kar L 111	7142, 8 × 10
Kar L 112	7136, 8 × 10
Kar L 113	7135, 8 × 10
Kar L 114	7137, 8 × 10
Kar L 115	7139, 8 × 10
Kar L 116	7140, 8 × 10
Kar L 117	7141, 8 × 10
Kar L 118	7143, 8 × 10
Kar L 119	7138, 8 × 10
Kar L 125	7091, 5 × 7
Kar L 125	8365, 5 × 7
Kar L 125	8369, 5 × 7
Kar L 126	8340, 8 × 10
Kar L 126	8374, 5 × 7
Kar L 128	8375, 5 × 7
Kar L 129	8448, 5 × 7
Kar L 130	8449, 5 × 7
Kar L 131	8342, 8 × 10
Kar L 131a	8364, 5 × 7
Kar L 131a	8369, 5 × 7

Karnak Temple (*cont.*)

Nelson Number/Description	Negative, Format
Kar L 131b	8374, 5 × 7
Kar L 132	8342, 8 × 10
Kar L 133	8446, 5 × 7
Kar L 134	8446, 5 × 7
Kar L 135	8338, 8 × 10
Kar L 136	8338, 8 × 10
Kar L 137	8338, 8 × 10
Kar L 138	8338, 8 × 10
Kar L 139	7089, 5 × 7
Kar L 139	7090, 5 × 7
Kar L 140	7089, 5 × 7
Kar L 140	7092, 5 × 7
Kar L 141	8366, 5 × 7
Kar L 141	8367, 5 × 7
Kar L 142	7066, 8 × 10
Kar L 143	6936, 8 × 10
Kar L 144	6936, 8 × 10
Kar L 145	6936, 8 × 10
Kar L 146	6936, 8 × 10
Kar L 147	8339, 8 × 10
Kar L 148	8339, 8 × 10
Kar L 149	8339, 8 × 10
Kar L 150	7065, 8 × 10
Kar L 150a	7065, 8 × 10
Kar L 151	7065, 8 × 10
Kar L 152	6935, 8 × 10
Kar L 153	6935, 8 × 10
Kar L 154a	8363, 5 × 7
Kar L 154b	8362, 5 × 7
Kar L 155	8337, 8 × 10
Kar L 156	8337, 8 × 10
Kar L 157	8368, 5 × 7
Kar L 158	8368, 5 × 7
Kar L 159	8360, 5 × 7
Kar L 160	8445, 5 × 7
Kar L 161	8361, 5 × 7
Kar L 162	8361, 5 × 7
Kar L 163	8361, 5 × 7
Kar N 151	8590, 8 × 10
Kar N 154	8591, 8 × 10
Kar N 154	8592, 8 × 10
Kar N 154	8593, 8 × 10
Kar N 155	8591, 8 × 10
Kar N 155	8592, 8 × 10
Kar N 155	8593, 8 × 10
Kar N 156	8591, 8 × 10
Kar N 156	8592, 8 × 10
Kar N 156	8593, 8 × 10
Kar N 160	8632, 8 × 10
Kar N 161	8610, 5 × 7
Kar N 161	8611, 5 × 7
Kar N 161	8612, 5 × 7
Kar N 161	8613, 5 × 7
Kar N 162	8610, 5 × 7
Kar N 162	8611, 5 × 7

Karnak Temple (*cont.*)

Nelson Number/Description	Negative, Format
Kar N 162	8612, 5 × 7
Kar N 162	8613, 5 × 7
Kar N 163	8610, 5 × 7
Kar N 163	8611, 5 × 7
Kar N 163	8612, 5 × 7
Kar N 163	8613, 5 × 7
Kar N 170	8594, 8 × 10
Kar N 171	8594, 8 × 10
Kar N 172	8594, 8 × 10
Kar N 173	8596, 8 × 10
Kar N 174	8596, 8 × 10
Kar N 175	8597, 8 × 10
Kar N 176	8597, 8 × 10
Kar N 177	8598, 8 × 10
Kar N 178	8598, 8 × 10
Kar N 179	8594, 8 × 10
Kar N 179	8599, 8 × 10
Kar N 180	8594, 8 × 10
Kar N 180	8599, 8 × 10
Kar N 181	8600, 8 × 10
Kar N 182	8600, 8 × 10
Kar N 183	8596, 8 × 10
Kar N 183	8597, 8 × 10
Kar N 183	8598, 8 × 10
Kar N 183	8599, 8 × 10
Kar N 183	8600, 8 × 10
Kar N 185	8601, 8 × 10
Kar N 185	8602, 8 × 10
Kar N 185	8603, 8 × 10
Kar N 185	8604, 8 × 10
Kar N 185	8614, 5 × 7
Kar N 186	8601, 8 × 10
Kar N 186	8602, 8 × 10
Kar N 186	8603, 8 × 10
Kar N 186	8604, 8 × 10
Kar N 186	8614, 5 × 7
Kar N 187	8601, 8 × 10
Kar N 187	8602, 8 × 10
Kar N 187	8603, 8 × 10
Kar N 187	8604, 8 × 10
Kar N 187	8614, 5 × 7
Kar N 190	8605, 8 × 10
Kar N 192	8606, 8 × 10
Kar N 192	8607, 8 × 10
Kar N 193	8606, 8 × 10
Kar N 193	8607, 8 × 10
Kar N 194	8606, 8 × 10
Kar N 194	8607, 8 × 10
Kar N 195	8608, 8 × 10
Kar N 195	8609, 8 × 10
Kar N 195a	8608, 8 × 10
Kar N 195a	8609, 8 × 10
Kar N 196	8608, 8 × 10
Kar N 196	8609, 8 × 10
Kar O 001	11075, 5 × 7

Karnak Temple (*cont.*)

Nelson Number/Description	Negative, Format
Kar O 001	11081, 5 × 7
Kar O 002	11076, 5 × 7
Kar O 002	11082, 5 × 7
Kar O 003	11077, 5 × 7
Kar O 004	11078, 5 × 7
Kar O 005	11079, 5 × 7
Kar O 005	11214, 5 × 7
Kar O 006	11080, 5 × 7
Kar O 029	8808, 8 × 10
Kar O 030	8809, 8 × 10
Kar O 031	5747, 8 × 10
Kar O 032	5748, 8 × 10
Kar O 033	5749, 8 × 10
Kar O 034	5750, 8 × 10
Kar O 035	5751, 8 × 10
Kar O 036	5728, 8 × 10
Kar O 037	5729, 8 × 10
Kar O 038	5730, 8 × 10
Kar O 039	5762, 8 × 10
Kar O 040	5724, 8 × 10
Kar O 041	5725, 8 × 10
Kar O 042	5726, 8 × 10
Kar O 043	5727, 8 × 10
Kar O 044	5746, 8 × 10
Kar O 044	13451, 5 × 7
Kar O 045	5752, 8 × 10
Kar O 046	8810, 8 × 10
Kar O 047	8807, 8 × 10
Kar O 048	8807, 8 × 10
Kar O 049	8811, 8 × 10
Kar O 050	8812, 8 × 10
Kar O 051	8811, 8 × 10
Kar O 052	8025, 8 × 10
Kar O 053	5218, 8 × 10
Kar O 054	8034, 8 × 10
Kar O 055	9082, 8 × 10
Kar O 056	9082, 8 × 10
Kar O 057	8025, 8 × 10
Kar O 058	8034, 8 × 10
Kar O 059	9082, 8 × 10
Kar O 060	9082, 8 × 10
Kar O 060	9083, 8 × 10
Kar O 061	9083, 8 × 10
Kar O 063	6195, 8 × 10
Kar O 064	8530, 8 × 10
Kar O 064	8531, 8 × 10
Kar O 065	8532, 8 × 10
Kar O 066	8533, 8 × 10
Kar O 066	8534, 8 × 10
Kar O 067	8534, 8 × 10
Kar O 067	8535, 8 × 10
Kar O 067	8536, 8 × 10
Kar O 068	8536, 8 × 10
Kar O 068	8537, 8 × 10
Kar O 069	3089, 8 × 10

Karnak Temple (*cont.*)

Nelson Number/Description	Negative, Format
Kar O 069	3090, 8 × 10
Kar O 069	3091, 8 × 10
Kar O 069	3092, 8 × 10
Kar O 069	3093, 8 × 10
Kar O 070	8538, 8 × 10
Kar O 070	8539, 8 × 10
Kar O 070	8736, 8 × 10
Kar O 074	13405, 5 × 7
Kar O 076	6206, 8 × 10
Kar O 076	13405, 5 × 7
Kar O 076E	8426, 5 × 7
Kar O 076W	8427, 5 × 7
Kar O 076W	8428, 5 × 7
Kar O 102	8744, 8 × 10
Kar O 102	8745, 8 × 10
Kar O 107	3448, 8 × 10
Kar O 108	3448, 8 × 10
Kar O 125	8336, 8 × 10
Kar O 126	8330, 8 × 10
Kar O 127	8330, 8 × 10
Kar O 128	8332, 8 × 10
Kar O 129	8328, 8 × 10
Kar O 130	8327, 8 × 10
Kar O 134	8331, 8 × 10
Kar O 135	8343, 8 × 10
Kar O 136	8344, 8 × 10
Kar O 137	8341, 8 × 10
Kar O 138	8341, 8 × 10
Kar O 139	8329, 8 × 10
Aerial photograph	10811, 5 × 7
Aerial photograph: Royal Air Force	11547, 8 × 10
Akoris Chapel: east wall, east face	11212, 5 × 7
Akoris Chapel: general view	11073, 5 × 7
Akoris Chapel: north doorway, east outer wall	11083, 5 × 7
Akoris Chapel: north wall, north face	11213, 5 × 7
Akoris Chapel: south wall and graffiti	11074, 5 × 7
Blocks of sanctuary of Hatshepsut	6553, 5 × 7
Blocks of sanctuary of Hatshepsut	6554, 5 × 7
Blocks of sanctuary of Hatshepsut	6555, 5 × 7
Blocks of sanctuary of Hatshepsut	6556, 5 × 7
Blocks of sanctuary of Hatshepsut	6557, 5 × 7
Blocks of sanctuary of Hatshepsut	6558, 5 × 7
Blocks of sanctuary of Hatshepsut	6559, 5 × 7
Blocks of sanctuary of Hatshepsut	6560, 5 × 7
Blocks of sanctuary of Hatshepsut	6561, 5 × 7
Blocks of sanctuary of Hatshepsut	6562, 5 × 7
Blocks of sanctuary of Hatshepsut	6563, 5 × 7
Blocks of sanctuary of Hatshepsut	6564, 5 × 7
Blocks of sanctuary of Hatshepsut	6565, 5 × 7
Blocks of sanctuary of Hatshepsut	6566, 5 × 7
Blocks of sanctuary of Hatshepsut	6567, 5 × 7
Blocks of sanctuary of Hatshepsut	6568, 5 × 7
Blocks of sanctuary of Hatshepsut	6569, 5 × 7
Blocks of sanctuary of Hatshepsut	6570, 5 × 7
Blocks of sanctuary of Hatshepsut	6571, 5 × 7

Karnak Temple (*cont.*)

Nelson Number/Description	Negative, Format
Blocks of sanctuary of Hatshepsut	6572, 5 × 7
Blocks of sanctuary of Hatshepsut	6573, 5 × 7
Blocks of sanctuary of Hatshepsut	6574, 5 × 7
Blocks of sanctuary of Hatshepsut	6575, 5 × 7
Blocks of sanctuary of Hatshepsut	6576, 5 × 7
Blocks of sanctuary of Hatshepsut	6577, 5 × 7
Blocks of sanctuary of Hatshepsut	6578, 5 × 7
Blocks of sanctuary of Hatshepsut	6579, 5 × 7
Blocks of sanctuary of Hatshepsut	6580, 5 × 7
Blocks of sanctuary of Hatshepsut	6581, 5 × 7
Blocks of sanctuary of Hatshepsut	6582, 5 × 7
Blocks of sanctuary of Hatshepsut	6583, 5 × 7
Blocks of sanctuary of Hatshepsut	6584, 5 × 7
Blocks of sanctuary of Hatshepsut	6585, 5 × 7
Blocks of sanctuary of Hatshepsut	6586, 5 × 7
Blocks of sanctuary of Hatshepsut	6587, 5 × 7
Blocks of sanctuary of Hatshepsut	6588, 5 × 7
Blocks of sanctuary of Hatshepsut	6589, 5 × 7
Blocks of sanctuary of Hatshepsut	6590, 5 × 7
Blocks of sanctuary of Hatshepsut	6591, 5 × 7
Blocks of sanctuary of Hatshepsut	6615, 5 × 7
Blocks of sanctuary of Hatshepsut	6616, 5 × 7
Blocks of sanctuary of Hatshepsut	6617, 5 × 7
Blocks of sanctuary of Hatshepsut	6618, 5 × 7
Blocks of sanctuary of Hatshepsut	6619, 5 × 7
Blocks of sanctuary of Hatshepsut	6620, 5 × 7
Blocks of sanctuary of Hatshepsut	6621, 5 × 7
Blocks of sanctuary of Hatshepsut	6622, 5 × 7
Blocks of sanctuary of Hatshepsut	6623, 5 × 7
Blocks of sanctuary of Hatshepsut	6624, 5 × 7
Blocks of sanctuary of Hatshepsut	6625, 5 × 7
Blocks of sanctuary of Hatshepsut	6626, 5 × 7
Blocks of sanctuary of Hatshepsut	6627, 5 × 7
Blocks of sanctuary of Hatshepsut	6628, 5 × 7
Blocks of sanctuary of Hatshepsut	6629, 5 × 7
Blocks of sanctuary of Hatshepsut	6630, 5 × 7
Blocks of sanctuary of Hatshepsut	6631, 5 × 7
Blocks of sanctuary of Hatshepsut	6632, 5 × 7
Blocks of sanctuary of Hatshepsut	6633, 5 × 7
Blocks of sanctuary of Hatshepsut	6634, 5 × 7
Blocks of sanctuary of Hatshepsut	6635, 5 × 7
Blocks of sanctuary of Hatshepsut	6636, 5 × 7
Blocks of sanctuary of Hatshepsut	6637, 5 × 7
Blocks of sanctuary of Hatshepsut	6638, 5 × 7
Blocks of sanctuary of Hatshepsut	6639, 5 × 7
Blocks of sanctuary of Hatshepsut	6640, 5 × 7
Blocks of sanctuary of Hatshepsut	6641, 5 × 7
Blocks of sanctuary of Hatshepsut	6642, 5 × 7
Blocks of sanctuary of Hatshepsut	6643, 5 × 7
Blocks of sanctuary of Hatshepsut	6644, 5 × 7
Blocks of sanctuary of Hatshepsut	6645, 5 × 7
Blocks of sanctuary of Hatshepsut	6646, 5 × 7
Blocks of sanctuary of Hatshepsut	6647, 5 × 7
Blocks of sanctuary of Hatshepsut	6648, 5 × 7
Blocks of sanctuary of Hatshepsut	6649, 5 × 7

Karnak Temple (*cont.*)

Nelson Number/Description	Negative, Format
Blocks of sanctuary of Hatshepsut	6650, 5 × 7
Blocks of sanctuary of Hatshepsut	6651, 5 × 7
Blocks of sanctuary of Hatshepsut	6652, 5 × 7
Blocks of sanctuary of Hatshepsut	6653, 5 × 7
Blocks of sanctuary of Hatshepsut	6654, 5 × 7
Blocks of sanctuary of Hatshepsut	6655, 5 × 7
Blocks of sanctuary of Hatshepsut	6656, 5 × 7
Blocks of sanctuary of Hatshepsut	6657, 5 × 7
Blocks of sanctuary of Hatshepsut	6658, 5 × 7
Blocks of sanctuary of Hatshepsut	6659, 5 × 7
Blocks of sanctuary of Hatshepsut	6660, 5 × 7
Blocks of sanctuary of Hatshepsut	6661, 5 × 7
Blocks of sanctuary of Hatshepsut	6662, 5 × 7
Blocks of sanctuary of Hatshepsut	6663, 5 × 7
Blocks of sanctuary of Hatshepsut	6664, 5 × 7
Blocks of sanctuary of Hatshepsut	6665, 5 × 7
Blocks of sanctuary of Hatshepsut	6666, 5 × 7
Blocks of sanctuary of Hatshepsut	6667, 5 × 7
Blocks of sanctuary of Hatshepsut	6683, 5 × 7
Blocks of sanctuary of Hatshepsut	6684, 5 × 7
Blocks of sanctuary of Hatshepsut	6685, 5 × 7
Blocks of sanctuary of Hatshepsut	6686, 5 × 7
Blocks of sanctuary of Hatshepsut	6687, 5 × 7
Blocks of sanctuary of Hatshepsut	6688, 5 × 7
Blocks of sanctuary of Hatshepsut	6689, 5 × 7
Blocks of sanctuary of Hatshepsut	6690, 5 × 7
Blocks of sanctuary of Hatshepsut	6691, 5 × 7
Blocks of sanctuary of Hatshepsut	6692, 5 × 7
Blocks of sanctuary of Hatshepsut	6693, 5 × 7
Blocks of sanctuary of Hatshepsut	6694, 5 × 7
Blocks of sanctuary of Hatshepsut	6695, 5 × 7
Blocks of sanctuary of Hatshepsut	6696, 5 × 7
Blocks of sanctuary of Hatshepsut	6697, 5 × 7
Blocks of sanctuary of Hatshepsut	6698, 5 × 7
Blocks of sanctuary of Hatshepsut	6699, 5 × 7
Blocks of sanctuary of Hatshepsut	6700, 5 × 7
Blocks of sanctuary of Hatshepsut	6701, 5 × 7
Blocks of sanctuary of Hatshepsut	6702, 5 × 7
Blocks of sanctuary of Hatshepsut	6703, 5 × 7
Blocks of sanctuary of Hatshepsut	6704, 5 × 7
Blocks of sanctuary of Hatshepsut	6705, 5 × 7
Blocks of sanctuary of Hatshepsut	6706, 5 × 7
Blocks of sanctuary of Hatshepsut	6707, 5 × 7
Blocks of sanctuary of Hatshepsut	6708, 5 × 7
Blocks of sanctuary of Hatshepsut	6709, 5 × 7
Blocks of sanctuary of Hatshepsut	6710, 5 × 7
Blocks of sanctuary of Hatshepsut	6711, 5 × 7
Blocks of sanctuary of Hatshepsut	6712, 5 × 7
Blocks of sanctuary of Hatshepsut	6713, 5 × 7
Blocks of sanctuary of Hatshepsut	6714, 5 × 7
Blocks of sanctuary of Hatshepsut	6715, 5 × 7
Blocks of sanctuary of Hatshepsut	6716, 5 × 7
Blocks of sanctuary of Hatshepsut	6717, 5 × 7
Blocks of sanctuary of Hatshepsut	6718, 5 × 7
Blocks of sanctuary of Hatshepsut	6719, 5 × 7

Karnak Temple (*cont.*)

Nelson Number/Description	Negative, Format
Blocks of sanctuary of Hatshepsut	6720, 5 × 7
Blocks of sanctuary of Hatshepsut	6721, 5 × 7
Blocks of sanctuary of Hatshepsut	6722, 5 × 7
Blocks of sanctuary of Hatshepsut	6723, 5 × 7
Blocks of sanctuary of Hatshepsut	6724, 5 × 7
Blocks of sanctuary of Hatshepsut	6725, 5 × 7
Blocks of sanctuary of Hatshepsut	6726, 5 × 7
Blocks of sanctuary of Hatshepsut	6727, 5 × 7
Blocks of sanctuary of Hatshepsut	6728, 5 × 7
Blocks of sanctuary of Hatshepsut	6729, 5 × 7
Blocks of sanctuary of Hatshepsut	6730, 5 × 7
Blocks of sanctuary of Hatshepsut	6731, 5 × 7
Blocks of sanctuary of Hatshepsut	6732, 5 × 7
Blocks of sanctuary of Hatshepsut	6733, 5 × 7
Blocks of sanctuary of Hatshepsut	6734, 5 × 7
Blocks of sanctuary of Hatshepsut	6735, 5 × 7
Blocks of sanctuary of Hatshepsut	6736, 5 × 7
Blocks of sanctuary of Hatshepsut	6737, 5 × 7
Blocks of sanctuary of Hatshepsut	6738, 5 × 7
Blocks of sanctuary of Hatshepsut	6739, 5 × 7
Blocks of sanctuary of Hatshepsut	6740, 5 × 7
Blocks of sanctuary of Hatshepsut	6741, 5 × 7
Blocks of sanctuary of Hatshepsut	6742, 5 × 7
Blocks of sanctuary of Hatshepsut	6743, 5 × 7
Blocks of sanctuary of Hatshepsut	6744, 5 × 7
Blocks of sanctuary of Hatshepsut	6745, 5 × 7
Blocks of sanctuary of Hatshepsut	6746, 5 × 7
Blocks of sanctuary of Hatshepsut	6747, 5 × 7
Blocks of sanctuary of Hatshepsut	6748, 5 × 7
Blocks of sanctuary of Hatshepsut	6749, 5 × 7
Blocks of sanctuary of Hatshepsut	6750, 5 × 7
Blocks of sanctuary of Hatshepsut	6751, 5 × 7
Blocks of sanctuary of Hatshepsut	6752, 5 × 7
Blocks of sanctuary of Hatshepsut	6753, 5 × 7
Blocks of sanctuary of Hatshepsut	6754, 5 × 7
Blocks of sanctuary of Hatshepsut	6755, 5 × 7
Blocks of sanctuary of Hatshepsut	6756, 5 × 7
Blocks of sanctuary of Hatshepsut	6757, 5 × 7
Blocks of sanctuary of Hatshepsut	6758, 5 × 7
Blocks of sanctuary of Hatshepsut	6759, 5 × 7
Blocks of sanctuary of Hatshepsut	7095, 5 × 7
Blocks of sanctuary of Hatshepsut	7096, 5 × 7
Blocks of sanctuary of Hatshepsut	7097, 5 × 7
Blocks of sanctuary of Hatshepsut	7098, 5 × 7
Blocks of sanctuary of Hatshepsut	7099, 5 × 7
Blocks of sanctuary of Hatshepsut	7100, 5 × 7
Blocks of sanctuary of Hatshepsut	7101, 5 × 7
Blocks of sanctuary of Hatshepsut	7102, 5 × 7
Blocks of sanctuary of Hatshepsut	7103, 5 × 7
Blocks of sanctuary of Hatshepsut	7104, 5 × 7
Blocks of sanctuary of Hatshepsut	7105, 5 × 7
Blocks of sanctuary of Hatshepsut	7106, 5 × 7
Blocks of sanctuary of Hatshepsut	7107, 5 × 7
Blocks of sanctuary of Hatshepsut	7108, 5 × 7
Blocks of sanctuary of Hatshepsut	7109, 5 × 7

Karnak Temple (*cont.*)

Nelson Number/Description	Negative, Format
Blocks of sanctuary of Hatshepsut	7110, 5 × 7
Blocks of sanctuary of Hatshepsut	7111, 5 × 7
Blocks of sanctuary of Hatshepsut	7112, 5 × 7
Blocks of sanctuary of Hatshepsut	7113, 5 × 7
Blocks of sanctuary of Hatshepsut	7114, 5 × 7
Blocks of sanctuary of Hatshepsut	7115, 5 × 7
Blocks of sanctuary of Hatshepsut	7116, 5 × 7
Blocks of sanctuary of Hatshepsut	7117, 5 × 7
Blocks of sanctuary of Hatshepsut	7118, 5 × 7
Blocks of sanctuary of Hatshepsut	7119, 5 × 7
Blocks of sanctuary of Hatshepsut	7120, 5 × 7
Blocks of sanctuary of Hatshepsut	7121, 5 × 7
Blocks of sanctuary of Hatshepsut	7122, 5 × 7
Blocks of sanctuary of Hatshepsut	7123, 5 × 7
Blocks of sanctuary of Hatshepsut	7124, 5 × 7
Blocks of sanctuary of Hatshepsut	7125, 5 × 7
Blocks of sanctuary of Hatshepsut	7126, 5 × 7
Blocks of sanctuary of Hatshepsut	7127, 5 × 7
Blocks of sanctuary of Hatshepsut	7128, 5 × 7
Blocks of sanctuary of Hatshepsut	7129, 5 × 7
Blocks of sanctuary of Hatshepsut	7130, 5 × 7
Columns: Karnak	3725, 8 × 10
East/west axis from Pylon I, before alabaster altar replaced in Taharqa Kiosk	13166, 5 × 7
General view	3212, 8 × 10
General view	5143, 11 × 14
General view	5693, 8 × 10
General view	5694, 8 × 10
General view	5703, 8 × 10
General view: Ramesses III Temple	5144, 11 × 14
General view: sphinxes between Pylon X and Mut Area	10268, 5 × 7
General view: sphinxes between Pylon X and Mut Area	10269, 5 × 7
General view: Temple of Karnak, Avenue of Sphinxes	5897, 8 × 10
Hatshepsut block	10267, 5 × 7
Hypostyle Hall	13559, 5 × 7
Hypostyle Hall: toward south along transverse axis, column 52 leaning (renumbered as 13378 variant)	13380, 5 × 7
Hypostyle Hall: photograph montage of west wall, south half	13231, 8 × 10
Kar B blocks	9769, 5 × 7
Kar B blocks	9770, 5 × 7
Kar B blocks	9774, 5 × 7
Kar B blocks	9775, 5 × 7
Kar B blocks	9776, 5 × 7
Kar B blocks	9777, 5 × 7
Kar B blocks	9778, 5 × 7
Kar B blocks	9779, 5 × 7
Kar B blocks	9780, 5 × 7
Kar B blocks	9781, 5 × 7
Kar B blocks	9782, 5 × 7
Kar B blocks	9783, 5 × 7
Kar B blocks	9784, 5 × 7
Kar B blocks	9785, 5 × 7

Karnak Temple (*cont.*)

Nelson Number/Description	Negative, Format
Kar B blocks	9786, 5 × 7
Kar B blocks	9787, 5 × 7
Kar B blocks	9788, 5 × 7
Kar B blocks	9789, 5 × 7
Kar B blocks	9805, 8 × 10
Kar B blocks	9885, 5 × 7
Kar B blocks	10435, 5 × 7
Kar C block	8520, 8 × 10
Kar C block	9887, 5 × 7
Kar D block	8509, 8 × 10
Kar D block	8510, 5 × 7
Kar D block	8511, 5 × 7
Kar D block	8522, 8 × 10
Kar D block	8547, 5 × 7
Kar D block	8580, 8 × 10
Kar D block	8581, 8 × 10
Kar D block: Thutmosis III annals	8512, 5 × 7
Kar D block: Thutmosis III annals	8513, 5 × 7
Kar D block: Thutmosis III annals	8514, 5 × 7
Kar D block: Thutmosis III annals	8515, 5 × 7
Kar D block: Thutmosis III annals	8516, 5 × 7
Kar D block: Thutmosis III annals	8517, 5 × 7
Kar D block: Thutmosis III annals	8518, 5 × 7
Kar D blocks	8508, 8 × 10
Kar G block	5733, 8 × 10
Kar G blocks	8528, 8 × 10
Kar G blocks	8529, 8 × 10
Kar G d blocks	5735, 8 × 10
Kar G d blocks	5736, 8 × 10
Kar H museum	7326, 8 × 10
Kar K roof 5	5565, 5 × 7
Kar K roof 6	5642, 8 × 10
Kar K stone	3088, 5 × 7
Kar L block	8527, 8 × 10
Kar L block	9356, 5 × 7
Loose block from central shrine of Thutmosis III	11322, 5 × 7
Loose block from central shrine of Thutmosis III	11323, 5 × 7
Loose blocks	10436, 5 × 7
Map	5231, 8 × 10
Mut Temple stone	5731, 8 × 10
Mut Temple stone	5738, 8 × 10?
Open-air museum, blocks of Amenhotep I	10032, 5 × 7
Plan	510, 8 × 10
Ptah Temple	13626, 5 × 7
Ptah Temple: block	6349, 8 × 10
Ptah Temple: block	6350, 8 × 10
Pylon I	10150, 5 × 7
Pylon I	10151, 5 × 7
Pylon II, general view	11208, 5 × 7
Pylon II, general view	11209, 5 × 7
Pylon II, general view	11210, 5 × 7
Sacred Lake	9888, 5 × 7
Shrine from southwest	10161, 5 × 7
Shrine from southwest	10162, 5 × 7
Shrine, south side, west end, upper	10163, 5 × 7

Karnak Temple (*cont.*)

Nelson Number/Description	Negative, Format
Temenos wall	9889, 5 × 7
Temenos wall	9890, 5 × 7
Unknown	5722, 8 × 10
Unknown	6050, 8 × 10
Unknown	7703, 3.5 × 4.5

Kasr el Aguz

Nelson Number/Description	Negative, Format
Kasr el Aguz 006	8960, 8 × 10
Kasr el Aguz 008	8971, 5 × 7
Kasr el Aguz 011	8972, 5 × 7
Kasr el Aguz 013	8961, 8 × 10
Kasr el Aguz 014	8961, 8 × 10
Kasr el Aguz 015	8961, 8 × 10
Kasr el Aguz 016	8963, 8 × 10
Kasr el Aguz 017	8962, 8 × 10
Kasr el Aguz 018	8963, 8 × 10
Kasr el Aguz 032	8964, 8 × 10
Kasr el Aguz 033	8973, 5 × 7
Kasr el Aguz 034	8974, 5 × 7
Kasr el Aguz 035	8965, 8 × 10
Kasr el Aguz 036	8964, 8 × 10
Kasr el Aguz 036	8982, 5 × 7
Kasr el Aguz 036	8983, 5 × 7
Kasr el Aguz 036	8984, 5 × 7
Kasr el Aguz 036	8987, 5 × 7
Kasr el Aguz 036	8988, 5 × 7
Kasr el Aguz 036	8989, 5 × 7
Kasr el Aguz 036	8991, 5 × 7
Kasr el Aguz 036	8992, 5 × 7
Kasr el Aguz 037	8964, 8 × 10
Kasr el Aguz 037	8973, 5 × 7
Kasr el Aguz 037	8974, 5 × 7
Kasr el Aguz 037	8975, 5 × 7
Kasr el Aguz 037	8977, 5 × 7
Kasr el Aguz 037	8978, 5 × 7
Kasr el Aguz 037	8979, 5 × 7
Kasr el Aguz 037	8980, 5 × 7
Kasr el Aguz 037	8981, 5 × 7
Kasr el Aguz 038	8975, 5 × 7
Kasr el Aguz 039	8976, 5 × 7
Kasr el Aguz 040	8977, 5 × 7
Kasr el Aguz 041	8966, 8 × 10
Kasr el Aguz 042	8978, 5 × 7
Kasr el Aguz 043	8965, 8 × 10
Kasr el Aguz 043	8966, 8 × 10
Kasr el Aguz 043	8967, 8 × 10
Kasr el Aguz 043	8976, 5 × 7
Kasr el Aguz 044	8965, 8 × 10
Kasr el Aguz 044	8966, 8 × 10
Kasr el Aguz 044	8967, 8 × 10
Kasr el Aguz 044	8976, 5 × 7
Kasr el Aguz 044	8985, 5 × 7

Kasr el Aguz (*cont.*)

Nelson Number/Description	Negative, Format
Kasr el Aguz 045	8979, 5 × 7
Kasr el Aguz 046	8980, 5 × 7
Kasr el Aguz 047	8981, 5 × 7
Kasr el Aguz 048	8982, 5 × 7
Kasr el Aguz 049	8983, 5 × 7
Kasr el Aguz 050	8984, 5 × 7
Kasr el Aguz 051	8967, 8 × 10
Kasr el Aguz 052	8985, 5 × 7
Kasr el Aguz 053	8986, 5 × 7
Kasr el Aguz 054	8968, 8 × 10
Kasr el Aguz 055	8985, 5 × 7
Kasr el Aguz 056	8986, 5 × 7
Kasr el Aguz 057	8987, 5 × 7
Kasr el Aguz 059	8988, 5 × 7
Kasr el Aguz 060	8989, 5 × 7
Kasr el Aguz 062	8969, 8 × 10
Kasr el Aguz 063	8990, 5 × 7
Kasr el Aguz 064	8968, 8 × 10
Kasr el Aguz 064	8969, 8 × 10
Kasr el Aguz 064	8986, 5 × 7
Kasr el Aguz 064	8990, 5 × 7
Kasr el Aguz 064	8993, 5 × 7
Kasr el Aguz 064	8994, 5 × 7
Kasr el Aguz 065	8968, 8 × 10
Kasr el Aguz 065	8969, 8 × 10
Kasr el Aguz 065	8990, 5 × 7
Kasr el Aguz 065	8993, 5 × 7
Kasr el Aguz 065	8994, 5 × 7
Kasr el Aguz 066	8991, 5 × 7
Kasr el Aguz 067	8992, 5 × 7
Kasr el Aguz 068	8993, 5 × 7
Kasr el Aguz 069	8994, 5 × 7
Kasr el Aguz 070	8970, 8 × 10
Plan	8269, 5 × 7

Kharga Oasis

Nelson Number/Description	Negative, Format
Map	7640, 8 × 10
Map	7641, 8 × 10
Map	7642, 8 × 10

Khonsu Temple

Nelson Number/Description	Negative, Format
Kh 001a	5812, 8 × 10
Kh 001b	5812, 8 × 10
Kh 001c	3123, 8 × 10
Kh 001c	5812, 8 × 10
Kh 001d	3123, 8 × 10
Kh 001e	3123, 8 × 10
Kh 001f	3123, 8 × 10
Kh 001g	5789, 8 × 10

Khonsu Temple (*cont.*)

Nelson Number/Description	Negative, Format
Kh 001k	5789, 8 × 10
Kh 001l	5789, 8 × 10
Kh 001m	5812, 8 × 10
Kh 001n	5812, 8 × 10
Kh 001o	3123, 8 × 10
Kh 001o	5812, 8 × 10
Kh 001p	3123, 8 × 10
Kh 001q	3123, 8 × 10
Kh 001r	3123, 8 × 10
Kh 002	8379, 8 × 10
Kh 002g	5789, 8 × 10
Kh 003	8380, 8 × 10
Kh 003g	5784, 8 × 10
Kh 004	8382, 8 × 10
Kh 005	8381, 8 × 10
Kh 005g	5783, 8 × 10
Kh 007	8379, 8 × 10
Kh 007	8380, 8 × 10
Kh 008	8381, 8 × 10
Kh 008	8382, 8 × 10
Kh 009	8380, 8 × 10
Kh 010	8380, 8 × 10
Kh 011	8379, 8 × 10
Kh 012	8379, 8 × 10
Kh 013	8380, 8 × 10
Kh 014	8380, 8 × 10
Kh 015	8380, 8 × 10
Kh 016	8379, 8 × 10
Kh 017	8379, 8 × 10
Kh 018	8380, 8 × 10
Kh 019	8380, 8 × 10
Kh 020	8380, 8 × 10
Kh 021	8379, 8 × 10
Kh 022	8379, 8 × 10
Kh 023	8380, 8 × 10
Kh 024	8380, 8 × 10
Kh 025	8379, 8 × 10
Kh 025	8380, 8 × 10
Kh 026	5816, 8 × 10
Kh 027	5816, 8 × 10
Kh 028	7367, 8 × 10
Kh 029	5816, 8 × 10
Kh 030	5816, 8 × 10
Kh 031	7367, 8 × 10
Kh 036	13395, 5 × 7
Kh 044	8381, 8 × 10
Kh 045	8381, 8 × 10
Kh 045	8382, 8 × 10
Kh 046	8382, 8 × 10
Kh 047	8382, 8 × 10
Kh 048	8381, 8 × 10
Kh 049	8381, 8 × 10
Kh 050	8381, 8 × 10
Kh 050	8382, 8 × 10
Kh 051	8382, 8 × 10

Khonsu Temple (*cont.*)

Nelson Number/Description	Negative, Format
Kh 052	8382, 8 × 10
Kh 053	8381, 8 × 10
Kh 054	8381, 8 × 10
Kh 055	8381, 8 × 10
Kh 055	8382, 8 × 10
Kh 056	8382, 8 × 10
Kh 057	8382, 8 × 10
Kh 058	8381, 8 × 10
Kh 059	8381, 8 × 10
Kh 060	8381, 8 × 10
Kh 060	8382, 8 × 10
Kh 061	5786, 8 × 10
Kh 062	5786, 8 × 10
Kh 063	5795, 8 × 10
Kh 064	5786, 8 × 10
Kh 065	5786, 8 × 10
Kh 066	5795, 8 × 10
Kh 074	12019, 8 × 10
Kh 074	12112, 8 × 10
Kh 074	12133, 8 × 10
Kh 074	12144, 5 × 7
Kh 078	4042, 8 × 10
Kh 078	12293, 8 × 10
Kh 078	12294, 8 × 10
Kh 079	4042, 8 × 10
Kh 079	12145, 5 × 7
Kh 079	12293, 8 × 10
Kh 079	12294, 8 × 10
Kh 080	7398, 8 × 10
Kh 080	12131, 8 × 10
Kh 081	12093, 8 × 10
Kh 100	12007, 8 × 10
Kh 100	12203, 8 × 10
Kh 100a	11967, 8 × 10
Kh 100a	12147, 5 × 7
Kh 100a	12148, 5 × 7
Kh 100a	12149, 5 × 7
Kh 100a	12182, 8 × 10
Kh 100a	12192, 5 × 7
Kh 100a	12193, 5 × 7
Kh 100a	12295, 8 × 10
Kh 100a	12297, 8 × 10
Kh 100b	11968, 8 × 10
Kh 100b	12147, 5 × 7
Kh 100b	12148, 5 × 7
Kh 100b	12149, 5 × 7
Kh 100b	12150, 5 × 7
Kh 100b	12182, 8 × 10
Kh 100b	12192, 5 × 7
Kh 100b	12193, 5 × 7
Kh 100b	12296, 8 × 10
Kh 100b	12297, 8 × 10
Kh 100c	11968, 8 × 10
Kh 100c	11969, 8 × 10
Kh 100c	12182, 8 × 10

Khonsu Temple (*cont.*)

Nelson Number/Description	Negative, Format
Kh 100c	12192, 5 × 7
Kh 100c	12193, 5 × 7
Kh 100c	12200, 8 × 10
Kh 100d	11969, 8 × 10
Kh 100d	11970, 8 × 10
Kh 100d	12182, 8 × 10
Kh 100d	12192, 5 × 7
Kh 100d	12193, 5 × 7
Kh 100d	12201, 8 × 10
Kh 100e	12137, 8 × 10
Kh 100e	12182, 8 × 10
Kh 100e	12192, 5 × 7
Kh 100e	12193, 5 × 7
Kh 100f	11970, 8 × 10
Kh 100f	11971, 8 × 10
Kh 100f	12113, 8 × 10
Kh 100f	12182, 8 × 10
Kh 100f	12192, 5 × 7
Kh 100f	12193, 5 × 7
Kh 100g	12113, 8 × 10
Kh 100g	12182, 8 × 10
Kh 100g	12192, 5 × 7
Kh 100g	12193, 5 × 7
Kh 100h	7356, 8 × 10
Kh 100h	11967, 8 × 10
Kh 100h	12146, 5 × 7
Kh 100h	12182, 8 × 10
Kh 100h	12192, 5 × 7
Kh 100h	12193, 5 × 7
Kh 100h	12295, 8 × 10
Kh 100h	12297, 8 × 10
Kh 100i	11971, 8 × 10
Kh 100i	12097, 8 × 10
Kh 100j	12095, 8 × 10
Kh 100j	12203, 8 × 10
Kh 100k	11972, 8 × 10
Kh 100k	12096, 8 × 10
Kh 100l	7356, 8 × 10
Kh 100l	11972, 8 × 10
Kh 100l	11973, 8 × 10
Kh 100m	11973, 8 × 10
Kh 100m	12056, 8 × 10
Kh 100n	7356, 8 × 10
Kh 100n	12056, 8 × 10
Kh 100o	12056, 8 × 10
Kh 100o	12094, 8 × 10
Kh 100o	12095, 8 × 10
Kh 100o	12096, 8 × 10
Kh 100o	12097, 8 × 10
Kh 100p	12113, 8 × 10
Kh 100p	12137, 8 × 10
Kh 100p	12200, 8 × 10
Kh 100p	12201, 8 × 10
Kh 101	7356, 8 × 10
Kh 101	12057, 8 × 10

Khonsu Temple (*cont.*)

Nelson Number/Description	Negative, Format
Kh 101	12124, 8 × 10
Kh 101	12202, 8 × 10
Kh 101i	12094, 8 × 10
Kh 102	7356, 8 × 10
Kh 102a	11971, 8 × 10
Kh 102a	12094, 8 × 10
Kh 102b	11971, 8 × 10
Kh 102b	12095, 8 × 10
Kh 102b	12203, 8 × 10
Kh 102c	11972, 8 × 10
Kh 102c	12096, 8 × 10
Kh 102d	11972, 8 × 10
Kh 102d	12097, 8 × 10
Kh 102e	11973, 8 × 10
Kh 102e	12056, 8 × 10
Kh 102f	11973, 8 × 10
Kh 102f	12056, 8 × 10
Kh 103	12058, 8 × 10
Kh 103	12114, 8 × 10
Kh 103	12148, 5 × 7
Kh 103	12149, 5 × 7
Kh 103	12204, 8 × 10
Kh 104a	11968, 8 × 10
Kh 104a	12148, 5 × 7
Kh 104a	12149, 5 × 7
Kh 104a	12150, 5 × 7
Kh 104a	12296, 8 × 10
Kh 104a	12297, 8 × 10
Kh 104b	11968, 8 × 10
Kh 104b	12200, 8 × 10
Kh 104c	11969, 8 × 10
Kh 104c	12201, 8 × 10
Kh 104d	11969, 8 × 10
Kh 104d	12137, 8 × 10
Kh 104e	11970, 8 × 10
Kh 104e	12113, 8 × 10
Kh 104f	11970, 8 × 10
Kh 104f	12113, 8 × 10
Kh 106	12025, 8 × 10
Kh 106	12026, 8 × 10
Kh 106	12205, 8 × 10
Kh 106b	7392, 8 × 10
Kh 106b	12134, 8 × 10
Kh 106c	12013, 8 × 10
Kh 106c	12027, 8 × 10
Kh 106c	12151, 5 × 7
Kh 106c	12152, 5 × 7
Kh 106c	12206, 8 × 10
Kh 107	12024, 8 × 10
Kh 107	12025, 8 × 10
Kh 107	12128, 8 × 10
Kh 107b	7390, 8 × 10
Kh 107b	12028, 8 × 10
Kh 107b	12153, 5 × 7
Kh 107b	12154, 5 × 7

Khonsu Temple (*cont.*)

Nelson Number/Description	Negative, Format
Kh 107b	12155, 5 × 7
Kh 107b	12207, 8 × 10
Kh 107c	12154, 5 × 7
Kh 107c	12155, 5 × 7
Kh 107c	12156, 5 × 7
Kh 107c	12157, 5 × 7
Kh 107c	12158, 5 × 7
Kh 107c	12160, 5 × 7
Kh 107c	12207, 8 × 10
Kh 108	12020, 8 × 10
Kh 108	12021, 8 × 10
Kh 108	12135, 8 × 10
Kh 108b	7392, 8 × 10
Kh 108b	12298, 8 × 10
Kh 108c	12027, 8 × 10
Kh 108c	12125, 8 × 10
Kh 109	12022, 8 × 10
Kh 109	12023, 8 × 10
Kh 109a	12299, 8 × 10
Kh 109b	7390, 8 × 10
Kh 109b	12159, 5 × 7
Kh 109b	12160, 5 × 7
Kh 109b	12161, 5 × 7
Kh 109b	12162, 5 × 7
Kh 109b	12115, 8 × 10
Kh 109c	12300, 8 × 10
Kh 110	6792, 8 × 10
Kh 111	6792, 8 × 10
Kh 111	12073, 8 × 10
Kh 112	6793, 8 × 10
Kh 112	12074, 8 × 10
Kh 113	6793, 8 × 10
Kh 113	12075, 8 × 10
Kh 114	6793, 8 × 10
Kh 114	12076, 8 × 10
Kh 115	6793, 8 × 10
Kh 115	12076, 8 × 10
Kh 116	6791, 8 × 10
Kh 116	12077, 8 × 10
Kh 117	6791, 8 × 10
Kh 117	12078, 8 × 10
Kh 118	6790, 8 × 10
Kh 118	12079, 8 × 10
Kh 119	6790, 8 × 10
Kh 119	11946, 8 × 10
Kh 119	12080, 8 × 10
Kh 120	6790, 8 × 10
Kh 120	12081, 8 × 10
Kh 121	6790, 8 × 10
Kh 121	12081, 8 × 10
Kh 126	6785, 8 × 10
Kh 126	11932, 8 × 10
Kh 127	6785, 8 × 10
Kh 127	11933, 8 × 10
Kh 128	6786, 8 × 10

Khonsu Temple (*cont.*)

Nelson Number/Description	Negative, Format
Kh 128	11934, 8 × 10
Kh 129	6786, 8 × 10
Kh 129	6787, 8 × 10
Kh 129	11935, 8 × 10
Kh 130	6787, 8 × 10
Kh 130	6788, 8 × 10
Kh 130	11936, 8 × 10
Kh 131	6788, 8 × 10
Kh 131	11937, 8 × 10
Kh 132	6789, 8 × 10
Kh 132	11938, 8 × 10
Kh 133	6780, 8 × 10
Kh 133	8045, 8 × 10
Kh 134	6780, 8 × 10
Kh 134	6781, 8 × 10
Kh 134	8045, 8 × 10
Kh 135	6781, 8 × 10
Kh 135	8046, 8 × 10
Kh 136	6782, 8 × 10
Kh 136	8046, 8 × 10
Kh 137	6784, 8 × 10
Kh 137a	6783, 8 × 10
Kh 137a	7052, 8 × 10
Kh 137b	7052, 8 × 10
Kh 138	6784, 8 × 10
Kh 138	7055, 8 × 10
Kh 139	6789, 8 × 10
Kh 139	7055, 8 × 10
Kh 140	3697, 8 × 10
Kh 140	4006, 8 × 10
Kh 140a	7056, 8 × 10
Kh 140b	7056, 8 × 10
Kh 141	4007, 8 × 10
Kh 141	7057, 8 × 10
Kh 142	4022, 8 × 10
Kh 142	12046, 8 × 10
Kh 143	4022, 8 × 10
Kh 143	12046, 8 × 10
Kh 144	4022, 8 × 10
Kh 144	12046, 8 × 10
Kh 145	3422, 8 × 10
Kh 145	3997, 8 × 10
Kh 146	3457, 8 × 10
Kh 146	3458, 8 × 10
Kh 146	6677, 8 × 10
Kh 147	3648, 8 × 10
Kh 147	12047, 8 × 10
Kh 148	3648, 8 × 10
Kh 148	12047, 8 × 10
Kh 149	3648, 8 × 10
Kh 149	12047, 8 × 10
Kh 152	7053, 8 × 10
Kh 153	7053, 8 × 10
Kh 153	7696, 8 × 10
Kh 153	7697, 8 × 10

Khonsu Temple (*cont.*)

Nelson Number/Description	Negative, Format
Kh 154	6798, 8 × 10
Kh 154	12082, 8 × 10
Kh 155	12046, 8 × 10
Kh 164	6779, 8 × 10
Kh 164	11907, 8 × 10
Kh 165	8575, 8 × 10
Kh 165	11908, 8 × 10
Kh 166	8576, 8 × 10
Kh 166	8577, 8 × 10
Kh 166	11909, 8 × 10
Kh 167	4005, 8 × 10
Kh 167	4025, 8 × 10
Kh 167b	7059, 8 × 10
Kh 168	4025, 8 × 10
Kh 168	4026, 8 × 10
Kh 168a	7058, 8 × 10
Kh 168b	7058, 8 × 10
Kh 169	3559, 8 × 10
Kh 169	7133, 8 × 10
Kh 170	3560, 8 × 10
Kh 170	3561, 8 × 10
Kh 170	7133, 8 × 10
Kh 171	3561, 8 × 10
Kh 172	3561, 8 × 10
Kh 172	6776, 8 × 10
Kh 172	6859, 8 × 10
Kh 172	6880, 5 × 7
Kh 172	6881, 5 × 7
Kh 172	12098, 8 × 10
Kh 175	12138, 8 × 10
Kh 176	6795, 8 × 10
Kh 177	6795, 8 × 10
Kh 177	12083, 8 × 10
Kh 178	6794, 8 × 10
Kh 178	12084, 8 × 10
Kh 179	6794, 8 × 10
Kh 179	12085, 8 × 10
Kh 180	6794, 8 × 10
Kh 180	12086, 8 × 10
Kh 181	6794, 8 × 10
Kh 181	12086, 8 × 10
Kh 182	6797, 8 × 10
Kh 183	6797, 8 × 10
Kh 183	12087, 8 × 10
Kh 184	6796, 8 × 10
Kh 184	12054, 8 × 10
Kh 185	6796, 8 × 10
Kh 185	12050, 8 × 10
Kh 186	6796, 8 × 10
Kh 186	12038, 8 × 10
Kh 186	12045, 8 × 10
Kh 187	6796, 8 × 10
Kh 187	12038, 8 × 10
Kh 187	12045, 8 × 10
Kh 192	6760, 8 × 10

Khonsu Temple (*cont.*)

Nelson Number/Description	Negative, Format
Kh 192	11964, 8 × 10
Kh 193	6761, 8 × 10
Kh 193	12032, 8 × 10
Kh 193	12052, 8 × 10
Kh 194	6761, 8 × 10
Kh 194	6762, 8 × 10
Kh 194	12040, 8 × 10
Kh 195	6762, 8 × 10
Kh 195	12041, 8 × 10
Kh 196	6763, 8 × 10
Kh 196	11965, 8 × 10
Kh 197	6763, 8 × 10
Kh 197	6764, 8 × 10
Kh 197	11939, 8 × 10
Kh 198	6764, 8 × 10
Kh 198	12044, 8 × 10
Kh 199	6765, 8 × 10
Kh 199	12039, 8 × 10
Kh 200	6765, 8 × 10
Kh 200	6766, 8 × 10
Kh 200	11940, 8 × 10
Kh 201	6775, 8 × 10
Kh 201	11941, 8 × 10
Kh 202	6775, 8 × 10
Kh 202	11941, 8 × 10
Kh 203	6774, 8 × 10
Kh 203	11942, 8 × 10
Kh 204	6773, 8 × 10
Kh 204	6774, 8 × 10
Kh 204	11942, 8 × 10
Kh 205	6773, 8 × 10
Kh 205	11920, 8 × 10
Kh 205	11943, 8 × 10
Kh 206	6772, 8 × 10
Kh 206	11944, 8 × 10
Kh 207	6772, 8 × 10
Kh 207	11944, 8 × 10
Kh 208	6771, 8 × 10
Kh 208	11966, 8 × 10
Kh 209	6770, 8 × 10
Kh 209	11910, 8 × 10
Kh 210	6769, 8 × 10
Kh 210	6770, 8 × 10
Kh 210	11911, 8 × 10
Kh 212	3425, 8 × 10
Kh 212	3595, 8 × 10
Kh 212	4020, 8 × 10
Kh 212	9599, 8 × 10
Kh 213	3455, 8 × 10
Kh 213	3456, 8 × 10
Kh 213	4020, 8 × 10
Kh 213	9599, 8 × 10
Kh 214	3455, 8 × 10
Kh 214	3596, 8 × 10
Kh 214	9600, 8 × 10

Khonsu Temple (*cont.*)		Khonsu Temple (*cont.*)	
Nelson Number/Description	*Negative, Format*	*Nelson Number/Description*	*Negative, Format*
Kh 215	10448, 8 × 10	Kh 241c	11974, 8 × 10
Kh 216	10448, 8 × 10	Kh 241c	12100, 8 × 10
Kh 217	10447, 8 × 10	Kh 241d	7342, 8 × 10
Kh 218	8492, 8 × 10	Kh 241d	11975, 8 × 10
Kh 218	10447, 8 × 10	Kh 241d	12101, 8 × 10
Kh 219	4043, 8 × 10	Kh 241e	7342, 8 × 10
Kh 219	4044, 8 × 10	Kh 241e	11975, 8 × 10
Kh 219	8492, 8 × 10	Kh 241e	12101, 8 × 10
Kh 219	11945, 8 × 10	Kh 241f	7342, 8 × 10
Kh 220	4043, 8 × 10	Kh 241f	11975, 8 × 10
Kh 220	4044, 8 × 10	Kh 241f	12118, 8 × 10
Kh 220	8492, 8 × 10	Kh 241h	11976, 8 × 10
Kh 220	11945, 8 × 10	Kh 241i	5500, 8 × 10
Kh 220	11946, 8 × 10	Kh 241i	11976, 8 × 10
Kh 221	12009, 8 × 10	Kh 241i	12100, 8 × 10
Kh 221	12088, 8 × 10	Kh 241j	7342, 8 × 10
Kh 222	12082, 8 × 10	Kh 241j	11976, 8 × 10
Kh 223	12008, 8 × 10	Kh 241j	12100, 8 × 10
Kh 223	12089, 8 × 10	Kh 241k	5500, 8 × 10
Kh 229	6767, 8 × 10	Kh 241k	7342, 8 × 10
Kh 229	11916, 8 × 10	Kh 241k	11977, 8 × 10
Kh 229	12043, 8 × 10	Kh 241k	12101, 8 × 10
Kh 230	6808, 8 × 10	Kh 241l	7342, 8 × 10
Kh 230	11917, 8 × 10	Kh 241l	11977, 8 × 10
Kh 230	11918, 8 × 10	Kh 241l	12101, 8 × 10
Kh 230	12042, 8 × 10	Kh 241m	7342, 8 × 10
Kh 231	11918, 8 × 10	Kh 241m	11977, 8 × 10
Kh 231	11919, 8 × 10	Kh 241m	12117, 8 × 10
Kh 231	12051, 8 × 10	Kh 242a	7397, 8 × 10
Kh 232	6778, 8 × 10	Kh 242a	12116, 8 × 10
Kh 232	8411, 8 × 10	Kh 242b	7397, 8 × 10
Kh 233	6800, 8 × 10	Kh 242b	12116, 8 × 10
Kh 233	8411, 8 × 10	Kh 251	5758, 8 × 10
Kh 234	6799, 8 × 10	Kh 251a	7421, 8 × 10
Kh 234	6800, 8 × 10	Kh 251a	11912, 8 × 10
Kh 234	8412, 8 × 10	Kh 251b	11912, 8 × 10
Kh 235	4035, 8 × 10	Kh 251b	7421, 8 × 10
Kh 235	4036, 8 × 10	Kh 251c	11912, 8 × 10
Kh 235	7404, 8 × 10	Kh 251c	7421, 8 × 10
Kh 236	4034, 8 × 10	Kh 251d	11979, 8 × 10
Kh 236	4035, 8 × 10	Kh 251d	12116, 8 × 10
Kh 236	6872, 5 × 7	Kh 251e	11978, 8 × 10
Kh 236	6873, 5 × 7	Kh 251e	12116, 8 × 10
Kh 236	7404, 8 × 10	Kh 251f	11979, 8 × 10
Kh 237	4036, 8 × 10	Kh 251f	12116, 8 × 10
Kh 237	7404, 8 × 10	Kh 251g	11978, 8 × 10
Kh 238	4036, 8 × 10	Kh 251g	12116, 8 × 10
Kh 238	7404, 8 × 10	Kh 252	12139, 8 × 10
Kh 241a	5500, 8 × 10	Kh 252	12208, 8 × 10
Kh 241a	11974, 8 × 10	Kh 253	5791, 8 × 10
Kh 241a	12099, 8 × 10	Kh 253	11879, 8 × 10
Kh 241b	5500, 8 × 10	Kh 254	5791, 8 × 10
Kh 241b	11974, 8 × 10	Kh 254	11879, 8 × 10
Kh 241b	12100, 8 × 10	Kh 256	7351, 8 × 10
Kh 241c	7342, 8 × 10	Kh 256	11880, 8 × 10

Khonsu Temple (*cont.*)

Nelson Number/Description	Negative, Format
Kh 257	7351, 8 × 10
Kh 257	11880, 8 × 10
Kh 257b	7359, 8 × 10
Kh 258	7359, 8 × 10
Kh 258	11881, 8 × 10
Kh 259	7348, 8 × 10
Kh 259	11881, 8 × 10
Kh 260	7348, 8 × 10
Kh 260	11947, 8 × 10
Kh 261	3451, 8 × 10
Kh 261a	7054, 8 × 10
Kh 261b	7054, 8 × 10
Kh 262	3450, 8 × 10
Kh 262	11734, 8 × 10
Kh 263	11818, 8 × 10
Kh 263	11819, 8 × 10
Kh 263	11820, 8 × 10
Kh 263	11913, 8 × 10
Kh 265	7362, 8 × 10
Kh 265	11948, 8 × 10
Kh 266	7363, 8 × 10
Kh 266	11948, 8 × 10
Kh 267	7363, 8 × 10
Kh 267	11949, 8 × 10
Kh 267b	7357, 8 × 10
Kh 268	7357, 8 × 10
Kh 268	11882, 8 × 10
Kh 269	3454, 8 × 10
Kh 269	7193, 8 × 10
Kh 270	3454, 8 × 10
Kh 270	7193, 8 × 10
Kh 271	3426, 8 × 10
Kh 271	7193, 8 × 10
Kh 272	3427, 8 × 10
Kh 272	7193, 8 × 10
Kh 272a	7193, 8 × 10
Kh 273	3427, 8 × 10
Kh 273	7193, 8 × 10
Kh 274	11821, 8 × 10
Kh 274	11913, 8 × 10
Kh 275	3427, 8 × 10
Kh 275	11822, 8 × 10
Kh 275	11913, 8 × 10
Kh 276	7353, 8 × 10
Kh 276	12209, 8 × 10
Kh 277	11986, 5 × 7
Kh 278	7353, 8 × 10
Kh 278	11883, 8 × 10
Kh 279	7353, 8 × 10
Kh 279	11883, 8 × 10
Kh 280	11823, 8 × 10
Kh 280	11950, 8 × 10
Kh 280b	7355, 8 × 10
Kh 281	7355, 8 × 10
Kh 281	11950, 8 × 10

Khonsu Temple (*cont.*)

Nelson Number/Description	Negative, Format
Kh 282	7360, 8 × 10
Kh 282	11951, 8 × 10
Kh 283	7358, 8 × 10
Kh 283	11952, 8 × 10
Kh 284	3432, 8 × 10
Kh 284	7194, 8 × 10
Kh 285	4038, 8 × 10
Kh 285a	3428, 8 × 10
Kh 285b	3432, 8 × 10
Kh 286	11822, 8 × 10
Kh 286	11824, 8 × 10
Kh 286	11913, 8 × 10
Kh 287	7347, 8 × 10
Kh 287	11987, 5 × 7
Kh 287	12209, 8 × 10
Kh 288	7347, 8 × 10
Kh 288	11884, 8 × 10
Kh 289	7347, 8 × 10
Kh 289	11884, 8 × 10
Kh 290	12119, 8 × 10
Kh 291	7352, 8 × 10
Kh 291	11828, 8 × 10
Kh 292	7354, 8 × 10
Kh 292	11829, 8 × 10
Kh 293	7354, 8 × 10
Kh 293	11830, 8 × 10
Kh 294	7350, 8 × 10
Kh 294	11885, 8 × 10
Kh 295	3452, 8 × 10
Kh 295	11831, 8 × 10
Kh 296	3459, 8 × 10
Kh 296	11735, 8 × 10
Kh 296	11832, 8 × 10
Kh 297	3459, 8 × 10
Kh 297	11833, 8 × 10
Kh 298	11819, 8 × 10
Kh 298	11825, 8 × 10
Kh 298	11914, 8 × 10
Kh 300	3429, 8 × 10
Kh 300	7093, 8 × 10
Kh 301	3453, 8 × 10
Kh 301	11886, 8 × 10
Kh 302	3453, 8 × 10
Kh 302	11887, 8 × 10
Kh 303	7361, 8 × 10
Kh 303	11888, 8 × 10
Kh 304	3430, 8 × 10
Kh 304	7181, 8 × 10
Kh 305	3431, 8 × 10
Kh 305	7181, 8 × 10
Kh 306	3308, 8 × 10
Kh 306	3765, 8 × 10
Kh 306a	3433, 8 × 10
Kh 306b	3434, 8 × 10
Kh 307	11826, 8 × 10

Khonsu Temple (*cont.*)

Nelson Number/Description	Negative, Format
Kh 307	11914, 8 × 10
Kh 309	12209, 8 × 10
Kh 310	7346, 8 × 10
Kh 310	11889, 8 × 10
Kh 311	7349, 8 × 10
Kh 311	11890, 8 × 10
Kh 311b	5790, 8 × 10
Kh 312	5790, 8 × 10
Kh 312	11891, 8 × 10
Kh 313	5794, 8 × 10
Kh 313	11892, 8 × 10
Kh 314	5794, 8 × 10
Kh 314	11892, 8 × 10
Kh 315	3449, 8 × 10
Kh 315	11834, 8 × 10
Kh 316	3449, 8 × 10
Kh 316	11834, 8 × 10
Kh 317	3423, 8 × 10
Kh 317	3424, 8 × 10
Kh 317	5997, 8 × 10
Kh 318	11820, 8 × 10
Kh 318	11827, 8 × 10
Kh 318	11914, 8 × 10
Kh 319	2523, 5 × 7
Kh 319	12102, 8 × 10
Kh 319a	11980, 8 × 10
Kh 319a	11981, 8 × 10
Kh 319a	11983, 8 × 10
Kh 319b	11980, 8 × 10
Kh 319b	11981, 8 × 10
Kh 319b	12103, 8 × 10
Kh 319c	11980, 8 × 10
Kh 319c	12103, 8 × 10
Kh 319d	11982, 8 × 10
Kh 319d	12104, 8 × 10
Kh 319e	11982, 8 × 10
Kh 319e	12104, 8 × 10
Kh 319f	11982, 8 × 10
Kh 319f	12105, 8 × 10
Kh 319g	12105, 8 × 10
Kh 319h	11981, 8 × 10
Kh 319h	11983, 8 × 10
Kh 319h	12103, 8 × 10
Kh 319i	11983, 8 × 10
Kh 319i	12103, 8 × 10
Kh 319j	12104, 8 × 10
Kh 319k	11984, 8 × 10
Kh 319k	12104, 8 × 10
Kh 319l	11984, 8 × 10
Kh 319l	12105, 8 × 10
Kh 319m	11984, 8 × 10
Kh 319m	12105, 8 × 10
Kh 319n	12106, 8 × 10
Kh 319o	12106, 8 × 10
Kh 320	12059, 8 × 10

Khonsu Temple (*cont.*)

Nelson Number/Description	Negative, Format
Kh 320	12120, 8 × 10
Kh 321	12059, 8 × 10
Kh 321	12120, 8 × 10
Kh 322a	12210, 8 × 10
Kh 322b	12210, 8 × 10
Kh 351	5759, 8 × 10
Kh 352	3980, 8 × 10
Kh 353	3980, 8 × 10
Kh 353	6017, 8 × 10
Kh 354	3980, 8 × 10
Kh 354	6017, 8 × 10
Kh 355	3349, 8 × 10
Kh 355	13386, 5 × 7
Kh 355	13393, 5 × 7
Kh 356	13386, 5 × 7
Kh 356	13393, 5 × 7
Kh 358	5448, 5 × 7
Kh 358	13392, 5 × 7
Kh 359	5804, 5 × 7
Kh 359	13392, 5 × 7
Kh 360	5492, 5 × 7
Kh 361	2525, 5 × 7
Kh 362	5497, 5 × 7
Kh 363	5498, 5 × 7
Kh 364	5496, 5 × 7
Kh 365	3435, 8 × 10
Kh 365	13392, 5 × 7
Kh 366	3335, 5 × 7
Kh 366	13383, 5 × 7
Kh 366	13392, 5 × 7
Kh 366	13397, 5 × 7
Kh 366	13402, 5 × 7
Kh 367	3336, 5 × 7
Kh 367	13397, 5 × 7
Kh 368	3337, 5 × 7
Kh 368	13397, 5 × 7
Kh 369	3338, 5 × 7
Kh 370	3339, 5 × 7
Kh 371	3436, 8 × 10
Kh 372	13383, 5 × 7
Kh 372	13397, 5 × 7
Kh 374	3305, 8 × 10
Kh 374	13404, 5 × 7
Kh 375	2699, 5 × 7
Kh 376	6016, 8 × 10
Kh 376	13404, 5 × 7
Kh 377	6015, 8 × 10
Kh 377	8629, 8 × 10
Kh 379	5760, 8 × 10
Kh 379a	8753, 8 × 10
Kh 379b	8753, 8 × 10
Kh 379c	8754, 8 × 10
Kh 379d	8754, 8 × 10
Kh 379e	8754, 8 × 10
Kh 379f	8754, 8 × 10

Khonsu Temple (*cont.*)

Nelson Number/Description	Negative, Format
Kh 379g	8753, 8 × 10
Kh 379h	8753, 8 × 10
Kh 379i	8754, 8 × 10
Kh 379j	8754, 8 × 10
Kh 379k	8754, 8 × 10
Kh 379l	8754, 8 × 10
Kh 379m	8753, 8 × 10
Kh 379n	8753, 8 × 10
Kh 382	6010, 8 × 10
Kh 383	6011, 8 × 10
Kh 384	5591, 5 × 7
Kh 385	5823, 5 × 7
Kh 386	8622, 5 × 7
Kh 387	8623, 5 × 7
Kh 388	5491, 5 × 7
Kh 391	6012, 8 × 10
Kh 391	7344, 8 × 10
Kh 392	7344, 8 × 10
Kh 393	6013, 8 × 10
Kh 393	7388, 8 × 10
Kh 394	6014, 8 × 10
Kh 394	7389, 8 × 10
Kh 397	5449, 5 × 7
Kh 398	5489, 5 × 7
Kh 399	5495, 5 × 7
Kh 400	5494, 5 × 7
Kh 402	3340, 5 × 7
Kh 403	3341, 5 × 7
Kh 404	3342, 5 × 7
Kh 404	13394, 5 × 7
Kh 405	3343, 5 × 7
Kh 410	5800, 8 × 10
Kh 411	5800, 8 × 10
Kh 412	5802, 8 × 10
Kh 413	5802, 8 × 10
Kh 414	5800, 8 × 10
Kh 421	7381, 8 × 10
Kh 422	7418, 8 × 10
Kh 423a	7381, 8 × 10
Kh 423b	7418, 8 × 10
Kh 425	7405, 8 × 10
Kh 426	7371, 8 × 10
Kh 427	7371, 8 × 10
Kh 428	7370, 8 × 10
Kh 429	7370, 8 × 10
Kh 430	7369, 8 × 10
Kh 431	7366, 8 × 10
Kh 432	7365, 8 × 10
Kh 433	7372, 8 × 10
Kh 434	7373, 8 × 10
Kh 435	7364, 8 × 10
Kh 436	7368, 8 × 10
Kh 437	7973, 8 × 10
Kh 443	5490, 5 × 7
Kh 444	5490, 5 × 7

Khonsu Temple (*cont.*)

Nelson Number/Description	Negative, Format
Kh 447	5810, 8 × 10
Kh 448	7400, 8 × 10
Kh 449	7384, 8 × 10
Kh 450	7386, 8 × 10
Kh 455	7378, 8 × 10
Kh 456	5781, 8 × 10
Kh 457	5781, 8 × 10
Kh 459	7380, 8 × 10
Kh 460	7380, 8 × 10
Kh 461	7379, 8 × 10
Kh 461	7380, 8 × 10
Kh 462	7410, 8 × 10
Kh 468	7407, 8 × 10
Kh 469	7935, 8 × 10
Kh 470	7385, 8 × 10
Kh 471	7936, 8 × 10
Kh 472	7383, 8 × 10
Kh 473	7403, 8 × 10
Kh 474	5775, 8 × 10
Kh 475	7396, 8 × 10
Kh 476	7382, 8 × 10
Kh 477	7401, 8 × 10
Kh 478	7420, 8 × 10
Kh 479	7399, 8 × 10
Kh 480	7420, 8 × 10
Kh 481	7399, 8 × 10
Kh 483	7345, 8 × 10
Kh 483	7374, 8 × 10
Kh 483	7375, 8 × 10
Kh 483	7376, 8 × 10
Kh 484	7409, 8 × 10
Kh 485	7376, 8 × 10
Kh 486	7374, 8 × 10
Kh 487	7419, 8 × 10
Kh 488	7375, 8 × 10
Kh 489	7377, 8 × 10
Kh 490	7345, 8 × 10
Kh 494	2526, 5 × 7
Kh 494	2531, 5 × 7
Kh 494	11084, 5 × 7
Kh 509	11893, 8 × 10
Kh 550	7417, 8 × 10
Kh 551	5771, 8 × 10
Kh 552	3265, 8 × 10
Kh 553	3265, 8 × 10
Kh 553	5996, 8 × 10
Kh 554	3265, 8 × 10
Kh 554	5996, 8 × 10
Kh 555	3220, 8 × 10
Kh 555	5995, 8 × 10
Kh 556	3220, 8 × 10
Kh 556	5995, 8 × 10
Kh 560	3266, 8 × 10
Kh 560	3267, 8 × 10
Kh 561	3268, 8 × 10

Khonsu Temple (*cont.*)

Nelson Number/Description	Negative, Format
Kh 562	3181, 8 × 10
Kh 563	3269, 8 × 10
Kh 563	3270, 8 × 10
Kh 564	3269, 8 × 10
Kh 564	3270, 8 × 10
Kh 565	3270, 8 × 10
Kh 566	3271, 8 × 10
Kh 567	3271, 8 × 10
Kh 568	3182, 8 × 10
Kh 569	3183, 8 × 10
Kh 570	3183, 8 × 10
Kh 571	3183, 8 × 10
Kh 573	3288, 8 × 10
Kh 574	3288, 8 × 10
Kh 575	3221, 8 × 10
Kh 576	3221, 8 × 10
Kh 577	3221, 8 × 10
Kh 578	3221, 8 × 10
Kh 580	3286, 8 × 10
Kh 580	3287, 8 × 10
Kh 581	3272, 8 × 10
Kh 582	3273, 8 × 10
Kh 583	3186, 8 × 10
Kh 583	3187, 8 × 10
Kh 584	3186, 8 × 10
Kh 584	3187, 8 × 10
Kh 586	3285, 8 × 10
Kh 587	3285, 8 × 10
Kh 588	3185, 8 × 10
Kh 589	3184, 8 × 10
Kh 590	3184, 8 × 10
Kh 592	5753, 8 × 10
Kh 593	5753, 8 × 10
Kh 594	5753, 8 × 10
Kh 597	7413, 8 × 10
Kh 606	3274, 8 × 10
Kh 607	3274, 8 × 10
Kh 608	3222, 8 × 10
Kh 608	3223, 8 × 10
Kh 608	8493, 8 × 10
Kh 608	9601, 8 × 10
Kh 609	3275, 8 × 10
Kh 610	3188, 8 × 10
Kh 610	3437, 5 × 7
Kh 611	3276, 8 × 10
Kh 611	7639, 8 × 10
Kh 612	3275, 8 × 10
Kh 615	3190, 8 × 10
Kh 616	3247, 8 × 10
Kh 616	3248, 8 × 10
Kh 617	3438, 8 × 10
Kh 618	3277, 8 × 10
Kh 618	3442, 8 × 10
Kh 619	3278, 8 × 10
Kh 620	3247, 8 × 10

Khonsu Temple (*cont.*)

Nelson Number/Description	Negative, Format
Kh 620	3439, 8 × 10
Kh 621	3189, 8 × 10
Kh 621	3190, 8 × 10
Kh 621	3482, 8 × 10
Kh 621a	3440, 8 × 10
Kh 621b	3441, 8 × 10
Kh 626	3224, 8 × 10
Kh 627	3225, 8 × 10
Kh 628	3226, 8 × 10
Kh 629	3227, 8 × 10
Kh 630	3191, 8 × 10
Kh 631	3230, 8 × 10
Kh 631	9085, 8 × 10
Kh 632	3229, 8 × 10
Kh 632	9086, 8 × 10
Kh 633	3228, 8 × 10
Kh 633	9087, 8 × 10
Kh 634	3193, 8 × 10
Kh 635	3192, 8 × 10
Kh 640	7408, 8 × 10
Kh 641	7408, 8 × 10
Kh 642	3233, 8 × 10
Kh 642	3703, 8 × 10
Kh 643	3231, 8 × 10
Kh 643	3703, 8 × 10
Kh 644	3249, 8 × 10
Kh 645	3232, 8 × 10
Kh 645	3234, 8 × 10
Kh 645	3704, 8 × 10
Kh 646	3249, 8 × 10
Kh 651	7402, 8 × 10
Kh 652	3283, 8 × 10
Kh 653a	7395, 8 × 10
Kh 653b	7394, 8 × 10
Kh 654	3284, 8 × 10
Kh 655	7393, 8 × 10
Kh 661	3281, 8 × 10
Kh 662	3282, 8 × 10
Kh 663	3302, 8 × 10
Kh 664	3303, 8 × 10
Kh 665	7416, 8 × 10
Kh 666	3304, 8 × 10
Kh 674	7411, 8 × 10
Kh 675	7415, 8 × 10
Kh 676	7414, 8 × 10
Kh 677	7412, 8 × 10
Kh 678	3280, 8 × 10
Kh 679	3279, 8 × 10
Kh 680	5801, 8 × 10
Kh 681	5801, 8 × 10
Kh 682	7406, 8 × 10
Kh 701	12012, 8 × 10
Kh 701	12014, 8 × 10
Kh 701	12015, 8 × 10
Kh 701	12127, 8 × 10

Khonsu Temple (*cont.*)

Nelson Number/Description	Negative, Format
Kh 701	12132, 8 × 10
Kh 701	12194, 5 × 7
Kh 701	12195, 5 × 7
Kh 701	14426, 5 × 7
Kh 701	14427, 4 × 5
Kh 701	14428, 5 × 7
Kh 701	15828, 5 × 7
Kh 702	12130, 8 × 10
Kh 703	12107, 8 × 10
Kh 704	12107, 8 × 10
Kh 704	12108, 8 × 10
Kh 705	12130, 8 × 10
Kh 706	11988, 5 × 7
Kh 706	11989, 5 × 7
Kh 706	11990, 5 × 7
Kh 706	11991, 5 × 7
Kh 706	11992, 5 × 7
Kh 706	11993, 5 × 7
Kh 706	11994, 5 × 7
Kh 706	12108, 8 × 10
Kh 707	11995, 5 × 7
Kh 707	11996, 5 × 7
Kh 707	11997, 5 × 7
Kh 707	12016, 8 × 10
Kh 707	12017, 8 × 10
Kh 707	12018, 8 × 10
Kh 707	12109, 8 × 10
Kh 708	12130, 8 × 10
Kh 709	12110, 8 × 10
Kh 709	12121, 8 × 10
Kh 710	12110, 8 × 10
Kh 710	12111, 8 × 10
Kh 711	12130, 8 × 10
Kh 712	12111, 8 × 10
Kh 713	7391, 8 × 10
Kh 713	11985, 8 × 10
Kh 713	12163, 5 × 7
Kh 713	12196, 5 × 7
Kh 713a	12301, 8 × 10
Kh 713b	12164, 5 × 7
Kh 713b	12301, 8 × 10
Kh 713c	12164, 5 × 7
Kh 713c	12211, 8 × 10
Kh 713d	12164, 5 × 7
Kh 713d	12165, 5 × 7
Kh 713d	12211, 8 × 10
Kh 713e	12165, 5 × 7
Kh 713e	12211, 8 × 10
Kh 713f	12165, 5 × 7
Kh 713f	12211, 8 × 10
Kh 720	12129, 8 × 10
Kh 721	5493, 5 × 7
Kh 721	12138, 8 × 10
Kh 722	12138, 8 × 10
Kh 723	12138, 8 × 10

Khonsu Temple (*cont.*)

Nelson Number/Description	Negative, Format
Kh 724	12129, 8 × 10
Kh 725	12121, 8 × 10
Kh 726	12121, 8 × 10
Kh 727	12129, 8 × 10
Kh 728	12138, 8 × 10
Kh 729	12121, 8 × 10
Kh 730	12063, 5 × 7
Kh 730	12064, 5 × 7
Kh 730	12069, 5 × 7
Kh 730	12169, 5 × 7
Kh 730	12212, 8 × 10
Kh 730N	12168, 5 × 7
Kh 730NE	12166, 5 × 7
Kh 730NW	12167, 5 × 7
Kh 734	3323, 8 × 10
Kh 738	3324, 8 × 10
Kh 738	5788, 8 × 10
Kh 739	3315, 8 × 10
Kh 739	7479, 8 × 10
Kh 740	3324, 8 × 10
Kh 741	5788, 8 × 10
Kh 742	5788, 8 × 10
Kh 743	5788, 8 × 10
Kh 744	5788, 8 × 10
Kh 745	5788, 8 × 10
Kh 746	5788, 8 × 10
Kh 747	3055, 8 × 10
Kh 748	3055, 8 × 10
Kh 749	3055, 8 × 10
Kh 750	3055, 8 × 10
Kh 751	3483, 8 × 10
Kh 752	3483, 8 × 10
Kh 753	3483, 8 × 10
Kh 754	3483, 8 × 10
Kh 755	3066, 8 × 10
Kh 756	3066, 8 × 10
Kh 757	3066, 8 × 10
Kh 758	3066, 8 × 10
Kh 759	3054, 8 × 10
Kh 760	3054, 8 × 10
Kh 761	3054, 8 × 10
Kh 762	3054, 8 × 10
Kh 763	5776, 8 × 10
Kh 764	5776, 8 × 10
Kh 765	5776, 8 × 10
Kh 766	5776, 8 × 10
Kh 767	5811, 8 × 10
Kh 768	5811, 8 × 10
Kh 769	2524, 5 × 7
Kh 769	5811, 8 × 10
Kh 770	5811, 8 × 10
Kh 771	5811, 8 × 10
Kh 772	5811, 8 × 10
Kh 774	3054, 8 × 10
Kh 774	3055, 8 × 10

Khonsu Temple (*cont.*)

Nelson Number/Description	Negative, Format
Kh 774	3066, 8 × 10
Kh 774	3483, 8 × 10
Kh 774	5776, 8 × 10
Kh 775	3323, 8 × 10
Kh 776	3315, 8 × 10
Kh 777	3315, 8 × 10
Kh 778	7479, 8 × 10
Kh 779	7479, 8 × 10
Kh 780	7479, 8 × 10
Kh 781	7479, 8 × 10
Kh 782	2688, 8 × 10
Kh 782	3241, 8 × 10
Kh 782	3899, 8 × 10
Kh 782	5499, 8 × 10
Kh 782	5796, 8 × 10
Kh 782	5798, 8 × 10
Kh 782	5799, 8 × 10
Kh 782	7343, 8 × 10
Kh 783	3899, 8 × 10
Kh 784	3899, 8 × 10
Kh 785	3899, 8 × 10
Kh 786	3899, 8 × 10
Kh 787	5499, 8 × 10
Kh 788	5499, 8 × 10
Kh 789	5499, 8 × 10
Kh 790	5499, 8 × 10
Kh 791	3241, 8 × 10
Kh 792	3241, 8 × 10
Kh 793	3241, 8 × 10
Kh 794	3241, 8 × 10
Kh 795	7343, 8 × 10
Kh 796	7343, 8 × 10
Kh 797a	7343, 8 × 10
Kh 798a	7343, 8 × 10
Kh 798b	5798, 8 × 10
Kh 799	5798, 8 × 10
Kh 799b	5798, 8 × 10
Kh 800	5798, 8 × 10
Kh 801	5798, 8 × 10
Kh 802	5798, 8 × 10
Kh 803	5796, 8 × 10
Kh 804	5796, 8 × 10
Kh 805	5796, 8 × 10
Kh 806	5796, 8 × 10
Kh 807	5799, 8 × 10
Kh 808	5799, 8 × 10
Kh 809	5799, 8 × 10
Kh 810	5799, 8 × 10
Kh 811	2688, 8 × 10
Kh 812	2688, 8 × 10
Kh 813	2688, 8 × 10
Kh 814	2688, 8 × 10
Kh 820	11998, 5 × 7
Kh 820	12119, 8 × 10
Kh 821	12302, 8 × 10

Khonsu Temple (*cont.*)

Nelson Number/Description	Negative, Format
Kh 822	11999, 5 × 7
Kh 822	12000, 5 × 7
Kh 822	12122, 8 × 10
Kh 824	12000, 5 × 7
Kh 824	12001, 5 × 7
Kh 824	12065, 5 × 7
Kh 824	12067, 5 × 7
Kh 825	12000, 5 × 7
Kh 825	12001, 5 × 7
Kh 827	11986, 5 × 7
Kh 827	12002, 5 × 7
Kh 827	12122, 8 × 10
Kh 828	12004, 5 × 7
Kh 828	12302, 8 × 10
Kh 829	11998, 5 × 7
Kh 829	12003, 5 × 7
Kh 829	12122, 8 × 10
Kh 830	12004, 5 × 7
Kh 830	12005, 5 × 7
Kh 830	12006, 5 × 7
Kh 830	12068, 5 × 7
Kh 831	12004, 5 × 7
Kh 831	12005, 5 × 7
Kh 831	12006, 5 × 7
Kh 831	12122, 8 × 10
Kh 831	12197, 5 × 7
Kh 832	12213, 8 × 10
Kh 832N	12170, 5 × 7
Kh 832S	12171, 5 × 7
Kh 833	12060, 8 × 10
Kh 833	12061, 8 × 10
Kh 833	12062, 8 × 10
Kh 833	12172, 5 × 7
Kh 833	12214, 8 × 10
Kh 833N	12173, 5 × 7
Kh 834	12174, 5 × 7
Kh 834	12213, 8 × 10
Kh 835	12175, 5 × 7
Kh 835	12176, 5 × 7
Kh 835	12136, 8 × 10
Kh 836	12123, 8 × 10
Kh 837	12123, 8 × 10
Kh 838	12177, 5 × 7
Kh 838	12210, 8 × 10
Kh 862	7387, 8 × 10
Kh 871	8751, 5 × 7
Kh 872	8751, 5 × 7
Kh 872	8752, 5 × 7
Kh 873	8751, 5 × 7
Kh 874	8752, 5 × 7
Kh 901	8737, 8 × 10
Kh 902	8737, 8 × 10
Kh 903	8737, 8 × 10
Kh 904	8737, 8 × 10
Kh 905	8737, 8 × 10

Khonsu Temple (*cont.*)

Nelson Number/Description	Negative, Format
Kh 906	8737, 8 × 10
Kh 907	8737, 8 × 10
Kh 908	8737, 8 × 10
Kh 909	8755, 8 × 10
Kh 910	8756, 8 × 10
Kh 911	8757, 8 × 10
Kh 912	8757, 8 × 10
Kh 913	8757, 8 × 10
Kh 914	8737, 8 × 10
Kh 915	8737, 8 × 10
Kh 916	8758, 8 × 10
Kh 917	8759, 8 × 10
Kh 918	8760, 8 × 10
Kh 919	8760, 8 × 10
Kh 920	8760, 8 × 10
Kh 921	8761, 8 × 10
Kh 922	8761, 8 × 10
Kh 923	5842, 8 × 10
Kh 924	5842, 8 × 10
Kh 925	5843, 8 × 10
Kh 926	5843, 8 × 10
Kh 929	5841, 8 × 10
Kh 929	8762, 8 × 10
Kh 931	8763, 8 × 10
Kh 932	8763, 8 × 10
Kh 933	5839, 8 × 10
Kh 934	5839, 8 × 10
Kh 935	5840, 8 × 10
Kh 936	5840, 8 × 10
Kh 938	8764, 8 × 10
Kh 939	8764, 8 × 10
Kh 940	5847, 8 × 10
Kh 941	5847, 8 × 10
Kh 942	5848, 8 × 10
Kh 943	5848, 8 × 10
Kh 943	8842, 5 × 7
Kh 944	8842, 5 × 7
Kh 946	5846, 8 × 10
Kh 946	8765, 8 × 10
Kh 948	8766, 8 × 10
Kh 949	8766, 8 × 10
Kh 950	5844, 8 × 10
Kh 951	5844, 8 × 10
Kh 952	5845, 8 × 10
Kh 953	5845, 8 × 10
Kh 953	8842, 5 × 7
Kh 954	8842, 5 × 7
Kh 955	5770, 8 × 10
Kh 955	13409, 5 × 7
Kh 956	5770, 8 × 10
Kh 956	13409, 5 × 7
Kh 957	5770, 8 × 10
Kh 957	13409, 5 × 7
Kh 958	5770, 8 × 10
Kh 958	13409, 5 × 7

Khonsu Temple (*cont.*)

Nelson Number/Description	Negative, Format
Kh 959	5770, 8 × 10
Kh 959	13409, 5 × 7
Kh 960	5770, 8 × 10
Kh 960	13409, 5 × 7
Kh 961	5770, 8 × 10
Kh 961	13409, 5 × 7
Kh 962	5770, 8 × 10
Kh 962	13409, 5 × 7
Kh 963	5770, 8 × 10
Kh 963	8767, 8 × 10
Kh 963	13409, 5 × 7
Kh 964	5770, 8 × 10
Kh 964	8768, 8 × 10
Kh 964	13409, 5 × 7
Kh 965	5770, 8 × 10
Kh 965	8769, 8 × 10
Kh 965	13409, 5 × 7
Kh 966	5770, 8 × 10
Kh 966	8769, 8 × 10
Kh 966	13409, 5 × 7
Kh 967	5770, 8 × 10
Kh 967	8769, 8 × 10
Kh 967	13409, 5 × 7
Kh 968	5770, 8 × 10
Kh 968	13409, 5 × 7
Kh 969	5770, 8 × 10
Kh 969	13409, 5 × 7
Kh 970	5770, 8 × 10
Kh 970	8770, 8 × 10
Kh 970	13409, 5 × 7
Kh 971	5770, 8 × 10
Kh 971	8771, 8 × 10
Kh 971	13409, 5 × 7
Kh 972	5770, 8 × 10
Kh 972	8772, 8 × 10
Kh 972	13409, 5 × 7
Kh 973	5770, 8 × 10
Kh 973	8772, 8 × 10
Kh 973	13409, 5 × 7
Kh 974	5770, 8 × 10
Kh 974	8772, 8 × 10
Kh 974	13409, 5 × 7
Kh Col. 001	7974, 5 × 7
Kh Col. 001	11921, 8 × 10
Kh Col. 001	12010, 8 × 10
Kh Col. 001	12011, 8 × 10
Kh Col. 001a	12090, 8 × 10
Kh Col. 001b	12091, 8 × 10
Kh Col. 002	11922, 8 × 10
Kh Col. 003	11954, 8 × 10
Kh Col. 004	11955, 8 × 10
Kh Col. 005	11923, 8 × 10
Kh Col. 007	11924, 8 × 10
Kh Col. 008	11956, 8 × 10
Kh Col. 009	11925, 8 × 10

Khonsu Temple (*cont.*)

Nelson Number/Description	Negative, Format
Kh Col. 010	11926, 8 × 10
Kh Col. 011	12030, 8 × 10
Kh Col. 012	12031, 8 × 10
Kh Col. 013	11957, 8 × 10
Kh Col. 014	12037, 8 × 10
Kh Col. 015	12053, 8 × 10
Kh Col. 016	12055, 8 × 10
Kh Col. 017	11958, 8 × 10
Kh Col. 018	7974, 5 × 7
Kh Col. 018	12029, 8 × 10
Kh Col. 019a	11959, 8 × 10
Kh Col. 019b	11960, 8 × 10
Kh Col. 019c	12071, 8 × 10
Kh Col. 020	12092, 8 × 10
Kh Col. 020a	11927, 8 × 10
Kh Col. 020b	11928, 8 × 10
Kh Col. 020c	11929, 8 × 10
Kh Col. 021	11961, 8 × 10
Kh Col. 022	11962, 8 × 10
Kh Col. 023	12072, 8 × 10
Kh Col. 024	11930, 8 × 10
Kh Col. 025a	12034, 8 × 10
Kh Col. 025b	12048, 8 × 10
Kh Col. 025c	12048, 8 × 10
Kh Col. 026a	12035, 8 × 10
Kh Col. 026b	12036, 8 × 10
Kh Col. 026c	12033, 8 × 10
Kh Col. 027	11931, 8 × 10
Kh Col. 028	11963, 8 × 10
Kh Col. 029	11899, 8 × 10
Kh Col. 030	11900, 8 × 10
Kh Col. 031	11901, 8 × 10
Kh Col. 032	11902, 8 × 10
Kh Col. 033	11903, 8 × 10
Kh Col. 034	11904, 8 × 10
Kh Col. 034SW	12188, 5 × 7
Kh Col. 035	11905, 8 × 10
Kh Col. 035NW	12189, 5 × 7
Kh Col. 036	11906, 8 × 10
Kh Col. 036SE	12190, 5 × 7
Kh Col. 036SE	12191, 5 × 7
East face	12183, 5 × 7
East face	12184, 5 × 7
East face	12185, 5 × 7
Exterior	14429, 5 × 7
Exterior	14430, 5 × 7
Exterior	14431, 5 × 7
Exterior	14432, 5 × 7
Exterior	14433, 5 × 7
Exterior	14434, 4 × 5
Exterior	14435, 5 × 7
First hypostyle hall, Ramesses XI column bases	13172, 2.25 × 2.25
First hypostyle hall, southeast corner	14422, 5 × 7
First hypostyle hall, southeast corner	14423, 5 × 7
First hypostyle hall, southeast corner	14424, 5 × 7

Khonsu Temple (*cont.*)

Nelson Number/Description	Negative, Format
First hypostyle hall, southeast corner	14425, 4 × 5
General view	3631, 11 × 14
General view	3632, 9 × 11
General view	3852, 11 × 14
General view	3853, 11 × 14
General view	5740, 8 × 10
General view	5741, 8 × 10
General view	5742, 8 × 10
General view	5743, 8 × 10
General view	5744, 8 × 10
General view	5745, 8 × 10
General view	5754, 8 × 10
General view	5755, 8 × 10
General view	5756, 8 × 10
General view	5757, 8 × 10
General view	5761, 8 × 10
General view	5769, 8 × 10
General view	7481, 8 × 10
General view	7482, 8 × 10
Hypostyle hall, baboon	13173, 2.25 × 2.25
Hypostyle hall, baboon	13174, 2.25 × 2.25
Interiors	14421, 5 × 7
Roof	7987, 5 × 7
Southeast corner of first hypostyle	12186, 5 × 7
Southeast corner of first hypostyle	12187, 5 × 7
View of hypostyle hall	12066, 5 × 7

Kom Ombo

Nelson Number/Description	Negative, Format
None	3095, 8 × 10

Luxor

Nelson Number/Description	Negative, Format
Aerial photograph: Royal Air Force	11546, 8 × 10
Aerial view of Luxor	13576, 5 × 7
Aerial view of Luxor	13579, 5 × 7
Aerial view of Luxor	13580, 5 × 7
Aerial view of Luxor	13580-A, 5 × 7
Aerial view of Luxor	13580-B, 5 × 7
Luxor from the Nile	13592, 5 × 7
View of city of Luxor	2482, 8 × 10
View of city of Luxor	2826, 8 × 10

Luxor Temple

Nelson Number/Description	Negative, Format
L A 011	13433, 5 × 7
L A 012	13433, 5 × 7
L A 013	13433, 5 × 7
L A 035	13399, 5 × 7

Luxor Temple (*cont.*)

Nelson Number/Description	Negative, Format
L A 044	10919, 8 × 10
L A 044	10920, 8 × 10
L A 045	9554, 8 × 10
L A 045	9555, 8 × 10
L A 045	9556, 8 × 10
L A 045	9557, 8 × 10
L A 045	10919, 8 × 10
L A 045	10920, 8 × 10
L A 045	10921, 8 × 10
L A 046	9554, 8 × 10
L A 046	10919, 8 × 10
L A 046	10920, 8 × 10
L A 046	10921, 8 × 10
L A 046	10922, 8 × 10
L A 046	10923, 8 × 10
L A 046	10924, 8 × 10
L A 046	13387, 5 × 7
L A 047	9554, 8 × 10
L A 047	9555, 8 × 10
L A 047	9556, 8 × 10
L A 047	9557, 8 × 10
L A 047	10919, 8 × 10
L A 047	10920, 8 × 10
L A 047	10921, 8 × 10
L A 047	10922, 8 × 10
L A 047	10923, 8 × 10
L A 047	10924, 8 × 10
L A 048	9554, 8 × 10
L A 048	9555, 8 × 10
L A 049	9556, 8 × 10
L A 049	9557, 8 × 10
L A 050	13726, 8 × 10
L A 051	9554, 8 × 10
L A 051	9555, 8 × 10
L A 051	9556, 8 × 10
L A 051	9557, 8 × 10
L A 051	13387, 5 × 7
L A 051	13389, 5 × 7
L A 051	13406, 5 × 7
L A 051	13407, 5 × 7
L A 052	3588, 8 × 10
L A 052	9557, 8 × 10
L A 052	12373, 5 × 7
L A 052	12374, 5 × 7
L A 052	13389, 5 × 7
L A 053	13276, 8 × 10
L A 053	12465, 8 × 10
L A 053	12466, 8 × 10
L A 054	13276, 8 × 10
L A 054	12465, 8 × 10
L A 054	12466, 8 × 10
L A 054	12470, 8 × 10
L A 054	12471, 8 × 10
L A 054	12472, 8 × 10
L A 054	12565, 5 × 7

Luxor Temple (*cont.*)

Nelson Number/Description	Negative, Format
L A 054	12566, 8 × 10
L A 055	12465, 8 × 10
L A 055	12466, 8 × 10
L A 055	12470, 8 × 10
L A 055	12471, 8 × 10
L A 055	12472, 8 × 10
L A 055	12565, 5 × 7
L A 055	12566, 8 × 10
L A 055	13276, 8 × 10
L A 060	12551, 8 × 10
L A 060	12961, 5 × 7
L A 060	12964, 5 × 7
L A 060	16005, 8 × 10
L A 062	12473, 8 × 10
L A 062	12543, 5 × 7
L A 062	12555, 8 × 10
L A 062	13738, 8 × 10
L A 062	13740, 8 × 10
L A 062	13742, 8 × 10
L A 062	13744, 8 × 10
L A 063	12568, 8 × 10
L A 063	12959, 5 × 7
L A 063	13459, 5 × 7
L A 063	13463, 5 × 7
L A 063	13756, 8 × 10
L A 064	12556, 8 × 10
L A 064	12557, 8 × 10
L A 064	12558, 5 × 7
L A 064	12559, 8 × 10
L A 064	12560, 5 × 7
L A 064	12568, 8 × 10
L A 064	13459, 5 × 7
L A 064	13463, 5 × 7
L A 064	16004, 8 × 10
L A 065	16018, 8 × 10
L A 066	12955, 5 × 7
L A 066	12956, 5 × 7
L A 066	12957, 5 × 7
L A 066	12958, 5 × 7
L A 066	12959, 5 × 7
L A 066	13113, 5 × 7
L A 066	13123, 5 × 7
L A 066	13275, 8 × 10
L A 066	13729, 8 × 10
L A 066	13730, 8 × 10
L A 066	13752, 8 × 10
L A 066	13766, 8 × 10
L A 066	13767, 8 × 10
L A 067	12567, 8 × 10
L A 067	12955, 5 × 7
L A 067	12956, 5 × 7
L A 067	12957, 5 × 7
L A 067	12958, 5 × 7
L A 067	12959, 5 × 7
L A 067	13113, 5 × 7

Luxor Temple (*cont.*)

Nelson Number/Description	Negative, Format
L A 067	13123, 5 × 7
L A 067	13275, 8 × 10
L A 067	13729, 8 × 10
L A 067	13730, 8 × 10
L A 067	13752, 8 × 10
L A 067	13766, 8 × 10
L A 067	13767, 8 × 10
L A 068	12567, 8 × 10
L A 068	12613, 8 × 10
L A 068	13275, 8 × 10
L A 069	12561, 8 × 10
L A 069	12562, 8 × 10
L A 069	12563, 8 × 10
L A 069	13275, 8 × 10
L A 070	12561, 8 × 10
L A 070	12562, 8 × 10
L A 070	12563, 8 × 10
L A 070	13275, 8 × 10
L A 070	13749, 8 × 10
L A 070	13750, 8 × 10
L A 070	16003, 4 × 5
L A 070a	9168, 8 × 10
L A 071	12564, 8 × 10
L A 081a	9216, 5 × 7
L A 135	13471, 5 × 7
L A 150	13433, 5 × 7
L A 151	13433, 5 × 7
L A 152	13433, 5 × 7
L A 153	13433, 5 × 7
L A 154	13477, 5 × 7
L A 155	13477, 5 × 7
L A 156	13459, 5 × 7
L A 156	13463, 5 × 7
L A 156	13477, 5 × 7
L A 157	12372, 5 × 7
L A 157	13459, 5 × 7
L A 157	13463, 5 × 7
L A 158	13471, 5 × 7
L A 159	13471, 5 × 7
L A 160	13471, 5 × 7
L A Col. 053	13471, 5 × 7
L A Col. 054	13471, 5 × 7
L A Col. 067	13471, 5 × 7
L A Col. 069	13471, 5 × 7
L A Col. 070	13471, 5 × 7
L A Col. 071	13471, 5 × 7
L B 028	3492, 8 × 10
L B 028	3493, 8 × 10
L B 034	3549, 8 × 10
L B 054	3548, 8 × 10
L B 074	3550, 8 × 10
L C	12291, 5 × 7
L C	12292, 5 × 7
L C	12461, 8 × 10
L C	12462, 8 × 10

Luxor Temple (*cont.*)

Nelson Number/Description	Negative, Format
L C	12464, 8 × 10
L C	12467, 8 × 10
L C	12468, 8 × 10
L C	14400, 5 × 7
L C	14401, 5 × 7
L C	14402, 5 × 7
L C	14403, 5 × 7
L C	14404, 5 × 7
L C	14405, 5 × 7
L C	14406, 5 × 7
L C	14407, 5 × 7
L C	14408, 5 × 7
L C	14409, 5 × 7
L C	14410, 5 × 7
L C	14411, 5 × 7
L C	14412, 5 × 7
L C	14413, 5 × 7
L C	14414, 5 × 7
L C	14415, 5 × 7
L C	14416, 5 × 7
L C	14417, 5 × 7
L C	14418, 5 × 7
L C	14419, 5 × 7
L C	15189, 8 × 10
L C	15189-a, 8 × 10
L C	15189-var e, 8 × 10
L C	15190, 4 × 5
L C	15191, 4 × 5
L C	15192, 4 × 5
L C	15193, 4 × 5
L C 001	13738, 8 × 10
L C 001	13740, 8 × 10
L C 001	13744, 8 × 10
L C 001	13751, 8 × 10
L C 002	13731, 8 × 10
L C 002	13732, 8 × 10
L C 002	13733, 8 × 10
L C 002	13734, 8 × 10
L C 002	13735, 8 × 10
L C 003	12553, 8 × 10
L C 003	13751, 8 × 10
L C 004	12553, 8 × 10
L C 004	13751, 8 × 10
L C 005	12553, 8 × 10
L C 005	12965, 5 × 7
L C 005	13751, 8 × 10
L C 006	12469, 8 × 10
L C 006	12553, 8 × 10
L C 006	12554, 8 × 10
L C 006	12555, 8 × 10
L C 006	16017, 8 × 10
L C 007	12463, 8 × 10
L C 007	12569, 8 × 10
L C 007	13731, 8 × 10
L C 007	13732, 8 × 10

Luxor Temple (*cont.*)		Luxor Temple (*cont.*)	
Nelson Number/Description	*Negative, Format*	*Nelson Number/Description*	*Negative, Format*
L C 007	13733, 8 × 10	L C 019	9058, 7 × 9
L C 007	13734, 8 × 10	L C 019	12279, 5 × 7
L C 007	13735, 8 × 10	L C 019	12280, 5 × 7
L C 007	16014, 8 × 10	L C 019	12344, 5 × 7
L C 008	13751, 8 × 10	L C 019	12345, 5 × 7
L C 009	13731, 8 × 10	L C 019	12346, 5 × 7
L C 009	13732, 8 × 10	L C 019	12370, 5 × 7
L C 009	13733, 8 × 10	L C 019	12371, 5 × 7
L C 009	13734, 8 × 10	L C 019	12439, 5 × 7
L C 009	13735, 8 × 10	L C 019	12440, 5 × 7
L C 011	13479, 5 × 7	L C 019	12441, 5 × 7
L C 015	12967, 5 × 7	L C 019	12442, 5 × 7
L C 015	12968, 5 × 7	L C 019	12443, 5 × 7
L C 015	12969, 5 × 7	L C 019	12452, 5 × 7
L C 015	12970, 5 × 7	L C 019	13007, 5 × 7
L C 015	12972, 5 × 7	L C 019	13226, 5 × 7
L C 015	12973, 5 × 7	L C 019	13524, 5 × 7
L C 015	13774, 8 × 10	L C 019	13525, 5 × 7
L C 016	12456, 8 × 10	L C 019	13526, 5 × 7
L C 016	12974, 5 × 7	L C 019	13527, 5 × 7
L C 016	12975, 5 × 7	L C 019	13528, 5 × 7
L C 016	12976, 5 × 7	L C 019	13745, 8 × 10
L C 016	12977, 5 × 7	L C 019	15671, 8 × 10
L C 016	15427, 8 × 10	L C 019	15691, 8 × 10
L C 016	15462, 8 × 10	L C 019	15692, 8 × 10
L C 017	12456, 8 × 10	L C 019	15693, 8 × 10
L C 017	12457, 8 × 10	L C 020	3514, 7 × 9
L C 017	12552, 8 × 10	L C 020	3515, 7 × 9
L C 018	3508, 7 × 9	L C 020	3516, 7 × 9
L C 018	3513, 7 × 9	L C 020	3517, 7 × 9
L C 018	9055, 7 × 9	L C 020	3518, 7 × 9
L C 018	9056, 7 × 9	L C 020	3519, 7 × 9
L C 018	12278, 5 × 7	L C 020	3541, 7 × 9
L C 018	12340, 5 × 7	L C 020	9059, 7 × 9
L C 018	12341, 5 × 7	L C 020	9060, 7 × 9
L C 018	12342, 5 × 7	L C 020	9061, 7 × 9
L C 018	12343, 5 × 7	L C 020	9062, 7 × 9
L C 018	12344, 5 × 7	L C 020	9063, 7 × 9
L C 018	12345, 5 × 7	L C 020	12280, 5 × 7
L C 018	12367, 5 × 7	L C 020	12281, 5 × 7
L C 018	12368, 5 × 7	L C 020	12282, 5 × 7
L C 018	12369, 5 × 7	L C 020	12283, 5 × 7
L C 018	12602, 8 × 10	L C 020	12347, 5 × 7
L C 018	12603, 8 × 10	L C 020	12348, 5 × 7
L C 018	13008, 5 × 7	L C 020	12349, 5 × 7
L C 018	13009, 8 × 10	L C 020	12350, 5 × 7
L C 018	15752, 8 × 10	L C 020	12351, 5 × 7
L C 018	15773, 8 × 10	L C 020	12352, 5 × 7
L C 018	15798, 8 × 10	L C 020	12353, 5 × 7
L C 019	3509, 7 × 9	L C 020	12371, 5 × 7
L C 019	3510, 7 × 9	L C 020	12436, 5 × 7
L C 019	3511, 7 × 9	L C 020	12438, 5 × 7
L C 019	3512, 7 × 9	L C 020	12444, 5 × 7
L C 019	3514, 7 × 9	L C 020	12445, 5 × 7
L C 019	9057, 7 × 9	L C 020	12446, 5 × 7

Luxor Temple (*cont.*)

Nelson Number/Description	Negative, Format
L C 020	12447, 5 × 7
L C 020	12448, 5 × 7
L C 020	12449, 5 × 7
L C 020	12450, 5 × 7
L C 020	12451, 5 × 7
L C 020	12604, 8 × 10
L C 020	12605, 8 × 10
L C 020	12606, 8 × 10
L C 020	13010, 5 × 7
L C 020	13169, 5 × 7
L C 020	13497, 8 × 10
L C 020	13498, 8 × 10
L C 020	15414, 8 × 10
L C 020	15415, 8 × 10
L C 020	15416, 8 × 10
L C 020	15417, 8 × 10
L C 020	15418, 8 × 10
L C 020	15419, 8 × 10
L C 020	15420, 8 × 10
L C 020	15421, 8 × 10
L C 020	15422, 8 × 10
L C 020	15423, 8 × 10
L C 020	15424, 8 × 10
L C 020	15425, 8 × 10
L C 020	15426, 8 × 10
L C 020	15429, 8 × 10
L C 020	15430, 8 × 10
L C 020	15431, 8 × 10
L C 020	15657, 8 × 10
L C 020	15658, 8 × 10
L C 020	15662, 8 × 10
L C 020	15670, 8 × 10
L C 020	15687, 8 × 10
L C 020	15688, 8 × 10
L C 020	15690, 8 × 10
L C 020	15760, 8 × 10
L C 021	3522, 7 × 9
L C 021	9064, 7 × 9
L C 021	12283, 5 × 7
L C 021	12284, 5 × 7
L C 021	12352, 5 × 7
L C 021	12353, 5 × 7
L C 021	12354, 5 × 7
L C 021	12428, 5 × 7
L C 021	12429, 5 × 7
L C 021	12433, 5 × 7
L C 021	12437, 5 × 7
L C 021	13545, 5 × 7
L C 021	15686, 8 × 10
L C 021	15689, 8 × 10
L C 021	15695, 8 × 10
L C 022	3520, 7 × 9
L C 022	3521, 7 × 9
L C 022	3522, 7 × 9
L C 022	3527, 7 × 9

Luxor Temple (*cont.*)

Nelson Number/Description	Negative, Format
L C 022	3528, 7 × 9
L C 022	9064, 7 × 9
L C 022	12284, 5 × 7
L C 022	12285, 5 × 7
L C 022	12355, 5 × 7
L C 022	12428, 5 × 7
L C 022	12430, 5 × 7
L C 022	12431, 5 × 7
L C 022	12432, 5 × 7
L C 022	12434, 5 × 7
L C 022	12435, 5 × 7
L C 022	13011, 5 × 7
L C 022	13545, 5 × 7
L C 022	15653, 8 × 10
L C 022	15654, 8 × 10
L C 022	15672, 8 × 10
L C 022	15680, 8 × 10
L C 022	15685, 8 × 10
L C 022	15751, 8 × 10
L C 022	15753, 8 × 10
L C 022	15758, 8 × 10
L C 022	15767, 8 × 10
L C 022	15785, 8 × 10
L C 023	13258, 8 × 10
L C 023	15815, 8 × 10
L C 024	13024, 5 × 7
L C 025	9558, 8 × 10
L C 025	12459, 8 × 10
L C 025	12542, 8 × 10
L C 025	13110, 5 × 7
L C 025	13256, 8 × 10
L C 025	13736, 8 × 10
L C 025	15757, 8 × 10
L C 025	15762, 8 × 10
L C 025	16027, 8 × 10
L C 026	9559, 8 × 10
L C 026	9560, 8 × 10
L C 026	12458, 8 × 10
L C 026	12607, 5 × 7
L C 026	12608, 8 × 10
L C 026	12609, 8 × 10
L C 026	12610, 8 × 10
L C 026	12611, 8 × 10
L C 026	12612, 8 × 10
L C 026	12981, 5 × 7
L C 026	12982, 5 × 7
L C 026	12983, 5 × 7
L C 026	12984, 5 × 7
L C 026	12985, 5 × 7
L C 026	12986, 5 × 7
L C 026	13122, 5 × 7
L C 026	13741, 8 × 10
L C 026	13743, 8 × 10
L C 026	13754, 8 × 10
L C 026	15804, 5 × 7

Luxor Temple (*cont.*)

Nelson Number/Description	Negative, Format
L C 027	12460, 8 × 10
L C 027	12544, 8 × 10
L C 027	12545, 8 × 10
L C 027	12979, 5 × 7
L C 027	12980, 5 × 7
L C 027	13257, 8 × 10
L C 027	15428, 8 × 10
L C 027	15804, 5 × 7
L C 027	15829, 8 × 10
L C 027	15830, 8 × 10
L C 027	15831, 8 × 10
L C 027	15832, 8 × 10
L C 027	15833, 8 × 10
L C 027	15834, 8 × 10
L C 027	15835, 8 × 10
L C 027	15836, 8 × 10
L C 027	16025, 8 × 10
L C 032	3536, 7 × 9
L C 032	12366, 5 × 7
L C 032	16008, 8 × 10
L C 032	16029, 8 × 10
L C 033	3536, 7 × 9
L C 033	12366, 5 × 7
L C 033	12537, 8 × 10
L C 033	12978, 5 × 7
L C 034	3526, 7 × 9
L C 034	3539, 7 × 9
L C 034	12236, 5 × 7
L C 034	12237, 5 × 7
L C 034	12238, 5 × 7
L C 034	12239, 5 × 7
L C 034	12240, 5 × 7
L C 034	12241, 5 × 7
L C 034	12242, 5 × 7
L C 034	12265, 5 × 7
L C 034	12266, 5 × 7
L C 034	12508, 5 × 7
L C 034	12509, 5 × 7
L C 034	12510, 5 × 7
L C 034	12511, 4.5 × 5
L C 034	12512, 5 × 7
L C 034	12513, 5 × 7
L C 034	12514, 5 × 7
L C 034	12515, 5 × 7
L C 034	12516, 5 × 7
L C 034	12517, 5 × 7
L C 034	12518, 5 × 7
L C 034	12519, 5 × 7
L C 034	12520, 5 × 7
L C 034	12521, 5 × 7
L C 034	12995, 5 × 7
L C 034	12996, 5 × 7
L C 034	12997, 5 × 7
L C 034	13546, 5 × 7
L C 034	13547, 5 × 7

Luxor Temple (*cont.*)

Nelson Number/Description	Negative, Format
L C 034	13548, 5 × 7
L C 034	15399, 8 × 10
L C 034	15400, 8 × 10
L C 034	15401, 8 × 10
L C 034	15402, 8 × 10
L C 034	15403, 8 × 10
L C 034	15404, 8 × 10
L C 034	15405, 8 × 10
L C 034	15406, 8 × 10
L C 034	15660, 8 × 10
L C 034	15665, 8 × 10
L C 034	15694, 8 × 10
L C 034	15697, 8 × 10
L C 034	15837, 8 × 10
L C 035	3525, 7 × 9
L C 035	3526, 7 × 9
L C 035	3534, 7 × 9
L C 035	12243, 5 × 7
L C 035	12244, 5 × 7
L C 035	12245, 5 × 7
L C 035	12265, 5 × 7
L C 035	12266, 5 × 7
L C 035	12267, 5 × 7
L C 035	12268, 5 × 7
L C 035	12269, 5 × 7
L C 035	13119, 4 × 5
L C 035	15407, 8 × 10
L C 035	15408, 8 × 10
L C 035	15764, 8 × 10
L C 036	3523, 7 × 9
L C 036	3524, 7 × 9
L C 036	3525, 7 × 9
L C 036	3529, 7 × 9
L C 036	3530, 7 × 9
L C 036	3538, 7 × 9
L C 036	3540, 7 × 9
L C 036	12246, 5 × 7
L C 036	12247, 5 × 7
L C 036	12248, 5 × 7
L C 036	12249, 5 × 7
L C 036	12250, 5 × 7
L C 036	12251, 5 × 7
L C 036	12252, 5 × 7
L C 036	12253, 5 × 7
L C 036	12254, 5 × 7
L C 036	12255, 5 × 7
L C 036	12256, 5 × 7
L C 036	12257, 5 × 7
L C 036	12258, 5 × 7
L C 036	12267, 5 × 7
L C 036	12268, 5 × 7
L C 036	12269, 5 × 7
L C 036	12270, 5 × 7
L C 036	12271, 5 × 7
L C 036	12272, 5 × 7

Luxor Temple (*cont.*)

Nelson Number/Description	Negative, Format
L C 036	12273, 5 × 7
L C 036	12327, 5 × 7
L C 036	12328, 5 × 7
L C 036	12329, 5 × 7
L C 036	12330, 5 × 7
L C 036	12331, 5 × 7
L C 036	12332, 5 × 7
L C 036	12333, 5 × 7
L C 036	12334, 5 × 7
L C 036	12574, 8 × 10
L C 036	12575, 8 × 10
L C 036	12576, 8 × 10
L C 036	12577, 8 × 10
L C 036	12578, 8 × 10
L C 036	12579, 8 × 10
L C 036	12580, 8 × 10
L C 036	12581, 8 × 10
L C 036	12582, 8 × 10
L C 036	12583, 8 × 10
L C 036	12584, 8 × 10
L C 036	12585, 8 × 10
L C 036	12586, 8 × 10
L C 036	12587, 8 × 10
L C 036	12588, 8 × 10
L C 036	12589, 8 × 10
L C 036	12590, 8 × 10
L C 036	12591, 8 × 10
L C 036	12592, 8 × 10
L C 036	12593, 8 × 10
L C 036	12998, 5 × 7
L C 036	12999, 8 × 10
L C 036	13004, 5 × 7
L C 036	13112, 5 × 7
L C 036	13117, 5 × 7
L C 036	13120, 4 × 5
L C 036	13791, 8 × 10
L C 036	15409, 8 × 10
L C 036	15410, 8 × 10
L C 036	15411, 8 × 10
L C 036	15412, 8 × 10
L C 036	15413, 8 × 10
L C 036	15432, 8 × 10
L C 036	15433, 8 × 10
L C 036	15655, 8 × 10
L C 036	15656, 8 × 10
L C 036	15661, 8 × 10
L C 036	15663, 8 × 10
L C 036	15664, 8 × 10
L C 036	15666, 8 × 10
L C 036	15667, 8 × 10
L C 036	15668, 8 × 10
L C 036	15669, 8 × 10
L C 036	15676, 8 × 10
L C 036	15677, 8 × 10
L C 036	15678, 8 × 10

Luxor Temple (*cont.*)

Nelson Number/Description	Negative, Format
L C 036	15679, 8 × 10
L C 036	15681, 8 × 10
L C 036	15682, 8 × 10
L C 036	15683, 8 × 10
L C 036	15684, 8 × 10
L C 036	15696, 8 × 10
L C 036	15698, 8 × 10
L C 036	15699, 8 × 10
L C 036	15739, 8 × 10
L C 036	15740, 8 × 10
L C 036	15741, 8 × 10
L C 036	15742, 8 × 10
L C 036	15743, 8 × 10
L C 036	15744, 8 × 10
L C 036	15745, 8 × 10
L C 036	15746, 8 × 10
L C 036	15747, 8 × 10
L C 036	15748, 8 × 10
L C 036	15749, 8 × 10
L C 036	15750, 8 × 10
L C 036	15754, 8 × 10
L C 036	15755, 8 × 10
L C 036	15756, 8 × 10
L C 036	15759, 8 × 10
L C 036	15761, 8 × 10
L C 036	15763, 8 × 10
L C 036	15765, 8 × 10
L C 036	15766, 8 × 10
L C 037	3495, 8 × 10
L C 037	3496, 8 × 10
L C 037	3531, 7 × 9
L C 037	3532, 7 × 9
L C 037	3533, 7 × 9
L C 037	12259, 5 × 7
L C 037	12260, 5 × 7
L C 037	12261, 5 × 7
L C 037	12262, 5 × 7
L C 037	12263, 5 × 7
L C 037	12273, 5 × 7
L C 037	12274, 5 × 7
L C 037	12334, 5 × 7
L C 037	12335, 5 × 7
L C 037	12336, 5 × 7
L C 037	12356, 5 × 7
L C 037	12357, 5 × 7
L C 037	12594, 8 × 10
L C 037	13000, 5 × 7
L C 037	13001, 5 × 7
L C 037	13002, 8 × 10
L C 037	13003, 5 × 7
L C 037	13765, 8 × 10
L C 037	13775, 8 × 10
L C 037	15770, 8 × 10
L C 037	15782, 8 × 10
L C 037	15783, 8 × 10

Luxor Temple (*cont.*)

Nelson Number/Description	Negative, Format
L C 037	15787, 8 × 10
L C 037	15799, 8 × 10
L C 038	3495, 8 × 10
L C 038	3497, 8 × 10
L C 038	3533, 7 × 9
L C 038	3535, 7 × 9
L C 038	3536, 7 × 9
L C 038	3537, 7 × 9
L C 038	12264, 5 × 7
L C 038	12274, 5 × 7
L C 038	12275, 5 × 7
L C 038	12276, 5 × 7
L C 038	12277, 5 × 7
L C 038	12337, 5 × 7
L C 038	12338, 5 × 7
L C 038	12339, 5 × 7
L C 038	12358, 5 × 7
L C 038	12359, 5 × 7
L C 038	12360, 5 × 7
L C 038	12361, 5 × 7
L C 038	12362, 5 × 7
L C 038	12363, 5 × 7
L C 038	12364, 5 × 7
L C 038	12365, 5 × 7
L C 038	12412, 8 × 10
L C 038	12413, 8 × 10
L C 038	12414, 8 × 10
L C 038	12415, 8 × 10
L C 038	12416, 8 × 10
L C 038	12417, 8 × 10
L C 038	12595, 8 × 10
L C 038	12596, 8 × 10
L C 038	12597, 8 × 10
L C 038	12598, 8 × 10
L C 038	12599, 8 × 10
L C 038	12600, 8 × 10
L C 038	12601, 8 × 10
L C 038	13005, 5 × 7
L C 038	13006, 5 × 7
L C 038	15659, 8 × 10
L C 038	15738, 8 × 10
L C 038	15771, 8 × 10
L C 038	15772, 8 × 10
L C 038	15774, 8 × 10
L C 038	15775, 8 × 10
L C 038	15786, 8 × 10
L C 038	15797, 8 × 10
L C 038	15800, 8 × 10
L C 039	3497, 8 × 10
L C 039	3536, 7 × 9
L C 039	13259, 8 × 10
L C 039	13764, 8 × 10
L C 039	15816, 8 × 10
L C 040	3497, 8 × 10
L C 040	3536, 7 × 9

Luxor Temple (*cont.*)

Nelson Number/Description	Negative, Format
L C 040	13024, 5 × 7
L C 041	12475, 8 × 10
L C 041	12547, 8 × 10
L C 042	12475, 8 × 10
L C 042	12547, 8 × 10
L C 042	16015, 8 × 10
L C 043	12475, 8 × 10
L C 043	12546, 8 × 10
L C 043	16006, 8 × 10
L C 044	12474, 8 × 10
L C 044	12548, 8 × 10
L C 044	12549, 8 × 10
L C 044	16019, 8 × 10
L C 045	12475, 8 × 10
L C 045	12547, 8 × 10
L C 045	12971, 5 × 7
L C 045	16009, 8 × 10
L C 045	16013, 8 × 10
L C 047	12411, 8 × 10
L C 046	12475, 8 × 10
L C 046	12547, 8 × 10
L C 047	12549, 8 × 10
L C 047	12550, 8 × 10
L C 047	12966, 8 × 10
L C 047	12988, 8 × 10
L C 047	13773, 8 × 10
L C 047	15673, 8 × 10
L C 047	15674, 8 × 10
L C 047	15675, 8 × 10
L C 047	15768, 8 × 10
L C 047	15769, 8 × 10
L C 046	16022, 8 × 10
L C 048	12486, 5 × 7
L C 048	12616, 8 × 10
L C 048	12617, 5 × 7
L C 048	12994, 5 × 7
L C 048	13723, 8 × 10
L C 048	13725, 8 × 10
L C 048	13755, 8 × 10
L C 048	14387, 8 × 10
L C 048	14388, 8 × 10
L C 048	16012, 8 × 10
L C 049	12487, 5 × 7
L C 049	12615, 8 × 10
L C 049	12989, 5 × 7
L C 049	12990, 5 × 7
L C 049	12991, 8 × 10
L C 049	12992, 5 × 7
L C 049	12993, 8 × 10
L C 049	13724, 8 × 10
L C 049	14389, 8 × 10
L C 050	12487, 5 × 7
L C 050	12615, 8 × 10
L C 050	12989, 5 × 7
L C 050	12990, 5 × 7

Luxor Temple (*cont.*)

Nelson Number/Description	Negative, Format
L C 050	12991, 8 × 10
L C 050	12992, 5 × 7
L C 050	14390, 8 × 10
L C 050	14391, 8 × 10
L C 050	16010, 8 × 10
L C 060	13086, 5 × 7
L C 060	13087, 5 × 7
L C 060	13088, 5 × 7
L C 060	13089, 5 × 7
L C 060	13090, 5 × 7
L C 060	13255, 8 × 10
L C 060	13468, 5 × 7
L C 061	13254, 8 × 10
L C 062	13253, 8 × 10
L C 063	13082, 5 × 7
L C 063	13083, 5 × 7
L C 063	13084, 5 × 7
L C 063	13085, 5 × 7
L C 063	13252, 8 × 10
L C 063	13462, 5 × 7
L C 063	13464, 5 × 7
L C 063	13470, 5 × 7
L C 075	12523, 5 × 7
L C 075	13538, 5 × 7
L C 076	12522, 5 × 7
L C 076	13039, 5 × 7
L C 076	13040, 5 × 7
L C 076	13041, 5 × 7
L C 076	13538, 5 × 7
L C 076	13720, 8 × 10
L C 077	12535, 8 × 10
L C 077	13538, 5 × 7
L C 077	13721, 8 × 10
L C 077	15395, 8 × 10
L C 078	12534, 8 × 10
L C 078	13066, 5 × 7
L C 078	13067, 5 × 7
L C 079	12532, 8 × 10
L C 079	12533, 8 × 10
L C 079	13064, 5 × 7
L C 079	13065, 5 × 7
L C 079	15397, 8 × 10
L C 080	12531, 8 × 10
L C 080	13057, 5 × 7
L C 080	13063, 5 × 7
L C 080	13717, 8 × 10
L C 080	15180, 8 × 10
L C 081	12530, 8 × 10
L C 081	13069, 5 × 7
L C 081	13715, 8 × 10
L C 081	15181, 8 × 10
L C 082	12529, 5 × 7
L C 082	13034, 5 × 7
L C 082	13035, 5 × 7
L C 082	13036, 5 × 7

Luxor Temple (*cont.*)

Nelson Number/Description	Negative, Format
L C 082	13716, 8 × 10
L C 083	12528, 5 × 7
L C 083	13037, 8 × 10
L C 083	13038, 5 × 7
L C 083	13200, 8 × 10
L C 083	13714, 8 × 10
L C 083	15838, 8 × 10
L C 083a	9091, 8 × 10
L C 083b	9092, 8 × 10
L C 084	12527, 5 × 7
L C 084	13042, 5 × 7
L C 084	13043, 5 × 7
L C 084	13044, 5 × 7
L C 084	13045, 5 × 7
L C 084	13046, 5 × 7
L C 084	13047, 5 × 7
L C 084	13115, 5 × 7
L C 084	13718, 8 × 10
L C 084	13777, 8 × 10
L C 085	12526, 5 × 7
L C 085	13048, 5 × 7
L C 085	13049, 5 × 7
L C 085	13050, 5 × 7
L C 085	13776, 8 × 10
L C 085	13779, 8 × 10
L C 085	15839, 8 × 10
L C 086	12485, 5 × 7
L C 086	12525, 5 × 7
L C 086	13051, 5 × 7
L C 086	13052, 5 × 7
L C 086	13053, 5 × 7
L C 086	13054, 5 × 7
L C 086	13055, 5 × 7
L C 086	13068, 5 × 7
L C 086	13778, 8 × 10
L C 086	15396, 8 × 10
L C 087	12524, 5 × 7
L C 087	13056, 5 × 7
L C 087	13158, 5 × 7
L C 087	13722, 8 × 10
L C 087	15398, 8 × 10
L C 088	12536, 8 × 10
L C 088	13058, 5 × 7
L C 088	13059, 5 × 7
L C 088	13060, 5 × 7
L C 088	13061, 5 × 7
L C 088	13719, 8 × 10
L C 095	13511, 8 × 10
L C 116	15434, 4 × 5
L C 116	15435, 4 × 5
L C 116	15436, 4 × 5
L C 116	15437, 4 × 5
L C 116	15438, 4 × 5
L C 116	15439, 4 × 5
L C 116	15440, 4 × 5

Luxor Temple (*cont.*)

Nelson Number/Description	Negative, Format
L C 116	15441, 4 × 5
L C 116	15442, 4 × 5
L C 116	15443, 4 × 5
L C 117	15526, 4 × 5
L C 117	15527, 4 × 5
L C 117	15528, 4 × 5
L C 117	15529, 4 × 5
L C 117	15530, 4 × 5
L C 117	15531, 4 × 5
L C 117	15532, 4 × 5
L C 117	15533, 4 × 5
L C 117	15534, 4 × 5
L C 117	15535, 4 × 5
L C 117	15536, 4 × 5
L C 117	15537, 4 × 5
L C 118	15444, 8 × 10
L C 118	15445, 8 × 10
L C 118	15446, 8 × 10
L C 118	15447, 8 × 10
L C 118	15448, 8 × 10
L C 118	15449, 8 × 10
L C 118	15450, 8 × 10
L C Col. 009	12485, 5 × 7
L C Col. 075W	13459, 5 × 7
L C Col. 075W	13462, 5 × 7
L C Col. 075W	13463, 5 × 7
L C Col. 075W	13464, 5 × 7
L C Col. 075W	13470, 5 × 7
L C Col. 076W	13462, 5 × 7
L C Col. 076W	13464, 5 × 7
L C Col. 076W	13470, 5 × 7
L C Col. 077W	13462, 5 × 7
L C Col. 077W	13464, 5 × 7
L C Col. 077W	13470, 5 × 7
L C Col. 078W	13462, 5 × 7
L C Col. 078W	13464, 5 × 7
L C Col. 078W	13470, 5 × 7
L C Col. 079W	13462, 5 × 7
L C Col. 079W	13464, 5 × 7
L C Col. 079W	13468, 5 × 7
L C Col. 079W	13470, 5 × 7
L C Col. 080W	13462, 5 × 7
L C Col. 080W	13464, 5 × 7
L C Col. 080W	13468, 5 × 7
L C Col. 080W	13470, 5 × 7
L C Col. 081W	13461, 5 × 7
L C Col. 081W	13462, 5 × 7
L C Col. 081W	13464, 5 × 7
L C Col. 081W	13466, 5 × 7
L C Col. 081W	13468, 5 × 7
L C Col. 081W	13470, 5 × 7
L C Col. 081W	13478, 5 × 7
L C Col. 082E	13467, 5 × 7
L C Col. 083E	13467, 5 × 7
L C Col. 084E	13467, 5 × 7

Luxor Temple (*cont.*)

Nelson Number/Description	Negative, Format
L C Col. 085E	13467, 5 × 7
L C Col. 086E	13467, 5 × 7
L C Col. 086E	13468, 5 × 7
L C Col. 087	13480, 5 × 7
L C Col. 087E	13467, 5 × 7
L C Col. 087E	13468, 5 × 7
L C Col. 088	13476, 5 × 7
L C Col. 088	13480, 5 × 7
L C Col. 088E	13461, 5 × 7
L C Col. 088E	13466, 5 × 7
L C Col. 088E	13467, 5 × 7
L C Col. 088E	13468, 5 × 7
L C Col. 088E	13478, 5 × 7
L C Col. 132	13479, 5 × 7
L C Col. 143	13479, 5 × 7
L C Col. 144	13479, 5 × 7
L C Col. 145	13479, 5 × 7
L C Col. 146	13479, 5 × 7
L C Col. 147	13479, 5 × 7
L C Col. 148	13479, 5 × 7
L C Col. 149	13479, 5 × 7
L C Col. 150	13479, 5 × 7
L C Col. 151	13479, 5 × 7
L D 004	9497, 8 × 10
L D 005	9497, 8 × 10
L D 006	9497, 8 × 10
L D 008	9498, 8 × 10
L D 008	9499, 8 × 10
L D 009	9498, 8 × 10
L D 009	9499, 8 × 10
L D 010	9498, 8 × 10
L D 011	9499, 8 × 10
L D 012	9500, 8 × 10
L D 013	9500, 8 × 10
L D 015	9500, 8 × 10
L D 016	9500, 8 × 10
L D 017	9501, 8 × 10
L D 018	9501, 8 × 10
L D 019	9501, 8 × 10
L D 031	6595, 5 × 7
L D 032	6600, 5 × 7
L D 032	6601, 5 × 7
L D 035	6602, 5 × 7
L D 037	6596, 5 × 7
L D 038	6592, 5 × 7
L D 039	6593, 5 × 7
L D 042	6597, 5 × 7
L D 202	6599, 5 × 7
L D 204	9481, 8 × 10
L D 205	9481, 8 × 10
L D 213	6594, 5 × 7
L D 214	6594, 5 × 7
L D 214	6598, 5 × 7
L D 215	6598, 5 × 7
L E 001	9169, 8 × 10

Luxor Temple (*cont.*)

Nelson Number/Description	Negative, Format
L E 002	9170, 8 × 10
L E 003	9217, 5 × 7
L E 004	9171, 8 × 10
L E 005	9172, 8 × 10
L E 006	9173, 8 × 10
L E 007	9174, 8 × 10
L E 019	9142, 8 × 10
L E 020	9142, 8 × 10
L E 021	9142, 8 × 10
L E 021	9143, 8 × 10
L E 022	9143, 8 × 10
L E 024	9142, 8 × 10
L E 025	9142, 8 × 10
L E 025	9143, 8 × 10
L E 026	9143, 8 × 10
L E 030	9502, 8 × 10
L E 030	9503, 8 × 10
L E 031	9459, 8 × 10
L E 031	9460, 8 × 10
L E 031	9461, 8 × 10
L E 031	9462, 8 × 10
L E 031	9477, 8 × 10
L E 031	9504, 8 × 10
L E 032	9431, 8 × 10
L E 032	9432, 8 × 10
L E 032	9433, 8 × 10
L E 032	9434, 8 × 10
L E 032	9435, 8 × 10
L E 032	9436, 8 × 10
L E 033	9504, 8 × 10
L E 034	9504, 8 × 10
L E 035	9463, 8 × 10
L E 037	9464, 8 × 10
L E 038	9465, 8 × 10
L E 038	9466, 8 × 10
L E 039	9466, 8 × 10
L E 039	9467, 8 × 10
L E 040	9467, 8 × 10
L E 040	9468, 8 × 10
L E 041	9468, 8 × 10
L E 042	9469, 8 × 10
L E 043	9470, 8 × 10
L E 043	9471, 8 × 10
L E 043	9472, 8 × 10
L E 044	9472, 8 × 10
L E 045	9473, 8 × 10
L E 046	9474, 8 × 10
L E 046	9475, 8 × 10
L E 046	9476, 8 × 10
L E 047	3614, 8 × 10
L E 047	9476, 8 × 10
L E 048	9477, 8 × 10
L E 049	9477, 8 × 10
L E 050	9478, 8 × 10
L E 051	6777, 8 × 10

Luxor Temple (*cont.*)

Nelson Number/Description	Negative, Format
L E 051	7051, 8 × 10
L E 051	9479, 8 × 10
L E 052	9480, 8 × 10
L E 053	9480, 8 × 10
L E 054	9480, 8 × 10
L E 055	9437, 8 × 10
L E 056	9437, 8 × 10
L E 057	9438, 8 × 10
L E 058	9439, 8 × 10
L E 060	9440, 8 × 10
L E 061	9440, 8 × 10
L E 061	9441, 8 × 10
L E 062	9441, 8 × 10
L E 062	9442, 8 × 10
L E 063	9442, 8 × 10
L E 063	9443, 8 × 10
L E 064	9443, 8 × 10
L E 065	9444, 8 × 10
L E 066	3542, 7 × 9
L E 066	9444, 8 × 10
L E 066	9445, 8 × 10
L E 067	3544, 7 × 9
L E 067	9445, 8 × 10
L E 067	9446, 8 × 10
L E 068	3543, 7 × 9
L E 068	9446, 8 × 10
L E 068	9447, 8 × 10
L E 069	9448, 8 × 10
L E 070	9448, 8 × 10
L E 070	9449, 8 × 10
L E 070	9450, 8 × 10
L E 071	3490, 8 × 10
L E 071	9450, 8 × 10
L E 071	9451, 8 × 10
L E 072	9451, 8 × 10
L E 073	9452, 8 × 10
L E 074	9453, 8 × 10
L E 075	9454, 8 × 10
L E 081	9402, 8 × 10
L E 082	9403, 8 × 10
L E 083	9404, 8 × 10
L E 084	9404, 8 × 10
L E 085	9405, 8 × 10
L E 086	9405, 8 × 10
L E 087	9406, 8 × 10
L E 088	9406, 8 × 10
L E 089	9407, 8 × 10
L E 089	9408, 8 × 10
L E 089	9409, 8 × 10
L E 089	9410, 8 × 10
L E 090	9411, 8 × 10
L E 091	9411, 8 × 10
L E 091	9412, 8 × 10
L E 092	9412, 8 × 10
L E 092	9413, 8 × 10

Luxor Temple (*cont.*)

Nelson Number/Description	Negative, Format
L E 093	9413, 8 × 10
L E 093	9414, 8 × 10
L E 094	9414, 8 × 10
L E 095	9415, 8 × 10
L E 096	9415, 8 × 10
L E 096	9416, 8 × 10
L E 096	9505, 8 × 10
L E 096a	9416, 8 × 10
L E 097	9416, 8 × 10
L E 097	9417, 8 × 10
L E 098	3507, 8 × 10
L E 098	9417, 8 × 10
L E 098	9418, 8 × 10
L E 100	9419, 8 × 10
L E 101	9419, 8 × 10
L E 102	9420, 8 × 10
L E 103	9421, 8 × 10
L E 103	9422, 8 × 10
L E 111	9423, 8 × 10
L E 112	9424, 8 × 10
L E 113	9175, 8 × 10
L E 114	9176, 8 × 10
L E 115	9176, 8 × 10
L E 115	9177, 8 × 10
L E 116	9177, 8 × 10
L E 116	9178, 8 × 10
L E 117	9178, 8 × 10
L E 118	9179, 8 × 10
L E 119	9179, 8 × 10
L E 120	9180, 8 × 10
L E 121	9180, 8 × 10
L E 121	9181, 8 × 10
L E 122	8286, 5 × 7
L E 122	9181, 8 × 10
L E 122	9182, 8 × 10
L E 123	9182, 8 × 10
L E 124	3547, 8 × 10
L E 124	9183, 8 × 10
L E 124	9184, 8 × 10
L E 125	3491, 8 × 10
L E 125	9184, 8 × 10
L E 126	9185, 8 × 10
L E 127	9185, 8 × 10
L E 127	9186, 8 × 10
L E 128	9186, 8 × 10
L E 129	9425, 8 × 10
L E 130	9425, 8 × 10
L E 131	9426, 8 × 10
L E 132	9426, 8 × 10
L E 133	9427, 8 × 10
L E 150	9428, 8 × 10
L E 150	9429, 8 × 10
L E 150	9430, 8 × 10
L E 151	9218, 5 × 7
L E 152	9218, 5 × 7

Luxor Temple (*cont.*)

Nelson Number/Description	Negative, Format
L E 153	9219, 5 × 7
L E 154	9219, 5 × 7
L E 155	9220, 5 × 7
L E 156	9220, 5 × 7
L E 157	9221, 5 × 7
L E 158	9221, 5 × 7
L E 159	9222, 5 × 7
L E 160	9222, 5 × 7
L E 161	9223, 5 × 7
L E 162	9223, 5 × 7
L E 163	9224, 5 × 7
L E 164	9224, 5 × 7
L E 164	13398, 5 × 7
L E 164	13403, 5 × 7
L E 165	9225, 5 × 7
L E 166	9225, 5 × 7
L E 167	9226, 5 × 7
L E 168	9226, 5 × 7
L E 176	9227, 5 × 7
L E 177	9227, 5 × 7
L E 178	9228, 5 × 7
L E 179	9228, 5 × 7
L E 180	9229, 5 × 7
L E 181	9229, 5 × 7
L E 182	9230, 5 × 7
L E 183	9230, 5 × 7
L E 184	9231, 5 × 7
L E 185	9231, 5 × 7
L E 186	9232, 5 × 7
L E 187	9232, 5 × 7
L E 188	9233, 5 × 7
L E 189	9233, 5 × 7
L E 190	9234, 5 × 7
L E 191	9234, 5 × 7
L E 192	9235, 5 × 7
L E 193	9235, 5 × 7
L E 197	9243, 8 × 10
L E 197	9244, 8 × 10
L E 197	9245, 8 × 10
L E 198	9243, 8 × 10
L E 199	9244, 8 × 10
L E 200	9245, 8 × 10
L E 201	9243, 8 × 10
L E 201	9244, 8 × 10
L E 201	9245, 8 × 10
L E 204	9246, 8 × 10
L E 204	9247, 8 × 10
L E 204	9248, 8 × 10
L E 205	9246, 8 × 10
L E 206	9247, 8 × 10
L E 207	9248, 8 × 10
L E 208	9246, 8 × 10
L E 208	9247, 8 × 10
L E 208	9248, 8 × 10
L E 220	9144, 8 × 10

Luxor Temple (*cont.*)

Nelson Number/Description	Negative, Format
L E 220	9145, 8 × 10
L E 220	9146, 8 × 10
L E 220	9147, 8 × 10
L E 221	9148, 8 × 10
L E 222	9148, 8 × 10
L E 222	9149, 8 × 10
L E 223	9149, 8 × 10
L E 224	9150, 8 × 10
L E 225	9151, 8 × 10
L E 226	9152, 8 × 10
L E 227	9152, 8 × 10
L E 227	9153, 8 × 10
L E 228	9153, 8 × 10
L E 229	9153, 8 × 10
L E 229	9154, 8 × 10
L E 230	9154, 8 × 10
L E 230	9155, 8 × 10
L E 231	9155, 8 × 10
L E 231	9156, 8 × 10
L E 232	9156, 8 × 10
L E 235	9506, 8 × 10
L E 236	9507, 8 × 10
L E 238	9508, 8 × 10
L E 238	9509, 8 × 10
L E 240	9187, 8 × 10
L E 240	9188, 8 × 10
L E 243	9157, 8 × 10
L E 244	9157, 8 × 10
L E 245	9158, 8 × 10
L E 246	9158, 8 × 10
L E 248	9159, 8 × 10
L E 249	9611, 8 × 10
L E 250	9159, 8 × 10
L E 252	9510, 8 × 10
L E 252	9561, 8 × 10
L E 252	9562, 8 × 10
L E 253	9563, 8 × 10
L E 254	9565, 8 × 10
L E 255	9511, 8 × 10
L E 256	9189, 8 × 10
L E 257	8464, 8 × 10
L E 258	9564, 8 × 10
L E 268	9162, 8 × 10
L E 269	9162, 8 × 10
L E 269	9164, 8 × 10
L E 270	9163, 8 × 10
L E 270	9164, 8 × 10
L E 271	9165, 8 × 10
L E 272	9161, 8 × 10
L E 272	9190, 8 × 10
L E 273	9190, 8 × 10
L E 274	9160, 8 × 10
L E 275	9160, 8 × 10
L E 275	9191, 8 × 10
L E 276	9191, 8 × 10

Luxor Temple (*cont.*)

Nelson Number/Description	Negative, Format
L E 276	9192, 8 × 10
L E 280	9193, 8 × 10
L E 281	9193, 8 × 10
L E 281	9194, 8 × 10
L E 282	9194, 8 × 10
L E 282	9195, 8 × 10
L E 283	9195, 8 × 10
L E 283	9196, 8 × 10
L E 284	9196, 8 × 10
L E 296	9197, 8 × 10
L E 297	9512, 8 × 10
L E 298	9198, 8 × 10
L E 299	9198, 8 × 10
L E 300	9198, 8 × 10
L E 300	9513, 8 × 10
L E 301	9513, 8 × 10
L E 302	9199, 8 × 10
L E 302	9514, 8 × 10
L E 303	9199, 8 × 10
L E 303	9514, 8 × 10
L E 303	9515, 8 × 10
L E 304	9515, 8 × 10
L E 310	9123, 8 × 10
L E 310	9124, 8 × 10
L E 311	9124, 8 × 10
L E 311	9125, 8 × 10
L E 312	9125, 8 × 10
L E 312	9126, 8 × 10
L E 313	9127, 8 × 10
L E 314	9127, 8 × 10
L E 314	9128, 8 × 10
L E 315	9128, 8 × 10
L E 315	9129, 8 × 10
L E 316	9129, 8 × 10
L E 316	9130, 8 × 10
L E 317	9130, 8 × 10
L E 318	9131, 8 × 10
L E 319	9131, 8 × 10
L E 319	9132, 8 × 10
L E 320	9132, 8 × 10
L E 321	9133, 8 × 10
L E 321	9134, 8 × 10
L E 322	9134, 8 × 10
L E 322	9135, 8 × 10
L E 323	9135, 8 × 10
L F 001	9138, 8 × 10
L F 002	9139, 8 × 10
L F 003	9138, 8 × 10
L F 003	9139, 8 × 10
L F 003	9140, 8 × 10
L F 003	9141, 8 × 10
L F 004	9140, 8 × 10
L F 005	9141, 8 × 10
L F 010	9612, 8 × 10
L F 011	9613, 8 × 10

Luxor Temple (*cont.*)

Nelson Number/Description	Negative, Format
L F 012	9613, 8 × 10
L F 013	9566, 8 × 10
L F 014	9567, 8 × 10
L F 015	9568, 8 × 10
L F 016	9569, 8 × 10
L F 017	9570, 8 × 10
L F 018	9570, 8 × 10
L F 018	9571, 8 × 10
L F 019	9571, 8 × 10
L F 019	9572, 8 × 10
L F 020	9572, 8 × 10
L F 022	9573, 8 × 10
L F 023	9574, 8 × 10
L F 024	6678, 5 × 7
L F 024	6681, 5 × 7
L F 024	6682, 5 × 7
L F 024	9575, 8 × 10
L F 024	9576, 8 × 10
L F 025	9577, 8 × 10
L F 026	6679, 5 × 7
L F 026	6680, 5 × 7
L F 026	9578, 8 × 10
L F 026	9579, 8 × 10
L F 027	9580, 8 × 10
L F 028	9581, 8 × 10
L F 028	9582, 8 × 10
L F 029	9516, 8 × 10
L F 030	9516, 8 × 10
L F 030	9517, 8 × 10
L F 030	9518, 8 × 10
L F 031	9519, 8 × 10
L F 032	9519, 8 × 10
L F 033	9520, 8 × 10
L F 034	9521, 8 × 10
L F 034a	9521, 8 × 10
L F 035	9522, 8 × 10
L F 036	9522, 8 × 10
L F 037	9523, 8 × 10
L F 040	9524, 8 × 10
L F 041	9524, 8 × 10
L F 042	9200, 8 × 10
L F 043	9525, 8 × 10
L F 044	9526, 8 × 10
L F 045	9526, 8 × 10
L F 045	9527, 8 × 10
L F 046	9527, 8 × 10
L F 046	9528, 8 × 10
L F 047	9528, 8 × 10
L F 048	9203, 8 × 10
L F 049	9203, 8 × 10
L F 049	9204, 8 × 10
L F 050	9204, 8 × 10
L F 051	9529, 8 × 10
L F 052	9201, 8 × 10
L F 053	9530, 8 × 10

Luxor Temple (*cont.*)

Nelson Number/Description	Negative, Format
L F 054	9531, 8 × 10
L F 054a	9527, 8 × 10
L F 055	9532, 8 × 10
L F 056	9532, 8 × 10
L F 057	9205, 8 × 10
L F 058	9205, 8 × 10
L F 058	9206, 8 × 10
L F 059	9206, 8 × 10
L F 060	9533, 8 × 10
L F 061	9202, 8 × 10
L F 062	9534, 8 × 10
L F 063	9535, 8 × 10
L F 064	9535, 8 × 10
L F 065	9536, 8 × 10
L F 066	9207, 8 × 10
L F 066	9537, 8 × 10
L F 067	9207, 8 × 10
L F 067	9208, 8 × 10
L F 068	9208, 8 × 10
L F 069	9614, 8 × 10
L F 070	9583, 8 × 10
L F 071	9584, 8 × 10
L F 080	9093, 8 × 10
L F 081	9093, 8 × 10
L F 081	9094, 8 × 10
L F 082a	9093, 8 × 10
L F 082b	9093, 8 × 10
L F 083	9093, 8 × 10
L F 083	9094, 8 × 10
L F 084	9095, 8 × 10
L F 085	9096, 8 × 10
L F 086	9096, 8 × 10
L F 086	9097, 8 × 10
L F 087	9098, 8 × 10
L F 088	9099, 8 × 10
L F 089	9096, 8 × 10
L F 090	9096, 8 × 10
L F 090	9097, 8 × 10
L F 091	9098, 8 × 10
L F 092	9099, 8 × 10
L F 100	9100, 8 × 10
L F 102	9101, 8 × 10
L F 103	9102, 8 × 10
L F 104	9103, 8 × 10
L F 105	9104, 8 × 10
L F 106	9105, 8 × 10
L F 107	9106, 8 × 10
L F 108	9106, 8 × 10
L F 108	9107, 8 × 10
L F 109	9107, 8 × 10
L F 110	9105, 8 × 10
L F 111	9105, 8 × 10
L F 111	9106, 8 × 10
L F 112	9106, 8 × 10
L F 113	9107, 8 × 10

Luxor Temple (*cont.*)		Luxor Temple (*cont.*)	
Nelson Number/Description	*Negative, Format*	*Nelson Number/Description*	*Negative, Format*
L F 114	9107, 8 × 10	L F 169	9215, 8 × 10
L F 115	9108, 8 × 10	L F 170	9215, 8 × 10
L F 116	9108, 8 × 10	L F 177	9602, 5 × 7
L F 120	9109, 8 × 10	L F 178	9602, 5 × 7
L F 121	9109, 8 × 10	L F 179	9538, 8 × 10
L F 122	9110, 8 × 10	L F 180	9538, 8 × 10
L F 123	9111, 8 × 10	L F 181	9538, 8 × 10
L F 124	9112, 8 × 10	L F 181	9539, 8 × 10
L F 125	9113, 8 × 10	L F 182	9539, 8 × 10
L F 126	8285, 5 × 7	L F 183	9539, 8 × 10
L F 126	9110, 8 × 10	L F 184	9540, 8 × 10
L F 126	9113, 8 × 10	L F 185	9540, 8 × 10
L F 127	8285, 5 × 7	L F 186	9541, 8 × 10
L F 127	9110, 8 × 10	L F 187	9542, 8 × 10
L F 128	9111, 8 × 10	L F 188	9542, 8 × 10
L F 128	9114, 8 × 10	L G	12286, 5 × 7
L F 129	9115, 8 × 10	L G	12287, 5 × 7
L F 130	9116, 8 × 10	L G	12288, 5 × 7
L F 131	9117, 8 × 10	L G	12289, 5 × 7
L F 132	9118, 8 × 10	L G	12290, 5 × 7
L F 133	9100, 8 × 10	L G 001	13438, 5 × 7
L F 133	9118, 8 × 10	L G 001	13460, 5 × 7
L F 134	9119, 8 × 10	L G 003	13438, 5 × 7
L F 135	9120, 8 × 10	L G 003	13460, 5 × 7
L F 136	9121, 8 × 10	L G 004	13460, 5 × 7
L F 136	9122, 8 × 10	L G 012	13460, 5 × 7
L F 142	9209, 8 × 10	L G 013	13460, 5 × 7
L F 143	9209, 8 × 10	L G 014	13460, 5 × 7
L F 144	9209, 8 × 10	L G 026	13460, 5 × 7
L F 150	9210, 8 × 10	L G 027	13460, 5 × 7
L F 151	9210, 8 × 10	L G 028	13460, 5 × 7
L F 151	9211, 8 × 10	L G 029	13460, 5 × 7
L F 152	9211, 8 × 10	L G 032	13465, 5 × 7
L F 152	9212, 8 × 10	L G 033	13465, 5 × 7
L F 153	9212, 8 × 10	L G 034	13465, 5 × 7
L F 153	9213, 8 × 10	L G 035	13465, 5 × 7
L F 154	9213, 8 × 10	L G 036	13465, 5 × 7
L F 155	9210, 8 × 10	L G 037	13465, 5 × 7
L F 156	9210, 8 × 10	L G 038	13465, 5 × 7
L F 156	9211, 8 × 10	L G 041	9587, 8 × 10
L F 157	9211, 8 × 10	L G 041	9588, 8 × 10
L F 157	9212, 8 × 10	L G 041	13465, 5 × 7
L F 158	9212, 8 × 10	L G 042	9588, 8 × 10
L F 158	9213, 8 × 10	L G 042	9589, 8 × 10
L F 159	9213, 8 × 10	L G 043	9589, 8 × 10
L F 160	9214, 8 × 10	L G 043	9590, 8 × 10
L F 161	9214, 8 × 10	L G 043	9591, 8 × 10
L F 162	9585, 8 × 10	L G 045	6035, 8 × 10
L F 163	9214, 8 × 10	L G 049	6034, 8 × 10
L F 164	9214, 8 × 10	L G 050	9592, 8 × 10
L F 165	9585, 8 × 10	L G 051	9593, 8 × 10
L F 166	9586, 8 × 10	L G 054	9594, 8 × 10
L F 167	9586, 8 × 10	L G 054	9595, 8 × 10
L F 168	9215, 8 × 10	L G 054	9596, 8 × 10
L F 168	9586, 8 × 10	L G 054	9597, 8 × 10

Luxor Temple (*cont.*)

Nelson Number/Description	Negative, Format
L G 055	9543, 8 × 10
L G 056	9544, 8 × 10
L G 056	9545, 8 × 10
L G 056	9546, 8 × 10
L G 056	9547, 8 × 10
L G 056	9548, 8 × 10
L G 056	9549, 8 × 10
L G 056	9550, 8 × 10
L G 056	9551, 8 × 10
L G 057	9551, 8 × 10
L G 057	9552, 8 × 10
L G 058	9553, 8 × 10
L G 059	9553, 8 × 10
L G 060a	9482, 8 × 10
L G 060a	9483, 8 × 10
L G 060b	9484, 8 × 10
L G 060b	9485, 8 × 10
L G 099	9486, 8 × 10
L G 100	9487, 8 × 10
L G 102a	9488, 8 × 10
L G 102a	9489, 8 × 10
L G 102a	9490, 8 × 10
L G 103	9491, 8 × 10
L G 104	9492, 8 × 10
L G 104	9603, 5 × 7
L G 104	13476, 5 × 7
L G 104	13480, 5 × 7
L G 105	9493, 8 × 10
L G 105	9494, 8 × 10
L G 105	9495, 8 × 10
L G 105	9496, 8 × 10
L G 105	13468, 5 × 7
L G 105	13476, 5 × 7
L G 105	13480, 5 × 7
L G 107	3498, 8 × 10
L G 108	3499, 8 × 10
L G 108	3500, 8 × 10
L G 108	3501, 8 × 10
L G 108	3502, 8 × 10
L G 108	3503, 8 × 10
L G 109	3504, 8 × 10
L G 109	3505, 8 × 10
L G 109	3506, 8 × 10
Aerial view	13600, 5 × 7
Amenhotep III Sun Court: east wall, fragment reconstruction of 13511	13512, 8 × 10
Amenhotep III Sun Court, toward southeast	13589, 5 × 7
Avenue of Sphinx, looking south towards pylon	13608, 5 × 7
Back of pylon, Ramesside court filled with houses	13458, 5 × 7
Block in Ramesside court	13737, 8 × 10
Colonnade from southeast	13570, 5 × 7
Colonnade in early 1860s: Houses of Mustafa Agha Ayat (right) and Qadi (Judge) of Esna (left). Oriental Institute print made from lantern slide (ex Breasted coll.) in 1982	13532, 5 × 7
Colonnade showing house built among columns	13555, 5 × 7

Luxor Temple (*cont.*)

Nelson Number/Description	Negative, Format
Colonnade: architraves	13139, 35 mm
Colonnade: architraves	13140, 35 mm
Colonnade: architraves	13141, 35 mm
Colonnade: architraves	13142, 35 mm
Colonnade: architraves	13143, 35 mm
Colonnade: architraves	13144, 35 mm
Colonnade: architraves	13145, 35 mm
Colonnade: architraves	13146, 35 mm
Colonnade: area of faded paint, Roman decoration of jambs of passageway between the Colonnade Hall and the court of Amenhotep III (L C 26)	12987, 5 × 7
Colonnade: area of faded paint, Roman decoration of jambs of passageway between the Colonnade Hall and the court of Amenhotep III (L C 26)	13100, 5 × 7
Colonnade: axis of temple from pylon roof, north view	13014, 5 × 7
Colonnade: block	12954, 5 × 7
Colonnade: breakage of capitals along central axis	13079, 5 × 7
Colonnade: capitals east and west of architrave	13080, 5 × 7
Colonnade: decoration over column capitals	13116, 5 × 7
Colonnade: east wall	16028, 8 × 10
Colonnade: east wall, south end, Amun barque scene (standards)	13519, 8 × 10
Colonnade: east wing of south gate from northeast	13020, 5 × 7
Colonnade: eastern exterior wall and join with Sun Court wall	13021, 5 × 7
Colonnade: eastern wall, upper extension	13026, 5 × 7
Colonnade: example of recut marginal text below Opet scenes	13753, 8 × 10
Colonnade: fallen architrave block, northeast end of Hall (view from above), preserving cartouches of Amenhotep III, part of Tutankhamun restoration inscription	15813, 2.25 × 2.25
Colonnade: fallen architrave block, northeast end of Hall (view from above), preserving cartouches of Amenhotep III, part of Tutankhamun restoration inscription	15814, 2.25 × 2.25
Colonnade: fragment (= throne) on top of west wall, south end	13111, 2.25 × 2.25
Colonnade: general view down axis from north	13016, 8 × 10
Colonnade: general view from pylon roof	13015, 5 × 7
Colonnade: general view, north/south axis	13017, 8 × 10
Colonnade: general view, northeastern passage/axis, northeastern exterior, Ramesses II statue	12614, 8 × 10
Colonnade: graffito on facade above roof of portico	13205, 5 × 7
Colonnade: graffito on facade above roof of portico	13206, 5 × 7
Colonnade: graffito on facade above roof of portico	13207, 5 × 7
Colonnade: graffito on facade above roof of portico	13208, 5 × 7
Colonnade: graffito on facade above roof of portico	13209, 5 × 7
Colonnade: graffito on facade above roof of portico	13210, 5 × 7

Luxor Temple (*cont.*)

Nelson Number/Description	Negative, Format
Colonnade: graffito on facade above roof of portico	13211, 5 × 7
Colonnade: graffito on facade above roof of portico	13212, 5 × 7
Colonnade: graffito on facade above roof of portico	13213, 5 × 7
Colonnade: graffito, loose block inside northeast wall	13022, 5 × 7
Colonnade: interior west wall from top of colonnade	13114, 5 × 7
Colonnade: join of northeast wall, with southeast wall of first court	15826, 5 × 7
Colonnade: join of southeast wall with Amenhotep III south wall, from southeast	13170, 8 × 10
Colonnade: join of southeast wall with south wall	13032, 5 × 7
Colonnade: join of southeast wall with south wall, top, inside	13033, 5 × 7
Colonnade: join of southwest corner with Amenhotep III court, from top of wall	13727, 8 × 10
Colonnade: join of southwest corner with Amenhotep III court, from top of wall	13728, 8 × 10
Colonnade: join of southwest corner with Amenhotep III court from top of wall	13739, 8 × 10
Colonnade: join of southwest wall with Amenhotep III south wall, view from northeast top	15825, 5 × 7
Colonnade: Late period fragment on colonnade wall	13070, 2.25 × 2.25
Colonnade: Late period fragment on colonnade wall	13071, 2.25 × 2.25
Colonnade: Late period fragment on colonnade wall	13072, 2.25 × 2.25
Colonnade: Late period fragment on colonnade wall	13073, 2.25 × 2.25
Colonnade: Late period fragment on colonnade wall	13074, 2.25 × 2.25
Colonnade: Late period fragment on colonnade wall	13075, 2.25 × 2.25
Colonnade: Late period fragment on colonnade wall	13076, 2.25 × 2.25
Colonnade: Late period fragment on colonnade wall	13077, 2.25 × 2.25
Colonnade: north/south axis	13154-a, 2.25 × 2.25
Colonnade: north/south axis	13154-b, 2.25 × 2.25
Colonnade: north/south axis from above	13152-a, 2.25 × 2.25
Colonnade: north/south axis from above	13152-b, 2.25 × 2.25
Colonnade: north/south axis from above	13152-c, 2.25 × 2.25
Colonnade: northeast exterior facade	12572, 8 × 10
Colonnade: northeast exterior facade (top)	12573, 8 × 10
Colonnade: northeast exterior facade	12571, 8 × 10
Colonnade: northeast exterior facade (right)	12570, 5 × 7
Colonnade: northeast facade showing bonding of Ramesside roof	13157-a, —
Colonnade: northeast facade showing bonding of Ramesside roof	13157-b, —
Colonnade: northeast facade showing bonding of Ramesside roof	13157-c, —
Colonnade: northeast tower, blocked-up west "doorway"	13118, 8 × 10

Nelson Number/Description	Negative, Format
Colonnade: northeastern wall, "hollow" thickness	13029, 5 × 7
Colonnade: northeastern wall, thickness and construction	13030, 5 × 7
Colonnade: northwest facade from above	13156, 2.25 × 2.25
Colonnade: Opet fragment group #1: east wall, Khonsu barge	15381, 8 × 10
Colonnade: Opet fragment group #2a: east wall, Khonsu barge; 2b: east wall, Khonsu barge towboats; 2c: east wall, Khonsu barge, inscription over Amun barge	15382, 8 × 10
Colonnade: Opet fragment group #3a: west wall, bottom row towboats; 3b: west wall, upper row towboats; east wall, pylons of Karnak Temple; 3c: end of Amun bark procession, beginning upper row towboats	15383, 8 × 10
Colonnade: Opet fragment group #4a: west wall, upper register towboats; 4b: west wall, upper register towboats	15384, 8 × 10
Colonnade: Opet fragment group #5a: west wall, Amun bark, Luxor Temple; 5b: west wall, Amun bark, Luxor Temple; 5c: west wall, king's barge	15385, 8 × 10
Colonnade: Opet fragment group #6a: west wall, Amun barge; 6b: horizontal inscription, running soldiers; 6c: horizontal inscription, running soldiers	15386, 8 × 10
Colonnade: Opet fragment group #7a: west wall, Amun bark procession; 7b: west wall, Amun bark procession; 7c: west wall, Amun bark procession, Luxor Temple portal, small bark procession	15387, 8 × 10
Colonnade: Opet fragment group #8a: east wall, upper register towboats; 8b: text;	15394, 8 × 10
Colonnade: Sety II fragment, block north of L A 53-55	12962, 5 × 7
Colonnade: Sety II fragment, block north of L A 53-55; detail of head of king	12963, 5 × 7
Colonnade: southwest side wall, "feet" graffito	13081, 2.25 × 2.25
Colonnade: "stairway" type massif inside northeast wall	13023, 5 × 7
Colonnade: top of Ramesses II scene, east exterior facade	12960, 5 × 7
Colonnade: view down the axis from north (pylon roof)	13012, 5 × 7
Colonnade: view from north down colonnade axis	13151, 5 × 7
Colonnade: view from northwest	13013, 5 × 7
Colonnade: view of southeastern corner, top	13028, 5 × 7
Colonnade: view of southeastern corner, top	13031, 5 × 7
Colonnade: west wall, clamp hole	13027, 5 × 7
Colonnade: west wall, WB, depiction of Karnak Temple, Pylon III, left half	13523, 5 × 7
Colossi of Ramesses II	13556, 5 × 7
Copy neg. from old photograph, entrance to room 8, view of Corinthian columns, apse	13186, 5 × 7
Copy neg. from old photograph, entrance to temple, obelisk	13187, 5 × 7
Copy neg. from old photograph, general view of temple	13185, 5 × 7
Copy neg. from old photograph, view of west side of Ramesses II court, showing standing colossi of king	13184, 5 × 7

Luxor Temple (*cont.*)

Nelson Number/Description	Negative, Format
Copy of Beato photograph, facade of temple	13217, 5 × 7
Copy of Bonfils photograph, about 1880, general view. Copy photograph from Collection Debbas, Harvard Semitic Museum, FD 126	13539, 5 × 7
Copy of Frith photograph of Colonnade	13247, 5 × 7
Copy of Sebah photograph, late 1860s-early 1870s, general view	13537, 5 × 7
Courtyard filled with modern houses	13469, 5 × 7
Demotic graffito, Phillip Arrhidaeus gateway	13204, 5 × 7
Demotic stela found in 1982 excavation, southeast corner, first court	13203, 5 × 7
First court of Ramesses II	13564, 5 × 7
First Court of Ramesses II: architrave, incomplete signs	13019, 5 × 7
First Court of Ramesses II: roof slab in facade	13018, 5 × 7
Fragment from quay	13091, 2.25 × 2.25
Fragment from quay	13092, 2.25 × 2.25
Fragment from quay	13093, 2.25 × 2.25
Fragment from quay	13094, 2.25 × 2.25
Fragment from quay	13095, 2.25 × 2.25
Fragment from quay	13096, 2.25 × 3.25
Fragment from quay	13097, 2.25 × 3.25
Fragment from quay	13098, 2.25 × 3.25
Fragment from quay	13099, 2.25 × 3.25
French house, Beato's house, and canal behind temple	13474, 5 × 7
Frith postcard: entrance to temple, section Kar G, Pylon I toward south, statues buried, 1857	13413, 5 × 7
General view from Colonnade south with Nile boats, view from west	13475, 5 × 7
General view	8429, 5 × 7
General view	8430, 5 × 7
General view	8431, 5 × 7
General view	8432, 5 × 7
General view (1988)	14420, 8 × 10
General view from west	12375, 5 × 7
General view of northeast from Nile	13572, 5 × 7
General view of northeast	13552, 8 × 10
General view of northeast toward mosque and pylon	13575, 5 × 7
General view of northwest over blockyard toward Colonnade Hall, mosque, and pylon	13565, 5 × 7
General view of south between seated statues and pylon toward temple	13591, 5 × 7
General view through pylon into temple, mudbrick houses in foreground	13554, 5 × 7
General view, main entrance to temple, great pylon, colossi of Ramesses II, and obelisk before clearance	13553, 5 × 7
House of Mustafa Agha Ayat	13569, 5 × 7
Houses built against Amenhotep III court	13473, 5 × 7
Luxor fragment	13910, 5 × 7
Luxor fragment 0001 Colonnade Hall, Opet register: upper register towboats, west wall. Drawing group #4b	12821, 5 × 7
Luxor fragment 0002 Colonnade Hall, 2nd register: west wall; Mut offering scene, Tut.	12618, 5 × 7

Luxor Temple (*cont.*)

Nelson Number/Description	Negative, Format
Luxor fragment 0003 Colonnade Hall, Opet register: upper register towboats, west wall. Drawing group #4a	12822, 5 × 7
Luxor fragment 0004, 0040, and 0389 Colonnade Hall, Opet register: Luxor Temple portal, west wall. Drawing group #7c	12900, 5 × 7
Luxor fragment 0005 Colonnade Hall, Opet register: upper register towboats, west wall. Drawing group #4b	12823, 5 × 7
Luxor fragment 0006 Colonnade Hall, Opet register: upper register towboats, west wall. Drawing group #4a	12824, 5 × 7
Luxor fragment 0007 Colonnade Hall, Opet register: upper register towboats, west wall. Drawing group #4a	12825, 5 × 7
Luxor fragment 0008 Colonnade Hall, Opet register: end of Amun bark procession, beginning upper row towboats. Drawing group #3c	12619, 5 × 7
Luxor fragment 0008 Colonnade Hall, Opet register: end of Amun bark procession, beginning upper row towboats. Drawing group #3c	12826, 5 × 7
Luxor fragment 0009 Colonnade Hall, Opet register: upper register towboats, west wall. Drawing group #4b	12827, 5 × 7
Luxor fragment 0010 Colonnade Hall, Opet register: Luxor Temple portal, west wall. Drawing group #7c	12828, 5 × 7
Luxor fragment 0011 Colonnade Hall, 2nd register: west wall; Mut offering scene, Tut.	12620, 5 × 7
Luxor fragment 0012 Colonnade Hall, Opet register: upper register towboats, west wall. Drawing group #4a	12829, 5 × 7
Luxor fragment 0013 and 0038 Colonnade Hall, Opet register: upper register towboats, west wall. Drawing group #4b	12621, 5 × 7
Luxor fragment 0013 and 0038 Opet register, upper register towboats, west wall. Drawing group #4b	12838, 5 × 7
Luxor fragment 0014 Colonnade Hall, 4th register: east wall; Tut.	12622, 5 × 7
Luxor fragment 0015 Colonnade Hall, Facade: text, east side	16044, 5 × 7
Luxor fragment 0017 Priest behind royal figure(?)	12623, 5 × 7
Luxor fragment 0018 Amenhotep III: offering list	12624, 5 × 7
Luxor fragment 0019 Colonnade Hall, Opet register: upper register towboats, west wall. Drawing group #4a	12830, 5 × 7
Luxor fragment 0020 Amenhotep III: offering list	12625, 5 × 7
Luxor fragment 0021 Amenhotep III: offering list	12626, 5 × 7
Luxor fragment 0022 small scale inscription	12627, 5 × 7
Luxor fragment 0024 Colonnade Hall, Opet register: bark of Amun procession, west wall. Drawing group #7a	12831, 5 × 7
Luxor fragment 0025 and 0026 Colonnade Hall, 2nd register: west wall; priests, Min procession, Sety I	12628, 5 × 7
Luxor fragment 0025, 0026, 0210, 0211, 0461, 0499 Colonnade Hall, 2nd register: west wall; Min procession, priests, Tut./Sety I	12952, 5 × 7
Luxor fragment 0027 Amenhotep III Sun Court: east wall; Amun bark	12832, 5 × 7
Luxor fragment 0028 Colonnade Hall, 2nd register: west wall; Mut offering scene, Tut.	13190, 5 × 7

Luxor Temple (*cont.*)

Nelson Number/Description	Negative, Format
Luxor fragment 0029 Colonnade Hall, Opet register: upper register towboats, west wall. Drawing group #4b	12833, 5 × 7
Luxor fragment 0030 Colonnade Hall, Opet register: small scale inscription	12629, 5 × 7
Luxor fragment 0031 Colonnade Hall, Opet register: bark of Amun procession, west wall. Drawing group #7b	12834, 5 × 7
Luxor fragment 0032 Colonnade Hall, Opet register: upper register towboats, west wall. Drawing group #4a	12835, 5 × 7
Luxor fragment 0033 Colonnade Hall, 2nd register: west wall; Tut.	12630, 5 × 7
Luxor fragment 0034 Colonnade Hall, Opet register: upper register towboats, west wall. Drawing group #4b	12631, 5 × 7
Luxor fragment 0035 Colonnade Hall, Opet register: upper register towboats, west wall. Drawing group #4b	12836, 5 × 7
Luxor fragment 0036 Colonnade Hall, Opet register: barge of Amun, west wall. Drawing group #6a	12837, 5 × 7
Luxor fragment 0039 Amenhotep III Sun Court: east wall; Amun bark scene	12632, 5 × 7
Luxor fragment 0041 Colonnade Hall, Opet register: Khonsu barge, east wall. Drawing group #1	12633, 5 × 7
Luxor fragment 0042 Colonnade Hall, Opet register: upper register towboats, west wall. Drawing group #4a	12839, 5 × 7
Luxor fragment 0043 Colonnade Hall, Opet register: upper register towboats, west wall. Drawing group #4a	12840, 5 × 7
Luxor fragment 0044 Colonnade Hall, Opet register: Khonsu barge, east wall. Drawing group #1	12841, 5 × 7
Luxor fragment 0045 King in *išd*- tree	13881, 5 × 7
Luxor fragment 0046 Colonnade Hall, Opet register: upper register towboats, west wall. Drawing group #4a	12842, 5 × 7
Luxor fragment 0047 Colonnade Hall, Opet register: Khonsu barge, east wall. Drawing group #1	12843, 5 × 7
Luxor fragment 0048 Colonnade Hall, upper register: Tut.	13191, 5 × 7
Luxor fragment 0049 Colonnade Hall, Opet register: bark of Amun procession, west wall. Drawing group #7a	12844, 5 × 7
Luxor fragment 0050 Colonnade Hall, 2nd register: west wall; Mut offering scene, Tut.	12634, 5 × 7
Luxor fragment 0051 Late period Thutmosis III rededication, priests, bark procession	12635, 5 × 7
Luxor fragment 0052 Colonnade Hall, Opet register: west wall; end of Amun bark procession, beginning upper row towboats. Drawing group #3c	12845, 5 × 7
Luxor fragment 0053 Colonnade Hall, Opet register: bark of Amun procession, west wall. Drawing group #7b	12846, 5 × 7
Luxor fragment 0054 Colonnade Hall, 3rd register: west wall, Tut.	14581, 5 × 7
Luxor fragment 0055 Colonnade Hall, 2nd register: west wall; priests, Min procession, Tut./Sety I	12636, 5 × 7

Luxor Temple (*cont.*)

Nelson Number/Description	Negative, Format
Luxor fragment 0056 Amenhotep III Sun Court: east wall; Amun bark scene	12637, 5 × 7
Luxor fragment 0057 Colonnade Hall, 3rd register?	13192, 5 × 7
Luxor fragment 0058 Colonnade Hall, Opet register: end of Amun bark procession, beginning upper row towboats. Drawing group #3c	12847, 5 × 7
Luxor fragment 0059 Colonnade Hall, upper register (possibly 4th): Tut.	14601, 5 × 7
Luxor fragment 0060 Colonnade Hall, Facade: lintel fragment; rightmost lintel scene	16061, 5 × 7
Luxor fragment 0061 Akhenaten talatat: water procession, sunk relief	12638-a, 5 × 7
Luxor fragment 0061 Akhenaten talatat: water procession, sunk relief	12638-b, 5 × 7
Luxor fragment 0062 Colonnade Hall, Opet register: Khonsu barge, inscription over Amun barge, east wall. Drawing group #2c	12639, 5 × 7
Luxor fragment 0062 Colonnade Hall, Opet register: Khonsu barge, inscription over Amun barge, east wall. Drawing group #2c	13193, 5 × 7
Luxor fragment 0064 Amenhotep III Sun Court: east wall; Amun bark scene	12848, 5 × 7
Luxor fragment 0065 Amenhotep III Sun Court: east wall; Amun bark scene	13194, 5 × 7
Luxor fragment 0066 Colonnade Hall, 2nd register: west wall; Theban Triad offering scene, Tut.	13195, 5 × 7
Luxor fragment 0067 Colonnade Hall, Opet register: upper register towboats, west wall. Drawing group #4a	12849, 5 × 7
Luxor fragment 0068 Akhenaten talatat	12640, 5 × 7
Luxor fragment 0069 Colonnade Hall, Opet register: upper register towboats, west wall. Drawing group #4a	12850, 5 × 7
Luxor fragment 0070 Colonnade Hall, Opet register: Temple Karnak pylons, east wall. Drawing group #3b	12851, 5 × 7
Luxor fragment 0071 Colonnade Hall, 2nd register: east wall, Tut.	14455, 5 × 7
Luxor fragment 0072 Colonnade Hall, Opet register: Amun bark, Luxor Temple, west wall. Drawing group #5a	12852, 5 × 7
Luxor fragment 0073 Tut. talatat: (Akhenaten reused talatat); military parade scene from Asiatic battle narrative	13913, 5 × 7
Luxor fragment 0074 and 0101 Colonnade Hall, 2nd register: west wall; Hathor behind king, Theban Triad offering scene	12641, 5 × 7
Luxor fragment 0076 Amenhotep III(?), small scale offering	12642, 5 × 7
Luxor fragment 0077 Colonnade Hall, Opet register: bottom row towboats, west wall. Drawing group #3a	12853, 5 × 7
Luxor fragment 0079 Colonnade Hall, Opet register: Khonsu barge towboats, east wall. Drawing group #2b	12854, 5 × 7
Luxor fragment 0080 Colonnade Hall, Opet register: Khonsu barge, east wall. Drawing group #1	12855, 5 × 7
Luxor fragment 0081 Colonnade Hall, Opet register: west wall; Karnak scene, Tut.	12643, 5 × 7

Luxor Temple (*cont.*)

Nelson Number/Description	Negative, Format
Luxor fragment 0082 Amenhotep III Sun Court?: restored bark, detail prow	12856, 5 × 7
Luxor fragment 0083 Colonnade Hall, Opet register: upper register towboats, east wall. Drawing group #8a	12857, 5 × 7
Luxor fragment 0084 Colonnade Hall, 2nd register: west wall; king, Theban Triad offering scene, Tut.	12644, 5 × 7
Luxor fragment 0085 Colonnade Hall, Facade: east doorjamb fragment; cartouches Ay usurped by Horemheb, possibly 4th jamb scene from bottom	12645, 5 × 7
Luxor fragment 0087 Colonnade Hall, Opet register: Khonsu barge towboats, east wall. Drawing group #2b	12858, 5 × 7
Luxor fragment 0088 Colonnade Hall, Facade: west doorjamb fragment; unrecut cartouches of Amenhotep III	12646, 5 × 7
Luxor fragment 0089 Colonnade Hall, Opet register: Amun bark, Luxor Temple, west wall. Drawing group #5b	12647, 5 × 7
Luxor fragment 0090 Colonnade Hall, Opet register: small scale inscriptions, Tut.	12648, 5 × 7
Luxor fragment 0091 Colonnade Hall, upper register: Sety I	12649, 5 × 7
Luxor fragment 0094 Colonnade Hall, Opet register; Khonsu barge, east wall. Drawing group #1	12650, 5 × 7
Luxor fragment 0095 Tut. talatat: (reused Akhenaten talatat); bark scene	12859, 5 × 7
Luxor fragment 0096 Colonnade Hall, Opet register: Khonsu barge, east wall. Drawing group #1	12860, 5 × 7
Luxor fragment 0097 front Sety I: small scale doorjamb block	12651-a, 5 × 7
Luxor fragment 0097 front Sety I: small scale doorjamb block	12651-b, 5 × 7
Luxor fragment 0097 front Sety I: small scale doorjamb block	12651-c, 5 × 7
Luxor fragment 0098 Colonnade Hall: cobra frieze, Tut./Sety I	15856, 5 × 7
Luxor fragment 0098 Colonnade Hall: uraeus frieze, Tut./Sety I	12652, 5 × 7
Luxor fragment 0099 Colonnade Hall, Opet register: upper register towboats, east wall. Drawing group #8a	12861, 5 × 7
Luxor fragment 0100 (joins 105) Colonnade Hall, 2nd register: Tut. cartouche	12653, 5 × 7
Luxor fragment 0102 Colonnade Hall, 2nd register: west wall; Theban Triad offering scene, Tut.	12654, 5 × 7
Luxor fragment 0103 Colonnade Hall, Opet register: upper register towboats, west wall. Drawing group #4a	12862, 5 × 7
Luxor fragment 0104 Colonnade Hall, 2nd register: west wall; Min procession, cartouches Amenhotep III, Tut.	12655, 5 × 7
Luxor fragment 0105 (joins 100) Colonnade Hall, 2nd register: Tut. cartouche	12656, 5 × 7
Luxor fragment 0106 Colonnade Hall, 4th register: east wall, Tut.	12657, 5 × 7
Luxor fragment 0107 Colonnade Hall, Opet register: Amun bark, Luxor Temple, west wall. Drawing group #5b	12658, 5 × 7

Luxor Temple (*cont.*)

Nelson Number/Description	Negative, Format
Luxor fragment 0108 (reverse see 35-313) Colonnade Hall, Facade: door thickness; Sety II cartouche frieze from west thickness, Ay carving. For reverse: see neg. 35-313 (plaster impression of Ramesses II decoration-door thickness, topmost register)	12659, 5 × 7
Luxor fragment 0109 Colonnade Hall, Facade: door thickness, Sety II, cartouche frieze from west thickness, Ay carving	12660, 5 × 7
Luxor fragment 0112 Colonnade Hall, Facade: lintel fragment; Tut./Ay carving, central text, part of right center Amun plumes, tip of Wadjit wing	12661, 5 × 7
Luxor fragment 0114 Colonnade Hall: Tut.	12662, 5 × 7
Luxor fragment 0115 Enshrined deities, possibly from Amenhotep III Mortuary Temple, reused in Luxor Temple	12938, 5 × 7
Luxor fragment 0116 Colonnade Hall: large scale inscription fragment, Tut.	12939, 5 × 7
Luxor fragment 0117 Colonnade Hall, Opet register: small scale inscription, Tut.	12940, 5 × 7
Luxor fragment 0118 Colonnade Hall, 2nd or 3rd register: west wall; king's legs (followed by goddess?)	12663, 5 × 7
Luxor fragment 0119 Colonnade Hall, upper register: Tut. Found in Colonnade Hall, north end	12664, 5 × 7
Luxor fragment 0120. Found in Colonnade Hall, north end	12665, 5 × 7
Luxor fragment 0123 Colonnade Hall, upper register: inscription fragment, Tut.	12941, 5 × 7
Luxor fragment 0124 Colonnade Hall: Tut.?	12863, 5 × 7
Luxor fragment 0125 Colonnade Hall, Opet register: King's barge, west wall. Drawing group #5c	12864, 5 × 7
Luxor fragment 0126 Colonnade Hall, 2nd register: west wall, Theban Triad offering scene	12666, 5 × 7
Luxor fragment 0127 Colonnade Hall, Opet register: barge of Amun, west wall. Drawing group #6a	13303, 5 × 7
Luxor fragment 0128 Colonnade Hall, upper register: Tut.	12942, 5 × 7
Luxor fragment 0129 Akhenaten talatat: rowers	12667, 5 × 7
Luxor fragment 0130 Akhenaten talatat: ship's rigging	12668, 5 × 7
Luxor fragment 0131 Colonnade Hall, upper register	12943, 5 × 7
Luxor fragment 0133 Tut. talatat: (reused Akhenaten talatat); cobra frieze	12865, 5 × 7
Luxor fragment 0134 Amenhotep III(?) legs of male figure	12944, 5 × 7
Luxor fragment 0135 Amenhotep III Sun Court: east wall; Amun bark scene	12866, 5 × 7
Luxor fragment 0138 Tut. talatat (reused Akhenaten talatat): bark, stern section	12669, 5 × 7
Luxor fragment 0139 Tutankhamun reused talatat	12867, 5 × 7
Luxor fragment 0139 Tutankhamun reused talatat	13885, 5 × 7
Luxor fragment 0141 Colonnade Hall, upper register: Tut.	12945, 5 × 7
Luxor fragment 0142 Colonnade Hall, 2nd register: west wall; Min procession, priest, Tut.	14295, 5 × 7
Luxor fragment 0144 Colonnade Hall, upper register: Tut.	12946, 5 × 7

Luxor Temple (*cont.*)

Nelson Number/Description	Negative, Format
Luxor fragment 0147 Tutankhamun reused talatat	13888, 5 × 7
Luxor fragment 0148 Colonnade Hall, Opet register: upper register towboats, west wall. Drawing group #4b	12670, 5 × 7
Luxor fragment 0148 Opet register, upper register towboats, west wall. Drawing group #4b	12868, 5 × 7
Luxor fragment 0149 Colonnade Hall, Opet register: Khonsu barge, east wall. Drawing group #1	14301, 5 × 7
Luxor fragment 0150 Colonnade Hall, Opet register: upper register towboats, west wall. Drawing group #4a	12869, 5 × 7
Luxor fragment 0151 Akhenaten talatat: ship's rigging	12671, 5 × 7
Luxor fragment 0152 Akhenaten talatat: ship's oars	12672, 5 × 7
Luxor fragment 0153 Colonnade Hall, upper register: Tut.	12948, 5 × 7
Luxor fragment 0154 Tut. talatat (reused Akhenaten talatat): offering list	12673, 5 × 7
Luxor fragment 0155 Colonnade Hall, upper register: Tut.	12674, 5 × 7
Luxor fragment 0157 Colonnade Hall, 2nd register: west wall; Min procession, text and uraeus of Amenhotep III figure, Tut.	12949, 5 × 7
Luxor fragment 0158 Colonnade Hall, 2nd register: west wall; Min procession, Tut./Sety I	12675, 5 × 7
Luxor fragment 0159 Amenhotep III Sun Court: east wall; Amun bark scene	12870, 5 × 7
Luxor fragment 0160 Colonnade Hall, 2nd register: east wall, enthronement scene, Tut.	12676-a, 5 × 7
Luxor fragment 0160 Colonnade Hall, 2nd register: east wall, enthronement scene, Tut.	12676-b, 5 × 7
Luxor fragment 0161 Colonnade Hall, 2nd register: west wall; *ka* figure, Tut.	12677, 5 × 7
Luxor fragment 0162 Amenhotep III Sun Court: east wall; Amun bark scene, stern aegis	12871, 5 × 7
Luxor fragment 0163 Colonnade Hall, 2nd register: west wall, Min procession, Tut.	12678, 5 × 7
Luxor fragments 0163, 0164, 0421, 0464, 0559, 0584: join Colonnade Hall, 2nd register: west wall; south, Min procession, priests carrying lettuce stand, Tut. (464 and 421 with Amenhotep III cartouche)	12953, 5 × 7
Luxor fragment 0164 Colonnade Hall, 2nd register: west wall, Min procession, Tut.	12679, 5 × 7
Luxor fragment 0165 Ramesses II: battle detail (horse trappings)	12680, 5 × 7
Luxor fragment 0166 Colonnade Hall, 2nd register: west wall; Min procession, Tut.	12681, 5 × 7
Luxor fragment 0167 Tut. cartouches usurped by Horemheb, interior portal, north wall (?)	12682, 5 × 7
Luxor fragment 0168 Ramesses II battle detail (soldiers)	12683, 5 × 7
Luxor fragment 0170 Colonnade Hall, 2nd register: Sety I	12684, 5 × 7
Luxor fragment 0172 Colonnade Hall, 2nd register: west wall, Min procession, Tut.	12685, 5 × 7
Luxor fragment 0173 Colonnade Hall, 2nd register: west wall, Mut offering scene, Tut.	12686, 5 × 7
Luxor fragment 0174 (joins 175) Colonnade Hall, 2nd register: west wall; Hathor behind king, Theban Triad offering scene, Tut.	12687, 5 × 7

Luxor Temple (*cont.*)

Nelson Number/Description	Negative, Format
Luxor fragment 0175 (joins 174) Colonnade Hall, 2nd register: west wall; Hathor behind king, Theban Triad offering scene, Tut.	12688, 5 × 7
Luxor fragment 0176 Amenhotep III Sun Court: east wall; Amun bark scene, stern aegis	12872, 5 × 7
Luxor fragment 0180 Reused Akhenaten talatat: Tut., possibly Horemheb; bark procession	12689, 5 × 7
Luxor fragment 0181 Reused Akhenaten talatat: Tut., possibly Horemheb; bark stern	12690, 5 × 7
Luxor fragment 0182 Akhenaten talatat: men rowing, sunk relief	12873, 5 × 7
Luxor fragment 0183 Amenhotep III Sun Court: east wall; Amun bark scene	12874, 5 × 7
Luxor fragment 0185 Colonnade Hall, Opet register: Khonsu barge, east wall. Drawing group #1	12875, 5 × 7
Luxor fragment 0186. Probably recarved Amenhotep III text referring to "king of the gods"	12950, 5 × 7
Luxor fragment 0190 Colonnade Hall, Opet register: Khonsu barge, east wall. Drawing group #1	13196, 5 × 7
Luxor fragment 0191 Colonnade Hall, Opet register: Khonsu barge towboats, east wall. Drawing group #2b	12691, 5 × 7
Luxor fragment 0192 Colonnade Hall, Opet register: Karnak Temple pylons, east wall. Drawing group #3b	12876, 5 × 7
Luxor fragment 0193 Colonnade Hall, Opet register: Khonsu barge, east wall. Drawing group #1	12877, 5 × 7
Luxor fragment 0194 Priests	12692, 5 × 7
Luxor fragment 0195 Amenhotep III Sun Court	12693, 5 × 7
Luxor fragment 0200 Colonnade Hall, Opet register: upper row towboats, west wall. Drawing group #3b	12878, 5 × 7
Luxor fragment 0202 Colonnade Hall, Opet register: bottom row towboats, west wall. Drawing group #3a	12694, 5 × 7
Luxor fragment 0203 Colonnade Hall, Opet register: upper register towboats, west wall. Drawing group #4a	12695, 5 × 7
Luxor fragment 0203 Colonnade Hall, Opet register: west wall; towboat group, Tut.	12879, 5 × 7
Luxor fragment 0204 Colonnade Hall, Opet register: small scale inscriptions, Tut.	12696, 5 × 7
Luxor fragment 0206 Colonnade Hall, upper register: Tut.	12697, 5 × 7
Luxor fragment 0209 Colonnade Hall, upper register: Tut.	12698, 5 × 7
Luxor fragment 0210 Colonnade Hall, 2nd register; west wall; Min procession, priests, Tut.	12699, 5 × 7
Luxor fragment 0211 Colonnade Hall, 2nd register; west wall; Min procession, priests, Tut.	12700, 5 × 7
Luxor fragment 0212 Colonnade Hall, Opet register: west wall; prow Amun bark, aegis, Tut./Sety I	12701, 5 × 7
Luxor fragment 0213 Colonnade Hall, Opet register: barge of Amun, west wall. Drawing group #6a	12880, 5 × 7
Luxor fragment 0214 Amenhotep III Sun Court: east wall; Amun bark scene	12881, 5 × 7
Luxor fragment 0215 Amenhotep III Sun Court: east wall; Amun bark scene, prow aegis	12702, 5 × 7

Luxor Temple (*cont.*)

Nelson Number/Description	Negative, Format
Luxor fragment 0216 Colonnade Hall, Tut./Sety I	14688, 5 × 7
Luxor fragment 0217 Colonnade Hall, 4th register: east wall, Tut.	12703, 5 × 7
Luxor fragment 0218 Amenhotep III Sun Court: east wall, Amun bark scene	12704, 5 × 7
Luxor fragment 0219 Colonnade Hall, Opet register: Khonsu barge, east wall. Drawing group #1	12882, 5 × 7
Luxor fragment 0220 King in *išd*-tree	13875, 5 × 7
Luxor fragment 0221 Amenhotep III? possibly Sun Court: west wall; Amun bark scene	12883, 5 × 7
Luxor fragment 0222 Thutmoside border decoration, possibly from Amenhotep II Chapel in 10th Pylon court, Karnak	12705, 5 × 7
Luxor fragment 0223 Colonnade Hall, upper register: Tut. cartouches	12706, 5 × 7
Luxor fragment 0224 Colonnade Hall, Opet register: Khonsu barge towboats, east wall. Drawing group #2b	15858, 5 × 7
Luxor fragment 0225 Priests	12707, 5 × 7
Luxor fragment 0227 Amenhotep III Sun Court: east wall; Amun bark scene	12885, 5 × 7
Luxor fragment 0228 Horemheb cartouche, pendant cobra, from a frieze, not Colonnade Hall	12708, 5 × 7
Luxor fragment 0229 Colonnade Hall, Opet register; east wall; Khonsu barge fragment group (same as 224)	12886, 5 × 7
Luxor fragment 0230 Colonnade Hall, upper register: double crown of goddess, Tut./Sety I	12887, 5 × 7
Luxor fragment 0231 Colonnade Hall, 2nd register: west wall, Min procession, priests, Tut./Sety I	12709, 5 × 7
Luxor fragment 0232 Colonnade Hall, Opet register: Luxor Temple portal, west wall. Drawing group #7c	12888, 5 × 7
Luxor fragment 0237 Colonnade Hall, Opet register: King's barge, west wall. Drawing group #5c	12889, 5 × 7
Luxor fragment 0241 Amenhotep III ? King running with oar	12710, 5 × 7
Luxor fragment 0242 possible Late period restoration of Thutmosis III shrine, parts of barks in procession with cartouche of Thutmosis III; group includes 243, 244, 288, 1279, 1280	12711, 5 × 7
Luxor fragment 0243 possible Late period restoration of Thutmosis III shrine, parts of barks in procession with cartouche of Thutmosis III; group includes 242, 244, 288, 1279, 1280	12712, 5 × 7
Luxor fragment 0244 possible Late period restoration of Thutmosis III shrine, parts of barks in procession with cartouche of Thutmosis III; group includes 242, 243, 288, 1279, 1280	12713, 5 × 7
Luxor fragment 0246 Colonnade Hall, 2nd register: west wall; Theban Triad offering scene, Tut.	12714, 5 × 7
Luxor fragment 0247 Colonnade Hall, 2nd register: west wall, Mut offering scene, Tut.	12715, 5 × 7
Luxor fragment 0249 Roman period bark procession detail	12716, 5 × 7
Luxor fragment 0257 Colonnade Hall, upper register: king running with oar	12717, 5 × 7

Luxor Temple (*cont.*)

Nelson Number/Description	Negative, Format
Luxor fragment 0261 Colonnade Hall, upper register: offering list, Tut./Sety I	12718, 5 × 7
Luxor fragment 0266 A and B: two carved surfaces Tut. talatat: (reused Akhenaten talatat): purification scene. Reverse-Akhenaten decoration, sunk relief figures	12719-a, 5 × 7
Luxor fragment 0266 A and B: two carved surfaces Tut. talatat: (reused Akhenaten talatat): purification scene. Reverse-Akhenaten decoration, sunk relief figures	12719-b, 5 × 7
Luxor fragment 0267 Tut. talatat (reused Akhenaten talatat): bark procession	12720-a, 5 × 7
Luxor fragment 0267 Tut. talatat (reused Akhenaten talatat): bark procession	12720-b, 5 × 7
Luxor fragment 0268 Tut. talatat (reused Akhenaten talatat): bark procession	12721, 5 × 7
Luxor fragment 0269 Colonnade Hall, 2nd register: Sety I	12722, 5 × 7
Luxor fragment 0270 Colonnade Hall, upper register: offering list, Tut./Sety I	12723, 5 × 7
Luxor fragment 0271 Colonnade Hall, Opet register: Khonsu barge, east wall. Drawing group #1	12890, 5 × 7
Luxor fragment 0272 Late period inscription	12724, 5 × 7
Luxor fragment 0273 Colonnade Hall, upper register: Tut.	12725, 5 × 7
Luxor fragment 0274 Colonnade Hall, 2nd register: west wall; Tut.	12726, 5 × 7
Luxor fragment 0275 Colonnade Hall: bark scene, Tut. (?)	12727, 5 × 7
Luxor fragment 0276 Colonnade Hall: inscription, Tut.(?)	12728, 5 × 7
Luxor fragment 0276 Colonnade Hall: small scale inscription, Tut.	13197, 5 × 7
Luxor fragment 0277 (joins 278) Colonnade Hall, 2nd register: west wall; Tut.	12729, 5 × 7
Luxor fragment 0278 (joins 277) Colonnade Hall, 2nd register: west wall; Tut.	12730, 5 × 7
Luxor fragment 0279 Tutankhamun reused talatat	13950, 5 × 7
Luxor fragment 0281 Late period (25th Dynasty?), running soldiers	12731, 5 × 7
Luxor fragment 0289 Late period, bark detail	12732, 5 × 7
Luxor fragment 0290 Colonnade Hall, 2nd register: west wall; Mut offering scene, Tut.	12733, 5 × 7
Luxor fragment 0294 Colonnade Hall, Opet register: Khonsu barge, inscription over Amun barge, east wall. Drawing group #2c	12734, 5 × 7
Luxor fragment 0297 Colonnade Hall, upper register: Tut.	12735, 5 × 7
Luxor fragment 0300 Colonnade Hall, upper register: Sety I (possibly Amenhotep III Sun Court restoration)	12736, 5 × 7
Luxor fragment 0313 Colonnade Hall, Opet register: Amun bark, Luxor Temple, west wall. Drawing group #5b	12737, 5 × 7
Luxor fragment 0315 Colonnade Hall, 2nd register: west wall; Mut offering scene, Tut.	13136, 5 × 7
Luxor fragment 0315 and 0318 Colonnade Hall, 2nd register: west wall; Mut offering scene, Tut.	12738, 5 × 7
Luxor fragment 0318 Colonnade Hall, 2nd register: west wall; Mut offering scene, Tut.	13137, 5 × 7
Luxor fragment 0326 Amenhotep III offering list	12739, 5 × 7

Luxor Temple (*cont.*)

Nelson Number/Description	Negative, Format
Luxor fragment 0331 Colonnade Hall, 4th register: Sety I	12740, 5 × 7
Luxor fragment 0335 Colonnade Hall, 2nd register: west wall; Mut offering scene, Tut.	12741, 5 × 7
Luxor fragment 0337 Colonnade Hall, Opet register: bark of Amun procession, west wall. Drawing group #7b	12891, 5 × 7
Luxor fragment 0339 Amenhotep III(?): temple proper, king with *ḥrp*-scepter	12892, 5 × 7
Luxor fragment 0340 Colonnade Hall, Opet register: small scale inscription, Tut.	12742, 5 × 7
Luxor fragment 0348 Amenhotep III Sun Court: east wall; Amun bark scene	12893, 5 × 7
Luxor fragment 0349 Colonnade Hall, 4th register: Tut./Sety I (?)	12743, 5 × 7
Luxor fragment 0350 Colonnade Hall, 2nd register: west wall; Mut offering scene, Tut.	12744, 5 × 7
Luxor fragment 0353 Colonnade Hall, upper register: usurped cartouches in text, Tut.	12745, 5 × 7
Luxor fragment 0354 Fragment with parallel to text of the Bentresh Stela	12746, 5 × 7
Luxor fragment 0354 Fragment with parallel to text of the Bentresh Stela	13990, 5 × 7
Luxor fragment 0355 Colonnade Hall, upper register: Tut./Sety I	12747, 5 × 7
Luxor fragment 0356 Colonnade Hall, upper register: Sety I	12748, 5 × 7
Luxor fragment 0357 Colonnade Hall, Opet register: horizontal inscription, running soldiers. Drawing group #6b	12749, 5 × 7
Luxor fragment 0359 Thutmosis II cartouche	12750, 5 × 7
Luxor fragment 0361 Colonnade Hall, upper register: offering list, Tut./Sety I	12751, 5 × 7
Luxor fragment 0363 Colonnade Hall: *išd*-tree group, Tut. (?)	12752, 5 × 7
Luxor fragment 0364 Ramesses II, bark procession, priest's feet	12753, 5 × 7
Luxor fragment 0369 Colonnade Hall, 2nd register: west wall; Mut offering scene, Tut.	12754, 5 × 7
Luxor fragment 0370 Colonnade Hall, 2nd register: west wall; Mut offering scene, Tut.	12755, 5 × 7
Luxor fragment 0372 Colonnade Hall, Opet register: Amun bark, Luxor Temple, west wall. Drawing group #5b	12756, 5 × 7
Luxor fragment 0373 Amenhotep III Sun Court: east wall; Amun bark scene	12894, 5 × 7
Luxor fragment 0374 Colonnade Hall, 2nd register: west wall; Theban Triad offering scene, Tut.	12757, 5 × 7
Luxor fragment 0375 Colonnade Hall, 2nd register: west wall; Theban Triad offering scene, Tut.	12758, 5 × 7
Luxor fragment 0376 Amenhotep III Sun Court: east wall; Amun bark scene	12895, 5 × 7
Luxor fragment 0379 Tut. talatat: (reused Akhenaten talatat); towboats	12896, 5 × 7
Luxor fragment 0380 Tut. talatat: (reused Akhenaten talatat), doorjamb fragment	12759, 5 × 7
Luxor fragment 0381 Colonnade Hall, Opet register: Amun bark, Luxor Temple, west wall. Drawing group #5a	12897, 5 × 7

Luxor Temple (*cont.*)

Nelson Number/Description	Negative, Format
Luxor fragment 0382 Colonnade Hall, 2nd register: west wall; Min procession, fans	12898, 5 × 7
Luxor fragment 0383 Colonnade Hall, 2nd register: west wall; Min procession, fans	12899, 5 × 7
Luxor fragment 0384 Tut. talatat: (reused Akhenaten talatat), divine barge	12760, 5 × 7
Luxor fragment 0384 B Tutankhamun reused talatat	13957, 5 × 7
Luxor fragment 0385 Colonnade Hall, 3rd register: west wall; Sety I	12761, 5 × 7
Luxor fragment 0395 Colonnade Hall, Opet register: upper register towboats, west wall. Drawing group #4b	12762, 5 × 7
Luxor fragment 0395 Tut. talatat: (reused Akhenaten talatat); ship's rigging	12901, 5 × 7
Luxor fragment 0396 Roman period, bark procession	12763, 5 × 7
Luxor fragment 0400 Amenhotep III Sun Court: east wall; Amun bark, stern aegis	12902, 5 × 7
Luxor fragment 0400 and 0401 Amenhotep III Sun Court: east wall; Amun bark, stern aegis	12903-a, 5 × 7
Luxor fragment 0400 and 0401 Amenhotep III Sun Court: east wall; Amun bark, stern aegis	12903-b, 5 × 7
Luxor fragment 0403 Amenhotep III Sun Court: east wall; Amun bark scene	14000, 5 × 7
Luxor fragment 0405 Colonnade Hall: Tut.	13304, 5 × 7
Luxor fragment 0406 Amenhotep III Sun Court: east wall; Amun bark scene	14001, 5 × 7
Luxor fragment 0407 Amenhotep III Sun Court: east wall; Amun bark scene	14002, 5 × 7
Luxor fragment 0408 Colonnade Hall, Opet register: Luxor Temple portal, west wall. Drawing group #7c	14003, 5 × 7
Luxor fragment 0409 Colonnade Hall, upper register: cobra frieze, Tut./Sety I	15983, 5 × 7
Luxor fragment 0410 Amenhotep III Sun Court: east wall; Amun bark, cabin decoration	12904, 5 × 7
Luxor fragment 0411 Amenhotep III Sun Court; east wall; Amun bark scene	12764, 5 × 7
Luxor fragment 0412 Colonnade Hall, 4th register: west wall; large scale offering list, Sety I	14571, 5 × 7
Luxor fragment 0413 Amenhotep III Sun Court; east wall; Amun bark scene	12765, 5 × 7
Luxor fragment 0414 Amenhotep III Sun Court: east wall; Amun bark, cabin veil	12905, 5 × 7
Luxor fragment 0415 (joins 429) Amenhotep III Temple proper; door lintel, winged sun disc	14005, 5 × 7
Luxor fragment 0416 Amenhotep III Sun Court: east wall; Amun bark, cabin veil	12906, 5 × 7
Luxor fragment 0418 Amenhotep III Sun Court: east wall; Amun bark, bottom prow aegis collar, offerings to right	12907, 5 × 7
Luxor fragment 0419 Colonnade Hall, Opet register: Luxor Temple portal, west wall. Drawing group #7c	12908, 5 × 7
Luxor fragment 0420 Amenhotep III Sun Court; east wall; Amun bark scene	12766, 5 × 7
Luxor fragment 0421 Colonnade Hall, 2nd register: west wall; Min procession, Tut.	12767, 5 × 7
Luxor fragment 0422 Colonnade Hall, Opet register: Khonsu barge, inscription over Amun barge, east wall. Drawing group #2c	13305, 5 × 7

Luxor Temple (*cont.*)

Nelson Number/Description	Negative, Format
Luxor fragment 0423 Colonnade Hall, 2nd register: west wall; Min procession, Tut./Sety I	14006, 5 × 7
Luxor fragment 0424 Colonnade Hall, 2nd register: west wall; Min procession, Tut./Sety I	14007, 5 × 7
Luxor fragment 0425 Colonnade Hall, 2nd register: west wall; Min procession, Tut.	12768, 5 × 7
Luxor fragment 0426 Amenhotep III Sun Court: east wall; Amun bark scene, stern aegis collar	14008, 5 × 7
Luxor fragment 0427 Colonnade Hall: Tut./Sety I	12769, 5 × 7
Luxor fragment 0429 (joins 0415) Amenhotep III Temple proper; door lintel, winged sun disc	14009, 5 × 7
Luxor fragment 0431 Amenhotep III Sun Court: east wall	14297, 5 × 7
Luxor fragment 0432 Colonnade Hall, Opet register: text. Drawing group #8b	13306, 5 × 7
Luxor fragment 0433 Colonnade Hall, 2nd register: west wall; Theban Triad offering scene, Tut.	14011, 5 × 7
Luxor fragment 0434 Amenhotep III Sun Court: east wall; Amun bark scene	12909, 5 × 7
Luxor fragment 0435 Colonnade Hall, Opet register: text. Drawing group #8b	14012, 5 × 7
Luxor fragment 0436 Colonnade Hall: Tut.	13307, 5 × 7
Luxor fragment 0440 Colonnade Hall, 2nd register: west wall; Mut offering scene, Tut.	14014, 5 × 7
Luxor fragment 0441 Colonnade Hall, 2nd register: Min procession, west wall	13880, 5 × 7
Luxor fragment 0443 Amenhotep III Sun Court: east wall	14017, 5 × 7
Luxor fragment 0444 Amenhotep III Sun Court: east wall	14018, 5 × 7
Luxor fragment 0445 Colonnade Hall, upper register: cobra frieze, Tut.	15981, 5 × 7
Luxor fragment 0446 Colonnade Hall, upper register: cobra frieze, Tut./Sety I	15980, 5 × 7
Luxor fragment 0447 Amenhotep III Sun Court: east wall; Amun bark scene	14019, 5 × 7
Luxor fragment 0448 Colonnade Hall, upper register: cobra frieze, Tut.	15982, 5 × 7
Luxor fragment 0449 Colonnade Hall: Tut./Sety I	14020, 5 × 7
Luxor fragment 0451 Colonnade Hall, upper register: Tut./Sety I	14021, 5 × 7
Luxor fragment 0452	15999, 5 × 7
Luxor fragment 0453 Colonnade Hall, Opet register: small scale inscription, Tut.	14306, 5 × 7
Luxor fragment 0454 Colonnade Hall, Opet register: text. Drawing group #8b	14022, 5 × 7
Luxor fragment 0455 Colonnade Hall, upper register: cobra frieze, Tut./Sety I	15985, 5 × 7
Luxor fragment 0457 Colonnade Hall, Opet register: barge of Amun, west wall. Drawing group #6a	12910, 5 × 7
Luxor fragment 0458 Amenhotep III Sun Court: east wall; Amun bark scene	12770, 5 × 7
Luxor fragment 0458 Amenhotep III Sun Court: east wall; Amun bark scene	12911, 5 × 7
Luxor fragment 0459 Colonnade Hall, Opet register: bark of Amun procession, west wall. Drawing group #7c	14690, 5 × 7
Luxor fragment 0460 Amenhotep III Sun Court: east wall; Amun bark scene	12771, 5 × 7

Luxor Temple (*cont.*)

Nelson Number/Description	Negative, Format
Luxor fragment 0461 Colonnade Hall, 2nd register: west wall; Min procession, Tut./Sety I	12772, 5 × 7
Luxor fragment 0462 Amenhotep III Sun Court: east wall; Amun bark scene	12773, 5 × 7
Luxor fragment 0463 Amenhotep III Sun Court: east wall; Amun bark scene, prow section	14024, 5 × 7
Luxor fragment 0464 Colonnade Hall, 2nd register: west wall; Min procession, cartouche Amenhotep III, Tut.	12774, 5 × 7
Luxor fragment 0465 Colonnade Hall, 2nd register: west wall; Min procession, standards, Tut./Sety I	12775, 5 × 7
Luxor fragment 0466 Colonnade Hall, Opet register: bark of Amun procession, west wall. Drawing group #7a	12912, 5 × 7
Luxor fragment 0467 Colonnade Hall, 3rd register: west wall; Tut./Sety I	14308, 5 × 7
Luxor fragment 0470 Colonnade Hall, Opet register: Khonsu barge, east wall. Drawing group #1	12776, 5 × 7
Luxor fragment 0471 Tut. talatat: (reused Akhenaten talatat), Amun bark on stand	12777, 5 × 7
Luxor fragment 0472 Colonnade Hall, upper register: Tut.(?)	12778, 5 × 7
Luxor fragment 0473 Colonnade Hall, Opet register: bark of Amun procession, west wall. Drawing group #7a	14026, 5 × 7
Luxor fragment 0475 Amenhotep III Sun Court: east wall; Amun bark scene	12913, 5 × 7
Luxor fragment 0476 Amenhotep III Sun Court: east wall; Amun bark scene, stern aegis	12914, 5 × 7
Luxor fragment 0477 Colonnade Hall, Opet register: bark of Amun procession, west wall. Drawing group #7c	12915, 5 × 7
Luxor fragment 0479 Colonnade Hall, Opet register: King's barge, west wall. Drawing group #5c	12916, 5 × 7
Luxor fragment 0480 Tut. talatat: (reused Akhenaten talatat), cobra shrine top	12779, 5 × 7
Luxor fragment 0481 Colonnade Hall, Opet register: end of Amun bark procession, beginning upper row towboats. Drawing group #3c	14027, 5 × 7
Luxor fragment 0482 Amenhotep III Sun Court: east wall; Amun bark scene	12917, 5 × 7
Luxor fragment 0483 Colonnade Hall, 2nd register: west wall; Min procession, standard, Tut./Sety I	12780, 5 × 7
Luxor fragment 0485 Tutankhamun reused talatat	13883, 5 × 7
Luxor fragment 0486 Colonnade Hall, Opet register: Khonsu barge east wall. Drawing group #2a	14029, 5 × 7
Luxor fragment 0487 Colonnade Hall, upper register: cobra frieze, Tut./Sety I	15973, 5 × 7
Luxor fragment 0488 (joins 677) Colonnade Hall, Opet register: west wall; horizontal inscription, running soldiers. Drawing group #6c	14575, 5 × 7
Luxor fragment 0489 Colonnade Hall, 4th register: east wall; cartouche, Tut.	14031, 5 × 7
Luxor fragment 0490 Colonnade Hall, 3rd register: south wall; Sety I	14032, 5 × 7
Luxor fragment 0491 Colonnade Hall, Opet register: Khonsu barge, east wall. Drawing group #1	12918, 5 × 7

Luxor Temple (*cont.*)

Nelson Number/Description	Negative, Format
Luxor fragment 0492 Amenhotep III Sun Court: east wall; Amun bark scene, prow aegis, offerings	12919, 5 × 7
Luxor fragment 0492, 0504, 0505: joined Amenhotep III Sun Court: east wall; Amun bark scene, prow aegis, offerings	12951, 5 × 7
Luxor fragment 0494 Colonnade Hall, 4th register(?): large scale offering list, Tut./Sety I	15872, 5 × 7
Luxor fragment 0497 A and B Colonnade Hall, 3rd register: west wall, head	14552, 5 × 7
Luxor fragment 0497 C Colonnade Hall, 3rd register: west wall, Tut.	14559, 5 × 7
Luxor fragment 0498 Colonnade Hall, Opet register: king's barge, west wall. Drawing group #5c	12781, 5 × 7
Luxor fragment 0499 Colonnade Hall, 2nd register: west wall; Min procession, standard, Tut./Sety I	12782, 5 × 7
Luxor fragment 0501 Colonnade Hall: fan, Tut.(?)	14034, 5 × 7
Luxor fragment 0502 Colonnade Hall, Opet register: end of Amun bark procession, beginning upper row towboats. Drawing group #3c	12920, 5 × 7
Luxor fragment 0503 Colonnade Hall, 2nd register: west wall; Min procession, cartouche, Tut./Sety I	12783, 5 × 7
Luxor fragment 0504 Amenhotep III Sun Court: east wall; Amun bark scene, prow aegis, offerings	12921, 5 × 7
Luxor fragment 0505 Amenhotep III Sun Court: east wall; Amun bark scene, prow aegis, offerings	12922, 5 × 7
Luxor fragment 0507 Colonnade Hall, Opet register: upper register towboats, west wall. Drawing group #4a	12923, 5 × 7
Luxor fragment 0508 Colonnade Hall, Opet register: small scale inscriptions, Tut.	14035, 5 × 7
Luxor fragment 0510 Colonnade Hall, Opet register: small bark procession, west wall. Drawing group #7c	12924, 5 × 7
Luxor fragment 0514 Colonnade Hall, 3rd register: south wall; Sety I	14037, 5 × 7
Luxor fragment 0515 Amenhotep III Sun Court: east wall; Amun bark scene	12784, 5 × 7
Luxor fragment 0516 Amenhotep III Sun Court: east wall, Amun bark scene	12785, 5 × 7
Luxor fragment 0517 Amenhotep III Sun Court: east wall, Amun bark scene	12786, 5 × 7
Luxor fragment 0518 Priests	12787, 5 × 7
Luxor fragment 0519 Amenhotep III Sun Court: east wall, Amun bark scene	12788, 5 × 7
Luxor fragment 0522 Colonnade Hall: cobra frieze, Tut./Sety I	15989, 5 × 7
Luxor fragment 0523 Amenhotep III Sun Court: east wall, Amun bark scene	12789, 5 × 7
Luxor fragment 0524 Amenhotep III Sun Court: east wall, Amun bark scene	12790, 5 × 7
Luxor fragment 0525 Amenhotep III Sun Court: east wall, Amun bark scene	12791, 5 × 7
Luxor fragment 0526 Indeterminate date, bark hull on barkstand	15929, 5 × 7
Luxor fragment 0530 Colonnade Hall, Opet register: end of Amun bark procession, beginning upper row towboats. Drawing group #3c	12925, 5 × 7
Luxor fragment 0531 Amenhotep III Sun Court: east wall, Amun bark scene	12792, 5 × 7

Luxor Temple (*cont.*)

Nelson Number/Description	Negative, Format
Luxor fragment 0535 Colonnade Hall, Opet register: bark of Amun procession, west wall. Drawing group #7c	12926, 5 × 7
Luxor fragment 0536 A Tutankhamun reused talatat	13943, 5 × 7
Luxor fragment 0536 B Tut. talatat: (reused Akhenaten talatat); Akhenaten sunk relief decoration, offering pile	13886, 5 × 7
Luxor fragment 0536 B Tut. talatat: (reused Akhenaten talatat); Akhenaten sunk relief decoration, offering pile	13892, 5 × 7
Luxor fragment 0537 Colonnade Hall, 3rd register: south wall; Sety I	14041, 5 × 7
Luxor fragment 0538 Colonnade Hall, 2nd register: west wall; Min procession, Amenhotep III cartouche, Tut.	14042, 5 × 7
Luxor fragment 0539 soldiers(?); Ramesses II(?)	14043, 5 × 7
Luxor fragment 0540 Amenhotep III Sun Court: east wall, Amun bark scene	14044, 5 × 7
Luxor fragment 0541 bark aegis collar	14045, 5 × 7
Luxor fragment 0542 Colonnade Hall, 2nd register: west wall; Min procession, priest arms, Tut./Sety I	14046, 5 × 7
Luxor fragment 0543 Colonnade Hall, Opet register: Khonsu barge, east wall. Drawing group #1	14047, 5 × 7
Luxor fragment 0545 Colonnade Hall, 2nd register	13955, 5 × 7
Luxor fragment 0546 Colonnade Hall, Opet register: horizontal inscription, running soldiers. Drawing group #6c	13308, 5 × 7
Luxor fragment 0547 Colonnade Hall, upper register: cobra frieze, Tut./Sety I(?)	15988, 5 × 7
Luxor fragment 0548 Colonnade Hall, Opet register: bottom row towboats, west wall. Drawing group #3a	12927, 5 × 7
Luxor fragment 0552 Colonnade Hall, upper register: west wall(?), Tut.	14051, 5 × 7
Luxor fragment 0554 Tutankhamun reused talatat	13962, 5 × 7
Luxor fragment 0555 Colonnade Hall, Opet register: bark of Amun procession, west wall. Drawing group #7b	12793, 5 × 7
Luxor fragment 0556 Colonnade Hall, Opet register: upper register towboats, west wall. Drawing group #4b	12929, 5 × 7
Luxor fragment 0557 Colonnade Hall, 2nd register: west wall; Min procession, priests, Tut./Sety I	12794, 5 × 7
Luxor fragment 0558 Colonnade Hall, Opet register: bark of Amun procession, west wall. Drawing group #7a	12930, 5 × 7
Luxor fragment 0558 Colonnade Hall, Opet register: bark of Amun procession, west wall. Drawing group #7a	14294, 5 × 7
Luxor fragment 0559 Colonnade Hall, 2nd register: west wall; Min procession, carrying lettuce, Tut.	12795, 5 × 7
Luxor fragment 0560 Colonnade Hall, 2nd register: west wall, Thoth	13903, 5 × 7
Luxor fragment 0561 Ramesses II, exterior west wall Luxor Temple, soldiers	12796, 5 × 7
Luxor fragment 0562 Colonnade Hall, Opet register: Khonsu barge, east wall. Drawing group #1	12931, 5 × 7

Luxor Temple (*cont.*)

Nelson Number/Description	Negative, Format
Luxor fragment 0563 Colonnade Hall, Opet register: bark of Amun procession, west wall. Drawing group #7a	12932, 5 × 7
Luxor fragment 0564 Amenhotep III Sun Court: east wall, Amun bark scene	12797, 5 × 7
Luxor fragment 0565 Colonnade Hall, Opet register: small scale inscriptions, Tut.	14054, 5 × 7
Luxor fragment 0566 Colonnade Hall, Opet register: end of Amun bark procession, beginning upper row towboats. Drawing group #3c	12933, 5 × 7
Luxor fragment 0567 Amenhotep III Sun Court: east wall; Amun bark scene	14055, 5 × 7
Luxor fragment 0568 Colonnade Hall, Opet register: king's barge, west wall. Drawing group #5c	12798, 5 × 7
Luxor fragment 0569 Colonnade Hall, upper register: cobra frieze, Tut.	12799, 5 × 7
Luxor fragment 0569 Colonnade Hall, upper register: cobra frieze, Tut./Sety I	15874, 5 × 7
Luxor fragment 0570 Colonnade Hall: Opet register: Amun bark, back aegis and corner, west wall, south end. Drawing group #5a	13917, 5 × 7
Luxor fragment 0572 Amenhotep III Sun Court: east wall, Amun bark scene	12800, 5 × 7
Luxor fragment 0573 Amenhotep III Sun Court: east wall; Amun bark scene	14057, 5 × 7
Luxor fragment 0575 Colonnade Hall, upper register: Tut.	14058, 5 × 7
Luxor fragment 0576 Colonnade Hall, 2nd register: west wall; Mut offering scene, king's crown, Tut.	12802, 5 × 7
Luxor fragment 0577 Colonnade Hall, Opet register: Khonsu barge, east wall. Drawing group #1	12934, 5 × 7
Luxor fragment 0578 Amenhotep III Sun Court: east wall, Amun bark scene	12803, 5 × 7
Luxor fragment 0580 Amenhotep III Sun Court: west wall, Amun bark scene	12804, 5 × 7
Luxor fragment 0581 Colonnade Hall: Tut.	13309, 5 × 7
Luxor fragment 0582 Colonnade Hall, 2nd register: west wall; Mut offering scene, king's crown, Tut.	12805, 5 × 7
Luxor fragment 0584 Colonnade Hall, 2nd register: west wall; Min procession, priests carrying lettuce, Tut.	12806, 5 × 7
Luxor fragment 0585 Colonnade Hall, 2nd register: west wall; Mut offering scene, king's crown, Tut.	12807, 5 × 7
Luxor fragment 0586 Colonnade Hall, 2nd register: west wall; Mut offering scene, king's crown, Tut.	12808, 5 × 7
Luxor fragment 0587 Colonnade Hall, Opet register: Khonsu barge, east wall. Drawing group #1	12935, 5 × 7
Luxor fragment 0588 Amenhotep III Sun Court: east wall; Amun bark scene, offering bouquets	12936, 5 × 7
Luxor fragment 0589 Colonnade Hall, Opet register: joins east wall, Tut.	12937, 5 × 7
Luxor fragment 0590 Colonnade Hall, upper register: cobra frieze, Tut./Sety I(?)	15964, 5 × 7
Luxor fragment 0591 Amenhotep III Sun Court: kings	14461, 5 × 7
Luxor fragment 0592 Colonnade Hall: Tut.	13310, 5 × 7

Luxor Temple (*cont.*)

Nelson Number/Description	Negative, Format
Luxor fragment 0593 Amenhotep III Sun Court: kings	14538, 5 × 7
Luxor fragment 0594 Amenhotep III Sun Court: east wall	13953, 5 × 7
Luxor fragment 0595 Amenhotep III Sun Court: east wall; Amun bark scene	14063, 5 × 7
Luxor fragment 0596 Amenhotep III Sun Court: east wall	14064, 5 × 7
Luxor fragment 0597 Amenhotep III Sun Court: east wall; Amun bark scene	14065, 5 × 7
Luxor fragment 0598 Colonnade Hall, 3rd register: west wall, Sety I	14550, 5 × 7
Luxor fragment 0599 Amenhotep III Sun Court: east wall; Amun bark scene	14067, 5 × 7
Luxor fragment 0601 Colonnade Hall, 2nd register: west wall; Min procession, standards, Tut./Sety I	12809, 5 × 7
Luxor fragment 0602 Amenhotep III Sun Court: east wall, Amun bark scene	12810, 5 × 7
Luxor fragment 0603 Colonnade Hall, 2nd register: west wall; Min procession, Amun-Ra-Kamutef head, Tut.	12811, 5 × 7
Luxor fragment 0604 Colonnade Hall, 2nd register: west wall; Min procession, arm of Amun-Ra-Kamutef, Tut.	12812, 5 × 7
Luxor fragment 0605 Colonnade Hall, 2nd register: west wall; Min procession, arm, and head of Amun-Ra-Kamutef, Tut.	12813, 5 × 7
Luxor fragment 0606 Colonnade Hall, 2nd register: west wall; Min procession, body of Amun-Ra Kamutef, Tut.	12814, 5 × 7
Luxor fragment 0607 Colonnade Hall, 2nd register: west wall; Min procession, phallus of Amun-Ra-Kamutef, Tut.	12815, 5 × 7
Luxor fragment 0608 Colonnade Hall, Opet register: end of Amun bark procession, beginning upper row towboats. Drawing group #3c	14069, 5 × 7
Luxor fragment 0609 Colonnade Hall, Opet register: upper register towboats, west wall. Drawing group #4b	14070, 5 × 7
Luxor fragment 0610 Colonnade Hall, 2nd register: west wall; Min procession, base of phallus, Amun-Ra-Kamutef	14071, 5 × 7
Luxor fragment 0611 Colonnade Hall: Tut.	14568, 5 × 7
Luxor fragment 0612 Colonnade Hall, Opet register: bark of Amun procession, west wall. Drawing group #7b	14307, 5 × 7
Luxor fragment 0613 Colonnade Hall, 2nd register: west wall; Min procession, fans	14072, 5 × 7
Luxor fragment 0614 Colonnade Hall, 2nd register: west wall; Min procession, priest, Tut.	14300, 5 × 7
Luxor fragment 0615 Colonnade Hall, Opet register: Khonsu barge towboats, east wall. Drawing group #2b	14073, 5 × 7
Luxor fragment 0617 Colonnade Hall, Opet register: bark of Amun procession, west wall. Drawing group #7a	14074, 5 × 7
Luxor fragment 0618 Colonnade Hall, Opet register: Khonsu barge, east wall. Drawing group #1	14075, 5 × 7
Luxor fragment 0619 Colonnade Hall, Opet register: horizontal inscription, running soldiers. Drawing group #6c	14076, 5 × 7

Luxor Temple (*cont.*)

Nelson Number/Description	Negative, Format
Luxor fragment 0620 Colonnade Hall, Opet register: Khonsu barge, east wall. Drawing group #2a	14077, 5 × 7
Luxor fragment 0621 Colonnade Hall, Opet register: small scale inscriptions, Tut.	14078, 5 × 7
Luxor fragment 0622 Tut.? Amenhotep III(?) small scale inscriptions	14079, 5 × 7
Luxor fragment 0623 Amenhotep III Sun Court(?) offering pile	15977, 5 × 7
Luxor fragment 0624 Colonnade Hall, Opet register: Khonsu barge towboats, east wall. Drawing group #2b	13311, 5 × 7
Luxor fragment 0625 Colonnade Hall, Opet register: east wall; Khonsu barge fragment group	14082, 5 × 7
Luxor fragment 0626 Colonnade Hall, Opet register: horizontal inscription, running soldiers. Drawing group #6b	13312, 5 × 7
Luxor fragment 0627 Colonnade Hall, Opet register: horizontal inscription, running soldiers. Drawing group #6b	13313, 5 × 7
Luxor fragment 0629 Colonnade Hall, 2nd register: west wall; Min procession, priest, Tut./Sety I	14086, 5 × 7
Luxor fragment 0630 Colonnade Hall, Opet register: small scale inscriptions, Tut.	14087, 5 × 7
Luxor fragment 0631 Colonnade Hall, 2nd register: west wall; Theban Triad offering scene, Tut.	14088, 5 × 7
Luxor fragment 0632 Amenhotep III Sun Court: east wall; Amun bark scene	14089, 5 × 7
Luxor fragment 0633 Colonnade Hall, 2nd register: west wall; Min procession, text, Tut.	14090, 5 × 7
Luxor fragment 0634 (joins 637) Colonnade Hall, 2nd register: west wall; Min procession, face of Amenhotep III, Tut.	14091, 5 × 7
Luxor fragment 0635 Amenhotep III Sun Court: east wall; Amun bark scene	14092, 5 × 7
Luxor fragment 0637 (joins 634) Colonnade Hall, 2nd register: west wall; Min procession, Tut.	14094, 5 × 7
Luxor fragment 0638 Colonnade Hall, 2nd register: west wall; Min procession, fan, Tut.	14095, 5 × 7
Luxor fragment 0639 Colonnade Hall, 2nd register: west wall, Min procession, fans, Tut.	14096, 5 × 7
Luxor fragment 0640 Colonnade Hall, 2nd register: north wall; standing Amun, goddess scene, Tut.	14097, 5 × 7
Luxor fragment 0641 Colonnade Hall, 2nd register: east wall; coronation scene, Tut.	14098, 5 × 7
Luxor fragment 0642 Colonnade Hall, Opet register: Khonsu barge, inscription over Amun barge, east wall. Drawing group #2c	14099, 5 × 7
Luxor fragment 0643 Colonnade Hall, 2nd register: north wall; standing Amun, goddess scene, Tut.	14100, 5 × 7
Luxor fragment 0644 Colonnade Hall, 2nd register: west wall, Tut.	14314, 5 × 7
Luxor fragment 0645 Colonnade Hall, 2nd register: north wall; standing Amun, goddess scene, Tut.	14101, 5 × 7
Luxor fragment 0646 Colonnade Hall, 2nd register: west wall; Tut.	14102, 5 × 7
Luxor fragment 0647 Amenhotep III Sun Court: east wall; Amun bark scene	14103, 5 × 7

Luxor Temple (*cont.*)

Nelson Number/Description	Negative, Format
Luxor fragment 0648 Colonnade Hall, 2nd register: west wall; Min procession, cartouches Amenhotep III, Tut.	14104, 5 × 7
Luxor fragment 0649 Colonnade Hall, 2nd register: west wall; Thoth with goddess, Tut.	14105, 5 × 7
Luxor fragment 0651 Colonnade Hall, 2nd register: west wall; Min procession, cartouches Amenhotep III, Tut.	14106, 5 × 7
Luxor fragment 0652 Colonnade Hall, 2nd register: west wall; Min procession, fans, Tut.	14107, 5 × 7
Luxor fragment 0653 Colonnade Hall, Opet register: Amun bark, Luxor Temple, west wall. Drawing group #5b	14108, 5 × 7
Luxor fragment 0654 Colonnade Hall, 2nd register: west wall; Min procession, top of Amenhotep III's *nemes*, Tut.	14109, 5 × 7
Luxor fragment 0655 Colonnade Hall, Opet register: Khonsu barge, east wall. Drawing group #1	14110, 5 × 7
Luxor fragment 0656 Colonnade Hall, 2nd register: east wall (joins wall), Tut.	14111, 5 × 7
Luxor fragment 0657 Colonnade Hall, Opet register: text. Drawing group #8b	14112, 5 × 7
Luxor fragment 0658 Colonnade Hall: Tut., small scale inscription	14113, 5 × 7
Luxor fragment 0659 Colonnade Hall, Opet register: small scale inscription, Tut.	14114, 5 × 7
Luxor fragment 0660 Colonnade Hall, Opet register: small scale inscription, Tut.	14115, 5 × 7
Luxor fragment 0661 Tut. talatat: (reused Akhenaten talatat)	14116, 5 × 7
Luxor fragment 0662 Colonnade Hall: offering pile, Tut./Sety I	15986, 5 × 7
Luxor fragment 0663 Colonnade Hall, Opet register: text. Drawing group #8b	14118, 5 × 7
Luxor fragment 0665 Colonnade Hall, Opet register: small scale inscription, Tut.	14120, 5 × 7
Luxor fragment 0666 Colonnade Hall, Opet register: small scale inscriptions, Tut.	14121, 5 × 7
Luxor fragment 0667 Colonnade Hall, Opet register: Khonsu barge, inscription over Amun barge, east wall. Drawing group #2c	14122, 5 × 7
Luxor fragment 0668 Colonnade Hall: Tut.	13314, 5 × 7
Luxor fragment 0669 Colonnade Hall, Opet register: small scale inscriptions, Tut.	14123, 5 × 7
Luxor fragment 0670 Colonnade Hall: small scale inscriptions, Tut.?	14124, 5 × 7
Luxor fragment 0672 Colonnade Hall, Opet register: Khonsu barge, inscription over Amun barge, east wall. Drawing group #2c	14125, 5 × 7
Luxor fragment 0673 Colonnade Hall, 2nd register: north wall; standing Amun, goddess scene, Tut.	14126, 5 × 7
Luxor fragment 0674 Colonnade Hall, Opet register: Khonsu barge towboats, east wall. Drawing group #2b	14127, 5 × 7
Luxor fragment 0675 Colonnade Hall, Opet register: Khonsu barge, inscription over Amun barge, east wall. Drawing group #2c	14311, 5 × 7
Luxor fragment 0676 Colonnade Hall, Opet register: Khonsu barge towboats, east wall. Drawing group #2b	14299, 5 × 7

Luxor Temple (*cont.*)

Nelson Number/Description	Negative, Format
Luxor fragment 0677 (joins 488) Colonnade Hall, Opet register: west wall; horizontal inscription, running soldiers. Drawing group #6c	14603, 5 × 7
Luxor fragment 0678 Colonnade Hall, Opet register: Khonsu barge, east wall. Drawing group #1	14129, 5 × 7
Luxor fragment 0679 Colonnade Hall, upper register: offering list, Tut./Sety I	14130, 5 × 7
Luxor fragment 0680 Amenhotep III? Tut.? small scale king, cartouches	14267, 5 × 7
Luxor fragment 0681 Colonnade Hall, 2nd register: west wall; Min procession, priest, text, Tut./Sety I	14131, 5 × 7
Luxor fragment 0682 A Colonnade Hall, Opet register: small scale inscriptions, Tut.	14132, 5 × 7
Luxor fragment 0682 A Colonnade Hall, Opet register: small scale inscriptions, Tut.	14132-a, 5 × 7
Luxor fragment 0682 A Colonnade Hall, Opet register: small scale inscriptions, Tut.	14132-b, 5 × 7
Luxor fragment 0684 Colonnade Hall, Opet register: Khonsu barge, inscription over Amun barge, east wall. Drawing group #2c	14133, 5 × 7
Luxor fragment 0686 Colonnade Hall, 4th register: east wall; cartouches, Tut.	14135, 5 × 7
Luxor fragment 0687 Colonnade Hall, 2nd register: west wall; Min procession, text, fanpoles, Tut.	14136, 5 × 7
Luxor fragment 0688 Colonnade Hall, 2nd register: west wall; Min procession, text, Tut.	14137, 5 × 7
Luxor fragment 0689 Colonnade Hall, 2nd register: west wall; Tut.	14302, 5 × 7
Luxor fragment 0690 Colonnade Hall, upper register: goddess head, Tut.	14138, 5 × 7
Luxor fragment 0691 Colonnade Hall, Opet register: Khonsu barge, east wall. Drawing group #1	14139, 5 × 7
Luxor fragment 0694 Colonnade Hall, 2nd register: Tut.; west wall	14694, 5 × 7
Luxor fragment 0695 Colonnade Hall, 2nd register: west wall; Theban Triad offering scene, Tut.	14140, 5 × 7
Luxor fragment 0696 Colonnade Hall, 2nd register: west wall; Min procession, fan pommel, Tut.	14141, 5 × 7
Luxor fragment 0697 Colonnade Hall, 2nd register: west wall; Min procession, priests, Tut./Sety I	14142, 5 × 7
Luxor fragment 0698 Colonnade Hall, 2nd register: west wall; Min procession, priests, Tut./Sety I	14298, 5 × 7
Luxor fragment 0706 Amenhotep III Sun Court: east wall; Amun bark scene	14143, 5 × 7
Luxor fragment 0711 Fragment with parallel to text of the Bentresh Stela	13986, 5 × 7
Luxor fragment 0715 Fragment with parallel to text of the Bentresh Stela	13972, 5 × 7
Luxor fragment 0716 Fragment with parallel to text of the Bentresh Stela	13976, 5 × 7
Luxor fragment 0724 Fragment with parallel to text of the Bentresh Stela	13985, 5 × 7
Luxor fragment 0724 Fragment with parallel to text of the Bentresh Stela	14332, 5 × 7

Luxor Temple (*cont.*)

Nelson Number/Description	Negative, Format
Luxor fragment 0725 Colonnade Hall, 2nd register: west wall; Mut offering scene, Tut.	14144, 5 × 7
Luxor fragment 0726 Fragment with parallel to text of the Bentresh Stela	13995, 5 × 7
Luxor fragment 0729 Fragment with parallel to text of the Bentresh Stela	14331, 5 × 7
Luxor fragment 0736 Fragment with parallel to text of the Bentresh Stela	13984, 5 × 7
Luxor fragment 0737 Fragment with parallel to text of the Bentresh Stela	13967, 5 × 7
Luxor fragment 0738 Fragment with parallel to text of the Bentresh Stela	13988, 5 × 7
Luxor fragment 0739 Fragment with parallel to text of the Bentresh Stela	13993, 5 × 7
Luxor fragment 0740 Fragment with parallel to text of the Bentresh Stela	13969, 5 × 7
Luxor fragment 0741 Fragment with parallel to text of the Bentresh Stela	13965, 5 × 7
Luxor fragment 0742 Fragment with parallel to text of the Bentresh Stela	13980, 5 × 7
Luxor fragment 0743 Fragment with parallel to text of the Bentresh Stela	13996, 5 × 7
Luxor fragment 0744 Fragment with parallel to text of the Bentresh Stela	13974, 5 × 7
Luxor fragment 0745 Fragment with parallel to text of the Bentresh Stela	13968, 5 × 7
Luxor fragment 0751 Fragment with parallel to text of the Bentresh Stela	13997, 5 × 7
Luxor fragment 0753 Fragment with parallel to text of the Bentresh Stela	13992, 5 × 7
Luxor fragment 0755 Fragment with parallel to text of the Bentresh Stela	13978, 5 × 7
Luxor fragment 0756 Fragment with parallel to text of the Bentresh Stela	13966, 5 × 7
Luxor fragment 0757 Fragment with parallel to text of the Bentresh Stela	13979, 5 × 7
Luxor fragment 0759 Fragment with parallel to text of the Bentresh Stela	13987, 5 × 7
Luxor fragment 0763 Colonnade Hall, 2nd register: west wall; Min procession, standard, Tut.	12816, 5 × 7
Luxor fragment 0764 Colonnade Hall, Opet register: Amun bark, Luxor Temple scene, back aegis and corner, west wall, south end. Drawing group #5a	13924, 5 × 7
Luxor fragment 0765 Fragment with parallel to text of the Bentresh Stela	13981, 5 × 7
Luxor fragment 0770 Colonnade Hall, 2nd register: west wall; Min procession, standard, Tut.	12817, 5 × 7
Luxor fragment 0777 Colonnade Hall, Opet register: bark of Amun procession, west wall. Drawing group #7a	14147, 5 × 7
Luxor fragment 0778 Colonnade Hall, 2nd register: west wall, Min procession, priest arms, Tut./Sety I	14484, 5 × 7
Luxor fragment 0778 Colonnade Hall, 2nd register: west wall; Min procession, priest arms, Tut./Sety I	14148, 5 × 7
Luxor fragment 0780 Fragment with parallel to text of the Bentresh Stela	13982, 5 × 7
Luxor fragment 0784 Fragment with parallel to text of the Bentresh Stela	13989, 5 × 7
Luxor fragment 0785 Amenhotep III Sun Court: kings	14543, 5 × 7

Luxor Temple (*cont.*)

Nelson Number/Description	Negative, Format
Luxor fragment 0786 Amenhotep III Sun Court: east wall; Amun bark scene	14151, 5 × 7
Luxor fragment 0787 Amenhotep III Sun Court: east wall; Amun bark scene	14152, 5 × 7
Luxor fragment 0792 Fragment with parallel to text of the Bentresh Stela	13971, 5 × 7
Luxor fragment 0795 Amenhotep III Sun Court: east wall; Amun bark scene	14153, 5 × 7
Luxor fragment 0827 Fragment with parallel to text of the Bentresh Stela	13977, 5 × 7
Luxor fragment 0828 Tutankhamun reused talatat	13884, 5 × 7
Luxor fragment 0832 Tutankhamun reused talatat	13882, 5 × 7
Luxor fragment 0839 Fragment with parallel to text of the Bentresh Stela	13999, 5 × 7
Luxor fragment 0840 Fragment with parallel to text of the Bentresh Stela	13994, 5 × 7
Luxor fragment 0851 Amenhotep III Sun Court: east wall	14155, 5 × 7
Luxor fragment 0856 Fragment with parallel to text of the Bentresh Stela	13983, 5 × 7
Luxor fragment 0871 Amenhotep III Sun Court: kings	14541, 5 × 7
Luxor fragment 0872 Amenhotep III Sun Court: east wall; Amun bark scene	14157, 5 × 7
Luxor fragment 0873 Amenhotep III Sun Court: east wall; Amun bark scene	14158, 5 × 7
Luxor fragment 0874 Amenhotep III Sun Court: east wall; Amun bark scene	14159, 5 × 7
Luxor fragment 0876 Colonnade Hall, 3rd register: west wall; Tut./Sety I	15463, 5 × 7
Luxor fragment 0877 Amenhotep III Sun Court: east wall; offering scene to immediate north of Amun bark scene	14161, 5 × 7
Luxor fragment 0882 Fragment with parallel to text of the Bentresh Stela	13991, 5 × 7
Luxor fragment 0883 Colonnade Hall, 2nd register: west wall; Mut offering scene, king's head, Tut.	14162, 5 × 7
Luxor fragment 0884 Colonnade Hall, 2nd register: north wall; standing Amun, goddess scene, Tut.	14163, 5 × 7
Luxor fragment 0885 Colonnade Hall, upper register: cobra frieze, Tut./Sety I(?)	15841, 5 × 7
Luxor fragment 0888 possible Late period restoration of Thutmosis III shrine, parts of barks in procession with cartouche of Thutmosis III; group includes 242, 243, 244, 1279, 1280	12818, 5 × 7
Luxor fragment 0891 kilt and knee of king	14165, 5 × 7
Luxor fragment 0893 Amenhotep III Sun Court: east wall; Amun bark scene	12819, 5 × 7
Luxor fragment 0906 Tutankhamun reused talatat	13890, 5 × 7
Luxor fragment 0908 A Tutankhamun reused talatat	13907, 5 × 7
Luxor fragment 0908 B Tut. talatat: (Akhenaten reused talatat); Tut. decoration, offering vessel	13914, 5 × 7
Luxor fragment 0908 C Tutankhamun reused talatat	13909, 5 × 7
Luxor fragment 0909 Amenhotep III Sun Court: kings	14459, 5 × 7
Luxor fragment 0910 Amenhotep III Sun Court: east wall; Amun bark scene	12820, 5 × 7

Luxor Temple (*cont.*)

Nelson Number/Description	Negative, Format
Luxor fragment 0912 Tutankhamun reused talatat	13894, 5 × 7
Luxor fragment 0918 Amenhotep III Sun Court: east wall	14169, 5 × 7
Luxor fragment 0939 Amenhotep III Sun Court: kings	14549, 5 × 7
Luxor fragment 0941 Amenhotep III Sun Court: east wall; Amun bark scene	14172, 5 × 7
Luxor fragment 0943 Amenhotep III Sun Court: kings	14560, 5 × 7
Luxor fragment 0955 Amenhotep III Sun Court: kings	14557, 5 × 7
Luxor fragment 0956 Amenhotep III Sun Court: kings	14460, 5 × 7
Luxor fragment 0957 Amenhotep III Sun Court: east wall; offering scene to immediate north of Amun bark scene	14176, 5 × 7
Luxor fragment 0958 Amenhotep III Sun Court: east wall; Amun bark scene	14177, 5 × 7
Luxor fragment 0959 Amenhotep III Sun Court: east wall; Amun bark scene	14178, 5 × 7
Luxor fragment 0979 Colonnade Hall, Opet register: Khonsu barge towboats, east wall. Drawing group #2b	14179, 5 × 7
Luxor fragment 0980 Colonnade Hall, 2nd register: west wall; Min procession, Tut./Sety I	14180, 5 × 7
Luxor fragment 0981 Colonnade Hall, upper register: papyrus bouquet, Tut./Sety I	15873, 5 × 7
Luxor fragment 0983 Ptolemaic bark	14597, 5 × 7
Luxor fragment 0984 Roman period: bark procession	14184, 5 × 7
Luxor fragment 0985 Roman period: bark procession	14185, 5 × 7
Luxor fragment 0986 (Late period)	14186, 5 × 7
Luxor fragment 0987 Ptolemaic bark	14574, 5 × 7
Luxor fragment 0988 Roman period: bark procession	13198, 5 × 7
Luxor fragment 0990 Ptolemaic bark	14486, 5 × 7
Luxor fragment 1000 Colonnade Hall, 2nd register: west wall; Min procession, priests, Tut./Sety I	14187, 5 × 7
Luxor fragment 1001 Colonnade Hall, upper register: Tut.	14188, 5 × 7
Luxor fragment 1003 Colonnade Hall, upper register: Tut.	14189, 5 × 7
Luxor fragment 1005 Colonnade Hall, 2nd register: west wall; Theban Triad offering scene, Tut.	14190, 5 × 7
Luxor fragment 1006 Colonnade Hall; Amun plumes, cobra frieze, Tut./Sety I	15849, 5 × 7
Luxor fragment 1007 Colonnade Hall, 2nd register	13956, 5 × 7
Luxor fragment 1008 Colonnade Hall, Opet register: text. Drawing group #8b	14192, 5 × 7
Luxor fragment 1009 Tut. talatat: (reused Akhenaten talatat); rowers on royal barge	14193, 5 × 7
Luxor fragment 1010 Colonnade Hall, 2nd register: west wall; Min procession, priests, Tut./Sety I	14194, 5 × 7
Luxor fragment 1011 Colonnade Hall, 2nd register: west wall; Thoth and goddess, Tut.	14195, 5 × 7
Luxor fragment 1012 Colonnade Hall: Tut./Sety I	14196, 5 × 7

Luxor Temple (*cont.*)

Nelson Number/Description	Negative, Format
Luxor fragment 1013 Amenhotep III Sun Court: east wall; Amun bark scene	14197, 5 × 7
Luxor fragment 1014 Colonnade Hall, Opet register: small scale inscriptions, Tut.	14198, 5 × 7
Luxor fragment 1015 Amenhotep III Sun Court: east wall; Amun bark scene	14199, 5 × 7
Luxor fragment 1016 Amenhotep III Sun Court: kings	14462, 5 × 7
Luxor Fragment 1017 Colonnade Hall, Opet register: west wall; south end, Tut./Sety I	15464, 5 × 7
Luxor fragment 1018 Colonnade Hall, 2nd register: west wall; Thoth and goddess, Tut.	14202, 5 × 7
Luxor fragment 1019 Amenhotep III Sun Court: kings	14562, 5 × 7
Luxor fragment 1021 Colonnade Hall, upper register: Tut.	14205, 5 × 7
Luxor fragment 1022 Amenhotep III Sun Court: kings	14555, 5 × 7
Luxor fragment 1023 Amenhotep III Sun Court: northeast corner bark scene (king)	14615, 5 × 7
Luxor fragment 1024 Colonnade Hall, 3rd register: south wall, Sety I	14208, 5 × 7
Luxor fragment 1025 Amenhotep III Sun Court: east wall; Amun bark scene	14209, 5 × 7
Luxor fragment 1027 Amenhotep III Sun Court: east wall; offering scene to immediate north of Amun bark scene	14211, 5 × 7
Luxor fragment 1028 Colonnade Hall, 2nd register; west wall; Thoth and goddess (Thoth wig), Tut.	14212, 5 × 7
Luxor fragment 1029 Colonnade Hall, upper register: Tut./Sety I	14548, 5 × 7
Luxor fragment 1030 Colonnade Hall: small scale inscription, Tut.?	14214, 5 × 7
Luxor fragment 1031 Amenhotep III Sun Court: east wall	13938, 5 × 7
Luxor fragment 1032 Colonnade Hall, Opet register: west wall; south end, Tut./Sety I	15465, 5 × 7
Luxor fragment 1033 Colonnade Hall, 2nd register	13876, 5 × 7
Luxor fragment 1034 Fragment with parallel to text of the Bentresh Stela	13973, 5 × 7
Luxor fragment 1035 Colonnade Hall, 2nd register: Sety I	14218, 5 × 7
Luxor fragment 1036 Fragment with parallel to text of the Bentresh Stela	13975, 5 × 7
Luxor fragment 1037 Amenhotep III Sun Court: kings	14561, 5 × 7
Luxor fragment 1038 Colonnade Hall, 3rd register: south wall, west side, Sety I	14546, 5 × 7
Luxor fragment 1039 Colonnade Hall, upper register: Amun-Ra-Kamutef hand, Tut.	14221, 5 × 7
Luxor fragment 1040 Amenhotep III Sun Court: kings	14491, 5 × 7
Luxor fragment 1041 Amenhotep III Sun Court: east wall; Amun bark scene	14223, 5 × 7
Luxor fragment 1042 Amenhotep III Sun Court: east wall; Amun bark scene	14224, 5 × 7
Luxor fragment 1043 Amenhotep III Sun Court: east wall	13964, 5 × 7
Luxor fragment 1044 Amenhotep III Sun Court: east wall; Amun bark scene	14226, 5 × 7

Luxor Temple (*cont.*)

Nelson Number/Description	Negative, Format
Luxor fragment 1045 Amenhotep III Sun Court: east wall; offering scene to immediate north of Amun bark scene	14227, 5 × 7
Luxor fragment 1046 Amenhotep III Sun Court: kings	14572, 5 × 7
Luxor fragment 1047 Amenhotep III Sun Court: east wall	13954, 5 × 7
Luxor fragment 1048 Amenhotep III Sun Court: east wall; Amun bark scene	14230, 5 × 7
Luxor fragment 1049 Amenhotep III Sun Court: kings	14573, 5 × 7
Luxor fragment 1050 Amenhotep III Sun Court: kings	14497, 5 × 7
Luxor fragment 1051 Colonnade Hall: north doorjamb, interior west side	13961, 5 × 7
Luxor fragment 1052 Amenhotep III Sun Court: east wall	13951, 5 × 7
Luxor fragment 1053 Amenhotep III Sun Court: kings	14556, 5 × 7
Luxor fragment 1054 Tutankhamun reused talatat	13960, 5 × 7
Luxor fragment 1055 Colonnade Hall, 3rd register: west wall; Tut./Sety I	14237, 5 × 7
Luxor fragment 1056 Amenhotep III Sun Court: east wall; Amun bark scene	14238, 5 × 7
Luxor fragment 1058 Colonnade Hall, 2nd register: west wall; Thoth and goddess, Tut.	14240, 5 × 7
Luxor fragment 1059 Amenhotep III Sun Court: east wall	14241, 5 × 7
Luxor fragment 1060 Colonnade Hall, 2nd register: west wall; Thoth and goddess, Tut.	14242, 5 × 7
Luxor fragment 1061 Colonnade Hall, 4th register: west wall; cartouches, Sety I	14243, 5 × 7
Luxor fragment 1062 Colonnade Hall, 2nd register	13958, 5 × 7
Luxor fragment 1063 Amenhotep III Sun Court: east wall; Amun bark scene	12947, 5 × 7
Luxor fragment 1063 Amenhotep III Sun Court: east wall; Amun bark scene	14245, 5 × 7
Luxor fragment 1064 Colonnade Hall, 2nd register: west wall; Theban Triad offering scene, Tut.	14246, 5 × 7
Luxor fragment 1065 Colonnade Hall, Opet register: bark of Amun procession, west wall. Drawing group #7b	14247, 5 × 7
Luxor fragment 1066 Colonnade Hall, 2nd register: west wall; Theban Triad offering scene, Tut.	14248, 5 × 7
Luxor fragment 1067 Colonnade Hall, Opet register: bark of Amun procession, west wall. Drawing group #7a	14249, 5 × 7
Luxor fragment 1068 Colonnade Hall, Opet register: bark of Amun procession, west wall. Drawing group #7a	14250, 5 × 7
Luxor fragment 1069 Colonnade Hall, Opet register: bark of Amun procession, west wall. Drawing group #7a	14251, 5 × 7
Luxor fragment 1070 Colonnade Hall, Opet register: bark of Amun procession, west wall. Drawing group #7a	14252, 5 × 7
Luxor fragment 1072 Colonnade Hall, 2nd register: west wall; Thoth and goddess, Tut.	14254, 5 × 7

Luxor Temple (*cont.*)

Nelson Number/Description	Negative, Format
Luxor fragment 1073 (joins 1074) Colonnade Hall, 2nd register: north wall; standing Amun and goddess, Tut.	14255, 5 × 7
Luxor fragment 1074 (joins 1073) Colonnade Hall, 2nd register: north wall; standing Amun and goddess, Tut.	14256, 5 × 7
Luxor fragment 1075 A and B Amenhotep III Sun Court: restored Amun figures	14585, 5 × 7
Luxor fragment 1078 Colonnade Hall: possibly Tut., upper register	14260, 5 × 7
Luxor fragment 1079 Amenhotep III Sun Court: restored Amun figures	14580, 5 × 7
Luxor fragment 1080 Colonnade Hall, 2nd register: west wall; Theban Triad offering scene, Tut.	14262, 5 × 7
Luxor fragment 1081 Amenhotep III Sun Court: restored Amun figures	14263, 5 × 7
Luxor fragment 1081 and 1110 Amenhotep III Sun Court: east wall; Amun-Ra-Kamutef flail	14691, 5 × 7
Luxor fragment 1082 Amenhotep III Sun Court: restored Amun figures	14593, 5 × 7
Luxor fragment 1083 Colonnade Hall, 2nd register: west wall; Theban Triad offering scene, Tut.	14265, 5 × 7
Luxor fragments 1084, 1085, and 1100: Colonnade Hall, 2nd register: west wall; Theban Triad offering scene, Tut.	14266, 5 × 7
Luxor fragment 1086 Colonnade Hall: Tut./Sety I	14268, 5 × 7
Luxor fragment 1087 Amenhotep III Sun Court: east wall; Amun bark scene	14269, 5 × 7
Luxor fragment 1088 Colonnade Hall, Opet register: Amun bark, Luxor Temple scene, back aegis and corner, west wall, south end. Drawing group #5a	13918, 5 × 7
Luxor fragment 1089 Indeterminate date, small scale inscription, top of disc crowning a deity	14271, 5 × 7
Luxor fragment 1090 Colonnade Hall, Opet register: Amun bark, Luxor Temple, west wall. Drawing group #5a	13930, 5 × 7
Luxor fragment 1090 Opet register, Amun bark, Luxor Temple, west wall. Drawing group #5a	14272, 5 × 7
Luxor fragment 1091 Colonnade Hall, 2nd register: west wall; Mut offering scene, Tut.	14273, 5 × 7
Luxor fragment 1092 and 1729 Amenhotep III Sun Court: east wall; lion goddess group 1729	14532, 5 × 7
Luxor fragment 1093 Amenhotep III Sun Court	14542, 5 × 7
Luxor fragment 1095 Colonnade Hall, Opet register: Khonsu barge, east wall. Drawing group #1	14277, 5 × 7
Luxor fragment 1098 Colonnade Hall: Tut.	13315, 5 × 7
Luxor fragment 1099 Colonnade Hall, Opet register: barge of Amun, west wall. Drawing group #6a	14281, 5 × 7
Luxor fragment 1102 Colonnade Hall: Sety I(?) Amenhotep III? goddess holding year sign	14284, 5 × 7
Luxor fragment 1103 Amenhotep III Sun Court: northeast corner bark scene (king)	14622, 5 × 7
Luxor fragment 1105 Colonnade Hall, Opet register: Amun bark, Luxor Temple, west wall. Drawing group #5b	14287, 5 × 7
Luxor fragment 1106 Colonnade Hall, 2nd register: north wall; standing Amun, Mut scene, Tut.	14288, 5 × 7

Luxor Temple (*cont.*)

Nelson Number/Description	Negative, Format
Luxor fragment 1107 Amenhotep III Sun Court: east wall	13935, 5 × 7
Luxor fragment 1108 Amenhotep III Sun Court: east wall	14290, 5 × 7
Luxor fragment 1109 Amenhotep III Sun Court: east wall	14291, 5 × 7
Luxor fragment 1111 Colonnade Hall, 3rd register: west wall, Sety I	14577, 5 × 7
Luxor fragment 1112 Colonnade Hall, 2nd register: west wall; Theban Triad offering scene, Tut.	14293, 5 × 7
Luxor fragment 1113 Colonnade Hall, 2nd register: west wall, Thoth	13893, 5 × 7
Luxor fragment 1115 Colonnade Hall, 4th register	13863, 5 × 7
Luxor fragment 1115 Colonnade Hall, 4th register: east wall; Tut.	13946, 5 × 7
Luxor fragment 1117 Colonnade Hall, upper register: Tut.	14304, 5 × 7
Luxor fragment 1118 Colonnade Hall, 2nd register: east wall, goddess, Tut.	14305, 5 × 7
Luxor fragment 1119 Colonnade Hall, 2nd register: north wall, west side, goddess, Tut.	14315, 5 × 7
Luxor fragment 1120 Colonnade Hall, 2nd register: north wall, west side, Amun kilt, Tut.	14303, 5 × 7
Luxor fragment 1124 Colonnade Hall, upper register, Tut.	14316, 5 × 7
Luxor fragment 1125 Colonnade Hall, 2nd register: west wall, Tut.	14313, 5 × 7
Luxor fragment 1126 Colonnade Hall, upper register, Tut.?	14282, 5 × 7
Luxor fragment 1127 Colonnade Hall, upper register, Tut.	14310, 5 × 7
Luxor fragment 1128 Colonnade Hall, upper register, Tut.	14309, 5 × 7
Luxor fragment 1129 Colonnade Hall, upper register, Tut.	14312, 5 × 7
Luxor fragment 1130 and 1136 Amenhotep III Sun Court: east wall, kings	14534, 5 × 7
Luxor fragment 1131 Colonnade Hall, 3rd register: west wall, Sety I	14317, 5 × 7
Luxor fragment 1132 Colonnade Hall, 2nd register: west wall, Tut.	13199, 5 × 7
Luxor fragment 1133 Colonnade Hall, upper register, Tut.	14318, 5 × 7
Luxor fragments 1134 and 1150 (join) Amenhotep III Sun Court: east wall	14662, 5 × 7
Luxor fragment 1135 (joins 1137, 1138, 1139, 1149) Amenhotep III Sun Court: east wall	13933, 5 × 7
Luxor fragment 1137 (joins 1138, 1139, 1135, 1149) Amenhotep III Sun Court: east wall	13939, 5 × 7
Luxor fragment 1138 (joins 1137, 1139, 1135, 1149) Amenhotep III Sun Court: east wall	13941, 5 × 7
Luxor fragment 1139 (joins 1137, 1138, 1135, 1149) Amenhotep III Sun Court: east wall	13945, 5 × 7
Luxor fragment 1140 Amenhotep III Sun Court: east wall	13937, 5 × 7
Luxor fragment 1141 Amenhotep III Sun Court: east wall	14004, 5 × 7
Luxor fragment 1142 Amenhotep III Sun Court: east wall	13936, 5 × 7

Luxor Temple (*cont.*)

Nelson Number/Description	Negative, Format
Luxor fragment 1143 Colonnade Hall, 2nd register: north wall, west side, Tut.	14010, 5 × 7
Luxor fragment 1144 Colonnade Hall, Opet register, small scale text, Tut.	14013, 5 × 7
Luxor fragment 1145 Colonnade Hall, 2nd register: west wall, Tut.	14015, 5 × 7
Luxor fragment 1146 Amenhotep III Sun Court: east wall	14016, 5 × 7
Luxor fragment 1147 Colonnade Hall, 2nd register: west wall, Min priest kilt, Tut./Sety I	14023, 5 × 7
Luxor fragment 1148 Amenhotep III Sun Court: east wall	14025, 5 × 7
Luxor fragment 1149 (joins 1137, 1138, 1139, 1135) Amenhotep III Sun Court: east wall	13932, 5 × 7
Luxor fragments 1151, 1152, and 1153 Colonnade Hall, 3rd register: Sety I; west wall	14700, 5 × 7
Luxor fragment 1154 Colonnade Hall, Opet register, Tut., small scale	14028, 5 × 7
Luxor fragment 1155 Fragment with parallel to text of the Bentresh Stela	13970, 5 × 7
Luxor fragment 1156 Amenhotep III Sun Court: east wall, Amenhotep III bark	14030, 5 × 7
Luxor fragment 1157 Colonnade Hall, Opet register, Tut.	14033, 5 × 7
Luxor fragment 1158 Colonnade Hall, Opet register: Khonsu barge towboats, east wall. Drawing group #2b	14036, 5 × 7
Luxor fragment 1159 Colonnade Hall, Opet register: Khonsu barge, inscription over Amun barge, east wall. Drawing group #2c	13316, 5 × 7
Luxor fragment 1160 Colonnade Hall, 4th register: west wall, Tut.	14038, 5 × 7
Luxor fragment 1162 Colonnade Hall, 2nd register: west wall, Tut.	14039, 5 × 7
Luxor fragment 1163 A Amenhotep III Sun Court: east wall, oars, Amun bark	14048, 5 × 7
Luxor fragment 1163 B Amenhotep III Sun Court: east wall, oars, Amun bark	14049, 5 × 7
Luxor fragment 1164 Colonnade Hall, Opet register: end of Amun bark procession, beginning upper row towboats. Drawing group #3c	14040, 5 × 7
Luxor fragment 1165 Colonnade Hall, 2nd register: north wall, west side, Tut.	14050, 5 × 7
Luxor fragment 1166 Colonnade Hall, Opet register, Tut.	14052, 5 × 7
Luxor fragment 1167 Colonnade Hall, Opet register: Khonsu barge, inscription over Amun barge, east wall. Drawing group #2c	14053, 5 × 7
Luxor fragment 1168 Colonnade Hall, 2nd register: west wall	14056, 5 × 7
Luxor fragment 1169 Colonnade Hall, 2nd register: west wall	14059, 5 × 7
Luxor fragment 1170 Colonnade Hall, 3rd register: west wall, Sety I	14693, 5 × 7
Luxor fragment 1171 (joins 1135, 1149, 1142) Amenhotep III Sun Court: east wall	13934, 5 × 7
Luxor fragment 1173 (joins 1644 back of Mut double crown) Colonnade Hall: Tut./Sety I; head of Khonsu with text	14605, 5 × 7
Luxor fragment 1175 Colonnade Hall, 4th register: Tut.	14060, 5 × 7

Luxor Temple (*cont.*)

Nelson Number/Description	Negative, Format
Luxor fragment 1176 Amenhotep III Sun Court: kings	14587, 5 × 7
Luxor fragment 1177 Colonnade Hall, upper register, Tut.	14061, 5 × 7
Luxor fragment 1179 Colonnade Hall, 2nd register: west wall, Tut.	14062, 5 × 7
Luxor fragment 1180 Colonnade Hall, 3rd register: west wall, Sety I	14066, 5 × 7
Luxor fragment 1181 A Colonnade Hall, upper register: Tut./Horemheb cartouches	14080, 5 × 7
Luxor fragment 1181 B Colonnade Hall, upper register: Tut./Horemheb cartouches	14081, 5 × 7
Luxor fragment 1183 Colonnade Hall, 3rd register: west wall, Sety I	15847, 5 × 7
Luxor fragment 1184 Colonnade Hall, 2nd register: west wall, Tut.	14083, 5 × 7
Luxor fragment 1185 Colonnade Hall, 2nd register: east wall, Tut.	14084, 5 × 7
Luxor fragment 1186 Colonnade Hall, 2nd register: west wall, Tut.	14085, 5 × 7
Luxor fragment 1187 Colonnade Hall, upper register: Tut.	14093, 5 × 7
Luxor fragment 1188 Colonnade Hall, 2nd register: west wall, Thoth	13902, 5 × 7
Luxor fragment 1190 Amenhotep III Sun Court: east wall	14117, 5 × 7
Luxor fragment 1191 Colonnade Hall, Opet register: end of Amun bark procession, beginning upper row towboats. Drawing group #3c	14119, 5 × 7
Luxor fragment 1192 Colonnade Hall, Opet register: Khonsu barge, east wall. Drawing group #2a	14128, 5 × 7
Luxor fragment 1193 Colonnade Hall, Opet register: upper register towboats, west wall. Drawing group #4b	14134, 5 × 7
Luxor fragment 1194 Colonnade Hall, 4th register: east wall, Tut.	14145, 5 × 7
Luxor fragment 1195 Colonnade Hall, 2nd register: west wall, Tut.	14146, 5 × 7
Luxor fragment 1196 Colonnade Hall, 2nd register: west wall, Tut.	14149, 5 × 7
Luxor fragment 1197 Colonnade Hall, 3rd register: west wall, Sety I	14594, 5 × 7
Luxor fragment 1199 Colonnade Hall, Opet register: end of Amun bark procession, beginning upper row towboats. Drawing group #3c	14150, 5 × 7
Luxor fragment 1200 Colonnade Hall, Opet register: upper register towboats, west wall. Drawing group #4b	14154, 5 × 7
Luxor fragment 1201 Colonnade Hall, Opet register: bark of Amun procession, west wall. Drawing group #7b	14156, 5 × 7
Luxor fragment 1202 Colonnade Hall, 2nd register: west wall, Tut.	14160, 5 × 7
Luxor fragment 1203 (joins 1212) Colonnade Hall, 2nd register: east wall, Tut.	14590, 5 × 7
Luxor fragment 1204 Amenhotep III Sun Court: kings, east wall	14537, 5 × 7
Luxor fragment 1205 Colonnade Hall, 2nd register: west wall, Tut.	14164, 5 × 7
Luxor fragment 1206 Colonnade Hall, upper register: Tut.	14166, 5 × 7

Luxor Temple (*cont.*)

Nelson Number/Description	Negative, Format
Luxor fragment 1207 Amenhotep III Sun Court: kings	14476, 5 × 7
Luxor fragment 1208 Colonnade Hall, Opet register: Tut.	14167, 5 × 7
Luxor fragment 1209 Colonnade Hall, upper register: Tut.	14168, 5 × 7
Luxor fragment 1210 Colonnade Hall, 2nd register: west wall, Tut.	14170, 5 × 7
Luxor fragment 1211 Colonnade Hall, upper register: king's ear, Tut./Sety I	15921, 5 × 7
Luxor fragment 1212 Colonnade Hall, 2nd register: Tut.; east wall (joins 1203)	14457, 5 × 7
Luxor fragment 1213 Colonnade Hall, Opet register: bark of Amun procession, west wall. Drawing group #7a	14171, 5 × 7
Luxor fragment 1214 Amenhotep III Sun Court: east wall, recarved Amun head	13915, 5 × 7
Luxor fragment 1215 Colonnade Hall, 2nd register: west wall, Tut.	14173, 5 × 7
Luxor fragment 1216 Colonnade Hall, 2nd register: west wall, Tut.	14174, 5 × 7
Luxor fragment 1217 Colonnade Hall, 2nd register: west wall, Tut.	14175, 5 × 7
Luxor fragment 1218 Colonnade Hall, 2nd register: west wall, Tut.	14181, 5 × 7
Luxor fragment 1219 Colonnade Hall, 3rd register: west wall, Sety I	14686, 5 × 7
Luxor fragment 1220 Colonnade Hall 2nd register: west wall, Tut.	14182, 5 × 7
Luxor fragment 1221 Colonnade Hall, 2nd register: west wall, Tut.	14183, 5 × 7
Luxor fragment 1222 Colonnade Hall, 2nd register: west wall, Tut.	14191, 5 × 7
Luxor fragment 1223 Colonnade Hall, 2nd register: west wall, Tut.	14200, 5 × 7
Luxor fragment 1224 Colonnade Hall, 2nd register: west wall, Tut.	13317, 5 × 7
Luxor fragment 1226 Colonnade Hall: upper register, Tut.?	14201, 5 × 7
Luxor fragment 1227 Colonnade Hall, 2nd register: west wall, Tut.	14203, 5 × 7
Luxor fragment 1228 Colonnade Hall, 2nd register: west wall, Tut., *ka* figure	14204, 5 × 7
Luxor fragment 1229 and 1230 Colonnade Hall, 3rd register: west wall, Sety I	14699, 5 × 7
Luxor fragment 1231 Colonnade Hall, 2nd register: west wall, Tut.	14206, 5 × 7
Luxor fragment 1232 Colonnade Hall, 2nd register: west wall, Tut.	14207, 5 × 7
Luxor fragment 1233 Colonnade Hall, 2nd register: west wall, Tut.	14210, 5 × 7
Luxor fragment 1234 Colonnade Hall, 2nd register: west wall, Tut.	14213, 5 × 7
Luxor fragment 1235 Colonnade Hall, 2nd register: west wall, Tut.	13318, 5 × 7
Luxor fragment 1236 Colonnade Hall, 2nd register: northwest corner, Tut.	14215, 5 × 7
Luxor fragment 1237 Tut. (?)	14216, 5 × 7
Luxor fragment 1238 Colonnade Hall, 2nd register: west wall, Tut.	14217, 5 × 7
Luxor fragment 1239 Colonnade Hall, 2nd register: west wall, Tut.	13319, 5 × 7

Luxor Temple (*cont.*)

Nelson Number/Description	Negative, Format
Luxor fragment 1240 Colonnade Hall, 2nd register: west wall, Tut.	14219, 5 × 7
Luxor fragment 1241 Colonnade Hall, 4th register: west wall, Sety I	14220, 5 × 7
Luxor fragment 1242 Colonnade Hall, 2nd register: west wall, Tut.	14222, 5 × 7
Luxor fragment 1243 Colonnade Hall, 2nd register: west wall, Tut.	14225, 5 × 7
Luxor fragment 1244 Colonnade Hall, 2nd register: west wall, Tut.	14228, 5 × 7
Luxor fragment 1245 Colonnade Hall, Opet register: horizontal inscription, running soldiers. Drawing group #6c	14229, 5 × 7
Luxor fragment 1246 Colonnade Hall, 2nd register: west wall, Tut.	14231, 5 × 7
Luxor fragment 1247 Colonnade Hall, 2nd register: west wall, Tut.	14232, 5 × 7
Luxor fragment 1248 Colonnade Hall, 2nd register: west wall, Tut.	14233, 5 × 7
Luxor fragment 1249 Colonnade Hall: upper register, offering list, Tut./Sety I	14234, 5 × 7
Luxor fragment 1249 Colonnade Hall, upper register: offering list, Tut.	15882, 5 × 7
Luxor fragment 1250 Colonnade Hall, 2nd register: west wall, Tut.	14235, 5 × 7
Luxor fragment 1251 Colonnade Hall, 2nd register: west wall, Tut.	14236, 5 × 7
Luxor fragment 1252 Colonnade Hall, 2nd register: west wall, Tut.	14239, 5 × 7
Luxor fragment 1253 Amenhotep III Sun Court	14244, 5 × 7
Luxor fragment 1254 Colonnade Hall: upper register, Sety I(?)	14253, 5 × 7
Luxor fragment 1255 Colonnade Hall, 2nd register: west wall, Tut.	14257, 5 × 7
Luxor fragment 1256 Colonnade Hall: Tut./Sety I; upper register	14258, 5 × 7
Luxor fragment 1257 Colonnade Hall: Tut./Sety I; upper register	14259, 5 × 7
Luxor fragment 1258 Colonnade Hall, 2nd register: Tut.; west wall	14261, 5 × 7
Luxor fragment 1259 Amenhotep III Sun Court: east wall	14264, 5 × 7
Luxor fragment 1260 Colonnade Hall, 3rd register: west wall, Sety I	14270, 5 × 7
Luxor fragment 1261 Tut. restoration of Amenhotep III cartouches	14274, 5 × 7
Luxor fragment 1263 Colonnade Hall, Opet register: end of Amun bark procession, beginning upper row towboats, west wall. Drawing group #3c	14275, 5 × 7
Luxor fragment 1264 Colonnade Hall: upper register, Tut.	14595, 5 × 7
Luxor fragment 1265 Colonnade Hall: Tut.?	14276, 5 × 7
Luxor fragment 1266 Amenhotep III Sun Court: east wall	14554, 5 × 7
Luxor fragment 1267 Colonnade Hall, 2nd register: Tut./Sety I; Min procession, west wall	14278, 5 × 7
Luxor fragment 1268 Colonnade Hall, Facade: text, east side; usurped prenomen Ay, 3rd register?	14279, 5 × 7
Luxor fragment 1269 Colonnade Hall, 2nd register	15848, 5 × 7
Luxor fragment 1270 Amenhotep III Sun Court	14280, 5 × 7

Luxor Temple (*cont.*)

Nelson Number/Description	Negative, Format
Luxor fragment 1271 Colonnade Hall, 3rd register: west wall, Tut./Sety I	14283, 5 × 7
Luxor fragment 1272 Amenhotep III Sun Court: east wall, aegis, Amenhotep III bark, oars	14285, 5 × 7
Luxor fragment 1273 Colonnade Hall: possibly Tut. talatat	14286, 5 × 7
Luxor fragment 1274 Amenhotep III Sun Court: east wall	14289, 5 × 7
Luxor fragment 1275 Tut. talatat	13277, 5 × 7
Luxor fragment 1275 reverse Tut. talatat, Akhenaten	13278, 5 × 7
Luxor fragment 1276 Amenhotep III Sun Court: east wall, *ka* standard	14292, 5 × 7
Luxor fragment 1277 Colonnade Hall, 2nd register: west wall, Tut.	13279, 5 × 7
Luxor fragment 1278 Amenhotep III Sun Court: east wall	13280, 5 × 7
Luxor fragment 1279 (joins 1280) possible Late period restoration of Thutmosis III shrine, parts of barks in procession with cartouche of Thutmosis III; part of group that includes 242, 243, 244, and 888	13281, 5 × 7
Luxor fragment 1280 (joins 1279) possible Late period restoration of Thutmosis III shrine, parts of barks in procession with cartouche of Thutmosis III; part of group that includes 242, 243, 244, and 888	13282, 5 × 7
Luxor fragment 1282 Amenhotep III Sun Court	13283, 5 × 7
Luxor fragment 1283 Colonnade Hall, 2nd register: west wall, Tut.	13284, 5 × 7
Luxor fragment 1284 Colonnade Hall: Tut.	13285, 5 × 7
Luxor fragment 1286 Colonnade Hall, 2nd register: east wall, king conducted by a god, Tut.	15979, 5 × 7
Luxor fragment 1287 Tutankhamun reused talatat	13908, 5 × 7
Luxor fragment 1288 Colonnade Hall, 2nd register: east wall	13959, 5 × 7
Luxor fragment 1289 Colonnade Hall: Tut.	13286, 5 × 7
Luxor fragment 1290 Colonnade Hall, 2nd register: west wall, Tut.	13287, 5 × 7
Luxor fragment 1291 Amenhotep III Sun Court: east wall	13288, 5 × 7
Luxor fragment 1292 Colonnade Hall, 2nd register: west wall, Tut.	13289, 5 × 7
Luxor fragment 1293 Colonnade Hall, 2nd register: west wall, Tut.	13290, 5 × 7
Luxor fragment 1294 Colonnade Hall, 2nd register: west wall, Tut.	13291, 5 × 7
Luxor fragment 1295 Colonnade Hall, 2nd register: east wall; Tut.	14600, 5 × 7
Luxor fragment 1296 Colonnade Hall, 2nd register: west wall, Tut.	13292, 5 × 7
Luxor fragment 1297 Colonnade Hall, 2nd register: northwest corner, Tut.	13293, 5 × 7
Luxor fragment 1298 Colonnade Hall, 2nd register: northwest corner, Tut.	13294, 5 × 7
Luxor fragment 1299 Colonnade Hall, 2nd register: northwest corner, Tut.	13320, 5 × 7
Luxor fragment 1300 Colonnade Hall, Opet register: Amun bark, Luxor Temple, west wall, south end. Drawing group #5b	13295, 5 × 7
Luxor fragment 1301 Amenhotep III Sun Court: east wall, kilt Amenhotep III	13321, 5 × 7

Luxor Temple (*cont.*)

Nelson Number/Description	Negative, Format
Luxor fragment 1302 Colonnade Hall, upper register: Tut.	15356, 5 × 7
Luxor fragment 1303 Colonnade Hall, upper register: Tut./Horemheb	15855, 5 × 7
Luxor fragment 1304 Colonnade Hall, upper register: Tut.	13296, 5 × 7
Luxor fragment 1305 Colonnade Hall: Tut.(?) Opet register?	13297, 5 × 7
Luxor fragment 1306 Colonnade Hall, upper register: Tut.	15317, 5 × 7
Luxor fragment 1307 Colonnade Hall: Tut.	13298, 5 × 7
Luxor fragment 1308 Amenhotep III Sun Court: east wall	13322, 5 × 7
Luxor fragment 1310 Colonnade Hall, 4th register: east wall, Tut.	13323, 5 × 7
Luxor fragment 1311 Amenhotep III Sun Court: lion goddess group, bark aegis	14507, 5 × 7
Luxor fragment 1314 Colonnade Hall, 3rd register: west wall, Sety I	14540, 5 × 7
Luxor fragment 1315 Colonnade Hall, 3rd register: west wall (left side Sety I, right side Tut.	14553, 5 × 7
Luxor fragment 1316 Colonnade Hall, 4th register: Tut.	13949, 5 × 7
Luxor fragment 1318 Colonnade Hall, 3rd register: west wall, Sety I	14522, 5 × 7
Luxor fragment 1319 Colonnade Hall, 3rd register: west wall, Sety I	14521, 5 × 7
Luxor fragment 1321 Colonnade Hall, Facade: 3rd register, east side; hand of colossal Amun figure grasping *wʒs* scepter, lotus bud of bouquet being offered by king	13869, 5 × 7
Luxor fragment 1322 Colonnade Hall, Facade: 3rd register, east side; lower part of hand of colossal Amun figure grasping *wʒs* scepter (same hand as 1321)	13868, 5 × 7
Luxor fragment 1323 Colonnade Hall, Facade: 2nd register, west side; text; joins 1335	13840, 5 × 7
Luxor fragment 1324 Colonnade Hall, Facade: 2nd register, west side; text behind Amun plumes; joins 1325, 1329, 1326; graffiti	13836, 5 × 7
Luxor fragment 1325 Colonnade Hall, Facade: 2nd register, west side; text behind Amun plumes; joins 1328, 1329, 1324	13837, 5 × 7
Luxor fragment 1326 Colonnade Hall, Facade: 2nd register, west side; text behind Amun plumes; joins 1329, 1330, 1327; graffiti	13838, 5 × 7
Luxor fragment 1327 Colonnade Hall, Facade: 2nd register, west side; text behind Amun plumes; joins 1326, 1331	13835, 5 × 7
Luxor fragment 1328 Colonnade Hall, Facade: 2nd register, west side; text behind Amun plumes; joins 1611, 1329, 1325	13832, 5 × 7
Luxor fragment 1329 Colonnade Hall Facade: 2nd register, west side; text behind Amun plumes; joins 1328, 1612, 1330, 1324, graffiti	13845, 5 × 7
Luxor fragment 1330 Colonnade Hall, Facade: 2nd register, west side; text behind Amun plumes; joins 1329, 1326, 1331; graffiti	13842, 5 × 7
Luxor fragment 1331 Colonnade Hall, Facade: 2nd register, west side; text behind Amun plumes; joins 1330, 1327; graffiti	13843, 5 × 7

Luxor Temple (*cont.*)

Nelson Number/Description	Negative, Format
Luxor fragment 1334 Colonnade Hall, Facade: 2nd register, west side; text over and in front of Amun plumes	13839, 5 × 7
Luxor fragment 1335 Colonnade Hall, Facade: 2nd register, west side; text, joins 1323	13830, 5 × 7
Luxor fragment 1338 Colonnade Hall, 3rd register: south wall; Sety I	13872, 5 × 7
Luxor fragment 1339 Colonnade Hall, 3rd register: west wall, Sety I	14698, 5 × 7
Luxor fragment 1340 Colonnade Hall, 3rd register: west wall; Great Ennead offering scene, Sety I	15879, 5 × 7
Luxor fragment 1341 Colonnade Hall, 3rd register: west wall; Great Ennead offering scene, Sety I	14483, 5 × 7
Luxor fragment 1342 Colonnade Hall, 3rd register: west wall, Great Ennead offering scene, Sety I	15903, 5 × 7
Luxor fragment 1350 Colonnade Hall, name frieze above 3rd register: west wall, Sety I	14850, 5 × 7
Luxor fragment 1351 Colonnade Hall, 3rd register: west wall, Sety I	14813, 5 × 7
Luxor fragment 1352 Colonnade Hall, name frieze above 3rd register: west wall, Sety I	14856, 5 × 7
Luxor fragment 1353 Colonnade Hall, name frieze above 3rd register: west wall, Sety I	14849, 5 × 7
Luxor fragments 1354 and 1829: 1354-Colonnade Hall: Sety I; 1829-Colonnade Hall, Opet register: horizontal inscription, running soldiers. Drawing group 6b	14875, 5 × 7
Luxor fragment 1355 Colonnade Hall, 3rd register: west wall, Sety I	14843, 5 × 7
Luxor fragment 1356 Colonnade Hall, 3rd register: west wall, Sety I	14852, 5 × 7
Luxor fragment 1357 Colonnade Hall, name frieze above 3rd register: west wall, Sety I	14868, 5 × 7
Luxor fragment 1358 Colonnade Hall, 3rd register: west wall, Sety I	14884, 5 × 7
Luxor fragment 1359 Colonnade Hall, 3rd register: west wall, Sety I	14854, 5 × 7
Luxor fragment 1361 Colonnade Hall, 3rd register: west wall, Sety I	14881, 5 × 7
Luxor fragments 1362, 1365, and 1503 Colonnade Hall, 3rd register: west wall, Sety I	14876, 5 × 7
Luxor fragments 1363, 1430, and 1465 (1430-red paint) Colonnade Hall, 3rd register: west wall, Sety I	14878, 5 × 7
Luxor fragment 1364 Colonnade Hall, name frieze above 3rd register: west wall, Sety I	14844, 5 × 7
Luxor fragment 1366 Colonnade Hall, 3rd register: west wall, Sety I	14872, 5 × 7
Luxor fragment 1367 Colonnade Hall, 3rd register: west wall, Sety I	14743, 5 × 7
Luxor fragment 1368 Colonnade Hall, 3rd register: west wall, Sety I	14746, 5 × 7
Luxor fragments 1369, 1375, 1406, and 1420 Colonnade Hall, 3rd register: west wall, Sety I	14855, 5 × 7
Luxor fragments 1370, 1395, 1401, and 1409 Colonnade Hall, 3rd register: west wall, Sety I	14874, 5 × 7
Luxor fragments 1372, 1393, and 1489: 1372-Colonnade Hall, Sety I; 1393 and 1489-Colonnade Hall, 3rd register: west wall, Sety I	14877, 5 × 7

Luxor Temple (*cont.*)

Nelson Number/Description	Negative, Format
Luxor fragment 1373 Colonnade Hall, 3rd register: west wall; Great Ennead offering scene, Sety I	14865, 5 × 7
Luxor fragment 1374 Colonnade Hall, 3rd register: west wall, Sety I	14847, 5 × 7
Luxor fragment 1377 Colonnade Hall, 3rd register: west wall, Sety I	14745, 5 × 7
Luxor fragment 1378 Colonnade Hall, 3rd register: west wall; Great Ennead offering scene, Sety I	14791, 5 × 7
Luxor fragment 1379 Colonnade Hall, 3rd register: west wall, Sety I	14859, 5 × 7
Luxor fragment 1380 Colonnade Hall, 3rd register: west wall, Sety I	14767, 5 × 7
Luxor fragment 1381 Colonnade Hall, 3rd register: west wall, Sety I	14764, 5 × 7
Luxor fragment 1382 Colonnade Hall, 3rd register: west wall, Sety I	14789, 5 × 7
Luxor fragment 1383 Colonnade Hall, 3rd register: west wall, Sety I	14761, 5 × 7
Luxor fragment 1384 Colonnade Hall, 3rd register: west wall, Sety I	14774, 5 × 7
Luxor fragment 1385 Colonnade Hall, 3rd register: west wall, Sety I	14771, 5 × 7
Luxor fragment 1386 Colonnade Hall, 3rd register: west wall, Sety I	14769, 5 × 7
Luxor fragment 1387 Colonnade Hall, 3rd register: west wall, Sety I	14785, 5 × 7
Luxor fragment 1388 Colonnade Hall, 3rd register: west wall, Sety I	14763, 5 × 7
Luxor fragment 1389 Colonnade Hall, 3rd register: west wall, Sety I	14786, 5 × 7
Luxor fragment 1390 Colonnade Hall, 3rd register: west wall, Sety I	14760, 5 × 7
Luxor fragment 1391 Colonnade Hall, 3rd register: west wall, Sety I	14815, 5 × 7
Luxor fragment 1392 Colonnade Hall, 3rd register: west wall, Sety I	14756, 5 × 7
Luxor fragment 1394 Colonnade Hall, 3rd register: west wall, Sety I	14846, 5 × 7
Luxor fragment 1396 Colonnade Hall, 3rd register: west wall, Sety I	14873, 5 × 7
Luxor fragment 1397 Colonnade Hall, 3rd register: west wall, Sety I	14753, 5 × 7
Luxor fragment 1398 Colonnade Hall, 3rd register: west wall, Sety I	14778, 5 × 7
Luxor fragment 1399 and 1413 Colonnade Hall, 3rd register: west wall, Sety I	14714, 5 × 7
Luxor fragments 1400, 1402, 1426, and 1449 Colonnade Hall, 3rd register: west wall, Sety I	14879, 5 × 7
Luxor fragment 1403 Colonnade Hall, 3rd register: west wall, Sety I	14819, 5 × 7
Luxor fragment 1404 Colonnade Hall, 3rd register: west wall, Sety I	14792, 5 × 7
Luxor fragment 1405 Colonnade Hall, 3rd register: west wall, Sety I	14788, 5 × 7
Luxor fragment 1407 Colonnade Hall: Sety I name frieze above 3rd register: west wall, south end	15226, 5 × 7
Luxor fragment 1408 Colonnade Hall, 3rd register: west wall, Sety I	14822, 5 × 7
Luxor fragment 1410 Colonnade Hall, 3rd register: west wall, Sety I	14765, 5 × 7

Luxor Temple (*cont.*)

Nelson Number/Description	Negative, Format
Luxor fragment 1411 Colonnade Hall, 3rd register: west wall, Sety I	14869, 5 × 7
Luxor fragment 1412 Colonnade Hall, 3rd register: west wall, Sety I	14864, 5 × 7
Luxor fragments 1415 and 1416 Colonnade Hall, 3rd register: west wall, Sety I	14811, 5 × 7
Luxor fragments 1418 and 1419 Colonnade Hall, 3rd register: west wall, Sety I	14860, 5 × 7
Luxor fragment 1421 Colonnade Hall, 3rd register: west wall, Sety I	14817, 5 × 7
Luxor fragment 1422 and 1429 Colonnade Hall, 3rd register: west wall, Sety I(?) 1429	14820, 5 × 7
Luxor fragment 1423 Colonnade Hall, 3rd register: west wall, Sety I	14784, 5 × 7
Luxor fragment 1424 Colonnade Hall, 3rd register: west wall, Sety I	14824, 5 × 7
Luxor fragment 1425 Colonnade Hall, name frieze above 3rd register: west wall, Sety I	14821, 5 × 7
Luxor fragment 1427 Colonnade Hall, 3rd register: west wall, Sety I	14790, 5 × 7
Luxor fragment 1428 Colonnade Hall, 3rd register: west wall, Sety I	14752, 5 × 7
Luxor fragment 1431 Colonnade Hall, name frieze above 3rd register: west wall, Sety I	14866, 5 × 7
Luxor fragment 1432 Colonnade Hall, 3rd register: west wall, Sety I	14758, 5 × 7
Luxor fragment 1433 Colonnade Hall, 3rd register: west wall, Sety I	14853, 5 × 7
Luxor fragment 1433 A Sety, small doorjamb, not Colonnade Hall	13911, 5 × 7
Luxor fragment 1434 Colonnade Hall, name frieze above 3rd register: west wall, Sety I	14737, 5 × 7
Luxor fragment 1435 Colonnade Hall, 3rd register: west wall, Sety I	14749, 5 × 7
Luxor fragment 1436 Colonnade Hall, 3rd register: west wall, Sety I	14751, 5 × 7
Luxor fragment 1437 Colonnade Hall, 3rd register: west wall, Sety I	14718, 5 × 7
Luxor fragment 1438 Colonnade Hall, 3rd register: west wall, Sety I	14723, 5 × 7
Luxor fragment 1439 Colonnade Hall, 3rd register: west wall, Sety I	14727, 5 × 7
Luxor fragments 1440 Colonnade Hall, 3rd register: west wall, Sety I	14744, 5 × 7
Luxor fragment 1441 Colonnade Hall, 3rd register: west wall, Sety I	14741, 5 × 7
Luxor fragment 1442 Colonnade Hall, 3rd register: west wall, Sety I	14725, 5 × 7
Luxor fragment 1443 Colonnade Hall, 3rd register: west wall, Sety I	14736, 5 × 7
Luxor fragment 1444 A Colonnade Hall, 3rd register: west wall, Sety I	14770, 5 × 7
Luxor fragment 1444 B Colonnade Hall, 3rd register: west wall, Sety I	14867, 5 × 7
Luxor fragment 1445 Colonnade Hall, 3rd register: west wall, Sety I	14779, 5 × 7
Luxor fragment 1446 Colonnade Hall, name frieze above 3rd register: west wall, Sety I	14728, 5 × 7
Luxor fragment 1447 Colonnade Hall, 3rd register: west wall, Sety I	14720, 5 × 7
Luxor fragment 1448 Colonnade Hall, 3rd register: west wall, Sety I	14721, 5 × 7

Luxor Temple (*cont.*)

Nelson Number/Description	Negative, Format
Luxor fragment 1450 Colonnade Hall, 3rd register: west wall, Sety I	14729, 5 × 7
Luxor fragment 1451 Colonnade Hall, 3rd register: west wall, Sety I	14812, 5 × 7
Luxor fragment 1452 B Colonnade Hall, 3rd register: west wall, Sety I	14793, 5 × 7
Luxor fragment 1453 Colonnade Hall, 3rd register: west wall, Sety I	14776, 5 × 7
Luxor fragment 1454 Colonnade Hall, 3rd register: west wall, Sety I	14773, 5 × 7
Luxor fragment 1455 Colonnade Hall, 3rd register: west wall, Sety I	14826, 5 × 7
Luxor fragment 1456 Colonnade Hall, 3rd register: west wall, Sety I	14842, 5 × 7
Luxor fragment 1457 Colonnade Hall, name frieze above 3rd register: west wall, Sety I	14818, 5 × 7
Luxor fragment 1458 Colonnade Hall, 2nd register: south wall, west side, Sety I	14722, 5 × 7
Luxor fragment 1459 Colonnade Hall, 3rd register: west wall, Sety I	14780, 5 × 7
Luxor fragment 1460 Colonnade Hall, name frieze above 3rd register: west wall, Sety I	14740, 5 × 7
Luxor fragment 1461 Colonnade Hall, 3rd register: west wall, Sety I	14781, 5 × 7
Luxor fragment 1462 Colonnade Hall, 3rd register: west wall, Sety I	14823, 5 × 7
Luxor fragment 1463 Colonnade Hall, name frieze above 3rd register: west wall, Sety I	14827, 5 × 7
Luxor fragment 1464 Colonnade Hall, 3rd register: west wall, Sety I	14848, 5 × 7
Luxor fragment 1466 Colonnade Hall, 3rd register: west wall, Sety I	14851, 5 × 7
Luxor fragment 1467, 1468, and 1475 Colonnade Hall, 3rd register: west wall, Sety I	14858, 5 × 7
Luxor fragment 1469 Colonnade Hall, 3rd register: west wall, Sety I	14768, 5 × 7
Luxor fragments 1470 and 1471 Colonnade Hall, 3rd register: west wall, Sety I	14726, 5 × 7
Luxor fragment 1472 Colonnade Hall, 3rd register: west wall, Sety I	14863, 5 × 7
Luxor fragment 1473 Colonnade Hall, 3rd register: west wall, Sety I	14782, 5 × 7
Luxor fragment 1474 Colonnade Hall, 3rd register: west wall, Sety I	14772, 5 × 7
Luxor fragment 1476 Colonnade Hall, 3rd register: west wall, Sety I	14775, 5 × 7
Luxor fragment 1477 Colonnade Hall, 3rd register: west wall, Sety I	14747, 5 × 7
Luxor fragment 1478 Colonnade Hall, 3rd register: west wall, Sety I	14757, 5 × 7
Luxor fragment 1479 Colonnade Hall, 3rd register: west wall, Sety I	14716, 5 × 7
Luxor fragment 1480 Colonnade Hall, 3rd register: west wall, Sety I	14814, 5 × 7
Luxor fragment 1481 Colonnade Hall, 3rd register: west wall, Sety I	14717, 5 × 7
Luxor fragment 1482 Colonnade Hall, 3rd register: west wall, Sety I	14715, 5 × 7
Luxor fragment 1483 Colonnade Hall, 3rd register: west wall, Sety I	14739, 5 × 7
Luxor fragment 1484 Colonnade Hall, 3rd register: west wall, Sety I	14748, 5 × 7

Luxor Temple (*cont.*)

Nelson Number/Description	Negative, Format
Luxor fragment 1485 Colonnade Hall, 3rd register: west wall, Sety I	14759, 5 × 7
Luxor fragment 1486 A Colonnade Hall, 3rd register: west wall, Sety I	14719, 5 × 7
Luxor fragment 1486 B Colonnade Hall, 3rd register: west wall, Sety I	14754, 5 × 7
Luxor fragment 1486 B Colonnade Hall, 3rd register: west wall, Sety I	14762, 5 × 7
Luxor fragment 1491 Colonnade Hall, 3rd register: west wall, Sety I	14845, 5 × 7
Luxor fragment 1492 Colonnade Hall, 3rd register: west wall, Sety I	14750, 5 × 7
Luxor fragment 1493 Colonnade Hall, 3rd register: west wall, Sety I	14777, 5 × 7
Luxor fragment 1494 Colonnade Hall, 3rd register: west wall, Sety I	14816, 5 × 7
Luxor fragment 1495 Colonnade Hall, 3rd register: west wall, Sety I	14787, 5 × 7
Luxor fragment 1496 Colonnade Hall, 3rd register: west wall, Sety I	14738, 5 × 7
Luxor fragment 1497 Colonnade Hall, 3rd register: west wall, Sety I	14825, 5 × 7
Luxor fragment 1498 Colonnade Hall, 3rd register: west wall, Sety I	14783, 5 × 7
Luxor fragment 1499 Colonnade Hall, 3rd register: west wall, Sety I	14766, 5 × 7
Luxor fragment 1500 Colonnade Hall, 3rd register: west wall, Sety I	14755, 5 × 7
Luxor fragments 1501 and 1502 Colonnade Hall, 3rd register: west wall, Sety I	14742, 5 × 7
Luxor fragment 1504 Colonnade Hall, 3rd register: west wall, Sety I	14862, 5 × 7
Luxor fragment 1505 Colonnade Hall, name frieze above 3rd register: west wall, Sety I	14870, 5 × 7
Luxor fragment 1506 Colonnade Hall, 3rd register: west wall, Sety I	14861, 5 × 7
Luxor fragment 1509 Colonnade Hall, 3rd register: west wall, Sety I	14506, 5 × 7
Luxor fragment 1510 Colonnade Hall, 3rd register: west wall, Sety I	14724, 5 × 7
Luxor fragment 1512 Colonnade Hall, 3rd register: west wall, Sety I	14539, 5 × 7
Luxor fragment 1514 Colonnade Hall, 3rd register: west wall, Sety I	14628, 5 × 7
Luxor fragment 1515 Colonnade Hall, 3rd register: west wall, Sety I	14510, 5 × 7
Luxor fragment 1516 Colonnade Hall, 3rd register: west wall, Sety I	14518, 5 × 7
Luxor fragment 1517 Colonnade Hall, Opet register: upper row towboats, west wall. Drawing group #4b	13877, 5 × 7
Luxor fragment 1521 Colonnade Hall, 2nd register: west wall, Tut.	14519, 5 × 7
Luxor fragment 1522 Colonnade Hall, 2nd register: west wall, Tut.	14625, 5 × 7
Luxor fragment 1523 Colonnade Hall, 2nd register: west wall, Thoth	13856, 5 × 7
Luxor fragment 1527 Colonnade Hall, 2nd register: west wall, Thoth	13827, 5 × 7
Luxor fragment 1528 Colonnade Temple, 2nd register: west wall, Thoth	13851, 5 × 7

Luxor Temple (*cont.*)

Nelson Number/Description	Negative, Format
Luxor fragment 1529 Colonnade Hall, 2nd register: west wall, Thoth	13823, 5 × 7
Luxor fragment 1530 Colonnade Hall, 2nd register	13864, 5 × 7
Luxor fragment 1531 Colonnade Hall, 2nd register: west wall, Tut.	14649, 5 × 7
Luxor fragment 1532 Colonnade Hall, 2nd register: west wall, Tut.	14578, 5 × 7
Luxor fragment 1534 Colonnade Hall, 2nd register: west wall, Tut.	14666, 5 × 7
Luxor fragment 1535 Colonnade Hall, 2nd register: west wall, Tut.	14679, 5 × 7
Luxor fragment 1536 Colonnade Hall, 2nd register	13848, 5 × 7
Luxor fragment 1537 Colonnade Hall, 2nd register	13846, 5 × 7
Luxor fragment 1538 A and B Colonnade Hall, 2nd register	13841, 5 × 7
Luxor fragment 1539 Colonnade Hall, 2nd register	13847, 5 × 7
Luxor fragment 1540 Colonnade Hall, 2nd register: west wall, Tut.	14670, 5 × 7
Luxor fragment 1541 Colonnade Hall, 2nd register: west wall, Tut.	14612, 5 × 7
Luxor fragment 1543 Colonnade Hall, 2nd register: Min procession, west wall	13889, 5 × 7
Luxor fragment 1544 Colonnade Hall, 2nd register: west wall, Sety I	14512, 5 × 7
Luxor fragment 1545 Colonnade Hall, 2nd register: west wall, Sety I	14511, 5 × 7
Luxor fragment 1546 Colonnade Hall, 2nd register: west wall, Sety I	14674, 5 × 7
Luxor fragment 1547 Colonnade Hall, 2nd register: west wall, Sety I	14465, 5 × 7
Luxor fragment 1548 Colonnade Hall, 2nd register: west wall, Sety I	14474, 5 × 7
Luxor fragment 1549 Colonnade Hall, 2nd register: west wall, Sety I	14513, 5 × 7
Luxor fragment 1550 Colonnade Hall, 2nd register: west wall, Sety I	14621, 5 × 7
Luxor fragment 1553 Colonnade Hall, 2nd register: Tut.; east wall	14463, 5 × 7
Luxor fragment 1556 Colonnade Hall, 2nd register: east wall, Tut.	14579, 5 × 7
Luxor fragments 1557 and 1558 Colonnade Hall, 2nd register: east wall, Tut.	14528, 5 × 7
Luxor fragments 1560 and 1561 Colonnade Hall, 2nd register: east wall, Tut.	14530, 5 × 7
Luxor fragment 1562 Colonnade Hall, 2nd register: east wall, Tut.	15976, 5 × 7
Luxor fragment 1564 Colonnade Hall, 2nd register: east wall; king conducted by a god, Tut.	15966, 5 × 7
Luxor fragment 1565 Colonnade Hall, 2nd register: east wall, king conducted by a god, Tut.	15978, 5 × 7
Luxor fragment 1566 Colonnade Hall, 2nd register: east wall; king conducted by a god, Tut.	15967, 5 × 7
Luxor fragment 1568 Colonnade Hall, 2nd register: east wall, Tut.	14630, 5 × 7
Luxor fragment 1569 Colonnade Hall, 2nd register: east wall, Tut.	14624, 5 × 7
Luxor fragment 1570 Colonnade Hall, 2nd register	13929, 5 × 7
Luxor fragment 1572 Colonnade Hall, 2nd register	13963, 5 × 7
Luxor fragment 1573 Colonnade Temple, 2nd register: east wall, Tut.	14480, 5 × 7

Luxor Temple (*cont.*)

Nelson Number/Description	Negative, Format
Luxor fragment 1574 Colonnade Hall, 2nd register: east wall, Tut.	14551, 5 × 7
Luxor fragment 1575 Colonnade Hall, 2nd register: east wall, Tut.	14678, 5 × 7
Luxor fragment 1577 Colonnade Hall, 2nd register	13867, 5 × 7
Luxor fragment 1578 Colonnade Hall, 2nd register: east wall, Sety I	14619, 5 × 7
Luxor fragment 1583 Colonnade Hall, 3rd register: east wall, Sety I	14613, 5 × 7
Luxor fragment 1584 Colonnade Hall, 3rd register: east wall; Tut.	13878, 5 × 7
Luxor fragment 1585 Colonnade Hall, 2nd register	13879, 5 × 7
Luxor fragment 1586 Colonnade Hall, 3rd register: east wall, Sety I	14500, 5 × 7
Luxor fragment 1587 Colonnade Hall, 3rd register: east wall, Sety I	14629, 5 × 7
Luxor fragment 1589 Colonnade Hall, 3rd register: east wall, Sety I	14586, 5 × 7
Luxor fragment 1595 Colonnade Hall, 3rd register: east wall, Sety I	14684, 5 × 7
Luxor fragment 1596 Colonnade Hall, 3rd register: east wall, Sety I	14677, 5 × 7
Luxor fragment 1600 Colonnade Hall, Facade: 2nd register, west side; text over and in front of Amun plumes; joins 1602, 1601	13862, 5 × 7
Luxor fragment 1601 Colonnade Hall, Facade: 2nd register, west side; text over and in front of Amun plumes; joins 1600, 1602	13850, 5 × 7
Luxor fragment 1602 Colonnade Hall, Facade: 2nd register, west side; text over and in front of Amun plumes; joins 1600, 1601	13833, 5 × 7
Luxor fragment 1603 Colonnade Hall, Facade: 2nd register, west side; text over and in front of Amun plumes; joins 1602, 1990	13822, 5 × 7
Luxor fragment 1604 Colonnade Hall, Facade: 3rd register, east side; text above Amun, joins 1605, 1608	13853, 5 × 7
Luxor fragment 1604 Colonnade Hall, Facade: 3rd register, east side; inscription, Tut./Ay	13947, 5 × 7
Luxor fragment 1605 Colonnade Hall, Facade: 3rd register, east side; text above Amun, joins 1604, 1608, 1606	13826, 5 × 7
Luxor fragment 1606 Colonnade Hall, Facade: 3rd register, east side	13942, 5 × 7
Luxor fragment 1606 Colonnade Hall, Facade: 3rd register, east side; text above Amun, joins 1605, 1608, 1609	13824, 5 × 7
Luxor fragment 1607 Colonnade Hall, Facade: 3rd register, east side; text above Amun, joins 1606, 1609	13834, 5 × 7
Luxor fragment 1608 Colonnade Hall, Facade: 3rd register, east side; text above Amun, joins 1604, 1605, 1606, 1609	13852, 5 × 7
Luxor fragment 1609 Colonnade Hall, Facade: 3rd register, east side; text above Amun, joins 1608, 1606, 1607	13828, 5 × 7
Luxor fragment 1610 Colonnade Hall, 2nd register: west wall, Thoth	13899, 5 × 7
Luxor fragment 1611 Colonnade Hall, Facade: 2nd register, west side; Amun plumes, joins 1612, 1328	13844, 5 × 7
Luxor fragment 1612 Colonnade Hall, Facade: 2nd register, west side; Amun plumes, joins 1611, 1329; graffiti	13849, 5 × 7

Luxor Temple (*cont.*)

Nelson Number/Description	Negative, Format
Luxor fragment 1614 Colonnade Hall: Tut.	14473, 5 × 7
Luxor fragment 1617 A Colonnade Hall, 2nd register	13857, 5 × 7
Luxor fragment 1617 B Colonnade Hall, 2nd register	13858, 5 × 7
Luxor fragment 1626 Colonnade Hall, 4th register: east wall, Sety I	14576, 5 × 7
Luxor fragment 1627 Colonnade Hall, 2nd register: east wall, Sety I	14683, 5 × 7
Luxor fragment 1628 Colonnade Hall, 3rd register: east wall, Sety I	14673, 5 × 7
Luxor fragment 1629 Colonnade Hall, Facade: 2nd register, east side; text above Khonsu's head, joins wall at L A 66	13873, 5 × 7
Luxor fragment 1630 Colonnade Hall, 2nd register	13874, 5 × 7
Luxor fragment 1632 Colonnade Hall, Facade: 2nd register, west side; traces of erased royal *ka* face, ear in raised relief, in Ramesside sunk relief name frieze beneath missing roof line	13825, 5 × 7
Luxor fragment 1633 Colonnade Hall, 2nd register	13865, 5 × 7
Luxor fragment 1634 Colonnade Hall, Opet register: bottom row towboats, west wall. Drawing group #3a	13855, 5 × 7
Luxor fragment 1635 Colonnade Hall, Opet register: bark of Amun procession, west wall. Drawing group #7b	13854, 5 × 7
Luxor fragment 1636 Colonnade Hall, Opet register: bark of Amun procession, west wall. Drawing group #7a	13871, 5 × 7
Luxor fragment 1637 Colonnade Hall, 2nd register	13831, 5 × 7
Luxor fragment 1638 Tut. reused talatat	13870, 5 × 7
Luxor fragment 1639 Colonnade Hall, 4th register: King grasping hoe	13829, 5 × 7
Luxor fragment 1640 Tut. reused talatat	13912, 5 × 7
Luxor fragment 1641 Tutankhamun reused talatat	13866, 5 × 7
Luxor fragment 1642 Tutankhamun reused talatat	13860, 5 × 7
Luxor fragment 1643 A Tutankhamun reused talatat	13861, 5 × 7
Luxor fragment 1643 B Tutankhamun reused talatat	13859, 5 × 7
Luxor fragment 1644 (joins 1173-head of Khonsu) Colonnade Hall: Tut./Sety I: back of double crown of Mut, text	14608, 5 × 7
Luxor fragment 1645 A Small Sety II doorjamb	13948, 5 × 7
Luxor fragment 1645 B Small Sety II doorjamb	13906, 5 × 7
Luxor fragment 1646 Tutankhamun reused talatat	13887, 5 × 7
Luxor fragment 1647 Tutankhamun reused talatat	13891, 5 × 7
Luxor fragment 1648 Tutankhamun reused talatat	13901, 5 × 7
Luxor fragment 1649 Tutankhamun reused talatat	13905, 5 × 7
Luxor fragment 1650 Colonnade Hall, Opet register: Amun bark, Luxor Temple scene, back aegis and corner, west wall, south end. Drawing group #5a	13916, 5 × 7
Luxor fragment 1651 A Tutankhamun reused talatat	13896, 5 × 7
Luxor fragment 1651 B Tutankhamun reused talatat	13952, 5 × 7
Luxor fragment 1652 A Tutankhamun reused talatat	13898, 5 × 7
Luxor fragment 1652 B Tutankhamun reused talatat	13904, 5 × 7
Luxor fragment 1653 Tutankhamun reused talatat	13895, 5 × 7
Luxor fragment 1654 A Tutankhamun reused talatat	13900, 5 × 7
Luxor fragment 1654 B Tutankhamun reused talatat	13897, 5 × 7
Luxor fragment 1655 Tutankhamun reused talatat	13920, 5 × 7
Luxor fragment 1657 Tutankhamun reused talatat	13927, 5 × 7
Luxor fragment 1658 Colonnade Hall, Opet register: Amun bark, Luxor Temple scene, back aegis and corner, west wall, south end. Drawing group #5a	13925, 5 × 7

Luxor Temple (*cont.*)

Nelson Number/Description	Negative, Format
Luxor fragment 1659 Colonnade Hall, Opet register: Amun bark, Luxor Temple scene, back aegis and corner, west wall, south end. Drawing group #5a	13922, 5 × 7
Luxor fragment 1660 Tutankhamun reused talatat	13931, 5 × 7
Luxor fragment 1661 Tutankhamun reused talatat	13921, 5 × 7
Luxor fragment 1662 A Tutankhamun reused talatat	13926, 5 × 7
Luxor fragment 1662 B Tutankhamun reused talatat	13928, 5 × 7
Luxor fragment 1663 Tutankhamun reused talatat	13919, 5 × 7
Luxor fragment 1665 Tutankhamun reused talatat	13923, 5 × 7
Luxor fragment 1666 Fragment with parallel to text of the Bentresh Stela	13998, 5 × 7
Luxor fragment 1674 Colonnade Hall, Opet register: Khonsu barge, east wall. Drawing group #1	14296, 5 × 7
Luxor fragment 1675 Amenhotep III Sun Court: east wall	13940, 5 × 7
Luxor fragment 1676 Amenhotep III Sun Court: east wall	13944, 5 × 7
Luxor fragment 1677 Amenhotep III Sun Court: east wall; Amun bark scene	12801, 5 × 7
Luxor fragments 1678 and 1683 Colonnàde Hall, 2nd register: east wall, Tut.	14527, 5 × 7
Luxor fragments 1678 and 1683 (join) Colonnade Hall, 2nd register: east wall; coronation scene, Tut.	14882, 5 × 7
Luxor fragment 1679 Amenhotep III Sun Court: northeast corner bark scene (king)	14515, 5 × 7
Luxor fragment 1680 Colonnade Hall, 3rd register: west wall, Sety I	14523, 5 × 7
Luxor fragment 1681 Colonnade Hall, Opet register: west wall; Amun bark, Luxor temple. Drawing group #5a	14544, 5 × 7
Luxor fragment 1682 Amenhotep III Sun Court	14475, 5 × 7
Luxor fragment 1684 Amenhotep III Sun Court	14479, 5 × 7
Luxor fragment 1685 Amenhotep III Sun Court	14509, 5 × 7
Luxor fragments 1686 and 1691 Colonnade Hall, 2nd register: east wall, Tut.	14531, 5 × 7
Luxor fragments 1687 and 1688 Colonnade Hall, 2nd register: east wall, Tut.	14529, 5 × 7
Luxor fragment 1689 Colonnade Hall: Tut.	14545, 5 × 7
Luxor fragment 1690 Colonnade Hall, Facade: west doorjamb fragment; goddess shoulder, wig, leftmost border (4th doorjamb scene from bottom[?], with 2217, 1970, and 2066)	14485, 5 × 7
Luxor fragment 1692 Colonnade Hall, 2nd register: east wall, Tut.	14536, 5 × 7
Luxor fragment 1693 Amenhotep III Sun Court: northeast corner bark scene	14508, 5 × 7
Luxor fragment 1694 interior lintel, central back to back text, part of right center unrecarved Amun plume; interior Colonnade Hall	14617, 5 × 7
Luxor fragment 1696 Colonnade Hall, Opet register: east wall, Tut.	14503, 5 × 7
Luxor fragment 1697 Colonnade Hall, 2nd register: east wall, Tut.	14623, 5 × 7
Luxor fragment 1698 Colonnade Hall, 2nd register: north wall, west side, Tut.	14616, 5 × 7
Luxor fragment 1699 Colonnade Hall, 4th register: east wall, Tut.	14584, 5 × 7
Luxor fragment 1700 Colonnade Hall, 2nd register: east wall, Tut.	14520, 5 × 7
Luxor fragment 1701 and 1702 Colonnade Hall, 2nd register: east wall, Tut.	14526, 5 × 7

Luxor Temple (*cont.*)

Nelson Number/Description	Negative, Format
Luxor fragment 1703 Colonnade Hall, 2nd register: east wall; fowling scene, Tut.	15329, 5 × 7
Luxor fragment 1704 Colonnade Hall, 2nd register: east wall, Sety I	14582, 5 × 7
Luxor fragment 1705 Colonnade Hall, 2nd register: east wall, Sety I	14482, 5 × 7
Luxor fragment 1706 Colonnade Hall, 2nd register: east wall, Sety I	14481, 5 × 7
Luxor fragment 1707 Amenhotep III Sun Court	14558, 5 × 7
Luxor fragment 1708 Amenhotep III Sun Court: restored Amun figures	14583, 5 × 7
Luxor fragment 1709 Colonnade Hall, 3rd register: east wall, Tut.	14517, 5 × 7
Luxor fragment 1710 (joins with 1709) Colonnade Hall, 3rd register: east wall, Tut.	14492, 5 × 7
Luxor fragment 1711 Colonnade Hall: Tut.	14514, 5 × 7
Luxor fragment 1713 Colonnade Hall, 2nd register: east wall, Tut.	14495, 5 × 7
Luxor fragment 1714 Colonnade Hall, upper register: (possibly over main or south doorways), large scale Heb Sed Scene	14494, 5 × 7
Luxor fragment 1716 Colonnade Hall, 2nd register: east wall, Tut.	14471, 5 × 7
Luxor fragment 1717 Colonnade Hall, 2nd register: east wall, Tut.	14499, 5 × 7
Luxor fragment 1718 A and B Colonnade Hall, 2nd register: east wall, Tut.	14535, 5 × 7
Luxor fragment 1719 Colonnade Hall, 2nd register: east wall, Tut.	14627, 5 × 7
Luxor fragment 1720 Amenhotep III Sun Court: northeast corner bark scene (king)	14620, 5 × 7
Luxor fragment 1721 Colonnade Hall, 3rd register: east wall, Sety I	14618, 5 × 7
Luxor fragment 1722 A and B Colonnade Hall	14525, 5 × 7
Luxor fragment 1723 A, B, and C Colonnade Hall	14533, 5 × 7
Luxor fragment 1724 Amenhotep III Sun Court: restored Amun figures	14477, 5 × 7
Luxor fragment 1725 Colonnade Hall: Tut.	14478, 5 × 7
Luxor fragment 1726 Colonnade Hall, 3rd register: west wall, Sety I	14498, 5 × 7
Luxor fragment 1727 Colonnade Hall, 3rd register: east wall, Sety I	14504, 5 × 7
Luxor fragment 1728 Colonnade Hall: lintel fragment, north doorway, Tut./Ay carving	14501, 5 × 7
Luxor fragment 1730 A and B Colonnade Hall: Tut./Sety I	14524, 5 × 7
Luxor fragment 1731 Amenhotep III Sun Court: northeast corner bark scene	14614, 5 × 7
Luxor fragment 1732 Amenhotep III Sun Court	14489, 5 × 7
Luxor fragment 1733 A Tut. talatat	14591, 5 × 7
Luxor fragment 1733 B Tut. talatat	14589, 5 × 7
Luxor fragment 1734 Tut. talatat	14502, 5 × 7
Luxor fragment 1735 Tut. talatat	14505, 5 × 7
Luxor fragment 1736 Colonnade Hall, 2nd register: west wall, Tut.	14611, 5 × 7
Luxor fragment 1737 A and B Colonnade Hall, Opet register: west wall, Tut.	14516, 5 × 7
Luxor fragment 1738 Colonnade Hall, 2nd register: east wall, Tut.	14496, 5 × 7
Luxor fragment 1739 Amenhotep III Sun Court: lion goddess group	14493, 5 × 7

Luxor Temple (*cont.*)

Nelson Number/Description	Negative, Format
Luxor fragment 1740 Amenhotep III Sun Court: restored Amun figures	14487, 5 × 7
Luxor fragment 1741 Amenhotep III Sun Court	14490, 5 × 7
Luxor fragment 1742 A Colonnade Hall, 3rd register: east wall, Tut.	14606, 5 × 7
Luxor fragment 1742 B Colonnade Hall, 3rd register: east wall, Tut.	14609, 5 × 7
Luxor fragment 1743 Colonnade Hall: Tut.	14566, 5 × 7
Luxor fragment 1744 Colonnade Hall, 2nd register: Tut.; east wall	14454, 5 × 7
Luxor fragment 1747 A Tut. talatat	14470, 5 × 7
Luxor fragment 1747 B Tut. talatat	14467, 5 × 7
Luxor fragment 1748 Tut. talatat	14458, 5 × 7
Luxor fragment 1750 Amenhotep III Sun Court	14464, 5 × 7
Luxor fragment 1751 A Tut. talatat	14468, 5 × 7
Luxor fragment 1751 B Tut. talatat	14469, 5 × 7
Luxor fragment 1751 C Tut. talatat	14472, 5 × 7
Luxor fragment 1751 D Tut. talatat	14466, 5 × 7
Luxor fragment 1752 Amenhotep III Sun Court: kings	14456, 5 × 7
Luxor fragment 1753 Colonnade Hall, 4th register: east wall, Sety I	14569, 5 × 7
Luxor fragment 1755 Colonnade Hall: Tut.	14610, 5 × 7
Luxor fragment 1756 Amenhotep III Sun Court: King, Amun, north wall Hypostyle, east side	14607, 5 × 7
Luxor fragment 1757 Amenhotep III Sun Court: King, Amun, north wall Hypostyle, east side	14599, 5 × 7
Luxor fragment 1758 Amenhotep III Sun Court: King, Amun, north wall Hypostyle, east side	14596, 5 × 7
Luxor fragment 1760 Colonnade Hall: Tut.	14602, 5 × 7
Luxor fragment 1761 Colonnade Hall: Tut./Sety I	14563, 5 × 7
Luxor fragment 1762 Colonnade Hall: Tut.	14570, 5 × 7
Luxor fragment 1763 Amenhotep III Sun Court: restored Amun figures	14565, 5 × 7
Luxor fragment 1764 Amenhotep III Sun Court: kings	14564, 5 × 7
Luxor fragment 1765 Amenhotep III Sun Court: King, Amun, north wall Hypostyle, east side	14567, 5 × 7
Luxor fragment 1768 A Amenhotep III Sun Court: restored Amun figures	14598, 5 × 7
Luxor fragment 1768 B Amenhotep III Sun Court: restored Amun figures	14588, 5 × 7
Luxor fragment 1769 Amenhotep III Sun Court	14696, 5 × 7
Luxor fragment 1770 Amenhotep III Sun Court: King, Amun, north wall Hypostyle, east side	14592, 5 × 7
Luxor fragment 1771 Colonnade Hall, 4th register: east wall, Sety I	14604, 5 × 7
Luxor fragment 1772 Amenhotep III Sun Court: restored Amun figures	14639, 5 × 7
Luxor fragment 1773 Colonnade Hall, upper register: Tut.	14638, 5 × 7
Luxor fragment 1775 Amenhotep III Sun Court	14635, 5 × 7
Luxor fragment 1776 Amenhotep III Sun Court	14634, 5 × 7
Luxor fragment 1777 Amenhotep III Sun Court	14641, 5 × 7
Luxor fragment 1778 Colonnade Hall, 2nd register: east wall, Sety I	14656, 5 × 7
Luxor fragment 1779 Colonnade Hall, 2nd register: east wall, Sety I	14644, 5 × 7
Luxor fragment 1780 Amenhotep III Sun Court: kings	14640, 5 × 7
Luxor fragment 1781 A Amenhotep III Sun Court: restored Amun figures	14682, 5 × 7

Luxor Temple (*cont.*)

Nelson Number/Description	Negative, Format
Luxor fragment 1781 B Amenhotep III Sun Court: restored Amun figures	14675, 5 × 7
Luxor fragment 1782 Colonnade Hall, 2nd register: east wall, Sety I	14643, 5 × 7
Luxor fragment 1783 Colonnade Hall, 4th register: north wall, west side, Tut.	14637, 5 × 7
Luxor fragment 1784 Amenhotep III Sun Court: kings	14632, 5 × 7
Luxor fragment 1787 Amenhotep III Sun Court	14654, 5 × 7
Luxor fragment 1788 Colonnade Hall: Tut.	14646, 5 × 7
Luxor fragment 1789 Amenhotep III Sun Court: kings	14642, 5 × 7
Luxor fragment 1790 Amenhotep III Sun Court: restored Amun figures	14647, 5 × 7
Luxor fragment 1791 Colonnade Hall: Tut.	14633, 5 × 7
Luxor fragment 1792 Colonnade Hall, 2nd register: east wall, Sety I	14645, 5 × 7
Luxor fragment 1793 Amenhotep III Sun Court: lion goddess group	14650, 5 × 7
Luxor fragment 1794 Colonnade Hall, 2nd register: east wall, Sety I	14653, 5 × 7
Luxor fragment 1795 Colonnade Hall, 2nd register: east wall, Sety I	14660, 5 × 7
Luxor fragment 1796 Colonnade Hall, 2nd register: east wall, Tut.	14651, 5 × 7
Luxor fragment 1797 Colonnade Hall, 2nd register: west wall, Tut.	14661, 5 × 7
Luxor fragment 1798 Amenhotep III Sun Court: restored Amun figures	14657, 5 × 7
Luxor fragment 1799 Amenhotep III Sun Court: north west area	14631, 5 × 7
Luxor fragment 1800 Colonnade Hall, Opet register: east wall, Tut.	14648, 5 × 7
Luxor fragment 1801 A Amenhotep III Sun Court: restored Amun figures	14658, 5 × 7
Luxor fragment 1801 B Amenhotep III Sun Court: restored Amun figures	14659, 5 × 7
Luxor fragment 1802 Colonnade Hall, 2nd register: east wall, Sety I	14652, 5 × 7
Luxor fragment 1803 Colonnade Hall, 4th register: north wall, west side, Tut.	14655, 5 × 7
Luxor fragment 1804 Colonnade Hall, 2nd register: west wall, Tut.	14636, 5 × 7
Luxor fragment 1806 Tut. talatat	14547, 5 × 7
Luxor fragment 1807 Amenhotep III Sun Court: kings	14664, 5 × 7
Luxor fragment 1808 Amenhotep III Sun Court: east wall	14668, 5 × 7
Luxor fragment 1809 Tut. talatat	14667, 5 × 7
Luxor fragment 1810 interior fourth register(?), east wall	14669, 5 × 7
Luxor fragment 1811 Colonnade Hall: Tut./Sety I	14671, 5 × 7
Luxor fragment 1812 Colonnade Hall, 4th register: east wall, Sety I	14680, 5 × 7
Luxor fragment 1813 Amenhotep III Sun Court: restored Amun figures	14663, 5 × 7
Luxor fragment 1814 Tut. talatat	14676, 5 × 7
Luxor fragment 1815 Amenhotep III Sun Court: east wall; reused as cornice in Christian period (see side view on negative 14685)	14681, 5 × 7
Luxor fragment 1815 B Amenhotep III Sun Court: east wall; view of reused block carved into cornice (see negative 14681 for adjacent Amenhotep III carving)	14685, 5 × 7

Luxor Temple (*cont.*)

Nelson Number/Description	Negative, Format
Luxor fragment 1816 Amenhotep III Sun Court: east wall	14672, 5 × 7
Luxor fragment 1817 winged sun disk over doorway	14665, 5 × 7
Luxor fragment 1818 Colonnade Hall: Tut.	14626, 5 × 7
Luxor fragment 1819 Colonnade Hall, 2nd register: east wall, Tut.	14687, 5 × 7
Luxor fragment 1820 vertical column line and portion of a king's *ḫprš*-crown to left; joins fragment 48 (front of *ḫprš*); interior Colonnade Hall, 3rd register	14692, 5 × 7
Luxor fragment 1821 Colonnade Hall: Tut.	14695, 5 × 7
Luxor fragment 1822 Colonnade Hall: Tut.	14689, 5 × 7
Luxor fragment 1823 Ptolemaic bark	14697, 5 × 7
Luxor fragment 1826 Colonnade Hall, 3rd register: west wall, Sety I	14871, 5 × 7
Luxor fragment 1827 Colonnade Hall, 3rd register: west wall, Sety I	14857, 5 × 7
Luxor fragment 1828 Colonnade Hall, 3rd register: west wall, Sety I	14883, 5 × 7
Luxor fragment 1830 A and B (two halves of same block) Colonnade Hall: nomen of Sety I facing prenomen of Amenhotep III, Sety I	14880, 5 × 7
Luxor fragment 1832 Colonnade Hall, possibly 2nd register: west wall; Min procession, Tut.	15337, 5 × 7
Luxor fragments 1833 and 2071: 1833-Amenhotep III Sun Court; 2071-Colonnade Hall: 3rd register: west wall, Tut./Sety I	15328, 5 × 7
Luxor fragment 1835 Colonnade Hall: Sety I; north pylon	15213, 5 × 7
Luxor fragment 1836 Colonnade Hall, upper register: offering list, Tut./Sety I	15466, 5 × 7
Luxor fragment 1837 Colonnade Hall: Tut./Sety I	15467, 5 × 7
Luxor fragment 1838 Colonnade Hall, 3rd register(?): west wall; Tut./Sety I	15880, 5 × 7
Luxor fragment 1839 Colonnade Hall, 3rd register: west wall; text, offering formulae, Tut./Sety I	15908, 5 × 7
Luxor fragment 1840 A hypostyle hall, west side, goddess' foot, Amenhotep III	15846, 5 × 7
Luxor fragment 1840 B hypostyle hall, west side, king's foot, Amenhotep III	15840, 5 × 7
Luxor fragment 1841 A Tut. talatat: text	15900, 5 × 7
Luxor fragment 1841 B Tut. talatat, reverse Akhenaten sun relief decoration, Aten rays over offerings	15901, 5 × 7
Luxor fragment 1842 Colonnade Hall, Facade: 3rd register, east side, and right-hand border, joins 2079	15877, 5 × 7
Luxor fragment 1843 Amenhotep III Sun Court: restored goddess wearing red crown	15924, 5 × 7
Luxor fragment 1844 Amenhotep III: hypostyle hall, west side, sky sign, and ground line	15868, 5 × 7
Luxor fragment 1845 Colonnade Hall: offering list, Tut./Sety I	15857, 5 × 7
Luxor fragment 1846 Amenhotep III: hypostyle hall(?) purification scene	15869, 5 × 7
Luxor fragment 1847 Colonnade Hall: offering list, Tut./Sety I	15913, 5 × 7
Luxor fragment 1848 Tut. talatat: purification text	15883, 5 × 7
Luxor fragment 1849 Amenhotep III: hypostyle hall, west side, purification scene	15914, 5 × 7
Luxor fragment 1850 Amenhotep III: hypostyle hall, purification scene	15904, 5 × 7

Luxor Temple (*cont.*)

Nelson Number/Description	Negative, Format
Luxor fragment 1853 Amenhotep III: hypostyle hall(?) purification scene	15866, 5 × 7
Luxor fragment 1854 Amenhotep III: hypostyle hall, purification scene	15895, 5 × 7
Luxor fragment 1855 (with 1856) Amenhotep III Sun Court: east wall	15300, 5 × 7
Luxor fragment 1856 (with 1855) Amenhotep III Sun Court: east wall	15296, 5 × 7
Luxor fragments 1857 and 1929 Amenhotep III Sun Court: east wall	15331, 5 × 7
Luxor fragment 1858 Colonnade Hall, 3rd register: west wall; Tut.	15996, 5 × 7
Luxor fragment 1859 Amenhotep III Sun Court	15953, 5 × 7
Luxor fragment 1860 Colonnade Hall, upper register: text, Tut.	15925, 5 × 7
Luxor fragment 1861 Amenhotep III Sun Court: goddess hand, shrine pole	15972, 5 × 7
Luxor fragment 1862 Amenhotep III Sun Court: east wall	15351, 5 × 7
Luxor fragment 1863 Amenhotep III Sun Court	15969, 5 × 7
Luxor fragment 1864 Amenhotep III Sun Court: sky sign, ground line above	15938, 5 × 7
Luxor fragment 1865 Colonnade Hall, upper register	15933, 5 × 7
Luxor fragment 1866 Amenhotep III Sun Court	15975, 5 × 7
Luxor fragment 1867 Amenhotep III(?) Sun Court	15860, 5 × 7
Luxor fragment 1868 Amenhotep III Sun Court	15909, 5 × 7
Luxor fragment 1869 Amenhotep III Sun Court	15954, 5 × 7
Luxor fragment 1870 (joins 1880) Colonnade Hall, upper register: (possibly 3rd register, south wall, west side), Amun plumes, Tut./Sety I	15992, 5 × 7
Luxor fragment 1871 Colonnade Hall, 3rd register: south wall; west side, Sety I	15487, 5 × 7
Luxor fragment 1872 Colonnade Hall, 3rd register: south wall; west side, text, Sety I(?)	15911, 5 × 7
Luxor fragment 1873 Colonnade Hall, 3rd register: west wall, Sety I	15931, 5 × 7
Luxor fragment 1874 Amenhotep III Sun Court: east wall	15295, 5 × 7
Luxor fragment 1876 Amenhotep III Sun Court: king's foot	15962, 5 × 7
Luxor fragment 1877 (joins 1878) Amenhotep III Sun Court: falcon wing	15934, 5 × 7
Luxor fragment 1878 (joins 1877, paint) Amenhotep III Sun Court: falcon wing	15932, 5 × 7
Luxor fragment 1879 Amenhotep III Sun Court: sky sign, hieroglyph below	15937, 5 × 7
Luxor fragment 1880 (joins 1870) Colonnade Hall, upper register: (possibly 3rd register, south wall, west side), Amun plumes, Tut./Sety I	15987, 5 × 7
Luxor fragment 1881 (joins 2178) Colonnade Hall, upper register: Tut./Sety I?	15468, 5 × 7
Luxor fragment 1883 Amenhotep III Sun Court: texts	15940, 5 × 7
Luxor fragment 1884 Amenhotep III Sun Court: east wall, pleated kilt, king	15945, 5 × 7
Luxor fragment 1885 Amenhotep III Sun Court: offering formulae	15910, 5 × 7
Luxor fragment 1886 Amenhotep III Sun Court: falcon wing, paint	15943, 5 × 7
Luxor fragment 1887 Amenhotep III Sun Court: restored deity's foot	15906, 5 × 7

Luxor Temple (*cont.*)

Nelson Number/Description	Negative, Format
Luxor fragment 1888 Amenhotep III Sun Court: sky sign, ground line above, foot of *ka* figure	15845, 5 × 7
Luxor fragment 1889 Amenhotep III Sun Court: king's foot	15852, 5 × 7
Luxor fragment 1890 Amenhotep III Sun Court: king's foot	15971, 5 × 7
Luxor fragment 1891 Amenhotep III Sun Court: restored deity's back leg, inscription	15956, 5 × 7
Luxor fragment 1892 (joins with 2178) Colonnade Hall: Tut.	15469, 5 × 7
Luxor fragment 1893 Amenhotep III Sun Court: ground line, goddess holding *rnp.t*-frond	15888, 5 × 7
Luxor fragment 1894 Colonnade Hall, upper register: Tut./Sety I (possibly 3rd register: south wall, west side)	15842, 5 × 7
Luxor fragment 1895 Amenhotep III Sun Court: east wall	15712, 5 × 7
Luxor fragment 1896 Amenhotep III Sun Court: east wall	15325, 5 × 7
Luxor fragments 1896 B and 2077 Amenhotep III Sun Court: east wall; 2077-falcon wing; 1896 B-text	15311, 5 × 7
Luxor fragment 1897 Tut./Sety I (?)	15935, 5 × 7
Luxor fragment 1898 Amenhotep III Sun Court: recarved goddess head, vulture crown	15959, 5 × 7
Luxor fragment 1899 Colonnade Hall, upper register: inscription, Tut./Sety I (?)	15965, 5 × 7
Luxor fragment 1900 Colonnade Hall, 3rd register: west wall; backside king, Sety I	15912, 5 × 7
Luxor fragment 1902 Colonnade Hall: 1st register(?), Tut./Sety I	15350, 5 × 7
Luxor fragment 1903 Amenhotep III? Sun Court: inscription	15927, 5 × 7
Luxor fragment 1904 Colonnade Hall, upper register: shrine poles, text, Tut./Sety I	15864, 5 × 7
Luxor fragment 1905 Amenhotep III Sun Court: text	15958, 5 × 7
Luxor fragment 1906 (joins 1907) Colonnade Hall, upper register: Tut.	15360, 5 × 7
Luxor fragment 1907 (joins 1906) Colonnade Hall, upper register: Tut.	15344, 5 × 7
Luxor fragment 1908 Amenhotep III Sun Court: falcon wing tips	15928, 5 × 7
Luxor fragment 1909 Colonnade Hall, 3rd register: east wall; Sety I	15892, 5 × 7
Luxor fragment 1911 Amenhotep III Sun Court	15936, 5 × 7
Luxor fragment 1912 Amenhotep III Sun Court	15926, 5 × 7
Luxor fragment 1913 Amenhotep III Sun Court	15292, 5 × 7
Luxor fragment 1914 Colonnade Hall: Sety I (?) possibly 3rd register, south wall, west side, bouquet	15316, 5 × 7
Luxor fragment 1915 Amenhotep III Sun Court: red crown, text to left	15310, 5 × 7
Luxor fragment 1917 Colonnade Hall, Facade: west doorjamb fragment; Tut./Ay, text of god, king's titulary, Wadjit wing (2nd or 4th doorjamb scene from bottom; 1st and 3rd scenes feature falcons)	15843, 5 × 7
Luxor fragment 1918 Colonnade Hall, Facade: west doorjamb fragment; Tut./Ay, text of god, king's titulary (continuation of 1917)	15963, 5 × 7
Luxor fragment 1920 Amenhotep III Sun Court: inscription	15893, 5 × 7
Luxor fragment 1921 Amenhotep III Sun Court: inscription	15897, 5 × 7
Luxor fragment 1922 Amenhotep III Sun Court: east wall	15309, 5 × 7

Luxor Temple (*cont.*)

Nelson Number/Description	Negative, Format
Luxor fragment 1923 Amenhotep III Sun Court: east wall	15352, 5 × 7
Luxor fragment 1926 Colonnade Hall, 3rd register: south wall; west side, Sety I	15323, 5 × 7
Luxor fragment 1927 Colonnade Hall, possibly 3rd register: south wall, west side, Sety I	15320, 5 × 7
Luxor fragment 1928 Amenhotep III Sun Court: east wall	15313, 5 × 7
Luxor fragment 1930 Colonnade Hall, 3rd register: west wall; Tut./Sety I	15307, 5 × 7
Luxor fragment 1931 Colonnade Hall, upper register: Tut.	15294, 5 × 7
Luxor fragment 1933 Amenhotep III Sun Court: east wall	15321, 5 × 7
Luxor fragment 1934 Amenhotep III Sun Court: east wall	15299, 5 × 7
Luxor fragment 1935 Amenhotep III block: reused (earlier) decoration	15648, 4 × 5
Luxor fragment 1935 Amenhotep III block: reused (earlier) decoration	15649, 4 × 5
Luxor fragment 1935 Amenhotep III block: reused (earlier) decoration	15650, 4 × 5
Luxor fragment 1935 Amenhotep III block: reused (earlier) decoration	15651, 4 × 5
Luxor fragment 1935 A Amenhotep III Sun Court: inscription, underside preserves blue paint with painted yellow stars, indicating the block was reused from an earlier monument	15949, 5 × 7
Luxor fragment 1935 B (underside of 1935 A) Amenhotep III Sun Court: painted stars on a blue ground, ceiling block of a monument reused by Amenhotep III in his Sun Court	15947, 5 × 7
Luxor fragment 1936 (blue paint) and 1950; 1936-Amenhotep III Sun Court: east wall; 1950-Amenhotep III	15319, 5 × 7
Luxor fragment 1937 Amenhotep III Sun Court: sky sign	15941, 5 × 7
Luxor fragment 1939 Colonnade Hall, upper register: sporran, Tut.	15297, 5 × 7
Luxor fragment 1940 (with 1941) Amenhotep III Sun Court: east wall	15340, 5 × 7
Luxor fragment 1941 (with 1940) Amenhotep III ? Sun Court, epithet of Amun	15291, 5 × 7
Luxor fragment 1942 Amenhotep III Sun Court: sky sign, ground line above	15991, 5 × 7
Luxor fragment 1943 Colonnade Hall, upper register: inscription, Tut.	15335, 5 × 7
Luxor fragment 1946 Amenhotep III Sun Court	15303, 5 × 7
Luxor fragment 1947 Amenhotep III Sun Court	15304, 5 × 7
Luxor fragment 1948 Amenhotep III Sun Court: restored inscriptions	15994, 5 × 7
Luxor fragment 1949 Colonnade Hall, Facade: text, west side; usurped cartouches Ay, 2nd register?	15355, 5 × 7
Luxor fragment 1951 Colonnade Hall: Tut./Sety I	15305, 5 × 7
Luxor fragment 1952 Colonnade Hall: name frieze above 3rd register, west wall, Sety I	15298, 5 × 7
Luxor fragment 1954 Amenhotep III Sun Court	15324, 5 × 7
Luxor fragment 1955 A-in focus on right side Amenhotep III (right side): back of hypostyle hall, main entrance to Temple proper, left (east jamb)	15997, 5 × 7

Luxor Temple (*cont.*)

Nelson Number/Description	Negative, Format
Luxor fragment 1955 B-in focus on right side (upside down) Amenhotep III (left side): back of hypostyle hall, main entrance to Temple proper, scene to left of left doorjamb, king before seated Amun, inscription	15998, 5 × 7
Luxor fragments 1956 and 2075: 1956-Sun Court, double crown, Amenhotep III(?); 2075- Colonnade Hall, upper register: standing male figure, back section with arm, streamer	15293, 5 × 7
Luxor fragment 1957 Amenhotep III Sun Court	15306, 5 × 7
Luxor fragment 1958 Colonnade Hall, upper register: inscription, Tut./Sety I	15330, 5 × 7
Luxor fragment 1959 Colonnade Hall, upper register: inscription, Tut.	15338, 5 × 7
Luxor fragment 1960 Amenhotep III Sun Court	15863, 5 × 7
Luxor fragment 1961 Amenhotep III(?) Horus name within column of text	15942, 5 × 7
Luxor fragment 1962 Amenhotep III Sun Court: sky sign	15709, 5 × 7
Luxor fragment 1963 Amenhotep III Sun Court	15705, 5 × 7
Luxor fragment 1968 Colonnade Hall, upper register: west wall; Tut.	15359, 5 × 7
Luxor fragment 1970 Colonnade Hall, Facade: west doorjamb fragment; upraised hand Amun-Ra-Kamutef figure (4th doorjamb scene from bottom[?])	15859, 5 × 7
Luxor fragment 1971 Amenhotep III: hypostyle hall(?) restored Amun plumes, text	15955, 5 × 7
Luxor fragment 1972 Colonnade Hall, 3rd register(?): west wall; text, Tut./Sety I	15923, 5 × 7
Luxor fragment 1974 Amenhotep III: Temple proper(?) purification scene	15353, 5 × 7
Luxor fragment 1976 Colonnade Hall, name frieze over 3rd register: east wall, Tut./Sety I	15948, 5 × 7
Luxor fragment 1977 Colonnade Hall, 3rd register: Sety I	15907, 5 × 7
Luxor fragment 1978 Colonnade Hall, upper register: east wall; Tut.	15357, 5 × 7
Luxor fragment 1979 Amenhotep III Sun Court	15902, 5 × 7
Luxor fragment 1980 Colonnade Hall, upper register: Tut./Sety I	15334, 5 × 7
Luxor fragment 1985 Colonnade Hall: Sety I; 3rd register	15470, 5 × 7
Luxor fragment 1986 Colonnade Hall: Sety I; 3rd register	15471, 5 × 7
Luxor fragment 1990 Colonnade Hall, Facade: 2nd register, west side; text, top of Amun plume; joins 1603, links fragment groups of text over Amun plumes and text group behind Amun plumes	15327, 5 × 7
Luxor fragment 1990 Colonnade Hall, Facade: 2nd register, west side; text, top of Amun plume; joins 1603, links fragment groups of text over Amun plumes and text group behind Amun plumes	16045, 5 × 7
Luxor fragment 1992 Colonnade Hall, upper register: south wall; east side, double shrine poles, text, Sety I	15970, 5 × 7
Luxor fragment 1997 Colonnade Hall, 3rd register: west wall; Great Ennead offering scene, Sety I	15264, 5 × 7
Luxor fragment 1998 Colonnade Hall, 3rd register: west wall; Sety I	15246, 5 × 7
Luxor fragment 1999 Colonnade Hall: Tut. name frieze above 3rd register, west wall	15235, 5 × 7
Luxor fragment 2000 Colonnade Hall, 3rd register: west wall, Tut./Sety I	15220, 5 × 7
Luxor fragment 2001 Amenhotep III Sun Court	15288, 5 × 7

Luxor Temple (*cont.*)

Nelson Number/Description	Negative, Format
Luxor fragment 2003 Amenhotep III(?)	15286, 5 × 7
Luxor fragment 2005 Colonnade Hall, 3rd register: west wall; Tut./Sety I	15290, 5 × 7
Luxor fragment 2006 Amenhotep III Sun Court(?)	15243, 5 × 7
Luxor fragment 2007 Colonnade Hall, 3rd register: west wall; Tut./Sety I	15282, 5 × 7
Luxor fragment 2008 Colonnade Hall, 3rd register: east wall; Tut.	15237, 5 × 7
Luxor fragment 2009 Amenhotep III Sun Court	15260, 5 × 7
Luxor fragment 2010 Colonnade Hall: *išd*-tree scene, Tut.(?)/Amenhotep III(?)	15265, 5 × 7
Luxor fragment 2011 Amenhotep III Sun Court: east wall	15216, 5 × 7
Luxor fragment 2012 Amenhotep III Sun Court: east wall	15217, 5 × 7
Luxor fragment 2013 Colonnade Hall: Tut.	15223, 5 × 7
Luxor fragment 2014 Colonnade Hall: *išd*-tree scene, Tut.(?)/Amenhotep III(?)	15249, 5 × 7
Luxor fragment 2015 Tut. talatat	15252, 5 × 7
Luxor fragment 2016 Colonnade Hall: name frieze above 3rd register, west wall(?), border element, Sety I	15251, 5 × 7
Luxor fragment 2017 Colonnade Hall: name frieze above 3rd register, west wall, Sety I	15241, 5 × 7
Luxor fragment 2018 Colonnade Hall, 3rd register: west wall; Great Ennead offering scene, Sety I	15245, 5 × 7
Luxor fragment 2019 Colonnade Hall: *išd*-tree scene, Tut./Amenhotep III	15261, 5 × 7
Luxor fragment 2020 (blue paint) Amenhotep III: hypostyle hall, sky sign, ground line above	15266, 5 × 7
Luxor fragment 2021 Colonnade Hall, upper register: inscription of offering king, scepter of deity, Tut.	15240, 5 × 7
Luxor fragment 2022 Colonnade Hall, 3rd register: west wall; Tut./Sety I	15215, 5 × 7
Luxor fragment 2023 Colonnade Hall: Tut. or Amenhotep III *išd*-tree scene	15218, 5 × 7
Luxor fragment 2024 Colonnade Hall, 3rd register: west wall; Great Ennead offering scene, Tut./Sety I	15257, 5 × 7
Luxor fragment 2025 Colonnade Hall, Facade: text	15250, 5 × 7
Luxor fragment 2026 Colonnade Hall: Tut. or Amenhotep III *išd*-tree scene	15238, 5 × 7
Luxor fragment 2027 Colonnade Hall: Tut. or Amenhotep III *išd*-tree scene	15236, 5 × 7
Luxor fragment 2028 Colonnade Hall: name frieze above 3rd register, west wall, Sety I	15258, 5 × 7
Luxor fragments 2029, 2034, and 2035: 2029-Amenhotep III Sun Court: hypostyle hall, west wall; 2034 and 2035-Colonnade Hall, 3rd register: west wall, Tut./Sety I	15231, 5 × 7
Luxor fragment 2030 Amenhotep III Sun Court: east wall, recarved Amun-Ra-Kamutef hand	15239, 5 × 7
Luxor fragment 2031 Colonnade Hall, upper register, Tut.	15259, 5 × 7
Luxor fragments 2032 and 2058: 2032-Colonnade Hall: *išd*-tree scene, Amenhotep III/Tut; 2058-Colonnade Hall, 3rd register, west wall, Sety I(?)	15233, 5 × 7
Luxor fragment 2033 Colonnade Hall, 3rd register: Tut./Sety I	15225, 5 × 7
Luxor fragments 2036 and 2038 Colonnade Hall, 3rd register: west wall, Tut.(?)/Sety I	15221, 5 × 7
Luxor fragment 2037 Colonnade Hall, 3rd register: possibly scepter of divinity, Sety I(?)	15230, 5 × 7

Luxor Temple (*cont.*)

Nelson Number/Description	Negative, Format
Luxor fragment 2039 Colonnade Hall, 3rd register: west wall, Tut./Sety I	15229, 5 × 7
Luxor fragment 2040 Tut. talatat	15214, 5 × 7
Luxor fragment 2041 Tut. talatat	15255, 5 × 7
Luxor fragment 2042 Amenhotep III Sun Court	15247, 5 × 7
Luxor fragment 2043 Colonnade Hall, upper register: east wall? Tut.	15242, 5 × 7
Luxor fragment 2044 Amenhotep III Sun Court: possibly east wall	15253, 5 × 7
Luxor fragment 2045 Amenhotep III Sun Court: hypostyle hall, west wall	15224, 5 × 7
Luxor fragment 2046 Colonnade Hall, 3rd register(?): west wall, Sety I	15228, 5 × 7
Luxor fragment 2047 Colonnade Hall, 2nd register: west wall; Thoth giving "years" to king, Tut.	15232, 5 × 7
Luxor fragment 2048 Colonnade Hall, 3rd register: west wall; Tut./Sety I	15248, 5 × 7
Luxor fragments 2049 and 2050 (join) Colonnade Hall, 4th register: Tut./ Sety I	15254, 5 × 7
Luxor fragments 2051 and 2052 (join) Colonnade Hall, 3rd register: Tut./Sety I	15234, 5 × 7
Luxor fragment 2053 Amenhotep III Sun Court: east wall; restored deity	15219, 5 × 7
Luxor fragment 2054 Amenhotep III Sun Court(?), restored text	15263, 5 × 7
Luxor fragment 2055 Ptolemaic(?)	15262, 5 × 7
Luxor fragment 2056 (blue paint) Colonnade Hall: Amun-Ra-Kamutef arm, Amenhotep III(?)/Sety I(?)	15244, 5 × 7
Luxor fragment 2057 Amenhotep III: hypostyle hall, west wall	15222, 5 × 7
Luxor fragment 2059 Colonnade Hall, 3rd register: west wall; Great Ennead offering scene, Sety I	15227, 5 × 7
Luxor fragment 2060 Colonnade Hall, upper register: *ka* figure, Tut.	15918, 5 × 7
Luxor fragment 2061 Late period, south portal? Nile god	15915, 5 × 7
Luxor fragments 2062 and 2063: 2062-Amenhotep III Sun Court; 2063-Amenhotep III / Sety I(?)	15326, 5 × 7
Luxor fragment 2064 Colonnade Hall: Tut. or Ay	15472, 5 × 7
Luxor fragment 2066 Colonnade Hall, Facade: west doorjamb fragment; head Amun-Ra-Kamutef figure, text (4th doorjamb scene from bottom[?]), Tut./Ay	15875, 5 × 7
Luxor fragment 2067 Colonnade Hall, 3rd register: east wall, Tut.	15844, 5 × 7
Luxor fragment 2068 Colonnade Hall, 4th register: Tut./Sety I	15957, 5 × 7
Luxor fragment 2069 Colonnade Hall, upper register: (possibly 3rd register, west wall), Tut./Sety I	15995, 5 × 7
Luxor fragment 2070 (joins 1389) Colonnade Hall, 3rd register: west wall; Great Ennead offering scene, Sety I	15990, 5 × 7
Luxor fragment 2072 Amenhotep III Sun Court	15968, 5 × 7
Luxor fragment 2073 Amenhotep III Sun Court	15960, 5 × 7
Luxor fragment 2074 Colonnade Hall, upper register: Tut./Sety I	15301, 5 × 7
Luxor fragment 2076 A Colonnade Hall, upper register: west wall; Tut./Sety I	15308, 5 × 7
Luxor fragment 2076 B Colonnade Hall, Opet register: south wall, west side, Sety I	15315, 5 × 7

Luxor Temple (*cont.*)

Nelson Number/Description	Negative, Format
Luxor fragment 2078 Colonnade Hall, 3rd register(?): west wall; falcon, Tut./Sety I	15939, 5 × 7
Luxor fragment 2079 Colonnade Hall, Facade: 3rd register, east side; joins 1842	15302, 5 × 7
Luxor fragment 2080 Tut. talatat (reused Akhenaten talatat): raised relief, battle related decoration, perhaps prisoners	15889, 5 × 7
Luxor fragment 2081 Amenhotep III Sun Court	15275, 5 × 7
Luxor fragment 2082 Amenhotep III Sun Court	15283, 5 × 7
Luxor fragment 2083 Amenhotep III Sun Court	15279, 5 × 7
Luxor fragment 2084 (blue paint) Amenhotep III Sun Court	15277, 5 × 7
Luxor fragment 2085 Amenhotep III Sun Court	15289, 5 × 7
Luxor fragment 2086 Amenhotep III: hypostyle hall	15212, 5 × 7
Luxor fragment 2087 Colonnade Hall, upper register: Tut./Sety I (possibly 2nd register, east wall)	15268, 5 × 7
Luxor fragment 2088 Amenhotep III Sun Court	15269, 5 × 7
Luxor fragment 2089 (joins 2094) Amenhotep III Sun Court: exterior northwest side door, doorjamb, west side	15273, 5 × 7
Luxor fragment 2090 Amenhotep III Sun Court	15285, 5 × 7
Luxor fragment 2091 Amenhotep III Sun Court	15280, 5 × 7
Luxor fragment 2092 Amenhotep III Sun Court	15276, 5 × 7
Luxor fragment 2093 Amenhotep III Sun Court	15287, 5 × 7
Luxor fragment 2094 (joins 2089) Amenhotep III Sun Court: exterior northwest side door, doorjamb, west side	15267, 5 × 7
Luxor fragment 2095 Amenhotep III Sun Court: restored deity	15284, 5 × 7
Luxor fragment 2096 Colonnade Hall, 3rd register: west wall; Tut./Sety I	15281, 5 × 7
Luxor fragment 2097 Colonnade Hall, Opet register: south wall; west side, Sety I	15272, 5 × 7
Luxor fragment 2098 Colonnade Hall, upper register: east side; double shrine poles, bouquet, Sety I	15946, 5 × 7
Luxor fragment 2099 Colonnade Hall, 3rd register: west wall; Sety I(?)	15917, 5 × 7
Luxor fragment 2100 Amenhotep III Sun Court: portal?	15256, 5 × 7
Luxor fragment 2107 Colonnade Hall, Facade: 2nd register, west side; text; plus left-hand border	16046, 5 × 7
Luxor fragment 2107 Colonnade Hall, Facade: 2nd register, west side; text, left-hand border	16046, 5 × 7
Luxor fragment 2107 Colonnade Hall, Facade: 2nd register, west side; text, left-hand border	16046, 5 × 7
Luxor fragment 2117 hypostyle hall(?) column of text, standard pole, Amenhotep III	15961, 5 × 7
Luxor fragment 2118 Amenhotep III: hypostyle hall, west side; king kilt, sporran	15916, 5 × 7
Luxor fragment 2119 Amenhotep III Sun Court	15876, 5 × 7
Luxor fragments 2120, 2121, 2122 hypostyle hall, west side, king's sporran, Amenhotep III	15867, 5 × 7
Luxor fragment 2123 Amenhotep III Sun Court: sky sign	15930, 5 × 7
Luxor fragment 2124 Colonnade Hall: border above name frieze, Tut./Sety I	15974, 5 × 7
Luxor fragment 2125 Colonnade Hall, Opet register: south wall; west side, Sety I	15473, 5 × 7

Luxor Temple (*cont.*)

Nelson Number/Description	Negative, Format
Luxor fragment 2126 Amenhotep III Sun Court: restored text, cartouche of Amenhotep III, made into cornice in Christian period	15944, 5 × 7
Luxor fragment 2127 Colonnade Hall, 3rd register: west wall; south end, Great Ennead offering scene, Sety I	15854, 5 × 7
Luxor fragment 2128 Amenhotep III: hypostyle hall, west end, restored Amun shoulders	15950, 5 × 7
Luxor fragment 2129 Amenhotep III Sun Court: south wall, east side; where wall abuts hypostyle hall	15993, 5 × 7
Luxor fragment 2133 Colonnade Hall, Facade: 2nd register, west side; text over and in front of Amun plumes; block line at bottom and text relate to 1334	15894, 5 × 7
Luxor fragment 2143 Colonnade Hall, Facade	15274, 5 × 7
Luxor fragment 2144 Amenhotep III Sun Court	15270, 5 × 7
Luxor fragment 2145 Colonnade Hall, upper register: Tut./Sety I	15271, 5 × 7
Luxor fragment 2146 Amenhotep III Sun Court: *Mrt*-chest, offerings	15278, 5 × 7
Luxor fragment 2147 Colonnade Hall, Opet register: south wall; west side, Sety I	15474, 5 × 7
Luxor fragment 2148 Amenhotep III Sun Court(?): Possibly Colonnade Hall, sky sign, text below	15314, 5 × 7
Luxor fragment 2150 Colonnade Hall, 3rd register: west wall, Tut./Sety I	15336, 5 × 7
Luxor fragment 2151 Colonnade Hall, 2nd register: east wall, Tut./Sety I	15312, 5 × 7
Luxor fragment 2152 Colonnade Hall, 3rd register: west wall, Sety I	15318, 5 × 7
Luxor fragment 2153 Colonnade Hall, 3rd register: west wall; Tut.	15322, 5 × 7
Luxor fragment 2155 Amenhotep III Sun Court	15339, 5 × 7
Luxor fragment 2157 (sunk relief) Amenhotep III Sun Court: exterior northwest side door, doorjamb, west side	15347, 5 × 7
Luxor fragment 2158 Amenhotep III Sun Court	15354, 5 × 7
Luxor fragment 2159 Colonnade Hall, upper register: Tut./Sety I	15345, 5 × 7
Luxor fragment 2160 Colonnade Hall, 3rd register: west wall, Sety I	15346, 5 × 7
Luxor fragment 2161 Colonnade Hall: Tut.; offering list	15358, 5 × 7
Luxor fragment 2162 Colonnade Hall, 3rd register: west wall, Sety I	15341, 5 × 7
Luxor fragment 2163 Amenhotep III Sun Court: back wig of restored deity	15343, 5 × 7
Luxor fragment 2164 Colonnade Hall, 3rd register: west wall; Tut./Sety I	15333, 5 × 7
Luxor fragment 2165 Amenhotep III Sun Court: text	15952, 5 × 7
Luxor fragments 2167 and 2173: 2167-Colonnade Hall, 2nd register: west wall; Theban Triad offering scene, Tut.; 2173-Amenhotep III Sun Court	15349, 5 × 7
Luxor fragment 2168 Colonnade Hall, possibly 3rd register: west wall; vulture, Tut./Sety I	15905, 5 × 7
Luxor fragment 2169 (blue paint) Amenhotep III Sun Court	15332, 5 × 7
Luxor fragment 2170 Colonnade Hall: Amenhotep III? Sety I(?)	15348, 5 × 7
Luxor fragment 2171 Colonnade Hall, upper register: Tut./Sety I	15342, 5 × 7
Luxor fragment 2172 Colonnade Hall, Facade: 3rd register, east side	15896, 5 × 7

Luxor Temple (*cont.*)

Nelson Number/Description	Negative, Format
Luxor fragment 2174 Colonnade Hall, 3rd register(?): west wall; Tut./Sety I	15984, 5 × 7
Luxor fragment 2175 Colonnade Hall, 3rd register: south wall; west side, Sety I	15475, 5 × 7
Luxor fragment 2178	12884, 5 × 7
Luxor fragment 2180 Colonnade Hall, Opet register: south wall; west side, Sety I	15476, 5 × 7
Luxor fragment 2181 Colonnade Hall, Opet register: west wall; Amun bark procession out of Karnak, priests, Tut.	15711, 5 × 7
Luxor fragment 2182 Colonnade Hall: offerings, Tut.	15713, 5 × 7
Luxor fragment 2183 Colonnade Hall, upper register: Tut./Sety I	15715, 5 × 7
Luxor fragment 2184 Late period recarving, possibly from back wall hypostyle hall	15862, 5 × 7
Luxor fragment 2186 Colonnade Hall, Opet register: small scale inscription, Tut.	15708, 5 × 7
Luxor fragment 2187 Colonnade Hall: hand of king holding bouquet, Tut./Sety I	15706, 5 × 7
Luxor fragment 2188 Colonnade Hall, Opet register: Tut.	15716, 5 × 7
Luxor fragment 2189 Colonnade Hall, upper register: sky sign, Tut.	15700, 5 × 7
Luxor fragment 2190 A Tut. talatat	15710, 5 × 7
Luxor fragment 2190 B Tut. talatat	15701, 5 × 7
Luxor fragment 2190 C Tut. talatat	15702, 5 × 7
Luxor fragment 2191 Colonnade Hall, Opet register: Tut.	15707, 5 × 7
Luxor fragment 2192 A and B Tut. talatat	15703, 5 × 7
Luxor fragment 2192 C Tut. talatat	15704, 5 × 7
Luxor fragment 2192 D Tut. talatat: Akhenaten side	15714, 5 × 7
Luxor fragment 2194 Colonnade Hall, upper register: Sety I	15718, 5 × 7
Luxor fragment 2195 Colonnade Hall, upper register: offerings, inscription (from same scene as 2194), Sety I	15717, 5 × 7
Luxor fragment 2196 Colonnade Hall, upper register: offering list, Sety I	15891, 5 × 7
Luxor fragment 2197 Colonnade Hall: offering list, Tut./Sety I	15898, 5 × 7
Luxor fragment 2198 Colonnade Hall, upper register: Tut.	15885, 5 × 7
Luxor fragment 2199 Colonnade Hall, 4th register: Tut./Sety I	15890, 5 × 7
Luxor fragment 2200 Colonnade Hall, 3rd register: west wall; Tut./Sety I	15886, 5 × 7
Luxor fragment 2201 Colonnade Hall, upper register: Tut./Sety I	15853, 5 × 7
Luxor fragment 2202 Colonnade Hall: offering pile, Tut./Sety I	15851, 5 × 7
Luxor fragment 2203 Colonnade Hall, upper register (probable 3rd register): text, Tut./Sety I	15850, 5 × 7
Luxor fragment 2204 Amenhotep III: head of king wearing *ḫprš*-crown	15881, 5 × 7
Luxor fragment 2205 Colonnade Hall, 4th register: west wall; Tut.	15878, 5 × 7
Luxor fragment 2206 Colonnade Hall, 3rd register(?): Tut./Sety I	15865, 5 × 7
Luxor fragment 2207 Colonnade Hall: vulture, Tut./Sety I	15920, 5 × 7

Luxor Temple (*cont.*)

Nelson Number/Description	Negative, Format
Luxor fragment 2208 Colonnade Hall: offering list, Tut./Sety I	15884, 5 × 7
Luxor fragment 2209 Colonnade Hall, 3rd register(?): upper cartouches, text, Tut.	15871, 5 × 7
Luxor fragment 2210 Colonnade Hall, 2nd register: offering list, text, Tut./Sety I	15861, 5 × 7
Luxor fragment 2211 Colonnade Hall: Tut., name frieze over 3rd register, east wall; usurped by Horemheb	15870, 5 × 7
Luxor fragment 2212 Colonnade Hall, 3rd register: west wall; Tut./Sety I	15899, 5 × 7
Luxor fragment 2213 Colonnade Hall: name frieze above 3rd register, border, Tut./Sety I	15887, 5 × 7
Luxor fragment 2214 Tut. talatat (reused Akhenaten talatat): kheker frieze	15922, 5 × 7
Luxor fragment 2215 Colonnade Hall: Tut./Sety I	15919, 5 × 7
Luxor fragment 2216 Tut. talatat (reused Akhenaten talatat): kheker frieze	15951, 5 × 7
Luxor fragment 2217 Colonnade Hall, Facade: west doorjamb fragment; Tut./Ay, scepter of goddess, lotus fan, same goddess as 1690 (4th doorjamb scene from bottom, part of the fragment-group strip to the right and the left [across the door space])	16001, 5 × 7
Luxor fragment 2220 (joins Luxor fragment 10, drawing group 7c) Colonnade Hall, Opet register: west wall; priests passing through Luxor Temple portal. Block fragment from Turin Museum (S 18057)	16002, 8 × 10
Luxor fragment 2221 Colonnade Hall, Facade: 2nd register, east side; text above Khonsu's head, to right of 1629; graffiti	16047, 5 × 7
Luxor fragment 2222 Colonnade Hall, Facade: 2nd register, east side; text above Khonsu's head, to right of 1629; graffiti	16048, 5 × 7
Luxor fragment 2223 Colonnade Hall, Facade: text, west side	16049, 5 × 7
Luxor fragment 2224 Colonnade Hall, Facade: 2nd register, east side; text above Khonsu's head, joining right side of 1629; block is a patch stone, dressed on all blank sides; graffiti	16050, 5 × 7
Luxor fragment 2225 Colonnade Hall: 4th interior register; text	16051, 5 × 7
Luxor fragment 2226 Colonnade Hall, Facade	16052, 5 × 7
Luxor fragment 2227 Colonnade Hall, Facade	16053, 5 × 7
Luxor fragment 2228	16054, 5 × 7
Luxor fragment 2229 Colonnade Hall, Facade: door thickness; Sety II, cartouche tops, east thickness scene	16062, 5 × 7
Luxor fragment 2230 Colonnade Hall, Facade: 1st register, west side; traces of erased raised-relief inscription and border above original standing Mut figure on far left within Ramesside sunk relief	16055, 5 × 7
Luxor fragment 2231 Colonnade Hall, Facade: 1st register, west side; traces of erased raised-relief inscription and border above original standing Mut figure on far left within Ramesside sunk relief	16059, 5 × 7
Luxor fragment 2232 Colonnade Hall, Facade: 2nd register, west side; traces of erased raised-relief podium of original Khonsu figure in the Ramesside sunk-relief decoration, small register below the name frieze (Amun plumes, epithets of Mut)	16060, 5 × 7

Luxor Temple (*cont.*)

Nelson Number/Description	Negative, Format
Luxor fragment 2233 Colonnade Hall, Facade: 2nd register, west side; traces of erased raised relief (inscription) in the Ramesside sunk-relief decoration, small register below the name frieze (top of king's *ḫprš*-crown)	16056, 5 × 7
Luxor fragment 2234 Colonnade Hall, Facade: 2nd register, west side	16057, 5 × 7
Luxor fragment 2235 Colonnade Hall, Facade: 2nd register, west side; traces of erased raised relief (leg of god Khonsu) in the Ramesside sunk-relief decoration, small register below the name frieze (text)	16058, 5 × 7
Luxor Temple and Haggag Mosque toward northeast	13563, 5 × 7
Middle Kingdom fragment, Amenemhat I	13138, 8 × 10
Northeast facade, Ramesses II statue, east tower, gateway	13109, 8 × 10
Obelisk	13153, 2.25 × 2.25
Obelisk and gate	13758, 8 × 10
Obelisk and gate	13759, 8 × 10
Obelisk and left side of Pylon 1	13757, 8 × 10
Rear court of Ramesses II, showing north end of colonnade, Zangaki No. 712	13605, 5 × 7
Southeast corner of Ramesses II court, north end of colonnade from court toward south, G. Lekegian No. 1077	13595, 5 × 7
Sun Court of Amenhotep III: east wall, interior	14899, 4 × 5
Sun Court of Amenhotep III: east wall, interior	14900, 4 × 5
Sun Court of Amenhotep III: east wall, interior	14885, 4 × 5
Sun Court of Amenhotep III: east wall, interior	14886, 4 × 5
Sun Court of Amenhotep III: east wall, interior	14902, 4 × 5
Sun Court of Amenhotep III: east wall, interior	14903, 4 × 5
Sun Court of Amenhotep III: east wall, interior	14904, 4 × 5
Sun Court of Amenhotep III: east wall, interior	14905, 4 × 5
Sun Court of Amenhotep III: east wall, interior	14906, 4 × 5
Sun Court of Amenhotep III: east wall, interior	14907, 4 × 5
Sun Court of Amenhotep III: east wall, interior	14908, 4 × 5
Sun Court of Amenhotep III: east wall, interior	14909, 4 × 5
Sun Court of Amenhotep III: east wall, interior	14887, 4 × 5
Sun Court of Amenhotep III: east wall, interior	14888, 4 × 5
Sun Court of Amenhotep III: east wall, interior	14889, 4 × 5
Sun Court of Amenhotep III: east wall, interior	14890, 4 × 5
Sun Court of Amenhotep III: east wall, interior	14891, 4 × 5
Sun Court of Amenhotep III: east wall, interior	14892, 4 × 5
Sun Court of Amenhotep III: east wall, interior	14893, 4 × 5
Sun Court of Amenhotep III: east wall, interior	14894, 4 × 5
Sun Court of Amenhotep III: east wall, interior	14895, 4 × 5
Sun Court of Amenhotep III: east wall, interior	14896, 4 × 5
Sun Court of Amenhotep III: east wall, interior	14897, 4 × 5
Sun Court of Amenhotep III: east wall, interior	14898, 4 × 5
Sun Court of Amenhotep III: east wall, interior	14901, 4 × 5
Sun Court of Amenhotep III: northeastern corner	13101, 5 × 7
Sun Court of Amenhotep III: northeastern corner	13102, 5 × 7
Sun Court of Amenhotep III: northeastern corner	13103, 5 × 7
Sun Court of Amenhotep III: northeastern corner	13104, 5 × 7
Sun Court of Amenhotep III: northeastern corner	13105, 5 × 7
Sun Court of Amenhotep III: northeastern corner	13106, 5 × 7

Luxor Temple (*cont.*)

Nelson Number/Description	Negative, Format
Sun Court of Amenhotep III: northeastern corner	13107, 5 × 7
Sun Court of Amenhotep III: northeastern corner	13108, 5 × 7
Sun Court: fallen roof block with graffiti, northwestern corner of Amenhotep III Sun Court	13062, 5 × 7
Temple facade	16030, 8 × 10
View from river toward east	13561, 5 × 7
View from West Bank	13557, 5 × 7
View from West Bank	13574, 5 × 7
View toward north along nave of Colonnade, during inundation	13599, 5 × 7
View of Colonnade from west, showing house built into colonnade	13568, 5 × 7
View of hypostyle hall through Amenhotep III Sun Court	13560, 5 × 7
View of temple toward east	13594, 5 × 7
View toward southwest across mosque and colonnade from top of first pylon	13603, 5 × 7
View of Colonnade Hall, Amenhotep III courtyard toward east, dahabiya in foreground	13598, 5 × 7

Medinet Habu

Nelson Number/Description	Negative, Format
General view from northeast, J. P. Sebah No. 768 MH B and D	13581, 5 × 7
General views of excavations in the 1920s	15817, 9.25 × 11.75
General views of excavations in the 1920s	15818, 9.25 × 11.75
General views of excavations in the 1920s	15819, 9.25 × 11.75
General views of excavations in the 1920s	15820, 9.25 × 11.75
General views of excavations in the 1920s	15821, 9.25 × 11.75
General views of excavations in the 1920s	15822, 9.25 × 11.75
General views of excavations in the 1920s	15823, 9.25 × 11.75
MH A 001	1, 5 × 7
MH A 001	398, 5 × 7
MH A 001	616, 8 × 10
MH A 001	962, 5 × 7
MH A 001	10983, 8 × 10
MH A 002	2, 5 × 7
MH A 002	299, 5 × 7
MH A 002	398, 5 × 7
MH A 002	617, 8 × 10
MH A 002	962, 5 × 7
MH A 002	10983, 8 × 10
MH A 003	3, 5 × 7
MH A 003	397, 5 × 7
MH A 003	646-a, 8 × 10
MH A 003	965, 8 × 10
MH A 003	10983, 8 × 10
MH A 004	4, 5 × 7
MH A 004	869, 5 × 7
MH A 004	960, 5 × 7
MH A 004	1065, 5 × 7
MH A 004	10983, 8 × 10
MH A 005	5, 5 × 7
MH A 005	396, 5 × 7

Medinet Habu (*cont.*)

Nelson Number/Description	Negative, Format
MH A 005	967, 8 × 10
MH A 005	1068, 5 × 7
MH A 005	10984, 8 × 10
MH A 006	6, 5 × 7
MH A 006	396, 5 × 7
MH A 006	738, 5 × 7
MH A 006	966, 8 × 10
MH A 006	1068, 5 × 7
MH A 006	10984, 8 × 10
MH A 007	622, 8 × 10
MH A 007	649, 5 × 7
MH A 007	747, 5 × 7
MH A 007	1065, 5 × 7
MH A 007	2018, 11 × 14
MH A 008	632, 8 × 10
MH A 008	743, 5 × 7
MH A 008	744, 5 × 7
MH A 008	745, 5 × 7
MH A 008	948, 8 × 10
MH A 008	974, 8 × 10
MH A 008	1062, 5 × 7
MH A 008	2019, 11 × 14
MH A 009	624, 8 × 10
MH A 009	650, 5 × 7
MH A 009	1062, 5 × 7
MH A 009	13422, 5 × 7
MH A 010	625, 8 × 10
MH A 010	968, 8 × 10
MH A 010	978, 8 × 10
MH A 010	1003, 8 × 10
MH A 010	1006, 8 × 10
MH A 010	1067, 5 × 7
MH A 011	572, 5 × 7
MH A 011	626, 8 × 10
MH A 011	647, 5 × 7
MH A 011	13420, 5 × 7
MH A 012	12, 5 × 7
MH A 012	627, 8 × 10
MH A 012	628, 8 × 10
MH A 012	768, 5 × 7
MH A 012	770, 8 × 10
MH A 012	946, 8 × 10
MH A 012	976, 8 × 10
MH A 012	977, 5 × 7
MH A 012	984, 8 × 10
MH A 012	1067, 5 × 7
MH A 012	13420, 5 × 7
MH A 013	13, 5 × 7
MH A 013	629, 8 × 10
MH A 013	648, 5 × 7
MH A 013	13327, 5 × 7
MH A 013	13373, 5 × 7
MH A 013	13420, 5 × 7
MH A 014	14, 5 × 7
MH A 014	64, 5 × 7

Medinet Habu (*cont.*)

Nelson Number/Description	Negative, Format
MH A 014	248, 5 × 7
MH A 014	630, 8 × 10
MH A 014	631, 8 × 10
MH A 014	674, 8 × 10
MH A 014	739, 5 × 7
MH A 014	763, 5 × 7
MH A 014	765, 5 × 7
MH A 014	771, 5 × 7
MH A 014	859, 5 × 7
MH A 014	860, 5 × 7
MH A 014	861, 5 × 7
MH A 014	862-a, 5 × 7
MH A 014	862-b, 5 × 7
MH A 014	863, 5 × 7
MH A 014	864, 8 × 10
MH A 014	878, 8 × 10
MH A 014	879, 8 × 10
MH A 014	956, 8 × 10
MH A 014	972, 8 × 10
MH A 014	973, 8 × 10
MH A 014	975, 8 × 10
MH A 014	979, 5 × 7
MH A 014	980, 8 × 10
MH A 014	995, 8 × 10
MH A 014	1066, 5 × 7
MH A 014	13327, 5 × 7
MH A 014	13328, 5 × 7
MH A 014	13330, 5 × 7
MH A 014	13373, 5 × 7
MH A 014	13418, 5 × 7
MH A 014	13420, 5 × 7
MH A 014	13455, 5 × 7
MH A 014	13472, 5 × 7
MH A 014	13582, 5 × 7
MH A 014	13622, 5 × 7
MH A 014	13624, 5 × 7
MH A 015	15, 5 × 7
MH A 015	724, 8 × 10
MH A 015	740, 5 × 7
MH A 015	741, 5 × 7
MH A 015	766, 5 × 7
MH A 015	989, 8 × 10
MH A 015	995, 8 × 10
MH A 015	1007, 8 × 10
MH A 015	13420, 5 × 7
MH A 015	13582, 5 × 7
MH A 016	16, 5 × 7
MH A 016	729, 8 × 10
MH A 016	748, 5 × 7
MH A 016	751, 5 × 7
MH A 016	1004, 8 × 10
MH A 017	17, 5 × 7
MH A 017	63, 5 × 7
MH A 017	2117, 8 × 10
MH A 017	13624, 5 × 7

Medinet Habu (*cont.*)

Nelson Number/Description	Negative, Format
MH A 018	18, 5 × 7
MH A 018	717, 5 × 7
MH A 019	20, 5 × 7
MH A 019	712, 5 × 7
MH A 019	713, 8 × 10
MH A 019	783, 5 × 7
MH A 019	886, 8 × 10
MH A 019	1008, 8 × 10
MH A 020	20, 5 × 7
MH A 020	22, 5 × 7
MH A 020	713, 8 × 10
MH A 020	769, 8 × 10
MH A 020	13424, 5 × 7
MH A 021	22, 5 × 7
MH A 021	778, 8 × 10
MH A 021	920, 8 × 10
MH A 021	929, 8 × 10
MH A 021	13424, 5 × 7
MH A 022	24, 5 × 7
MH A 022	353, 8 × 10
MH A 022	897, 8 × 10
MH A 022	930, 8 × 10
MH A 022	931, 8 × 10
MH A 022	1536, 8 × 10
MH A 022	2043, 11 × 14
MH A 023	26, 5 × 7
MH A 023	1177, 8 × 10
MH A 023	1190, 8 × 10
MH A 023	1971, 11 × 14
MH A 024	19, 5 × 7
MH A 024	717, 5 × 7
MH A 025	21, 5 × 7
MH A 025	712, 5 × 7
MH A 025	713, 8 × 10
MH A 025	730, 8 × 10
MH A 025	900, 8 × 10
MH A 025	969, 8 × 10
MH A 025	1948, 11 × 14
MH A 025	2009, 11 × 14
MH A 026	23, 5 × 7
MH A 026	713, 8 × 10
MH A 026	735, 8 × 10
MH A 026	906, 8 × 10
MH A 026	13424, 5 × 7
MH A 027	23, 5 × 7
MH A 027	735, 8 × 10
MH A 027	905, 8 × 10
MH A 027	920, 8 × 10
MH A 027	1990, 11 × 14
MH A 027	2010, 11 × 14
MH A 027	13424, 5 × 7
MH A 028	25, 5 × 7
MH A 028	556, 8 × 10
MH A 028	897, 8 × 10
MH A 028	1155, 8 × 10

Medinet Habu (*cont.*)

Nelson Number/Description	Negative, Format
MH A 028	1156, 8 × 10
MH A 028	1157, 8 × 10
MH A 028	1158, 8 × 10
MH A 028	1159, 8 × 10
MH A 028	2043, 11 × 14
MH A 029	27, 5 × 7
MH A 029	495, 8 × 10
MH A 029	1160, 8 × 10
MH A 029	1161, 8 × 10
MH A 029	1163, 8 × 10
MH A 029	1164, 8 × 10
MH A 029	1165, 8 × 10
MH A 029	1254, 8 × 10
MH A 029	1972, 11 × 14
MH A 029	13623, 5 × 7
MH A 030	591, 8 × 10
MH A 030	2119, 8 × 10
MH A 031	29, 5 × 7
MH A 031	82, 5 × 7
MH A 031	99, 5 × 7
MH A 031	958-a, 8 × 10
MH A 032	30, 5 × 7
MH A 032	98, 8 × 10
MH A 032	1510, 8 × 10
MH A 032	2145, 11 × 14
MH A 033	98, 8 × 10
MH A 033	1510, 8 × 10
MH A 033	2145, 11 × 14
MH A 033	13617, 5 × 7
MH A 034	867, 8 × 10
MH A 034	908, 8 × 10
MH A 034	2148, 11 × 14
MH A 035	31, 5 × 7
MH A 035	97, 8 × 10
MH A 035	2201, 8 × 10
MH A 035	2202, 8 × 10
MH A 035	2217, 8 × 10
MH A 035	2224, 8 × 10
MH A 035	2227, 8 × 10
MH A 035	6258, 8 × 10
MH A 035	7675, 8 × 10
MH A 036	79, 5 × 7
MH A 036	773, 8 × 10
MH A 036	909, 5 × 7
MH A 036	2147, 11 × 14
MH A 037	32, 5 × 7
MH A 037	96, 8 × 10
MH A 037	1201, 8 × 10
MH A 037	2146, 11 × 14
MH A 038	2122, 8 × 10
MH A 038a	1508, 8 × 10
MH A 038a	1511, 8 × 10
MH A 038b	1508, 8 × 10
MH A 038b	1511, 8 × 10
MH A 038c	1509, 8 × 10

Medinet Habu (*cont.*)

Nelson Number/Description	Negative, Format
MH A 038d	1509, 8 × 10
MH A 039	33, 5 × 7
MH A 039	81, 5 × 7
MH A 039	95, 8 × 10
MH A 039	782, 8 × 10
MH A 039	1975, 11 × 14
MH A 039	1989, 11 × 14
MH A 039	13324, 5 × 7
MH A 039	13425, 5 × 7
MH A 039	13611, 5 × 7
MH A 040	35, 8 × 10
MH A 040	36, 8 × 10
MH A 040	1213, 8 × 10
MH A 040	2142, 8 × 10
MH A 040	2143, 8 × 10
MH A 040	7511, 5 × 7
MH A 040	13344, 5 × 7
MH A 040	13447, 5 × 7
MH A 040	13593, 5 × 7
MH A 041	35, 8 × 10
MH A 041	36, 8 × 10
MH A 041	981, 8 × 10
MH A 041	1012, 8 × 10
MH A 041	1389, 8 × 10
MH A 041	13344, 5 × 7
MH A 041	13447, 5 × 7
MH A 041	13593, 5 × 7
MH A 042	38, 5 × 7
MH A 042	147, 8 × 10
MH A 042	917, 8 × 10
MH A 042	13609, 5 × 7
MH A 043	39, 5 × 7
MH A 043	146, 8 × 10
MH A 043	147, 8 × 10
MH A 043	197, 5 × 7
MH A 043	1956, 8 × 10
MH A 043	13615, 5 × 7
MH A 044	40, 5 × 7
MH A 044	146, 8 × 10
MH A 044	1612, 8 × 10
MH A 045	41, 5 × 7
MH A 045	146, 8 × 10
MH A 045	2118, 8 × 10
MH A 046	37, 5 × 7
MH A 046	42, 5 × 7
MH A 046	48, 8 × 10
MH A 046	49, 8 × 10
MH A 046	50, 8 × 10
MH A 046	51, 8 × 10
MH A 046	52, 8 × 10
MH A 046	53, 8 × 10
MH A 046	54, 8 × 10
MH A 046	55, 8 × 10
MH A 046	56, 8 × 10
MH A 046	57, 8 × 10

Medinet Habu (*cont.*)

Nelson Number/Description	Negative, Format
MH A 046	58, 8 × 10
MH A 046	59, 8 × 10
MH A 046	83, 8 × 10
MH A 046	84, 8 × 10
MH A 046	146, 8 × 10
MH A 046	147, 8 × 10
MH A 046	399, 8 × 10
MH A 046	400, 8 × 10
MH A 046	2088, 8 × 10
MH A 046	2094, 8 × 10
MH A 046	2388, 11 × 14
MH A 046	2389, 11 × 14
MH A 046	2390, 11 × 14
MH A 046	2407, 11 × 14
MH A 046	2408, 11 × 14
MH A 046	2409, 8 × 10
MH A 046	2410, 8 × 10
MH A 046	2423, 5 × 7
MH A 046	2424, 5 × 7
MH A 046	2425, 5 × 7
MH A 046	2426, 5 × 7
MH A 046	2429, 5 × 7
MH A 046	2430, 5 × 7
MH A 046	2431, 5 × 7
MH A 046	2432, 5 × 7
MH A 046	2433, 5 × 7
MH A 046	2434, 5 × 7
MH A 046	2435, 5 × 7
MH A 046	2436, 5 × 7
MH A 046	2441-a, 5 × 7
MH A 046	2441-b, 5 × 7
MH A 046	2442-a, 5 × 7
MH A 046	2442-b, 5 × 7
MH A 046	2450, 11 × 14
MH A 046	2492, 8 × 10
MH A 046	2532, 11 × 14
MH A 046	2612, 11 × 14
MH A 046	2613, 11 × 14
MH A 046	2614, 11 × 14
MH A 046	2615, 11 × 14
MH A 046	2616, 11 × 14
MH A 046	2617, 11 × 14
MH A 046	2618, 11 × 14
MH A 046	2619, 11 × 14
MH A 046	2620, 11 × 14
MH A 046	2621, 11 × 14
MH A 046	2655, 5 × 7
MH A 046	2656, 5 × 7
MH A 046	2657, 5 × 7
MH A 046	2658, 5 × 7
MH A 046	2659, 5 × 7
MH A 046	2660, 5 × 7
MH A 046	2668, 11 × 14
MH A 046	2670, 11 × 14
MH A 046	2677, 5 × 7

Medinet Habu (*cont.*)

Nelson Number/Description	Negative, Format
MH A 047	249, 5 × 7
MH A 047	2589, 8 × 10
MH A 047	11215, 5 × 7
MH A 047	11450, 8 × 10
MH A 048	553, 5 × 7
MH A 048	554, 5 × 7
MH A 048	560, 5 × 7
MH A 048	561, 5 × 7
MH A 048	564, 5 × 7
MH A 048	567, 5 × 7
MH A 048	568, 5 × 7
MH A 048	569, 5 × 7
MH A 048	570, 5 × 7
MH A 048	571, 5 × 7
MH A 048	577, 5 × 7
MH A 048	11452, 8 × 10
MH A 048	11509, 8 × 10
MH A 048	11510, 8 × 10
MH A 048	11511, 8 × 10
MH A 048	11512, 8 × 10
MH A 048	11513, 8 × 10
MH A 048	11514, 8 × 10
MH A 048	13330, 5 × 7
MH A 048	13455, 5 × 7
MH A 049	43, 5 × 7
MH A 049	44, 5 × 7
MH A 049	45, 5 × 7
MH A 049	46, 5 × 7
MH A 049	146, 8 × 10
MH A 049	147, 8 × 10
MH A 049	562, 5 × 7
MH A 049	563, 5 × 7
MH A 049	565, 5 × 7
MH A 049	566, 5 × 7
MH A 049	579, 5 × 7
MH A 049	585, 8 × 10
MH A 049	586, 8 × 10
MH A 049	587, 8 × 10
MH A 049	588, 8 × 10
MH A 049	589, 8 × 10
MH A 049	590, 8 × 10
MH A 049	592, 8 × 10
MH A 049	593, 8 × 10
MH A 049	2096, 8 × 10
MH A 049	2097, 8 × 10
MH A 049	2106, 8 × 10
MH A 049	2107, 8 × 10
MH A 049	2108, 8 × 10
MH A 049	2109, 8 × 10
MH A 049	2111, 8 × 10
MH A 049	2112, 8 × 10
MH A 049	2113, 8 × 10
MH A 049	7663, 8 × 10
MH A 049	7664, 8 × 10
MH A 049	7665, 8 × 10

Medinet Habu (cont.)

Nelson Number/Description	Negative, Format
MH A 049	7666, 8 × 10
MH A 049	7667, 8 × 10
MH A 049	7668, 8 × 10
MH A 049	7669, 8 × 10
MH A 049	7670, 8 × 10
MH A 049	7671, 8 × 10
MH A 049	7672, 8 × 10
MH A 049	7673, 8 × 10
MH A 049	8482, 8 × 10
MH A 049	8483, 8 × 10
MH A 049	8484, 8 × 10
MH A 049	8485, 8 × 10
MH A 049	8486, 8 × 10
MH A 049	8487, 8 × 10
MH A 049	11451, 8 × 10
MH A 049	11453, 8 × 10
MH A 049	11468, 8 × 10
MH A 049	11469, 8 × 10
MH A 049	11470, 8 × 10
MH A 049	11471, 8 × 10
MH A 049	11472, 8 × 10
MH A 049	11473, 8 × 10
MH A 049	11474, 8 × 10
MH A 051	1252, 8 × 10
MH A 051	2164, 8 × 10
MH A 051	6259, 8 × 10
MH A 051	6530, 8 × 10
MH A 052	549, 8 × 10
MH A 052	1249, 8 × 10
MH A 052	2165, 8 × 10
MH A 052	6531, 8 × 10
MH A 053	2133, 8 × 10
MH A 053	2135, 8 × 10
MH A 053	2158, 8 × 10
MH A 053	6614, 8 × 10
MH A 053	15602, 8 × 10
MH A 054	1533, 8 × 10
MH A 054	2163, 8 × 10
MH A 054	6550, 8 × 10
MH A 055	2134, 8 × 10
MH A 055	2136, 8 × 10
MH A 055	6613, 8 × 10
MH A 055	11235, 8 × 10
MH A 055	15602, 8 × 10
MH A 056	6387, 8 × 10
MH A 056	8803, 8 × 10
MH A 056	11235, 8 × 10
MH A 057	6388, 8 × 10
MH A 057	8803, 8 × 10
MH A 058	8349, 8 × 10
MH A 058	8803, 8 × 10
MH A 059	8348, 8 × 10
MH A 059	8803, 8 × 10
MH A 060	8347, 8 × 10
MH A 060	8803, 8 × 10

Medinet Habu (cont.)

Nelson Number/Description	Negative, Format
MH A 061	8346, 8 × 10
MH A 061	8803, 8 × 10
MH A 062	8345, 8 × 10
MH A 062	8803, 8 × 10
MH A 063	6336, 8 × 10
MH A 063	9678, 8 × 10
MH A 064	6337, 8 × 10
MH A 064	9678, 8 × 10
MH A 065	6547, 8 × 10
MH A 065	9678, 8 × 10
MH A 066	6546, 8 × 10
MH A 066	6548, 8 × 10
MH A 066	9678, 8 × 10
MH A 067	6390, 8 × 10
MH A 067	6391, 8 × 10
MH A 067	10250, 8 × 10
MH A 067a	10123, 8 × 10
MH A 067b	10124, 8 × 10
MH A 068	6389, 8 × 10
MH A 068	6392, 8 × 10
MH A 068	10125, 8 × 10
MH A 068	10126, 8 × 10
MH A 068	10251, 8 × 10
MH A 068a	11252, 8 × 10
MH A 069	239, 5 × 7
MH A 069	1216, 8 × 10
MH A 069	2159, 8 × 10
MH A 069	2221, 8 × 10
MH A 069	2223, 8 × 10
MH A 069	6396, 8 × 10
MH A 069	6397, 8 × 10
MH A 069	7638, 8 × 10
MH A 070	1505, 8 × 10
MH A 070	2220, 8 × 10
MH A 070	6260, 8 × 10
MH A 070	6672, 8 × 10
MH A 071	1211, 8 × 10
MH A 071	2205, 8 × 10
MH A 071	6260, 8 × 10
MH A 071	6672, 8 × 10
MH A 072	251, 5 × 7
MH A 072	1212, 8 × 10
MH A 072	6260, 8 × 10
MH A 072	6395, 8 × 10
MH A 072	6398, 8 × 10
MH A 072	7972, 8 × 10
MH A 072	15605, 8 × 10
MH A 073	250, 5 × 7
MH A 073	1212, 8 × 10
MH A 073	6261, 8 × 10
MH A 073	6399, 8 × 10
MH A 073	6400, 8 × 10
MH A 073	7972, 8 × 10
MH A 073	15604, 8 × 10
MH A 073	15606, 8 × 10

Medinet Habu (*cont.*)

Nelson Number/Description	Negative, Format
MH A 074	1506, 8 × 10
MH A 074	1507, 8 × 10
MH A 074	1849, 8 × 10
MH A 074	2103, 8 × 10
MH A 074	6261, 8 × 10
MH A 074	6672, 8 × 10
MH A 075	238, 5 × 7
MH A 075	1215, 8 × 10
MH A 075	2175, 8 × 10
MH A 075	2176, 8 × 10
MH A 075	2203, 8 × 10
MH A 075	6393, 8 × 10
MH A 075	6394, 8 × 10
MH A 075	7638, 8 × 10
MH A 076	362, 5 × 7
MH A 076	7425, 8 × 10
MH A 076	10252, 8 × 10
MH A 077	361, 5 × 7
MH A 077	7494, 8 × 10
MH A 077	10252, 8 × 10
MH A 078	252, 5 × 7
MH A 078	6267, 8 × 10
MH A 078	10253, 8 × 10
MH A 079	253, 5 × 7
MH A 079	2229, 8 × 10
MH A 079	10253, 8 × 10
MH A 080	255, 5 × 7
MH A 080	2126-a, 8 × 10
MH A 080	6266, 8 × 10
MH A 080	6535, 8 × 10
MH A 081	254, 5 × 7
MH A 081	2123, 8 × 10
MH A 081	2128, 8 × 10
MH A 081	3023, 8 × 10
MH A 082	901, 8 × 10
MH A 082	2115, 8 × 10
MH A 082	2451, 8 × 10
MH A 083	2116, 8 × 10
MH A 083	2588, 8 × 10
MH A 083	3136, 8 × 10
MH A 084	285, 5 × 7
MH A 084	2126, 8 × 10
MH A 084	6225, 8 × 10
MH A 084	6534, 8 × 10
MH A 085	284, 5 × 7
MH A 085	2127, 8 × 10
MH A 085	6668, 8 × 10
MH A 086	283, 5 × 7
MH A 086	2124, 8 × 10
MH A 086	2125, 8 × 10
MH A 086	2228, 8 × 10
MH A 086	2643, 8 × 10
MH A 087	282, 5 × 7
MH A 087	2587, 8 × 10
MH A 087	6224, 8 × 10

Medinet Habu (*cont.*)

Nelson Number/Description	Negative, Format
MH A 087	6533, 8 × 10
MH A 088	1270, 8 × 10
MH A 088	6227, 8 × 10
MH A 088	10254, 8 × 10
MH A 089	1269, 8 × 10
MH A 089	6226, 8 × 10
MH A 089	10254, 8 × 10
MH A 090	122, 8 × 10
MH A 090	127, 5 × 7
MH A 090	2177, 8 × 10
MH A 090	2178, 8 × 10
MH A 090	2199, 8 × 10
MH A 090	2200, 8 × 10
MH A 090	2232, 8 × 10
MH A 090	10452, 8 × 10
MH A 091	119, 5 × 7
MH A 091	731, 8 × 10
MH A 091	732, 8 × 10
MH A 091	733, 8 × 10
MH A 091	1130, 8 × 10
MH A 091	1973, 11 × 14
MH A 091	2044, 11 × 14
MH A 091	2045, 11 × 14
MH A 091	2130, 11 × 14
MH A 091	2131, 11 × 14
MH A 092	119, 5 × 7
MH A 092	642, 8 × 10
MH A 092	645, 8 × 10
MH A 092	646, 8 × 10
MH A 092	893, 8 × 10
MH A 092	901, 8 × 10
MH A 092	918, 8 × 10
MH A 092	1130, 8 × 10
MH A 092	2230, 8 × 10
MH A 093	139, 5 × 7
MH A 093	6287, 5 × 7
MH A 093	6288, 5 × 7
MH A 094	272, 8 × 10
MH A 094	273, 8 × 10
MH A 094	781, 5 × 7
MH A 094	882, 8 × 10
MH A 094	959, 8 × 10
MH A 094	961, 5 × 7
MH A 094	1015, 8 × 10
MH A 094	1133, 8 × 10
MH A 094	1135, 8 × 10
MH A 094	1138, 8 × 10
MH A 094	1139, 8 × 10
MH A 094	1144, 8 × 10
MH A 094	1244, 8 × 10
MH A 094	1245, 8 × 10
MH A 094	1246, 8 × 10
MH A 094	1247, 8 × 10
MH A 094	6303, 5 × 7
MH A 094	6304, 5 × 7

Medinet Habu (*cont.*)

Nelson Number/Description	Negative, Format
MH A 094	13366, 5 × 7
MH A 095	269, 8 × 10
MH A 095	270, 8 × 10
MH A 095	1132, 8 × 10
MH A 095	1537, 8 × 10
MH A 095	1542, 8 × 10
MH A 095	6305, 5 × 7
MH A 095	13437, 5 × 7
MH A 096	268, 8 × 10
MH A 096	269, 8 × 10
MH A 096	907, 8 × 10
MH A 096	1131, 8 × 10
MH A 096	1136, 8 × 10
MH A 096	1137, 8 × 10
MH A 096	6306, 5 × 7
MH A 096	6307, 5 × 7
MH A 096	13429, 5 × 7
MH A 097	266, 8 × 10
MH A 097	267, 8 × 10
MH A 097	779, 5 × 7
MH A 097	985, 8 × 10
MH A 097	6308, 5 × 7
MH A 097	6309, 5 × 7
MH A 098	280, 8 × 10
MH A 098	281, 8 × 10
MH A 098	1210, 8 × 10
MH A 098	2161, 8 × 10
MH A 099	280, 8 × 10
MH A 099	1209, 8 × 10
MH A 099	2161, 8 × 10
MH A 100	1209, 8 × 10
MH A 100	2161, 8 × 10
MH A 101	2161, 8 × 10
MH A 101	6289, 5 × 7
MH A 102	278, 8 × 10
MH A 102	610, 8 × 10
MH A 102	2161, 8 × 10
MH A 103	278, 8 × 10
MH A 103	2161, 8 × 10
MH A 104	1850, 8 × 10
MH A 104	6255, 8 × 10
MH A 105	1853, 8 × 10
MH A 105	2823, 8 × 10
MH A 105	6255, 8 × 10
MH A 106	1852, 8 × 10
MH A 106	6255, 8 × 10
MH A 107	1851, 8 × 10
MH A 107	1852, 8 × 10
MH A 107	6256, 8 × 10
MH A 108	1851, 8 × 10
MH A 108	6256, 8 × 10
MH A 109	2121, 8 × 10
MH A 110	130, 5 × 7
MH A 111	100, 8 × 10
MH A 111	101, 8 × 10

Medinet Habu (*cont.*)

Nelson Number/Description	Negative, Format
MH A 111	901, 8 × 10
MH A 111	1005, 8 × 10
MH A 111	6269, 8 × 10
MH A 111	13329, 5 × 7
MH A 111	13369, 5 × 7
MH A 112	123, 8 × 10
MH A 112	575, 5 × 7
MH A 112	6544, 8 × 10
MH A 112	10188, 8 × 10
MH A 112	10189, 8 × 10
MH A 112	10237, 5 × 7
MH A 112	10405, 8 × 10
MH A 112	13371, 5 × 7
MH A 112a	11226, 5 × 7
MH A 112a	11253, 8 × 10
MH A 112n	10238, 5 × 7
MH A 112n	10453, 8 × 10
MH A 113	102, 8 × 10
MH A 113	125, 5 × 7
MH A 113	902, 8 × 10
MH A 113	6270, 8 × 10
MH A 113	6290, 5 × 7
MH A 113	13367, 5 × 7
MH A 113	13369, 5 × 7
MH A 113	13371, 5 × 7
MH A 114	116, 5 × 7
MH A 114	1154, 8 × 10
MH A 115	257, 8 × 10
MH A 115	742, 8 × 10
MH A 115	753, 8 × 10
MH A 115	934, 8 × 10
MH A 115	935, 8 × 10
MH A 115	936, 8 × 10
MH A 115	1153, 8 × 10
MH A 115	1178, 8 × 10
MH A 115	1199, 8 × 10
MH A 115	1202, 8 × 10
MH A 115	2186, 8 × 10
MH A 115	6292, 5 × 7
MH A 115	6293, 5 × 7
MH A 115	6294, 5 × 7
MH A 115	10705, 8 × 10
MH A 116	261, 8 × 10
MH A 116	634, 8 × 10
MH A 116	639, 8 × 10
MH A 116	714, 8 × 10
MH A 116	755, 8 × 10
MH A 116	757, 5 × 7
MH A 116	938, 8 × 10
MH A 116	939, 8 × 10
MH A 116	1188, 8 × 10
MH A 116	1189, 8 × 10
MH A 116	1232, 8 × 10
MH A 116	1233, 8 × 10
MH A 116	1525, 8 × 10

Medinet Habu (*cont.*)

Medinet Habu (*cont.*)

Nelson Number/Description	Negative, Format	Nelson Number/Description	Negative, Format
MH A 116	1526, 8 × 10	MH A 121	1151, 8 × 10
MH A 116	1527, 8 × 10	MH A 121	1152, 8 × 10
MH A 116	1528, 8 × 10	MH A 121	1162, 8 × 10
MH A 116	1632, 8 × 10	MH A 121	1974, 11 × 14
MH A 116	1906, 8 × 10	MH A 121	2132, 11 × 14
MH A 116	1907, 8 × 10	MH A 121	2151, 8 × 10
MH A 116	1908, 8 × 10	MH A 121	2152, 8 × 10
MH A 116	1909, 8 × 10	MH A 121	2153, 8 × 10
MH A 116	6295, 5 × 7	MH A 121	2154, 8 × 10
MH A 116	6296, 5 × 7	MH A 121	2155, 8 × 10
MH A 116	6297, 5 × 7	MH A 121	2156, 8 × 10
MH A 116	10705, 8 × 10	MH A 121	13428, 5 × 7
MH A 117	759, 5 × 7	MH A 121	13587, 5 × 7
MH A 117	760, 5 × 7	MH A 121	13612, 5 × 7
MH A 117	941, 8 × 10	MH A 122a	149, 5 × 7
MH A 117	942, 8 × 10	MH A 122b	103, 5 × 7
MH A 117	944, 8 × 10	MH A 123a	128, 5 × 7
MH A 117	1183, 8 × 10	MH A 123b	104, 5 × 7
MH A 117	1193, 8 × 10	MH A 124a	114, 5 × 7
MH A 117	1194, 8 × 10	MH A 124b	105, 5 × 7
MH A 117	1195, 8 × 10	MH A 125a	113, 5 × 7
MH A 117	1196, 8 × 10	MH A 125b	106, 5 × 7
MH A 117	1222, 8 × 10	MH A 126a	107, 5 × 7
MH A 117	1248, 8 × 10	MH A 126b	111, 5 × 7
MH A 117	1255, 8 × 10	MH A 127a	108, 5 × 7
MH A 117	1271, 8 × 10	MH A 127b	112, 5 × 7
MH A 117	2036, 8 × 10	MH A 128a	109, 5 × 7
MH A 117	2037, 8 × 10	MH A 128b	129, 5 × 7
MH A 117	2038, 8 × 10	MH A 129a	110, 5 × 7
MH A 117	2039, 8 × 10	MH A 129b	148, 5 × 7
MH A 117	2040, 8 × 10	MH A 130	137, 5 × 7
MH A 117	2041, 8 × 10	MH A 130	420, 8 × 10
MH A 117	6298, 5 × 7	MH A 131	137, 5 × 7
MH A 117	6299, 5 × 7	MH A 132	136, 5 × 7
MH A 117	6300, 5 × 7	MH A 133	134, 5 × 7
MH A 117	6301, 5 × 7	MH A 133	135, 5 × 7
MH A 117	15601, 8 × 10	MH A 133	420, 8 × 10
MH A 118	118, 5 × 7	MH A 134	134, 5 × 7
MH A 118	6302, 5 × 7	MH A 134	135, 5 × 7
MH A 119	121, 8 × 10	MH A 134	420, 8 × 10
MH A 120	121, 8 × 10	MH A 135	132, 5 × 7
MH A 120	2001, 8 × 10	MH A 135	133, 5 × 7
MH A 120	2033, 8 × 10	MH A 136	131, 5 × 7
MH A 121	121, 8 × 10	MH A 136	132, 5 × 7
MH A 121	126, 5 × 7	MH A 136	133, 5 × 7
MH A 121	899, 8 × 10	MH A 137	1147, 8 × 10
MH A 121	945, 8 × 10	MH A 137	1180, 8 × 10
MH A 121	1134, 8 × 10	MH A 137	1191, 8 × 10
MH A 121	1140, 8 × 10	MH A 137	1205, 8 × 10
MH A 121	1141, 8 × 10	MH A 137	1226, 8 × 10
MH A 121	1142, 5 × 7	MH A 138	754, 8 × 10
MH A 121	1143, 8 × 10	MH A 138	1184, 8 × 10
MH A 121	1145, 8 × 10	MH A 138	1203, 8 × 10
MH A 121	1149, 8 × 10	MH A 138	1204, 8 × 10
MH A 121	1150, 8 × 10	MH A 138	1224, 8 × 10

Medinet Habu (*cont.*)

Nelson Number/Description	Negative, Format
MH A 139	1179, 8 × 10
MH A 139	1181, 8 × 10
MH A 139	1185, 8 × 10
MH A 139	1225, 8 × 10
MH A 139	1504, 8 × 10
MH A 139	1949, 8 × 10
MH A 139	1951, 8 × 10
MH A 139	2144, 8 × 10
MH A 139	2149, 8 × 10
MH A 140	356, 8 × 10
MH A 140	596, 8 × 10
MH A 140	910, 8 × 10
MH A 140	911, 8 × 10
MH A 140	2216, 8 × 10
MH A 140	3332, 8 × 10
MH A 140	6362, 8 × 10
MH A 140	6363, 8 × 10
MH A 140	7459, 8 × 10
MH A 140	7950, 8 × 10
MH A 140	13331, 5 × 7
MH A 140	13333, 5 × 7
MH A 140	13346, 5 × 7
MH A 140	13356, 5 × 7
MH A 140	13621, 5 × 7
MH A 141	357, 8 × 10
MH A 141	912, 8 × 10
MH A 141	3301, 8 × 10
MH A 141	13333, 5 × 7
MH A 141	13356, 5 × 7
MH A 142	328, 8 × 10
MH A 142	329, 8 × 10
MH A 142	358, 8 × 10
MH A 142	359, 8 × 10
MH A 142	360, —
MH A 142	913, 8 × 10
MH A 142	915, 8 × 10
MH A 142	925, 5 × 7
MH A 142	926, 5 × 7
MH A 142	2234, 8 × 10
MH A 142	2235, 8 × 10
MH A 142	2445, 5 × 7
MH A 142	3038, 8 × 10
MH A 142	3861, 8 × 10
MH A 142	3865, 8 × 10
MH A 142	6273, 8 × 10
MH A 142	6338, 8 × 10
MH A 142	6364, 8 × 10
MH A 142	6365, 8 × 10
MH A 142	7674, 8 × 10
MH A 143	330, 5 × 7
MH A 143	927, 8 × 10
MH A 143	3854, 8 × 10
MH A 143	3873, 8 × 10
MH A 143	6367, 8 × 10
MH A 143	7268, 8 × 10

Medinet Habu (*cont.*)

Nelson Number/Description	Negative, Format
MH A 143	7270, 8 × 10
MH A 143	7995, 8 × 10
MH A 143	7997, 8 × 10
MH A 144	331, 8 × 10
MH A 144	928, 8 × 10
MH A 144	3855, 8 × 10
MH A 144	6366, 8 × 10
MH A 144	6527, 8 × 10
MH A 144	7269, 8 × 10
MH A 144	13336, 5 × 7
MH A 145	350, 8 × 10
MH A 145	351, 8 × 10
MH A 145	352, 8 × 10
MH A 145	887, 8 × 10
MH A 145	888, 5 × 7
MH A 145	2191, 8 × 10
MH A 145	2192, 8 × 10
MH A 145	2373, 8 × 10
MH A 145	2374, 8 × 10
MH A 145	2375, 8 × 10
MH A 145	2376, 8 × 10
MH A 145	3562, 8 × 10
MH A 145	3649, 8 × 10
MH A 145	4021, 8 × 10
MH A 145	4024, 8 × 10
MH A 145	7266, 8 × 10
MH A 145	13331, 5 × 7
MH A 145	13333, 5 × 7
MH A 145	13346, 5 × 7
MH A 145	13356, 5 × 7
MH A 145	13621, 5 × 7
MH A 146	347, 8 × 10
MH A 146	348, 8 × 10
MH A 146	349, 8 × 10
MH A 146	595, 8 × 10
MH A 146	891, 8 × 10
MH A 146	892, 8 × 10
MH A 146	2376, 8 × 10
MH A 146	2377, 8 × 10
MH A 146	2378, 8 × 10
MH A 146	2379, 8 × 10
MH A 146	3743, 8 × 10
MH A 146	4039, 8 × 10
MH A 146	6274, 8 × 10
MH A 146	6275, 8 × 10
MH A 146	15600, 8 × 10
MH A 147	346, 8 × 10
MH A 147	594, 8 × 10
MH A 147	894, 8 × 10
MH A 147	2380, 8 × 10
MH A 147	4040, 8 × 10
MH A 148	342, 8 × 10
MH A 148	343, 8 × 10
MH A 148	344, 8 × 10
MH A 148	721, 8 × 10

Medinet Habu (*cont.*)

Nelson Number/Description	Negative, Format
MH A 148	2399, 8 × 10
MH A 148	2400, 8 × 10
MH A 148	2401, 8 × 10
MH A 148	2402, 8 × 10
MH A 148	6028, 8 × 10
MH A 148	6029, 8 × 10
MH A 148	6030, 8 × 10
MH A 148	6031, 8 × 10
MH A 148	6276, 8 × 10
MH A 148	6539, 8 × 10
MH A 148	6603, 5 × 7
MH A 148a	3876, 8 × 10
MH A 148b	3875, 8 × 10
MH A 149	337, 8 × 10
MH A 149	338, 8 × 10
MH A 149	734, 8 × 10
MH A 149	919, 8 × 10
MH A 149	932, 8 × 10
MH A 150	294, 8 × 10
MH A 150	603, 5 × 7
MH A 150	604, 5 × 7
MH A 150	720, 8 × 10
MH A 150	726, 8 × 10
MH A 150	736, 5 × 7
MH A 150	737, 5 × 7
MH A 150	953, 8 × 10
MH A 150	954, 8 × 10
MH A 150	955, 8 × 10
MH A 150	957, 8 × 10
MH A 150	958, 8 × 10
MH A 150	963, 8 × 10
MH A 150	964, 8 × 10
MH A 150	971, 5 × 7
MH A 150	1001, 8 × 10
MH A 150	2157, 8 × 10
MH A 150	13347, 5 × 7
MH A 150	13352, 5 × 7
MH A 150	13408, 5 × 7
MH A 150	13454, 5 × 7
MH A 150	13456, 5 × 7
MH A 150	13604, 5 × 7
MH A 150	13616, 5 × 7
MH A 151	338, 8 × 10
MH A 151	612, 8 × 10
MH A 151	614, 8 × 10
MH A 151	877, 5 × 7
MH A 151	988, 8 × 10
MH A 152	340, 8 × 10
MH A 152	612, 8 × 10
MH A 152	613, 8 × 10
MH A 152	623, 8 × 10
MH A 152	13336, 5 × 7
MH A 153	294, 8 × 10
MH A 153	295, 8 × 10
MH A 153	296, 8 × 10

Medinet Habu (*cont.*)

Nelson Number/Description	Negative, Format
MH A 153	297, 8 × 10
MH A 153	298, 8 × 10
MH A 153	606, 5 × 7
MH A 153	607, 5 × 7
MH A 153	608, 8 × 10
MH A 153	609, 5 × 7
MH A 153	749, 8 × 10
MH A 153	780, 8 × 10
MH A 153	4045, 8 × 10
MH A 154	700, 8 × 10
MH A 154	1635, 8 × 10
MH A 154	2114, 8 × 10
MH A 154	3037, 8 × 10
MH A 154	3558, 8 × 10
MH A 154	3904, 8 × 10
MH A 154	4001, 8 × 10
MH A 155	701, 8 × 10
MH A 155	3564, 8 × 10
MH A 155	4001, 8 × 10
MH A 156	702, 8 × 10
MH A 156	3563, 8 × 10
MH A 156	3741, 8 × 10
MH A 156	3926, 8 × 10
MH A 156	3999, 8 × 10
MH A 156a	3925, 8 × 10
MH A 156b	3924, 8 × 10
MH A 157	703, 8 × 10
MH A 157	704, 8 × 10
MH A 157	4000, 8 × 10
MH A 158	704, 8 × 10
MH A 158	705, 8 × 10
MH A 158	706, 8 × 10
MH A 158	4002, 8 × 10
MH A 158	7953, 8 × 10
MH A 158	13456, 5 × 7
MH A 159	335, 8 × 10
MH A 159	336, 8 × 10
MH A 159	921, 8 × 10
MH A 159	922, 5 × 7
MH A 159	923, 5 × 7
MH A 159	924, 8 × 10
MH A 159	1388, 8 × 10
MH A 159	2241, 8 × 10
MH A 159	2381, 8 × 10
MH A 159	3937, 8 × 10
MH A 159	3938, 8 × 10
MH A 159	6032, 8 × 10
MH A 159	6536, 8 × 10
MH A 159	6537, 8 × 10
MH A 159	6538, 8 × 10
MH A 159	7253, 5 × 7
MH A 159a	3041, 8 × 10
MH A 159b	3042, 8 × 10
MH A 159c	3043, 8 × 10
MH A 159d	3044, 8 × 10

Medinet Habu (*cont.*)

Nelson Number/Description	Negative, Format
MH A 159d	3930, 8 × 10
MH A 160	10132, 8 × 10
MH A 160a	10033, 5 × 7
MH A 160b	7216, 5 × 7
MH A 160b	7529, 5 × 7
MH A 160b	10034, 5 × 7
MH A 160c	7522, 5 × 7
MH A 160c	10035, 5 × 7
MH A 161	10132, 8 × 10
MH A 161a	7600, 5 × 7
MH A 161a	10036, 5 × 7
MH A 161b	7433, 8 × 10
MH A 161b	10037, 5 × 7
MH A 161c	7432, 8 × 10
MH A 161c	10038, 5 × 7
MH A 162	218, 5 × 7
MH A 162	219, 5 × 7
MH A 162	1597, 8 × 10
MH A 162	2391, 8 × 10
MH A 162	10133, 8 × 10
MH A 162a	10039, 5 × 7
MH A 162b	7238, 5 × 7
MH A 162b	7519, 5 × 7
MH A 162b	10040, 5 × 7
MH A 162c	7966, 5 × 7
MH A 162c	10041, 5 × 7
MH A 163	576, 5 × 7
MH A 163	1597, 8 × 10
MH A 163	10133, 8 × 10
MH A 163a	10042, 5 × 7
MH A 163b	7218, 5 × 7
MH A 163b	7508, 5 × 7
MH A 163b	10043, 5 × 7
MH A 163c	7515, 5 × 7
MH A 163c	10044, 5 × 7
MH A 164	1597, 8 × 10
MH A 164	10134, 8 × 10
MH A 164a	7598, 5 × 7
MH A 164a	10045, 5 × 7
MH A 164b	7429, 8 × 10
MH A 164b	10046, 5 × 7
MH A 164c	7434, 8 × 10
MH A 164c	10047, 5 × 7
MH A 165	218, 5 × 7
MH A 165	219, 5 × 7
MH A 165	1597, 8 × 10
MH A 165	2392, 8 × 10
MH A 165	10134, 8 × 10
MH A 165a	10048, 5 × 7
MH A 165b	7239, 5 × 7
MH A 165b	7533, 5 × 7
MH A 165b	10049, 5 × 7
MH A 165c	10050, 5 × 7
MH A 166	230, 5 × 7
MH A 166	231, 5 × 7

Medinet Habu (*cont.*)

Nelson Number/Description	Negative, Format
MH A 166	1597, 8 × 10
MH A 166	2393, 8 × 10
MH A 166	10135, 8 × 10
MH A 166a	10051, 5 × 7
MH A 166b	7250, 5 × 7
MH A 166b	7535, 5 × 7
MH A 166b	10052, 5 × 7
MH A 166c	7968, 5 × 7
MH A 166c	10053, 5 × 7
MH A 167	1597, 8 × 10
MH A 167	10135, 8 × 10
MH A 167a	7604, 5 × 7
MH A 167a	10054, 5 × 7
MH A 167b	7566, 8 × 10
MH A 167b	10055, 5 × 7
MH A 167c	7565, 8 × 10
MH A 167c	10056, 5 × 7
MH A 168	220, 5 × 7
MH A 168	221, 5 × 7
MH A 168	1597, 8 × 10
MH A 168	10136, 8 × 10
MH A 168a	10057, 5 × 7
MH A 168b	7236, 5 × 7
MH A 168b	7516, 5 × 7
MH A 168b	10058, 5 × 7
MH A 168c	2398, 8 × 10
MH A 168c	7971, 5 × 7
MH A 168c	10059, 5 × 7
MH A 169	230, 5 × 7
MH A 169	231, 5 × 7
MH A 169	2394, 8 × 10
MH A 169	1597, 8 × 10
MH A 169	10136, 8 × 10
MH A 169a	7220, 5 × 7
MH A 169a	10060, 5 × 7
MH A 169b	7249, 5 × 7
MH A 169b	10061, 5 × 7
MH A 169c	7470, 5 × 7
MH A 169c	10062, 5 × 7
MH A 170	1597, 8 × 10
MH A 170	10137, 8 × 10
MH A 170a	7605, 5 × 7
MH A 170a	10063, 5 × 7
MH A 170b	7569, 8 × 10
MH A 170b	10064, 5 × 7
MH A 170c	7568, 8 × 10
MH A 170c	10065, 5 × 7
MH A 171	220, 5 × 7
MH A 171	221, 5 × 7
MH A 171	1597, 8 × 10
MH A 171	10137, 8 × 10
MH A 171a	10066, 5 × 7
MH A 171b	7231, 5 × 7
MH A 171b	7524, 5 × 7
MH A 171b	10066, 5 × 7

Medinet Habu (*cont.*)

Nelson Number/Description	Negative, Format
MH A 171c	7472, 5 × 7
MH A 171c	7520, 5 × 7
MH A 171c	10067, 5 × 7
MH A 172	228, 5 × 7
MH A 172	229, 5 × 7
MH A 172	1597, 8 × 10
MH A 172	2395, 8 × 10
MH A 172	10138, 8 × 10
MH A 172a	7228, 5 × 7
MH A 172a	10068, 5 × 7
MH A 172b	7237, 5 × 7
MH A 172b	10068, 5 × 7
MH A 172c	7967, 5 × 7
MH A 172c	10069, 5 × 7
MH A 173	1597, 8 × 10
MH A 173	10138, 8 × 10
MH A 173a	7606, 5 × 7
MH A 173a	10070, 5 × 7
MH A 173b	7572, 8 × 10
MH A 173b	10071, 5 × 7
MH A 173c	7571, 8 × 10
MH A 173c	10072, 5 × 7
MH A 174	222, 5 × 7
MH A 174	1597, 8 × 10
MH A 174	10139, 8 × 10
MH A 174a	7232, 5 × 7
MH A 174a	10073, 5 × 7
MH A 174b	7532, 5 × 7
MH A 174b	10074, 5 × 7
MH A 174c	7471, 5 × 7
MH A 174c	7530, 5 × 7
MH A 174c	10075, 5 × 7
MH A 175	228, 5 × 7
MH A 175	1352, 8 × 10
MH A 175	1597, 8 × 10
MH A 175	10139, 8 × 10
MH A 175a	7222, 5 × 7
MH A 175a	10076, 5 × 7
MH A 175b	7225, 5 × 7
MH A 175b	10077, 5 × 7
MH A 175c	7970, 5 × 7
MH A 175c	10078, 5 × 7
MH A 176	1352, 8 × 10
MH A 176	1597, 8 × 10
MH A 176	10140, 8 × 10
MH A 176a	7609, 5 × 7
MH A 176a	10079, 5 × 7
MH A 176b	7570, 8 × 10
MH A 176b	10080, 5 × 7
MH A 176c	7567, 8 × 10
MH A 176c	10081, 5 × 7
MH A 177	222, 5 × 7
MH A 177	223, 5 × 7
MH A 177	1597, 8 × 10
MH A 177	10140, 8 × 10

Medinet Habu (*cont.*)

Nelson Number/Description	Negative, Format
MH A 177a	10082, 5 × 7
MH A 177b	7233, 5 × 7
MH A 177b	7523, 5 × 7
MH A 177b	10083, 5 × 7
MH A 177c	7469, 5 × 7
MH A 177c	7518, 5 × 7
MH A 177c	10084, 5 × 7
MH A 178	226, 5 × 7
MH A 178	227, 5 × 7
MH A 178	1597, 8 × 10
MH A 178	2396, 8 × 10
MH A 178	2397, 8 × 10
MH A 178	10141, 8 × 10
MH A 178a	7221, 5 × 7
MH A 178a	10085, 5 × 7
MH A 178b	7234, 5 × 7
MH A 178b	10086, 5 × 7
MH A 178c	7969, 5 × 7
MH A 178c	10087, 5 × 7
MH A 179	1597, 8 × 10
MH A 179	10141, 8 × 10
MH A 179a	7608, 5 × 7
MH A 179a	10088, 5 × 7
MH A 179b	7976, 8 × 10
MH A 179b	10089, 5 × 7
MH A 179c	7430, 8 × 10
MH A 179c	10090, 5 × 7
MH A 180	224, 5 × 7
MH A 180	10142, 8 × 10
MH A 180a	10091, 5 × 7
MH A 180b	7215, 5 × 7
MH A 180b	10092, 5 × 7
MH A 180c	7599, 5 × 7
MH A 180c	10093, 5 × 7
MH A 181	226, 5 × 7
MH A 181	2382, 8 × 10
MH A 181	10142, 8 × 10
MH A 181a	7230, 5 × 7
MH A 181a	10094, 5 × 7
MH A 181b	7235, 5 × 7
MH A 181b	10095, 5 × 7
MH A 181c	10096, 5 × 7
MH A 182	10143, 8 × 10
MH A 182a	7607, 5 × 7
MH A 182a	10097, 5 × 7
MH A 182b	7435, 8 × 10
MH A 182b	10098, 5 × 7
MH A 182c	7431, 8 × 10
MH A 182c	10099, 5 × 7
MH A 183	10143, 8 × 10
MH A 183a	7526, 5 × 7
MH A 183a	10100, 5 × 7
MH A 183b	7525, 5 × 7
MH A 183b	10101, 5 × 7
MH A 183c	7517, 5 × 7

Medinet Habu (*cont.*)

Nelson Number/Description	Negative, Format
MH A 183c	10102, 5 × 7
MH A 184	1229, 8 × 10
MH A 184	10980, 8 × 10
MH A 185	10896, 5 × 7
MH A 185	10980, 8 × 10
MH A 186	1231, 8 × 10
MH A 186	10980, 8 × 10
MH A 187	10897, 5 × 7
MH A 187	10980, 8 × 10
MH A 188	188, 5 × 7
MH A 188	189, 5 × 7
MH A 188	11063, 8 × 10
MH A 189	183, 5 × 7
MH A 189	186, 5 × 7
MH A 189	11064, 8 × 10
MH A 190	184, 5 × 7
MH A 190	185, 5 × 7
MH A 190	11065, 8 × 10
MH A 191	182, 5 × 7
MH A 191	187, 5 × 7
MH A 191	11066, 8 × 10
MH A 192	245, 5 × 7
MH A 192	1223, 8 × 10
MH A 192	10859, 5 × 7
MH A 192	10899, 5 × 7
MH A 192	10970, 8 × 10
MH A 192	11244, 8 × 10
MH A 193	243, 5 × 7
MH A 193	1220, 8 × 10
MH A 193	10864, 5 × 7
MH A 193	10898, 5 × 7
MH A 193	10900, 5 × 7
MH A 193	10970, 8 × 10
MH A 193	11244, 8 × 10
MH A 194	159, 5 × 7
MH A 194	160, 5 × 7
MH A 194	10997, 8 × 10
MH A 195	157, 5 × 7
MH A 195	158, 5 × 7
MH A 195	10998, 8 × 10
MH A 196	155, 5 × 7
MH A 196	156, 5 × 7
MH A 196	10999, 8 × 10
MH A 197	153, 5 × 7
MH A 197	154, 5 × 7
MH A 197	11000, 8 × 10
MH A 198	151, 5 × 7
MH A 198	152, 5 × 7
MH A 198	161, 5 × 7
MH A 198	11001, 8 × 10
MH A 199	164, 5 × 7
MH A 199	171, 5 × 7
MH A 199	7426, 8 × 10
MH A 199	10020, 8 × 10
MH A 199a	7227, 5 × 7

Medinet Habu (*cont.*)

Nelson Number/Description	Negative, Format
MH A 199a	7513, 5 × 7
MH A 199a	9935, 8 × 10
MH A 199b	9935, 8 × 10
MH A 200	10012, 8 × 10
MH A 200a	7961, 5 × 7
MH A 200a	9896, 5 × 7
MH A 200b	7502, 5 × 7
MH A 200b	9897, 5 × 7
MH A 200c	7962, 5 × 7
MH A 200c	9898, 5 × 7
MH A 201	322, 8 × 10
MH A 201	323, 8 × 10
MH A 201	10012, 8 × 10
MH A 201a	7561, 8 × 10
MH A 201a	9936, 8 × 10
MH A 201b	7560, 8 × 10
MH A 201b	9936, 8 × 10
MH A 201c	9936, 8 × 10
MH A 202	172, 5 × 7
MH A 202	10012, 8 × 10
MH A 202a	9899, 5 × 7
MH A 202b	3025, 8 × 10
MH A 202b	7251, 5 × 7
MH A 202b	7965, 5 × 7
MH A 202b	9900, 5 × 7
MH A 202c	9900, 5 × 7
MH A 203	163, 5 × 7
MH A 203	10013, 8 × 10
MH A 203a	9901, 5 × 7
MH A 203b	7224, 5 × 7
MH A 203b	7537, 5 × 7
MH A 203b	9902, 5 × 7
MH A 203c	9902, 5 × 7
MH A 204	322, 8 × 10
MH A 204	323, 8 × 10
MH A 204	10013, 8 × 10
MH A 204a	7561, 8 × 10
MH A 204a	9937, 8 × 10
MH A 204b	7560, 8 × 10
MH A 204b	9937, 8 × 10
MH A 204c	9937, 8 × 10
MH A 205	173, 5 × 7
MH A 205	174, 5 × 7
MH A 205	7245, 5 × 7
MH A 205	10013, 8 × 10
MH A 205a	7534, 5 × 7
MH A 205a	9903, 5 × 7
MH A 205b	3032, 8 × 10
MH A 205b	9904, 5 × 7
MH A 205c	9904, 5 × 7
MH A 206	165, 5 × 7
MH A 206	166, 5 × 7
MH A 206	10014, 8 × 10
MH A 206a	9905, 5 × 7
MH A 206b	7223, 5 × 7

Medinet Habu (*cont.*)

Nelson Number/Description	Negative, Format
MH A 206b	7521, 5 × 7
MH A 206b	9906, 5 × 7
MH A 206c	9906, 5 × 7
MH A 207	320, 8 × 10
MH A 207	321, 8 × 10
MH A 207	10014, 8 × 10
MH A 207a	7586, 8 × 10
MH A 207a	9938, 8 × 10
MH A 207b	7590, 8 × 10
MH A 207b	9938, 8 × 10
MH A 207c	9938, 8 × 10
MH A 207d	9907, 5 × 7
MH A 207d	10020, 8 × 10
MH A 208	173, 5 × 7
MH A 208	174, 5 × 7
MH A 208	7246, 5 × 7
MH A 208	10014, 8 × 10
MH A 208a	7503, 5 × 7
MH A 208a	9908, 5 × 7
MH A 208b	3033, 8 × 10
MH A 208b	9909, 5 × 7
MH A 208c	9909, 5 × 7
MH A 208d	9910, 5 × 7
MH A 208d	10020, 8 × 10
MH A 209	165, 5 × 7
MH A 209	166, 5 × 7
MH A 209	10015, 8 × 10
MH A 209a	7610, 5 × 7
MH A 209a	9911, 5 × 7
MH A 209b	3036, 8 × 10
MH A 209b	7963, 5 × 7
MH A 209b	9912, 5 × 7
MH A 209c	9912, 5 × 7
MH A 210	320, 8 × 10
MH A 210	321, 8 × 10
MH A 210	10015, 8 × 10
MH A 210a	7586, 8 × 10
MH A 210a	9939, 8 × 10
MH A 210b	7590, 8 × 10
MH A 210b	9939, 8 × 10
MH A 210c	9939, 8 × 10
MH A 211	175, 5 × 7
MH A 211	176, 5 × 7
MH A 211	10015, 8 × 10
MH A 211a	7509, 5 × 7
MH A 211a	9913, 5 × 7
MH A 211b	3034, 8 × 10
MH A 211b	9913, 5 × 7
MH A 211c	3034, 8 × 10
MH A 211c	9913, 5 × 7
MH A 212	167, 5 × 7
MH A 212	168, 5 × 7
MH A 212	10016, 8 × 10
MH A 212a	9915, 5 × 7
MH A 212b	7219, 5 × 7

Medinet Habu (*cont.*)

Nelson Number/Description	Negative, Format
MH A 212b	9916, 5 × 7
MH A 212c	3035, 8 × 10
MH A 212c	9916, 5 × 7
MH A 213	318, 8 × 10
MH A 213	319, 8 × 10
MH A 213	10016, 8 × 10
MH A 213a	7591, 8 × 10
MH A 213a	9940, 8 × 10
MH A 213b	7589, 8 × 10
MH A 213b	9940, 8 × 10
MH A 213c	9940, 8 × 10
MH A 214	175, 5 × 7
MH A 214	176, 5 × 7
MH A 214	10016, 8 × 10
MH A 214a	7507, 5 × 7
MH A 214a	9917, 5 × 7
MH A 214b	7504, 5 × 7
MH A 214b	9918, 5 × 7
MH A 214c	9918, 5 × 7
MH A 215	167, 5 × 7
MH A 215	168, 5 × 7
MH A 215	7247, 5 × 7
MH A 215	10017, 8 × 10
MH A 215a	9919, 5 × 7
MH A 215b	7248, 5 × 7
MH A 215b	7531, 5 × 7
MH A 215b	9920, 5 × 7
MH A 215c	9920, 5 × 7
MH A 216	318, 8 × 10
MH A 216	319, 8 × 10
MH A 216	10017, 8 × 10
MH A 216	10020, 8 × 10
MH A 216a	7591, 8 × 10
MH A 216a	9941, 8 × 10
MH A 216b	7589, 8 × 10
MH A 216b	9941, 8 × 10
MH A 216c	9941, 8 × 10
MH A 217	178, 5 × 7
MH A 217	179, 5 × 7
MH A 217	10017, 8 × 10
MH A 217a	7510, 5 × 7
MH A 217a	9921, 5 × 7
MH A 217b	7506, 5 × 7
MH A 217b	9922, 5 × 7
MH A 217c	9922, 5 × 7
MH A 218	169, 5 × 7
MH A 218	170, 5 × 7
MH A 218	7243, 5 × 7
MH A 218	7473, 5 × 7
MH A 218	10018, 8 × 10
MH A 218a	9923, 5 × 7
MH A 218b	7214, 5 × 7
MH A 218b	9924, 5 × 7
MH A 218c	9924, 5 × 7
MH A 219	316, 8 × 10

Medinet Habu (*cont.*)

Nelson Number/Description	Negative, Format
MH A 219	317, 8 × 10
MH A 219	10018, 8 × 10
MH A 219a	7588, 8 × 10
MH A 219a	9942, 8 × 10
MH A 219b	7587, 8 × 10
MH A 219b	9942, 8 × 10
MH A 219c	9942, 8 × 10
MH A 220	178, 5 × 7
MH A 220	179, 5 × 7
MH A 220	10018, 8 × 10
MH A 220a	7505, 5 × 7
MH A 220a	9925, 5 × 7
MH A 220b	7512, 5 × 7
MH A 220b	9926, 5 × 7
MH A 220c	9926, 5 × 7
MH A 221	169, 5 × 7
MH A 221	170, 5 × 7
MH A 221	7244, 5 × 7
MH A 221	10019, 8 × 10
MH A 221a	9927, 5 × 7
MH A 221b	3024, 8 × 10
MH A 221b	7229, 5 × 7
MH A 221b	7964, 5 × 7
MH A 221b	9928, 5 × 7
MH A 221c	9928, 5 × 7
MH A 222	316, 8 × 10
MH A 222	317, 8 × 10
MH A 222	10019, 8 × 10
MH A 222a	7588, 8 × 10
MH A 222a	9943, 8 × 10
MH A 222b	7587, 8 × 10
MH A 222b	9943, 8 × 10
MH A 222c	9943, 8 × 10
MH A 223	10019, 8 × 10
MH A 223a	7514, 5 × 7
MH A 223a	9929, 5 × 7
MH A 223b	7612, 5 × 7
MH A 223b	9930, 5 × 7
MH A 223c	9930, 5 × 7
MH A 224	9931, 5 × 7
MH A 224	10021, 8 × 10
MH A 225	9932, 5 × 7
MH A 225	10021, 8 × 10
MH A 226	325, 8 × 10
MH A 226	363, 5 × 7
MH A 226	364, 5 × 7
MH A 226	365, 5 × 7
MH A 226	10770, 8 × 10
MH A 226a	10764, 5 × 7
MH A 226a	10765, 5 × 7
MH A 226a	10766, 5 × 7
MH A 226b	10767, 5 × 7
MH A 226b	10768, 5 × 7
MH A 227	366, 5 × 7
MH A 227	367, 5 × 7

Medinet Habu (*cont.*)

Nelson Number/Description	Negative, Format
MH A 227	368, 5 × 7
MH A 227	10770, 8 × 10
MH A 227a	10759, 5 × 7
MH A 227a	10760, 5 × 7
MH A 227a	10761, 5 × 7
MH A 227b	10762, 5 × 7
MH A 227b	10763, 5 × 7
MH A 228	369, 5 × 7
MH A 228	370, 5 × 7
MH A 228	371, 5 × 7
MH A 228	10771, 8 × 10
MH A 228	11128, 5 × 7
MH A 228a	10754, 5 × 7
MH A 228a	10755, 5 × 7
MH A 228a	10756, 5 × 7
MH A 228b	10757, 5 × 7
MH A 228b	10758, 5 × 7
MH A 229	372, 5 × 7
MH A 229	373, 5 × 7
MH A 229	374, 5 × 7
MH A 229	10771, 8 × 10
MH A 229a	10749, 5 × 7
MH A 229a	10750, 5 × 7
MH A 229a	10751, 5 × 7
MH A 229b	10752, 5 × 7
MH A 229b	10753, 5 × 7
MH A 230	375, 5 × 7
MH A 230	376, 5 × 7
MH A 230	377, 5 × 7
MH A 230	10978, 8 × 10
MH A 230	11129, 5 × 7
MH A 230a	10727, 5 × 7
MH A 230a	10728, 5 × 7
MH A 230a	10729, 5 × 7
MH A 230b	10730, 5 × 7
MH A 230b	10731, 5 × 7
MH A 231	378, 5 × 7
MH A 231	379, 5 × 7
MH A 231	380, 5 × 7
MH A 231	10978, 8 × 10
MH A 231a	10732, 5 × 7
MH A 231a	10733, 5 × 7
MH A 231a	10734, 5 × 7
MH A 231b	10735, 5 × 7
MH A 231b	10736, 5 × 7
MH A 232	381, 5 × 7
MH A 232	382, 5 × 7
MH A 232	383, 5 × 7
MH A 232	10979, 8 × 10
MH A 232a	10737, 5 × 7
MH A 232a	10738, 5 × 7
MH A 232a	10739, 5 × 7
MH A 232b	10740, 5 × 7
MH A 232b	10741, 5 × 7
MH A 233	384, 5 × 7

Medinet Habu (*cont.*)

Nelson Number/Description	Negative, Format
MH A 233	385, 5 × 7
MH A 233	386, 5 × 7
MH A 233	10979, 8 × 10
MH A 233a	10742, 5 × 7
MH A 233a	10743, 5 × 7
MH A 233a	10744, 5 × 7
MH A 233a	10745, 5 × 7
MH A 233a	10746, 5 × 7
MH A 233b	10747, 5 × 7
MH A 233b	10748, 5 × 7
MH A 250	324, 5 × 7
MH A 250	3927, 8 × 10
MH A 250a	7651, 8 × 10
MH A 250a	9947, 8 × 10
MH A 250b	7652, 8 × 10
MH A 250b	8405, 8 × 10
MH A 250b	9947, 8 × 10
MH A 251	7426, 8 × 10
MH A 251	10020, 8 × 10
MH A 251a	8406, 8 × 10
MH A 251b	8405, 8 × 10
MH A 252	326, 8 × 10
MH A 252	573, 5 × 7
MH A 252	9948, 8 × 10
MH A 252a	7662, 8 × 10
MH A 252a	8406, 8 × 10
MH A 252b	7661, 8 × 10
MH A 252b	9806, 8 × 10
MH A 253	308, 8 × 10
MH A 253	3921, 8 × 10
MH A 253	3928, 8 × 10
MH A 253	9799, 8 × 10
MH A 254	308, 8 × 10
MH A 254	309, 8 × 10
MH A 254	3921, 8 × 10
MH A 254	9799, 8 × 10
MH A 255	309, 8 × 10
MH A 255	310, 8 × 10
MH A 255	3860, 8 × 10
MH A 255	3863, 8 × 10
MH A 255	9800, 8 × 10
MH A 256	3860, 8 × 10
MH A 256	3864, 8 × 10
MH A 256	9801, 8 × 10
MH A 257	310, 8 × 10
MH A 257	311, 8 × 10
MH A 257	3864, 8 × 10
MH A 257	9801, 8 × 10
MH A 258	311, 8 × 10
MH A 258	3862, 8 × 10
MH A 258	9801, 8 × 10
MH A 259	312, 8 × 10
MH A 259	3046, 8 × 10
MH A 259	3813, 8 × 10
MH A 259	7979, 8 × 10

Medinet Habu (*cont.*)

Nelson Number/Description	Negative, Format
MH A 260	312, 8 × 10
MH A 260	313, 8 × 10
MH A 260	3814, 8 × 10
MH A 260	7979, 8 × 10
MH A 261	313, 8 × 10
MH A 261	3857, 8 × 10
MH A 261	7977, 8 × 10
MH A 261a	9944, 8 × 10
MH A 261b	9944, 8 × 10
MH A 262	314, 8 × 10
MH A 262	3856, 8 × 10
MH A 262	3857, 8 × 10
MH A 262	7977, 8 × 10
MH A 263	314, 8 × 10
MH A 263	3859, 8 × 10
MH A 263	7978, 8 × 10
MH A 263	11599, 8 × 10
MH A 264	3859, 8 × 10
MH A 264	7978, 8 × 10
MH A 264	11599, 8 × 10
MH A 265	306, 8 × 10
MH A 265	307, 8 × 10
MH A 265	3922, 8 × 10
MH A 265	7952, 8 × 10
MH A 265	7958, 8 × 10
MH A 265	8467, 8 × 10
MH A 266	306, 8 × 10
MH A 266	3922, 8 × 10
MH A 266	7952, 8 × 10
MH A 266	8467, 8 × 10
MH A 266	11599, 8 × 10
MH A 267	305, 8 × 10
MH A 267	3920, 8 × 10
MH A 267	7701, 3.5 × 4.5
MH A 267	7702, 3.5 × 4.5
MH A 267	8468, 8 × 10
MH A 268	304, 8 × 10
MH A 268	305, 8 × 10
MH A 268	3835, 8 × 10
MH A 268	3920, 8 × 10
MH A 268	8468, 8 × 10
MH A 269	302, 8 × 10
MH A 269	303, 8 × 10
MH A 269	3834, 8 × 10
MH A 269	8466, 8 × 10
MH A 269b	3849, 8 × 10
MH A 270	301, 8 × 10
MH A 270	302, 8 × 10
MH A 270	3849, 8 × 10
MH A 270	8465, 8 × 10
MH A 271	300, 8 × 10
MH A 271	301, 8 × 10
MH A 271	3848, 8 × 10
MH A 271	8465, 8 × 10
MH A 271a	3847, 8 × 10

Medinet Habu (*cont.*)

Nelson Number/Description	Negative, Format
MH A 271b	3846, 8 × 10
MH A 272	300, 8 × 10
MH A 272	3846, 8 × 10
MH A 272	8465, 8 × 10
MH A 273	242, 5 × 7
MH A 273a	8407, 8 × 10
MH A 273a	9948, 8 × 10
MH A 273b	8408, 8 × 10
MH A 273b	9807, 8 × 10
MH A 274	7427, 8 × 10
MH A 274	10021, 8 × 10
MH A 274a	7559, 8 × 10
MH A 274a	9945, 8 × 10
MH A 274b	9945, 8 × 10
MH A 275	244, 5 × 7
MH A 275	3929, 8 × 10
MH A 275a	7448, 8 × 10
MH A 275a	10128, 8 × 10
MH A 275b	7448, 8 × 10
MH A 275b	9679, 8 × 10
MH A 276	164, 5 × 7
MH A 276	171, 5 × 7
MH A 276	7427, 8 × 10
MH A 276	10021, 8 × 10
MH A 276a	7559, 8 × 10
MH A 276a	9933, 5 × 7
MH A 276b	7226, 5 × 7
MH A 276b	9934, 5 × 7
MH A 276c	9934, 5 × 7
MH A 277	10711, 5 × 7
MH A 278	10712, 5 × 7
MH A 279	236, 5 × 7
MH A 279	237, 5 × 7
MH A 279	341, 8 × 10
MH A 279	6339, 8 × 10
MH A 279	10129, 8 × 10
MH A 280	236, 5 × 7
MH A 280	237, 5 × 7
MH A 280	341, 8 × 10
MH A 280	2172, 8 × 10
MH A 280	2173, 8 × 10
MH A 280	2174, 8 × 10
MH A 280	7450, 8 × 10
MH A 280	7455, 8 × 10
MH A 280	10167, 5 × 7
MH A 280	10166, 5 × 7
MH A 280	10190, 8 × 10
MH A 280	15210, 5 × 7
MH A 280	15211, 5 × 7
MH A 280	15211-var, 5 × 7
MH A 281	789, 5 × 7
MH A 281	790, 5 × 7
MH A 281	796, 5 × 7
MH A 281	1009, 5 × 7
MH A 281	1010, 8 × 10

Medinet Habu (*cont.*)

Nelson Number/Description	Negative, Format
MH A 281	1011, 8 × 10
MH A 281	7440, 8 × 10
MH A 281	7457, 8 × 10
MH A 281	7458, 8 × 10
MH A 281	10406, 8 × 10
MH A 281a	10239, 5 × 7
MH A 281a	10407, 8 × 10
MH A 281b	7491, 8 × 10
MH A 281b	10240, 5 × 7
MH A 281b	10407, 8 × 10
MH A 281c	7476, 8 × 10
MH A 281c	10241, 5 × 7
MH A 281c	10407, 8 × 10
MH A 281d	7428, 8 × 10
MH A 281d	7476, 8 × 10
MH A 281d	10242, 5 × 7
MH A 281d	10407, 8 × 10
MH A 281e	7476, 8 × 10
MH A 281e	10243, 5 × 7
MH A 281e	10408, 8 × 10
MH A 281f	7476, 8 × 10
MH A 281f	10244, 5 × 7
MH A 281f	10408, 8 × 10
MH A 281g	7476, 8 × 10
MH A 281g	10245, 5 × 7
MH A 281g	10561, 8 × 10
MH A 281h	7476, 8 × 10
MH A 281h	7491, 8 × 10
MH A 281h	10245, 5 × 7
MH A 281h	10561, 8 × 10
MH A 281i	7476, 8 × 10
MH A 281i	10246, 5 × 7
MH A 281i	10408, 8 × 10
MH A 281j	7428, 8 × 10
MH A 281j	10247, 5 × 7
MH A 281j	10408, 8 × 10
MH A 281k	10248, 5 × 7
MH A 281k	10561, 8 × 10
MH A 281l	10248, 5 × 7
MH A 281l	10561, 8 × 10
MH A 282	124, 5 × 7
MH A 285a	11598, 8 × 10
MH A 286	9726, 8 × 10
MH A 286	9727, 8 × 10
MH A 286	9728, 8 × 10
MH A 286	9729, 8 × 10
MH A 286a	7198, 8 × 10
MH A 286a	9949, 8 × 10
MH A 286b	3953, 8 × 10
MH A 286b	7199, 8 × 10
MH A 286b	9949, 8 × 10
MH A 286c	7196, 8 × 10
MH A 286c	9950, 8 × 10
MH A 286d	7200, 8 × 10
MH A 286d	9950, 8 × 10

Medinet Habu (*cont.*)

Nelson Number/Description	Negative, Format
MH A 286e	7242, 5 × 7
MH A 286e	9951, 8 × 10
MH A 286f	7240, 5 × 7
MH A 286f	9951, 8 × 10
MH A 286g	7241, 5 × 7
MH A 286g	9951, 8 × 10
MH A 286h	9895, 5 × 7
MH A 286h	9951, 8 × 10
MH A 287	9730, 8 × 10
MH A 287	9731, 8 × 10
MH A 287	9732, 8 × 10
MH A 287	9733, 8 × 10
MH A 287	9757, 5 × 7
MH A 287	9758, 5 × 7
MH A 287	9759, 5 × 7
MH A 287	9760, 5 × 7
MH A 287	9761, 5 × 7
MH A 287	9762, 5 × 7
MH A 287a	7202, 8 × 10
MH A 287a	10255, 8 × 10
MH A 287b	7203, 8 × 10
MH A 287b	10255, 8 × 10
MH A 287c	7201, 8 × 10
MH A 287c	10256, 8 × 10
MH A 287d	7197, 8 × 10
MH A 287d	10256, 8 × 10
MH A 287e	10257, 8 × 10
MH A 287f	10257, 8 × 10
MH A 288	4009, 5 × 7
MH A 288	11251, 8 × 10
MH A 288a	11216, 5 × 7
MH A 288b	11217, 5 × 7
MH A 288c	11216, 5 × 7
MH A 288d	11217, 5 × 7
MH A 289a	11218, 5 × 7
MH A 289a	11219, 5 × 7
MH A 289a	11253, 8 × 10
MH A 289b	11220, 5 × 7
MH A 289b	11220, 5 × 7
MH A 289b	11253, 8 × 10
MH A 289b	11221, 5 × 7
MH A 289c	11222, 5 × 7
MH A 289c	11253, 8 × 10
MH A 289d	11223, 5 × 7
MH A 289d	11253, 8 × 10
MH A 290c	11224, 5 × 7
MH A 290c	11253, 8 × 10
MH A 290d	11225, 5 × 7
MH A 290d	11253, 8 × 10
MH A 300	10682, 8 × 10
MH A 301	10682, 8 × 10
MH A 302	410, 8 × 10
MH A 302	7456, 8 × 10
MH A 302	10130, 8 × 10
MH A 302	13341, 5 × 7

Medinet Habu (*cont.*)

Nelson Number/Description	Negative, Format
MH A 303	410, 8 × 10
MH A 303	7456, 8 × 10
MH A 303	10130, 8 × 10
MH A 303	13341, 5 × 7
MH A 304	410, 8 × 10
MH A 304	411, 8 × 10
MH A 304	7443, 8 × 10
MH A 304	10130, 8 × 10
MH A 304	13341, 5 × 7
MH A 305	410, 8 × 10
MH A 305	411, 8 × 10
MH A 305	7464, 8 × 10
MH A 305	9808, 8 × 10
MH A 305	13341, 5 × 7
MH A 306	410, 8 × 10
MH A 306	411, 8 × 10
MH A 306	7465, 8 × 10
MH A 306	9808, 8 × 10
MH A 306	13341, 5 × 7
MH A 307	411, 8 × 10
MH A 307	7436, 8 × 10
MH A 307	9808, 8 × 10
MH A 307	13341, 5 × 7
MH A 308	411, 8 × 10
MH A 308	7564, 8 × 10
MH A 308	9845, 8 × 10
MH A 308	10449, 8 × 10
MH A 308	13341, 5 × 7
MH A 309	411, 8 × 10
MH A 309	7564, 8 × 10
MH A 309	9845, 8 × 10
MH A 309	10449, 8 × 10
MH A 309	13341, 5 × 7
MH A 310	7654, 8 × 10
MH A 310	9845, 8 × 10
MH A 310a	10449, 8 × 10
MH A 310b	10449, 8 × 10
MH A 311	412, 8 × 10
MH A 311	7653, 8 × 10
MH A 311	9845, 8 × 10
MH A 311	10449, 8 × 10
MH A 311	13341, 5 × 7
MH A 312	412, 8 × 10
MH A 312	7653, 8 × 10
MH A 312	9845, 8 × 10
MH A 312	10449, 8 × 10
MH A 312	13341, 5 × 7
MH A 313	412, 8 × 10
MH A 313	7994, 8 × 10
MH A 313	7996, 8 × 10
MH A 313	9952, 8 × 10
MH A 313	13341, 5 × 7
MH A 314	412, 8 × 10
MH A 314	7992, 8 × 10
MH A 314	7996, 8 × 10

Medinet Habu (*cont.*)

Nelson Number/Description	Negative, Format
MH A 314	9952, 8 × 10
MH A 314	13341, 5 × 7
MH A 315	7992, 8 × 10
MH A 315	7993, 8 × 10
MH A 315	9952, 8 × 10
MH A 315	13341, 5 × 7
MH A 316	7993, 8 × 10
MH A 316	9952, 8 × 10
MH A 316	13341, 5 × 7
MH A 317	412, 8 × 10
MH A 317	7992, 8 × 10
MH A 317	7994, 8 × 10
MH A 317	7996, 8 × 10
MH A 317	10131, 8 × 10
MH A 317	13341, 5 × 7
MH A 318	7993, 8 × 10
MH A 318	10131, 8 × 10
MH A 318	13341, 5 × 7
MH A 319	401, 8 × 10
MH A 319	10422, 8 × 10
MH A 319	10562, 8 × 10
MH A 320	401, 8 × 10
MH A 320	10422, 8 × 10
MH A 320	10562, 8 × 10
MH A 321	8633, 8 × 10
MH A 321	10423, 8 × 10
MH A 321	10562, 8 × 10
MH A 322	8633, 8 × 10
MH A 322	10423, 8 × 10
MH A 322	10562, 8 × 10
MH A 323	8633, 8 × 10
MH A 323	8634, 8 × 10
MH A 323	10423, 8 × 10
MH A 323	10562, 8 × 10
MH A 324	401, 8 × 10
MH A 324	7438, 8 × 10
MH A 324	9953, 8 × 10
MH A 324	10422, 8 × 10
MH A 324	10713, 5 × 7
MH A 324	13618, 5 × 7
MH A 325	8633, 8 × 10
MH A 325	8634, 8 × 10
MH A 326	404, 5 × 7
MH A 326	10432, 5 × 7
MH A 326	10678, 5 × 7
MH A 329	2652, 8 × 10
MH A 329	7483, 8 × 10
MH A 329	9848, 8 × 10
MH A 329	10563, 8 × 10
MH A 329	13341, 5 × 7
MH A 330	406, 8 × 10
MH A 330	7484, 8 × 10
MH A 330	9849, 8 × 10
MH A 330	10563, 8 × 10
MH A 330	13341, 5 × 7

Medinet Habu (*cont.*)

Nelson Number/Description	Negative, Format
MH A 331	7449, 8 × 10
MH A 331	9850, 8 × 10
MH A 331	10564, 8 × 10
MH A 331	13341, 5 × 7
MH A 332	7454, 8 × 10
MH A 332	9851, 8 × 10
MH A 332	10564, 8 × 10
MH A 332	13341, 5 × 7
MH A 333	7453, 8 × 10
MH A 333	9852, 8 × 10
MH A 333	10564, 8 × 10
MH A 333	13341, 5 × 7
MH A 334	2633, 8 × 10
MH A 334	10453, 8 × 10
MH A 334a	6676, 8 × 10
MH A 334a	6278, 8 × 10
MH A 334b	6279, 8 × 10
MH A 335	2592, 8 × 10
MH A 335	3058, 8 × 10
MH A 336	686, 8 × 10
MH A 336	2593, 8 × 10
MH A 336	3058, 8 × 10
MH A 337	688, 8 × 10
MH A 337	2594, 8 × 10
MH A 337	3058, 8 × 10
MH A 338	817, 8 × 10
MH A 338	2595, 8 × 10
MH A 338	3984, 8 × 10
MH A 339	687, 8 × 10
MH A 339	2533, 8 × 10
MH A 339	3059, 8 × 10
MH A 340	685, 8 × 10
MH A 340	2534, 8 × 10
MH A 340	3059, 8 × 10
MH A 341	2591, 8 × 10
MH A 341	3059, 8 × 10
MH A 341	11256, 8 × 10
MH A 342	6062, 8 × 10
MH A 343	2596, 8 × 10
MH A 343	2650, 8 × 10
MH A 344	6043, 8 × 10
MH A 344	6361, 8 × 10
MH A 345	2411, 8 × 10
MH A 345	2475, 8 × 10
MH A 345	6404, 8 × 10
MH A 346	6063, 8 × 10
MH A 346	11256, 8 × 10
MH A 347	2597, 8 × 10
MH A 347	3872, 8 × 10
MH A 348	2626, 8 × 10
MH A 348	2637, 8 × 10
MH A 349	1186, 8 × 10
MH A 349	2598, 8 × 10
MH A 349	2624, 8 × 10
MH A 349	2638, 8 × 10

Medinet Habu (*cont.*)

Nelson Number/Description	Negative, Format
MH A 350	6064, 8 × 10
MH A 350	11256, 8 × 10
MH A 351	2599, 8 × 10
MH A 351	3851, 8 × 10
MH A 352	2622, 8 × 10
MH A 352	3135, 8 × 10
MH A 352	3235, 8 × 10
MH A 353	2600, 8 × 10
MH A 353	3060, 8 × 10
MH A 353	3137, 8 × 10
MH A 354	6065, 8 × 10
MH A 354	11256, 8 × 10
MH A 354	11258, 8 × 10
MH A 355	2601, 8 × 10
MH A 355	2667, 8 × 10
MH A 355	3331, 8 × 10
MH A 355a	4029, 8 × 10
MH A 355b	4004, 8 × 10
MH A 356	6042, 8 × 10
MH A 356	6669, 8 × 10
MH A 357	2602, 8 × 10
MH A 357	2603, 8 × 10
MH A 357	6532, 8 × 10
MH A 360	2839, 8 × 10
MH A 360	10565, 8 × 10
MH A 361	10424, 8 × 10
MH A 361	10566, 8 × 10
MH A 362	2829, 8 × 10
MH A 362	2830, 8 × 10
MH A 362	2831, 8 × 10
MH A 362	10567, 8 × 10
MH A 364	500, 8 × 10
MH A 364	501, 8 × 10
MH A 364	9853, 8 × 10
MH A 364	11192, 8 × 10
MH A 365	834, 5 × 7
MH A 365	9857, 8 × 10
MH A 365	11192, 8 × 10
MH A 366	836, 5 × 7
MH A 366	9854, 8 × 10
MH A 366	11192, 8 × 10
MH A 367	835, 5 × 7
MH A 367	836, 5 × 7
MH A 367	9854, 8 × 10
MH A 367	11192, 8 × 10
MH A 368	500, 8 × 10
MH A 368	501, 8 × 10
MH A 368	10925, 8 × 10
MH A 368a	10925, 8 × 10
MH A 369	497, 8 × 10
MH A 369	3900, 8 × 10
MH A 369	9855, 8 × 10
MH A 369	10780, 8 × 10
MH A 370	497, 8 × 10
MH A 370	3902, 8 × 10

Medinet Habu (*cont.*)

Nelson Number/Description	Negative, Format
MH A 370	9855, 8 × 10
MH A 370	10780, 8 × 10
MH A 371	497, 8 × 10
MH A 371	3902, 8 × 10
MH A 371	9855, 8 × 10
MH A 371	10780, 8 × 10
MH A 372	498, 8 × 10
MH A 372	6239, 8 × 10
MH A 372	10781, 8 × 10
MH A 373	498, 8 × 10
MH A 373	10781, 8 × 10
MH A 374	499, 8 × 10
MH A 374	3919, 8 × 10
MH A 374	6240, 8 × 10
MH A 374	10782, 8 × 10
MH A 374	11086, 8 × 10
MH A 375	499, 8 × 10
MH A 375	3919, 8 × 10
MH A 375	10782, 8 × 10
MH A 376	499, 8 × 10
MH A 376	3918, 8 × 10
MH A 376	10782, 8 × 10
MH A 377	7562, 8 × 10
MH A 377	10718, 8 × 10
MH A 377	13368, 5 × 7
MH A 377a	11007, 5 × 7
MH A 377a	11193, 8 × 10
MH A 378	10718, 8 × 10
MH A 378a	7926, 5 × 7
MH A 378a	11008, 5 × 7
MH A 378a	11165, 5 × 7
MH A 378b	7925, 5 × 7
MH A 378b	11163, 5 × 7
MH A 378b	11193, 8 × 10
MH A 378c	7603, 5 × 7
MH A 378c	11164, 5 × 7
MH A 378c	11193, 8 × 10
MH A 379	7545, 8 × 10
MH A 379	7546, 8 × 10
MH A 379	7551, 8 × 10
MH A 379	10550, 8 × 10
MH A 379	10551, 8 × 10
MH A 379a	7602, 5 × 7
MH A 379a	11193, 8 × 10
MH A 380	7547, 8 × 10
MH A 380	7550, 8 × 10
MH A 380	7552, 8 × 10
MH A 380	10552, 8 × 10
MH A 380	10553, 8 × 10
MH A 380	11087, 8 × 10
MH A 381	694, 8 × 10
MH A 381	2487, 8 × 10
MH A 381a	2604, 8 × 10
MH A 382	693, 8 × 10
MH A 382	694, 8 × 10

Medinet Habu (*cont.*)		Medinet Habu (*cont.*)	
Nelson Number/Description	*Negative, Format*	*Nelson Number/Description*	*Negative, Format*
MH A 382	2654, 8 × 10	MH A 406	7460, 8 × 10
MH A 383	691, 8 × 10	MH A 406	7636, 8 × 10
MH A 383	2483, 8 × 10	MH A 407	695, 8 × 10
MH A 383	2590, 8 × 10	MH A 407	10613, 8 × 10
MH A 383	2641, 8 × 10	MH A 407	11228, 5 × 7
MH A 384	691, 8 × 10	MH A 407	11257, 8 × 10
MH A 384	692, 8 × 10	MH A 407a	8635, 8 × 10
MH A 384	2483, 8 × 10	MH A 408a	8686, 8 × 10
MH A 384	2484, 8 × 10	MH A 408a	8687, 8 × 10
MH A 384	2535, 8 × 10	MH A 408a	10614, 8 × 10
MH A 384	2536, 8 × 10	MH A 408b	8687, 8 × 10
MH A 384	2605, 8 × 10	MH A 408b	8688, 8 × 10
MH A 384	2641, 8 × 10	MH A 408b	10614, 8 × 10
MH A 385	692, 8 × 10	MH A 409	681, 8 × 10
MH A 385	2484, 8 × 10	MH A 409	10613, 8 × 10
MH A 385	2641, 8 × 10	MH A 409	11229, 5 × 7
MH A 386	689, 8 × 10	MH A 409a	7474, 5 × 7
MH A 386	10772, 8 × 10	MH A 409b	7475, 5 × 7
MH A 386a	10772, 8 × 10	MH A 410a	8689, 8 × 10
MH A 387	690, 8 × 10	MH A 410a	10615, 8 × 10
MH A 387	2653, 8 × 10	MH A 410b	8690, 8 × 10
MH A 388	803, 8 × 10	MH A 410b	8691, 8 × 10
MH A 388	2488, 8 × 10	MH A 410b	10615, 8 × 10
MH A 389	803, 8 × 10	MH A 411	698, 8 × 10
MH A 389	2489, 8 × 10	MH A 411	11257, 8 × 10
MH A 389	2498, 5 × 7	MH A 411a	8636, 8 × 10
MH A 390	2490, 8 × 10	MH A 411a	10701, 8 × 10
MH A 391	803, 8 × 10	MH A 412	677, 8 × 10
MH A 391a	2485, 8 × 10	MH A 412	6052, 8 × 10
MH A 391b	2486, 8 × 10	MH A 412	10679, 5 × 7
MH A 392	2623, 8 × 10	MH A 412	10702, 8 × 10
MH A 393	2634, 8 × 10	MH A 413	678, 8 × 10
MH A 394	2631, 8 × 10	MH A 413	6052, 8 × 10
MH A 395	2491, 8 × 10	MH A 413	10702, 8 × 10
MH A 396	2629, 8 × 10	MH A 414	683, 8 × 10
MH A 397	2630, 8 × 10	MH A 414	10701, 8 × 10
MH A 398	2632, 8 × 10	MH A 415	6040, 8 × 10
MH A 399	2627, 8 × 10	MH A 415a	7548, 8 × 10
MH A 400	2628, 8 × 10	MH A 415a	10616, 8 × 10
MH A 401	2636, 8 × 10	MH A 415b	10616, 8 × 10
MH A 402	699, 8 × 10	MH A 416	787, 8 × 10
MH A 402	7493, 8 × 10	MH A 416	11230, 5 × 7
MH A 402	11227, 5 × 7	MH A 416	11257, 8 × 10
MH A 402	11257, 8 × 10	MH A 417	679, 8 × 10
MH A 403	696, 8 × 10	MH A 417	680, 8 × 10
MH A 403	697, 8 × 10	MH A 417	6037, 8 × 10
MH A 403	7327, 8 × 10	MH A 417	6038, 8 × 10
MH A 403	7328, 8 × 10	MH A 417	6039, 8 × 10
MH A 403	7637, 8 × 10	MH A 417	7267, 8 × 10
MH A 404	682, 8 × 10	MH A 418	684, 8 × 10
MH A 404	7656, 8 × 10	MH A 418	10788, 8 × 10
MH A 404a	7451, 8 × 10	MH A 418	10792, 5 × 7
MH A 404b	7452, 8 × 10	MH A 419	6025, 8 × 10
MH A 405	7461, 8 × 10	MH A 419	6026, 8 × 10
MH A 405	7636, 8 × 10	MH A 419	6027, 8 × 10

Medinet Habu (*cont.*)

Nelson Number/Description	Negative, Format
MH A 419	7334, 8 × 10
MH A 420	496, 8 × 10
MH A 420	10554, 8 × 10
MH A 420	10984, 8 × 10
MH A 420a	11022, 5 × 7
MH A 420c	11194, 8 × 10
MH A 421	494, 8 × 10
MH A 421	3923, 8 × 10
MH A 421	6058, 8 × 10
MH A 421	6066, 5 × 7
MH A 421	6067, 5 × 7
MH A 421	6068, 5 × 7
MH A 421	10556, 8 × 10
MH A 421	10719, 8 × 10
MH A 421a	10554, 8 × 10
MH A 421a	10555, 8 × 10
MH A 421a	10983, 8 × 10
MH A 421a	10984, 8 × 10
MH A 422	6041, 8 × 10
MH A 422	6059, 8 × 10
MH A 422	6069, 5 × 7
MH A 422	10601, 8 × 10
MH A 422	10602, 8 × 10
MH A 422	10720, 8 × 10
MH A 422a	10983, 8 × 10
MH A 423	725, 5 × 7
MH A 423	6070, 5 × 7
MH A 423	6071, 5 × 7
MH A 423	6076, 8 × 10
MH A 423	10721, 8 × 10
MH A 423a	10983, 8 × 10
MH A 424	493, 8 × 10
MH A 424	3917, 8 × 10
MH A 424	10722, 8 × 10
MH A 425	493, 8 × 10
MH A 425	800, 8 × 10
MH A 425	3827, 8 × 10
MH A 425	10985, 8 × 10
MH A 425a	10984, 8 × 10
MH A 426	10986, 8 × 10
MH A 427	6061, 8 × 10
MH A 427	10773, 8 × 10
MH A 427	10986, 8 × 10
MH A 428	10793, 5 × 7
MH A 428	10987, 8 × 10
MH A 429	6060, 8 × 10
MH A 429	10774, 8 × 10
MH A 429	10775, 8 × 10
MH A 429	10987, 8 × 10
MH A 431	8637, 8 × 10
MH A 431	9856, 8 × 10
MH A 431	11088, 8 × 10
MH A 432	828, 5 × 7
MH A 432	8626, 5 × 7
MH A 432	9857, 8 × 10

Medinet Habu (*cont.*)

Nelson Number/Description	Negative, Format
MH A 432	11130, 5 × 7
MH A 432	11194, 8 × 10
MH A 432a	11194, 8 × 10
MH A 434	491, 8 × 10
MH A 434	795, 5 × 7
MH A 434	3759, 8 × 10
MH A 434	10557, 8 × 10
MH A 434	10723, 8 × 10
MH A 435	491, 8 × 10
MH A 435	10557, 8 × 10
MH A 435	10723, 8 × 10
MH A 436	491, 8 × 10
MH A 436	785, 5 × 7
MH A 436	3826, 8 × 10
MH A 436	10723, 8 × 10
MH A 437	489, 8 × 10
MH A 437	3829, 8 × 10
MH A 437	9809, 8 × 10
MH A 437	9858, 8 × 10
MH A 437	10724, 8 × 10
MH A 438	490, 8 × 10
MH A 438	3850, 8 × 10
MH A 438	6053, 8 × 10
MH A 438	9859, 8 × 10
MH A 438	10789, 8 × 10
MH A 438	15806, 8 × 10
MH A 438	15810, 8 × 10
MH A 439	490, 8 × 10
MH A 439	3762, 8 × 10
MH A 439	6053, 8 × 10
MH A 439	10725, 8 × 10
MH A 440	492, 8 × 10
MH A 440	3760, 8 × 10
MH A 440	10790, 8 × 10
MH A 441	11009, 5 × 7
MH A 441	11085, 8 × 10
MH A 442	476, 8 × 10
MH A 442	3758, 8 × 10
MH A 442	11002, 8 × 10
MH A 443	477, 8 × 10
MH A 443	7543, 8 × 10
MH A 443	11002, 8 × 10
MH A 444	475, 8 × 10
MH A 444	3756, 8 × 10
MH A 444	11003, 8 × 10
MH A 445	473, 8 × 10
MH A 445	3749, 8 × 10
MH A 445	11010, 5 × 7
MH A 445	11195, 8 × 10
MH A 446	473, 8 × 10
MH A 446	3825, 8 × 10
MH A 446	9860, 8 × 10
MH A 446	10910, 5 × 7
MH A 447	473, 8 × 10
MH A 447	949, 8 × 10

Medinet Habu (*cont.*)

Nelson Number/Description	Negative, Format
MH A 447	3761, 8 × 10
MH A 447	11023, 5 × 7
MH A 447	11195, 8 × 10
MH A 448	474, 8 × 10
MH A 448	3764, 8 × 10
MH A 448	10911, 8 × 10
MH A 449	483, 8 × 10
MH A 449	8118, 8 × 10
MH A 449	10912, 8 × 10
MH A 450	487, 8 × 10
MH A 450	9680, 8 × 10
MH A 450	11067, 8 × 10
MH A 451	486, 8 × 10
MH A 451	9681, 8 × 10
MH A 451	11067, 8 × 10
MH A 452	486, 8 × 10
MH A 452	9682, 8 × 10
MH A 452	11067, 8 × 10
MH A 453	482, 8 × 10
MH A 453	3747, 8 × 10
MH A 453	10913, 8 × 10
MH A 454	484, 8 × 10
MH A 454	6238, 8 × 10
MH A 454	7954, 8 × 10
MH A 454	7955, 8 × 10
MH A 454	9683, 8 × 10
MH A 454	11004, 8 × 10
MH A 454	15808, 8 × 10
MH A 455	484, 8 × 10
MH A 455	485, 8 × 10
MH A 455	9684, 8 × 10
MH A 455	11004, 8 × 10
MH A 456	485, 8 × 10
MH A 456	9685, 8 × 10
MH A 456	11004, 8 × 10
MH A 457	488, 8 × 10
MH A 457	2480, 8 × 10
MH A 457	2481, 8 × 10
MH A 457	11072, 8 × 10
MH A 458	479, 8 × 10
MH A 458	480, 8 × 10
MH A 458	481, 8 × 10
MH A 458	3871, 5 × 7
MH A 458	9874, 5 × 7
MH A 458	11195, 8 × 10
MH A 458a	9763, 5 × 7
MH A 458a	11195, 8 × 10
MH A 459	472, 8 × 10
MH A 459	9810, 8 × 10
MH A 459	15807, 8 × 10
MH A 459	10971, 8 × 10
MH A 460	471, 8 × 10
MH A 460	3753, 8 × 10
MH A 460	9754, 8 × 10
MH A 460	9811, 8 × 10

Medinet Habu (*cont.*)

Nelson Number/Description	Negative, Format
MH A 460	10914, 8 × 10
MH A 460	15811, 8 × 10
MH A 461	469, 8 × 10
MH A 461	3737, 8 × 10
MH A 461	9812, 8 × 10
MH A 461	10915, 8 × 10
MH A 461	15809, 8 × 10
MH A 462	470, 8 × 10
MH A 462	3754, 8 × 10
MH A 462	9813, 8 × 10
MH A 462	10916, 8 × 10
MH A 462	15812, 8 × 10
MH A 463	478, 8 × 10
MH A 463	3896, 5 × 7
MH A 463	11011, 5 × 7
MH A 463	11195, 8 × 10
MH A 464	468, 8 × 10
MH A 464	2403, 8 × 10
MH A 464	3738, 8 × 10
MH A 464	3763, 8 × 10
MH A 464	10972, 8 × 10
MH A 465	467, 8 × 10
MH A 465	3755, 8 × 10
MH A 465	10988, 8 × 10
MH A 466	465, 8 × 10
MH A 466	3566, 8 × 10
MH A 466	10973, 8 × 10
MH A 467	466, 8 × 10
MH A 467	3752, 8 × 10
MH A 467	10989, 8 × 10
MH A 468	444, 8 × 10
MH A 468	10558, 8 × 10
MH A 468	10603, 8 × 10
MH A 468	10619, 8 × 10
MH A 469	445, 8 × 10
MH A 469	9861, 8 × 10
MH A 469	10617, 8 × 10
MH A 469	11193, 8 × 10
MH A 469a	11012, 5 × 7
MH A 470	445, 8 × 10
MH A 470	7497, 8 × 10
MH A 470	10714, 5 × 7
MH A 470	11193, 8 × 10
MH A 470a	10714, 5 × 7
MH A 470a	11193, 8 × 10
MH A 471	446, 8 × 10
MH A 471a	10680, 5 × 7
MH A 471a	11193, 8 × 10
MH A 472	446, 8 × 10
MH A 472	9862, 8 × 10
MH A 472	10621, 8 × 10
MH A 473	8638, 8 × 10
MH A 473	10620, 8 × 10
MH A 474	443, 8 × 10
MH A 474	9863, 8 × 10

Medinet Habu (*cont.*)

Nelson Number/Description	Negative, Format
MH A 474	10620, 8 × 10
MH A 475	502, 8 × 10
MH A 475	7444, 8 × 10
MH A 475	7446, 8 × 10
MH A 475	7959, 8 × 10
MH A 476	506, 8 × 10
MH A 476	788, 8 × 10
MH A 476	7439, 8 × 10
MH A 476	7951, 8 × 10
MH A 476	7986, 8 × 10
MH A 477	506, 8 × 10
MH A 477	788, 8 × 10
MH A 477	7445, 8 × 10
MH A 477	7498, 8 × 10
MH A 477	7951, 8 × 10
MH A 477	7986, 8 × 10
MH A 478	503, 8 × 10
MH A 478	788, 8 × 10
MH A 478	7500, 8 × 10
MH A 478	7960, 8 × 10
MH A 479	503, 8 × 10
MH A 479	504, 8 × 10
MH A 479	788, 8 × 10
MH A 479	7960, 8 × 10
MH A 480	503, 8 × 10
MH A 480	504, 8 × 10
MH A 480	505, 8 × 10
MH A 480	788, 8 × 10
MH A 480	7492, 8 × 10
MH A 480	7957, 8 × 10
MH A 481	503, 8 × 10
MH A 481	504, 8 × 10
MH A 481	507, 8 × 10
MH A 481	788, 8 × 10
MH A 481	7563, 8 × 10
MH A 481	8409, 8 × 10
MH A 482	502, 8 × 10
MH A 482	503, 8 × 10
MH A 482	504, 8 × 10
MH A 482	788, 8 × 10
MH A 482	7444, 8 × 10
MH A 482	7959, 8 × 10
MH A 483	502, 8 × 10
MH A 483	503, 8 × 10
MH A 483	504, 8 × 10
MH A 483	788, 8 × 10
MH A 483	7444, 8 × 10
MH A 483	7959, 8 × 10
MH A 484	503, 8 × 10
MH A 484	504, 8 × 10
MH A 484	788, 8 × 10
MH A 484	7439, 8 × 10
MH A 484	7497, 8 × 10
MH A 484	7951, 8 × 10
MH A 484	7985, 8 × 10

Medinet Habu (*cont.*)

Nelson Number/Description	Negative, Format
MH A 485	503, 8 × 10
MH A 485	504, 8 × 10
MH A 485	506, 8 × 10
MH A 485	788, 8 × 10
MH A 485	7439, 8 × 10
MH A 485	7498, 8 × 10
MH A 485	7951, 8 × 10
MH A 485	7985, 8 × 10
MH A 486	503, 8 × 10
MH A 486	504, 8 × 10
MH A 486	506, 8 × 10
MH A 486	7445, 8 × 10
MH A 486	7498, 8 × 10
MH A 486	7984, 8 × 10
MH A 487	503, 8 × 10
MH A 487	504, 8 × 10
MH A 487	506, 8 × 10
MH A 487	512, 8 × 10
MH A 487	7447, 8 × 10
MH A 487	7984, 8 × 10
MH A 488	503, 8 × 10
MH A 488	504, 8 × 10
MH A 488	511, 8 × 10
MH A 488	7496, 8 × 10
MH A 488	7983, 8 × 10
MH A 489	503, 8 × 10
MH A 489	504, 8 × 10
MH A 489	7501, 8 × 10
MH A 489	7983, 8 × 10
MH A 490	503, 8 × 10
MH A 490	504, 8 × 10
MH A 490	7496, 8 × 10
MH A 490	7983, 8 × 10
MH A 491	503, 8 × 10
MH A 491	504, 8 × 10
MH A 491	511, 8 × 10
MH A 491	512, 8 × 10
MH A 491	7983, 8 × 10
MH A 491a	7501, 8 × 10
MH A 491b	7496, 8 × 10
MH A 492	503, 8 × 10
MH A 492	504, 8 × 10
MH A 492	505, 8 × 10
MH A 492	7492, 8 × 10
MH A 492	7957, 8 × 10
MH A 493	503, 8 × 10
MH A 493	504, 8 × 10
MH A 493	7499, 8 × 10
MH A 493	7957, 8 × 10
MH A 494	503, 8 × 10
MH A 494	7499, 8 × 10
MH A 494	7960, 8 × 10
MH A 495	7500, 8 × 10
MH A 495	7960, 8 × 10
MH A 496	507, 8 × 10

Medinet Habu (*cont.*)

Nelson Number/Description	Negative, Format
MH A 496	10618, 8 × 10
MH A 497	508, 8 × 10
MH A 497	7437, 8 × 10
MH A 497	10618, 8 × 10
MH A 498	10412, 8 × 10
MH A 498	10618, 8 × 10
MH A 498a	10413, 8 × 10
MH A 499	509, 8 × 10
MH A 499	10425, 8 × 10
MH A 499	10618, 8 × 10
MH A 500	7495, 8 × 10
MH A 500	10621, 8 × 10
MH A 501	516, 8 × 10
MH A 501	7538, 5 × 7
MH A 501	10414, 8 × 10
MH A 501	10622, 8 × 10
MH A 502	516, 8 × 10
MH A 502	7490, 8 × 10
MH A 502	10414, 8 × 10
MH A 502	10426, 8 × 10
MH A 502	10427, 8 × 10
MH A 502	10622, 8 × 10
MH A 503	514, 8 × 10
MH A 503	7441, 8 × 10
MH A 503	10623, 8 × 10
MH A 504	515, 8 × 10
MH A 504	7544, 8 × 10
MH A 504	10428, 8 × 10
MH A 504	10429, 8 × 10
MH A 504	10430, 8 × 10
MH A 504	10624, 8 × 10
MH A 505	513, 8 × 10
MH A 505	7442, 8 × 10
MH A 505	10623, 8 × 10
MH A 506	10715, 5 × 7
MH A 507	10716, 5 × 7
MH A 508	10717, 5 × 7
MH A 511	11024, 5 × 7
MH A 511	11194, 8 × 10
MH A 511b	10959, 5 × 7
MH A 511b	11194, 8 × 10
MH A 513a	814, 5 × 7
MH A 513a	11013, 5 × 7
MH A 513a	11197, 8 × 10
MH A 514	825, 5 × 7
MH A 514a	11025, 5 × 7
MH A 514a	11198, 8 × 10
MH A 515	11205, 8 × 10
MH A 520	838, 5 × 7
MH A 520	9875, 5 × 7
MH A 520	11199, 8 × 10
MH A 521	11012, 5 × 7
MH A 521	11197, 8 × 10
MH A 522	544, 8 × 10
MH A 522	545, 8 × 10

Medinet Habu (*cont.*)

Nelson Number/Description	Negative, Format
MH A 522	11197, 8 × 10
MH A 522	807, 5 × 7
MH A 524	11026, 5 × 7
MH A 524	11199, 8 × 10
MH A 525	11013, 5 × 7
MH A 525	11014, 5 × 7
MH A 525	11196, 8 × 10
MH A 526	952, 8 × 10
MH A 526	9864, 8 × 10
MH A 526	11089, 8 × 10
MH A 527	950, 8 × 10
MH A 527	9865, 8 × 10
MH A 527	11090, 8 × 10
MH A 528	837, 5 × 7
MH A 529	424, 8 × 10
MH A 529	8119, 8 × 10
MH A 529	11091, 8 × 10
MH A 529a	11231, 5 × 7
MH A 529c	11252, 8 × 10
MH A 530	424, 8 × 10
MH A 530	8119, 8 × 10
MH A 530	11091, 8 × 10
MH A 531	833, 5 × 7
MH A 531	11015, 5 × 7
MH A 531	11187, 8 × 10
MH A 531b	673, 5 × 7
MH A 532	818, 5 × 7
MH A 532	819, 5 × 7
MH A 532	9853, 8 × 10
MH A 532	11014, 5 × 7
MH A 532	11188, 8 × 10
MH A 534	415, 8 × 10
MH A 534	9876, 5 × 7
MH A 534	11092, 8 × 10
MH A 535	786, 8 × 10
MH A 535	844, 5 × 7
MH A 535	9877, 5 × 7
MH A 535	11197, 8 × 10
MH A 536	11012, 5 × 7
MH A 536	11197, 8 × 10
MH A 536a	845, 5 × 7
MH A 536a	9878, 5 × 7
MH A 536a	11027, 5 × 7
MH A 536a	11197, 8 × 10
MH A 537	11028, 5 × 7
MH A 537	11189, 8 × 10
MH A 538	8700, 5 × 7
MH A 538	9866, 8 × 10
MH A 538	11190, 8 × 10
MH A 539	843, 5 × 7
MH A 539	9880, 5 × 7
MH A 539	11197, 8 × 10
MH A 539a	11027, 5 × 7
MH A 539a	11197, 8 × 10
MH A 540	812, 5 × 7

Medinet Habu (*cont.*)

Nelson Number/Description	Negative, Format
MH A 540	11016, 5 × 7
MH A 540	11131, 5 × 7
MH A 540	11198, 8 × 10
MH A 541	417, 8 × 10
MH A 541	9867, 8 × 10
MH A 541	11093, 8 × 10
MH A 542	9868, 8 × 10
MH A 542	11132, 5 × 7
MH A 542	11198, 8 × 10
MH A 542a	8701, 5 × 7
MH A 542a	10960, 5 × 7
MH A 542a	11017, 5 × 7
MH A 542a	11198, 8 × 10
MH A 543	521, 8 × 10
MH A 543	3866, 8 × 10
MH A 543	11018, 5 × 7
MH A 543	11198, 8 × 10
MH A 544	518, 8 × 10
MH A 544	8692, 8 × 10
MH A 544	8693, 8 × 10
MH A 544	10776, 8 × 10
MH A 544	10777, 8 × 10
MH A 544	11094, 8 × 10
MH A 545	517, 8 × 10
MH A 545	11095, 8 × 10
MH A 546	520, 8 × 10
MH A 546	8640, 8 × 10
MH A 546	8641, 8 × 10
MH A 546	10778, 8 × 10
MH A 546	10779, 8 × 10
MH A 546	11096, 8 × 10
MH A 547	519, 8 × 10
MH A 547	10990, 8 × 10
MH A 548	522, 8 × 10
MH A 548	523, 8 × 10
MH A 548	8642, 8 × 10
MH A 548	10991, 8 × 10
MH A 549	522, 8 × 10
MH A 549	523, 8 × 10
MH A 549	8643, 8 × 10
MH A 549	10991, 8 × 10
MH A 550	525, 8 × 10
MH A 550	11133, 5 × 7
MH A 550	11198, 8 × 10
MH A 551	524, 8 × 10
MH A 551	8644, 8 × 10
MH A 551	11068, 8 × 10
MH A 552	11019, 5 × 7
MH A 552	11097, 8 × 10
MH A 553	8645, 8 × 10
MH A 553	11005, 8 × 10
MH A 554a	822, 5 × 7
MH A 554a	11017, 5 × 7
MH A 554a	813, 5 × 7
MH A 554q	11197, 8 × 10

Medinet Habu (*cont.*)

Nelson Number/Description	Negative, Format
MH A 555	418, 8 × 10
MH A 555	419, 8 × 10
MH A 555	823, 5 × 7
MH A 555	824, 5 × 7
MH A 555	8646, 8 × 10
MH A 555	8647, 8 × 10
MH A 555	9869, 8 × 10
MH A 556	842, 5 × 7
MH A 556	8627, 5 × 7
MH A 556	9875, 5 × 7
MH A 557	8648, 8 × 10
MH A 557	9881, 5 × 7
MH A 557	11235, 8 × 10
MH A 557a	8649, 8 × 10
MH A 557a	9879, 5 × 7
MH A 558	418, 8 × 10
MH A 558	419, 8 × 10
MH A 558	9869, 8 × 10
MH A 558a	810, 5 × 7
MH A 558a	8639, 8 × 10
MH A 558a	11199, 8 × 10
MH A 558b	809, 5 × 7
MH A 558b	8639, 8 × 10
MH A 558b	11199, 8 × 10
MH A 558c	808, 5 × 7
MH A 558c	8639, 8 × 10
MH A 558c	11199, 8 × 10
MH A 558d	8639, 8 × 10
MH A 558d	11199, 8 × 10
MH A 559	670, 5 × 7
MH A 560	671, 5 × 7
MH A 561	805, 5 × 7
MH A 562	669, 5 × 7
MH A 562	9882, 5 × 7
MH A 563	826, 5 × 7
MH A 564	672, 5 × 7
MH A 565	804, 5 × 7
MH A 566	667, 5 × 7
MH A 567	827, 5 × 7
MH A 568	660, 5 × 7
MH A 568	11199, 8 × 10
MH A 569	544, 8 × 10
MH A 569	545, 8 × 10
MH A 569	9883, 5 × 7
MH A 570	664, 5 × 7
MH A 572	663, 5 × 7
MH A 573	806, 5 × 7
MH A 575	811, 5 × 7
MH A 575	10961, 5 × 7
MH A 575	11020, 5 × 7
MH A 575	11196, 8 × 10
MH A 576	665, 5 × 7
MH A 576	11134, 5 × 7
MH A 576	11135, 5 × 7
MH A 576	11200, 8 × 10

Medinet Habu (*cont.*)

Nelson Number/Description	Negative, Format
MH A 577	841, 5 × 7
MH A 577	3026, 8 × 10
MH A 577	9871, 8 × 10
MH A 577	11196, 8 × 10
MH A 578	840, 5 × 7
MH A 578	3026, 8 × 10
MH A 578	9871, 8 × 10
MH A 578	11196, 8 × 10
MH A 579	839, 5 × 7
MH A 579	840, 5 × 7
MH A 579	3026, 8 × 10
MH A 579	9871, 8 × 10
MH A 579	11196, 8 × 10
MH A 580	839, 5 × 7
MH A 580	3026, 8 × 10
MH A 580	9871, 8 × 10
MH A 580	11196, 8 × 10
MH A 581	661, 5 × 7
MH A 581	8699, 5 × 7
MH A 581	11166, 5 × 7
MH A 581	11200, 8 × 10
MH A 582	11200, 8 × 10
MH A 583	666, 5 × 7
MH A 583	11020, 5 × 7
MH A 583	11167, 5 × 7
MH A 583	11200, 8 × 10
MH A 585	832, 5 × 7
MH A 585	9854, 8 × 10
MH A 585	11196, 8 × 10
MH A 586	423, 5 × 7
MH A 586	11136, 5 × 7
MH A 586	11137, 5 × 7
MH A 586	11201, 8 × 10
MH A 587	820, 5 × 7
MH A 587	11016, 5 × 7
MH A 587	11196, 8 × 10
MH A 588	11138, 5 × 7
MH A 588	11139, 5 × 7
MH A 588	11201, 8 × 10
MH A 589	10784, 8 × 10
MH A 589a	3652, 8 × 10
MH A 589b	3572, 8 × 10
MH A 590	3729, 8 × 10
MH A 590	11140, 5 × 7
MH A 590	11201, 8 × 10
MH A 591	10783, 8 × 10
MH A 591a	3651, 8 × 10
MH A 591b	3650, 8 × 10
MH A 592	791, 5 × 7
MH A 592	3723, 8 × 10
MH A 592	11141, 5 × 7
MH A 592	11199, 8 × 10
MH A 592	11201, 8 × 10
MH A 593	448, 8 × 10
MH A 593	3097, 8 × 10

Medinet Habu (*cont.*)

Nelson Number/Description	Negative, Format
MH A 593	3674, 8 × 10
MH A 593	7254, 8 × 10
MH A 594	450, 8 × 10
MH A 594	3675, 8 × 10
MH A 594	10791, 8 × 10
MH A 595	449, 8 × 10
MH A 595	3051, 5 × 7
MH A 595	3098, 8 × 10
MH A 595	3696, 8 × 10
MH A 595	10926, 8 × 10
MH A 596	662, 5 × 7
MH A 596	11142, 5 × 7
MH A 596	11143, 5 × 7
MH A 596	11200, 8 × 10
MH A 597	821, 5 × 7
MH A 597	10962, 5 × 7
MH A 597	11007, 5 × 7
MH A 597	11202, 8 × 10
MH A 597a	10963, 5 × 7
MH A 597a	11021, 5 × 7
MH A 597a	11202, 8 × 10
MH A 598	11144, 5 × 7
MH A 598	11145, 5 × 7
MH A 598	11203, 8 × 10
MH A 599	9871, 8 × 10
MH A 599	11202, 8 × 10
MH A 600	9871, 8 × 10
MH A 600	11202, 8 × 10
MH A 601	531, 8 × 10
MH A 601	11146, 5 × 7
MH A 601	11203, 8 × 10
MH A 602	527, 8 × 10
MH A 602	8650, 8 × 10
MH A 602	10992, 8 × 10
MH A 603	528, 8 × 10
MH A 603	3052, 5 × 7
MH A 603	3565, 8 × 10
MH A 603	10992, 8 × 10
MH A 604	532, 8 × 10
MH A 604	11147, 5 × 7
MH A 604	11148, 5 × 7
MH A 604	11203, 8 × 10
MH A 605	529, 8 × 10
MH A 605	8651, 8 × 10
MH A 605	11069, 8 × 10
MH A 606	530, 8 × 10
MH A 606	3053, 5 × 7
MH A 606	8652, 8 × 10
MH A 606	11069, 8 × 10
MH A 607	546, 8 × 10
MH A 607	11149, 5 × 7
MH A 607	11203, 8 × 10
MH A 608	534, 8 × 10
MH A 608	8695, 8 × 10
MH A 609	533, 8 × 10

Medinet Habu (*cont.*)

Nelson Number/Description	Negative, Format
MH A 609	11556, 5 × 7
MH A 609	11575, 8 × 10
MH A 610	535, 8 × 10
MH A 610	8694, 8 × 10
MH A 610	11070, 8 × 10
MH A 611	10964, 5 × 7
MH A 611	11236, 8 × 10
MH A 612	422, 5 × 7
MH A 612	11150, 5 × 7
MH A 612	11151, 5 × 7
MH A 612	11204, 8 × 10
MH A 613	829, 5 × 7
MH A 613	830, 5 × 7
MH A 613	8653, 8 × 10
MH A 613	9870, 8 × 10
MH A 613	11205, 8 × 10
MH A 614	830, 5 × 7
MH A 614	831, 5 × 7
MH A 614	8653, 8 × 10
MH A 614	9870, 8 × 10
MH A 614	11205, 8 × 10
MH A 615	668, 5 × 7
MH A 615	11168, 5 × 7
MH A 616	10965, 5 × 7
MH A 616	11236, 8 × 10
MH A 617	460, 8 × 10
MH A 617	3837, 8 × 10
MH A 617	10685, 8 × 10
MH A 617	10927, 8 × 10
MH A 617a	11152, 5 × 7
MH A 617a	11153, 5 × 7
MH A 617a	11204, 8 × 10
MH A 618	459, 8 × 10
MH A 618	3838, 8 × 10
MH A 618	10686, 8 × 10
MH A 618	10927, 8 × 10
MH A 619	458, 8 × 10
MH A 619	3836, 8 × 10
MH A 619	10687, 8 × 10
MH A 619	10928, 8 × 10
MH A 620	457, 8 × 10
MH A 620	3828, 8 × 10
MH A 620	10688, 8 × 10
MH A 620	10928, 8 × 10
MH A 621	3730, 8 × 10
MH A 621	10917, 8 × 10
MH A 622	453, 8 × 10
MH A 622	3731, 8 × 10
MH A 622	10689, 8 × 10
MH A 622	10929, 8 × 10
MH A 623	454, 8 × 10
MH A 623	3746, 8 × 10
MH A 623	10690, 8 × 10
MH A 623	10929, 8 × 10
MH A 624	455, 8 × 10

Medinet Habu (*cont.*)

Nelson Number/Description	Negative, Format
MH A 624	3745, 8 × 10
MH A 624	10691, 8 × 10
MH A 624	10930, 8 × 10
MH A 625	456, 8 × 10
MH A 625	3748, 8 × 10
MH A 625	10692, 8 × 10
MH A 625	10930, 8 × 10
MH A 626	10966, 5 × 7
MH A 626	10967, 5 × 7
MH A 626	11236, 8 × 10
MH A 626a	10968, 5 × 7
MH A 626a	10969, 5 × 7
MH A 627	10969, 5 × 7
MH A 627	11236, 8 × 10
MH A 628	8702, 5 × 7
MH A 628	11168, 5 × 7
MH A 628	11205, 8 × 10
MH A 629	9870, 8 × 10
MH A 629	11205, 8 × 10
MH A 630	9870, 8 × 10
MH A 630	11205, 8 × 10
MH A 631	421, 5 × 7
MH A 631	11154, 5 × 7
MH A 631	11155, 5 × 7
MH A 631	11204, 8 × 10
MH A 632	547, 8 × 10
MH A 632	11156, 5 × 7
MH A 632	11204, 8 × 10
MH A 633	3868, 8 × 10
MH A 633	3869, 8 × 10
MH A 633	10974, 8 × 10
MH A 633a	543, 8 × 10
MH A 633a	10693, 8 × 10
MH A 633b	542, 8 × 10
MH A 633b	10694, 8 × 10
MH A 634	3867, 8 × 10
MH A 634	3870, 8 × 10
MH A 634	10975, 8 × 10
MH A 634a	541, 8 × 10
MH A 634a	10695, 8 × 10
MH A 634b	540, 8 × 10
MH A 634b	10696, 8 × 10
MH A 635	10794, 5 × 7
MH A 635	10918, 8 × 10
MH A 636	8696, 8 × 10
MH A 636	10976, 8 × 10
MH A 636a	536, 8 × 10
MH A 636a	10697, 8 × 10
MH A 636b	537, 8 × 10
MH A 636b	10698, 8 × 10
MH A 637	8696, 8 × 10
MH A 637	8697, 8 × 10
MH A 637	10977, 8 × 10
MH A 637a	538, 8 × 10
MH A 637a	10699, 8 × 10

Medinet Habu (*cont.*)

Nelson Number/Description	Negative, Format
MH A 637b	539, 8 × 10
MH A 637b	10700, 8 × 10
MH A 650	6057, 8 × 10
MH A 650	10931, 8 × 10
MH A 650	10993, 8 × 10
MH A 651	3963, 8 × 10
MH A 651	10932, 8 × 10
MH A 651	10994, 8 × 10
MH A 652	428, 8 × 10
MH A 652	429, 8 × 10
MH A 652	3963, 8 × 10
MH A 652	10932, 8 × 10
MH A 652	10994, 8 × 10
MH A 653	428, 8 × 10
MH A 653	429, 8 × 10
MH A 653	3555, 8 × 10
MH A 653	10933, 8 × 10
MH A 653	11259, 8 × 10
MH A 654	428, 8 × 10
MH A 654	429, 8 × 10
MH A 654	3555, 8 × 10
MH A 654	10933, 8 × 10
MH A 654	11259, 8 × 10
MH A 655	428, 8 × 10
MH A 655	429, 8 × 10
MH A 655	3556, 8 × 10
MH A 655	10934, 8 × 10
MH A 655	11260, 8 × 10
MH A 656	428, 8 × 10
MH A 656	429, 8 × 10
MH A 656	3556, 8 × 10
MH A 656	10935, 8 × 10
MH A 656	11260, 8 × 10
MH A 657	428, 8 × 10
MH A 657	429, 8 × 10
MH A 657	3936, 8 × 10
MH A 657	10935, 8 × 10
MH A 657	11261, 8 × 10
MH A 658	3936, 8 × 10
MH A 658	10936, 8 × 10
MH A 658	11261, 8 × 10
MH A 659	3568, 8 × 10
MH A 659	10936, 8 × 10
MH A 659	11465, 8 × 10
MH A 659	15603, 8 × 10
MH A 660	3568, 8 × 10
MH A 660	10937, 8 × 10
MH A 660	11262, 8 × 10
MH A 660	15603, 8 × 10
MH A 661	3935, 8 × 10
MH A 661	10937, 8 × 10
MH A 661	11262, 8 × 10
MH A 662	3935, 8 × 10
MH A 662	10938, 8 × 10
MH A 662	11454, 8 × 10

Medinet Habu (*cont.*)

Nelson Number/Description	Negative, Format
MH A 663	3569, 8 × 10
MH A 663	10938, 8 × 10
MH A 663	11454, 8 × 10
MH A 663	15603, 8 × 10
MH A 664	3569, 8 × 10
MH A 664	10939, 8 × 10
MH A 664	11466, 8 × 10
MH A 664	15603, 8 × 10
MH A 665	3831, 8 × 10
MH A 665	10939, 8 × 10
MH A 665	11466, 8 × 10
MH A 665	15603, 8 × 10
MH A 666	3831, 8 × 10
MH A 666	10940, 8 × 10
MH A 666	11467, 8 × 10
MH A 666	15603, 8 × 10
MH A 667	3567, 8 × 10
MH A 667	10940, 8 × 10
MH A 667	11467, 8 × 10
MH A 667	15603, 8 × 10
MH A 668	3567, 8 × 10
MH A 668	10941, 8 × 10
MH A 668	11455, 8 × 10
MH A 668	15603, 8 × 10
MH A 669	3554, 8 × 10
MH A 669	10941, 8 × 10
MH A 669	10942, 8 × 10
MH A 669	11455, 8 × 10
MH A 669	15603, 8 × 10
MH A 670	433, 8 × 10
MH A 670	435, 8 × 10
MH A 670	3554, 8 × 10
MH A 670	10942, 8 × 10
MH A 670	11456, 8 × 10
MH A 670	15603, 8 × 10
MH A 671	433, 8 × 10
MH A 671	435, 8 × 10
MH A 671	3552, 8 × 10
MH A 671	10943, 8 × 10
MH A 671	11456, 8 × 10
MH A 672	435, 8 × 10
MH A 672	3553, 8 × 10
MH A 672	10944, 8 × 10
MH A 672	11457, 8 × 10
MH A 673	435, 8 × 10
MH A 673	3551, 8 × 10
MH A 673	10945, 8 × 10
MH A 673	11291, 8 × 10
MH A 674	435, 8 × 10
MH A 674	3551, 8 × 10
MH A 674	10946, 8 × 10
MH A 674	11291, 8 × 10
MH A 675	435, 8 × 10
MH A 675	3750, 8 × 10
MH A 675	11263, 8 × 10

Medinet Habu (*cont.*)

Nelson Number/Description	Negative, Format
MH A 675a	3551, 8 × 10
MH A 675a	10946, 8 × 10
MH A 675b	10947, 8 × 10
MH A 676	3750, 8 × 10
MH A 676	10947, 8 × 10
MH A 676	11263, 8 × 10
MH A 677	3750, 8 × 10
MH A 677	10948, 8 × 10
MH A 677	11264, 8 × 10
MH A 678	3751, 8 × 10
MH A 678	10948, 8 × 10
MH A 678	11265, 8 × 10
MH A 679	441, 8 × 10
MH A 679	3751, 8 × 10
MH A 679	10949, 8 × 10
MH A 679	11265, 8 × 10
MH A 679a	10949, 8 × 10
MH A 679a	11265, 8 × 10
MH A 680	441, 8 × 10
MH A 680	6054, 8 × 10
MH A 680	10950, 8 × 10
MH A 680	10995, 8 × 10
MH A 681	6055, 8 × 10
MH A 681	10951, 8 × 10
MH A 681	10996, 8 × 10
MH A 682	3940, 8 × 10
MH A 682	6056, 8 × 10
MH A 682	10797, 5 × 7
MH A 682	11292, 8 × 10
MH A 683	3940, 8 × 10
MH A 683	10798, 5 × 7
MH A 683	11293, 8 × 10
MH A 684	439, 8 × 10
MH A 684	3571, 8 × 10
MH A 684	10799, 5 × 7
MH A 684	11266, 8 × 10
MH A 685	3571, 8 × 10
MH A 685	10799, 5 × 7
MH A 685	11266, 8 × 10
MH A 686	439, 8 × 10
MH A 686	3570, 8 × 10
MH A 686	10800, 5 × 7
MH A 686	11267, 8 × 10
MH A 687	439, 8 × 10
MH A 687	3570, 8 × 10
MH A 687	3939, 8 × 10
MH A 687	10800, 5 × 7
MH A 687	11267, 8 × 10
MH A 688	3939, 8 × 10
MH A 688	11458, 8 × 10
MH A 689	3833, 8 × 10
MH A 689	10952, 8 × 10
MH A 689	11458, 8 × 10
MH A 690	3833, 8 × 10
MH A 690	10952, 8 × 10

Medinet Habu (*cont.*)

Nelson Number/Description	Negative, Format
MH A 690	11459, 8 × 10
MH A 691	3832, 8 × 10
MH A 691	10953, 8 × 10
MH A 691	11459, 8 × 10
MH A 692	436, 8 × 10
MH A 692	437, 8 × 10
MH A 692	3832, 8 × 10
MH A 692	10953, 8 × 10
MH A 692	11294, 8 × 10
MH A 693	436, 8 × 10
MH A 693	437, 8 × 10
MH A 693	3830, 8 × 10
MH A 693	10954, 8 × 10
MH A 693	11294, 8 × 10
MH A 694	436, 8 × 10
MH A 694	437, 8 × 10
MH A 694	3830, 8 × 10
MH A 694	10954, 8 × 10
MH A 694	11294, 8 × 10
MH A 695	436, 8 × 10
MH A 695	437, 8 × 10
MH A 695	3858, 8 × 10
MH A 695	10955, 8 × 10
MH A 695	11460, 8 × 10
MH A 696	436, 8 × 10
MH A 696	437, 8 × 10
MH A 696	3858, 8 × 10
MH A 696	10955, 8 × 10
MH A 696	11460, 8 × 10
MH A 697	436, 8 × 10
MH A 697	437, 8 × 10
MH A 697	3934, 8 × 10
MH A 697	10956, 8 × 10
MH A 697	11461, 8 × 10
MH A 698	436, 8 × 10
MH A 698	437, 8 × 10
MH A 698	3934, 8 × 10
MH A 698	10956, 8 × 10
MH A 698	11461, 8 × 10
MH A 699	436, 8 × 10
MH A 699	437, 8 × 10
MH A 699	3721, 8 × 10
MH A 699	10801, 5 × 7
MH A 699	11462, 8 × 10
MH A 700	436, 8 × 10
MH A 700	437, 8 × 10
MH A 700	3721, 8 × 10
MH A 700	10801, 5 × 7
MH A 700	11462, 8 × 10
MH A 701	436, 8 × 10
MH A 701	437, 8 × 10
MH A 701	3722, 8 × 10
MH A 701	10802, 5 × 7
MH A 701	11463, 8 × 10
MH A 702	436, 8 × 10

Medinet Habu (*cont.*)		Medinet Habu (*cont.*)	
Nelson Number/Description	*Negative, Format*	*Nelson Number/Description*	*Negative, Format*
MH A 702	437, 8 × 10	MH A 731	9457, 8 × 10
MH A 702	880, 8 × 10	MH A 731	10451, 8 × 10
MH A 702	3722, 8 × 10	MH A 732	1515, 8 × 10
MH A 702	10802, 5 × 7	MH A 732	9457, 8 × 10
MH A 702	11463, 8 × 10	MH A 732	10451, 8 × 10
MH A 703	3933, 8 × 10	MH A 733	7422, 8 × 10
MH A 703	10803, 5 × 7	MH A 733	11519, 5 × 7
MH A 703	11268, 8 × 10	MH A 733	11539, 8 × 10
MH A 704	3933, 8 × 10	MH A 734	10795, 5 × 7
MH A 704	10803, 5 × 7	MH A 734	11520, 5 × 7
MH A 704	11268, 8 × 10	MH A 734	11521, 5 × 7
MH A 705	3933, 8 × 10	MH A 734	11540, 8 × 10
MH A 705	10804, 5 × 7	MH A 735	10796, 5 × 7
MH A 705	11268, 8 × 10	MH A 735	11522, 5 × 7
MH A 706	7468, 5 × 7	MH A 735	11541, 8 × 10
MH A 706	10568, 8 × 10	MH A 736	11448, 5 × 7
MH A 707	7466, 5 × 7	MH A 736	11523, 5 × 7
MH A 707	11516, 5 × 7	MH A 736	11524, 5 × 7
MH A 707	11538, 8 × 10	MH A 736	11541, 8 × 10
MH A 710	8383, 8 × 10	MH A 740	2671, 11 × 14
MH A 710	10568, 8 × 10	MH A 741	34, 5 × 7
MH A 711a	2034, 8 × 10	MH A 741	2675, 11 × 14
MH A 712	7478, 8 × 10	MH A 742	2672, 11 × 14
MH A 712	10568, 8 × 10	MH A 742	2673, 11 × 14
MH A 713	10454, 8 × 10	MH A 743	47, 5 × 7
MH A 713	10568, 8 × 10	MH A 743	2674, 11 × 14
MH A 714	7467, 5 × 7	MH A 802	13422, 5 × 7
MH A 714	11517, 5 × 7	MH A 804	917-a, 8 × 10
MH A 714	11538, 8 × 10	MH A 805	1518, 8 × 10
MH A 718	9458, 8 × 10	MH A 805	1524, 8 × 10
MH A 719	1217, 8 × 10	MH A 807	903, 8 × 10
MH A 719	9458, 8 × 10	MH A 807	1521, 8 × 10
MH A 719	10450, 8 × 10	MH A 807	1522, 8 × 10
MH A 720	1512, 8 × 10	MH A 807	1523, 8 × 10
MH A 720	9458, 8 × 10	MH A 808	903, 8 × 10
MH A 720	10450, 8 × 10	MH A 808	1521, 8 × 10
MH A 721	8711, 5 × 7	MH A 808	1522, 8 × 10
MH A 724	9458, 8 × 10	MH A 808	1523, 8 × 10
MH A 724	10450, 8 × 10	MH A 809	903, 8 × 10
MH A 724a	10127, 8 × 10	MH A 809	1521, 8 × 10
MH A 724a	10250, 8 × 10	MH A 809	1522, 8 × 10
MH A 725	9458, 8 × 10	MH A 809	1523, 8 × 10
MH A 725	10450, 8 × 10	MH A 810	903, 8 × 10
MH A 725a	6545, 8 × 10	MH A 810	13623, 5 × 7
MH A 725c	11252, 8 × 10	MH A 814	146, 8 × 10
MH A 728	1514, 8 × 10	MH A 814	147, 8 × 10
MH A 728	9457, 8 × 10	MH A 815	13593, 5 × 7
MH A 728	10451, 8 × 10	MH A 816	10703, 8 × 10
MH A 729	1516, 8 × 10	MH A 816	10726, 8 × 10
MH A 729	9457, 8 × 10	MH A 817	10703, 8 × 10
MH A 729	10451, 8 × 10	MH A 818	10785, 8 × 10
MH A 730	7423, 8 × 10	MH A 819a	3839-a, 5 × 7
MH A 730	11518, 5 × 7	MH A 819a	3839-b, 5 × 7
MH A 730	11539, 8 × 10	MH A 819b	3839-a, 5 × 7
MH A 731	1517, 8 × 10	MH A 819b	3839-b, 5 × 7

Medinet Habu (*cont.*)

Nelson Number/Description	Negative, Format
MH A 819c	3840-a, 5 × 7
MH A 819c	3840-b, 5 × 7
MH A 819d	3840-a, 5 × 7
MH A 819d	3840-b, 5 × 7
MH A 819e	3845-a, 5 × 7
MH A 819e	3845-b, 5 × 7
MH A 819f	3845-a, 5 × 7
MH A 819f	3845-b, 5 × 7
MH A 819g	3844-a, 5 × 7
MH A 819g	3844-b, 5 × 7
MH A 819h	3844-a, 5 × 7
MH A 819h	3844-b, 5 × 7
MH A 820	10726, 8 × 10
MH A 820	13372, 5 × 7
MH A 820a	3804-a, 5 × 7
MH A 820b	3804-b, 5 × 7
MH A 820c	3805-b, 5 × 7
MH A 820d	3805-a, 5 × 7
MH A 821	11269, 8 × 10
MH A 822	901, 8 × 10
MH A 822	6269, 8 × 10
MH A 822	10704, 8 × 10
MH A 822	13329, 5 × 7
MH A 822	13369, 5 × 7
MH A 823	10411, 8 × 10
MH A 823	13369, 5 × 7
MH A 823a	142, 5 × 7
MH A 823a	143, 5 × 7
MH A 823a	3807-b, 5 × 7
MH A 823a	6268, 8 × 10
MH A 823b	140, 5 × 7
MH A 823b	141, 5 × 7
MH A 823b	1250, 8 × 10
MH A 823b	3806-b, 5 × 7
MH A 823c	142, 5 × 7
MH A 823c	143, 5 × 7
MH A 823c	3807-a, 5 × 7
MH A 823c	6268, 8 × 10
MH A 823d	140, 5 × 7
MH A 823d	141, 5 × 7
MH A 823d	1251, 8 × 10
MH A 823d	3808-a, 5 × 7
MH A 823e	10191, 5 × 7
MH A 823f	10191, 5 × 7
MH A 824	3808-b, 5 × 7
MH A 824	6270, 8 × 10
MH A 824	6290, 5 × 7
MH A 824	10704, 8 × 10
MH A 824	13369, 5 × 7
MH A 824	902, 8 × 10
MH A 825	3806-a, 5 × 7
MH A 825	11269, 8 × 10
MH A 825	902, 8 × 10
MH A 826	10726, 8 × 10
MH A 826	13420, 5 × 7

Medinet Habu (*cont.*)

Nelson Number/Description	Negative, Format
MH A 827c	6272, 8 × 10
MH A 828	10785, 8 × 10
MH A 829	6272, 8 × 10
MH A 830	10705, 8 × 10
MH A 831	10705, 8 × 10
MH A 831a	3810-a, 5 × 7
MH A 831b	3810-b, 5 × 7
MH A 831c	3812-b, 5 × 7
MH A 831d	3811-a, 5 × 7
MH A 832	10705, 8 × 10
MH A 832	10853, 5 × 7
MH A 833	2102, 8 × 10
MH A 833a	8481, 8 × 10
MH A 833b	9080, 5 × 7
MH A 833c	9079, 5 × 7
MH A 833d	9078, 5 × 7
MH A 834	6401, 8 × 10
MH A 834	6541, 8 × 10
MH A 834a	3809-b, 5 × 7
MH A 834c	3812-a, 5 × 7
MH A 834d	3811-b, 5 × 7
MH A 835	6291, 5 × 7
MH A 837	3809-a, 5 × 7
MH A 837	6271, 8 × 10
MH A 837	11206, 8 × 10
MH A 838	11247, 8 × 10
MH A 838	13336, 5 × 7
MH A 839	10814, 5 × 7
MH A 839	10815, 5 × 7
MH A 839	11247, 8 × 10
MH A 839	11248, 8 × 10
MH A 839	13336, 5 × 7
MH A 840	10857, 5 × 7
MH A 840	11246, 8 × 10
MH A 840	11247, 8 × 10
MH A 840	13336, 5 × 7
MH A 841	10816, 5 × 7
MH A 841	10817, 5 × 7
MH A 841	11247, 8 × 10
MH A 841	13336, 5 × 7
MH A 842	11098, 8 × 10
MH A 843	3584, 8 × 10
MH A 843	11098, 8 × 10
MH A 843	15197, 5 × 7
MH A 844	196, 5 × 7
MH A 844	3582, 8 × 10
MH A 844	11098, 8 × 10
MH A 845	195, 5 × 7
MH A 845	3581, 8 × 10
MH A 845	11098, 8 × 10
MH A 845	15198, 5 × 7
MH A 846	194, 5 × 7
MH A 846	3579, 8 × 10
MH A 846	11098, 8 × 10
MH A 846	13619, 5 × 7

Medinet Habu (*cont.*)

Nelson Number/Description	Negative, Format
MH A 846	15199, 5 × 7
MH A 847	193, 5 × 7
MH A 847	3573, 8 × 10
MH A 847	11098, 8 × 10
MH A 847	13619, 5 × 7
MH A 847	15200, 5 × 7
MH A 848	192, 5 × 7
MH A 848	3574, 8 × 10
MH A 848	11098, 8 × 10
MH A 848	13619, 5 × 7
MH A 848	15201, 5 × 7
MH A 849	191, 5 × 7
MH A 849	3742, 8 × 10
MH A 849	11098, 8 × 10
MH A 849	15202, 5 × 7
MH A 850	3585, 8 × 10
MH A 850	11098, 8 × 10
MH A 850	11237, 8 × 10
MH A 850	15203, 5 × 7
MH A 851	190, 5 × 7
MH A 851	197, 5 × 7
MH A 851	7424, 8 × 10
MH A 851	11191, 8 × 10
MH A 852	180, 8 × 10
MH A 852	792, 8 × 10
MH A 852	3575, 8 × 10
MH A 852	11191, 8 × 10
MH A 852	15204, 5 × 7
MH A 853	180, 8 × 10
MH A 853	792, 8 × 10
MH A 853	3576, 8 × 10
MH A 853	11191, 8 × 10
MH A 853	15205, 5 × 7
MH A 854	180, 8 × 10
MH A 854	793, 8 × 10
MH A 854	3577, 8 × 10
MH A 854	11191, 8 × 10
MH A 854	15206, 5 × 7
MH A 855	793, 8 × 10
MH A 855	3586, 8 × 10
MH A 855	10901, 5 × 7
MH A 856	181, 8 × 10
MH A 856	793, 8 × 10
MH A 856	3578, 8 × 10
MH A 856	11191, 8 × 10
MH A 856	15207, 5 × 7
MH A 857	181, 8 × 10
MH A 857	794, 8 × 10
MH A 857	3580, 8 × 10
MH A 857	11191, 8 × 10
MH A 857	15208, 5 × 7
MH A 858	181, 8 × 10
MH A 858	794, 8 × 10
MH A 858	3583, 8 × 10
MH A 858	11191, 8 × 10

Medinet Habu (*cont.*)

Nelson Number/Description	Negative, Format
MH A 858	15209, 5 × 7
MH A 859	7463, 8 × 10
MH A 859	11191, 8 × 10
MH A 859	11237, 8 × 10
MH A 860	201, 5 × 7
MH A 860	202, 5 × 7
MH A 860	3626, 5 × 7
MH A 860a	1261, 8 × 10
MH A 860a	9954, 8 × 10
MH A 860b	6237, 8 × 10
MH A 860c	7554, 8 × 10
MH A 860c	10258, 8 × 10
MH A 861	209, 8 × 10
MH A 861	210, 8 × 10
MH A 861a	1262, 8 × 10
MH A 861a	2226, 8 × 10
MH A 861a	9954, 8 × 10
MH A 861c	7553, 8 × 10
MH A 861c	7555, 8 × 10
MH A 861c	10258, 8 × 10
MH A 862	117, 5 × 7
MH A 862a	9954, 8 × 10
MH A 862c	6402, 8 × 10
MH A 862c	10258, 8 × 10
MH A 863	115, 5 × 7
MH A 863a	1261, 8 × 10
MH A 863a	1262, 8 × 10
MH A 863a	9954, 8 × 10
MH A 863b	10704, 8 × 10
MH A 863c	7542, 8 × 10
MH A 863c	10258, 8 × 10
MH A 865	10850, 5 × 7
MH A 865	10851, 5 × 7
MH A 865	10852, 5 × 7
MH A 865	10853, 5 × 7
MH A 865	10854, 5 × 7
MH A 865	10855, 5 × 7
MH A 865	11245, 8 × 10
MH A 866	10855, 5 × 7
MH A 866	11254, 8 × 10
MH A 866a	3842-a, 5 × 7
MH A 866a	3842-b, 5 × 7
MH A 866b	3842-a, 5 × 7
MH A 866b	3842-b, 5 × 7
MH A 866c	3843-a, 5 × 7
MH A 866c	3843-b, 5 × 7
MH A 866d	3843-a, 5 × 7
MH A 866d	3843-b, 5 × 7
MH A 867	10855, 5 × 7
MH A 867	10856, 5 × 7
MH A 867	10857, 5 × 7
MH A 867	10858, 5 × 7
MH A 867	11245, 8 × 10
MH A 868	11254, 8 × 10
MH A 868a	3888-a, 5 × 7

Medinet Habu (*cont.*)

Nelson Number/Description	Negative, Format
MH A 868a	3888-b, 5 × 7
MH A 868b	3886-a, 5 × 7
MH A 868b	3886-b, 5 × 7
MH A 868c	3886-a, 5 × 7
MH A 868c	3886-b, 5 × 7
MH A 868d	3888-a, 5 × 7
MH A 868d	3888-b, 5 × 7
MH A 869	247, 5 × 7
MH A 869	1259, 8 × 10
MH A 869	6271, 8 × 10
MH A 869	11206, 8 × 10
MH A 869a	6271, 8 × 10
MH A 869a	11206, 8 × 10
MH A 870	11249, 8 × 10
MH A 870	11250, 8 × 10
MH A 870	13356, 5 × 7
MH A 870	13621, 5 × 7
MH A 871	10818, 5 × 7
MH A 871	10819, 5 × 7
MH A 871	10820, 5 × 7
MH A 871	10821, 5 × 7
MH A 871	11250, 8 × 10
MH A 871	13356, 5 × 7
MH A 872	10859, 5 × 7
MH A 872	10860, 5 × 7
MH A 872	10861, 5 × 7
MH A 872	10862, 5 × 7
MH A 872	11246, 8 × 10
MH A 873	11232, 5 × 7
MH A 873	11254, 8 × 10
MH A 873a	11232, 5 × 7
MH A 873b	11232, 5 × 7
MH A 873c	3841-a, 5 × 7
MH A 873c	3841-b, 5 × 7
MH A 873d	3841-a, 5 × 7
MH A 873d	3841-b, 5 × 7
MH A 874	11254, 8 × 10
MH A 874a	11233, 5 × 7
MH A 874b	11233, 5 × 7
MH A 874c	3889-a, 5 × 7
MH A 874c	3889-b, 5 × 7
MH A 874d	3887-a, 5 × 7
MH A 874d	3887-b, 5 × 7
MH A 874e	3889-a, 5 × 7
MH A 874e	3889-b, 5 × 7
MH A 874f	3887-a, 5 × 7
MH A 874f	3887-b, 5 × 7
MH A 875	10863, 5 × 7
MH A 875	10864, 5 × 7
MH A 875	10865, 5 × 7
MH A 875	10866, 5 × 7
MH A 875	10867, 5 × 7
MH A 875	11246, 8 × 10
MH A 876	11248, 8 × 10
MH A 877	10822, 5 × 7

Medinet Habu (*cont.*)

Nelson Number/Description	Negative, Format
MH A 877	10823, 5 × 7
MH A 877	10824, 5 × 7
MH A 877	10825, 5 × 7
MH A 877	13619, 5 × 7
MH A 877a	11248, 8 × 10
MH A 877a	11249, 8 × 10
MH A 877b	11249, 8 × 10
MH A 878	180, 8 × 10
MH A 878	198, 5 × 7
MH A 878	200, 8 × 10
MH A 878	10850, 5 × 7
MH A 878	10868, 5 × 7
MH A 878	10869, 5 × 7
MH A 878	10870, 5 × 7
MH A 878	10871, 5 × 7
MH A 878	10872, 5 × 7
MH A 878	10873, 5 × 7
MH A 878	11071, 8 × 10
MH A 878	11244, 8 × 10
MH A 878	13336, 5 × 7
MH A 878	13359, 5 × 7
MH A 878	13619, 5 × 7
MH A 879	181, 8 × 10
MH A 879	198, 5 × 7
MH A 879	10854, 5 × 7
MH A 879	10873, 5 × 7
MH A 879	10874, 5 × 7
MH A 879	10875, 5 × 7
MH A 879	10881, 5 × 7
MH A 879	11071, 8 × 10
MH A 879	11244, 8 × 10
MH A 879	11245, 8 × 10
MH A 879	13336, 5 × 7
MH A 879	13356, 5 × 7
MH A 880	3804-a, 5 × 7
MH A 880	3804-b, 5 × 7
MH A 880	11255, 8 × 10
MH A 880c	3805-a, 5 × 7
MH A 880c	3805-b, 5 × 7
MH A 880d	3805-a, 5 × 7
MH A 880d	3805-b, 5 × 7
MH A 881	10876, 5 × 7
MH A 881	10877, 5 × 7
MH A 881	10878, 5 × 7
MH A 881	11101, 8 × 10
MH A 882	10879, 5 × 7
MH A 882	10880, 5 × 7
MH A 882	11101, 8 × 10
MH A 883	11255, 8 × 10
MH A 883a	3807-a, 5 × 7
MH A 883a	3807-b, 5 × 7
MH A 883b	3806-a, 5 × 7
MH A 883b	3806-b, 5 × 7
MH A 883c	3807-a, 5 × 7
MH A 883c	3807-b, 5 × 7

Medinet Habu (*cont.*)

Nelson Number/Description	Negative, Format
MH A 883d	3808-a, 5 × 7
MH A 883d	3808-b, 5 × 7
MH A 884	10881, 5 × 7
MH A 884	10882, 5 × 7
MH A 884	10883, 5 × 7
MH A 884	10884, 5 × 7
MH A 884	10885, 5 × 7
MH A 884	11101, 8 × 10
MH A 885	11099, 8 × 10
MH A 886	9726, 8 × 10
MH A 886	9727, 8 × 10
MH A 886	9728, 8 × 10
MH A 886	9729, 8 × 10
MH A 886a	9949, 8 × 10
MH A 886a	9950, 8 × 10
MH A 886b	9949, 8 × 10
MH A 886b	9950, 8 × 10
MH A 886e	9951, 8 × 10
MH A 887	10880, 5 × 7
MH A 887	10892, 5 × 7
MH A 887	11250, 8 × 10
MH A 888	11250, 8 × 10
MH A 889	11255, 8 × 10
MH A 889a	3806-a, 5 × 7
MH A 889a	3806-b, 5 × 7
MH A 889a	3808-a, 5 × 7
MH A 889a	3808-b, 5 × 7
MH A 890	10885, 5 × 7
MH A 890	10886, 5 × 7
MH A 890	11100, 8 × 10
MH A 891	3799, 5 × 7
MH A 891	11206, 8 × 10
MH A 892	10876, 5 × 7
MH A 892	11100, 8 × 10
MH A 893	246, 5 × 7
MH A 893	3744, 8 × 10
MH A 893	11206, 8 × 10
MH A 894	11100, 8 × 10
MH A 896	10863, 5 × 7
MH A 896	10886, 5 × 7
MH A 896	11100, 8 × 10
MH A 897	11250, 8 × 10
MH A 898	10890, 5 × 7
MH A 898	11250, 8 × 10
MH A 899	11255, 8 × 10
MH A 899a	3810-a, 5 × 7
MH A 899a	3810-b, 5 × 7
MH A 899b	3810-a, 5 × 7
MH A 899b	3810-b, 5 × 7
MH A 899c	3812-a, 5 × 7
MH A 899c	3812-b, 5 × 7
MH A 899d	3811-a, 5 × 7
MH A 899d	3811-b, 5 × 7
MH A 900	10878, 5 × 7
MH A 900	10887, 5 × 7

Medinet Habu (*cont.*)

Nelson Number/Description	Negative, Format
MH A 900	10888, 5 × 7
MH A 900	10889, 5 × 7
MH A 900	11100, 8 × 10
MH A 901	10889, 5 × 7
MH A 901	10890, 5 × 7
MH A 901	10891, 5 × 7
MH A 901	11100, 8 × 10
MH A 902	11255, 8 × 10
MH A 902a	3809-b, 5 × 7
MH A 902a	3809-a, 5 × 7
MH A 902b	3803-a, 5 × 7
MH A 902b	3803-b, 5 × 7
MH A 902c	3812-a, 5 × 7
MH A 902c	3812-b, 5 × 7
MH A 902d	3811-a, 5 × 7
MH A 902d	3811-b, 5 × 7
MH A 903	10892, 5 × 7
MH A 903	10893, 5 × 7
MH A 903	10894, 5 × 7
MH A 903	10895, 5 × 7
MH A 903	11100, 8 × 10
MH A 903	11101, 8 × 10
MH A 905	9730, 8 × 10
MH A 905	9731, 8 × 10
MH A 905	9732, 8 × 10
MH A 905	9733, 8 × 10
MH A 905a	10255, 8 × 10
MH A 905b	10255, 8 × 10
MH A 905c	10256, 8 × 10
MH A 905d	10256, 8 × 10
MH A 906	11255, 8 × 10
MH A 906a	3803-a, 5 × 7
MH A 906a	3803-b, 5 × 7
MH A 906b	3809-a, 5 × 7
MH A 906b	3809-b, 5 × 7
MH A Col. 001	209, 8 × 10
MH A Col. 001	210, 8 × 10
MH A Col. 001	6228, 8 × 10
MH A Col. 001	6334, 8 × 10
MH A Col. 001	6351, 5 × 7
MH A Col. 001	6353, 5 × 7
MH A Col. 001	10249, 8 × 10
MH A Col. 001E	3616, 5 × 7
MH A Col. 001E	3630, 5 × 7
MH A Col. 001E	3882, 5 × 7
MH A Col. 001W	3619, 5 × 7
MH A Col. 001W	3630, 5 × 7
MH A Col. 001W	3882, 5 × 7
MH A Col. 001W	6229, 8 × 10
MH A Col. 002	207, 5 × 7
MH A Col. 002	211, 8 × 10
MH A Col. 002	212, 8 × 10
MH A Col. 002	6335, 8 × 10
MH A Col. 002	6352, 5 × 7
MH A Col. 002	6353, 5 × 7

Medinet Habu (*cont.*)

Nelson Number/Description	Negative, Format
MH A Col. 002	6405, 5 × 7
MH A Col. 002	10249, 8 × 10
MH A Col. 002E	3617, 5 × 7
MH A Col. 002W	3620, 5 × 7
MH A Col. 002W	3880, 5 × 7
MH A Col. 002W	6231, 8 × 10
MH A Col. 003	205, 5 × 7
MH A Col. 003	206, 5 × 7
MH A Col. 003	211, 8 × 10
MH A Col. 003	212, 8 × 10
MH A Col. 003	6265, 8 × 10
MH A Col. 003	6354, 5 × 7
MH A Col. 003	10249, 8 × 10
MH A Col. 003N	3795, 5 × 7
MH A Col. 003E	3880, 5 × 7
MH A Col. 003W	3625, 5 × 7
MH A Col. 003W	3881, 5 × 7
MH A Col. 003W	6232, 8 × 10
MH A Col. 004	205, 5 × 7
MH A Col. 004	206, 5 × 7
MH A Col. 004	213, 8 × 10
MH A Col. 004	214, 8 × 10
MH A Col. 004	6234, 8 × 10
MH A Col. 004	6235, 8 × 10
MH A Col. 004	6355, 5 × 7
MH A Col. 004	10249, 8 × 10
MH A Col. 004N	3796, 5 × 7
MH A Col. 004E	3622, 5 × 7
MH A Col. 004E	3881, 5 × 7
MH A Col. 004W	3629, 5 × 7
MH A Col. 004W	3879, 5 × 7
MH A Col. 005	203, 5 × 7
MH A Col. 005	204, 5 × 7
MH A Col. 005	213, 8 × 10
MH A Col. 005	214, 8 × 10
MH A Col. 005	6356, 5 × 7
MH A Col. 005	6360, 5 × 7
MH A Col. 005	10249, 8 × 10
MH A Col. 005E	3618, 5 × 7
MH A Col. 005E	3879, 5 × 7
MH A Col. 005E	6233, 8 × 10
MH A Col. 005W	3628, 5 × 7
MH A Col. 005W	3883, 5 × 7
MH A Col. 005W	6236, 8 × 10
MH A Col. 006	203, 5 × 7
MH A Col. 006	204, 5 × 7
MH A Col. 006	6077, 8 × 10
MH A Col. 006	6262, 8 × 10
MH A Col. 006	6263, 8 × 10
MH A Col. 006	6264, 8 × 10
MH A Col. 006	6357, 5 × 7
MH A Col. 006	6358, 5 × 7
MH A Col. 006	10249, 8 × 10
MH A Col. 006N	3793, 5 × 7
MH A Col. 006E	3624, 5 × 7

Medinet Habu (*cont.*)

Nelson Number/Description	Negative, Format
MH A Col. 006E	3883, 5 × 7
MH A Col. 006E	6230, 8 × 10
MH A Col. 006W	215, 8 × 10
MH A Col. 006W	3627, 5 × 7
MH A Col. 006W	3885, 5 × 7
MH A Col. 007	201, 5 × 7
MH A Col. 007	202, 5 × 7
MH A Col. 007	6078, 8 × 10
MH A Col. 007	6358, 5 × 7
MH A Col. 007	6359, 5 × 7
MH A Col. 007	6403, 8 × 10
MH A Col. 007	10249, 8 × 10
MH A Col. 007N	3792, 5 × 7
MH A Col. 007N	3798, 5 × 7
MH A Col. 007E	3621, 5 × 7
MH A Col. 007E	3623, 5 × 7
MH A Col. 007E	3885, 5 × 7
MH A Col. 007E	6526, 8 × 10
MH A Col. 007W	3884, 5 × 7
MH A Col. 008	10787, 8 × 10
MH A Col. 009	10787, 8 × 10
MH A Col. 010	10787, 8 × 10
MH A Col. 010	11240, 8 × 10
MH A Col. 011	2187, 8 × 10
MH A Col. 011	2188, 8 × 10
MH A Col. 011	10787, 8 × 10
MH A Col. 012	10787, 8 × 10
MH A Col. 013	10787, 8 × 10
MH A Col. 014	10787, 8 × 10
MH A Col. 015	10787, 8 × 10
MH A Col. 016a	10826, 5 × 7
MH A Col. 016a	10830, 5 × 7
MH A Col. 016b	10826, 5 × 7
MH A Col. 016b	10827, 5 × 7
MH A Col. 016c	10826, 5 × 7
MH A Col. 016d	10826, 5 × 7
MH A Col. 016e	10826, 5 × 7
MH A Col. 016e	10827, 5 × 7
MH A Col. 016e	10828, 5 × 7
MH A Col. 016f	10826, 5 × 7
MH A Col. 016f	10829, 5 × 7
MH A Col. 016g	10826, 5 × 7
MH A Col. 016g	10827, 5 × 7
MH A Col. 016h	10826, 5 × 7
MH A Col. 016i	10826, 5 × 7
MH A Col. 016j	10826, 5 × 7
MH A Col. 016j	10830, 5 × 7
MH A Col. 017a	10830, 5 × 7
MH A Col. 017b	10831, 5 × 7
MH A Col. 017c	10833, 5 × 7
MH A Col. 017d	10829, 5 × 7
MH A Col. 017e	10832, 5 × 7
MH A Col. 017f	10832, 5 × 7
MH A Col. 017g	10833, 5 × 7
MH A Col. 017h	10831, 5 × 7

Medinet Habu (*cont.*)

Nelson Number/Description	Negative, Format
MH A Col. 017j	10830, 5 × 7
MH A Col. 017S	3884, 5 × 7
MH A Col. 018b	10834, 5 × 7
MH A Col. 018c	10833, 5 × 7
MH A Col. 018d	10835, 5 × 7
MH A Col. 018e	10821, 5 × 7
MH A Col. 018f	10835, 5 × 7
MH A Col. 018g	10833, 5 × 7
MH A Col. 018h	10834, 5 × 7
MH A Col. 019a	10836, 5 × 7
MH A Col. 019b	10837, 5 × 7
MH A Col. 019c	10836, 5 × 7
MH A Col. 019d	10958, 5 × 7
MH A Col. 019e	10838, 5 × 7
MH A Col. 019f	10838, 5 × 7
MH A Col. 019g	10836, 5 × 7
MH A Col. 019h	10837, 5 × 7
MH A Col. 019j	10839, 5 × 7
MH A Col. 020	13356, 5 × 7
MH A Col. 020	13449, 5 × 7
MH A Col. 021	13356, 5 × 7
MH A Col. 021	13449, 5 × 7
MH A Col. 022	13356, 5 × 7
MH A Col. 022	13449, 5 × 7
MH A Col. 024	10902, 5 × 7
MH A Col. 025	10902, 5 × 7
MH A Col. 025	10904, 5 × 7
MH A Col. 025	10903, 5 × 7
MH A Col. 026	10903, 5 × 7
MH A Col. 026	10904, 5 × 7
MH A Col. 027	10903, 5 × 7
MH A Col. 027	10904, 5 × 7
MH A Col. 027	10905, 5 × 7
MH A Col. 027	10906, 5 × 7
MH A Col. 028	11129, 5 × 7
MH A Col. 028	11207, 8 × 10
MH A Col. 028a	10727, 5 × 7
MH A Col. 028a	10728, 5 × 7
MH A Col. 028a	10729, 5 × 7
MH A Col. 028b	10730, 5 × 7
MH A Col. 028b	10731, 5 × 7
MH A Col. 029a	7527, 5 × 7
MH A Col. 029a	10732, 5 × 7
MH A Col. 029a	10733, 5 × 7
MH A Col. 029a	10734, 5 × 7
MH A Col. 029b	10735, 5 × 7
MH A Col. 029b	10736, 5 × 7
MH A Col. 030a	10737, 5 × 7
MH A Col. 030a	10738, 5 × 7
MH A Col. 030a	10739, 5 × 7
MH A Col. 030b	10740, 5 × 7
MH A Col. 030b	10741, 5 × 7
MH A Col. 031	3874, 8 × 10
MH A Col. 031a	10742, 5 × 7
MH A Col. 031a	10743, 5 × 7

Medinet Habu (*cont.*)

Nelson Number/Description	Negative, Format
MH A Col. 031a	10744, 5 × 7
MH A Col. 031a	10745, 5 × 7
MH A Col. 031a	10746, 5 × 7
MH A Col. 031a	7528, 5 × 7
MH A Col. 031b	7991, 5 × 7
MH A Col. 031b	10747, 5 × 7
MH A Col. 031b	10748, 5 × 7
MH A Col. 032 d	10841, 5 × 7
MH A Col. 032b	10840, 5 × 7
MH A Col. 032c	10842, 5 × 7
MH A Col. 032e	10841, 5 × 7
MH A Col. 032e	10843, 5 × 7
MH A Col. 032f	10828, 5 × 7
MH A Col. 032f	10843, 5 × 7
MH A Col. 032g	10842, 5 × 7
MH A Col. 032h	10840, 5 × 7
MH A Col. 033a	10845, 5 × 7
MH A Col. 033c	10842, 5 × 7
MH A Col. 033d	10844, 5 × 7
MH A Col. 033g	10842, 5 × 7
MH A Col. 033j	10845, 5 × 7
MH A Col. 034a	10845, 5 × 7
MH A Col. 034d	10846, 5 × 7
MH A Col. 034e	10846, 5 × 7
MH A Col. 034f	10844, 5 × 7
MH A Col. 034g	10839, 5 × 7
MH A Col. 034h	10849, 5 × 7
MH A Col. 034j	10845, 5 × 7
MH A Col. 035c	10839, 5 × 7
MH A Col. 035d	10847, 5 × 7
MH A Col. 035e	10848, 5 × 7
MH A Col. 035f	10847, 5 × 7
MH A Col. 035g	10839, 5 × 7
MH A Col. 035h	10849, 5 × 7
MH A Col. 036	13359, 5 × 7
MH A Col. 037	11162, 5 × 7
MH A Col. 037	13359, 5 × 7
MH A Col. 038	13359, 5 × 7
MH A Col. 041	4009, 5 × 7
MH A Col. 041	10902, 5 × 7
MH A Col. 042	10902, 5 × 7
MH A Col. 042	10908, 5 × 7
MH A Col. 042	10909, 5 × 7
MH A Col. 043	10907, 5 × 7
MH A Col. 043	10908, 5 × 7
MH A Col. 043	10909, 5 × 7
MH A Col. 044	10907, 5 × 7
MH A Col. 044	10908, 5 × 7
MH A Col. 044	10909, 5 × 7
MH A Col. 045a	10749, 5 × 7
MH A Col. 045a	10750, 5 × 7
MH A Col. 045a	10751, 5 × 7
MH A Col. 045b	10752, 5 × 7
MH A Col. 045b	10753, 5 × 7
MH A Col. 046	11128, 5 × 7

Medinet Habu (*cont.*)

Nelson Number/Description	Negative, Format
MH A Col. 046	11207, 8 × 10
MH A Col. 046a	10754, 5 × 7
MH A Col. 046a	10755, 5 × 7
MH A Col. 046a	10756, 5 × 7
MH A Col. 046b	10757, 5 × 7
MH A Col. 046b	10758, 5 × 7
MH A Col. 047a	10759, 5 × 7
MH A Col. 047a	10760, 5 × 7
MH A Col. 047a	10761, 5 × 7
MH A Col. 047b	10762, 5 × 7
MH A Col. 047b	10763, 5 × 7
MH A Col. 048a	10764, 5 × 7
MH A Col. 048a	10765, 5 × 7
MH A Col. 048a	10766, 5 × 7
MH A Col. 048b	7536, 5 × 7
MH A Col. 048b	10767, 5 × 7
MH A Col. 048b	10768, 5 × 7
MH A Col. 051	11157, 5 × 7
MH A Col. 051	11207, 8 × 10
MH A Col. 053	11241, 8 × 10
MH A Col. 054	11241, 8 × 10
MH A Col. 055	11158, 5 × 7
MH A Col. 055	11207, 8 × 10
MH A Col. 055	11241, 8 × 10
MH A Col. 056	11241, 8 × 10
MH A Col. 057N	11239, 8 × 10
MH A Col. 057S	11239, 8 × 10
MH A Col. 058N	11240, 8 × 10
MH A Col. 058S	11240, 8 × 10
MH A Col. 059N	11240, 8 × 10
MH A Col. 059S	11240, 8 × 10
MH A Col. 064	11159, 5 × 7
MH A Col. 064	11207, 8 × 10
MH A Col. 065	11242, —
MH A Col. 067	11242, —
MH A Col. 068	11242, —
MH A Col. 068N	11242, —
MH A Col. 068S	11242, —
MH A Col. 071	11160, 5 × 7
MH A Col. 071	11207, 8 × 10
MH A Col. 071N	11243, 8 × 10
MH A Col. 071S	11243, 8 × 10
MH A Col. 072N	11243, 8 × 10
MH A Col. 072S	11243, 8 × 10
MH A Col. 075	11161, 5 × 7
MH A Col. 075	11207, 8 × 10
MH A Col. 087	11207, 8 × 10
MH A Pil. 001	10786, 8 × 10
MH A Pil. 002	10786, 8 × 10
MH A Pil. 003	10786, 8 × 10
MH A Pil. 003	13372, 5 × 7
MH A Pil. 004	10786, 8 × 10
MH A Pil. 004	13372, 5 × 7
MH A Pil. 005	10786, 8 × 10
MH A Pil. 005	13372, 5 × 7

Medinet Habu (*cont.*)

Nelson Number/Description	Negative, Format
MH A Pil. 006	10786, 8 × 10
MH A Pil. 006	13372, 5 × 7
MH A Pil. 007	10786, 8 × 10
MH A Pil. 007	13372, 5 × 7
MH A Pil. 016	13336, 5 × 7
MH A Pil. 017	13336, 5 × 7
MH A Pil. 026	13356, 5 × 7
MH A Pil. 027	13356, 5 × 7
MH A Pil. 032	13336, 5 × 7
MH A Pil. 042	13359, 5 × 7
MH A Pil. 043	13359, 5 × 7
MH A Pil. 044	13359, 5 × 7
MH A fragment 004	240, 5 × 7
MH A fragment 004	241, 5 × 7
MH A fragment 005	234, 5 × 7
MH A fragment 005	235, 5 × 7
MH B	13227, 5 × 7
MH B	13228, 5 × 7
MH B	13229, 5 × 7
MH B	13230, 5 × 7
MH B 001	1387, 8 × 10
MH B 001	15379, 8 × 10
MH B 002	707, 5 × 7
MH B 002	708, 5 × 7
MH B 002	709, 5 × 7
MH B 002	710, 5 × 7
MH B 002	1380, 8 × 10
MH B 003	707, 5 × 7
MH B 003	708, 5 × 7
MH B 003	709, 5 × 7
MH B 003	710, 5 × 7
MH B 003	1380, 8 × 10
MH B 004	707, 5 × 7
MH B 004	708, 5 × 7
MH B 004	709, 5 × 7
MH B 004	710, 5 × 7
MH B 004	1380, 8 × 10
MH B 005	1375, 8 × 10
MH B 005	1376, 8 × 10
MH B 005	1383, 8 × 10
MH B 005	1384, 8 × 10
MH B 005	1385, 8 × 10
MH B 005	1386, 8 × 10
MH B 005	15376, 8 × 10
MH B 005	15378, 8 × 10
MH B 006	1375, 8 × 10
MH B 006	1376, 8 × 10
MH B 006	1383, 8 × 10
MH B 006	1384, 8 × 10
MH B 006	1385, 8 × 10
MH B 006	1386, 8 × 10
MH B 006	15376, 8 × 10
MH B 006	15378, 8 × 10
MH B 007	1375, 8 × 10
MH B 007	1376, 8 × 10

Medinet Habu (*cont.*)

Nelson Number/Description	Negative, Format
MH B 007	1383, 8 × 10
MH B 007	1384, 8 × 10
MH B 007	1385, 8 × 10
MH B 007	1386, 8 × 10
MH B 007	15376, 8 × 10
MH B 007	15378, 8 × 10
MH B 008	709, 5 × 7
MH B 009	709, 5 × 7
MH B 010	709, 5 × 7
MH B 010	710, 5 × 7
MH B 011	710, 5 × 7
MH B 012	1385, 8 × 10
MH B 013	1385, 8 × 10
MH B 013	15376, 8 × 10
MH B 014	1386, 8 × 10
MH B 014	15376, 8 × 10
MH B 015	1386, 8 × 10
MH B 015	15376, 8 × 10
MH B 016	1309, 8 × 10
MH B 016	15545, 8 × 10
MH B 017	1308, 8 × 10
MH B 017	15388, 8 × 10
MH B 017	15389, 8 × 10
MH B 018	1307, 8 × 10
MH B 018	15389, 8 × 10
MH B 019	1306, 8 × 10
MH B 019	15390, 8 × 10
MH B 020	1304, 8 × 10
MH B 020	1305, 8 × 10
MH B 020	15391, 8 × 10
MH B 020	15392, 8 × 10
MH B 021	1303, 8 × 10
MH B 021	15393, 8 × 10
MH B 022	1303, 8 × 10
MH B 022	15393, 8 × 10
MH B 023	1313, 8 × 10
MH B 023	15546, 8 × 10
MH B 024	1283, 8 × 10
MH B 024	8173, 8 × 10
MH B 024	13660, 8 × 10
MH B 024	14345, 8 × 10
MH B 024	14345, 8 × 10
MH B 024	14346, 8 × 10
MH B 024	14347, 8 × 10
MH B 024	14840, 8 × 10
MH B 025	1283, 8 × 10
MH B 025	8173, 8 × 10
MH B 025	13692, 8 × 10
MH B 025	14345, 8 × 10
MH B 025	14840, 8 × 10
MH B 025	14841, 8 × 10
MH B 026	1283, 8 × 10
MH B 026	8173, 8 × 10
MH B 026	13649, 8 × 10
MH B 026	14840, 8 × 10

Medinet Habu (*cont.*)

Nelson Number/Description	Negative, Format
MH B 026	14841, 8 × 10
MH B 027	1284, 8 × 10
MH B 027	8156, 8 × 10
MH B 027	13657, 8 × 10
MH B 027	14357, 8 × 10
MH B 028	1285, 8 × 10
MH B 028	8163, 8 × 10
MH B 028	13661, 8 × 10
MH B 028	14365, 8 × 10
MH B 029	1280, 8 × 10
MH B 029	14832, 8 × 10
MH B 029	13648, 8 × 10
MH B 030	1280, 8 × 10
MH B 030	13655, 8 × 10
MH B 030	13685, 8 × 10
MH B 030	15182, 8 × 10
MH B 030	15185, 8 × 10
MH B 030	15186, 8 × 10
MH B 031	1280, 8 × 10
MH B 031	13655, 8 × 10
MH B 031	13685, 8 × 10
MH B 031	15182, 8 × 10
MH B 031	15185, 8 × 10
MH B 031	15186, 8 × 10
MH B 032	13659, 8 × 10
MH B 032	14368, 8 × 10
MH B 033	1281, 8 × 10
MH B 033	8164, 8 × 10
MH B 033	13656, 8 × 10
MH B 033	14370, 8 × 10
MH B 034	1282, 8 × 10
MH B 034	8148, 8 × 10
MH B 034	13658, 8 × 10
MH B 034	14386, 8 × 10
MH B 034	14830, 8 × 10
MH B 035	1282, 8 × 10
MH B 035	8148, 8 × 10
MH B 035	13658, 8 × 10
MH B 035	13684, 8 × 10
MH B 035	14386, 8 × 10
MH B 035	14830, 8 × 10
MH B 036	1276, 8 × 10
MH B 036	13676, 8 × 10
MH B 036	14831, 8 × 10
MH B 037	1276, 8 × 10
MH B 037	13677, 8 × 10
MH B 037	14340, 8 × 10
MH B 037	15183, 8 × 10
MH B 037	15184, 8 × 10
MH B 038	1276, 8 × 10
MH B 038	13680, 8 × 10
MH B 038	14835, 8 × 10
MH B 039	1275, 8 × 10
MH B 039	13682, 8 × 10
MH B 039	14337, 8 × 10

Medinet Habu (*cont.*)

Nelson Number/Description	Negative, Format
MH B 039	14338, 8 × 10
MH B 039	14339, 8 × 10
MH B 040	1275, 8 × 10
MH B 040	13683, 8 × 10
MH B 040	14369, 8 × 10
MH B 041	1274, 8 × 10
MH B 041	13673, 8 × 10
MH B 041	14358, 8 × 10
MH B 042	1274, 8 × 10
MH B 042	13688, 8 × 10
MH B 042	14364, 8 × 10
MH B 043	1273, 8 × 10
MH B 043	13675, 8 × 10
MH B 043	14371, 8 × 10
MH B 044	1273, 8 × 10
MH B 044	13674, 8 × 10
MH B 044	14353, 8 × 10
MH B 045	1277, 8 × 10
MH B 045	14341, 8 × 10
MH B 045	14342, 8 × 10
MH B 045	14343, 8 × 10
MH B 046	1278, 8 × 10
MH B 046	13711, 8 × 10
MH B 046	14355, 8 × 10
MH B 047	1278, 8 × 10
MH B 047	13712, 8 × 10
MH B 047	14367, 8 × 10
MH B 048	1279, 8 × 10
MH B 048	13713, 8 × 10
MH B 048	14359, 8 × 10
MH B 049	1279, 8 × 10
MH B 049	13768, 8 × 10
MH B 049	13769, 8 × 10
MH B 049	14348, 8 × 10
MH B 050	13643, 5 × 7
MH B 050	13645, 5 × 7
MH B 051	13642, 5 × 7
MH B 051	13644, 5 × 7
MH B 052	1277, 8 × 10
MH B 052	13710, 8 × 10
MH B 052	13770, 8 × 10
MH B 052	13771, 8 × 10
MH B 052	13772, 8 × 10
MH B 052	14349, 8 × 10
MH B 053	1295, 8 × 10
MH B 053	13690, 8 × 10
MH B 053	14350, 8 × 10
MH B 054	1295, 8 × 10
MH B 054	1296, 8 × 10
MH B 054	8157, 8 × 10
MH B 054	13678, 8 × 10
MH B 054	13817, 8 × 10
MH B 054	14361, 8 × 10
MH B 055	1296, 8 × 10
MH B 055	8155, 8 × 10

Medinet Habu (*cont.*)

Nelson Number/Description	Negative, Format
MH B 055	13679, 8 × 10
MH B 055	13819-b, 8 × 10
MH B 056	1291, 8 × 10
MH B 056	13671, 8 × 10
MH B 057	1291, 8 × 10
MH B 057	13671, 8 × 10
MH B 057	13687, 8 × 10
MH B 057	13689, 8 × 10
MH B 057	13691, 8 × 10
MH B 057	14382, 8 × 10
MH B 057	14383, 8 × 10
MH B 057	14833, 8 × 10
MH B 058	1291, 8 × 10
MH B 058	13691, 8 × 10
MH B 058	14382, 8 × 10
MH B 059	1292, 8 × 10
MH B 059	8171, 8 × 10
MH B 059	13698, 8 × 10
MH B 059	13816, 8 × 10
MH B 059	14360, 8 × 10
MH B 060	1292, 8 × 10
MH B 060	8171, 8 × 10
MH B 060	13697, 8 × 10
MH B 060	13814, 8 × 10
MH B 061	1293, 8 × 10
MH B 061	13700, 8 × 10
MH B 061	13818-a, 8 × 10
MH B 062	1293, 8 × 10
MH B 062	2832, 8 × 10
MH B 062	13681, 8 × 10
MH B 062	14380, 8 × 10
MH B 062	14381, 8 × 10
MH B 063	1294, 8 × 10
MH B 063	8174, 8 × 10
MH B 063	13699, 8 × 10
MH B 063	13812, 8 × 10
MH B 063	14379, 8 × 10
MH B 063	14379-a, 8 × 10
MH B 064	1294, 8 × 10
MH B 064	8174, 8 × 10
MH B 064	13702, 8 × 10
MH B 065	13672, 8 × 10
MH B 065	14344, 8 × 10
MH B 065	14351, 8 × 10
MH B 066	1288, 8 × 10
MH B 066	13694, 8 × 10
MH B 066	13811, 8 × 10
MH B 066	14356, 8 × 10
MH B 067	1287, 8 × 10
MH B 067	1288, 8 × 10
MH B 067	13499, 8 × 10
MH B 067	13701, 8 × 10
MH B 067	13815, 8 × 10
MH B 067	15188, 8 × 10
MH B 068	1286, 8 × 10

Medinet Habu (*cont.*)		Medinet Habu (*cont.*)	
Nelson Number/Description	*Negative, Format*	*Nelson Number/Description*	*Negative, Format*
MH B 068	13216, 5 × 7	MH B 077	14354, 8 × 10
MH B 068	13686, 8 × 10	MH B 078	1297, 8 × 10
MH B 068	13693, 8 × 10	MH B 078	1298, 8 × 10
MH B 068	13803, 8 × 10	MH B 078	7556, 8 × 10
MH B 069	1286, 8 × 10	MH B 078	7557, 8 × 10
MH B 069	13216, 5 × 7	MH B 078	7592, 8 × 10
MH B 069	13686, 8 × 10	MH B 078	13650, 8 × 10
MH B 069	13696, 8 × 10	MH B 078	13652, 8 × 10
MH B 069	13792, 8 × 10	MH B 078	13709, 8 × 10
MH B 069	13793, 8 × 10	MH B 078	14366, 8 × 10
MH B 069	13794, 8 × 10	MH B 078	14828, 8 × 10
MH B 069	13795, 8 × 10	MH B 078	14839, 8 × 10
MH B 070	1290, 8 × 10	MH B 081	708, 5 × 7
MH B 070	13695, 8 × 10	MH B 082	1311, 8 × 10
MH B 070	13804, 8 × 10	MH B 082	15547, 8 × 10
MH B 070	14362, 8 × 10	MH B 082	15591, 8 × 10
MH B 070	14363, 8 × 10	MH B 083	7682, 5 × 7
MH B 071	1289, 8 × 10	MH B 083	15548, 8 × 10
MH B 071	13703, 8 × 10	MH B 084	1310, 8 × 10
MH B 071	13813, 8 × 10	MH B 084	15549, 8 × 10
MH B 071	15187, 8 × 10	MH B 085	707, 5 × 7
MH B 072	1302, 8 × 10	MH B 085	708, 5 × 7
MH B 072	13706, 8 × 10	MH B 086	1314, 8 × 10
MH B 072	14373, 8 × 10	MH B 086	15550, 8 × 10
MH B 072	14374, 8 × 10	MH B 086	15590, 8 × 10
MH B 072	14834, 8 × 10	MH B 087	7683, 5 × 7
MH B 073	1302, 8 × 10	MH B 087	15551, 8 × 10
MH B 074	1302, 8 × 10	MH B 088	15552, 8 × 10
MH B 074	13707, 8 × 10	MH B 088	1549, 8 × 10
MH B 074	14384, 8 × 10	MH B 089	707, 5 × 7
MH B 074	14385, 8 × 10	MH B 090	1315, 8 × 10
MH B 075	1300, 8 × 10	MH B 090	15553, 8 × 10
MH B 075	1301, 8 × 10	MH B 091	7684, 5 × 7
MH B 075	3047, 8 × 10	MH B 091	15554, 8 × 10
MH B 075	3048, 8 × 10	MH B 092	1550, 8 × 10
MH B 075	3049, 8 × 10	MH B 092	15555, 8 × 10
MH B 075	7694, 8 × 10	MH B 093	1380, 8 × 10
MH B 075	13651, 8 × 10	MH B 094	1317, 8 × 10
MH B 075	13653, 8 × 10	MH B 094	15556, 8 × 10
MH B 075	13708, 8 × 10	MH B 095	7685, 5 × 7
MH B 075	14375, 8 × 10	MH B 095	15557, 8 × 10
MH B 075	14376, 8 × 10	MH B 096	1316, 8 × 10
MH B 075	14377, 8 × 10	MH B 096	15558, 8 × 10
MH B 075	14378-a, 8 × 10	MH B 097	1333, 8 × 10
MH B 075	14836, 8 × 10	MH B 097	1380, 8 × 10
MH B 075	14837, 8 × 10	MH B 097	1381, 8 × 10
MH B 076	1299, 8 × 10	MH B 098	1319, 8 × 10
MH B 076	7333, 8 × 10	MH B 098	15559, 8 × 10
MH B 076	13647, 8 × 10	MH B 099	1913, 8 × 10
MH B 076	13654, 8 × 10	MH B 099	7686, 5 × 7
MH B 076	14352, 8 × 10	MH B 099	15560, 8 × 10
MH B 077	1299, 8 × 10	MH B 100	1318, 8 × 10
MH B 077	7333, 8 × 10	MH B 100	15561, 8 × 10
MH B 077	13646, 8 × 10	MH B 101	1381, 8 × 10
MH B 077	13654, 8 × 10	MH B 103	1321, 8 × 10

Medinet Habu (*cont.*)

Nelson Number/Description	Negative, Format
MH B 103	15562, 8 × 10
MH B 104	1320, 8 × 10
MH B 104	15563, 8 × 10
MH B 105	1312, 8 × 10
MH B 105	15564, 8 × 10
MH B 107	1321, 8 × 10
MH B 107	15565, 8 × 10
MH B 108	1913, 8 × 10
MH B 108	7678, 5 × 7
MH B 108	15566, 8 × 10
MH B 108b	7695, 5 × 7
MH B 109	1312, 8 × 10
MH B 109	15567, 8 × 10
MH B 110	1378, 8 × 10
MH B 110	15370, 8 × 10
MH B 111	1322, 8 × 10
MH B 111	15568, 8 × 10
MH B 111	15592, 8 × 10
MH B 112	7681, 5 × 7
MH B 112	15569, 8 × 10
MH B 113	1322, 8 × 10
MH B 113	15570, 8 × 10
MH B 114	1378, 8 × 10
MH B 114	15370, 8 × 10
MH B 115	1323, 8 × 10
MH B 115	15571, 8 × 10
MH B 116	7679, 5 × 7
MH B 116	15572, 8 × 10
MH B 117	1324, 8 × 10
MH B 117	15573, 8 × 10
MH B 119	1323, 8 × 10
MH B 119	15574, 8 × 10
MH B 120	7680, 5 × 7
MH B 120	15575, 8 × 10
MH B 121	1324, 8 × 10
MH B 121	15576, 8 × 10
MH B 125	1376, 8 × 10
MH B 125a	1375, 8 × 10
MH B 127	1552, 8 × 10
MH B 127	7687, 5 × 7
MH B 127	15577, 8 × 10
MH B 128	1551, 8 × 10
MH B 128	7689, 5 × 7
MH B 128	15578, 8 × 10
MH B 129	1376, 8 × 10
MH B 130	1325, 8 × 10
MH B 130	15579, 8 × 10
MH B 131	1912, 8 × 10
MH B 131	7690, 5 × 7
MH B 131	15580, 8 × 10
MH B 132	1326, 8 × 10
MH B 132	7691, 5 × 7
MH B 132	15581, 8 × 10
MH B 133	1383, 8 × 10
MH B 133	15378, 8 × 10

Medinet Habu (*cont.*)

Nelson Number/Description	Negative, Format
MH B 134	1327, 8 × 10
MH B 134	15582, 8 × 10
MH B 135	1912, 8 × 10
MH B 135	7688, 5 × 7
MH B 135	15583, 8 × 10
MH B 136	1328, 8 × 10
MH B 136	7692, 5 × 7
MH B 136	15584, 8 × 10
MH B 137	1383, 8 × 10
MH B 137	15378, 8 × 10
MH B 138	1329, 8 × 10
MH B 138	15585, 8 × 10
MH B 139	7677, 5 × 7
MH B 139	15586, 8 × 10
MH B 140	1330, 8 × 10
MH B 140	15587, 8 × 10
MH B 141	1384, 8 × 10
MH B 141	15378, 8 × 10
MH B 142	1331, 8 × 10
MH B 142	15593, 8 × 10
MH B 143	7676, 5 × 7
MH B 143	15588, 8 × 10
MH B 144	1332, 8 × 10
MH B 144	15589, 8 × 10
MH B 150	1335, 8 × 10
MH B 150	1336, 8 × 10
MH B 150	1337, 8 × 10
MH B 150	1338, 8 × 10
MH B 150	15721, 8 × 10
MH B 150	15722, 8 × 10
MH B 150	15723, 8 × 10
MH B 150	15735, 8 × 10
MH B 150	15736, 8 × 10
MH B 150	15737, 8 × 10
MH B 151	1334, 8 × 10
MH B 151	1335, 8 × 10
MH B 151	15730, 8 × 10
MH B 151	15731, 8 × 10
MH B 151	15732, 8 × 10
MH B 151	15733, 8 × 10
MH B 151	15734, 8 × 10
MH B 152	1339, 8 × 10
MH B 152	1340, 8 × 10
MH B 152	1341, 8 × 10
MH B 152	15724, 8 × 10
MH B 152	15725, 8 × 10
MH B 152	15726, 8 × 10
MH B 152	15727, 8 × 10
MH B 152	15728, 8 × 10
MH B 152	15729, 8 × 10
MH B 153	1341, 8 × 10
MH B 153	1377, 8 × 10
MH B 154	1351, 8 × 10
MH B 154	3162, 8 × 10
MH B 154	5971, 8 × 10

Medinet Habu (*cont.*)

Nelson Number/Description	Negative, Format
MH B 155	1548, 8 × 10
MH B 156	1353, 8 × 10
MH B 156	3163, 8 × 10
MH B 156	5970, 8 × 10
MH B 157	1354, 8 × 10
MH B 157	3027, 8 × 10
MH B 157	3096, 8 × 10
MH B 158	1355, 8 × 10
MH B 158	3030, 8 × 10
MH B 158	3096, 8 × 10
MH B 159	1356, 8 × 10
MH B 159	3029, 8 × 10
MH B 159	3096, 8 × 10
MH B 160	1357, 8 × 10
MH B 160	3028, 8 × 10
MH B 161	1358, 8 × 10
MH B 161	3099, 8 × 10
MH B 162	1359, 8 × 10
MH B 162	3100, 8 × 10
MH B 163	1342, 8 × 10
MH B 163	8154, 8 × 10
MH B 164	1343, 8 × 10
MH B 164	8169, 8 × 10
MH B 165	1345, 8 × 10
MH B 165	8146, 8 × 10
MH B 166	1346, 8 × 10
MH B 166	8172, 8 × 10
MH B 167	1347, 8 × 10
MH B 167	8175, 8 × 10
MH B 168	1348, 8 × 10
MH B 168	8158, 8 × 10
MH B 169	1349, 8 × 10
MH B 169	8159, 8 × 10
MH B 169	8479, 8 × 10
MH B 169	8480, 8 × 10
MH B 170	1350, 8 × 10
MH B 170	2842, 8 × 10
MH B 170	3213, 8 × 10
MH B 178	1367, 8 × 10
MH B 178	8147, 8 × 10
MH B 180	1368, 8 × 10
MH B 180	8120, 8 × 10
MH B 181	1368, 8 × 10
MH B 181	8120, 8 × 10
MH B 182	1369, 8 × 10
MH B 182a	8139, 8 × 10
MH B 182b	8140, 8 × 10
MH B 183	1370, 8 × 10
MH B 183	8141, 8 × 10
MH B 184	1370, 8 × 10
MH B 184	8142, 8 × 10
MH B 185	1371, 8 × 10
MH B 185	8116, 8 × 10
MH B 186	1371, 8 × 10
MH B 186	1372, 8 × 10

Medinet Habu (*cont.*)

Nelson Number/Description	Negative, Format
MH B 186	8117, 8 × 10
MH B 186	7341, 8 × 10
MH B 187	1372, 8 × 10
MH B 187	7329, 8 × 10
MH B 187	7341, 8 × 10
MH B 187	8121, 8 × 10
MH B 188	1373, 8 × 10
MH B 188	8123, 8 × 10
MH B 189	1373, 8 × 10
MH B 189	1543, 8 × 10
MH B 189	8123, 8 × 10
MH B 190	1374, 8 × 10
MH B 190	1543, 8 × 10
MH B 190	8122, 8 × 10
MH B 191	1374, 8 × 10
MH B 191	1543, 8 × 10
MH B 191	8122, 8 × 10
MH B 192	1344, 8 × 10
MH B 193	1344, 8 × 10
MH B 194	1360, 8 × 10
MH B 194	2537, 8 × 10
MH B 194	2538, 5 × 7
MH B 194a	1464, 8 × 10
MH B 196	7693, 8 × 10
MH B 197	7693, 8 × 10
MH B 198	1362, 8 × 10
MH B 198a	8143, 8 × 10
MH B 198b	8144, 8 × 10
MH B 199	1361, 8 × 10
MH B 199	1362, 8 × 10
MH B 199	8145, 8 × 10
MH B 200	1361, 8 × 10
MH B 200	8145, 8 × 10
MH B 201	1361, 8 × 10
MH B 201	8150, 8 × 10
MH B 202	1361, 8 × 10
MH B 202	8150, 8 × 10
MH B 203	1366, 8 × 10
MH B 203	1544, 8 × 10
MH B 203	8152, 8 × 10
MH B 204	1365, 8 × 10
MH B 204	1366, 8 × 10
MH B 204	1544, 8 × 10
MH B 204	8151, 8 × 10
MH B 205	1365, 8 × 10
MH B 205	8151, 8 × 10
MH B 206	1363, 8 × 10
MH B 206	1364, 8 × 10
MH B 206a	8162, 8 × 10
MH B 206b	8161, 8 × 10
MH B 206c	8160, 8 × 10
MH B 207	1378, 8 × 10
MH B 207	15370, 8 × 10
MH B 212	15370, 8 × 10
MH B 213	15370, 8 × 10

Medinet Habu (*cont.*)

Nelson Number/Description	Negative, Format
MH B 214	1382, 8 × 10
MH B 215	951, 8 × 10
MH B 217	1442, 8 × 10
MH B 218	1482, 8 × 10
MH B 219	1482, 8 × 10
MH B 221	1399, 8 × 10
MH B 222	1561, 8 × 10
MH B 223	1438, 8 × 10
MH B 223	1442, 8 × 10
MH B 224	1502, 8 × 10
MH B 224	3981, 8 × 10
MH B 225	1502, 8 × 10
MH B 225	3981, 8 × 10
MH B 226	1474, 8 × 10
MH B 227	1474, 8 × 10
MH B 230	1502, 8 × 10
MH B 231	1502, 8 × 10
MH B 232a	1469, 8 × 10
MH B 232b	1420, 8 × 10
MH B 234	1490, 8 × 10
MH B 235	1490, 8 × 10
MH B 236	1503, 8 × 10
MH B 238	1561, 8 × 10
MH B 239	1561, 8 × 10
MH B 240	1472, 8 × 10
MH B 241	1467, 8 × 10
MH B 242	1495, 8 × 10
MH B 243	1491, 8 × 10
MH B 244	1491, 8 × 10
MH B 245	1461, 8 × 10
MH B 246	1465, 8 × 10
MH B 247	1458, 8 × 10
MH B 248	1458, 8 × 10
MH B 249	1572, 8 × 10
MH B 250	1447, 8 × 10
MH B 251	1459, 8 × 10
MH B 252	1478, 8 × 10
MH B 253	1480, 8 × 10
MH B 254	1479, 8 × 10
MH B 255	1379, 8 × 10
MH B 256	1468, 8 × 10
MH B 257	1466, 8 × 10
MH B 258	1468, 8 × 10
MH B 259	1470, 8 × 10
MH B 260	1470, 8 × 10
MH B 261	1487, 8 × 10
MH B 262	1466, 8 × 10
MH B 263	1487, 8 × 10
MH B 264	1481, 8 × 10
MH B 265	1481, 8 × 10
MH B 266	1475, 8 × 10
MH B 267	1475, 8 × 10
MH B 268	1475, 8 × 10
MH B 269	1471, 8 × 10
MH B 270	1471, 8 × 10

Medinet Habu (*cont.*)

Nelson Number/Description	Negative, Format
MH B 271	1471, 8 × 10
MH B 272	1496, 8 × 10
MH B 273	1496, 8 × 10
MH B 300	1445, 8 × 10
MH B 300	13325, 5 × 7
MH B 300	13354, 5 × 7
MH B 300	13481, 5 × 7
MH B 300	13802, 8 × 10
MH B 301	1416, 8 × 10
MH B 301	1451, 8 × 10
MH B 301	1453, 8 × 10
MH B 301	1476, 8 × 10
MH B 301	13325, 5 × 7
MH B 301	13354, 5 × 7
MH B 301	13481, 5 × 7
MH B 301	13802, 8 × 10
MH B 302	1407, 8 × 10
MH B 302	1419, 8 × 10
MH B 302	1448, 8 × 10
MH B 302	1499, 8 × 10
MH B 302	13325, 5 × 7
MH B 302	13354, 5 × 7
MH B 302	13481, 5 × 7
MH B 302	13802, 8 × 10
MH B 303	1454, 8 × 10
MH B 303	1488, 8 × 10
MH B 303	13325, 5 × 7
MH B 303	13354, 5 × 7
MH B 303	13481, 5 × 7
MH B 303	13802, 8 × 10
MH B 304	1412, 8 × 10
MH B 304	1446, 8 × 10
MH B 304	1452, 8 × 10
MH B 304	1488, 8 × 10
MH B 304	13325, 5 × 7
MH B 304	13354, 5 × 7
MH B 304	13481, 5 × 7
MH B 304	13802, 8 × 10
MH B 305	1554, 8 × 10
MH B 305	1556, 8 × 10
MH B 305	13325, 5 × 7
MH B 305	13354, 5 × 7
MH B 305	13481, 5 × 7
MH B 305	13802, 8 × 10
MH B 306	1557, 8 × 10
MH B 306	13325, 5 × 7
MH B 306	13354, 5 × 7
MH B 306	13481, 5 × 7
MH B 306	13802, 8 × 10
MH B 307	1402, 8 × 10
MH B 308	1402, 8 × 10
MH B 309	1398, 8 × 10
MH B 309	13325, 5 × 7
MH B 309	13354, 5 × 7
MH B 309	13481, 5 × 7

Medinet Habu (*cont.*)

Nelson Number/Description	Negative, Format
MH B 309	13802, 8 × 10
MH B 310	1415, 8 × 10
MH B 310	13325, 5 × 7
MH B 310	13354, 5 × 7
MH B 310	13481, 5 × 7
MH B 310	13802, 8 × 10
MH B 311	1401, 8 × 10
MH B 311	7462, 8 × 10
MH B 312	1441, 8 × 10
MH B 313	1576, 8 × 10
MH B 314	1911, 8 × 10
MH B 315	1560, 8 × 10
MH B 316	1911, 8 × 10
MH B 317	1562, 8 × 10
MH B 318	1562, 8 × 10
MH B 319	13482, 5 × 7
MH B 319	13483, 5 × 7
MH B 319	13484, 5 × 7
MH B 320	13482, 5 × 7
MH B 320	13485, 5 × 7
MH B 320	13486, 5 × 7
MH C 001	1129, 8 × 10
MH C 001	1623, 8 × 10
MH C 001	1625, 8 × 10
MH C 002	1129, 8 × 10
MH C 002	1592, 8 × 10
MH C 003	1129, 8 × 10
MH C 003	1623, 8 × 10
MH C 004	1129, 8 × 10
MH C 004	1626, 8 × 10
MH C 005	1129, 8 × 10
MH C 005	1626, 8 × 10
MH C 006	1129, 8 × 10
MH C 006	1625, 8 × 10
MH C 007	1129, 8 × 10
MH C 007	1610, 8 × 10
MH C 008	1129, 8 × 10
MH C 008	1610, 8 × 10
MH C 010	2042, 8 × 10
MH C 011	1602, 8 × 10
MH C 012	1602, 8 × 10
MH C 013	1611, 8 × 10
MH C 014	1611, 8 × 10
MH C 015	1580, 8 × 10
MH C 015	1599, 8 × 10
MH C 015	2098, 8 × 10
MH C 016	1580, 8 × 10
MH C 016	1599, 8 × 10
MH C 016	2098, 8 × 10
MH C 017	1580, 8 × 10
MH C 017	1581, 8 × 10
MH C 017	2098, 8 × 10
MH C 018	1580, 8 × 10
MH C 018	1599, 8 × 10
MH C 018	2098, 8 × 10

Medinet Habu (*cont.*)

Nelson Number/Description	Negative, Format
MH C 019	1580, 8 × 10
MH C 019	1599, 8 × 10
MH C 019	2098, 8 × 10
MH C 020	1580, 8 × 10
MH C 020	1581, 8 × 10
MH C 020	2098, 8 × 10
MH C 021	1128, 8 × 10
MH C 021	1594, 8 × 10
MH C 022	1128, 8 × 10
MH C 022	1594, 8 × 10
MH C 023	1128, 8 × 10
MH C 023	1594, 8 × 10
MH C 024	1128, 8 × 10
MH C 024	1588, 8 × 10
MH C 025	1128, 8 × 10
MH C 025	1604, 8 × 10
MH C 026	1128, 8 × 10
MH C 026	1604, 8 × 10
MH C 027	1609, 8 × 10
MH C 028	1609, 8 × 10
MH C 029	1609, 8 × 10
MH C 030	1609, 8 × 10
MH C 031	1609, 8 × 10
MH C 032	1609, 8 × 10
MH C 034	1617, 8 × 10
MH C 035	1617, 8 × 10
MH C 041	7940, 8 × 10
MH C 042	7940, 8 × 10
MH C 043	7946, 8 × 10
MH C 044	7940, 8 × 10
MH C 045	9734, 8 × 10
MH C 046	9734, 8 × 10
MH C 047	9734, 8 × 10
MH C 048	9735, 8 × 10
MH C 048	9734, 8 × 10
MH C 049	9735, 8 × 10
MH C 050	9735, 8 × 10
MH C 051	9735, 8 × 10
MH C 052	9736, 8 × 10
MH C 053	9736, 8 × 10
MH C 054	9736, 8 × 10
MH C 054	9737, 8 × 10
MH C 055	9737, 8 × 10
MH C 056	9737, 8 × 10
MH C 057	9737, 8 × 10
MH C 060	9734, 8 × 10
MH C 060	9735, 8 × 10
MH C 060	9736, 8 × 10
MH C 060	9737, 8 × 10
MH C 061	9737, 8 × 10
MH C 062	9737, 8 × 10
MH C 063	8351, 8 × 10
MH C 063	9686, 8 × 10
MH C 063	9687, 8 × 10
MH C 063	9688, 8 × 10

Medinet Habu (*cont.*)

Nelson Number/Description	Negative, Format
MH C 063	9738, 8 × 10
MH C 065	9739, 8 × 10
MH C 066	9739, 8 × 10
MH C 067	9739, 8 × 10
MH C 068	9739, 8 × 10
MH C 069	9739, 8 × 10
MH C 070	9739, 8 × 10
MH C 071	9740, 8 × 10
MH C 072	9741, 8 × 10
MH C 073	9741, 8 × 10
MH C 074	9739, 8 × 10
MH C 075	9689, 8 × 10
MH C 075	9690, 8 × 10
MH C 076	9741, 8 × 10
MH C 077	9691, 8 × 10
MH C 077	9692, 8 × 10
MH C 080	9742, 8 × 10
MH C 081	9742, 8 × 10
MH C 082	9742, 8 × 10
MH C 083	9742, 8 × 10
MH C 083	9743, 8 × 10
MH C 084	9742, 8 × 10
MH C 084	9743, 8 × 10
MH C 085	9743, 8 × 10
MH C 086	9743, 8 × 10
MH C 087	9744, 8 × 10
MH C 088	9744, 8 × 10
MH C 089	9744, 8 × 10
MH C 089	9745, 8 × 10
MH C 090	9744, 8 × 10
MH C 090	9745, 8 × 10
MH C 091	9745, 8 × 10
MH C 092	9742, 8 × 10
MH C 092	9743, 8 × 10
MH C 092	9744, 8 × 10
MH C 092	9745, 8 × 10
MH C 093	9693, 8 × 10
MH C 093	9746, 8 × 10
MH C 094	9694, 8 × 10
MH C 094	9695, 8 × 10
MH C 095	7947, 8 × 10
MH C 096	7947, 8 × 10
MH C 097	7921, 5 × 7
MH C 097	7922, 5 × 7
MH C 100	1596, 8 × 10
MH C 101	7949, 8 × 10
MH C 102	7944, 8 × 10
MH C 103	8324, 8 × 10
MH C 103	9747, 8 × 10
MH C 103	9748, 8 × 10
MH C 103	9749, 8 × 10
MH C 104	8324, 8 × 10
MH C 104	9747, 8 × 10
MH C 104	9748, 8 × 10
MH C 104	9749, 8 × 10

Medinet Habu (*cont.*)

Nelson Number/Description	Negative, Format
MH C 105	7941, 8 × 10
MH C 106	7941, 8 × 10
MH C 107	8384, 8 × 10
MH C 108	8352, 8 × 10
MH C 108	8384, 8 × 10
MH C 109	8352, 8 × 10
MH C 111	9750, 8 × 10
MH C 111	9751, 8 × 10
MH C 112	9750, 8 × 10
MH C 117	9751, 8 × 10
MH C 118	9697, 8 × 10
MH C 119	9696, 8 × 10
MH C 125	9752, 8 × 10
MH C 125	9753, 8 × 10
MH C 126	9753, 8 × 10
MH C 127	9753, 8 × 10
MH C 128	9752, 8 × 10
MH C 128	9753, 8 × 10
MH C 129	9752, 8 × 10
MH C 130	9752, 8 × 10
MH C 131	8385, 8 × 10
MH C 132	8385, 8 × 10
MH C 133	8387, 8 × 10
MH C 134	8386, 8 × 10
MH C 134	8387, 8 × 10
MH C 135	8386, 8 × 10
MH C 136	7948, 8 × 10
MH C 137	723, 8 × 10
MH C 137	7942, 8 × 10
MH C 141	8353, 8 × 10
MH C 142	1127, 8 × 10
MH C 143	1127, 8 × 10
MH C 144	1127, 8 × 10
MH C 145	8354, 8 × 10
MH C 148	1585, 8 × 10
MH C 148	1621, 8 × 10
MH C 149	1621, 8 × 10
MH C 150	1585, 8 × 10
MH C 151	1585, 8 × 10
MH C 152	1584, 8 × 10
MH C 153	1586, 8 × 10
MH C 170	1624, 8 × 10
MH C 171	1624, 8 × 10
MH C 172	1624, 8 × 10
MH C 173	1630, 8 × 10
MH C 175	1629, 8 × 10
MH C 176	1627, 8 × 10
MH C 180	1628, 8 × 10
MH C 181	1628, 8 × 10
MH C 182	1628, 8 × 10
MH C 183	1587, 8 × 10
MH C 184	1603, 8 × 10
MH C 185	1603, 8 × 10
MH C 186	1619, 8 × 10
MH C 187	1619, 8 × 10

Medinet Habu (*cont.*)

Nelson Number/Description	Negative, Format
MH C 188	1606, 8 × 10
MH C 189	1606, 8 × 10
MH C 190	1606, 8 × 10
MH C 191	1590, 8 × 10
MH C 192	1593, 8 × 10
MH C 193	1595, 8 × 10
MH C 194a	1600, 8 × 10
MH C 194b	1600, 8 × 10
MH C 195	1601, 8 × 10
MH C 201	7943, 8 × 10
MH C 202	1598, 8 × 10
MH C 203	1598, 8 × 10
MH C 204	1598, 8 × 10
MH C 205	7945, 8 × 10
MH C 211	7924, 5 × 7
MH C 212	1605, 8 × 10
MH C 213	1605, 8 × 10
MH C 214	1605, 8 × 10
MH C 215	7923, 5 × 7
MH C 221	8333, 8 × 10
MH C 222	8333, 8 × 10
MH C 223	8334, 8 × 10
MH C 224	8333, 8 × 10
MH C 225	8334, 8 × 10
MH C 226	1615, 8 × 10
MH C 227	1607, 8 × 10
MH C 228	1608, 8 × 10
MH C 228	8318, 8 × 10
MH C 229	1608, 8 × 10
MH C 229	8318, 8 × 10
MH C 230	1607, 8 × 10
MH C 230	8318, 8 × 10
MH D	13588, 5 × 7
MH D	13597, 5 × 7
MH D	13620, 5 × 7
MH D	15805, 8 × 10
MH D 001	2067, 8 × 10
MH D 001	11299, 8 × 10
MH D 001	11791, 8 × 10
MH D 001	13334, 5 × 7
MH D 001	13338, 5 × 7
MH D 001	13390, 5 × 7
MH D 001	13457, 5 × 7
MH D 001	13544, 5 × 7
MH D 002	2067, 8 × 10
MH D 002	11299, 8 × 10
MH D 002	11791, 8 × 10
MH D 002	13334, 5 × 7
MH D 002	13338, 5 × 7
MH D 002	13390, 5 × 7
MH D 002	13457, 5 × 7
MH D 003	2068, 8 × 10
MH D 003	11300, 8 × 10
MH D 003	11722, 8 × 10
MH D 003	13334, 5 × 7

Medinet Habu (*cont.*)

Nelson Number/Description	Negative, Format
MH D 003	13338, 5 × 7
MH D 003	13390, 5 × 7
MH D 003	13457, 5 × 7
MH D 004	2068, 8 × 10
MH D 004	11300, 8 × 10
MH D 004	11722, 8 × 10
MH D 004	13334, 5 × 7
MH D 004	13338, 5 × 7
MH D 004	13390, 5 × 7
MH D 005	13334, 5 × 7
MH D 005	13338, 5 × 7
MH D 005	13390, 5 × 7
MH D 005	13457, 5 × 7
MH D 006	13334, 5 × 7
MH D 006	13338, 5 × 7
MH D 006	13390, 5 × 7
MH D 006	13457, 5 × 7
MH D 009	2064, 8 × 10
MH D 009	11301, 8 × 10
MH D 009	11648, 8 × 10
MH D 010	2064, 8 × 10
MH D 010	11301, 8 × 10
MH D 010	11648, 8 × 10
MH D 011	2064, 8 × 10
MH D 011	11301, 8 × 10
MH D 011	11648, 8 × 10
MH D 012	2071, 8 × 10
MH D 012	11302, 8 × 10
MH D 012	11649, 8 × 10
MH D 013	2071, 8 × 10
MH D 013	11302, 8 × 10
MH D 013	11649, 8 × 10
MH D 014	2071, 8 × 10
MH D 014	11302, 8 × 10
MH D 014	11649, 8 × 10
MH D 015	816, 8 × 10
MH D 015	11303, 8 × 10
MH D 015	11650, 8 × 10
MH D 016	816, 8 × 10
MH D 016	11303, 8 × 10
MH D 016	11650, 8 × 10
MH D 017	816, 8 × 10
MH D 017	11303, 8 × 10
MH D 017	11650, 8 × 10
MH D 018	815, 8 × 10
MH D 018	1563, 8 × 10
MH D 018	11304, 8 × 10
MH D 018	11651, 8 × 10
MH D 019	815, 8 × 10
MH D 019	1563, 8 × 10
MH D 019	11304, 8 × 10
MH D 019	11651, 8 × 10
MH D 020	815, 8 × 10
MH D 020	1563, 8 × 10
MH D 020	11304, 8 × 10

Medinet Habu (*cont.*)

Nelson Number/Description	Negative, Format
MH D 020	11651, 8 × 10
MH D 031	802, 8 × 10
MH D 031	11274, 8 × 10
MH D 031	11652, 8 × 10
MH D 031	13334, 5 × 7
MH D 031	13338, 5 × 7
MH D 031	13390, 5 × 7
MH D 031	13457, 5 × 7
MH D 032	802, 8 × 10
MH D 032	11274, 8 × 10
MH D 032	11275, 8 × 10
MH D 032	11652, 8 × 10
MH D 032	13334, 5 × 7
MH D 032	13338, 5 × 7
MH D 032	13362, 5 × 7
MH D 032	13390, 5 × 7
MH D 032	13457, 5 × 7
MH D 033	802, 8 × 10
MH D 033	866, 5 × 7
MH D 033	2104, 8 × 10
MH D 033	11274, 8 × 10
MH D 033	11464, 8 × 10
MH D 033	13334, 5 × 7
MH D 033	13338, 5 × 7
MH D 033	13362, 5 × 7
MH D 033	13390, 5 × 7
MH D 033	13457, 5 × 7
MH D 034	802, 8 × 10
MH D 034	866, 5 × 7
MH D 034	2104, 8 × 10
MH D 034	11305, 8 × 10
MH D 034	11619, 8 × 10
MH D 034	13334, 5 × 7
MH D 034	13338, 5 × 7
MH D 034	13362, 5 × 7
MH D 034	13390, 5 × 7
MH D 034	13457, 5 × 7
MH D 035	802, 8 × 10
MH D 035	2061, 8 × 10
MH D 035	2104, 8 × 10
MH D 035	11311, 5 × 7
MH D 035	13334, 5 × 7
MH D 035	13338, 5 × 7
MH D 035	13362, 5 × 7
MH D 035	13390, 5 × 7
MH D 035	13457, 5 × 7
MH D 036	801, 8 × 10
MH D 036	11276, 8 × 10
MH D 036	11565, 8 × 10
MH D 036	13334, 5 × 7
MH D 036	13338, 5 × 7
MH D 036	13362, 5 × 7
MH D 036	13390, 5 × 7
MH D 036	13457, 5 × 7
MH D 037	801, 8 × 10

Medinet Habu (*cont.*)

Nelson Number/Description	Negative, Format
MH D 037	2105, 8 × 10
MH D 037	11276, 8 × 10
MH D 037	11565, 8 × 10
MH D 037	13334, 5 × 7
MH D 037	13338, 5 × 7
MH D 037	13362, 5 × 7
MH D 037	13390, 5 × 7
MH D 037	13457, 5 × 7
MH D 038	801, 8 × 10
MH D 038	2062, 8 × 10
MH D 038	2062, 8 × 10
MH D 038	2105, 8 × 10
MH D 038	11276, 8 × 10
MH D 038	11464, 8 × 10
MH D 038	13334, 5 × 7
MH D 038	13338, 5 × 7
MH D 038	13362, 5 × 7
MH D 038	13390, 5 × 7
MH D 038	13457, 5 × 7
MH D 039	801, 8 × 10
MH D 039	2105, 8 × 10
MH D 039	11306, 8 × 10
MH D 039	11619, 8 × 10
MH D 039	13334, 5 × 7
MH D 039	13338, 5 × 7
MH D 039	13362, 5 × 7
MH D 039	13390, 5 × 7
MH D 039	13457, 5 × 7
MH D 040	2062, 8 × 10
MH D 040	11307, 8 × 10
MH D 040	11621, 8 × 10
MH D 040	13334, 5 × 7
MH D 040	13338, 5 × 7
MH D 040	13362, 5 × 7
MH D 040	13390, 5 × 7
MH D 040	13457, 5 × 7
MH D 050	1966, 8 × 10
MH D 050	1967, 8 × 10
MH D 050	11653, 8 × 10
MH D 051	676, 8 × 10
MH D 051	1966, 8 × 10
MH D 051	1967, 8 × 10
MH D 051	11653, 8 × 10
MH D 052	635, 8 × 10
MH D 052	11723, 8 × 10
MH D 053	635, 8 × 10
MH D 053	2065, 8 × 10
MH D 053	11308, 8 × 10
MH D 054	635, 8 × 10
MH D 054	2065, 8 × 10
MH D 054	11308, 8 × 10
MH D 055	2065, 8 × 10
MH D 055	11308, 8 × 10
MH D 056	2065, 8 × 10
MH D 056	11308, 8 × 10

Medinet Habu (*cont.*)

Nelson Number/Description	Negative, Format
MH D 057	2000, 8 × 10
MH D 057a	11312, 5 × 7
MH D 058	850, 8 × 10
MH D 058	1964, 8 × 10
MH D 058	11675, 8 × 10
MH D 059	850, 8 × 10
MH D 059	1964, 8 × 10
MH D 059	11675, 8 × 10
MH D 060	850, 8 × 10
MH D 060	1964, 8 × 10
MH D 060	11675, 8 × 10
MH D 061	846, 8 × 10
MH D 061	11673, 8 × 10
MH D 062	846, 8 × 10
MH D 062	11313, 5 × 7
MH D 062	11314, 5 × 7
MH D 063	846, 8 × 10
MH D 063	11313, 5 × 7
MH D 063	11314, 5 × 7
MH D 065	1987, 8 × 10
MH D 065	2047, 8 × 10
MH D 066	1987, 8 × 10
MH D 066	2047, 8 × 10
MH D 067	2047, 8 × 10
MH D 068	2047, 8 × 10
MH D 068	11315, 5 × 7
MH D 069	2047, 8 × 10
MH D 069	11315, 5 × 7
MH D 070	658, 8 × 10
MH D 071	658, 8 × 10
MH D 071	1962, 8 × 10
MH D 071	1963, 8 × 10
MH D 071	11316, 5 × 7
MH D 071	11324, 8 × 10
MH D 072	658, 8 × 10
MH D 072	1962, 8 × 10
MH D 072	1963, 8 × 10
MH D 072	11316, 5 × 7
MH D 072	11324, 8 × 10
MH D 073	658, 8 × 10
MH D 073	1962, 8 × 10
MH D 073	1963, 8 × 10
MH D 073	1977, 8 × 10
MH D 073	11316, 5 × 7
MH D 073	11324, 8 × 10
MH D 074	658, 8 × 10
MH D 074	1962, 8 × 10
MH D 074	1963, 8 × 10
MH D 074	1977, 8 × 10
MH D 074	2006, 8 × 10
MH D 074	11316, 5 × 7
MH D 074	11324, 8 × 10
MH D 075	658, 8 × 10
MH D 075	1962, 8 × 10
MH D 075	1963, 8 × 10

Medinet Habu (*cont.*)

Nelson Number/Description	Negative, Format
MH D 075	1977, 8 × 10
MH D 075	11316, 5 × 7
MH D 075	11324, 8 × 10
MH D 076	658, 8 × 10
MH D 076	1962, 8 × 10
MH D 076	1963, 8 × 10
MH D 076	1977, 8 × 10
MH D 076	11316, 5 × 7
MH D 076	11324, 8 × 10
MH D 077	658, 8 × 10
MH D 077	1962, 8 × 10
MH D 077	1963, 8 × 10
MH D 077	1977, 8 × 10
MH D 077	11316, 5 × 7
MH D 077	11324, 8 × 10
MH D 078	658, 8 × 10
MH D 078	1962, 8 × 10
MH D 078	1963, 8 × 10
MH D 078	1977, 8 × 10
MH D 078	11316, 5 × 7
MH D 078	11324, 8 × 10
MH D 079	658, 8 × 10
MH D 079	1977, 8 × 10
MH D 079	11316, 5 × 7
MH D 079	11324, 8 × 10
MH D 080	638, 8 × 10
MH D 080	11814, 8 × 10
MH D 080	11844, 8 × 10
MH D 080	11654, 8 × 10
MH D 080	13453, 5 × 7
MH D 081	2063, 8 × 10
MH D 081	11309, 8 × 10
MH D 081	11655, 8 × 10
MH D 081	13453, 5 × 7
MH D 082	2063, 8 × 10
MH D 082	11309, 8 × 10
MH D 082	11655, 8 × 10
MH D 082	13453, 5 × 7
MH D 085	848, 8 × 10
MH D 085	11656, 8 × 10
MH D 085	13457, 5 × 7
MH D 085	13390, 5 × 7
MH D 085	13334, 5 × 7
MH D 085	13338, 5 × 7
MH D 086	848, 8 × 10
MH D 086	11549, 8 × 10
MH D 086	11656, 8 × 10
MH D 086	13457, 5 × 7
MH D 086	13390, 5 × 7
MH D 086	13334, 5 × 7
MH D 086	13338, 5 × 7
MH D 087	848, 8 × 10
MH D 087	11549, 8 × 10
MH D 087	11656, 8 × 10
MH D 087	13334, 5 × 7

Medinet Habu (*cont.*)

Nelson Number/Description	Negative, Format
MH D 087	13338, 5 × 7
MH D 087	13390, 5 × 7
MH D 087	13457, 5 × 7
MH D 088	848, 8 × 10
MH D 088	11549, 8 × 10
MH D 088	11656, 8 × 10
MH D 088	11657, 8 × 10
MH D 088	13334, 5 × 7
MH D 088	13338, 5 × 7
MH D 088	13390, 5 × 7
MH D 088	13457, 5 × 7
MH D 089	11549, 8 × 10
MH D 089	11657, 8 × 10
MH D 089	13334, 5 × 7
MH D 089	13338, 5 × 7
MH D 089	13390, 5 × 7
MH D 089	13457, 5 × 7
MH D 090	11549, 8 × 10
MH D 090	11657, 8 × 10
MH D 090	13334, 5 × 7
MH D 090	13338, 5 × 7
MH D 090	13390, 5 × 7
MH D 090	13457, 5 × 7
MH D 091	11549, 8 × 10
MH D 091	11550, 8 × 10
MH D 091	11657, 8 × 10
MH D 091	13334, 5 × 7
MH D 091	13338, 5 × 7
MH D 091	13390, 5 × 7
MH D 091	13457, 5 × 7
MH D 092	847, 8 × 10
MH D 092	848, 8 × 10
MH D 092	11657, 8 × 10
MH D 092	13334, 5 × 7
MH D 092	13338, 5 × 7
MH D 092	13390, 5 × 7
MH D 092	13452, 5 × 7
MH D 092	13452, 5 × 7
MH D 092	13457, 5 × 7
MH D 093	847, 8 × 10
MH D 093	13334, 5 × 7
MH D 093	13338, 5 × 7
MH D 093	13390, 5 × 7
MH D 093	13453, 5 × 7
MH D 093	13457, 5 × 7
MH D 093a	848, 8 × 10
MH D 093a	11550, 8 × 10
MH D 093b	848, 8 × 10
MH D 093b	11550, 8 × 10
MH D 093b	11657, 8 × 10
MH D 093c	11552, 8 × 10
MH D 093c	11620, 8 × 10
MH D 093d	11552, 8 × 10
MH D 093d	11620, 8 × 10
MH D 093e	11552, 8 × 10

Medinet Habu (*cont.*)

Nelson Number/Description	Negative, Format
MH D 093e	11620, 8 × 10
MH D 093f	11552, 8 × 10
MH D 093f	11620, 8 × 10
MH D 093g	11551, 8 × 10
MH D 093g	11620, 8 × 10
MH D 093h	11551, 8 × 10
MH D 093h	11620, 8 × 10
MH D 093i	11551, 8 × 10
MH D 093i	11620, 8 × 10
MH D 093j	11551, 8 × 10
MH D 093j	11620, 8 × 10
MH D 095	1965, 8 × 10
MH D 095	11317, 5 × 7
MH D 095	11325, 8 × 10
MH D 096	1965, 8 × 10
MH D 096	11317, 5 × 7
MH D 096	11325, 8 × 10
MH D 097	659, 8 × 10
MH D 097	1965, 8 × 10
MH D 097	2004, 8 × 10
MH D 097	11317, 5 × 7
MH D 097	11325, 8 × 10
MH D 098	659, 8 × 10
MH D 098	1961, 8 × 10
MH D 098	1965, 8 × 10
MH D 098	11317, 5 × 7
MH D 098	11325, 8 × 10
MH D 099	659, 8 × 10
MH D 099	1961, 8 × 10
MH D 099	1965, 8 × 10
MH D 099	11317, 5 × 7
MH D 099	11325, 8 × 10
MH D 100	659, 8 × 10
MH D 100	1961, 8 × 10
MH D 100	1965, 8 × 10
MH D 100	11317, 5 × 7
MH D 100	11325, 8 × 10
MH D 101	659, 8 × 10
MH D 101	1961, 8 × 10
MH D 101	11317, 5 × 7
MH D 101	11325, 8 × 10
MH D 102	659, 8 × 10
MH D 102	1961, 8 × 10
MH D 102	11317, 5 × 7
MH D 102	11325, 8 × 10
MH D 103	659, 8 × 10
MH D 103	1961, 8 × 10
MH D 103	11317, 5 × 7
MH D 103	11325, 8 × 10
MH D 104	637, 8 × 10
MH D 104	11658, 8 × 10
MH D 105	11310, 8 × 10
MH D 105	11621, 8 × 10
MH D 106	11310, 8 × 10
MH D 106	11621, 8 × 10

Medinet Habu (*cont.*)

Nelson Number/Description	Negative, Format
MH D 108	2048, 8 × 10
MH D 109	2048, 8 × 10
MH D 110	2048, 8 × 10
MH D 110	11318, 5 × 7
MH D 110	11621, 8 × 10
MH D 111	2048, 8 × 10
MH D 111	11318, 5 × 7
MH D 111	11621, 8 × 10
MH D 115	1968, 8 × 10
MH D 115	1969, 8 × 10
MH D 115	11529, 5 × 7
MH D 115	11622, 8 × 10
MH D 116	1968, 8 × 10
MH D 116	1969, 8 × 10
MH D 116	11529, 5 × 7
MH D 116	11622, 8 × 10
MH D 117	849, 8 × 10
MH D 117	1968, 8 × 10
MH D 117	1969, 8 × 10
MH D 117	11529, 5 × 7
MH D 117	11622, 8 × 10
MH D 117	11623, 8 × 10
MH D 118	849, 8 × 10
MH D 118	1968, 8 × 10
MH D 118	11623, 8 × 10
MH D 119	11277, 8 × 10
MH D 119	11624, 8 × 10
MH D 120	11319, 5 × 7
MH D 120	11320, 5 × 7
MH D 120	11621, 8 × 10
MH D 121	11319, 5 × 7
MH D 121	11320, 5 × 7
MH D 121	11621, 8 × 10
MH D 122	2000, 8 × 10
MH D 122	11621, 8 × 10
MH D 122a	11321, 5 × 7
MH D 123	1976, 8 × 10
MH D 123	11684, 8 × 10
MH D 124	675, 8 × 10
MH D 124	1976, 8 × 10
MH D 124	11684, 8 × 10
MH D 125	636, 8 × 10
MH D 125	11278, 8 × 10
MH D 125	11724, 8 × 10
MH D 125	13342, 5 × 7
MH D 126	636, 8 × 10
MH D 126	11278, 8 × 10
MH D 126	11310, 8 × 10
MH D 126	11621, 8 × 10
MH D 127	11278, 8 × 10
MH D 127	11310, 8 × 10
MH D 127	11621, 8 × 10
MH D 128	11310, 8 × 10
MH D 128	11621, 8 × 10
MH D 129	11310, 8 × 10

Medinet Habu (*cont.*)

Nelson Number/Description	Negative, Format
MH D 129	11621, 8 × 10
MH D 135	2057, 8 × 10
MH D 135	11279, 8 × 10
MH D 135	11566, 8 × 10
MH D 135	13453, 5 × 7
MH D 136	2057, 8 × 10
MH D 136	2058, 8 × 10
MH D 136	11279, 8 × 10
MH D 136	11566, 8 × 10
MH D 136	13453, 5 × 7
MH D 137	2058, 8 × 10
MH D 137	11279, 8 × 10
MH D 137	11566, 8 × 10
MH D 137	13453, 5 × 7
MH D 138	2058, 8 × 10
MH D 138	11279, 8 × 10
MH D 138	11566, 8 × 10
MH D 138	13453, 5 × 7
MH D 139	2049, 8 × 10
MH D 139	11567, 8 × 10
MH D 140	2049, 8 × 10
MH D 140	11567, 8 × 10
MH D 141	2055, 8 × 10
MH D 141	11280, 8 × 10
MH D 141	11568, 8 × 10
MH D 142	2056, 8 × 10
MH D 142	11280, 8 × 10
MH D 142	11568, 8 × 10
MH D 143	2056, 8 × 10
MH D 143	11280, 8 × 10
MH D 143	11568, 8 × 10
MH D 144	2059, 8 × 10
MH D 144	11281, 8 × 10
MH D 144	11569, 8 × 10
MH D 145	2059, 8 × 10
MH D 145	2060, 8 × 10
MH D 145	11281, 8 × 10
MH D 145	11569, 8 × 10
MH D 146	2060, 8 × 10
MH D 146	11281, 8 × 10
MH D 146	11569, 8 × 10
MH D 147	2060, 8 × 10
MH D 147	11281, 8 × 10
MH D 147	11569, 8 × 10
MH D 148	2050, 8 × 10
MH D 148	11625, 8 × 10
MH D 149	2050, 8 × 10
MH D 149	11625, 8 × 10
MH D 150	2050, 8 × 10
MH D 150	11625, 8 × 10
MH D 151	2054, 8 × 10
MH D 151	11282, 8 × 10
MH D 151	11570, 8 × 10
MH D 152	2051, 8 × 10
MH D 152	11282, 8 × 10

Medinet Habu (*cont.*)

Nelson Number/Description	Negative, Format
MH D 152	11570, 8 × 10
MH D 153	11282, 8 × 10
MH D 153	11570, 8 × 10
MH D 154	2051, 8 × 10
MH D 154	11282, 8 × 10
MH D 154	11570, 8 × 10
MH D 155	2007, 8 × 10
MH D 155	11725, 8 × 10
MH D 158	2051, 8 × 10
MH D 160	853, 8 × 10
MH D 160	1597, 8 × 10
MH D 160	11553, 8 × 10
MH D 160	11726, 8 × 10
MH D 161	851, 8 × 10
MH D 161	853, 8 × 10
MH D 161	1597, 8 × 10
MH D 161	11553, 8 × 10
MH D 161	11726, 8 × 10
MH D 162	851, 8 × 10
MH D 162	853, 8 × 10
MH D 162	11553, 8 × 10
MH D 162	11726, 8 × 10
MH D 163	851, 8 × 10
MH D 163	853, 8 × 10
MH D 163	11553, 8 × 10
MH D 163	11726, 8 × 10
MH D 164	851, 8 × 10
MH D 164	853, 8 × 10
MH D 164	11553, 8 × 10
MH D 164	11726, 8 × 10
MH D 165	851, 8 × 10
MH D 165	853, 8 × 10
MH D 165	11553, 8 × 10
MH D 165	11726, 8 × 10
MH D 166	641, 8 × 10
MH D 166	851, 8 × 10
MH D 166	853, 8 × 10
MH D 166	11553, 8 × 10
MH D 166	11726, 8 × 10
MH D 167	641, 8 × 10
MH D 167	851, 8 × 10
MH D 167	853, 8 × 10
MH D 167	11680, 8 × 10
MH D 167	11727, 8 × 10
MH D 168	641, 8 × 10
MH D 168	851, 8 × 10
MH D 168	853, 8 × 10
MH D 168	11680, 8 × 10
MH D 168	11727, 8 × 10
MH D 169	641, 8 × 10
MH D 169	851, 8 × 10
MH D 169	853, 8 × 10
MH D 169	11680, 8 × 10
MH D 169	11727, 8 × 10
MH D 170	641, 8 × 10

Medinet Habu (*cont.*)

Nelson Number/Description	Negative, Format
MH D 170	851, 8 × 10
MH D 170	853, 8 × 10
MH D 170	11680, 8 × 10
MH D 170	11727, 8 × 10
MH D 171	640, 8 × 10
MH D 171	641, 8 × 10
MH D 171	643, 8 × 10
MH D 171	851, 8 × 10
MH D 171	853, 8 × 10
MH D 171	11685, 8 × 10
MH D 172	640, 8 × 10
MH D 172	641, 8 × 10
MH D 172	643, 8 × 10
MH D 172	851, 8 × 10
MH D 172	853, 8 × 10
MH D 172	11685, 8 × 10
MH D 173	640, 8 × 10
MH D 173	641, 8 × 10
MH D 173	643, 8 × 10
MH D 173	851, 8 × 10
MH D 173	853, 8 × 10
MH D 173	11685, 8 × 10
MH D 174	643, 8 × 10
MH D 174	644, 8 × 10
MH D 174	851, 8 × 10
MH D 174	853, 8 × 10
MH D 174	11283, 8 × 10
MH D 174	11571, 8 × 10
MH D 175	643, 8 × 10
MH D 175	644, 8 × 10
MH D 175	851, 8 × 10
MH D 175	853, 8 × 10
MH D 175	11283, 8 × 10
MH D 175	11571, 8 × 10
MH D 176	643, 8 × 10
MH D 176	644, 8 × 10
MH D 176	851, 8 × 10
MH D 176	853, 8 × 10
MH D 176	11283, 8 × 10
MH D 176	11571, 8 × 10
MH D 177	643, 8 × 10
MH D 177	644, 8 × 10
MH D 177	851, 8 × 10
MH D 177	853, 8 × 10
MH D 177	11284, 8 × 10
MH D 177	11572, 8 × 10
MH D 178	643, 8 × 10
MH D 178	644, 8 × 10
MH D 178	851, 8 × 10
MH D 178	853, 8 × 10
MH D 178	11284, 8 × 10
MH D 178	11572, 8 × 10
MH D 179	643, 8 × 10
MH D 179	644, 8 × 10
MH D 179	851, 8 × 10

Medinet Habu (*cont.*)		Medinet Habu (*cont.*)	
Nelson Number/Description	*Negative, Format*	*Nelson Number/Description*	*Negative, Format*
MH D 179	853, 8 × 10	MH D 197	2016, 8 × 10
MH D 179	11284, 8 × 10	MH D 197	11730, 8 × 10
MH D 179	11572, 8 × 10	MH D 198	854, 8 × 10
MH D 184	855, 8 × 10	MH D 198	1622, 8 × 10
MH D 184	1394, 8 × 10	MH D 198	2013, 8 × 10
MH D 184	1456, 8 × 10	MH D 198	2014, 8 × 10
MH D 184	11686, 8 × 10	MH D 198	2016, 8 × 10
MH D 185	855, 8 × 10	MH D 198	11730, 8 × 10
MH D 185	1394, 8 × 10	MH D 199	854, 8 × 10
MH D 185	1456, 8 × 10	MH D 199	1403, 8 × 10
MH D 185	2014, 8 × 10	MH D 199	2014, 8 × 10
MH D 185	11686, 8 × 10	MH D 199	2016, 8 × 10
MH D 186	855, 8 × 10	MH D 199	11731, 8 × 10
MH D 186	1394, 8 × 10	MH D 205	2027, 8 × 10
MH D 186	1456, 8 × 10	MH D 206	2027, 8 × 10
MH D 186	2014, 8 × 10	MH D 206	11661, 5 × 7
MH D 186	11686, 8 × 10	MH D 206	11738, 8 × 10
MH D 187	855, 8 × 10	MH D 207	2027, 8 × 10
MH D 187	1394, 8 × 10	MH D 208	2027, 8 × 10
MH D 187	1456, 8 × 10	MH D 208	11662, 5 × 7
MH D 187	1489, 8 × 10	MH D 208	11794, 8 × 10
MH D 187	2014, 8 × 10	MH D 208	14392, 5 × 7
MH D 187	11686, 8 × 10	MH D 208	14395, 5 × 7
MH D 188	2005, 8 × 10	MH D 209	1565, 8 × 10
MH D 188	2014, 8 × 10	MH D 209	2027, 8 × 10
MH D 189	2014, 8 × 10	MH D 209	11815, 8 × 10
MH D 189	11530, 5 × 7	MH D 209	11845, 8 × 10
MH D 189	11626, 8 × 10	MH D 210	1565, 8 × 10
MH D 190	2014, 8 × 10	MH D 210	2027, 8 × 10
MH D 190	11536, 5 × 7	MH D 210	11815, 8 × 10
MH D 190	11627, 8 × 10	MH D 210	11845, 8 × 10
MH D 191	2014, 8 × 10	MH D 211	1564, 8 × 10
MH D 191	2015, 8 × 10	MH D 211	1614, 8 × 10
MH D 191	11792, 8 × 10	MH D 211	2027, 8 × 10
MH D 192	2014, 8 × 10	MH D 211	11732, 8 × 10
MH D 193	2002, 8 × 10	MH D 212	2027, 8 × 10
MH D 193	2014, 8 × 10	MH D 212	11660, 5 × 7
MH D 193	11531, 5 × 7	MH D 212	11687, 8 × 10
MH D 193	11737, 8 × 10	MH D 213	2027, 8 × 10
MH D 194	1998, 8 × 10	MH D 213	11660, 5 × 7
MH D 194	2014, 8 × 10	MH D 213	11687, 8 × 10
MH D 194	11728, 8 × 10	MH D 214	1564, 8 × 10
MH D 195	854, 8 × 10	MH D 214	2027, 8 × 10
MH D 195	2013, 8 × 10	MH D 214	11688, 8 × 10
MH D 195	2014, 8 × 10	MH D 215	1591, 8 × 10
MH D 195	2016, 8 × 10	MH D 215	2027, 8 × 10
MH D 195	11729, 8 × 10	MH D 216	1591, 8 × 10
MH D 195	13788, 5 × 7	MH D 216	2027, 8 × 10
MH D 196	854, 8 × 10	MH D 217	2027, 8 × 10
MH D 196	1396, 8 × 10	MH D 217	2075, 8 × 10
MH D 196	2014, 8 × 10	MH D 217	11311, 5 × 7
MH D 196	2016, 8 × 10	MH D 226	11689, 8 × 10
MH D 196	11793, 8 × 10	MH D 232	2138, 8 × 10
MH D 197	2013, 8 × 10	MH D 252	1986, 8 × 10
MH D 197	2014, 8 × 10	MH D 252	1997, 8 × 10

Medinet Habu (*cont.*)		Medinet Habu (*cont.*)	
Nelson Number/Description	*Negative, Format*	*Nelson Number/Description*	*Negative, Format*
MH D 252	11690, 8 × 10	MH D 278	1991, 8 × 10
MH D 253a	1995, 8 × 10	MH D 278	11844, 8 × 10
MH D 253a	11674, 8 × 10	MH D 279	1984, 8 × 10
MH D 253b	1986, 8 × 10	MH D 279	11442, 5 × 7
MH D 253b	1997, 8 × 10	MH D 279	11443, 5 × 7
MH D 253b	11690, 8 × 10	MH D 279	11444, 5 × 7
MH D 254a	1995, 8 × 10	MH D 279	11573, 8 × 10
MH D 254a	11674, 8 × 10	MH D 280a	1983, 8 × 10
MH D 254a	11692, 8 × 10	MH D 280a	11443, 5 × 7
MH D 254b	1996, 8 × 10	MH D 280a	11573, 8 × 10
MH D 255	1995, 8 × 10	MH D 280b	1992, 8 × 10
MH D 255	11674, 8 × 10	MH D 280b	11536, 5 × 7
MH D 256	1996, 8 × 10	MH D 280b	11574, 8 × 10
MH D 256	11692, 8 × 10	MH D 280b	11627, 8 × 10
MH D 257	1994, 8 × 10	MH D 281a	1985, 8 × 10
MH D 257	11691, 8 × 10	MH D 281a	11444, 5 × 7
MH D 258	1994, 8 × 10	MH D 281a	11573, 8 × 10
MH D 258	11691, 8 × 10	MH D 281b	1970, 8 × 10
MH D 259a	1994, 8 × 10	MH D 282	2003, 8 × 10
MH D 259a	11691, 8 × 10	MH D 282a	1999, 8 × 10
MH D 259b	1986, 8 × 10	MH D 282a	11628, 8 × 10
MH D 259b	1997, 8 × 10	MH D 282b	1988, 8 × 10
MH D 259b	11690, 8 × 10	MH D 282b	11574, 8 × 10
MH D 261a	2139, 8 × 10	MH D 285a	1558, 8 × 10
MH D 261b	2140, 8 × 10	MH D 285a	11445, 5 × 7
MH D 262	11617, 5 × 7	MH D 285a	11446, 5 × 7
MH D 263	1978, 8 × 10	MH D 285b	1993, 8 × 10
MH D 263	1979, 8 × 10	MH D 285b	11447, 5 × 7
MH D 263	11435, 5 × 7	MH D 285b	11629, 8 × 10
MH D 263	11436, 5 × 7	MH E 035	1575, 8 × 10
MH D 263	11437, 5 × 7	MH E 036	1425, 8 × 10
MH D 264a	11436, 5 × 7	MH E 037	1425, 8 × 10
MH D 264b	11438, 5 × 7	MH E 041	8357, 5 × 7
MH D 264b	11733, 8 × 10	MH E 042	8312, 5 × 7
MH D 265	2053, 8 × 10	MH E 044	8309, 5 × 7
MH D 265	11439, 5 × 7	MH E 060	8335, 8 × 10
MH D 265	11693, 8 × 10	MH E 060	8358, 5 × 7
MH D 266	11437, 5 × 7	MH E 061	8335, 8 × 10
MH D 267	2052, 8 × 10	MH E 061	8359, 5 × 7
MH D 267a	11440, 5 × 7	MH E 062	8291, 8 × 10
MH D 267a	11618, 5 × 7	MH E 062	8355, 5 × 7
MH D 267a	11733, 8 × 10	MH E 062	8356, 5 × 7
MH D 267b	11441, 5 × 7	MH E 063	8291, 8 × 10
MH D 267b	11693, 8 × 10	MH E 063	8355, 5 × 7
MH D 270	11515, 8 × 10	MH E 063	8356, 5 × 7
MH D 271	2141, 8 × 10	MH E 076	8311, 5 × 7
MH D 272	11532, 5 × 7	MH E 077	8313, 5 × 7
MH D 273	11533, 5 × 7	MH E 078	8313, 5 × 7
MH D 274	2029, 8 × 10	MH E 079	8310, 5 × 7
MH D 275	11534, 5 × 7	MH E 080	1424, 8 × 10
MH D 275	15824, 5 × 7	MH E 081	1430, 8 × 10
MH D 275	11795, 8 × 10	MH E 085	1400, 8 × 10
MH D 276	11535, 5 × 7	MH E 086	1411, 8 × 10
MH D 276	11796, 8 × 10	MH E 090	1395, 8 × 10
MH D 277	2028, 8 × 10	MH E 091	719, 8 × 10

Medinet Habu (*cont.*)

Nelson Number/Description	Negative, Format
MH E 091	1410, 8 × 10
MH E 093	1566, 8 × 10
MH E 093	8350, 8 × 10
MH E 094	1566, 8 × 10
MH E 094	8350, 8 × 10
MH E 095	1583, 8 × 10
MH E 095	8350, 8 × 10
MH E 096	1583, 8 × 10
MH E 096	8350, 8 × 10
MH E 100	2074, 8 × 10
MH E 100	2084, 8 × 10
MH E 100	2085, 8 × 10
MH E 100	2086, 8 × 10
MH E 100	8319, 8 × 10
MH E 100	8320, 8 × 10
MH E 100	8321, 8 × 10
MH E 100	8322, 8 × 10
MH E 100	8325, 8 × 10
MH E 100	8326, 8 × 10
MH E 100	9698, 8 × 10
MH E 100	9699, 8 × 10
MH E 100	9700, 8 × 10
MH E 100	9701, 8 × 10
MH E 100	9702, 8 × 10
MH E 100	9703, 8 × 10
MH E 100	9704, 8 × 10
MH E 100	9705, 8 × 10
MH E 100	9707, 8 × 10
MH E 100	9708, 8 × 10
MH E 100	9709, 8 × 10
MH E 100	9710, 8 × 10
MH E 100	9711, 8 × 10
MH E 100	9713, 8 × 10
MH E 100	9714, 8 × 10
MH E 100	9715, 8 × 10
MH E 100	9846, 8 × 10
MH E 101	2074, 8 × 10
MH E 101	2082, 8 × 10
MH E 101	2083, 8 × 10
MH E 101	9846, 8 × 10
MH E 102	2074, 8 × 10
MH E 102	9846, 8 × 10
MH E 103	2082, 8 × 10
MH E 103	9698, 8 × 10
MH E 104	2082, 8 × 10
MH E 104	9699, 8 × 10
MH E 105	2083, 8 × 10
MH E 105	9700, 8 × 10
MH E 106	2083, 8 × 10
MH E 106	9701, 8 × 10
MH E 107	8322, 8 × 10
MH E 107	9702, 8 × 10
MH E 108	8319, 8 × 10
MH E 108	8322, 8 × 10
MH E 108	9702, 8 × 10

Medinet Habu (*cont.*)

Nelson Number/Description	Negative, Format
MH E 108	9703, 8 × 10
MH E 109	8319, 8 × 10
MH E 109	9703, 8 × 10
MH E 110	8319, 8 × 10
MH E 110	9704, 8 × 10
MH E 111	8320, 8 × 10
MH E 111	9704, 8 × 10
MH E 112	8320, 8 × 10
MH E 112	9705, 8 × 10
MH E 113	8320, 8 × 10
MH E 113	9705, 8 × 10
MH E 114	8323, 8 × 10
MH E 114	9706, 8 × 10
MH E 115	8323, 8 × 10
MH E 115	9707, 8 × 10
MH E 116	8321, 8 × 10
MH E 116	9707, 8 × 10
MH E 117	8321, 8 × 10
MH E 117	9708, 8 × 10
MH E 118	8321, 8 × 10
MH E 118	8326, 8 × 10
MH E 118	9709, 8 × 10
MH E 119	8326, 8 × 10
MH E 119	9709, 8 × 10
MH E 120	8325, 8 × 10
MH E 120	8326, 8 × 10
MH E 120	9710, 8 × 10
MH E 121	8325, 8 × 10
MH E 121	9711, 8 × 10
MH E 122	2085, 8 × 10
MH E 122	8325, 8 × 10
MH E 122	9711, 8 × 10
MH E 123	2085, 8 × 10
MH E 123	9711, 8 × 10
MH E 123	9712, 8 × 10
MH E 124	2085, 8 × 10
MH E 124	9712, 8 × 10
MH E 125	2084, 8 × 10
MH E 125	9713, 8 × 10
MH E 126	2084, 8 × 10
MH E 126	9713, 8 × 10
MH E 127	2084, 8 × 10
MH E 127	9714, 8 × 10
MH E 128	2086, 8 × 10
MH E 128	9714, 8 × 10
MH E 129	2086, 8 × 10
MH E 129	9715, 8 × 10
MH E 130	2074, 8 × 10
MH E 130	2082, 8 × 10
MH E 130	2083, 8 × 10
MH E 130	8319, 8 × 10
MH E 130	8320, 8 × 10
MH E 130	8322, 8 × 10
MH E 130	9698, 8 × 10
MH E 130	9699, 8 × 10

Medinet Habu (*cont.*)

Nelson Number/Description	Negative, Format
MH E 130	9700, 8 × 10
MH E 130	9701, 8 × 10
MH E 130	9713, 8 × 10
MH E 130	9846, 8 × 10
MH E 134	2066, 8 × 10
MH E 134	2072, 8 × 10
MH E 134	2073, 8 × 10
MH E 134	2079, 8 × 10
MH E 134	2080, 8 × 10
MH E 134	2081, 8 × 10
MH E 134	9716, 8 × 10
MH E 134	9717, 8 × 10
MH E 134	9718, 8 × 10
MH E 134	9719, 8 × 10
MH E 134	9720, 8 × 10
MH E 134	9721, 8 × 10
MH E 134	9722, 8 × 10
MH E 134	9723, 8 × 10
MH E 134	9724, 8 × 10
MH E 134	9725, 8 × 10
MH E 134	10409, 8 × 10
MH E 135	2066, 8 × 10
MH E 135	9716, 8 × 10
MH E 136	2073, 8 × 10
MH E 136	9717, 8 × 10
MH E 137	2073, 8 × 10
MH E 137	9718, 8 × 10
MH E 138	2072, 8 × 10
MH E 138	9719, 8 × 10
MH E 138	10409, 8 × 10
MH E 139	2072, 8 × 10
MH E 139	9720, 8 × 10
MH E 139	10409, 8 × 10
MH E 140	2081, 8 × 10
MH E 140	9720, 8 × 10
MH E 140	10409, 8 × 10
MH E 141	2081, 8 × 10
MH E 141	9721, 8 × 10
MH E 142	2081, 8 × 10
MH E 142	9722, 8 × 10
MH E 143	2080, 8 × 10
MH E 143	9723, 8 × 10
MH E 144	2080, 8 × 10
MH E 144	9723, 8 × 10
MH E 145	2079, 8 × 10
MH E 145	2080, 8 × 10
MH E 145	9724, 8 × 10
MH E 146	2079, 8 × 10
MH E 146	9725, 8 × 10
MH E 147	2079, 8 × 10
MH E 147	9847, 8 × 10
MH E 148	9847, 8 × 10
MH E 149	9847, 8 × 10
Bark pedestal, front	11554, 5 × 7
Bark pedestal, front and rear	11548, 8 × 10

Medinet Habu (*cont.*)

Nelson Number/Description	Negative, Format
Bark pedestal, rear	11555, 5 × 7
Court, sunrise from pylon, view of Small Temple	13805, 8 × 10
Court, sunrise from pylon, view of Small Temple	13806, 8 × 10
Court, sunrise from pylon, view of Small Temple	13807, 8 × 10
Court, sunrise from pylon, view of Small Temple	13808, 8 × 10
Court, sunset from pylon, view of Small Temple	13809, 8 × 10
Decorative elements	1848, 8 × 10
Decorative elements	2190, 8 × 10
Destroyed quay area, reused block #1316	2215, 8 × 10
Exterior	15362, 8 × 10
Exterior	15363, 8 × 10
Exterior	15364, 8 × 10
Exterior	15365, 8 × 10
Exterior	15366, 8 × 10
Exterior	15367, 8 × 10
Exterior	15368, 4 × 5
Exterior	15369, 4 × 5
Exterior	15371, 4 × 5
Exterior	15372, 4 × 5
Exterior	15373, 4 × 5
Exterior	15374, 4 × 5
Exterior	15375, 8 × 10
Exterior	15376, 8 × 10
Exterior	15377, 8 × 10
Exterior	15380, 8 × 10
General view	65, 5 × 7
General view	66, 5 × 7
General view	145, 8 × 10
General view	150, 8 × 10
General view	199, 8 × 10
General view	217, 5 × 7
General view	287, 8 × 10
General view	288, 8 × 10
General view	289, 8 × 10
General view	290, 8 × 10
General view	291, 8 × 10
General view	292, 8 × 10
General view	583, 5 × 7
General view	601, 8 × 10
General view	727, 8 × 10
General view	728, 8 × 10
General view	774, 5 × 7
General view	775, 5 × 7
General view	776, 5 × 7
General view	777, 5 × 7
General view	857, 8 × 10
General view	858, 5 × 7
General view	970, 8 × 10
General view	990, 8 × 10
General view	991, 8 × 10
General view	992, 8 × 10
General view	997, 5 × 7
General view	998, 8 × 10
General view	999, 8 × 10
General view	1000, 8 × 10

Medinet Habu (*cont.*)

Nelson Number/Description	Negative, Format
General view	1055, 8 × 10
General view	1056, 8 × 10
General view	1057, 8 × 10
General view	1058, 8 × 10
General view	1059, 8 × 10
General view	1069, 5 × 7
General view	1109, 5 × 7
General view	1116, 5 × 7
General view	1253, 8 × 10
General view	1260, 8 × 10
General view	1263, 11 × 14
General view	1264, 11 × 14
General view	1265, 11 × 14
General view	1272, 11 × 14
General view	2020, 11 × 14
General view	2021, 11 × 14
General view	2022, 11 × 14
General view	2023, 11 × 14
General view	2024, 11 × 14
General view	2025, 11 × 14
General view	2026, 11 × 14
General view	2069, 11 × 14
General view	2070, 11 × 14
General view	2197, 8 × 10
General view	2198, 8 × 10
General view	2404, 11 × 14
General view	2406, 8 × 10
General view	2412, 8 × 10
General view	2635, 8 × 10
General view	2676, 8 × 10
General view	2803, 5 × 7
General view	2804, 5 × 7
General view	2805, 5 × 7
General view	2806, 5 × 7
General view	2807, 5 × 7
General view	2808, 5 × 7
General view	2809, 5 × 7
General view	2810, 5 × 7
General view	2828, 5 × 7
General view	3557, 8 × 10
General view	6277, 8 × 10
General view	7480, 8 × 10
General view	9065, 5 × 7
General view	9066, 5 × 7
General view	9067, 5 × 7
General view	9068, 5 × 7
General view	9069, 5 × 7
General view	10706, 8 × 10
General view	10707, 8 × 10
General view	10708, 8 × 10
General view	10709, 8 × 10
General view	10710, 8 × 10
General view	13585, 5 × 7
General view	13586, 5 × 7
General view	13613, 5 × 7

Medinet Habu (*cont.*)

Nelson Number/Description	Negative, Format
General view from desert	872, 8 × 10
General view from desert	874, 8 × 10
General view from west MH B and D	13606, 5 × 7
General view front	11816, 8 × 10
General view front	11846, 8 × 10
General view front	11847, 8 × 10
General view rear	11817, 8 × 10
Aerial photograph: general view	2799, 5 × 7
Aerial photograph: general view	2800, 5 × 7
Aerial photograph: general view	2801, 5 × 7
Aerial photograph: general view	2802, 5 × 7
General view, first court, east	2129, 11 × 14
General view, first court, north	2453, 11 × 14
General view, first court, north	2454, 11 × 14
General view of southeast toward Main Gate	2611, 11 × 14
General view, north wall, Pylon I and II	2193, 11 × 14
General view, rear, north side	11273, 8 × 10
General view, rear, south side	11272, 8 × 10
General view, second court	2166, 11 × 14
General view, second court	2167, 11 × 14
General view, second court	2168, 11 × 14
General view, second court	2169, 11 × 14
General view, second court	2170, 11 × 14
General view, second court	2171, 11 × 14
General view, second court, south	797, 5 × 7
General view, second court, west	602, 8 × 10
General view, second court, west	2189, 11 × 14
General view, south wall, Pylon I, II	2405, 11 × 14
Hypostyle Hall	2669, 11 × 14
Hypostyle Hall	13583, 5 × 7
Loose block Ramesses III	8628, 5 × 7
MH 1045: reused block	1427, 8 × 10
MH 1090: reused block	1405, 8 × 10
MH 1097: reused block	1477, 8 × 10
MH 1102: reused block	1473, 8 × 10
MH 1102: reused block	1571, 8 × 10
MH 1102: reused block	1574, 8 × 10
MH 1103: reused block	1417, 8 × 10
MH 1103: reused block	1422, 8 × 10
MH 1103: reused block	1423, 8 × 10
MH 1103: reused block	1449, 8 × 10
MH 1103: reused block	1450, 8 × 10
MH 1103: reused block	1455, 8 × 10
MH 1103: reused block	1460, 8 × 10
MH 1104: reused block	1492, 8 × 10
MH 1104: reused block	1494, 8 × 10
MH 1104: reused block	1570, 8 × 10
MH 1105: reused block	1462, 8 × 10
MH 1105: reused block	1501, 8 × 10
MH 1106: reused block	1431, 8 × 10
MH 1106: reused block	1437, 8 × 10
MH 1106: reused block	1485, 8 × 10
MH 1106: reused block	1493, 8 × 10
MH 1106: reused block	1498, 8 × 10
MH 1106: reused block	1547, 8 × 10

Medinet Habu (*cont.*)

Nelson Number/Description	Negative, Format
MH 1106: reused block	2413, 8 × 10
MH 1106: reused block	2414, 8 × 10
MH 1106: reused block	2415, 8 × 10
MH 1106: reused block	2416, 8 × 10
MH 1106: reused block	2422, 8 × 10
MH 1106: reused block	2443, 5 × 7
MH 1106: reused block	2444, 5 × 7
MH 1106: reused block	2473, 8 × 10
MH 1106: reused block	2499, 5 × 7
MH 1106: reused block	2500, 5 × 7
MH 1106: reused block	2501, 5 × 7
MH 1106: reused block	2502, 5 × 7
MH 1106: reused block	2503, 5 × 7
MH 1107: reused block	1457, 8 × 10
MH 1107: reused block	1463, 8 × 10
MH 1107: reused block	1567, 8 × 10
MH 1107: reused block	1568, 8 × 10
MH 1108: reused block	1413, 8 × 10
MH 1108: reused block	1414, 8 × 10
MH 1108: reused block	1484, 8 × 10
MH 1108: reused block	2474, 8 × 10
MH 1108: reused block	2504, 5 × 7
MH 1108: reused block	2505, 5 × 7
MH 1109: reused block	1397, 8 × 10
MH 1110: reused block	1418, 8 × 10
MH 1110: reused block	1436, 8 × 10
MH 1110: reused block	1439, 8 × 10
MH 1110: reused block	2421, 8 × 10
MH 1110: reused block	2438, 5 × 7
MH 1111: reused block	1409, 8 × 10
MH 1111: reused block	1432, 8 × 10
MH 1112: reused block	1429, 8 × 10
MH 1112: reused block	1440, 8 × 10
MH 1112: reused block	1569, 8 × 10
MH 1113: reused block	1408, 8 × 10
MH 1113: reused block	1559, 8 × 10
MH 1113: reused block	1582, 8 × 10
MH 1113: reused block	2437, 5 × 7
MH 1113: reused block	2506, 5 × 7
MH 1114: reused block	1434, 8 × 10
MH 1117: reused block	1404, 8 × 10
MH 1118: reused block	1426, 8 × 10
MH 1118: reused block	1433, 8 × 10
MH 1119: reused block	1483, 8 × 10
MH 1119: reused block	1486, 8 × 10
MH 1120: reused block	1435, 8 × 10
MH 1127: reused block	1573, 8 × 10
MH 1127: reused block	1577, 8 × 10
MH 1127: reused block	1579, 8 × 10
MH 1139: reused block	1578, 8 × 10
MH 1142: reused block	718, 8 × 10
MH 1142: reused block	2417, 8 × 10
MH 1142: reused block	2418, 5 × 7
MH 1187: reused block	1620, 8 × 10
MH 1188: reused block	1421, 8 × 10

Medinet Habu (*cont.*)

Nelson Number/Description	Negative, Format
MH 1210: reused block	1618, 8 × 10
MH 1339: reused block	1546, 8 × 10
MH 1392: reused block	2076, 8 × 10
MH 1392: reused block	2077, 8 × 10
MH 1501: hieroglyphic detail	865, 5 × 7
MH 1502: hieroglyphic detail	1002, 5 × 7
MH 1503: hieroglyphic detail	1016, 5 × 7
MH 1504: hieroglyphic detail	1017, 5 × 7
MH 1505: hieroglyphic detail	1018, 5 × 7
MH 1506: hieroglyphic detail	1019, 5 × 7
MH 1507: hieroglyphic detail	1020, 5 × 7
MH 1508: hieroglyphic detail	1021, 5 × 7
MH 1509: hieroglyphic detail	1022, 5 × 7
MH 1510: hieroglyphic detail	1023, 5 × 7
MH 1511: hieroglyphic detail	1024, 5 × 7
MH 1512: hieroglyphic detail	1025, 5 × 7
MH 1513: hieroglyphic detail	1026, 5 × 7
MH 1514: hieroglyphic detail	1027, 5 × 7
MH 1515: hieroglyphic detail	1028, 5 × 7
MH 1516: hieroglyphic detail	1029, 5 × 7
MH 1517: hieroglyphic detail	1030, 5 × 7
MH 1518: hieroglyphic detail	1031, 5 × 7
MH 1519: hieroglyphic detail	1032, 5 × 7
MH 1520: hieroglyphic detail	1033, 5 × 7
MH 1521: hieroglyphic detail	1034, 5 × 7
MH 1522: hieroglyphic detail	1035, 5 × 7
MH 1523: hieroglyphic detail	1036, 5 × 7
MH 1524: hieroglyphic detail	1014, 5 × 7
MH 1525: hieroglyphic detail	1013, 8 × 10
MH 1526: hieroglyphic detail	1390, 8 × 10
MH 1527: hieroglyphic detail	1214, 8 × 10
MH 1528: hieroglyphic detail	1218, 8 × 10
MH 1529: hieroglyphic detail	1219, 8 × 10
MH 1530: hieroglyphic detail	1221, 8 × 10
MH 1531: hieroglyphic detail	1235, 8 × 10
MH 1532: hieroglyphic detail	1236, 8 × 10
MH 1533: hieroglyphic detail	1237, 8 × 10
MH 1534: hieroglyphic detail	1238, 8 × 10
MH 1535: hieroglyphic detail	1239, 8 × 10
MH 1536: hieroglyphic detail	1240, 8 × 10
MH 1537: hieroglyphic detail	1241, 8 × 10
MH 1538: hieroglyphic detail	1242, 8 × 10
MH 1539: hieroglyphic detail	1243, 8 × 10
MH 1541: hieroglyphic detail	767, 5 × 7
MH 1542: hieroglyphic detail	876, 5 × 7
Miscellaneous blocks	2095, 8 × 10
Miscellaneous details	5870, 5 × 7
Miscellaneous details	5871, 5 × 7
Miscellaneous details	5872, 5 × 7
Miscellaneous details	5873, 5 × 7
Miscellaneous details	5874, 5 × 7
Miscellaneous details	5879, 5 × 7
Miscellaneous details	5880, 5 × 7
Miscellaneous details	5881, 5 × 7
Miscellaneous details	5882, 5 × 7

Medinet Habu (*cont.*)

Nelson Number/Description	Negative, Format
Miscellaneous details	5883, 5 × 7
Miscellaneous details	5884, 5 × 7
Miscellaneous details	5885, 5 × 7
Miscellaneous details	5886, 5 × 7
Miscellaneous details	5887, 5 × 7
Miscellaneous details	5888, 5 × 7
Miscellaneous details	5889, 5 × 7
Miscellaneous details	5890, 5 × 7
Miscellaneous details	5891, 5 × 7
Miscellaneous details	5895, 5 × 7
Miscellaneous details	5896, 5 × 7
Miscellaneous view	387, 5 × 7
Miscellaneous view	388, 5 × 7
Miscellaneous view	389, 5 × 7
Miscellaneous view	390, 5 × 7
Miscellaneous view	391, 5 × 7
Miscellaneous view	392, 5 × 7
Miscellaneous view	393, 5 × 7
Miscellaneous view	395, 5 × 7
Miscellaneous view	651, 5 × 7
Miscellaneous view	652, 5 × 7
Miscellaneous view	653, 5 × 7
Miscellaneous view	654, 5 × 7
Miscellaneous view	655, 5 × 7
Miscellaneous view	657, 5 × 7
Miscellaneous view	9070, 5 × 7
Miscellaneous view	9071, 5 × 7
Miscellaneous views of western cliffs and valley	873, 5 × 7
None	993, 8 × 10
None	1217, 8 × 10
None	1406, 8 × 10
None	2508, 5 × 7
None	2509, 5 × 7
None	2510, 5 × 7
None	2511, 5 × 7
None	2512, 5 × 7
None	2513, 5 × 7
None	2514, 5 × 7
None	2515, 5 × 7
None	2516, 5 × 7
Portico west of second court toward north	13610, 5 × 7
Pylon I	6540, 8 × 10
Pylon toward west	13607, 5 × 7
Reused block in foundation of Small Temple Temporary number-exterior wall reused block #37. Raised relief, Hathor	16099, 4 × 5
Reused block in foundations of God's Wives of Amun Chapel Temporary number-reused block 94.1.A. Sunk relief	16106, 5 × 7
Reused block in foundations of God's Wives of Amun Chapel Temporary number-reused block 94.1.B. Sunk relief	16122, 5 × 7
Reused block in foundations of God's Wives of Amun Chapel Temporary number-reused block 94.10.A. Raised relief	16113, 5 × 7

Medinet Habu (*cont.*)

Nelson Number/Description	Negative, Format
Reused block in foundations of God's Wives of Amun Chapel Temporary number-reused block 94.10.B. Sunk relief	16119, 5 × 7
Reused block in foundations of God's Wives of Amun Chapel Temporary number-reused block 94.11. Raised relief	16120, 5 × 7
Reused block in foundations of God's Wives of Amun Chapel Temporary number-reused block 94.12. Raised relief	16121, 5 × 7
Reused block in foundations of God's Wives of Amun Chapel Temporary number-reused block 94.13. Raised relief	16112, 5 × 7
Reused block in foundations of God's Wives of Amun Chapel Temporary number-reused block 94.2.A. Raised relief	16105, 5 × 7
Reused block in foundations of God's Wives of Amun Chapel Temporary number-reused block 94.2.B. Sunk relief	16123, 5 × 7
Reused block in foundations of God's Wives of Amun Chapel Temporary number-reused block 94.3.A Left side raised relief, right side sunk relief	16102, 5 × 7
Reused block in foundations of God's Wives of Amun Chapel Temporary number-reused block 94.3.B. Raised relief, traces of red paint	16118, 5 × 7
Reused block in foundations of God's Wives of Amun Chapel Temporary number-reused block 94.4.A. Raised relief	16103, 5 × 7
Reused block in foundations of God's Wives of Amun Chapel Temporary number-reused block 94.5.A. Raised relief	16104, 5 × 7
Reused block in foundations of God's Wives of Amun Chapel Temporary number-reused block 94.5.B. Raised relief	16110, 5 × 7
Reused block in foundations of God's Wives of Amun Chapel Temporary number-reused block 94.6. Raised relief	16108, 5 × 7
Reused block in foundations of God's Wives of Amun Chapel Temporary number-reused block 94.7. Raised relief	16111, 5 × 7
Reused block in foundations of God's Wives of Amun Chapel Temporary number-reused block 94.8.A. Raised relief	16107, 5 × 7
Reused block in foundations of God's Wives of Amun Chapel Temporary number-reused block 94.8.B. Raised relief	16109, 5 × 7
Reused block in foundations of God's Wives of Amun Chapel Temporary number-reused block 94.8.C. Raised relief	16117, 5 × 7
Reused block in foundations of God's Wives of Amun Chapel Temporary number-reused block 94.9.A. Raised relief on left side (traces red, blue paint), sunk relief on right side	16114, 5 × 7
Reused block in foundations of God's Wives of Amun Chapel Temporary number-reused block 94.9.B. Raised relief, traces of red and blue paint	16115, 5 × 7
Reused block in foundations of God's Wives of Amun Chapel Temporary number-reused block 94.9.C. Raised relief, badly deteriorated, some traces of text	16116, 5 × 7
Reused block in Ptolemaic foundation of Small Temple Temporary number-MH B Wall A reused block #1, part of #2. Raised relief	16079, 4 × 5

Medinet Habu (*cont.*)

Nelson Number/Description	Negative, Format
Reused block in Ptolemaic foundation of Small Temple Temporary number-MH B Wall A reused block #2. Raised relief, painted (traces of blue), badly salted	16080, 4 × 5
Reused block in Ptolemaic foundation of Small Temple Temporary number-MH B Wall A reused block #3. Raised relief	16074, 4 × 5
Reused block in Ptolemaic foundation of Small Temple Temporary number-MH B Wall A reused block #4. Sunk relief, painted	16081, 4 × 5
Reused block in Ptolemaic foundation of Small Temple Temporary number-MH B Wall A reused block #5. Sunk relief, painted	16082, 4 × 5
Reused block in Ptolemaic foundation of Small Temple Temporary number-MH B Wall A reused block #6. Sunk relief, painted, traces of yellow	16093, 4 × 5
Reused block in Ptolemaic foundation of Small Temple Temporary number-MH B Wall A reused block #7. Raised relief, painted	16089, 4 × 5
Reused block in Ptolemaic foundation of Small Temple Temporary number-MH B Wall A reused block #8. Raised relief	16090, 4 × 5
Reused block in Ptolemaic foundation of Small Temple Temporary number-MH B Wall A reused block #9. Sunk relief	16092, 4 × 5
Reused block in Ptolemaic foundation of Small Temple Temporary number-MH B Wall B reused block #13. Raised relief	16091, 4 × 5
Reused block in Ptolemaic foundation of Small Temple Temporary number-MH B Wall B reused block #14. Raised relief	16088, 4 × 5
Reused block in Ptolemaic foundation of Small Temple Temporary number-MH B Wall B reused block #16. Sunk relief	16065, 4 × 5
Reused block in Ptolemaic foundation of Small Temple Temporary number-MH B Wall B reused block #18. Raised relief. See also negative 16064	16094, 4 × 5
Reused block in Ptolemaic foundation of Small Temple Temporary number-MH B Wall B reused block #19. Sunk relief, painted	16084, 4 × 5
Reused block in Ptolemaic foundation of Small Temple Temporary number-MH B Wall B reused block #20. Raised relief	16087, 4 × 5
Reused block in Ptolemaic foundation of Small Temple Temporary number-MH B Wall B reused block #21 and 22: 21-raised relief, painted, 22-sunk relief	16083, 4 × 5
Reused block in Ptolemaic foundation of Small Temple Temporary number-MH B Wall B reused block #23. Raised relief, painted	16086, 4 × 5
Reused block in Ptolemaic foundation of Small Temple Temporary number-MH B Wall B reused block #24. Raised relief	16085, 4 × 5
Reused block in Ptolemaic foundation of Small Temple Temporary number-MH B Wall B reused block #25. Raised relief, painted	16063, 4 x 5
Reused block in Ptolemaic foundation of Small Temple Temporary number-MH B Wall B reused block #25. Raised relief, painted	16063, 4 x 5
Reused block in Ptolemaic foundation of Small Temple Temporary number-MH B Wall B reused blocks #17 and 18: 17-sunk relief, 18-raised relief	16064, 4 × 5

Medinet Habu (*cont.*)

Nelson Number/Description	Negative, Format
Reused block in Ptolemaic foundation of Small Temple Temporary number-MH B Wall C reused block #27. Sunk relief	16071, 4 × 5
Reused block in Ptolemaic foundation of Small Temple Temporary number-MH B Wall C reused block #28. Sunk relief	16072, 4 × 5
Reused block in Ptolemaic foundation of Small Temple Temporary number-MH B Wall C reused block #29. Raised relief	16073, 4 × 5
Reused block in Ptolemaic foundation of Small Temple Temporary number-MH B Wall C reused block #30. Sunk relief, trace of blue paint	16076, 4 × 5
Reused block in Ptolemaic foundation of Small Temple Temporary number-MH B Wall C reused block #31. Raised relief	16097, 4 × 5
Reused block in Ptolemaic foundation of Small Temple Temporary number-MH B Wall C reused block #32. Raised relief, painted	16075, 4 × 5
Reused block in Ptolemaic foundation of Small Temple Temporary number-MH B Wall C reused block #33 A. Sunk relief, painted. Also see negative 16077	16078, 4 × 5
Reused block in Ptolemaic foundation of Small Temple Temporary number-MH B Wall C reused block #33 B. Sunk relief, painted. Also see negative 16078	16077, 4 × 5
Reused block in Ptolemaic foundation of Small Temple Temporary number-MH B Wall C reused block #34, part of #35. Raised relief	16095, 4 × 5
Reused block in Ptolemaic foundation of Small Temple Temporary number-MH B Wall C reused block #35. Raised relief	16096, 4 × 5
Reused block in Ptolemaic foundation of Small Temple Temporary number-MH B Wall C reused block #36. Sunk relief	16098, 4 × 5
Reused block in Ptolemaic foundation of Small Temple Temporary number-MH Wall B reused block #10. Sunk relief, painted (traces of blue)	16069, 4 × 5
Reused block in Ptolemaic foundation of Small Temple Temporary number-MH Wall B reused block #11. Sunk relief, painted	16068, 4 × 5
Reused block in Ptolemaic foundation of Small Temple Temporary number-MH Wall B reused block #12. Sunk relief	16067, 4 × 5
Reused block in Ptolemaic foundation of Small Temple Temporary number-MH Wall B reused block #15. Sunk relief	16066, 4 × 5
Reused block in Ptolemaic foundation of Small Temple Temporary number-MH Wall C reused block #26. Sunk relief	16070, 4 × 5
Reused block in Ptolemaic foundation of Well Temporary number-reused column block #38A-half of block Papyrus bud column with raised relief, Amenhotep III	16100, 4 × 5
Reused block in Ptolemaic foundation of Well Temporary number-reused column block #38B-half of block Papyrus bud column with raised relief, Amenhotep III	16101, 4 × 5
Reused blocks #1043 and 1044	1444, 8 × 10
Reused blocks #1046, 1047	1428, 8 × 10
Reused blocks #1130 and 1186	1616, 8 × 10
Roman Forecourt: northeast corner outside north wall, reused blocks	13641, 5 × 7

Medinet Habu (*cont.*)

Nelson Number/Description	Negative, Format
Second court, east	6542, 8 × 10
Second court, J. P. Sebah No. 775	13596, 5 × 7
Second court, J. P. Sebah No. 776	13625, 5 × 7
Second court, J. P. Sebah No. 777	13584, 5 × 7
Second court, toward north	1538, 11 × 14
Second court, north	6543, 8 × 10
Second court, southwest corner	13627, 5 × 7
Second court, southwest side	13571, 5 × 7
Section D east face	856, 8 × 10
Small Temple	13125, 5 × 7
Small Temple from southwest pylon	13126, 5 × 7
Small Temple, facade	13127, 5 × 7
Small Temple, facade	13128, 5 × 7
Small Temple: exterior	13801, 8 × 10
Small Temple: exterior	13810, 8 × 10
Small Temple: exterior view, from top of pylon	13799, 8 × 10
Small Temple: exterior view, from top of pylon	13800, 8 × 10
Small Temple: exterior view, toward south	13798, 8 × 10
Small Temple: exterior view, toward southeast	13796, 8 × 10
Small Temple: exterior view, toward southeast (var neg.)	13797, 8 × 10
Small Temple: floor excavation, Room 2, toward east	13704, 8 × 10
Small Temple: floor excavation, Room 2, toward west	13705, 8 × 10
Small Temple: forecourt, reused blocks	13634, 5 × 7
Small Temple: forecourt, reused blocks	13635, 5 × 7
Small Temple: forecourt, reused blocks	13636, 5 × 7
Small Temple: forecourt, reused blocks	13637, 5 × 7
Small Temple: forecourt, reused blocks	13638, 5 × 7
Small Temple: forecourt, reused blocks	13639, 5 × 7
Small Temple: forecourt, reused blocks	13640, 5 × 7
Small Temple: interior, naos room	15195, 4 × 5
Small Temple: interior, naos room	15196, 4 × 5
Small Temple: interior, naos, full view	15194, 4 × 5
Small Temple: northwest outside corner and doorjamb. Same angle as albumen print taken by J. B. Greene; see also Hölscher, The Excavation of Medinet Habu II, Taharka Gateway, p. 35, fig. 32	13662, 8 × 10
Small Temple: room 5, floor excavation, left side (door)	13667, 8 × 10
Small Temple: room 5, floor excavation, left side of naos	13669, 8 × 10
Small Temple: room 5, floor excavation, right side	13668, 8 × 10
Small Temple: room 5, floor excavation, right side of naos	13670, 8 × 10
Small Temple: Taharka gateway, northwest corner, copy of original albumen print taken in 1853 by J. B. Greene	13495, 5 × 7
Small Temple: Taharka gateway, northwest corner, same view as 13495, in February, 1985	13496, 5 × 7
Small Temple: Taharka gateway, northwest corner, same view as 13495, in February, 1985	13496-a, 5 × 7
Statue group opposite MH B 141	13487, 5 × 7
Statue group opposite MH B 141, back pillar	13488, 5 × 7
Statue group opposite MH B 141, view from northwest	13489, 5 × 7

Medinet Habu (*cont.*)

Nelson Number/Description	Negative, Format
Statue group opposite MH B 141, without meter stick	13490, 5 × 7
Stone	1227, 8 × 10
Stone	1228, 8 × 10
Stone	1230, 8 × 10
Stone	1234, 8 × 10
Stone 2, 3	2420, 5 × 7
Stone 11	1497, 8 × 10
Stone 12	1500, 8 × 10
Stone 13	1555, 8 × 10
Stone 14	1589, 8 × 10
Stone 15	1802, 8 × 1
Stone 15	2150, 8 × 10
Stone 17	2012, 8 × 10
Stone 18	2222, 8 × 10
Stone 19	2225, 8 × 10
Stone 20	2642, 8 × 10
Stone 56	1553, 5 × 7
Stone 1540	764, 5 × 7
Stones	3143, 8 × 10
Stones	3144, 8 × 10
Stones	3145, 8 × 10
Stones	3146, 8 × 10
Stones	3147, 8 × 10
Stones	3148, 8 × 10
Stones	3149, 8 × 10
Stones	3150, 8 × 10
Stones	3151, 8 × 10
Stones	3877, 8 × 10
Stones	3878, 8 × 10
Stones	3890, 8 × 10
Stones	3891, 8 × 10
Stones	3892, 8 × 10
Stones	3944, 8 × 10
Stones	3945, 8 × 10
Stones	3946, 8 × 10
Stones	3947, 8 × 10
Stones	3948, 8 × 10
Stones	3954, 8 × 10
Stones	3955, 8 × 10
Stones from excavation	9755, 8 × 10
Stones from excavation	9756, 8 × 10
Stones from excavation	9764, 5 × 7
Terrace	10681, 8 × 10
Third hypostyle hall, back of south statue group	11449, 5 × 7
Third hypostyle hall, north statue group	11525, 5 × 7
Third hypostyle hall, north statue group, back	11526, 5 × 7
Third hypostyle hall, south and north statue groups	11542, 8 × 10
Third hypostyle hall, south and north statue groups, backs	11543, 8 × 10
Third hypostyle hall, south statue group, back	11527, 5 × 7
Third hypostyle hall, south statue group, back	11528, 5 × 7
View from north	13558, 5 × 7
View south along terrace between pillars and columns	1108, 5 × 7

Montu Temple

Nelson Number/Description	Negative, Format
Montu 042	8489, 8 × 10
Montu 043	8489, 8 × 10
Montu 044	8489, 8 × 10
Montu 045	8489, 8 × 10
Montu 046	8489, 8 × 10
Montu 047	8489, 8 × 10
Montu 048	8489, 8 × 10
Montu 049	8489, 8 × 10
Montu 050	8489, 8 × 10
Montu 051	8489, 8 × 10
Montu 052	8489, 8 × 10
Montu 053	8489, 8 × 10
Montu 054	8489, 8 × 10
Montu 055	8489, 8 × 10

Mut Temple

Nelson Number/Description	Negative, Format
Mut A 005	6343, 8 × 10
Mut A 005	6344, 8 × 10
Mut A 040	8393, 5 × 7
Mut A 041	8393, 5 × 7
Mut A 042	8393, 5 × 7
Mut A 045	8392, 5 × 7
Mut A 046	8392, 5 × 7
Mut B 008	13401, 5 × 7
Mut B 019	8391, 5 × 7
Mut B 020	8391, 5 × 7
Mut B 021	8391, 5 × 7
Mut B 056	10153, 5 × 7
Mut B 086	10152, 5 × 7
Mut C 007	8450, 5 × 7
Mut C 008	8389, 5 × 7
Mut C 009	8389, 5 × 7
Mut C 010	8390, 5 × 7
Mut C 011	8388, 5 × 7
Mut D 001	3194, 8 × 10
Mut D 001	5919, 8 × 10
Mut D 002	3073, 5 × 7
Mut D 002	3255, 8 × 10
Mut D 002	5933, 8 × 10
Mut D 002	5934, 8 × 10
Mut D 002a	3195, 8 × 10
Mut D 002b	3196, 8 × 10
Mut D 003	3197, 8 × 10
Mut D 003	3256, 8 × 10
Mut D 003	3418, 8 × 10
Mut D 003	5935, 8 × 10
Mut D 003	5936, 8 × 10
Mut D 004	3197, 8 × 10
Mut D 004	3198, 8 × 10
Mut D 004	3257, 8 × 10
Mut D 004	3794, 5 × 7
Mut D 004	5937, 8 × 10

Mut Temple (*cont.*)

Nelson Number/Description	Negative, Format
Mut D 005	3101, 5 × 7
Mut D 005	3198, 8 × 10
Mut D 005	3199, 8 × 10
Mut D 005	3258, 8 × 10
Mut D 005	5938, 8 × 10
Mut D 006	3200, 8 × 10
Mut D 006	3259, 8 × 10
Mut D 006	5939, 8 × 10
Mut D 007	3201, 8 × 10
Mut D 007	3202, 8 × 10
Mut D 007	3260, 8 × 10
Mut D 007	5940, 8 × 10
Mut D 007	5941, 8 × 10
Mut D 008	3261, 8 × 10
Mut D 008	5942, 8 × 10
Mut D 008	5943, 8 × 10
Mut D 008a	3203, 8 × 10
Mut D 008b	3204, 8 × 10
Mut D 009	3094, 8 × 10
Mut D 010	3205, 8 × 10
Mut D 010	5917, 8 × 10
Mut D 011	3206, 8 × 10
Mut D 011	5917, 8 × 10
Mut D 012	3206, 8 × 10
Mut D 012	5917, 8 × 10
Mut D 013	3207, 8 × 10
Mut D 013	5917, 8 × 10
Mut D 014	3208, 8 × 10
Mut D 014	5918, 8 × 10
Mut D 015	3209, 8 × 10
Mut D 015	5918, 8 × 10
Mut D 016	3210, 8 × 10
Mut D 016	5918, 8 × 10
Mut D 017	5918, 8 × 10
Mut D 018	5918, 8 × 10
Mut D 018	5917, 8 × 10
Mut D 019	5918, 8 × 10
Mut D 020	3211, 8 × 10
Mut D 024	3102, 5 × 7
Mut D 025	3103, 5 × 7
Mut D 025	5914, 8 × 10
Mut D 025a	3104, 5 × 7
Mut D 026	3177, 8 × 10
Mut D 026	3178, 8 × 10
Mut D 026	3264, 8 × 10
Mut D 027	3177, 8 × 10
Mut D 027	3178, 8 × 10
Mut D 030	3105, 5 × 7
Mut D 031a	3072, 5 × 7
Mut D 032	3106, 5 × 7
Mut D 034	3107, 5 × 7
Mut D 035	3108, 5 × 7
Mut D 035a	3109, 5 × 7
Mut D 036	3110, 5 × 7
Mut D 040	3111, 5 × 7

Mut Temple (*cont.*)

Nelson Number/Description	Negative, Format
Mut D 041	3112, 5 × 7
Mut D 042	3113, 5 × 7
Mut D 043	3114, 8 × 10
Mut D 044	3115, 5 × 7
Mut D 045	3116, 5 × 7
Mut D 045	5920, 8 × 10
Mut D 046	5913, 8 × 10
Mut D 047	5905, 8 × 10
Mut D 047	5921, 8 × 10
Mut D 048	3117, 5 × 7
Mut D 048	5905, 8 × 10
Mut D 049	5922, 8 × 10
Mut D 050	3069, 5 × 7
Mut D 050	5922, 8 × 10
Mut D 051	3068, 5 × 7
Mut D 051	5922, 8 × 10
Mut D 052	3070, 5 × 7
Mut D 052	5922, 8 × 10
Mut D 053	5922, 8 × 10
Mut D 054	3071, 5 × 7
General view toward north	15594, 11 × 14
General view toward west	5900, 11 × 14
North room east of sanctuary of Amun, south door to shrine of Mut, east jamb	3118, 5 × 7
Ramesses III Temple: west statue	10981, 5 × 7
Ramesses III Temple: west statue	10982, 5 × 7
Ramesses Temple	5916, 11 × 14
Stone	3074, 5 × 7
Stone	3075, 5 × 7
Stone	3076, 5 × 7
Stone	3077, 5 × 7
Stone	3078, 5 × 7
Stone	3079, 5 × 7
Stone	3080, 5 × 7
Stone	3119, 5 × 7
Stone	5902, 8 × 10
Stone	5903, 8 × 10
Stone	5904, 8 × 10
Stone	5923, 5 × 7
Stone	5924, 5 × 7
Stone	5925, 5 × 7
Stone	5926, 5 × 7
Stone	5927, 5 × 7
Stone	5928, 5 × 7
Stone	5929, 5 × 7
Stone	5930, 5 × 7
Stone	5957, 5 × 7
Stone	5958, 5 × 7
Stone	5959, 5 × 7
Stone	5960, 5 × 7
Stone	5961, 5 × 7
Stone	5962, 5 × 7
Stone	5963, 5 × 7
Stone	5964, 5 × 7
Stone	5965, 5 × 7
Stone	5966, 5 × 7

Mut Temple (*cont.*)

Nelson Number/Description	Negative, Format
Stone	5967, 5 × 7
Stone	5968, 5 × 7
Stone	5969, 5 × 7

Nag Hammadi

Nelson Number/Description	Negative, Format
Tomb, inner room, ceiling	10226, 5 × 7
Tomb, inner room, ceiling	10227, 5 × 7
Tomb, inner room, ceiling	10228, 5 × 7
Tomb, inner room, ceiling	10229, 5 × 7
Tomb, inner room, ceiling	10230, 5 × 7
Tomb, inner room, ceiling	10231, 5 × 7
Tomb, inner room, ceiling	10232, 5 × 7
Tomb, inner room, ceiling	10233, 5 × 7
Tomb, inner room, ceiling	10234, 5 × 7
Tomb, inner room, ceiling	10235, 5 × 7
Tomb, inner room, ceiling	11290, 8 × 10
Tomb, outer room, ceiling	10220, 5 × 7
Tomb, outer room, ceiling	10221, 5 × 7
Tomb, outer room, ceiling	10222, 5 × 7
Tomb, outer room, ceiling	10223, 5 × 7
Tomb, outer room, ceiling	10224, 5 × 7
Tomb, outer room, ceiling	10225, 5 × 7
Tomb, outer room, ceiling	11289, 8 × 10

Philae

Nelson Number/Description	Negative, Format
Photograph by the Preussische Akademie der Wissenschaften zu Berlin in Berlin Museum	10559, 8 × 10
Plan of Temple of Isis	8271, 5 × 7

Qift

Nelson Number/Description	Negative, Format
Block	7252, 5 × 7
General view	7280, 5 × 7
General view	7281, 5 × 7
None	8707, 5 × 7
None	8708, 5 × 7
None	8709, 5 × 7

Ramesseum

Nelson Number/Description	Negative, Format
None	7335, 8 × 10
None	7336, 8 × 10
None	7337, 8 × 10
None	7338, 8 × 10
None	7339, 8 × 10
R 016	7279, 8 × 10

Ramesseum (*cont.*)

Nelson Number/Description	Negative, Format
R 017	7278, 8 × 10
R 017	8469, 8 × 10
R 017	8470, 8 × 10
R 017	8471, 8 × 10
R 017	8472, 8 × 10
R 018	7278, 8 × 10
R 018	8469, 8 × 10
R 018	8470, 8 × 10
R 018	8471, 8 × 10
R 018	8472, 8 × 10
R 021	7279, 8 × 10
R 021	8473, 8 × 10
R 022	7279, 8 × 10
R 022	8473, 8 × 10
R 022	8474, 8 × 10
R 023	7279, 8 × 10
R 023	8473, 8 × 10
R 024	8474, 8 × 10
R 024	9072, 5 × 7
R 025	8474, 8 × 10
R 031a	8863, 8 × 10
R 035	7277, 8 × 10
R 036	7277, 8 × 10
R 037	7277, 8 × 10
R 040	6989, 8 × 10
R 041	6987, 8 × 10
R 041	7276, 8 × 10
R 042	6988, 8 × 10
R 042	7265, 8 × 10
R 043	8857, 8 × 10
R 043	8858, 8 × 10
R 043	8859, 8 × 10
R 043	8860, 8 × 10
R 043	8861, 8 × 10
R 043	8862, 8 × 10
R 043	8869, 5 × 7
R 075	8719, 8 × 10
R 077	8864, 8 × 10
R 078	8865, 8 × 10
R 079	8865, 8 × 10
R 080	8719, 8 × 10
R 080	8720, 8 × 10
R 081	8720, 8 × 10
R 082	8719, 8 × 10
R 082	8720, 8 × 10
R 100	8717, 5 × 7
R 102a	8863, 8 × 10
R 102b	8863, 8 × 10
R 103	8867, 8 × 10
R 104	8867, 8 × 10
R 105	8868, 8 × 10
R 106	8868, 8 × 10
R 121	8721, 8 × 10
R 122	8721, 8 × 10
R 122	8722, 8 × 10

Ramesseum (*cont.*)

Nelson Number/Description	Negative, Format
R 131	8723, 8 × 10
R 132	8723, 8 × 10
R 133	8718, 5 × 7
R 133	8724, 8 × 10
R 133	8725, 8 × 10
R 161a	7263, 8 × 10
R 162a	5180, 8 × 10
R 163b	7264, 8 × 10
R 164a	7262, 8 × 10
R 164b	7264, 8 × 10
R 165	8726, 8 × 10
R 165	8866, 8 × 10
R 166	8726, 8 × 10
R 166	8866, 8 × 10
R 167	8855, 8 × 10
R 168	8856, 8 × 10
R 169	8856, 8 × 10
R 180	9088, 8 × 10
R 180	9089, 8 × 10
R 181	8727, 8 × 10
R 181	8728, 8 × 10
R 181	9456, 8 × 10
R 182	9089, 8 × 10
R 182	9090, 8 × 10
R 202	8729, 8 × 10
R 202	8730, 8 × 10
R 206	8731, 8 × 10
R 206	8732, 8 × 10
R 207	8730, 8 × 10
R 208	8730, 8 × 10
R 209	8730, 8 × 10
R 210	8733, 8 × 10
R 220	10569, 5 × 7
R Pil. 012l	8870, 5 × 7
R Pil. 012o	8871, 5 × 7
R Pil. 013n	8872, 5 × 7
R Pil. 013o	8873, 5 × 7
R Pil. 014k	8879, 5 × 7
R Pil. 014l	8874, 5 × 7
R Pil. 014n	8875, 5 × 7
R Pil. 014o	8876, 5 × 7
R Pil. 015l	8877, 5 × 7
R Pil. 015o	8878, 5 × 7
R Pil. 020h	8712, 5 × 7
R Pil. 020i	8712, 5 × 7
R Pil. 020k	8713, 5 × 7
R Pil. 020l	8713, 5 × 7
R Pil. 020n	8880, 5 × 7
R Pil. 020o	8880, 5 × 7
R Pil. 021h	8714, 5 × 7
R Pil. 021i	8714, 5 × 7
R Pil. 021k	8715, 5 × 7
R Pil. 021n	8881, 5 × 7
R Pil. 021o	8881, 5 × 7
R Pil. 022h	8716, 5 × 7

Ramesseum (*cont.*)

Nelson Number/Description	Negative, Format
R Pil. 022k	8882, 5 × 7
R Pil. 022l	8882, 5 × 7
R Pil. 022n	8883, 5 × 7
R Pil. 023k	8884, 5 × 7
R Pil. 023n	8885, 5 × 7
R Pil. 023o	8885, 5 × 7
Unknown	8149, 8 × 10

Saqqara

Nelson Number/Description	Negative, Format
Block fragments in Antiquities Department storehouse	14730, 8 × 10
Block fragments in Antiquities Department storehouse	14731, 8 × 10
Block fragments in Antiquities Department storehouse	14732, 8 × 10
Block fragments in Antiquities Department storehouse	14733, 8 × 10
Block fragments in Antiquities Department storehouse	14734, 8 × 10
Block fragments in Antiquities Department storehouse	14735, 8 × 10
Number 7: stone in Antiquities Department Storehouse at Saqqara (Caroline Ransom Williams)	15595, 8 × 10
Number 8: stone in Antiquities Department Storehouse at Saqqara (Caroline Ransom Williams)	15596, 8 × 10
Number 9: stone in Antiquities Department Storehouse at Saqqara (Caroline Ransom Williams)	15597, 8 × 10
Number 10: stone in Antiquities Department Storehouse at Saqqara (Caroline Ransom Williams)	15598, 8 × 10
Number 11: stone in Antiquities Department Storehouse at Saqqara (Caroline Ransom Williams)	15599, 8 × 10
Plan: Tomb of Mereruka	2387, 5 × 7
Tomb of Idut: room 2	15541, 8 × 10
Tomb of Idut: room 2	15542, 8 × 10
Tomb of Idut: room 2	15544, 8 × 10
Tomb of Idut: room 2, west	15543, 8 × 10
Tomb of Mereruka: A1	14920, 8 × 10
Tomb of Mereruka: A1, east	14913, 8 × 10
Tomb of Mereruka: A1, east	15043, 8 × 10
Tomb of Mereruka: A1, east	15045, 8 × 10
Tomb of Mereruka: A1, north var 14912	14916, 8 × 10
Tomb of Mereruka: A1, north (color)	14911, 8 × 10
Tomb of Mereruka: A1, north	14912, 8 × 10
Tomb of Mereruka: A1, north	14914, 8 × 10
Tomb of Mereruka: A1, north	14917, 8 × 10
Tomb of Mereruka: A1, north	15048, 8 × 10
Tomb of Mereruka: A1, north, scene 1	15046, 8 × 10
Tomb of Mereruka: A1, north, scene 2	15049, 8 × 10
Tomb of Mereruka: A1, north, scene 2	15047, 8 × 10
Tomb of Mereruka: A1, north, scene 2, detail	14919, 8 × 10

Saqqara (*cont.*)

Nelson Number/Description	Negative, Format
Tomb of Mereruka: A1, south	14915, 8 × 10
Tomb of Mereruka: A1, south	14918, 8 × 10
Tomb of Mereruka: A1, south, scene 2	15050, 8 × 10
Tomb of Mereruka: A1, west	14910, 8 × 10
Tomb of Mereruka: A1, west	15044, 8 × 10
Tomb of Mereruka: A1, 2, 3, east, jamb	15165, 8 × 10
Tomb of Mereruka: A1, 2, 3, west, jamb	15164, 8 × 10
Tomb of Mereruka: A3, east	15051, 8 × 10
Tomb of Mereruka: A3, east, scene 1	15053, 8 × 10
Tomb of Mereruka: A3, north	14921, 8 × 10
Tomb of Mereruka: A3, north	15054, 8 × 10
Tomb of Mereruka: A3, south	14922, 8 × 10
Tomb of Mereruka: A3, south	15055, 8 × 10
Tomb of Mereruka: A3, west	14923, 8 × 10
Tomb of Mereruka: A3, west	15056, 8 × 10
Tomb of Mereruka: A3, west, scene 2	15052, 8 × 10
Tomb of Mereruka: A3, 4, east, jamb	15166, 8 × 10
Tomb of Mereruka: A3, 4, west, jamb	15167, 8 × 10
Tomb of Mereruka: A4, east	14924, 8 × 10
Tomb of Mereruka: A4, east	14926, 8 × 10
Tomb of Mereruka: A4, east	15059, 8 × 10
Tomb of Mereruka: A4, east	15060, 8 × 10
Tomb of Mereruka: A4, east	15062, 8 × 10
Tomb of Mereruka: A4, north	15063, 8 × 10
Tomb of Mereruka: A4, south	14925, 8 × 10
Tomb of Mereruka: A4, south	15057, 8 × 10
Tomb of Mereruka: A4, west	14927, 8 × 10
Tomb of Mereruka: A4, west	14928, 8 × 10
Tomb of Mereruka: A4, west	15058, 8 × 10
Tomb of Mereruka: A4, west	15061, 8 × 10
Tomb of Mereruka: A4, west	15064, 8 × 10
Tomb of Mereruka: A4, 5, 6, north, jamb	15169, 8 × 10
Tomb of Mereruka: A4, 5, 6, south, jamb	15170, 8 × 10
Tomb of Mereruka: A4, 5, 6, 7, 8, 9, 10, 11, east, jamb	15173, 8 × 10
Tomb of Mereruka: A4, 5, south, jamb	15168, 8 × 10
Tomb of Mereruka: A6, east	14935, 8 × 10
Tomb of Mereruka: A6, east	15075, 8 × 10
Tomb of Mereruka: A6, north	14936, 8 × 10
Tomb of Mereruka: A6, north	14937, 8 × 10
Tomb of Mereruka: A6, north	14938, 8 × 10
Tomb of Mereruka: A6, north	14939, 8 × 10
Tomb of Mereruka: A6, north	15071, 8 × 10
Tomb of Mereruka: A6, north	15072, 8 × 10
Tomb of Mereruka: A6, north	15073, 8 × 10
Tomb of Mereruka: A6, north	15074, 8 × 10
Tomb of Mereruka: A6, south	14930, 8 × 10
Tomb of Mereruka: A6, south	14931, 8 × 10
Tomb of Mereruka: A6, south	14932, 8 × 10
Tomb of Mereruka: A6, south	14933, 8 × 10
Tomb of Mereruka: A6, south	15065, 8 × 10
Tomb of Mereruka: A6, south	15068, 8 × 10
Tomb of Mereruka: A6, south	15069, 8 × 10
Tomb of Mereruka: A6, south	15070, 8 × 10
Tomb of Mereruka: A6, west	14929, 8 × 10

Saqqara (*cont.*)

Nelson Number/Description	Negative, Format
Tomb of Mereruka: A6, west	14934, 8 × 10
Tomb of Mereruka: A6, west	15066, 8 × 10
Tomb of Mereruka: A6, west	15067, 8 × 10
Tomb of Mereruka: A6, 7, 8, east, jamb	15172, 8 × 10
Tomb of Mereruka A6, 7, 8, west, jamb	15171, 8 × 10
Tomb of Mereruka: A8	14943, 8 × 10
Tomb of Mereruka: A8	15032, 8 × 10
Tomb of Mereruka: A8, east	14944, 8 × 10
Tomb of Mereruka: A8, east	15077, 8 × 10
Tomb of Mereruka: A8, north	14940, 8 × 10
Tomb of Mereruka: A8, north	14941, 8 × 10
Tomb of Mereruka: A8, north	14942, 8 × 10
Tomb of Mereruka: A8, north	15029, 8 × 10
Tomb of Mereruka: A8, north	15078, 8 × 10
Tomb of Mereruka A8, north	15079, 8 × 10
Tomb of Mereruka: A8, north	15080, 8 × 10
Tomb of Mereruka: A8, north	15081, 8 × 10
Tomb of Mereruka: A8, north, scene 2	15033, 8 × 10
Tomb of Mereruka: A8, south	15023, 8 × 10
Tomb of Mereruka: A8, south	15024, 8 × 10
Tomb of Mereruka: A8, south	15030, 8 × 10
Tomb of Mereruka: A8, south	15031, 8 × 10
Tomb of Mereruka: A8, south	15034, 8 × 10
Tomb of Mereruka: A8, south	15082, 8 × 10
Tomb of Mereruka: A8, south	15083, 8 × 10
Tomb of Mereruka: A8, south	15084, 8 × 10
Tomb of Mereruka: A8, south	15085, 8 × 10
Tomb of Mereruka: A8, south	15086, 8 × 10
Tomb of Mereruka: A8, south	15087, 8 × 10
Tomb of Mereruka: A8, south, bottom center	15027, 8 × 10
Tomb of Mereruka: A8, south, bottom right	15026, 8 × 10
Tomb of Mereruka: A8, south, bottom right	15028, 8 × 10
Tomb of Mereruka: A8, south, bottom right	15035, 8 × 10
Tomb of Mereruka: A8, south, bottom right	15036, 8 × 10
Tomb of Mereruka: A8, south, detail	15025, 8 × 10
Tomb of Mereruka: A8, west	15076, 8 × 10
Tomb of Mereruka: A8, 9, east, jamb	15177, 8 × 10
Tomb of Mereruka: A8, 9, west, jamb	15178, 8 × 10
Tomb of Mereruka: A9, east	14949, 8 × 10
Tomb of Mereruka: A9, east	14950, 8 × 10
Tomb of Mereruka: A9, east	14951, 8 × 10
Tomb of Mereruka: A9, east	14952, 8 × 10
Tomb of Mereruka: A9, east	15089, 8 × 10
Tomb of Mereruka: A9, east	15090, 8 × 10
Tomb of Mereruka: A9, east	15091, 8 × 10
Tomb of Mereruka: A9, east	15096, 8 × 10
Tomb of Mereruka: A9, north	14953, 8 × 10
Tomb of Mereruka: A9, north	15088, 8 × 10
Tomb of Mereruka: A9, south	14948, 8 × 10
Tomb of Mereruka: A9, south	15092, 8 × 10
Tomb of Mereruka: A9, west	14945, 8 × 10
Tomb of Mereruka: A9, west	14946, 8 × 10
Tomb of Mereruka: A9, west	14947, 8 × 10
Tomb of Mereruka: A9, west	15093, 8 × 10
Tomb of Mereruka: A9, west	15094, 8 × 10

Saqqara (*cont.*)

Nelson Number/Description	Negative, Format
Tomb of Mereruka: A9, west	15095, 8 × 10
Tomb of Mereruka: A9, west	15097, 8 × 10
Tomb of Mereruka: A10, east	14959, 8 × 10
Tomb of Mereruka: A10, east	14963, 8 × 10
Tomb of Mereruka A10, east	15105, 8 × 10
Tomb of Mereruka: A10, east, lower	15100, 8 × 10
Tomb of Mereruka: A10, east, upper	15101, 8 × 10
Tomb of Mereruka: A10, north	14964, 8 × 10
Tomb of Mereruka: A10, north	14965, 8 × 10
Tomb of Mereruka: A10, north	15104, 8 × 10
Tomb of Mereruka: A10, north, lower	15103, 8 × 10
Tomb of Mereruka: A10, north, upper	15102, 8 × 10
Tomb of Mereruka: A10, pillar 1, east	14967, 8 × 10
Tomb of Mereruka: A10, pillar 1, east	15111, 8 × 10
Tomb of Mereruka A10, pillar 1, west	14966, 8 × 10
Tomb of Mereruka: A10, pillar 1, west	15112, 8 × 10
Tomb of Mereruka: A10, pillar 2, east	14968, 8 × 10
Tomb of Mereruka: A10, pillar 2, east	15113, 8 × 10
Tomb of Mereruka: A10, pillar 2, west	14969, 8 × 10
Tomb of Mereruka: A10, pillar 2, west	15114, 8 × 10
Tomb of Mereruka: A10, south	14956, 8 × 10
Tomb of Mereruka: A10, south	14957, 8 × 10
Tomb of Mereruka: A10, south	14960, 8 × 10
Tomb of Mereruka: A10, south	14961, 8 × 10
Tomb of Mereruka: A10, south	14962, 8 × 10
Tomb of Mereruka: A10, south	15106, 8 × 10
Tomb of Mereruka: A10, south	15108, 8 × 10
Tomb of Mereruka: A10, south	15109, 8 × 10
Tomb of Mereruka: A10, west	14954, 8 × 10
Tomb of Mereruka: A10, west	14955, 8 × 10
Tomb of Mereruka: A10, west	14958, 8 × 10
Tomb of Mereruka: A10, west	15098, 8 × 10
Tomb of Mereruka: A10, west	15099, 8 × 10
Tomb of Mereruka: A10, west	15107, 8 × 10
Tomb of Mereruka: A10, west	15110, 8 × 10
Tomb of Mereruka: A11, east	14972, 8 × 10
Tomb of Mereruka: A11, east	15115, 8 × 10
Tomb of Mereruka: A11, east	15118, 8 × 10
Tomb of Mereruka: A11, north	14971, 8 × 10
Tomb of Mereruka: A11, north	15116, 8 × 10
Tomb of Mereruka: A11, north	15119, 8 × 10
Tomb of Mereruka: A11, south	15117, 8 × 10
Tomb of Mereruka: A11, west	14970, 8 × 10
Tomb of Mereruka: A11, west	15120, 8 × 10
Tomb of Mereruka: A11, 12, north, jamb	15176, 8 × 10
Tomb of Mereruka: A11, 12, south, jamb	15175, 8 × 10
Tomb of Mereruka: A11, 12, 13, east, jamb	15179, 8 × 10
Tomb of Mereruka: A11, 12, 13, west, jamb	15174, 8 × 10
Tomb of Mereruka: A12, east	14976, 8 × 10
Tomb of Mereruka: A12, east	15124, 8 × 10
Tomb of Mereruka: A12, north	14974, 8 × 10
Tomb of Mereruka: A12, north	14975, 8 × 10
Tomb of Mereruka: A12, north	15121, 8 × 10
Tomb of Mereruka: A12, north	15122, 8 × 10
Tomb of Mereruka: A12, south	14977, 8 × 10

Saqqara (*cont.*)

Nelson Number/Description	Negative, Format
Tomb of Mereruka: A12, south	14978, 8 × 10
Tomb of Mereruka: A12, south	15123, 8 × 10
Tomb of Mereruka: A12, west	14973, 8 × 10
Tomb of Mereruka: A12, west	15125, 8 × 10
Tomb of Mereruka: A13, altar	15161, 8 × 10
Tomb of Mereruka: A13, altar, east	15163, 8 × 10
Tomb of Mereruka: A13, altar, west	15162, 8 × 10
Tomb of Mereruka: A13, east	14994, 8 × 10
Tomb of Mereruka: A13, east	14995, 8 × 10
Tomb of Mereruka: A13, east	14996, 8 × 10
Tomb of Mereruka: A13, east	15004, 8 × 10
Tomb of Mereruka: A13, east	15132, 8 × 10
Tomb of Mereruka: A13, east	15133, 8 × 10
Tomb of Mereruka: A13, east	15134, 8 × 10
Tomb of Mereruka: A13, east	15135, 8 × 10
Tomb of Mereruka: A13, east	15136, 8 × 10
Tomb of Mereruka: A13, west	15130, 8 × 10
Tomb of Mereruka: A13, north	14987, 8 × 10
Tomb of Mereruka: A13, north	14988, 8 × 10
Tomb of Mereruka: A13, north	14989, 8 × 10
Tomb of Mereruka: A13, north	14990, 8 × 10
Tomb of Mereruka: A13, north	14991, 8 × 10
Tomb of Mereruka: A13, north	14992, 8 × 10
Tomb of Mereruka: A13, north	14993, 8 × 10
Tomb of Mereruka: A13, north	15002, 8 × 10
Tomb of Mereruka: A13, north	15003, 8 × 10
Tomb of Mereruka: A13, north	15142, 8 × 10
Tomb of Mereruka: A13, north	15143, 8 × 10
Tomb of Mereruka: A13, north	15144, 8 × 10
Tomb of Mereruka: A13, north	15145, 8 × 10
Tomb of Mereruka: A13, north	15146, 8 × 10
Tomb of Mereruka: A13, north	15150, 8 × 10
Tomb of Mereruka: A13, north	15151, 8 × 10
Tomb of Mereruka: A13, north	15152, 8 × 10
Tomb of Mereruka: A13, north	15153, 8 × 10
Tomb of Mereruka: A13, pillar 1, north	15011, 8 × 10
Tomb of Mereruka: A13, pillar 1, south	15010, 8 × 10
Tomb of Mereruka: A13, pillar 2, east	15013, 8 × 10
Tomb of Mereruka: A13, pillar 2, north	15014, 8 × 10
Tomb of Mereruka: A13, pillar 2, south	15012, 8 × 10
Tomb of Mereruka: A13, pillar 2, west	15015, 8 × 10
Tomb of Mereruka: A13, pillar 3, east	15022, 8 × 10
Tomb of Mereruka: A13, pillar 3, east	15018, 8 × 10
Tomb of Mereruka: A13, pillar 3, east	15019, 8 × 10
Tomb of Mereruka: A13, pillar 3, south	15016, 8 × 10
Tomb of Mereruka: A13, pillar 3, south	15020, 8 × 10
Tomb of Mereruka: A13, pillar 3, west	15017, 8 × 10
Tomb of Mereruka: A13, pillar 3, west	15021, 8 × 10
Tomb of Mereruka: A13, pillar 3, east	15149, 8 × 10
Tomb of Mereruka: A13, pillar 3, west	15148, 8 × 10
Tomb of Mereruka: A13, south	14997, 8 × 10
Tomb of Mereruka: A13, south	14998, 8 × 10
Tomb of Mereruka: A13, south	14999, 8 × 10
Tomb of Mereruka: A13, south	15000, 8 × 10
Tomb of Mereruka: A13, south	15001, 8 × 10

Saqqara (*cont.*)

Nelson Number/Description	Negative, Format
Tomb of Mereruka: A13, south	15005, 8 × 10
Tomb of Mereruka: A13, south	15006, 8 × 10
Tomb of Mereruka: A13, south	15007, 8 × 10
Tomb of Mereruka: A13, south	15008, 8 × 10
Tomb of Mereruka: A13, south	15009, 8 × 10
Tomb of Mereruka: A13, south	15137, 8 × 10
Tomb of Mereruka: A13, south	15138, 8 × 10
Tomb of Mereruka: A13, south	15139, 8 × 10
Tomb of Mereruka: A13, south	15140, 8 × 10
Tomb of Mereruka: A13, south	15141, 8 × 10
Tomb of Mereruka: A13, south	15154, 8 × 10
Tomb of Mereruka: A13, south	15155, 8 × 10
Tomb of Mereruka: A13, south	15156, 8 × 10
Tomb of Mereruka: A13, south	15157, 8 × 10
Tomb of Mereruka: A13, south	15158, 8 × 10
Tomb of Mereruka: A13, west	14979, 8 × 10
Tomb of Mereruka: A13, west	14980, 8 × 10
Tomb of Mereruka: A13, west	14981, 8 × 10
Tomb of Mereruka: A13, west	14982, 8 × 10
Tomb of Mereruka: A13, west	14983, 8 × 10
Tomb of Mereruka: A13, west	14984, 8 × 10
Tomb of Mereruka: A13, west	14985, 8 × 10
Tomb of Mereruka: A13, west	14986, 8 × 10
Tomb of Mereruka: A13, west	15126, 8 × 10
Tomb of Mereruka: A13, west	15127, 8 × 10
Tomb of Mereruka: A13, west	15128, 8 × 10
Tomb of Mereruka: A13, west	15129, 8 × 10
Tomb of Mereruka: A13, west	15131, 8 × 10
Tomb of Mereruka: A15, A17, A18	15159, 8 × 10
Tomb of Mereruka: A19, A20	15160, 8 × 10

Shanhur

Nelson Number/Description	Negative, Format
Ceiling	11285, 8 × 10
None	8703, 5 × 7
None	8704, 5 × 7
None	8705, 5 × 7
None	8706, 5 × 7

Soleb Temple

Nelson Number/Description	Negative, Format
None	2700, 8 × 10
None	2701, 8 × 10
None	2751, 8 × 10
None	2752, 8 × 10
None	2753, 8 × 10
None	2754, 5 × 7
None	2755, 5 × 7
None	2756, 5 × 7
None	2757, 5 × 7
None	2758, 5 × 7

Theban Tombs

Nelson Number/Description	Negative, Format
TT 1: Tomb of Sennedjem	3350, 8 × 10
TT 1: Tomb of Sennedjem	3351, 8 × 10
TT 1: Tomb of Sennedjem	3352, 8 × 10
TT 1: Tomb of Sennedjem	3353, 8 × 10
TT 1: Tomb of Sennedjem	3354, 8 × 10
TT 1: Tomb of Sennedjem	3355, 8 × 10
TT 13: Tomb of Shuroy	2977, 7 × 9
TT 13: Tomb of Shuroy	10306, 5 × 7
TT 13: Tomb of Shuroy	10307, 5 × 7
TT 13: Tomb of Shuroy	10308, 5 × 7
TT 13: Tomb of Shuroy	10309, 5 × 7
TT 14: Tomb of Huy	10324, 5 × 7
TT 14: Tomb of Huy	10325, 5 × 7
TT 16: Tomb of Panehesy	10296, 5 × 7
TT 16: Tomb of Panehesy	10297, 5 × 7
TT 16: Tomb of Panehesy	10298, 5 × 7
TT 16: Tomb of Panehesy	10299, 5 × 7
TT 16: Tomb of Panehesy	10300, 5 × 7
TT 16: Tomb of Panehesy	10301, 5 × 7
TT 16: Tomb of Panehesy	10302, 5 × 7
TT 16: Tomb of Panehesy	10303, 5 × 7
TT 16: Tomb of Panehesy	10304, 5 × 7
TT 17: Tomb of Nebamun	10284, 5 × 7
TT 17: Tomb of Nebamun	10285, 5 × 7
TT 17: Tomb of Nebamun	10286, 5 × 7
TT 17: Tomb of Nebamun	10287, 5 × 7
TT 17: Tomb of Nebamun	10288, 5 × 7
TT 17: Tomb of Nebamun	10289, 5 × 7
TT 17: Tomb of Nebamun	10290, 5 × 7
TT 18: Tomb of Baki	10310, 5 × 7
TT 19: Tomb of Amenmose	10345, 5 × 7
TT 19: Tomb of Amenmose	10346, 5 × 7
TT 19: Tomb of Amenmose	10347, 5 × 7
TT 21: Tomb of User	10367, 5 × 7
TT 21: Tomb of User	10368, 5 × 7
TT 21: Tomb of User	10369, 5 × 7
TT 21: Tomb of User	10370, 5 × 7
TT 21: Tomb of User	10371, 5 × 7
TT 21: Tomb of User	10372, 5 × 7
TT 30: Tomb of Khonsumose	3994, 5 × 7
TT 30: Tomb of Khonsumose	3995, 5 × 7
TT 31: Tomb of Khonsu-Ta	2983, 8 × 10
TT 31: Tomb of Khonsu-Ta	2982, 8 × 10
TT 31: Tomb of Khonsu-Ta	2984, 8 × 10
TT 31: Tomb of Khonsu-Ta	2985, 8 × 10
TT 31: Tomb of Khonsu-Ta	2986, 8 × 10
TT 31: Tomb of Khonsu-Ta	7791, 3.5 × 4.5
TT 31: Tomb of Khonsu-Ta	7792, 3.5 × 4.5
TT 31: Tomb of Khonsu-Ta	7793, 3.5 × 4.5
TT 31: Tomb of Khonsu-Ta	7794, 3.5 × 4.5
TT 31: Tomb of Khonsu-Ta	7795, 3.5 × 4.5
TT 31: Tomb of Khonsu-Ta	7796, 3.5 × 4.5
TT 31: Tomb of Khonsu-Ta	7797, 3.5 × 4.5
TT 31: Tomb of Khonsu-Ta	7798, 3.5 × 4.5
TT 31: Tomb of Khonsu-Ta	7799, 3.5 × 4.5

Theban Tombs (*cont.*)

Nelson Number/Description	Negative, Format
TT 31: Tomb of Khonsu-Ta	7800, 3.5 × 4.5
TT 31: Tomb of Khonsu-Ta	7801, 3.5 × 4.5
TT 31: Tomb of Khonsu-Ta	7802, 3.5 × 4.5
TT 31: Tomb of Khonsu-Ta	7803, 3.5 × 4.5
TT 31: Tomb of Khonsu-Ta	7804, 3.5 × 4.5
TT 31: Tomb of Khonsu-Ta	7805, 3.5 × 4.5
TT 31: Tomb of Khonsu-Ta	7806, 3.5 × 4.5
TT 31: Tomb of Khonsu-Ta	7807, 3.5 × 4.5
TT 31: Tomb of Khonsu-Ta	7808, 3.5 × 4.5
TT 31: Tomb of Khonsu-Ta	7809, 3.5 × 4.5
TT 33: Tomb of Pedamenemopet	3976, 8 × 10
TT 33: Tomb of Pedamenemopet	3977, 8 × 10
TT 33: Tomb of Pedamenemopet	3978, 8 × 10
TT 33: Tomb of Pedamenemopet	3979, 8 × 10
TT 33: Tomb of Pedamenemopet: hall 22, ceiling	9790, 5 × 7
TT 33: Tomb of Pedamenemopet: hall 22, ceiling	9791, 5 × 7
TT 33: Tomb of Pedamenemopet: hall 22, ceiling	9792, 5 × 7
TT 33: Tomb of Pedamenemopet: hall 22, ceiling	9793, 5 × 7
TT 33: Tomb of Pedamenemopet: hall 22, ceiling	9794, 5 × 7
TT 33: Tomb of Pedamenemopet: hall 22, ceiling	9795, 5 × 7
TT 33: Tomb of Pedamenemopet: hall 22, ceiling	9796, 5 × 7
TT 33: Tomb of Pedamenemopet: hall 22, ceiling	9797, 5 × 7
TT 33: Tomb of Pedamenemopet: hall 22, ceiling	9798, 5 × 7
TT 33: Tomb of Pedamenemopet: hall 22, side walls, Amduat text	10455, 5 × 7
TT 33: Tomb of Pedamenemopet: hall 22, side walls, Amduat text	10456, 5 × 7
TT 33: Tomb of Pedamenemopet: hall 22, side walls, Amduat text	10457, 5 × 7
TT 33: Tomb of Pedamenemopet: hall 22, side walls, Amduat text	10461, 5 × 7
TT 33: Tomb of Pedamenemopet: hall 22, side walls, Amduat text	10462, 5 × 7
TT 33: Tomb of Pedamenemopet: hall 22, side walls, Amduat text	10463, 5 × 7
TT 33: Tomb of Pedamenemopet: hall 22, side walls, Amduat text	10464, 5 × 7
TT 33: Tomb of Pedamenemopet: hall 22, side walls, Amduat text	10465, 5 × 7
TT 33: Tomb of Pedamenemopet: hall 22, side walls, Amduat text	10466, 5 × 7
TT 33: Tomb of Pedamenemopet: hall 22, Amduat	14394, 5 × 7
TT 34: Tomb of Montuemhat: sarcophagus chamber, ceiling	10115, 5 × 7
TT 34: Tomb of Montuemhat: sarcophagus chamber, ceiling	10116, 5 × 7
TT 34: Tomb of Montuemhat: sarcophagus chamber, ceiling	10117, 5 × 7
TT 34: Tomb of Montuemhat: sarcophagus chamber, ceiling	10118, 5 × 7
TT 34: Tomb of Montuemhat: sarcophagus chamber, ceiling	10119, 5 × 7
TT 34: Tomb of Montuemhat: sarcophagus chamber, ceiling	10120, 5 × 7
TT 34: Tomb of Montuemhat: sarcophagus chamber, ceiling	10121, 5 × 7
TT 34: Tomb of Montuemhat: sarcophagus chamber, ceiling	10122, 5 × 7

Theban Tombs (*cont.*)

Nelson Number/Description	Negative, Format
TT 40: Tomb of Amenhotep-Huy	10376, 5 × 7
TT 40: Tomb of Amenhotep-Huy	10377, 5 × 7
TT 40: Tomb of Amenhotep-Huy	10378, 5 × 7
TT 40: Tomb of Amenhotep-Huy	10379, 5 × 7
TT 40: Tomb of Amenhotep-Huy	10380, 5 × 7
TT 40: Tomb of Amenhotep-Huy	10381, 5 × 7
TT 40: Tomb of Amenhotep-Huy	10382, 5 × 7
TT 40: Tomb of Amenhotep-Huy	10383, 5 × 7
TT 40: Tomb of Amenhotep-Huy	10384, 5 × 7
TT 40: Tomb of Amenhotep-Huy	10385, 5 × 7
TT 40: Tomb of Amenhotep-Huy	10386, 5 × 7
TT 45: Tomb of Djehuty/Djehutyemheb	6087, 8 × 10
TT 45: Tomb of Djehuty/Djehutyemheb	7761, 3.5 × 4.5
TT 45: Tomb of Djehuty/Djehutyemheb	7762, 3.5 × 4.5
TT 45: Tomb of Djehuty/Djehutyemheb	10584, 5 × 7
TT 45: Tomb of Djehuty/Djehutyemheb	10585, 5 × 7
TT 45: Tomb of Djehuty/Djehutyemheb	10586, 5 × 7
TT 45: Tomb of Djehuty/Djehutyemheb	10587, 5 × 7
TT 45: Tomb of Djehuty/Djehutyemheb: ceiling	6420, 5 × 7
TT 45: Tomb of Djehuty/Djehutyemheb: hall, east wall	6086, 8 × 10
TT 45: Tomb of Djehuty/Djehutyemheb: hall, east wall	6094, 8 × 10
TT 45: Tomb of Djehuty/Djehutyemheb: hall, east wall	6095, 8 × 10
TT 45: Tomb of Djehuty/Djehutyemheb: hall, north wall	6093, 8 × 10
TT 45: Tomb of Djehuty/Djehutyemheb: hall, south wall	6088, 8 × 10
TT 45: Tomb of Djehuty/Djehutyemheb: hall, west wall	6089, 8 × 10
TT 45: Tomb of Djehuty/Djehutyemheb: hall, west wall	6090, 8 × 10
TT 45: Tomb of Djehuty/Djehutyemheb: hall, west wall	6091, 8 × 10
TT 45: Tomb of Djehuty/Djehutyemheb: hall, west wall	6092, 8 × 10
TT 49: Tomb of Neferhotep (chief scribe of Amun)	2987, 8 × 10
TT 49: Tomb of Neferhotep (chief scribe of Amun)	2988, 8 × 10
TT 49: Tomb of Neferhotep (chief scribe of Amun)	2989, 8 × 10
TT 50: Tomb of Neferhotep (divine father of Amun-Ra)	2990, 8 × 10
TT 50: Tomb of Neferhotep (divine father of Amun-Ra): upper register of south wall of the transverse hall	13590, 8 × 10
TT 53: Tomb of Amenemhat: false door	6139, 7 × 9
TT 53: Tomb of Amenemhat: hall	6138, 7 × 9
TT 53: Tomb of Amenemhat: hall	6421, 5 × 7
TT 53: Tomb of Amenemhat: hall	6422, 5 × 7
TT 53: Tomb of Amenemhat: hall	6423, 5 × 7
TT 53: Tomb of Amenemhat: hall	6424, 5 × 7
TT 53: Tomb of Amenemhat: hall	6425, 5 × 7
TT 53: Tomb of Amenemhat: hall	6426, 5 × 7
TT 53: Tomb of Amenemhat: hall	6427, 5 × 7
TT 53: Tomb of Amenemhat: hall	6428, 5 × 7
TT 53: Tomb of Amenemhat: hall	6429, 5 × 7
TT 53: Tomb of Amenemhat: hall	6430, 5 × 7

Theban Tombs (*cont.*)

Nelson Number/Description	Negative, Format
TT 53: Tomb of Amenemhat: hall	6431, 5 × 7
TT 53: Tomb of Amenemhat: hall	6432, 5 × 7
TT 53: Tomb of Amenemhat: hall	6433, 5 × 7
TT 53: Tomb of Amenemhat: passage	6434, 5 × 7
TT 53: Tomb of Amenemhat: passage	6435, 5 × 7
TT 53: Tomb of Amenemhat: passage	6436, 5 × 7
TT 53: Tomb of Amenemhat: passage	6437, 5 × 7
TT 53: Tomb of Amenemhat: passage	6438, 5 × 7
TT 53: Tomb of Amenemhat: passage	6439, 5 × 7
TT 53: Tomb of Amenemhat: passage	6440, 5 × 7
TT 53: Tomb of Amenemhat: passage	6441, 5 × 7
TT 53: Tomb of Amenemhat: passage	6442, 5 × 7
TT 53: Tomb of Amenemhat: passage	6443, 5 × 7
TT 53: Tomb of Amenemhat: passage	6444, 5 × 7
TT 53: Tomb of Amenemhat: wall painting	6445, 5 × 7
TT 53: Tomb of Amenemhat: wall painting	6446, 5 × 7
TT 53: Tomb of Amenemhat: wall painting	6447, 5 × 7
TT 54: Tomb of Huy	7763, 3.5 × 4.5
TT 54: Tomb of Huy	7764, 3.5 × 4.5
TT 54: Tomb of Huy	7765, 3.5 × 4.5
TT 54: Tomb of Huy	7766, 3.5 × 4.5
TT 54: Tomb of Huy	7767, 3.5 × 4.5
TT 54: Tomb of Huy	7768, 3.5 × 4.5
TT 54: Tomb of Huy	7769, 3.5 × 4.5
TT 54: Tomb of Huy	7770, 3.5 × 4.5
TT 54: Tomb of Huy	7771, 3.5 × 4.5
TT 54: Tomb of Huy	7772, 3.5 × 4.5
TT 54: Tomb of Huy	7773, 3.5 × 4.5
TT 54: Tomb of Huy	7774, 3.5 × 4.5
TT 54: Tomb of Huy	7775, 3.5 × 4.5
TT 54: Tomb of Huy	7776, 3.5 × 4.5
TT 54: Tomb of Huy	7777, 3.5 × 4.5
TT 54: Tomb of Huy	7778, 3.5 × 4.5
TT 54: Tomb of Huy	7779, 3.5 × 4.5
TT 54: Tomb of Huy	7780, 3.5 × 4.5
TT 54: Tomb of Huy	7781, 3.5 × 4.5
TT 54: Tomb of Huy	7782, 3.5 × 4.5
TT 54: Tomb of Huy	7783, 3.5 × 4.5
TT 54: Tomb of Huy	7784, 3.5 × 4.5
TT 54: Tomb of Huy: wall painting	6448, 5 × 7
TT 54: Tomb of Huy: wall painting	6449, 5 × 7
TT 54: Tomb of Huy: wall painting	6450, 5 × 7
TT 54: Tomb of Huy: wall painting	6451, 5 × 7
TT 54: Tomb of Huy: wall painting	6452, 5 × 7
TT 54: Tomb of Huy: wall painting	6453, 5 × 7
TT 54: Tomb of Huy: wall painting	6454, 5 × 7
TT 54: Tomb of Huy: wall painting	6455, 5 × 7
TT 54: Tomb of Huy: wall painting	6456, 5 × 7
TT 54: Tomb of Huy: wall painting	6457, 5 × 7
TT 54: Tomb of Huy: wall painting	6458, 5 × 7
TT 54: Tomb of Huy: wall painting	6459, 5 × 7
TT 55: Tomb of Ramose	2843, 8 × 10
TT 55: Tomb of Ramose	2844, 8 × 10
TT 55: Tomb of Ramose	2845, 8 × 10
TT 55: Tomb of Ramose	3344, 8 × 10

Theban Tombs (*cont.*)

Nelson Number/Description	Negative, Format
TT 55: Tomb of Ramose	3345, 8 × 10
TT 55: Tomb of Ramose	3346, 8 × 10
TT 55: Tomb of Ramose	3347, 8 × 10
TT 55: Tomb of Ramose	3348, 8 × 10
TT 55: Tomb of Ramose	6372, 8 × 10
TT 55: Tomb of Ramose	6373, 8 × 10
TT 55: Tomb of Ramose	6374, 8 × 10
TT 55: Tomb of Ramose	6375, 8 × 10
TT 55: Tomb of Ramose	6376, 8 × 10
TT 55: Tomb of Ramose	6377, 8 × 10
TT 55: Tomb of Ramose	6378, 8 × 10
TT 55: Tomb of Ramose	6379, 8 × 10
TT 55: Tomb of Ramose	6380, 8 × 10
TT 55: Tomb of Ramose	6381, 8 × 10
TT 55: Tomb of Ramose	8491, 8 × 10
TT 55: Tomb of Ramose: entrance	7340, —
TT 55: Tomb of Ramose: exterior	7273, 8 × 10
TT 55: Tomb of Ramose: hall, east wall	7323, —
TT 55: Tomb of Ramose: hall, east wall	7324, —
TT 55: Tomb of Ramose: inner doorway	7195, 8 × 10
TT 55: Tomb of Ramose: relief	7272, 8 × 10
TT 55: Tomb of Ramose: relief	7275, 8 × 10
TT 55: Tomb of Ramose: relief	7321, 8 × 10
TT 55: Tomb of Ramose: relief	7322, —
TT 55: Tomb of Ramose: relief	7330, —
TT 55: Tomb of Ramose: relief	7331, —
TT 55: Tomb of Ramose: relief, hall	7274, 8 × 10
TT 55: Tomb of Ramose	7271, 8 × 10
TT 56: Tomb of Userhat	2846, 8 × 10
TT 56: Tomb of Userhat	2847, 8 × 10
TT 56: Tomb of Userhat	2848, 8 × 10
TT 56: Tomb of Userhat	2849, 8 × 10
TT 56: Tomb of Userhat	2850, 8 × 10
TT 56: Tomb of Userhat	2851, 8 × 10
TT 56: Tomb of Userhat	2852, 8 × 10
TT 56: Tomb of Userhat	2852-a, 8 × 10
TT 56: Tomb of Userhat	2991, 8 × 10
TT 56: Tomb of Userhat	2992, 8 × 10
TT 56: Tomb of Userhat: false door	6141, 7 × 9
TT 56: Tomb of Userhat: mural painting	6460, 5 × 7
TT 56: Tomb of Userhat: mural painting	6461, 5 × 7
TT 56: Tomb of Userhat: mural painting	6462, 5 × 7
TT 56: Tomb of Userhat: mural painting	6463, 5 × 7
TT 56: Tomb of Userhat: mural painting	6464, 5 × 7
TT 56: Tomb of Userhat: mural painting	6465, 5 × 7
TT 56: Tomb of Userhat: mural painting	6466, 5 × 7
TT 56: Tomb of Userhat: stela	6140, 7 × 9
TT 57: Tomb of Khaemhat	2993, 8 × 10
TT 57: Tomb of Khaemhat	2994, 8 × 10
TT 57: Tomb of Khaemhat	2995, 8 × 10
TT 63: Tomb of Sobekhotep	2853, 8 × 10
TT 63: Tomb of Sobekhotep	2854, 8 × 10
TT 63: Tomb of Sobekhotep	10339, 5 × 7
TT 63: Tomb of Sobekhotep	10340, 5 × 7
TT 63: Tomb of Sobekhotep	10341, 5 × 7

Theban Tombs (*cont.*)

Nelson Number/Description	Negative, Format
TT 63: Tomb of Sobekhotep	10342, 5 × 7
TT 63: Tomb of Sobekhotep	10343, 5 × 7
TT 63: Tomb of Sobekhotep	10344, 5 × 7
TT 64: Tomb of Heqaerneheh	2996, 8 × 10
TT 65: Tomb of Nebamun/Imiseba	2855, 8 × 10
TT 65: Tomb of Nebamun/Imiseba	2856, 8 × 10
TT 65: Tomb of Nebamun/Imiseba	2857, 8 × 10
TT 65: Tomb of Nebamun/Imiseba	2858, 8 × 10
TT 65: Tomb of Nebamun/Imiseba	10348, 5 × 7
TT 65: Tomb of Nebamun/Imiseba	10349, 5 × 7
TT 65: Tomb of Nebamun/Imiseba	10350, 5 × 7
TT 65: Tomb of Nebamun/Imiseba	10351, 5 × 7
TT 65: Tomb of Nebamun/Imiseba	10352, 5 × 7
TT 65: Tomb of Nebamun/Imiseba	10353, 5 × 7
TT 65: Tomb of Nebamun/Imiseba	10354, 5 × 7
TT 65: Tomb of Nebamun/Imiseba	10355, 5 × 7
TT 65: Tomb of Nebamun/Imiseba	10356, 5 × 7
TT 65: Tomb of Nebamun/Imiseba	10357, 5 × 7
TT 65: Tomb of Nebamun/Imiseba	10358, 5 × 7
TT 65: Tomb of Nebamun/Imiseba	10359, 5 × 7
TT 65: Tomb of Nebamun/Imiseba: main chamber, ceiling in front of entrance to second chamber	3001, 8 × 10
TT 65: Tomb of Nebamun/Imiseba: main chamber, east wall	3000, 8 × 10
TT 65: Tomb of Nebamun/Imiseba: main chamber, east wall, right half	2997, 8 × 10
TT 65: Tomb of Nebamun/Imiseba: main chamber, south wall, left half	2999, 8 × 10
TT 65: Tomb of Nebamun/Imiseba: main chamber, south wall, right half	2998, 8 × 10
TT 65: Tomb of Nebamun/Imiseba: painting by Nina Davies	3985, 8 × 10
TT 65: Tomb of Nebamun/Imiseba: painting by Nina Davies	3986, 8 × 10
TT 65: Tomb of Nebamun/Imiseba: painting by Nina Davies	3987, 8 × 10
TT 65: Tomb of Nebamun/Imiseba: painting by Nina Davies	3989, 8 × 10
TT 65: Tomb of Nebamun/Imiseba: painting by Nina Davies	3990, 8 × 10
TT 65: Tomb of Nebamun/Imiseba: painting by Nina Davies	3991, 8 × 10
TT 65: Tomb of Nebamun/Imiseba: painting by Nina Davies	3992, 8 × 10
TT 65: Tomb of Nebamun/Imiseba: painting by Nina Davies	3993, 8 × 10
TT 65: Tomb of Nebamun/Imiseba: painting by Nina Davies	3988, 8 × 10
TT 66: Tomb of Hepu	10360, 5 × 7
TT 66: Tomb of Hepu	10361, 5 × 7
TT 66: Tomb of Hepu	10362, 5 × 7
TT 66: Tomb of Hepu	10363, 5 × 7
TT 66: Tomb of Hepu	10364, 5 × 7
TT 66: Tomb of Hepu	10365, 5 × 7
TT 66: Tomb of Hepu	10366, 5 × 7
TT 69: Tomb of Menna	2867, 8 × 10
TT 69: Tomb of Menna	2868, 8 × 10

Theban Tombs (*cont.*)

Nelson Number/Description	Negative, Format
TT 69: Tomb of Menna	2869, 8 × 10
TT 69: Tomb of Menna	2870, 8 × 10
TT 69: Tomb of Menna	2871, 8 × 10
TT 69: Tomb of Menna	2871-a, 8 × 10
TT 69: Tomb of Menna	2872, 8 × 10
TT 69: Tomb of Menna	2873, 8 × 10
TT 69: Tomb of Menna	2874, 8 × 10
TT 69: Tomb of Menna	2875, 8 × 10
TT 69: Tomb of Menna	2876, 8 × 10
TT 69: Tomb of Menna	2877, 8 × 10
TT 69: Tomb of Menna	2878, 8 × 10
TT 69: Tomb of Menna	2878-a, 8 × 10
TT 69: Tomb of Menna	2878-b, 8 × 10
TT 69: Tomb of Menna	2879, 8 × 10
TT 69: Tomb of Menna	2880, 8 × 10
TT 69: Tomb of Menna	2881, 8 × 10
TT 69: Tomb of Menna	2882, 8 × 10
TT 69: Tomb of Menna	2883, 8 × 10
TT 69: Tomb of Menna	2883-a, 8 × 10
TT 69: Tomb of Menna	2884, 8 × 10
TT 69: Tomb of Menna	2885, 8 × 10
TT 69: Tomb of Menna	2886, 8 × 10
TT 69: Tomb of Menna	2887, 8 × 10
TT 69: Tomb of Menna	2888, 8 × 10
TT 73: Tomb of Amenhotep	10334, 5 × 7
TT 74: Tomb of Tjanuny	2889, 8 × 10
TT 74: Tomb of Tjanuny	2890, 8 × 10
TT 74: Tomb of Tjanuny	2891, 8 × 10
TT 74: Tomb of Tjanuny	2892, 8 × 10
TT 74: Tomb of Tjanuny	10336, 5 × 7
TT 74: Tomb of Tjanuny	10337, 5 × 7
TT 74: Tomb of Tjanuny	10338, 5 × 7
TT 75: Tomb of Amenhotep-Sase	2893, 8 × 10
TT 75: Tomb of Amenhotep-Sase	2894, 8 × 10
TT 75: Tomb of Amenhotep-Sase	2895, 8 × 10
TT 75: Tomb of Amenhotep-Sase	2896, 8 × 10
TT 75: Tomb of Amenhotep-Sase	2897, 8 × 10
TT 75: Tomb of Amenhotep-Sase	2898, 8 × 10
TT 75: Tomb of Amenhotep-Sase	3002, 8 × 10
TT 75: Tomb of Amenhotep-Sase	3003, 8 × 10
TT 76: Tomb of Tjenuna	2899, 8 × 10
TT 76: Tomb of Tjenuna	2900, 8 × 10
TT 76: Tomb of Tjenuna	2901, 8 × 10
TT 78: Tomb of Horemheb	2902, 8 × 10
TT 78: Tomb of Horemheb	2903, 8 × 10
TT 78: Tomb of Horemheb	2904, 8 × 10
TT 78: Tomb of Horemheb	3004, 8 × 10
TT 78: Tomb of Horemheb	7863, 5 × 7
TT 78: Tomb of Horemheb	7864, 5 × 7
TT 78: Tomb of Horemheb	7865, 5 × 7
TT 78: Tomb of Horemheb	7866, 5 × 7
TT 78: Tomb of Horemheb	7867, 5 × 7
TT 78: Tomb of Horemheb	7868, 5 × 7
TT 78: Tomb of Horemheb	7869, 5 × 7
TT 78: Tomb of Horemheb	7870, 5 × 7

Theban Tombs (*cont.*)

Nelson Number/Description	Negative, Format
TT 78: Tomb of Horemheb	7871, 5 × 7
TT 78: Tomb of Horemheb	7872, 5 × 7
TT 78: Tomb of Horemheb	7873, 5 × 7
TT 78: Tomb of Horemheb	7874, 5 × 7
TT 78: Tomb of Horemheb	7875, 5 × 7
TT 78: Tomb of Horemheb	7876, 5 × 7
TT 78: Tomb of Horemheb	7877, 5 × 7
TT 78: Tomb of Horemheb	7878, 5 × 7
TT 78: Tomb of Horemheb	7879, 5 × 7
TT 78: Tomb of Horemheb	7880, 5 × 7
TT 78: Tomb of Horemheb	7881, 5 × 7
TT 78: Tomb of Horemheb	7882, 5 × 7
TT 78: Tomb of Horemheb	7883, 5 × 7
TT 78: Tomb of Horemheb	7884, 5 × 7
TT 78: Tomb of Horemheb	7885, 5 × 7
TT 78: Tomb of Horemheb	7886, 5 × 7
TT 78: Tomb of Horemheb: central, west wall	6098, 8 × 10
TT 78: Tomb of Horemheb: hall, north wall	6143, 7 × 9
TT 78: Tomb of Horemheb: hall, south wall	6142, 7 × 9
TT 78: Tomb of Horemheb: north end	6096, 8 × 10
TT 78: Tomb of Horemheb: north end, west wall	6097, 8 × 10
TT 78: Tomb of Horemheb: north end, west wall	6103, 8 × 10
TT 78: Tomb of Horemheb: north end, west wall	6104, 8 × 10
TT 78: Tomb of Horemheb: south central, east wall	6102, 8 × 10
TT 78: Tomb of Horemheb: south end, passage	6099, 8 × 10
TT 78: Tomb of Horemheb: south end, passage	6100, 8 × 10
TT 78: Tomb of Horemheb: west wall, passage	6101, 8 × 10
TT 79: Tomb of Menkheper	2905, 8 × 10
TT 79: Tomb of Menkheper	2906, 8 × 10
TT 79: Tomb of Menkheper	2907, 8 × 10
TT 79: Tomb of Menkheper: left of entrance	6467, 5 × 7
TT 79: Tomb of Menkheper: left of entrance	6468, 5 × 7
TT 79: Tomb of Menkheper: left of entrance	6469, 5 × 7
TT 79: Tomb of Menkheper: left of entrance	6470, 5 × 7
TT 79: Tomb of Menkheper: left of entrance	6471, 5 × 7
TT 79: Tomb of Menkheper: left of entrance	6472, 5 × 7
TT 80: Tomb of Djehutynefer	3005, 8 × 10
TT 80: Tomb of Djehutynefer: hall, right of door	6105, 8 × 10
TT 80: Tomb of Djehutynefer: hall, right of door	6106, 8 × 10
TT 80: Tomb of Djehutynefer: hall, right of door	6107, 8 × 10
TT 80: Tomb of Djehutynefer: hall, right of door	6108, 8 × 10
TT 80: Tomb of Djehutynefer: passage	6110, 8 × 10
TT 80: Tomb of Djehutynefer: passage, left of entrance	6112, 8 × 10
TT 80: Tomb of Djehutynefer: passage, left of entrance	6113, 8 × 10
TT 80: Tomb of Djehutynefer: passage, right of entrance	6111, 8 × 10
TT 80: Tomb of Djehutynefer: passage, right of entrance	6153, 8 × 10
TT 80: Tomb of Djehutynefer: wall painting	6109, 8 × 10
TT 81: Tomb of Ineni	2908, 8 × 10
TT 81: Tomb of Ineni	2909, 8 × 10
TT 81: Tomb of Ineni	2910, 8 × 10
TT 81: Tomb of Ineni	2911, 8 × 10

Theban Tombs (*cont.*)

Nelson Number/Description	Negative, Format
TT 81: Tomb of Ineni	2912, 8 × 10
TT 81: Tomb of Ineni	2913, 8 × 10
TT 81: Tomb of Ineni	2914, 8 × 10
TT 81: Tomb of Ineni	10810, 5 × 7
TT 81: Tomb of Ineni: back of portico	6114, 8 × 10
TT 81: Tomb of Ineni: back of portico	6115, 8 × 10
TT 84: Tomb of Yamunedjeh	2915, 8 × 10
TT 84: Tomb of Yamunedjeh	2916, 8 × 10
TT 84: Tomb of Yamunedjeh: mural	6116, 8 × 10
TT 84: Tomb of Yamunedjeh: mural	6117, 8 × 10
TT 84: Tomb of Yamunedjeh: mural	6118, 8 × 10
TT 84: Tomb of Yamunedjeh: mural	6119, 8 × 10
TT 85: Tomb of Amenemheb-Mahu	2917, 8 × 10
TT 85: Tomb of Amenemheb-Mahu	2918, 8 × 10
TT 85: Tomb of Amenemheb-Mahu	2919, 8 × 10
TT 85: Tomb of Amenemheb-Mahu	2920, 8 × 10
TT 85: Tomb of Amenemheb-Mahu	2921, 8 × 10
TT 85: Tomb of Amenemheb-Mahu	2922, 8 × 10
TT 85: Tomb of Amenemheb-Mahu	2923, 8 × 10
TT 85: Tomb of Amenemheb-Mahu	2924, 8 × 10
TT 85: Tomb of Amenemheb-Mahu	2925, 8 × 10
TT 85: Tomb of Amenemheb-Mahu	2926, 8 × 10
TT 85: Tomb of Amenemheb-Mahu	2927, 8 × 10
TT 85: Tomb of Amenemheb-Mahu	2928, 8 × 10
TT 85: Tomb of Amenemheb-Mahu	2929, 8 × 10
TT 85: Tomb of Amenemheb-Mahu	2930, 8 × 10
TT 85: Tomb of Amenemheb-Mahu	2931, 8 × 10
TT 85: Tomb of Amenemheb-Mahu	2932, 8 × 10
TT 85: Tomb of Amenemheb-Mahu	2933, 8 × 10
TT 86: Tomb of Menkheperraseneb	2934, 8 × 10
TT 86: Tomb of Menkheperraseneb	2935, 8 × 10
TT 86: Tomb of Menkheperraseneb	2936, 8 × 10
TT 86: Tomb of Menkheperraseneb	2937, 8 × 10
TT 86: Tomb of Menkheperraseneb	2938, 8 × 10
TT 86: Tomb of Menkheperraseneb	2939, 8 × 10
TT 86: Tomb of Menkheperraseneb	2940, 8 × 10
TT 86: Tomb of Menkheperraseneb	2941, 8 × 10
TT 86: Tomb of Menkheperraseneb	2942, 8 × 10
TT 86: Tomb of Menkheperraseneb	7887, 5 × 7
TT 86: Tomb of Menkheperraseneb	7888, 5 × 7
TT 86: Tomb of Menkheperraseneb	7889, 5 × 7
TT 86: Tomb of Menkheperraseneb	7890, 5 × 7
TT 86: Tomb of Menkheperraseneb	7891, 5 × 7
TT 86: Tomb of Menkheperraseneb	7892, 5 × 7
TT 86: Tomb of Menkheperraseneb	7893, 5 × 7
TT 86: Tomb of Menkheperraseneb	7894, 5 × 7
TT 86: Tomb of Menkheperraseneb	7895, 5 × 7
TT 86: Tomb of Menkheperraseneb	7896, 5 × 7
TT 86: Tomb of Menkheperraseneb	7897, 5 × 7
TT 86: Tomb of Menkheperraseneb	7898, 5 × 7
TT 86: Tomb of Menkheperraseneb	7899, 5 × 7
TT 86: Tomb of Menkheperraseneb	9955, 5 × 7
TT 86: Tomb of Menkheperraseneb: hall	6473, 5 × 7
TT 86: Tomb of Menkheperraseneb: hall	6474, 5 × 7
TT 88: Tomb of Pehsukher-Tjenunu	3006, 8 × 10

Theban Tombs (*cont.*)

Nelson Number/Description	Negative, Format
TT 88: Tomb of Pehsukher-Tjenunu: hall	6120, 8 × 10
TT 88: Tomb of Pehsukher-Tjenunu: hall	6121, 8 × 10
TT 88: Tomb of Pehsukher-Tjenunu: hall, left side	6145, 7 × 9
TT 88: Tomb of Pehsukher-Tjenunu: hall, right side	6144, 7 × 9
TT 88: Tomb of Pehsukher-Tjenunu: kheker frieze	6475, 5 × 7
TT 88: Tomb of Pehsukher-Tjenunu: wall painting	6476, 5 × 7
TT 88: Tomb of Pehsukher-Tjenunu: wall painting	6477, 5 × 7
TT 89: Tomb of Amenmose	2943, 8 × 10
TT 89: Tomb of Amenmose	2944, 8 × 10
TT 89: Tomb of Amenmose	2945, 8 × 10
TT 89: Tomb of Amenmose	2946, 8 × 10
TT 89: Tomb of Amenmose	2947, 8 × 10
TT 89: Tomb of Amenmose	2948, 8 × 10
TT 89: Tomb of Amenmose: wall painting	6146, 7 × 9
TT 92: Tomb of Suemniut	2949, 8 × 10
TT 92: Tomb of Suemniut	2950, 8 × 10
TT 92: Tomb of Suemniut	2951, 8 × 10
TT 92: Tomb of Suemniut	2952, 8 × 10
TT 92: Tomb of Suemniut	2953, 8 × 10
TT 92: Tomb of Suemniut	2974, 7 × 9
TT 92: Tomb of Suemniut	2975, 7 × 9
TT 92: Tomb of Suemniut	2976, 7 × 9
TT 92: Tomb of Suemniut: hall	6124, 8 × 10
TT 92: Tomb of Suemniut: inner hall	6126, 8 × 10
TT 92: Tomb of Suemniut: inner hall	6127, 8 × 10
TT 92: Tomb of Suemniut: inner hall	6132, 8 × 10
TT 92: Tomb of Suemniut: inner hall	6133, 8 × 10
TT 92: Tomb of Suemniut: inner hall	6134, 8 × 10
TT 92: Tomb of Suemniut: inner hall	6135, 8 × 10
TT 92: Tomb of Suemniut: inner passage	6147, 7 × 9
TT 92: Tomb of Suemniut: inner passage	6148, 7 × 9
TT 92: Tomb of Suemniut: inside niche	6131, 8 × 10
TT 92: Tomb of Suemniut: relief	6122, 8 × 10
TT 92: Tomb of Suemniut: right side	6129, 8 × 10
TT 92: Tomb of Suemniut: right side, upper	6130, 8 × 10
TT 92: Tomb of Suemniut: wall of passage	6149, 7 × 9
TT 92: Tomb of Suemniut: wall painting	6123, 8 × 10
TT 92: Tomb of Suemniut: wall painting	6125, 8 × 10
TT 92: Tomb of Suemniut: wall painting	6128, 8 × 10
TT 93: Tomb of Kenamun	9956, 5 × 7
TT 93: Tomb of Kenamun	9957, 5 × 7
TT 93: Tomb of Kenamun	9958, 5 × 7
TT 93: Tomb of Kenamun	9959, 5 × 7
TT 93: Tomb of Kenamun	9960, 5 × 7
TT 93: Tomb of Kenamun	9961, 5 × 7
TT 93: Tomb of Kenamun	9962, 5 × 7
TT 93: Tomb of Kenamun	9963, 5 × 7
TT 93: Tomb of Kenamun	9964, 5 × 7
TT 93: Tomb of Kenamun	9965, 5 × 7
TT 93: Tomb of Kenamun	9966, 5 × 7
TT 93: Tomb of Kenamun	9967, 5 × 7
TT 93: Tomb of Kenamun	9968, 5 × 7
TT 93: Tomb of Kenamun	9969, 5 × 7
TT 93: Tomb of Kenamun	9970, 5 × 7
TT 93: Tomb of Kenamun	9971, 5 × 7

Theban Tombs (*cont.*)

Nelson Number/Description	Negative, Format
TT 93: Tomb of Kenamun	9972, 5 × 7
TT 93: Tomb of Kenamun	9973, 5 × 7
TT 93: Tomb of Kenamun	9974, 5 × 7
TT 93: Tomb of Kenamun	9975, 5 × 7
TT 93: Tomb of Kenamun	9976, 5 × 7
TT 93: Tomb of Kenamun	9977, 5 × 7
TT 93: Tomb of Kenamun	9978, 5 × 7
TT 93: Tomb of Kenamun	9979, 5 × 7
TT 93: Tomb of Kenamun	9980, 5 × 7
TT 93: Tomb of Kenamun	9981, 5 × 7
TT 93: Tomb of Kenamun	9982, 5 × 7
TT 93: Tomb of Kenamun	9983, 5 × 7
TT 93: Tomb of Kenamun	9984, 5 × 7
TT 93: Tomb of Kenamun	9985, 5 × 7
TT 96: Tomb of Sennefer	3356, 8 × 10
TT 96: Tomb of Sennefer	3357, 8 × 10
TT 96: Tomb of Sennefer	3358, 8 × 10
TT 96: Tomb of Sennefer	3359, 8 × 10
TT 96: Tomb of Sennefer	3360, 8 × 10
TT 96: Tomb of Sennefer	3361, 8 × 10
TT 96: Tomb of Sennefer	3362, 8 × 10
TT 96: Tomb of Sennefer	3363, 8 × 10
TT 96: Tomb of Sennefer	3364, 8 × 10
TT 96: Tomb of Sennefer	3365, 8 × 10
TT 96: Tomb of Sennefer	3366, 8 × 10
TT 100: Tomb of Rekhmire	9986, 5 × 7
TT 100: Tomb of Rekhmire	9987, 5 × 7
TT 100: Tomb of Rekhmire	9988, 5 × 7
TT 100: Tomb of Rekhmire	9989, 5 × 7
TT 100: Tomb of Rekhmire	9990, 5 × 7
TT 100: Tomb of Rekhmire	9991, 5 × 7
TT 100: Tomb of Rekhmire	9992, 5 × 7
TT 100: Tomb of Rekhmire	9993, 5 × 7
TT 100: Tomb of Rekhmire	9994, 5 × 7
TT 100: Tomb of Rekhmire	9995, 5 × 7
TT 100: Tomb of Rekhmire	9996, 5 × 7
TT 100: Tomb of Rekhmire	9997, 5 × 7
TT 100: Tomb of Rekhmire	9998, 5 × 7
TT 100: Tomb of Rekhmire	9999, 5 × 7
TT 100: Tomb of Rekhmire	10000, 5 × 7
TT 100: Tomb of Rekhmire	10001, 5 × 7
TT 100: Tomb of Rekhmire	10002, 5 × 7
TT 100: Tomb of Rekhmire	10003, 5 × 7
TT 100: Tomb of Rekhmire	10004, 5 × 7
TT 100: Tomb of Rekhmire	10005, 5 × 7
TT 100: Tomb of Rekhmire	10006, 5 × 7
TT 101: Tomb of Tjaenro	2954, 8 × 10
TT 101: Tomb of Tjaenro	3007, 8 × 10
TT 101: Tomb of Tjaenro	4010, 5 × 7
TT 101: Tomb of Tjaenro	4011, 5 × 7
TT 101: Tomb of Tjaenro	4012, 5 × 7
TT 101: Tomb of Tjaenro	4013, 5 × 7
TT 101: Tomb of Tjaenro	4014, 5 × 7
TT 101: Tomb of Tjaenro	4015, 5 × 7
TT 101: Tomb of Tjaenro	4016, 5 × 7

Theban Tombs (*cont.*)

Nelson Number/Description	Negative, Format
TT 101: Tomb of Tjaenro	4017, 5 × 7
TT 101: Tomb of Tjaenro	4018, 5 × 7
TT 101: Tomb of Tjaenro	4019, 5 × 7
TT 107: Tomb of Nefersekheru: overview of court	12488, 4 × 5
TT 123: Tomb of Amenemhat: lower part of passage	6481, 5 × 7
TT 123: Tomb of Amenemhat: lower wall of passage	6478, 5 × 7
TT 123: Tomb of Amenemhat: passage	6482, 5 × 7
TT 123: Tomb of Amenemhat: passage	6483, 5 × 7
TT 123: Tomb of Amenemhat: passage	6484, 5 × 7
TT 123: Tomb of Amenemhat: passage	6486, 5 × 7
TT 123: Tomb of Amenemhat: passage	6487, 5 × 7
TT 123: Tomb of Amenemhat: passage	6488, 5 × 7
TT 123: Tomb of Amenemhat: passage	6489, 5 × 7
TT 123: Tomb of Amenemhat: passage	6490, 5 × 7
TT 123: Tomb of Amenemhat: passage	6491, 5 × 7
TT 123: Tomb of Amenemhat: passage	6492, 5 × 7
TT 123: Tomb of Amenemhat: passage	6493, 5 × 7
TT 123: Tomb of Amenemhat: relief	6485, 5 × 7
TT 123: Tomb of Amenemhat: upper wall of passage	6479, 5 × 7
TT 123: Tomb of Amenemhat: upper wall of passage	6480, 5 × 7
TT 125: Tomb of Duawyneheh: relief	6495, 5 × 7
TT 125: Tomb of Duawyneheh: relief	6496, 5 × 7
TT 125: Tomb of Duawyneheh: relief	6497, 5 × 7
TT 125: Tomb of Duawyneheh: stela	6494, 5 × 7
TT 125: Tomb of Duawyneheh: wall painting	6498, 5 × 7
TT 125: Tomb of Duawyneheh: wall painting	6499, 5 × 7
TT 127: Tomb of Seniemiah	3473, 8 × 10
TT 127: Tomb of Seniemiah	3474, 8 × 10
TT 127: Tomb of Seniemiah	3475, 8 × 10
TT 127: Tomb of Seniemiah	3476, 8 × 10
TT 127: Tomb of Seniemiah	3477, 8 × 10
TT 127: Tomb of Seniemiah	3478, 8 × 10
TT 127: Tomb of Seniemiah	3479, 8 × 10
TT 127: Tomb of Seniemiah	3480, 8 × 10
TT 127: Tomb of Seniemiah	3481, 8 × 10
TT 127: Tomb of Seniemiah	3484, 8 × 10
TT 131: Tomb of Amenuser	10262, 5 × 7
TT 131: Tomb of Amenuser	10263, 5 × 7
TT 131: Tomb of Amenuser	10264, 5 × 7
TT 131: Tomb of Amenuser	10265, 5 × 7
TT 131: Tomb of Amenuser	10266, 5 × 7
TT 132: Tomb of Ramose	10597, 5 × 7
TT 132: Tomb of Ramose	10598, 5 × 7
TT 132: Tomb of Ramose	10599, 5 × 7
TT 132: Tomb of Ramose	10600, 5 × 7
TT 138: Tomb of Nedjemger	2978, 7 × 9
TT 138: Tomb of Nedjemger	7785, 3.5 × 4.5
TT 138: Tomb of Nedjemger	7786, 3.5 × 4.5
TT 138: Tomb of Nedjemger	7787, 3.5 × 4.5
TT 138: Tomb of Nedjemger	7788, 3.5 × 4.5
TT 138: Tomb of Nedjemger	7789, 3.5 × 4.5
TT 138: Tomb of Nedjemger	7790, 3.5 × 4.5

Theban Tombs (*cont.*)

Nelson Number/Description	Negative, Format
TT 139: Tomb of Pairy: doorway to niche	6150, 7 × 9
TT 139: Tomb of Pairy: painting	6136, 8 × 10
TT 139: Tomb of Pairy: painting	6151, 7 × 9
TT 139: Tomb of Pairy: painting	6152, 7 × 9
TT 141: Tomb of Bakenkhonsu	10292, 5 × 7
TT 144: Tomb of Nenu	10270, 5 × 7
TT 145: Tomb of Nebamun	10281, 5 × 7
TT 145: Tomb of Nebamun	10282, 5 × 7
TT 145: Tomb of Nebamun	10283, 5 × 7
TT 148: Tomb of Amenemopet	3911, 8 × 10
TT 148: Tomb of Amenemopet	3912, 8 × 10
TT 148: Tomb of Amenemopet	3913, 8 × 10
TT 148: Tomb of Amenemopet	3914, 8 × 10
TT 148: Tomb of Amenemopet	3915, 8 × 10
TT 148: Tomb of Amenemopet	3916, 8 × 10
TT 148: Tomb of Amenemopet	10333, 5 × 7
TT 151: Tomb of Haty	2979, 7 × 9
TT 154: Tomb of Tati	10311, 5 × 7
TT 154: Tomb of Tati	10312, 5 × 7
TT 155: Tomb of Intef	10313, 5 × 7
TT 155: Tomb of Intef	10314, 5 × 7
TT 155: Tomb of Intef	10315, 5 × 7
TT 158: Tomb of Tjanefer	3015, 8 × 10
TT 158: Tomb of Tjanefer	3016, 8 × 10
TT 158: Tomb of Tjanefer	3599, 8 × 10
TT 158: Tomb of Tjanefer	3600, 8 × 10
TT 158: Tomb of Tjanefer	3601, 8 × 10
TT 158: Tomb of Tjanefer	3602, 8 × 10
TT 158: Tomb of Tjanefer	3603, 8 × 10
TT 158: Tomb of Tjanefer	3604, 8 × 10
TT 158: Tomb of Tjanefer	3605, 8 × 10
TT 158: Tomb of Tjanefer	3606, 8 × 10
TT 158: Tomb of Tjanefer	3607, 8 × 10
TT 158: Tomb of Tjanefer	3608, 8 × 10
TT 158: Tomb of Tjanefer	3609, 8 × 10
TT 158: Tomb of Tjanefer	3610, 8 × 10
TT 158: Tomb of Tjanefer	3611, 8 × 10
TT 158: Tomb of Tjanefer	3612, 8 × 10
TT 158: Tomb of Tjanefer	3613, 8 × 10
TT 158: Tomb of Tjanefer	3633, 8 × 10
TT 158: Tomb of Tjanefer	3634, 8 × 10
TT 158: Tomb of Tjanefer	3635, 8 × 10
TT 158: Tomb of Tjanefer	3636, 8 × 10
TT 158: Tomb of Tjanefer	3637, 8 × 10
TT 158: Tomb of Tjanefer	3638, 8 × 10
TT 158: Tomb of Tjanefer	3639, 8 × 10
TT 158: Tomb of Tjanefer	3640, 8 × 10
TT 158: Tomb of Tjanefer	3641, 8 × 10
TT 158: Tomb of Tjanefer	3642, 8 × 10
TT 158: Tomb of Tjanefer	3643, 8 × 10
TT 158: Tomb of Tjanefer	3644, 8 × 10
TT 158: Tomb of Tjanefer	3645, 8 × 10
TT 158: Tomb of Tjanefer	3662, 5 × 7
TT 158: Tomb of Tjanefer	3663, 5 × 7
TT 158: Tomb of Tjanefer	3664, 5 × 7

Theban Tombs (*cont.*)

Nelson Number/Description	Negative, Format
TT 158: Tomb of Tjanefer	3665, 5 × 7
TT 158: Tomb of Tjanefer	3666, 5 × 7
TT 158: Tomb of Tjanefer	3667, 5 × 7
TT 158: Tomb of Tjanefer	3668, 5 × 7
TT 158: Tomb of Tjanefer	3709, 5 × 7
TT 158: Tomb of Tjanefer	3710, 5 × 7
TT 158: Tomb of Tjanefer	3711, 5 × 7
TT 158: Tomb of Tjanefer	3712, 5 × 7
TT 158: Tomb of Tjanefer	3713, 5 × 7
TT 158: Tomb of Tjanefer	3714, 5 × 7
TT 158: Tomb of Tjanefer	3715, 5 × 7
TT 158: Tomb of Tjanefer	3716, 5 × 7
TT 158: Tomb of Tjanefer	3717, 5 × 7
TT 158: Tomb of Tjanefer	3897, 5 × 7
TT 158: Tomb of Tjanefer	3898, 5 × 7
TT 158: Tomb of Tjanefer	3901, 8 × 10
TT 158: Tomb of Tjanefer	3903, 8 × 10
TT 158: Tomb of Tjanefer	3905, 8 × 10
TT 158: Tomb of Tjanefer	3906, 8 × 10
TT 158: Tomb of Tjanefer	3907, 8 × 10
TT 158: Tomb of Tjanefer	3908, 8 × 10
TT 158: Tomb of Tjanefer	3909, 8 × 10
TT 158: Tomb of Tjanefer	3910, 8 × 10
TT 158: Tomb of Tjanefer	3957, 5 × 7
TT 158: Tomb of Tjanefer	3958, 5 × 7
TT 158: Tomb of Tjanefer	3959, 5 × 7
TT 158: Tomb of Tjanefer	3960, 5 × 7
TT 158: Tomb of Tjanefer	3961, 5 × 7
TT 158: Tomb of Tjanefer	3962, 5 × 7
TT 158: Tomb of Tjanefer	3970, 5 × 7
TT 158: Tomb of Tjanefer	3971, 5 × 7
TT 158: Tomb of Tjanefer	3972, 5 × 7
TT 158: Tomb of Tjanefer: exterior, east end	3008, 8 × 10
TT 158: Tomb of Tjanefer: exterior, north wall, west of doorway	3010, 8 × 10
TT 158: Tomb of Tjanefer: exterior, west end	3009, 8 × 10
TT 158: Tomb of Tjanefer: fragments	3597, 8 × 10
TT 158: Tomb of Tjanefer: fragments	3598, 8 × 10
TT 158: Tomb of Tjanefer: passage, left side, bottom	3011, 8 × 10
TT 158: Tomb of Tjanefer: passage, left side, bottom	3012, 8 × 10
TT 158: Tomb of Tjanefer: passage, left side, second section from bottom	3013, 8 × 10
TT 158: Tomb of Tjanefer: passage, left side, third section from bottom	3014, 8 × 10
TT 161: Tomb of Nakht	10294, 5 × 7
TT 161: Tomb of Nakht	10295, 5 × 7
TT 178: Tomb of Neferrenpet (Kenro)	3949, 8 × 10
TT 178: Tomb of Neferrenpet (Kenro)	3950, 8 × 10
TT 178: Tomb of Neferrenpet (Kenro)	3951, 8 × 10
TT 178: Tomb of Neferrenpet (Kenro)	3952, 8 × 10
TT 181: Tomb of Nebamun	2955, 8 × 10
TT 181: Tomb of Nebamun	2956, 8 × 10
TT 181: Tomb of Nebamun	2957, 8 × 10
TT 181: Tomb of Nebamun	2958, 8 × 10

Theban Tombs (*cont.*)

Nelson Number/Description	Negative, Format
TT 192: Tomb of Kheruef	9814, 8 × 10
TT 192: Tomb of Kheruef	9815, 8 × 10
TT 192: Tomb of Kheruef	9816, 8 × 10
TT 192: Tomb of Kheruef	9817, 8 × 10
TT 192: Tomb of Kheruef	9818, 8 × 10
TT 192: Tomb of Kheruef	9819, 8 × 10
TT 192: Tomb of Kheruef	9820, 8 × 10
TT 192: Tomb of Kheruef	9821, 8 × 10
TT 192: Tomb of Kheruef	9822, 8 × 10
TT 192: Tomb of Kheruef	9823, 8 × 10
TT 192: Tomb of Kheruef	9824, 8 × 10
TT 192: Tomb of Kheruef	9825, 8 × 10
TT 192: Tomb of Kheruef	9826, 8 × 10
TT 192: Tomb of Kheruef	9827, 8 × 10
TT 192: Tomb of Kheruef	9828, 8 × 10
TT 192: Tomb of Kheruef	9829, 8 × 10
TT 192: Tomb of Kheruef	9830, 8 × 10
TT 192: Tomb of Kheruef	9831, 8 × 10
TT 192: Tomb of Kheruef	9832, 8 × 10
TT 192: Tomb of Kheruef	9833, 8 × 10
TT 192: Tomb of Kheruef	9834, 8 × 10
TT 192: Tomb of Kheruef	9835, 8 × 10
TT 192: Tomb of Kheruef	9836, 8 × 10
TT 192: Tomb of Kheruef	9837, 8 × 10
TT 192: Tomb of Kheruef	9838, 8 × 10
TT 192: Tomb of Kheruef	9839, 8 × 10
TT 192: Tomb of Kheruef	9840, 8 × 10
TT 192: Tomb of Kheruef	9841, 8 × 10
TT 192: Tomb of Kheruef	9842, 8 × 10
TT 192: Tomb of Kheruef	9843, 8 × 10
TT 192: Tomb of Kheruef	9844, 8 × 10
TT 192: Tomb of Kheruef	9891, 5 × 7
TT 192: Tomb of Kheruef	11579, 5 × 7
TT 192: Tomb of Kheruef	11580, 5 × 7
TT 192: Tomb of Kheruef	11581, 5 × 7
TT 192: Tomb of Kheruef	11582, 5 × 7
TT 192: Tomb of Kheruef	11591, 8 × 10
TT 192: Tomb of Kheruef	11592, 8 × 10
TT 192: Tomb of Kheruef	11593, 8 × 10
TT 192: Tomb of Kheruef	11594, 8 × 10
TT 192: Tomb of Kheruef	11595, 8 × 10
TT 192: Tomb of Kheruef	11596, 8 × 10
TT 192: Tomb of Kheruef	11597, 8 × 10
TT 192: Tomb of Kheruef	11600, 8 × 10
TT 192: Tomb of Kheruef	11601, 8 × 10
TT 192: Tomb of Kheruef	11602, 8 × 10
TT 192: Tomb of Kheruef	11603, 8 × 10
TT 192: Tomb of Kheruef	11604, 8 × 10
TT 192: Tomb of Kheruef	11605, 8 × 10
TT 192: Tomb of Kheruef	11606, 8 × 10
TT 192: Tomb of Kheruef	11607, 8 × 10
TT 192: Tomb of Kheruef	11739, 8 × 10
TT 192: Tomb of Kheruef	11740, 8 × 10
TT 192: Tomb of Kheruef	11741, 8 × 10
TT 192: Tomb of Kheruef	11742, 8 × 10

Theban Tombs (*cont.*)

Nelson Number/Description	Negative, Format
TT 192: Tomb of Kheruef	11743, 8 × 10
TT 192: Tomb of Kheruef	11744, 8 × 10
TT 192: Tomb of Kheruef	11745, 8 × 10
TT 192: Tomb of Kheruef	11746, 8 × 10
TT 192: Tomb of Kheruef	11747, 8 × 10
TT 192: Tomb of Kheruef	11748, 8 × 10
TT 192: Tomb of Kheruef	11749, 8 × 10
TT 192: Tomb of Kheruef	11750, 8 × 10
TT 192: Tomb of Kheruef	11751, 8 × 10
TT 192: Tomb of Kheruef	11752, 8 × 10
TT 192: Tomb of Kheruef	11753, 8 × 10
TT 192: Tomb of Kheruef	11754, 8 × 10
TT 192: Tomb of Kheruef	11755, 8 × 10
TT 192: Tomb of Kheruef	11756, 8 × 10
TT 192: Tomb of Kheruef	11757, 8 × 10
TT 192: Tomb of Kheruef	11758, 8 × 10
TT 192: Tomb of Kheruef	11759, 8 × 10
TT 192: Tomb of Kheruef	11760, 8 × 10
TT 192: Tomb of Kheruef	11843, 8 × 10
TT 192: Tomb of Kheruef, entrance	11036, 5 × 7
TT 192: Tomb of Kheruef: black statue parts and red quartzite statue fragments	11898, 8 × 10
TT 192: Tomb of Kheruef: black statue, footboard, right side	11635, 5 × 7
TT 192: Tomb of Kheruef: black statue, footboard, right side	11636, 5 × 7
TT 192: Tomb of Kheruef: black statue, inscriptions on right side	11633, 5 × 7
TT 192: Tomb of Kheruef: black statue, lap	11634, 5 × 7
TT 192: Tomb of Kheruef: black statue, left side, front	11897, 8 × 10
TT 192: Tomb of Kheruef: black statue, right side, front	11896, 8 × 10
TT 192: Tomb of Kheruef: ceiling, back passage	11698, 5 × 7
TT 192: Tomb of Kheruef: ceiling, front	11696, 5 × 7
TT 192: Tomb of Kheruef: ceiling, north portico, #1	11704, 5 × 7
TT 192: Tomb of Kheruef: ceiling, north portico, #2	11705, 5 × 7
TT 192: Tomb of Kheruef: ceiling, south portico, #1	11699, 5 × 7
TT 192: Tomb of Kheruef: ceiling, south portico, #2	11700, 5 × 7
TT 192: Tomb of Kheruef: ceiling, south portico, #3	11701, 5 × 7
TT 192: Tomb of Kheruef: ceiling, south portico, #4	11702, 5 × 7
TT 192: Tomb of Kheruef: ceiling, south portico, fragments	11703, 5 × 7
TT 192: Tomb of Kheruef: clearance, pigment chest	11630, 5 × 7
TT 192: Tomb of Kheruef: clearance, inscription inside lid of pigment chest	11632, 5 × 7
TT 192: Tomb of Kheruef: clearance, pigments	11631, 5 × 7
TT 192: Tomb of Kheruef: columns	11797, 5 × 7
TT 192: Tomb of Kheruef: columns	11798, 5 × 7
TT 192: Tomb of Kheruef: columns	11799, 5 × 7
TT 192: Tomb of Kheruef: columns	11800, 5 × 7

Theban Tombs (*cont.*)

Nelson Number/Description	Negative, Format
TT 192: Tomb of Kheruef: columns	11801, 5 × 7
TT 192: Tomb of Kheruef: columns 1-4 (of Column 1 wide)	11761, 5 × 7
TT 192: Tomb of Kheruef: columns 5-11 (of Column 1 narrow)	11762, 5 × 7
TT 192: Tomb of Kheruef: columns 12-21 (of Column 1 narrow)	11763, 5 × 7
TT 192: Tomb of Kheruef: columns 22-40 (miscellaneous fragments of group B)	11764, 5 × 7
TT 192: Tomb of Kheruef: columns 41-46 (miscellaneous fragments of group B); 49 (group J); 50 (group J); 51-52 (from south column of inscription, standing column to north of central axis); 53-67 (groups D-I)	11765, 5 × 7
TT 192: Tomb of Kheruef: columns 47 (group B0; 48 (group I); 68, 78 (group D-I0); 89-94 (column 6)	11766, 5 × 7
TT 192: Tomb of Kheruef: columns 69-80 (groups D-I); 81-88 (column 6); 81, 83, 87 (join from column 6)	11767, 5 × 7
TT 192: Tomb of Kheruef: columns 83, 81-87 (join) from column 6; 96 abc, 98, 100, 101 (column 7); 98 ab (column 7); 99 ab (column 7a); 100 abc (column 7)	11768, 5 × 7
TT 192: Tomb of Kheruef: columns 98 ab (column 7); 172	11782, 5 × 7
TT 192: Tomb of Kheruef: columns 99 ab (column 7 a); 100 abc (column 7); 155 abc (column 2); 167 (column 3	11781, 5 × 7
TT 192: Tomb of Kheruef: columns 102-103 (column 7); 97, 104 (column 7); 105 (column 6; 106-108 (group C)	11769, 5 × 7
TT 192: Tomb of Kheruef: columns 109 abc (column 8)	11770, 5 × 7
TT 192: Tomb of Kheruef: columns 110, 111, 114, 116 ab, 117, 118 ab, 119, 120, 121, 122 (group C)	11771, 5 × 7
TT 192: Tomb of Kheruef: columns 123, 124, 125 (column 6); 113, 115 (group C); 126 (column 2 A); 127 (column 2)	11772, 5 × 7
TT 192: Tomb of Kheruef: columns 138 (column 4 a); 137, 138, 139, 140 abc, 141 ab, 142, 143 ab (column 4)	11773, 5 × 7
TT 192: Tomb of Kheruef: columns 144 ab, 145 ab, 146 (column 5)	11774, 5 × 7
TT 192: Tomb of Kheruef: columns 147, 148, 149 ab, 151 ab (column 4); 152, 153, 154 (column 2); 156, 157, 158, 159 ab, 160, 161 ab (group K)	11775, 5 × 7
TT 192: Tomb of Kheruef: columns 162 ab, 163 (column 3); 150 (column 4); 165 (column 2)	11776, 5 × 7
TT 192: Tomb of Kheruef: columns 164 abcde (column 3)	11777, 5 × 7
TT 192: Tomb of Kheruef: columns 166 abcde (column 2)	11778, 5 × 7
TT 192: Tomb of Kheruef: columns 168, 169 (column 2)	11779, 5 × 7
TT 192: Tomb of Kheruef: columns 170 ab, 171 (column 2)	11780, 5 × 7
TT 192: Tomb of Kheruef: columns, fragment	11802, 5 × 7
TT 192: Tomb of Kheruef: columns, fragment	11803, 5 × 7
TT 192: Tomb of Kheruef: columns, fragment	11804, 5 × 7
TT 192: Tomb of Kheruef: columns, fragment	11805, 5 × 7

Theban Tombs (*cont.*)

Nelson Number/Description	Negative, Format
TT 192: Tomb of Kheruef: columns, fragment	11806, 5 × 7
TT 192: Tomb of Kheruef: columns, fragment	11807, 5 × 7
TT 192: Tomb of Kheruef: columns, fragment	11808, 5 × 7
TT 192: Tomb of Kheruef: columns, fragment	11809, 5 × 7
TT 192: Tomb of Kheruef: columns, fragment	11810, 5 × 7
TT 192: Tomb of Kheruef: columns, fragment	11811, 5 × 7
TT 192: Tomb of Kheruef: columns, restoration	11298, 8·× 10
TT 192: Tomb of Kheruef: court	11868, 5 × 7
TT 192: Tomb of Kheruef: court	11868-a, 5 × 7
TT 192: Tomb of Kheruef: court, first pillared hall	11894, 8 × 10
TT 192: Tomb of Kheruef: court, west A	11867, 5 × 7
TT 192: Tomb of Kheruef: east column of inscription, low	11788, 5 × 7
TT 192: Tomb of Kheruef: entrance	11029, 5 × 7
TT 192: Tomb of Kheruef: entrance	11030, 5 × 7
TT 192: Tomb of Kheruef: entrance	11031, 5 × 7
TT 192: Tomb of Kheruef: entrance	11032, 5 × 7
TT 192: Tomb of Kheruef: entrance	11033, 5 × 7
TT 192: Tomb of Kheruef: entrance	11034, 5 × 7
TT 192: Tomb of Kheruef: entrance	11035, 5 × 7
TT 192: Tomb of Kheruef: entrance	11037, 5 × 7
TT 192: Tomb of Kheruef: entrance	11038, 5 × 7
TT 192: Tomb of Kheruef: entrance	11039, 5 × 7
TT 192: Tomb of Kheruef: entrance	11040, 5 × 7
TT 192: Tomb of Kheruef: entrance	11863, 5 × 7
TT 192: Tomb of Kheruef: entrance	11864, 5 × 7
TT 192: Tomb of Kheruef: entrance	11865, 5 × 7
TT 192: Tomb of Kheruef: entrance	11866, 5 × 7
TT 192: Tomb of Kheruef: entry	11645, 5 × 7
TT 192: Tomb of Kheruef: entry	11646, 5 × 7
TT 192: Tomb of Kheruef: entry	11647, 5 × 7
TT 192: Tomb of Kheruef: entry, fragment	11812, 5 × 7
TT 192: Tomb of Kheruef: fragment	11640, 5 × 7
TT 192: Tomb of Kheruef: fragments	11557, 5 × 7
TT 192: Tomb of Kheruef: fragments	11558, 5 × 7
TT 192: Tomb of Kheruef: fragments	11559, 5 × 7
TT 192: Tomb of Kheruef: fragments	11560, 5 × 7
TT 192: Tomb of Kheruef: fragments	11561, 5 × 7
TT 192: Tomb of Kheruef: fragments	11562, 5 × 7
TT 192: Tomb of Kheruef: fragments	11563, 5 × 7
TT 192: Tomb of Kheruef: fragments	11564, 5 × 7
TT 192: Tomb of Kheruef: fragments	11637, 5 × 7
TT 192: Tomb of Kheruef: fragments	11638, 5 × 7
TT 192: Tomb of Kheruef: fragments	11639, 5 × 7
TT 192: Tomb of Kheruef: fragments	11641, 5 × 7
TT 192: Tomb of Kheruef: fragments	11642, 5 × 7
TT 192: Tomb of Kheruef: fragments	11643, 5 × 7
TT 192: Tomb of Kheruef: fragments	11644, 5 × 7
TT 192: Tomb of Kheruef: fragments	11849, 5 × 7
TT 192: Tomb of Kheruef: fragments	11850, 5 × 7
TT 192: Tomb of Kheruef: fragments	11851, 5 × 7
TT 192: Tomb of Kheruef: fragments	11853, 5 × 7
TT 192: Tomb of Kheruef: fragments	11854, 5 × 7
TT 192: Tomb of Kheruef: fragments	11855, 5 × 7
TT 192: Tomb of Kheruef: fragments	11856, 5 × 7

Theban Tombs (*cont.*)

Nelson Number/Description	Negative, Format
TT 192: Tomb of Kheruef: fragments	11857, 5 × 7
TT 192: Tomb of Kheruef: frieze, north portico, southeast corner	11852, 5 × 7
TT 192: Tomb of Kheruef: front entry, detail word square	11697, 5 × 7
TT 192: Tomb of Kheruef: graffiti	11041, 5 × 7
TT 192: Tomb of Kheruef: graffiti	11042, 5 × 7
TT 192: Tomb of Kheruef: graffito	11860, 5 × 7
TT 192: Tomb of Kheruef: graffito	11861, 5 × 7
TT 192: Tomb of Kheruef: ground plan	11295, 8 × 10
TT 192: Tomb of Kheruef: ground plan and elevation	11296, 8 × 10
TT 192: Tomb of Kheruef: ground plan and elevation, restoration	11297, 8 × 10
TT 192: Tomb of Kheruef: marginal inscription	11813, 5 × 7
TT 192: Tomb of Kheruef: name from entrance to hall, south reveal	11858, 5 × 7
TT 192: Tomb of Kheruef: name from entrance to hall, south reveal	11859, 5 × 7
TT 192: Tomb of Kheruef: north presentation, detail	11708, 5 × 7
TT 192: Tomb of Kheruef: northern throne scene, detail	11706, 5 × 7
TT 192: Tomb of Kheruef: northern throne scene, detail	11707, 5 × 7
TT 192: Tomb of Kheruef: red quartzite head	11895, 8 × 10
TT 192: Tomb of Kheruef: several stones from entry	11616, 5 × 7
TT 192: Tomb of Kheruef: south column of inscription, low	11787, 5 × 7
TT 192: Tomb of Kheruef: south column of inscription, middle	11786, 5 × 7
TT 192: Tomb of Kheruef: south presentation, detail	11709, 5 × 7
TT 192: Tomb of Kheruef: squared-off surface	11862, 5 × 7
TT 192: Tomb of Kheruef: stone from entry	11611, 5 × 7
TT 192: Tomb of Kheruef: stone from entry	11612, 5 × 7
TT 192: Tomb of Kheruef: stone from entry	11613, 5 × 7
TT 192: Tomb of Kheruef: stone from entry	11614, 5 × 7
TT 192: Tomb of Kheruef: stone from entry	11615, 5 × 7
TT 192: Tomb of Kheruef: west column of inscription, high	11783, 5 × 7
TT 192: Tomb of Kheruef: west column of inscription, low	11785, 5 × 7
TT 192: Tomb of Kheruef: west column of inscription, middle	11784, 5 × 7
TT 192: Tomb of Kheruef: word square, first version	11848, 8 × 10
TT 194: Tomb of Djehutyemheb	11043, 5 × 7
TT 194: Tomb of Djehutyemheb	11044, 5 × 7
TT 194: Tomb of Djehutyemheb	11045, 5 × 7
TT 194: Tomb of Djehutyemheb	11046, 5 × 7
TT 194: Tomb of Djehutyemheb	11047, 5 × 7
TT 194: Tomb of Djehutyemheb	11048, 5 × 7
TT 194: Tomb of Djehutyemheb	11049, 5 × 7
TT 194: Tomb of Djehutyemheb	11050, 5 × 7
TT 194: Tomb of Djehutyemheb	11051, 5 × 7
TT 194: Tomb of Djehutyemheb	11052, 5 × 7
TT 194: Tomb of Djehutyemheb	11053, 5 × 7

Theban Tombs (*cont.*)

Nelson Number/Description	Negative, Format
TT 194: Tomb of Djehutyemheb	11054, 5 × 7
TT 194: Tomb of Djehutyemheb	11055, 5 × 7
TT 194: Tomb of Djehutyemheb	11056, 5 × 7
TT 194: Tomb of Djehutyemheb	11057, 5 × 7
TT 194: Tomb of Djehutyemheb	11058, 5 × 7
TT 194: Tomb of Djehutyemheb	11059, 5 × 7
TT 194: Tomb of Djehutyemheb	11060, 5 × 7
TT 194: Tomb of Djehutyemheb	11061, 5 × 7
TT 194: Tomb of Djehutyemheb	11062, 5 × 7
TT 200: Tomb of Dedi	2959, 8 × 10
TT 201: Tomb of Ra	2960, 8 × 10
TT 221: Tomb of Horimin	7749, 3.5 × 4.5
TT 221: Tomb of Horimin	7750, 3.5 × 4.5
TT 221: Tomb of Horimin	7751, 3.5 × 4.5
TT 221: Tomb of Horimin	7752, 3.5 × 4.5
TT 221: Tomb of Horimin	7753, 3.5 × 4.5
TT 221: Tomb of Horimin	7754, 3.5 × 4.5
TT 221: Tomb of Horimin	7755, 3.5 × 4.5
TT 222: Tomb of Heqamaatranakht (Turo)	7853, 5 × 7
TT 222: Tomb of Heqamaatranakht (Turo)	7854, 5 × 7
TT 222: Tomb of Heqamaatranakht (Turo)	7855, 5 × 7
TT 222: Tomb of Heqamaatranakht (Turo)	8176, 8 × 10
TT 232: Tomb of Tjerwas: ceiling	10651, 5 × 7
TT 253: Tomb of Khnummose	2961, 8 × 10
TT 254: Tomb of Mose	2962, 8 × 10
TT 254: Tomb of Mose	2963, 8 × 10
TT 254: Tomb of Mose	2964, 8 × 10
TT 254: Tomb of Mose	2965, 8 × 10
TT 255: Tomb of Roy	10326, 5 × 7
TT 255: Tomb of Roy	10327, 5 × 7
TT 255: Tomb of Roy	10328, 5 × 7
TT 255: Tomb of Roy	10329, 5 × 7
TT 255: Tomb of Roy	10330, 5 × 7
TT 255: Tomb of Roy	10331, 5 × 7
TT 255: Tomb of Roy	10332, 5 × 7
TT 260: Tomb of User	10271, 5 × 7
TT 260: Tomb of User	10272, 5 × 7
TT 260: Tomb of User	10273, 5 × 7
TT 260: Tomb of User	10274, 5 × 7
TT 261: Tomb of Khaemwaset	2980, 7 × 9
TT 261: Tomb of Khaemwaset	2981, 7 × 9
TT 261: Tomb of Khaemwaset	10275, 5 × 7
TT 261: Tomb of Khaemwaset	10276, 5 × 7
TT 261: Tomb of Khaemwaset	10277, 5 × 7
TT 261: Tomb of Khaemwaset	10278, 5 × 7
TT 261: Tomb of Khaemwaset	10279, 5 × 7
TT 261: Tomb of Khaemwaset	10280, 5 × 7
TT 271: Tomb of Nay	7756, 3.5 × 4.5
TT 271: Tomb of Nay	7757, 3.5 × 4.5
TT 271: Tomb of Nay	7758, 3.5 × 4.5
TT 271: Tomb of Nay	7759, 3.5 × 4.5
TT 271: Tomb of Nay	7760, 3.5 × 4.5
TT 272: Tomb of Khaemopet	7724, 3.5 × 4.5
TT 272: Tomb of Khaemopet	7725, 3.5 × 4.5
TT 272: Tomb of Khaemopet	7726, 3.5 × 4.5

Theban Tombs (*cont.*)

Nelson Number/Description	Negative, Format
TT 272: Tomb of Khaemopet	7727, 3.5 × 4.5
TT 272: Tomb of Khaemopet	7728, 3.5 × 4.5
TT 272: Tomb of Khaemopet	7729, 3.5 × 4.5
TT 272: Tomb of Khaemopet	7730, 3.5 × 4.5
TT 272: Tomb of Khaemopet	7731, 3.5 × 4.5
TT 272: Tomb of Khaemopet	7732, 3.5 × 4.5
TT 272: Tomb of Khaemopet	7733, 3.5 × 4.5
TT 272: Tomb of Khaemopet	7734, 3.5 × 4.5
TT 272: Tomb of Khaemopet	7735, 3.5 × 4.5
TT 273: Tomb of Sayemitef	7736, 3.5 × 4.5
TT 273: Tomb of Sayemitef	7737, 3.5 × 4.5
TT 273: Tomb of Sayemitef	7738, 3.5 × 4.5
TT 273: Tomb of Sayemitef	7739, 3.5 × 4.5
TT 273: Tomb of Sayemitef	7740, 3.5 × 4.5
TT 273: Tomb of Sayemitef	7741, 3.5 × 4.5
TT 273: Tomb of Sayemitef	7742, 3.5 × 4.5
TT 273: Tomb of Sayemitef	7743, 3.5 × 4.5
TT 273: Tomb of Sayemitef	7744, 3.5 × 4.5
TT 273: Tomb of Sayemitef	7745, 3.5 × 4.5
TT 273: Tomb of Sayemitef	7746, 3.5 × 4.5
TT 273: Tomb of Sayemitef	7747, 3.5 × 4.5
TT 273: Tomb of Sayemitef	7748, 3.5 × 4.5
TT 276: Tomb of Amenemopet	2966, 8 × 10
TT 276: Tomb of Amenemopet	2967, 8 × 10
TT 276: Tomb of Amenemopet	2968, 8 × 10
TT 276: Tomb of Amenemopet	2969, 8 × 10
TT 276: Tomb of Amenemopet	3018, 5 × 7
TT 276: Tomb of Amenemopet	10387, 5 × 7
TT 276: Tomb of Amenemopet	10388, 5 × 7
TT 276: Tomb of Amenemopet	10389, 5 × 7
TT 276: Tomb of Amenemopet	10390, 5 × 7
TT 276: Tomb of Amenemopet	10391, 5 × 7
TT 276: Tomb of Amenemopet	10392, 5 × 7
TT 276: Tomb of Amenemopet	10393, 5 × 7
TT 276: Tomb of Amenemopet	10394, 5 × 7
TT 276: Tomb of Amenemopet	10395, 5 × 7
TT 276: Tomb of Amenemopet	10396, 5 × 7
TT 277: Tomb of Amenemonet	2866, 8 × 10
TT 277: Tomb of Amenemonet	2970, 8 × 10
TT 277: Tomb of Amenemonet	2971, 8 × 10
TT 277: Tomb of Amenemonet	2972, 8 × 10
TT 277: Tomb of Amenemonet	2973, 8 × 10
TT 277: Tomb of Amenemonet	7704, 3.5 × 4.5
TT 277: Tomb of Amenemonet	7705, 3.5 × 4.5
TT 277: Tomb of Amenemonet	7706, 3.5 × 4.5
TT 277: Tomb of Amenemonet	7707, 3.5 × 4.5
TT 277: Tomb of Amenemonet	7708, 3.5 × 4.5
TT 277: Tomb of Amenemonet	7709, 3.5 × 4.5
TT 277: Tomb of Amenemonet	7710, 3.5 × 4.5
TT 277: Tomb of Amenemonet	7711, 3.5 × 4.5
TT 277: Tomb of Amenemonet	7712, 3.5 × 4.5
TT 277: Tomb of Amenemonet	7713, 3.5 × 4.5
TT 277: Tomb of Amenemonet	7714, 3.5 × 4.5
TT 277: Tomb of Amenemonet	10397, 5 × 7
TT 277: Tomb of Amenemonet	10398, 5 × 7

Theban Tombs (*cont.*)

Nelson Number/Description	Negative, Format
TT 277: Tomb of Amenemonet	10399, 5 × 7
TT 277: Tomb of Amenemonet	10400, 5 × 7
TT 277: Tomb of Amenemonet	10401, 5 × 7
TT 277: Tomb of Amenemonet	10402, 5 × 7
TT 277: Tomb of Amenemonet	10403, 5 × 7
TT 277: Tomb of Amenemonet	10404, 5 × 7
TT 278: Tomb of Amenemheb	7715, 3.5 × 4.5
TT 278: Tomb of Amenemheb	7716, 3.5 × 4.5
TT 278: Tomb of Amenemheb	7717, 3.5 × 4.5
TT 278: Tomb of Amenemheb	7718, 3.5 × 4.5
TT 278: Tomb of Amenemheb	7719, 3.5 × 4.5
TT 278: Tomb of Amenemheb	7720, 3.5 × 4.5
TT 278: Tomb of Amenemheb	7721, 3.5 × 4.5
TT 278: Tomb of Amenemheb	7722, 3.5 × 4.5
TT 278: Tomb of Amenemheb	7723, 3.5 × 4.5
TT 341: Tomb of Nakhtamun	3367, 8 × 10
TT 341: Tomb of Nakhtamun	3368, 8 × 10
TT 341: Tomb of Nakhtamun	3369, 8 × 10
TT 341: Tomb of Nakhtamun	3370, 8 × 10
TT 341: Tomb of Nakhtamun	3371, 8 × 10
TT 341: Tomb of Nakhtamun	3372, 8 × 10
TT 341: Tomb of Nakhtamun	3373, 8 × 10
TT 341: Tomb of Nakhtamun	3374, 8 × 10
TT 341: Tomb of Nakhtamun	3375, 8 × 10
TT 341: Tomb of Nakhtamun	3376, 8 × 10
TT 341: Tomb of Nakhtamun	3377, 8 × 10
TT 341: Tomb of Nakhtamun	3461, 8 × 10
TT 341: Tomb of Nakhtamun	7860, 5 × 7
TT 341: Tomb of Nakhtamun	7861, 5 × 7
TT 341: Tomb of Nakhtamun	7862, 5 × 7
TT 341: Tomb of Nakhtamun	10588, 5 × 7
TT 341: Tomb of Nakhtamun	10589, 5 × 7
TT 341: Tomb of Nakhtamun	10590, 5 × 7
TT 341: Tomb of Nakhtamun	10591, 5 × 7
TT 341: Tomb of Nakhtamun	10592, 5 × 7
TT 341: Tomb of Nakhtamun	10593, 5 × 7
TT 341: Tomb of Nakhtamun	10594, 5 × 7
TT 341: Tomb of Nakhtamun	10595, 5 × 7
TT 341: Tomb of Nakhtamun	10596, 5 × 7
TT 341: Tomb of Nakhtamun: wall painting	6137, 8 × 10
TT 343: Tomb of Benia-Paheqamen	7810, 3.5 × 4.5
TT 343: Tomb of Benia-Paheqamen	7811, 3.5 × 4.5
TT 343: Tomb of Benia-Paheqamen	7812, 3.5 × 4.5
TT 343: Tomb of Benia-Paheqamen	7813, 3.5 × 4.5
TT 343: Tomb of Benia-Paheqamen	7814, 3.5 × 4.5
TT 343: Tomb of Benia-Paheqamen	7815, 3.5 × 4.5
TT 343: Tomb of Benia-Paheqamen	7816, 3.5 × 4.5
TT 343: Tomb of Benia-Paheqamen	7817, 3.5 × 4.5
TT 343: Tomb of Benia-Paheqamen	7818, 3.5 × 4.5
TT 343: Tomb of Benia-Paheqamen	7819, 3.5 × 4.5
TT 343: Tomb of Benia-Paheqamen	7820, 3.5 × 4.5
TT 343: Tomb of Benia-Paheqamen	7821, 3.5 × 4.5
TT 343: Tomb of Benia-Paheqamen	7822, 3.5 × 4.5
TT 343: Tomb of Benia-Paheqamen	7823, 3.5 × 4.5
TT 343: Tomb of Benia-Paheqamen	7824, 3.5 × 4.5

Theban Tombs (*cont.*)

Nelson Number/Description	Negative, Format
TT 343: Tomb of Benia-Paheqamen	7825, 3.5 × 4.5
TT 343: Tomb of Benia-Paheqamen	7826, 3.5 × 4.5
TT 343: Tomb of Benia-Paheqamen	7827, 3.5 × 4.5
TT 343: Tomb of Benia-Paheqamen	7828, 3.5 × 4.5
TT 343: Tomb of Benia-Paheqamen	7829, 3.5 × 4.5
TT 343: Tomb of Benia-Paheqamen	7830, 3.5 × 4.5
TT 343: Tomb of Benia-Paheqamen	7831, 3.5 × 4.5
TT 343: Tomb of Benia-Paheqamen	7832, 3.5 × 4.5
TT 365: Tomb of Nefermenu	3017, 5 × 7
TT 372: Tomb of Amenkhau	7856, 5 × 7
TT 372: Tomb of Amenkhau	7857, 5 × 7
TT 372: Tomb of Amenkhau	7858, 5 × 7
TT 372: Tomb of Amenkhau	7859, 5 × 7
TT 373: Tomb of Amenmose	10604, 5 × 7
TT 373: Tomb of Amenmose	10605, 5 × 7
TT 373: Tomb of Amenmose	10606, 5 × 7
TT 373: Tomb of Amenmose	10607, 5 × 7
TT 373: Tomb of Amenmose	10608, 5 × 7
TT 373: Tomb of Amenmose	10609, 5 × 7
TT 373: Tomb of Amenmose	10610, 5 × 7
TT 373: Tomb of Amenmose	10611, 5 × 7
TT 373: Tomb of Amenmose	10612, 5 × 7
TT 409: Tomb of Samut-Kyky	11169, 5 × 7
TT 409: Tomb of Samut-Kyky	11170, 5 × 7
TT 409: Tomb of Samut-Kyky	11171, 5 × 7
TT 409: Tomb of Samut-Kyky	11172, 5 × 7
TT 409: Tomb of Samut-Kyky	11173, 5 × 7
TT 409: Tomb of Samut-Kyky	11174, 5 × 7
TT 409: Tomb of Samut-Kyky	11175, 5 × 7
TT 409: Tomb of Samut-Kyky	11176, 5 × 7
TT 409: Tomb of Samut-Kyky	11177, 5 × 7
TT 409: Tomb of Samut-Kyky	11178, 5 × 7
TT 409: Tomb of Samut-Kyky	11179, 5 × 7
TT 409: Tomb of Samut-Kyky	11180, 5 × 7
TT 409: Tomb of Samut-Kyky	11181, 5 × 7
TT 409: Tomb of Samut-Kyky	11182, 5 × 7
TT 409: Tomb of Samut-Kyky	11183, 5 × 7
TT 409: Tomb of Samut-Kyky	11184, 5 × 7
TT 409: Tomb of Samut-Kyky	11185, 5 × 7
TT 409: Tomb of Samut-Kyky	11186, 5 × 7
Unknown	6208, 8 × 10
Unknown	10318, 5 × 7
Unknown	10319, 5 × 7
Unknown	10320, 5 × 7
Unknown	10321, 5 × 7
Unknown	10322, 5 × 7
Unknown	10323, 5 × 7

Thebes

Nelson Number/Description	Negative, Format
Aerial photograph: Royal Air Force	11544, 8 × 10
Map of Thebes	11610, 8 × 10

Tuna el Gebel

Nelson Number/Description	Negative, Format
Subterranean Galleries, ceiling	9380, 5 × 7
Subterranean Galleries, ceiling	9381, 5 × 7
Subterranean Galleries, ceiling	9382, 5 × 7
Subterranean Galleries, ceiling	9383, 5 × 7
Subterranean Galleries, ceiling	9384, 5 × 7
Subterranean Galleries, ceiling	9385, 5 × 7
Subterranean Galleries, ceiling	9386, 5 × 7
Subterranean Galleries, ceiling	9387, 5 × 7
Subterranean Galleries, ceiling	9388, 5 × 7
Subterranean Galleries, ceiling	9389, 5 × 7
Subterranean Galleries, ceiling	9390, 5 × 7
Subterranean Galleries, ceiling	9391, 5 × 7
Subterranean Galleries, ceiling	9392, 5 × 7
Subterranean Galleries, ceiling	9393, 5 × 7
Subterranean Galleries, ceiling	9394, 5 × 7
Subterranean Galleries, ceiling	9395, 5 × 7

Valley of the Kings

Nelson Number/Description	Negative, Format
Tomb 01, Ramesses VII: hall B, ceiling	9330, 5 × 7
Tomb 01, Ramesses VII: hall B, ceiling	9331, 5 × 7
Tomb 01, Ramesses VII: hall B, ceiling	9332, 5 × 7
Tomb 01, Ramesses VII: hall B, ceiling	9296, 5 × 7
Tomb 01, Ramesses VII: hall B, ceiling	9297, 5 × 7
Tomb 01, Ramesses VII: hall B, ceiling	9298, 5 × 7
Tomb 01, Ramesses VII: hall B, ceiling	9299, 5 × 7
Tomb 01, Ramesses VII: hall A	9604, 5 × 7
Tomb 01, Ramesses VII: hall A	9605, 5 × 7
Tomb 01, Ramesses VII: hall A	9606, 5 × 7
Tomb 01, Ramesses VII: hall A	9607, 5 × 7
Tomb 01, Ramesses VII: hall A	9608, 5 × 7
Tomb 01, Ramesses VII: hall A	9609, 5 × 7
Tomb 01, Ramesses VII: hall A	9610, 5 × 7
Tomb 01, Ramesses VII: hall B, ceiling	9300, 5 × 7
Tomb 01, Ramesses VII: hall B, ceiling	9301, 5 × 7
Tomb 01, Ramesses VII: hall B, ceiling	9302, 5 × 7
Tomb 01, Ramesses VII: hall B, ceiling	9303, 5 × 7
Tomb 01, Ramesses VII: hall B, ceiling	9304, 5 × 7
Tomb 01, Ramesses VII: hall B, ceiling	9305, 5 × 7
Tomb 01, Ramesses VII: hall B, ceiling	9306, 5 × 7
Tomb 01, Ramesses VII: hall B, ceiling	9307, 5 × 7
Tomb 01, Ramesses VII: hall B, ceiling	9308, 5 × 7
Tomb 01, Ramesses VII: hall B, ceiling	9309, 5 × 7
Tomb 01, Ramesses VII: hall B, ceiling	9310, 5 × 7
Tomb 01, Ramesses VII: hall B, ceiling	9311, 5 × 7
Tomb 01, Ramesses VII: hall B, ceiling	9312, 5 × 7
Tomb 01, Ramesses VII: hall B, ceiling	9342, 5 × 7
Tomb 01, Tomb of Ramesses VII: hall B, ceiling	9329, 5 × 7
Tomb 02, Ramesses IV	8435, 8 × 10
Tomb 02, Ramesses IV	8436, 8 × 10
Tomb 02, Ramesses IV	8437, 8 × 10
Tomb 02, Ramesses IV	8438, 8 × 10
Tomb 02, Ramesses IV	8439, 8 × 10

Valley of the Kings (*cont.*)

Nelson Number/Description	Negative, Format
Tomb 02, Ramesses IV: corridor A, 2, Litany of Ra	13410, 5 × 7
Tomb 02, Ramesses IV: entrance, corridor A, 2, 3, Litany of Ra	13421, 5 × 7
Tomb 02, Ramesses IV: hall E, ceiling	9333, 5 × 7
Tomb 02, Ramesses IV: hall E, ceiling	9334, 5 × 7
Tomb 02, Ramesses IV: hall E, ceiling	9335, 5 × 7
Tomb 02, Ramesses IV: hall E, ceiling	9336, 5 × 7
Tomb 02, Ramesses IV: hall E, ceiling	9337, 5 × 7
Tomb 02, Ramesses IV: hall E, ceiling	9338, 5 × 7
Tomb 02, Ramesses IV: hall E, ceiling	9339, 5 × 7
Tomb 02, Ramesses IV: hall E, ceiling	9290, 5 × 7
Tomb 02, Ramesses IV: hall E, ceiling	9291, 5 × 7
Tomb 02, Ramesses IV: hall E, ceiling	9292, 5 × 7
Tomb 02, Ramesses IV: hall E, ceiling	9293, 5 × 7
Tomb 02, Ramesses IV: hall E, ceiling	9294, 5 × 7
Tomb 02, Ramesses IV: hall E, ceiling (montage)	11103, 8 × 10
Tomb 06, Ramesses IX: corridor B, 15, east end of south wall	13340, 5 × 7
Tomb 06, Ramesses IX: corridor B, 15, south wall	13343, 5 × 7
Tomb 06, Ramesses IX: entrance, view from corridor A into B	13365, 5 × 7
Tomb 06, Ramesses IX: entrance, view from corridor A into B	13419, 5 × 7
Tomb 06, Ramesses IX: entrance, view through corridor B into C	13445, 5 × 7
Tomb 06, Ramesses IX: hall B, ceiling	9282, 5 × 7
Tomb 06, Ramesses IX: hall B, ceiling	9283, 5 × 7
Tomb 06, Ramesses IX: hall B, ceiling	9284, 5 × 7
Tomb 06, Ramesses IX: hall B, ceiling	9285, 5 × 7
Tomb 06, Ramesses IX: hall B, ceiling	9286, 5 × 7
Tomb 06, Ramesses IX: hall B, ceiling	9287, 5 × 7
Tomb 06, Ramesses IX: hall B, ceiling	9288, 5 × 7
Tomb 06, Ramesses IX: hall B, ceiling	9289, 5 × 7
Tomb 06, Ramesses IX: hall B, ceiling	9343, 5 × 7
Tomb 06, Ramesses IX: hall B, ceiling	9344, 5 × 7
Tomb 06, Ramesses IX: hall B, ceiling	9345, 5 × 7
Tomb 06, Ramesses IX: hall B, ceiling	9346, 5 × 7
Tomb 06, Ramesses IX: hall B, ceiling	9347, 5 × 7
Tomb 06, Ramesses IX: hall B, ceiling	9348, 5 × 7
Tomb 06, Ramesses IX: hall B, ceiling	9349, 5 × 7
Tomb 06, Ramesses IX: hall B, ceiling	9350, 5 × 7
Tomb 06, Ramesses IX: hall B, ceiling	9351, 5 × 7
Tomb 06, Ramesses IX: hall B, ceiling	9352, 5 × 7
Tomb 06, Ramesses IX: middle register, west end of north wall	13364, 5 × 7
Tomb 06, Ramesses VI: hall A, ceiling	9353, 5 × 7
Tomb 07, Ramesses II	10805, 5 × 7
Tomb 07, Ramesses II	10806, 5 × 7
Tomb 07, Ramesses II: hall A, left side	10633, 5 × 7
Tomb 07, Ramesses II: hall A, left side	10634, 5 × 7
Tomb 07, Ramesses II: hall A, left side	10635, 5 × 7
Tomb 07, Ramesses II: hall A, left side	10636, 5 × 7
Tomb 07, Ramesses II: hall A, left side	10637, 5 × 7
Tomb 07, Ramesses II: hall A, left side	10638, 5 × 7
Tomb 07, Ramesses II: hall A, left side	10639, 5 × 7
Tomb 07, Ramesses II: hall A, left side	10640, 5 × 7

Valley of the Kings (*cont.*)

Nelson Number/Description	Negative, Format
Tomb 07, Ramesses II: hall A, right side	10625, 5 × 7
Tomb 07, Ramesses II: hall A, right side	10626, 5 × 7
Tomb 07, Ramesses II: hall A, right side	10627, 5 × 7
Tomb 07, Ramesses II: hall A, right side	10628, 5 × 7
Tomb 07, Ramesses II: hall A, right side	10629, 5 × 7
Tomb 07, Ramesses II: hall A, right side	10630, 5 × 7
Tomb 07, Ramesses II: hall A, right side	10631, 5 × 7
Tomb 07, Ramesses II: hall A, right side	10632, 5 × 7
Tomb 08, Merneptah	10807, 5 × 7
Tomb 08, Merneptah	10808, 5 × 7
Tomb 08, Merneptah: hall A, left side	10652, 5 × 7
Tomb 08, Merneptah: hall A, left side	10653, 5 × 7
Tomb 08, Merneptah: hall A, left side	10654, 5 × 7
Tomb 08, Merneptah: hall A, left side	10655, 5 × 7
Tomb 08, Merneptah: hall A, left side	10656, 5 × 7
Tomb 08, Merneptah: hall A, left side	10657, 5 × 7
Tomb 08, Merneptah: hall A, right side	10658, 5 × 7
Tomb 08, Merneptah: hall A, right side	10659, 5 × 7
Tomb 08, Merneptah: hall A, right side	10660, 5 × 7
Tomb 08, Merneptah: hall A, right side	10661, 5 × 7
Tomb 08, Merneptah: hall A, right side	10662, 5 × 7
Tomb 08, Merneptah: hall A, right side	10663, 5 × 7
Tomb 08, Merneptah: hall A, right side	10664, 5 × 7
Tomb 08, Merneptah: hall J, ceiling	9313, 5 × 7
Tomb 08, Merneptah: hall J, ceiling	9314, 5 × 7
Tomb 08, Merneptah: hall J, ceiling	9315, 5 × 7
Tomb 08, Merneptah: hall J, ceiling	9316, 5 × 7
Tomb 08, Merneptah: hall J, ceiling	9317, 5 × 7
Tomb 08, Merneptah: hall J, ceiling	9318, 5 × 7
Tomb 09, Ramesses VI: east, north section; pillars C and D, walls 17, 19	13361, 5 × 7
Tomb 09, Ramesses VI: hall A, ceiling	9249, 5 × 7
Tomb 09, Ramesses VI: hall A, ceiling	9250, 5 × 7
Tomb 09, Ramesses VI: hall A, ceiling	9251, 5 × 7
Tomb 09, Ramesses VI: hall A, ceiling	9252, 5 × 7
Tomb 09, Ramesses VI: hall A, ceiling	9253, 5 × 7
Tomb 09, Ramesses VI: hall A, ceiling	9254, 5 × 7
Tomb 09, Ramesses VI: hall A, ceiling	9255, 5 × 7
Tomb 09, Ramesses VI: hall A, ceiling	9354, 5 × 7
Tomb 09, Ramesses VI: hall A, ceiling	9355, 5 × 7
Tomb 09, Ramesses VI: hall B, ceiling	9256, 5 × 7
Tomb 09, Ramesses VI: hall B, ceiling	9257, 5 × 7
Tomb 09, Ramesses VI: hall B, ceiling	9258, 5 × 7
Tomb 09, Ramesses VI: hall B, ceiling	9259, 5 × 7
Tomb 09, Ramesses VI: hall B, ceiling	9260, 5 × 7
Tomb 09, Ramesses VI: hall B, ceiling	9261, 5 × 7
Tomb 09, Ramesses VI: hall E, ceiling	9262, 5 × 7
Tomb 09, Ramesses VI: hall E, ceiling	9263, 5 × 7
Tomb 09, Ramesses VI: hall E, ceiling	9264, 5 × 7
Tomb 09, Ramesses VI: hall E, ceiling	9265, 5 × 7
Tomb 09, Ramesses VI: hall E, ceiling	9266, 5 × 7
Tomb 09, Ramesses VI: hall E, ceiling	9267, 5 × 7
Tomb 09, Ramesses VI: hall E, ceiling	9268, 5 × 7
Tomb 09, Ramesses VI: hall E, ceiling	9269, 5 × 7
Tomb 09, Ramesses VI: hall E, ceiling	9270, 5 × 7

Valley of the Kings (*cont.*)

Nelson Number/Description	Negative, Format
Tomb 09, Ramesses VI: hall E, ceiling	9271, 5 × 7
Tomb 09, Ramesses VI: hall E, ceiling	9272, 5 × 7
Tomb 09, Ramesses VI: hall E, ceiling	9273, 5 × 7
Tomb 09, Ramesses VI: hall E, ceiling	9274, 5 × 7
Tomb 09, Ramesses VI: hall E, ceiling	9275, 5 × 7
Tomb 09, Ramesses VI: hall E, ceiling	9276, 5 × 7
Tomb 09, Ramesses VI: hall F, north side, #24, 6th and 7th Divisions of Amduat	13360, 5 × 7
Tomb 09, Ramesses VI: hall J	9277, 5 × 7
Tomb 09, Ramesses VI: hall J	9278, 5 × 7
Tomb 09, Ramesses VI; hall J	9279, 5 × 7
Tomb 09, Ramesses VI: hall J	9280, 5 × 7
Tomb 09, Ramesses VI: hall J	9281, 5 × 7
Tomb 11, Ramesses III	3389, 8 × 10
Tomb 11, Ramesses III	3390, 8 × 10
Tomb 11, Ramesses III	3391, 8 × 10
Tomb 11, Ramesses III	3392, 8 × 10
Tomb 11, Ramesses III	3393, 8 × 10
Tomb 11, Ramesses III	3394, 8 × 10
Tomb 11, Ramesses III	3395, 8 × 10
Tomb 11, Ramesses III	3396, 8 × 10
Tomb 11, Ramesses III	3397, 8 × 10
Tomb 11, Ramesses III	3398, 8 × 10
Tomb 11, Ramesses III	3399, 8 × 10
Tomb 11, Ramesses III	3400, 8 × 10
Tomb 11, Ramesses III	3401, 8 × 10
Tomb 11, Ramesses III	3402, 8 × 10
Tomb 11, Ramesses III	3403, 8 × 10
Tomb 11, Ramesses III	3404, 8 × 10
Tomb 11, Ramesses III	3405, 8 × 10
Tomb 11, Ramesses III	3406, 8 × 10
Tomb 11, Ramesses III	3407, 8 × 10
Tomb 11, Ramesses III	3408, 8 × 10
Tomb 11, Ramesses III	3409, 8 × 10
Tomb 11, Ramesses III	3460, 8 × 10
Tomb 11, Ramesses III	6500, 8 × 10
Tomb 11, Ramesses III	6500-a, 8 × 10
Tomb 11, Ramesses III	6501, 8 × 10
Tomb 11, Ramesses III	6502, 8 × 10
Tomb 11, Ramesses III	6503, 8 × 10
Tomb 11, Ramesses III	6504, 8 × 10
Tomb 11, Ramesses III	6505, 8 × 10
Tomb 11, Ramesses III	6506, 8 × 10
Tomb 11, Ramesses III	6507, 8 × 10
Tomb 11, Ramesses III	6508, 8 × 10
Tomb 11, Ramesses III	6509, 8 × 10
Tomb 11, Ramesses III	6510, 8 × 10
Tomb 11, Ramesses III	6511, 8 × 10
Tomb 11, Ramesses III	6512, 8 × 10
Tomb 11, Ramesses III	6513, 8 × 10
Tomb 11, Ramesses III	6514, 8 × 10
Tomb 11, Ramesses III	6515, 8 × 10
Tomb 11, Ramesses III	6516, 8 × 10
Tomb 11, Ramesses III	6517, 8 × 10
Tomb 11, Ramesses III	6518, 8 × 10

Valley of the Kings (*cont.*)

Nelson Number/Description	Negative, Format
Tomb 11, Ramesses III	6519, 8 × 10
Tomb 11, Ramesses III	6520, 8 × 10
Tomb 11, Ramesses III	6521, 8 × 10
Tomb 11, Ramesses III	6522, 8 × 10
Tomb 11, Ramesses III	6523, 8 × 10
Tomb 11, Ramesses III	6524, 8 × 10
Tomb 11, Ramesses III	7833, 8 × 10
Tomb 11, Ramesses III	7834, 8 × 10
Tomb 11, Ramesses III	7835, 8 × 10
Tomb 11, Ramesses III	7836, 8 × 10
Tomb 11, Ramesses III	7837, 8 × 10
Tomb 11, Ramesses III	7838, 8 × 10
Tomb 11, Ramesses III	7839, 8 × 10
Tomb 11, Ramesses III	7840, 8 × 10
Tomb 11, Ramesses III	7841, 8 × 10
Tomb 11, Ramesses III	7842, 8 × 10
Tomb 11, Ramesses III	7843, 8 × 10
Tomb 11, Ramesses III	7844, 8 × 10
Tomb 11, Ramesses III	7845, 8 × 10
Tomb 11, Ramesses III	7846, 8 × 10
Tomb 11, Ramesses III	7847, 8 × 10
Tomb 11, Ramesses III	7848, 8 × 10
Tomb 11, Ramesses III	7849, 8 × 10
Tomb 11, Ramesses III	7850, 8 × 10
Tomb 11, Ramesses III	7851, 8 × 10
Tomb 11, Ramesses III	7852, 8 × 10
Tomb 11, Ramesses III	10809, 5 × 7
Tomb 14, Tausert	10011, 5 × 7
Tomb 14, Tausert	10374, 5 × 7
Tomb 14, Tausert	10375, 5 × 7
Tomb 14, Tausert: hall J, ceiling	9319, 5 × 7
Tomb 14, Tausert: hall J, ceiling	9320, 5 × 7
Tomb 14, Tausert: hall J, ceiling	9321, 5 × 7
Tomb 14, Tausert: hall J, ceiling	9322, 5 × 7
Tomb 14, Tausert: hall J, ceiling	9323, 5 × 7
Tomb 14, Tausert: hall J, ceiling	9324, 5 × 7
Tomb 14, Tausert: hall L, ceiling	9325, 5 × 7
Tomb 14, Tausert: hall L, ceiling	9326, 5 × 7
Tomb 14, Tausert: hall L, ceiling	9327, 5 × 7
Tomb 14, Tausert: hall L, ceiling	9328, 5 × 7
Tomb 15, Sety II: corridor A, 3, north end of west wall, second scene from entrance	13423, 5 × 7
Tomb 15, Sety II: hall A, left side	10641, 5 × 7
Tomb 15, Sety II: hall A, left side	10642, 5 × 7
Tomb 15, Sety II: hall A, left side	10643, 5 × 7
Tomb 15, Sety II: hall A, left side	10644, 5 × 7
Tomb 15, Sety II: hall A, left side	10645, 5 × 7
Tomb 15, Sety II: hall A, right side	10646, 5 × 7
Tomb 15, Sety II: hall A, right side	10647, 5 × 7
Tomb 15, Sety II: hall A, right side	10648, 5 × 7
Tomb 15, Sety II: hall A, right side	10649, 5 × 7
Tomb 15, Sety II: hall A, right side	10650, 5 × 7
Tomb 15, Sety II: reliefs, corridor A, 2 (north end of east wall, in front of the Litany of Ra)	13339, 5 × 7
Tomb 16, Ramesses I	10007, 5 × 7

Valley of the Kings (*cont.*)

Nelson Number/Description	Negative, Format
Tomb 16, Ramesses I	10008, 5 × 7
Tomb 16, Ramesses I	10009, 5 × 7
Tomb 16, Ramesses I	10010, 5 × 7
Tomb 17, Sety I	10570, 5 × 7
Tomb 17, Sety I	10571, 5 × 7
Tomb 17, Sety I	10572, 5 × 7
Tomb 17, Sety I	10573, 5 × 7
Tomb 17, Sety I	10574, 5 × 7
Tomb 17, Sety I	10575, 5 × 7
Tomb 17, Sety I	10576, 5 × 7
Tomb 17, Sety I	10577, 5 × 7
Tomb 17, Sety I	10578, 5 × 7
Tomb 17, Sety I	10579, 5 × 7
Tomb 17, Sety I	10580, 5 × 7
Tomb 17, Sety I	10581, 5 × 7
Tomb 17, Sety I	10582, 5 × 7
Tomb 17, Sety I	10583, 5 × 7
Tomb 17, Sety I: chamber F, 19, ninth division of the Amduat	13432, 5 × 7
Tomb 17, Sety I: corridor 1, 31	13349, 5 × 7
Tomb 17, Sety I: corridor H, 26	13363, 5 × 7
Tomb 17, Sety I: hall J, 33	13370, 5 × 7
Tomb 17, Sety I: hall J, 34	13435, 5 × 7
Tomb 17, Sety I: hall J, pillar A (b)	13443, 5 × 7
Tomb 17, Sety I: hall K, ceiling	9396, 5 × 7
Tomb 17, Sety I: hall K, ceiling	9397, 5 × 7
Tomb 17, Sety I: hall K, ceiling	9398, 5 × 7
Tomb 17, Sety I: hall K, ceiling	9399, 5 × 7
Tomb 17, Sety I: hall K, ceiling	9400, 5 × 7
Tomb 17, Sety I: hall K, ceiling	9401, 5 × 7
Tomb 17, Sety I: painting, room F, pillar B, side b	13446, 5 × 7
Tomb 17, Sety I: relief, side room N, 45	13417, 5 × 7
Tomb 17, Sety I: side room N, 45	13353, 5 × 7
Tomb 17, Sety I: side room N, 46	13357, 5 × 7
Tomb 17, Sety I: side room N, 46	13426, 5 × 7
Tomb 17, Sety I: side room N, 46	13440, 5 × 7
Tomb 23, Ay	6411, 5 × 7
Tomb 23, Ay	6412, 5 × 7
Tomb 23, Ay	6413, 5 × 7
Tomb 23, Ay	6414, 5 × 7
Tomb 23, Ay	6415, 5 × 7
Tomb 23, Ay	6416, 5 × 7
Tomb 23, Ay	6417, 5 × 7
Tomb 23, Ay	6418, 5 × 7
Tomb 23, Ay	6419, 5 × 7
Tomb 47, Siptah: hall A, left side	10665, 5 × 7
Tomb 47, Siptah: hall A, left side	10666, 5 × 7
Tomb 47, Siptah: hall A, left side	10667, 5 × 7
Tomb 47, Siptah: hall A, left side	10668, 5 × 7
Tomb 47, Siptah: hall A, left side	10669, 5 × 7
Tomb 47, Siptah: hall A, left side	10670, 5 × 7
Tomb 47, Siptah: hall A, right side	10671, 5 × 7
Tomb 47, Siptah: hall A, right side	10672, 5 × 7
Tomb 47, Siptah: hall A, right side	10673, 5 × 7
Tomb 47, Siptah: hall A, right side	10674, 5 × 7

Valley of the Kings (*cont.*)

Nelson Number/Description	Negative, Format
Tomb 47, Siptah: hall A, right side	10675, 5 × 7
Tomb 47, Siptah: hall A, right side	10676, 5 × 7
Tomb 47, Siptah: hall A, right side	10677, 5 × 7
Tomb 62, Tutankhamun: east wall	6410, 5 × 7
Tomb 62, Tutankhamun: wall painting	6406, 5 × 7
Tomb 62, Tutankhamun: wall painting	6407, 5 × 7
Tomb 62, Tutankhamun: wall painting	6408, 5 × 7
Tomb 62, Tutankhamun: wall painting	6409, 5 × 7

Valley of the Queens

Nelson Number/Description	Negative, Format
Tomb 66, Nefertari	2859, 8 × 10
Tomb 66, Nefertari	2860, 8 × 10
Tomb 66, Nefertari	2861, 8 × 10
Tomb 66, Nefertari	2862, 8 × 10
Tomb 66, Nefertari	2863, 8 × 10
Tomb 66, Nefertari	2864, 8 × 10
Tomb 66, Nefertari	2865, 8 × 10
Tomb 66, Nefertari	3378, 8 × 10
Tomb 66, Nefertari	3379, 8 × 10
Tomb 66, Nefertari	3380, 8 × 10
Tomb 66, Nefertari	3381, 8 × 10
Tomb 66, Nefertari	3382, 8 × 10
Tomb 66, Nefertari	3383, 8 × 10
Tomb 66, Nefertari	3384, 8 × 10
Tomb 66, Nefertari	3385, 8 × 10
Tomb 66, Nefertari	3386, 8 × 10
Tomb 66, Nefertari	3387, 8 × 10
Tomb 66, Nefertari	3388, 8 × 10
Tomb 66, Nefertari	3462, 8 × 10

Wadi Abu Kua (Wadi Hammamat)

Nelson Number/Description	Negative, Format
None	6072, 5 × 7
None	6073, 5 × 7

Western Thebes

Nelson Number/Description	Negative, Format
Aerial photograph: Royal Air Force	11545, 8 × 10
Colossi of Amenhotep III	1037, 5 × 7
Colossi of Amenhotep III	1038, 5 × 7
Colossus of Amenhotep III: south side	13431, 5 × 7
Miscellaneous view	584, 5 × 7
Miscellaneous view, western cliffs	2827, 8 × 10
River and western cliffs	2759, 7 × 9

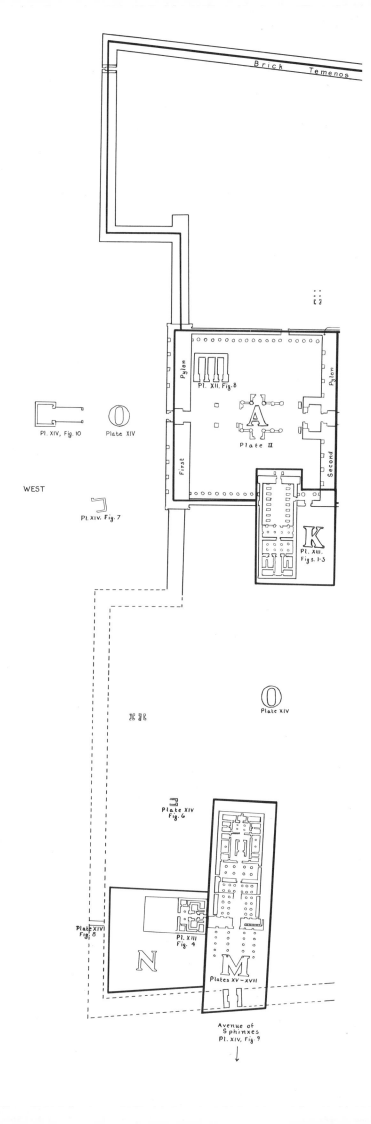

Brick   Temenos

Pylon

Pl. XII. Fig. 8

Pylon

Pl. XIV, Fig. 10   Plate XIV

A

Plate II

First

Second

WEST

Pl. XIV. Fig. 7

K

Pl. XIII.
Figs. 1-3

O
Plate XIV

Plate XIV
Fig. 6

Plate XIV
Fig. 8

Pl. XIII
Fig. 4

N

M

Plates XV–XVII

Avenue of
Sphinxes
Pl. XIV, Fig. 9

Plate 1

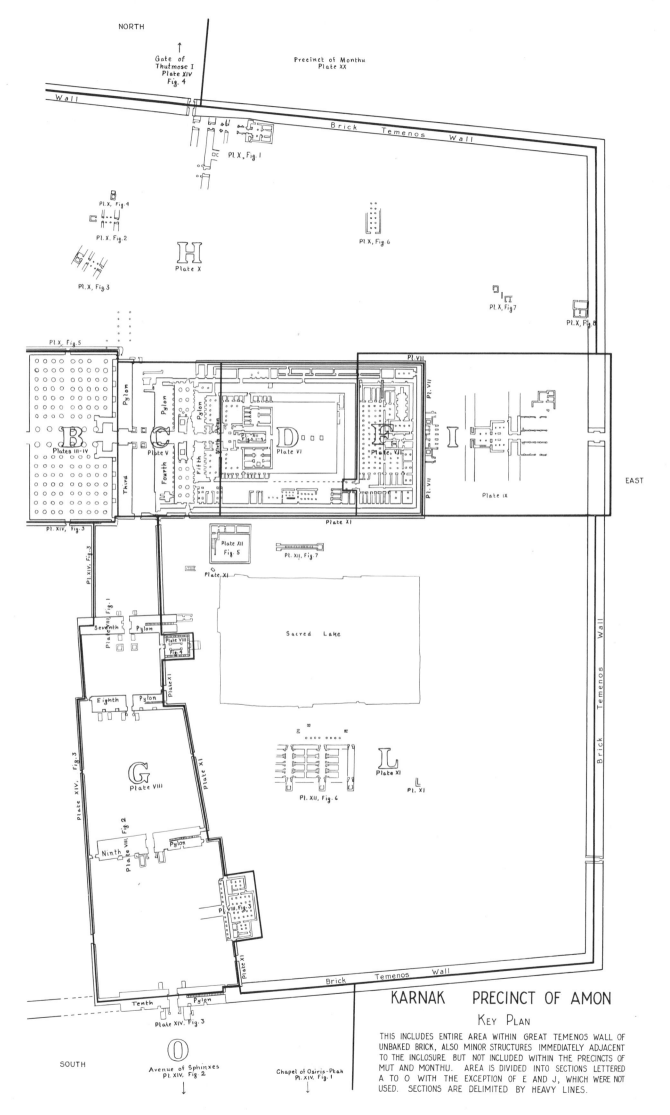

NORTH

Gate of
Thutmose I
Plate XIV
Fig. 4

Precinct of Monthu
Plate XX

Wall

Brick Temenos Wall

Pl. X, Fig. 1

Pl. X, Fig. 4

Pl. X. Fig. 2

Pl. X, Fig. 6

Pl. X, Fig. 3

H
Plate X

Pl. X, Fig. 7

Pl. X, Fig. 8

Pl. X, Fig. 5

Pl. VII

Pl. VII

B
Plates III-IV

C
Plate V

D
Plate VI

E
Plate VII

I
Plate IX

Third Pylon

Pylon

Pylon

Pl. XII, 1

Fourth

Fifth

Sixth Pylon

Pl. VII

EAST

Pl. XIV, Fig. 3

Plate XI

Plate XII
Fig. 5

Pl. XII, Fig. 7

Plate XI

Pl. XIV, Fig. 3

Pl. XIV, Fig. 1

Seventh

Pylon

Plate VIII
Fig. 4

Sacred Lake

Place III, Fig. 1

Plate XI

Brick Temenos Wall

Eighth

Pylon

Plate XI

Plate XIV, Fig. 3

G
Plate VIII

L
Plate XI

Plate VIII, Fig. 2

L
Pl. XI

Pl. XII, Fig. 6

Ninth

Pylon

Plate VIII, Fig. 3

Plate XI

Brick Temenos Wall

Tenth

Pylon

KARNAK   PRECINCT OF AMON

Plate XIV, Fig. 3

Key Plan

SOUTH

O

Avenue of Sphinxes
Pl. XIV, Fig. 2

Chapel of Osiris-Ptah
Pl. XIV, Fig. 1

THIS INCLUDES ENTIRE AREA WITHIN GREAT TEMENOS WALL OF
UNBAKED BRICK, ALSO MINOR STRUCTURES IMMEDIATELY ADJACENT
TO THE INCLOSURE BUT NOT INCLUDED WITHIN THE PRECINCTS OF
MUT AND MONTHU. AREA IS DIVIDED INTO SECTIONS LETTERED
A TO O WITH THE EXCEPTION OF E AND J, WHICH WERE NOT
USED. SECTIONS ARE DELIMITED BY HEAVY LINES.

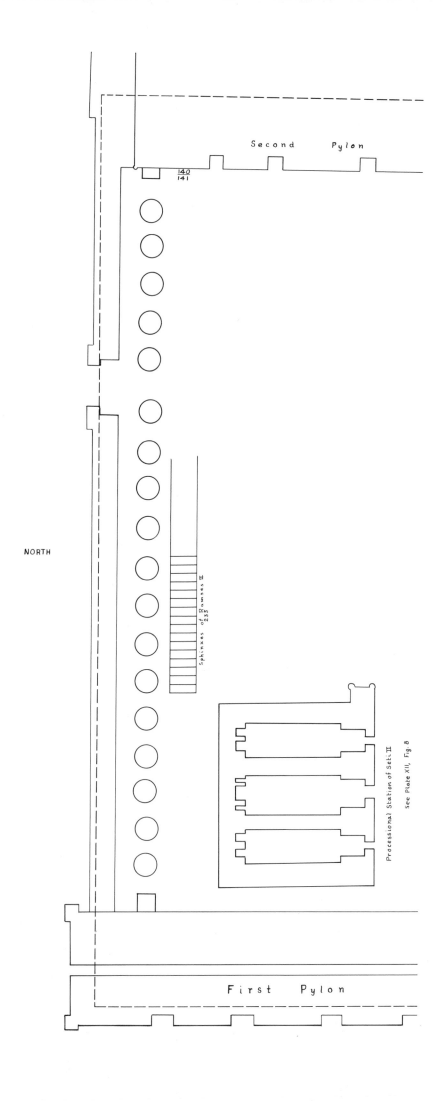

NORTH

Second   Pylon

140/141

Sphinxes of Ramses II
235

Processional Station of Seti II

See Plate XII, Fig. 8

First   Pylon

Plate 2

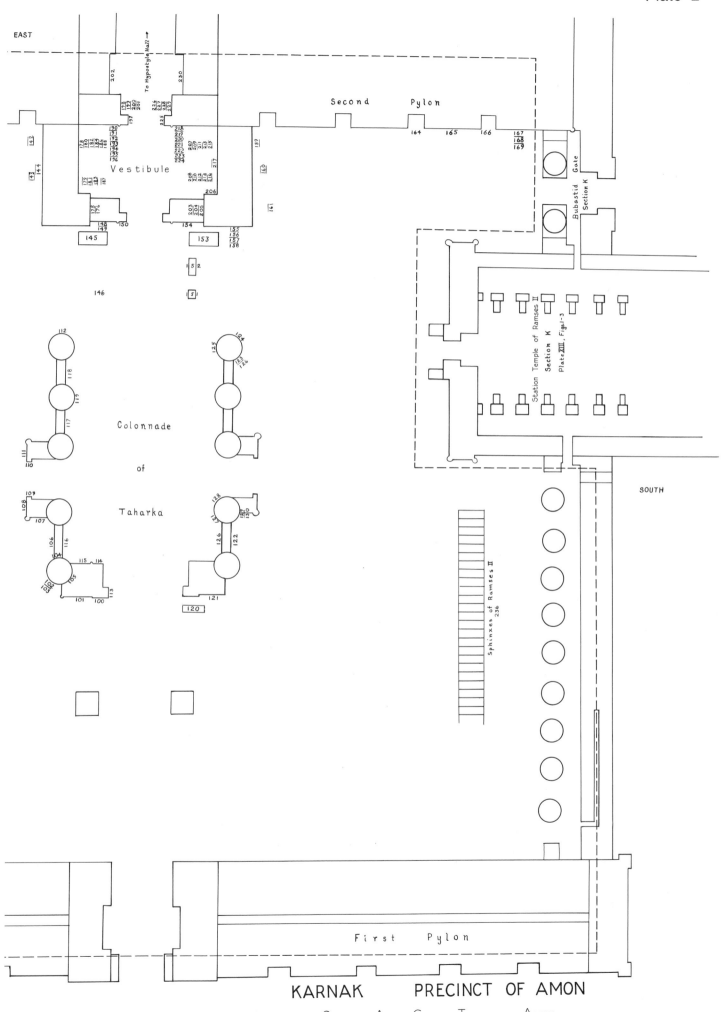

KARNAK   PRECINCT OF AMON

Section A   Great Temple of Amon

FIRST COURT OF TEMPLE

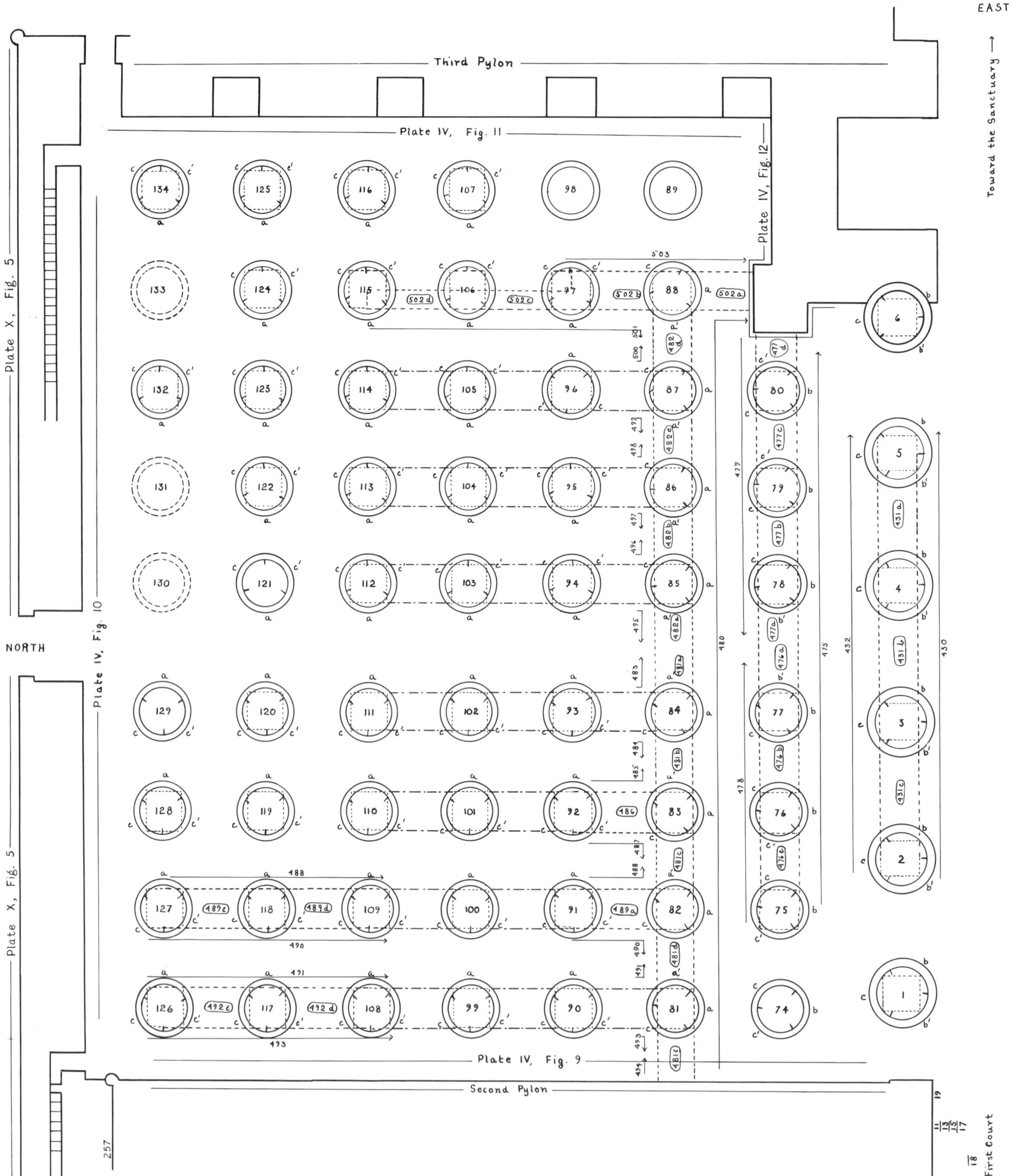

EAST

Toward the Sanctuary →

Third Pylon

Plate IV, Fig. 11

Plate IV, Fig. 12

Plate X, Fig. 5

Plate IV, Fig. 10

NORTH

Plate X, Fig. 5

| 134 | 125 | 116 | 107 | 98 | 89 |

| 133 | 124 | 115 | 106 | 97 | 88 | 6 |

| 132 | 123 | 114 | 105 | 96 | 87 | 80 |

| 131 | 122 | 113 | 104 | 95 | 86 | 79 | 5 |

| 130 | 121 | 112 | 103 | 94 | 85 | 78 | 4 |

| 129 | 120 | 111 | 102 | 93 | 84 | 77 | 3 |

| 128 | 119 | 110 | 101 | 92 | 83 | 76 | 2 |

| 127 | 118 | 109 | 100 | 91 | 82 | 75 | |

| 126 | 117 | 108 | 99 | 90 | 81 | 74 | 1 |

502d 502c 502b 502a 503 501 500

482e 477d 492e 492d 491 490 489a 489d 489c 488 487 486 485 484 483 482a 482b 482c 481a 481b 481c 481d 477a 477b 477c 476a 476b 476c 431a 431b 431c 493

478 480 475 432 430 479

Plate IV, Fig. 9

Second Pylon

257 19

Entrance from First Court

WEST

Columns 89, 98, 119-124, and 133 had fallen prior to the excavation of
the Hypostyle Hall. Of these 119-124 were re-erected by Legrain. Columns 90, 94-96, and 99-105 fell October 3, 1899, and were re-erected by
Legrain. Of columns 89 and 98 only base and small portion of column below reliefs survive. Columns 130, 131, and 133 have been entirely removed. Site of
columns 130 and 131 is now occupied by drainage tank. Column 96 has been re-
erected in reverse position; relief "a" should face west, not east as at present.
Upper portion of column 103, as now re-erected, does not belong with lower portion (possibly interchanged with No. 104). Architraves which fell with the columns in 1899 are indicated thus:—·—·—·—. In so far as restored they are now
covered with cement and show no inscriptions.

Plate 3

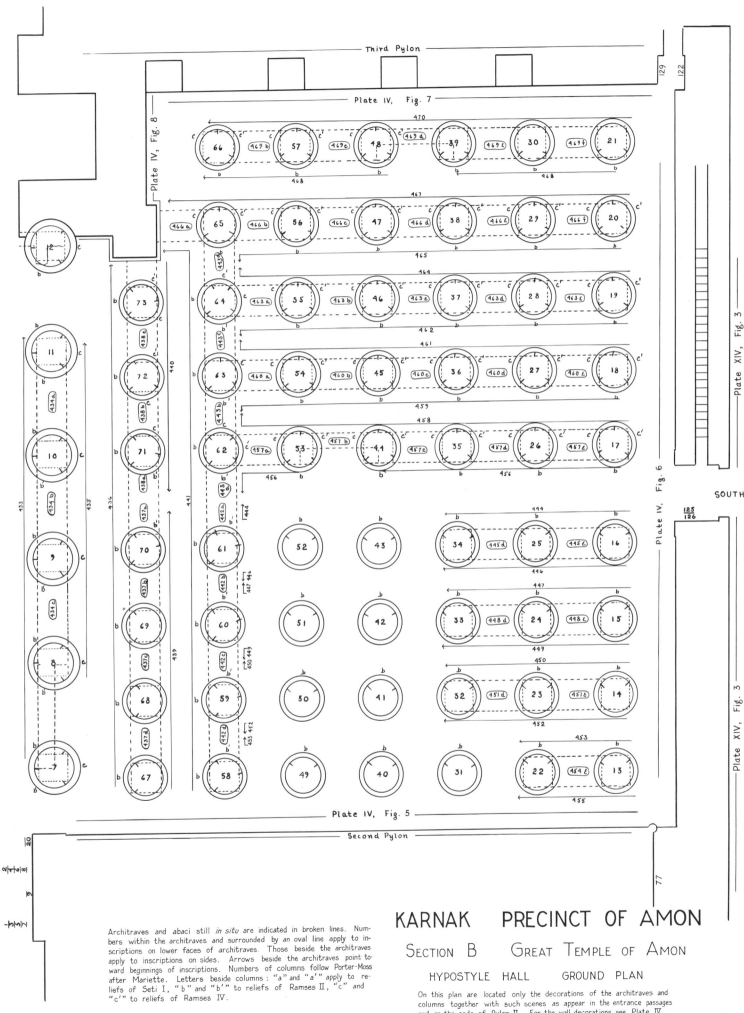

Third Pylon

Plate IV, Fig. 7

Plate IV, Fig. 8

Plate XIV, Fig. 3

Plate IV, Fig. 6

SOUTH

Plate XIV, Fig. 3

Plate IV, Fig. 5

Second Pylon

Architraves and abaci still *in situ* are indicated in broken lines. Numbers within the architraves and surrounded by an oval line apply to inscriptions on lower faces of architraves. Those beside the architraves apply to inscriptions on sides. Arrows beside the architraves point toward beginnings of inscriptions. Numbers of columns follow Porter-Moss after Mariette. Letters beside columns: "a" and "a'" apply to reliefs of Seti I, "b" and "b'" to reliefs of Ramses II, "c" and "c'" to reliefs of Ramses IV.

KARNAK   PRECINCT OF AMON

SECTION B   GREAT TEMPLE OF AMON

HYPOSTYLE HALL   GROUND PLAN

On this plan are located only the decorations of the architraves and columns together with such scenes as appear in the entrance passages and on the ends of Pylon II. For the wall decorations see Plate IV.

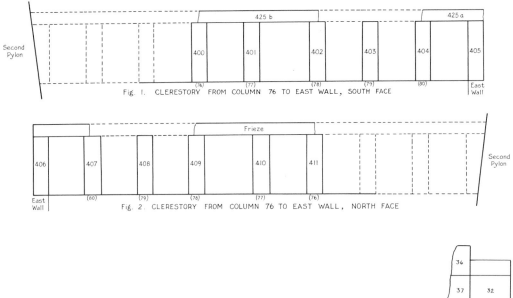

Fig. 1. CLERESTORY FROM COLUMN 76 TO EAST WALL, SOUTH FACE

Fig. 2. CLERESTORY FROM COLUMN 76 TO EAST WALL, NORTH FACE

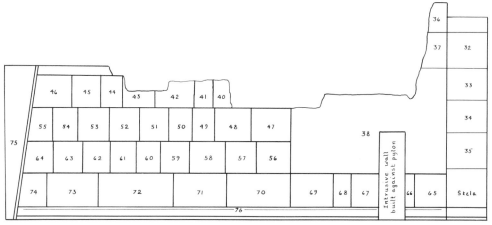

Fig. 5. WEST WALL. SOUTH HALF

Fig. 6. SOUTH WALL

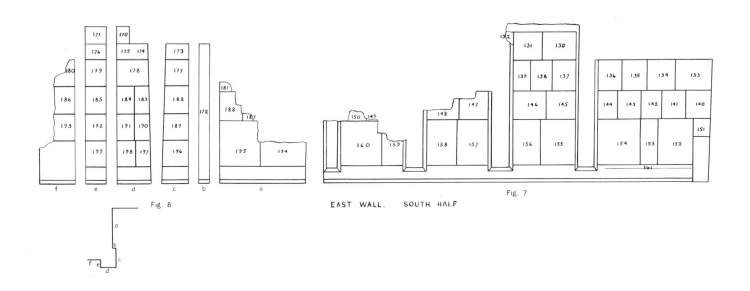

Fig. 8

Fig. 7

EAST WALL. SOUTH HALF

Plate 4

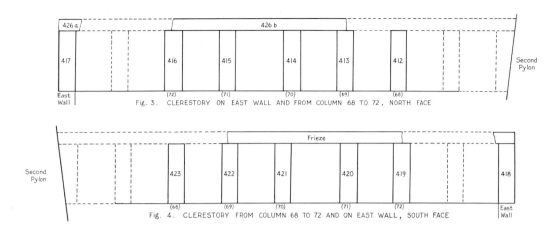

Fig. 3. CLERESTORY ON EAST WALL AND FROM COLUMN 68 TO 72, NORTH FACE

Fig. 4. CLERESTORY FROM COLUMN 68 TO 72 AND ON EAST WALL, SOUTH FACE

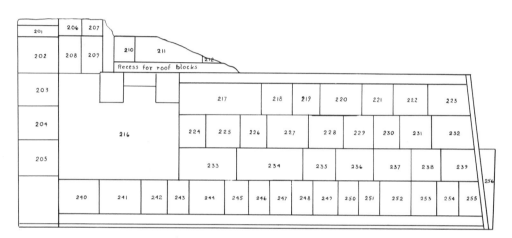

Fig. 9. WEST WALL. NORTH HALF

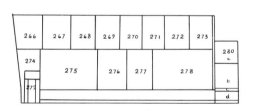
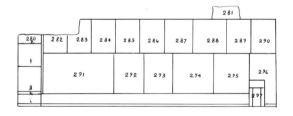

Fig. 10. NORTH WALL

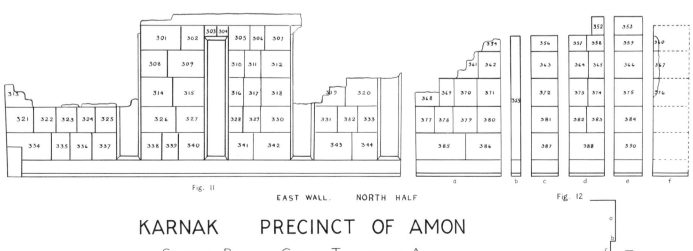

Fig. 11   Fig. 12

EAST WALL. NORTH HALF

KARNAK   PRECINCT OF AMON
Section B   Great Temple of Amon
HYPOSTYLE HALL   WALLS AND CLERESTORY

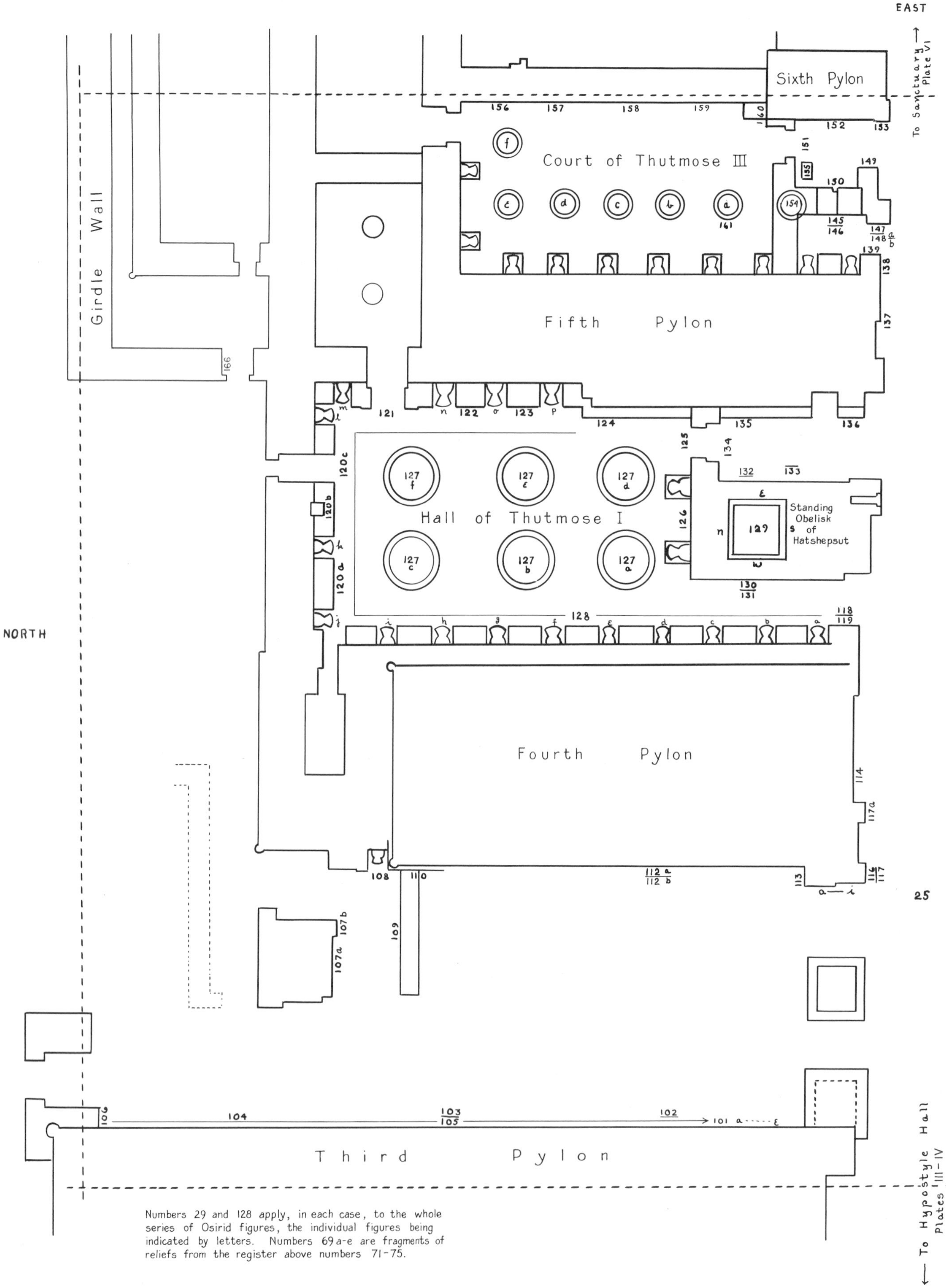

EAST

To Sanctuary
Plate VI

Sixth Pylon

156   157   158   159   160   152   153

151

f

Court of Thutmose III

149

135

150

c   d   c   b   a   154

145
146

147
148

161

139

138

Fifth   Pylon

137

166

m
l   121   n   122   o   123   p   124   135   136

125   134

120c

127   127   127
f   e   d

132   133

126   129   n   Standing
Obelisk
of
Hatshepsut

120b

Hall of Thutmose I

120a

127   127   127
c   b   a

130
131

i   j   i   h   g   f   128   e   d   c   b   a   118
119

NORTH

Fourth   Pylon

114

117a

116
117

108   110   112 a
112 b   113   a — i

25

107b

109

107a

106   104   103
105   102   101 a i

To Hypostyle Hall
Plates III–IV

Third   Pylon

Numbers 29 and 128 apply, in each case, to the whole
series of Osirid figures, the individual figures being
indicated by letters. Numbers 69 a-e are fragments of
reliefs from the register above numbers 71-75.

Plate 5

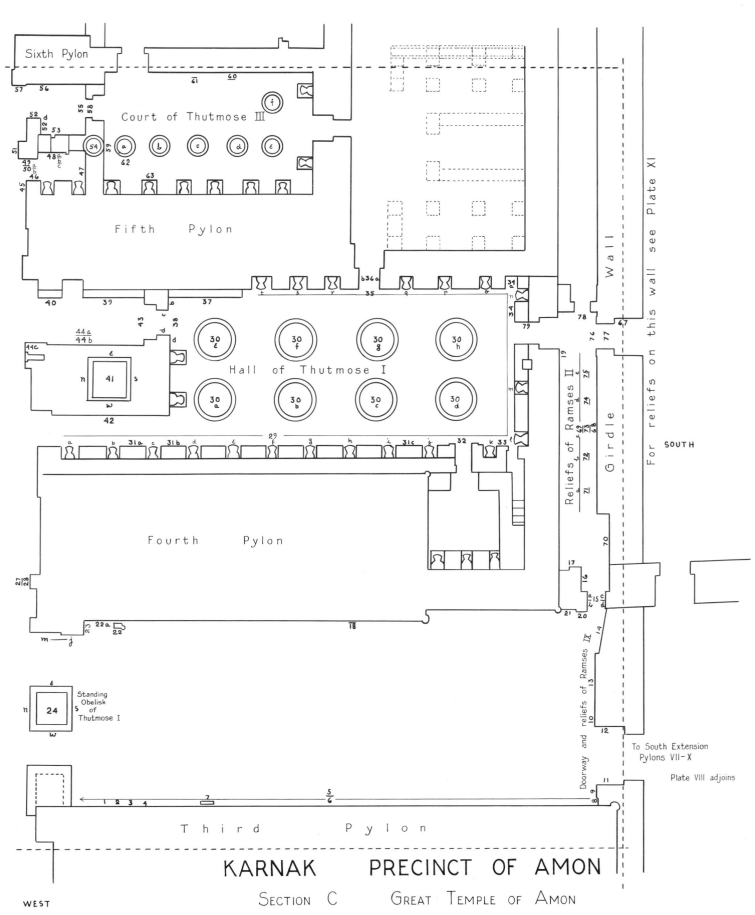

Sixth Pylon

57 56

52 52 d
53
51 48
49 46 47
50 c
45

Court of Thutmose III

61 60

f

54 59 a b c d e
42

63

Fifth   Pylon

40 39 b 37 35 q p o

44 a
44 b 43 d 38
44 c d
41
n s
w
42

30 e 30 f 30 g 30 h

Hall of Thutmose I

30 a 30 b 30 c 30 d

29

a b 31a c 31b d e f g h i 31c j 32 k 33

Fourth   Pylon

27
28

23 22a
m j 22

18

24
Standing
Obelisk
of
Thutmose I
n s
w

Wall

For reliefs on this wall see Plate XI

Girdle

Reliefs of Ramses II

19
25
24
73
68
72
71
70

78
76 77 67
79
34
n
p
m

17
16
15
20 21
14

Doorway and reliefs of Ramses IX

13
10
12

SOUTH

To South Extension
Pylons VII-X

Plate VIII adjoins

1 2 3 4

7

5
6

8 9
11

Third   Pylon

KARNAK   PRECINCT   OF   AMON

Section C   Great Temple of Amon

COURTS AND PYLONS OF THE EIGHTEENTH DYNASTY BETWEEN THE HYPOSTYLE
HALL AND THE SANCTUARY COMPLEX

WEST

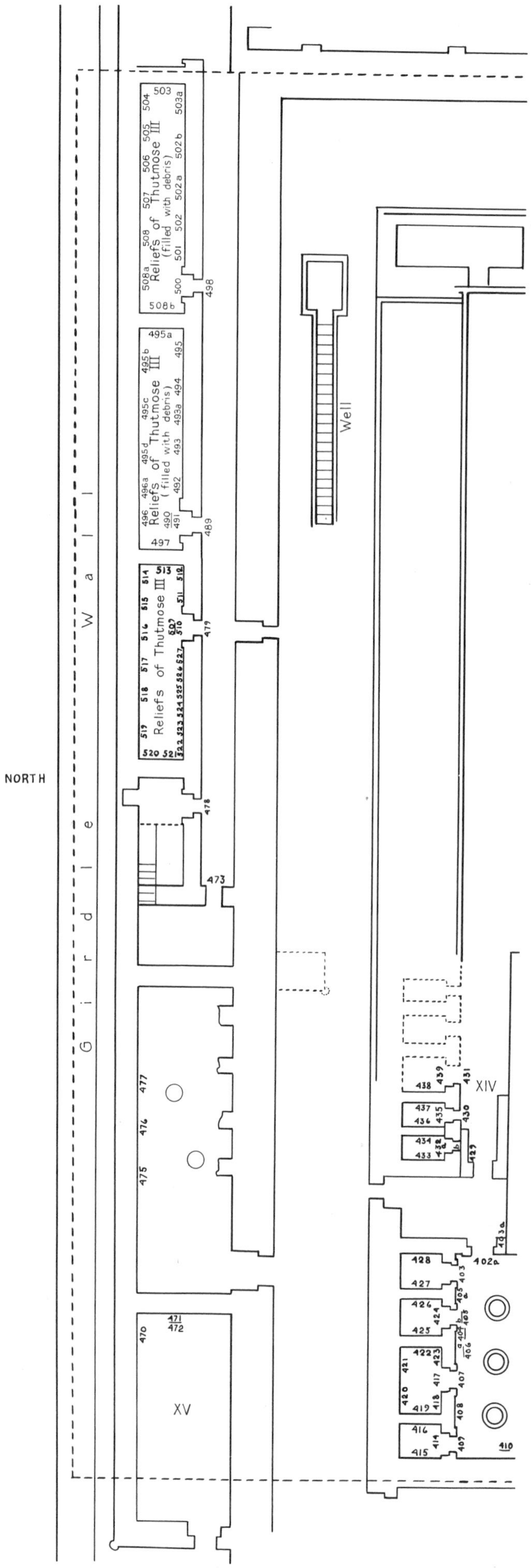

NORTH

Girdle wall

Well

XV

XIV

Reliefs of Thutmose III
(filled with debris)

503
503a
503b
504
505
506
507
508
508a
508b
500 501 502 502a 502b
498

Reliefs of Thutmose III
(filled with debris)

495a
495b
495c
495d
496
496a
490 491 492 493 493a 494 495
497
489

Reliefs of Thutmose III

513
514
515
516
517
518
519
507 510 511 512
479
520 521 522 523 524 525 526 527

478
473
477
476 475
474
471 472
470

438 439 431
437 435
436 430
434 432
433 b
429

428
427
426 424
425 b 403
422 423 a 405 404 402b
421 417 406 403a
420 418 407 402
416 419 408
414 409
415 410

Plate 6

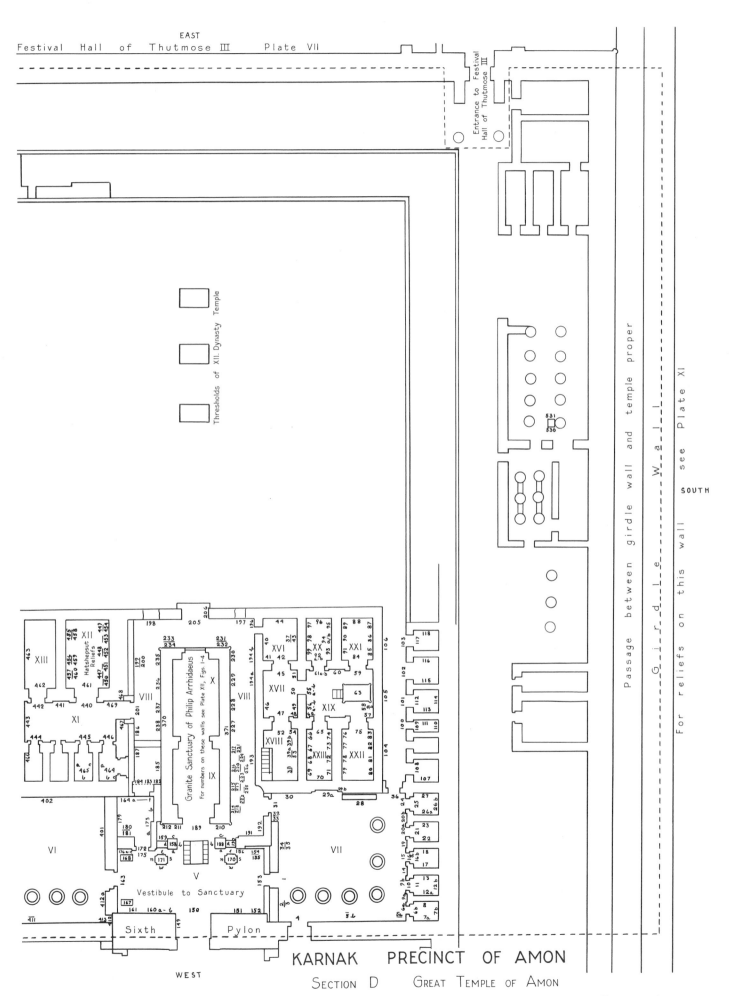

EAST

Festival Hall of Thutmose III Plate VII

Entrance to Festival Hall of Thutmose III

Thresholds of XII. Dynasty Temple

Passage between girdle wall and temple proper

Girdle Wall

For reliefs on this wall see Plate XI

SOUTH

KARNAK PRECINCT OF AMON

SECTION D GREAT TEMPLE OF AMON

SANCTUARY COMPLEX BETWEEN PYLON VI AND THE FESTIVAL HALL OF THUTMOSE III

WEST

Sixth Pylon

Vestibule to Sanctuary

Granite Sanctuary of Philip Arrhidaeus

For numbers on these walls see Plate XII, Figs. 1-4

Hatshepsut Reliefs

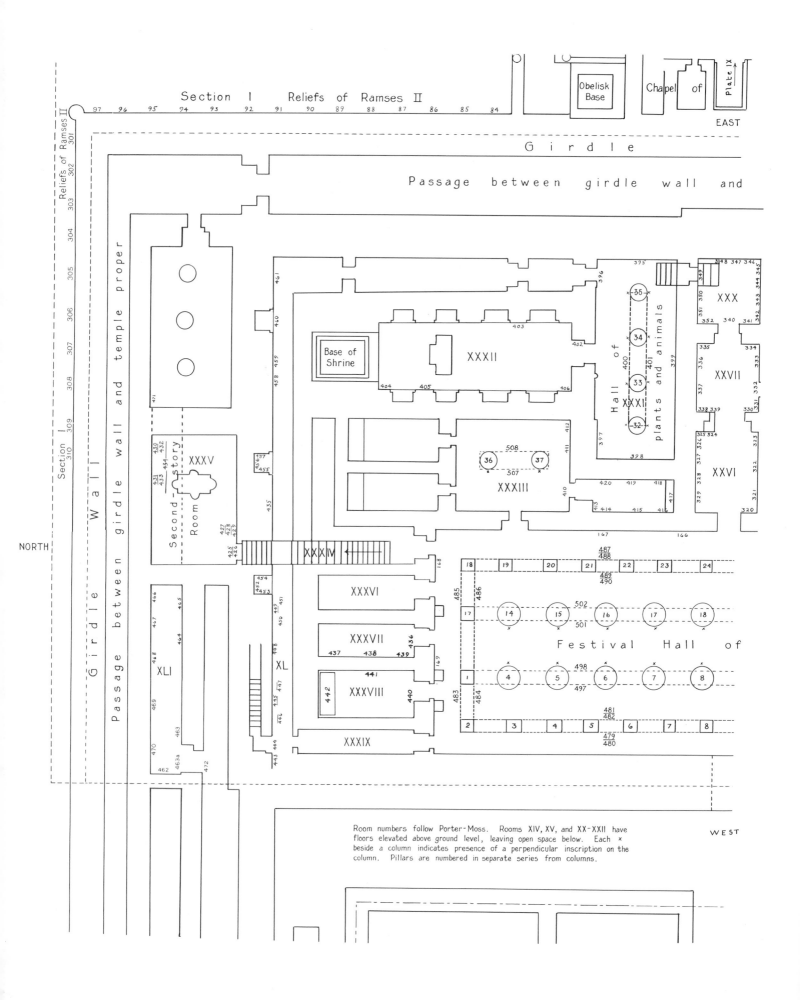

Section I   Reliefs of Ramses II

Reliefs of Ramses II

97 96 95 94 93 92 91 90 89 88 87 86 85 84

301 302 303 304 305 306 307 308 309 310

Obelisk Base

Chapel of

Plate IX

EAST

G i r d l e

Passage between girdle wall and

NORTH

Girdle Wall

Passage between girdle wall and temple proper

Section I

461 460 459 458 456 457 455 435 454 452 453 450 451 449 448 447 445 442 444 443

471

Base of Shrine

404 405 406

403

402

XXXII

XXXV

Second-story Room

430 432 431 434 435 433

427 428 429 425 426

XXXIV

XXXVI

XXXVII
437 438 439 436

XXXVIII
441 442 440

XXXIX

468 467 466 465 469 464 463 470 462 463a 472

XLI

XL

395

396

348 347 346 349 350 351 352 340 341 352 343 344 345

XXX

XXXI XXXII XXXI

35 34 33 32

Hall of plants and animals

397 398 399 400 401

402

335 336 337 338 339

XXVII 333 334 331 332 330

508 507 36 37

XXXIII

412 411 410

420 419 418 415 414 415 416 417

167 166

325 324 327 326 329 328 323 321 322 320

XXVI

487 488 489 490

18 19 20 21 22 23 24

485 486

17 14 15 16 17 18

502 501

483 484

1 4 5 6 7 8

498 497

2 3 4 5 6 7 8

481 482 479 480

168

169

Festival Hall of

WEST

Room numbers follow Porter-Moss. Rooms XIV, XV, and XX–XXII have floors elevated above ground level, leaving open space below. Each × beside a column indicates presence of a perpendicular inscription on the column. Pillars are numbered in separate series from columns.

Plate 7

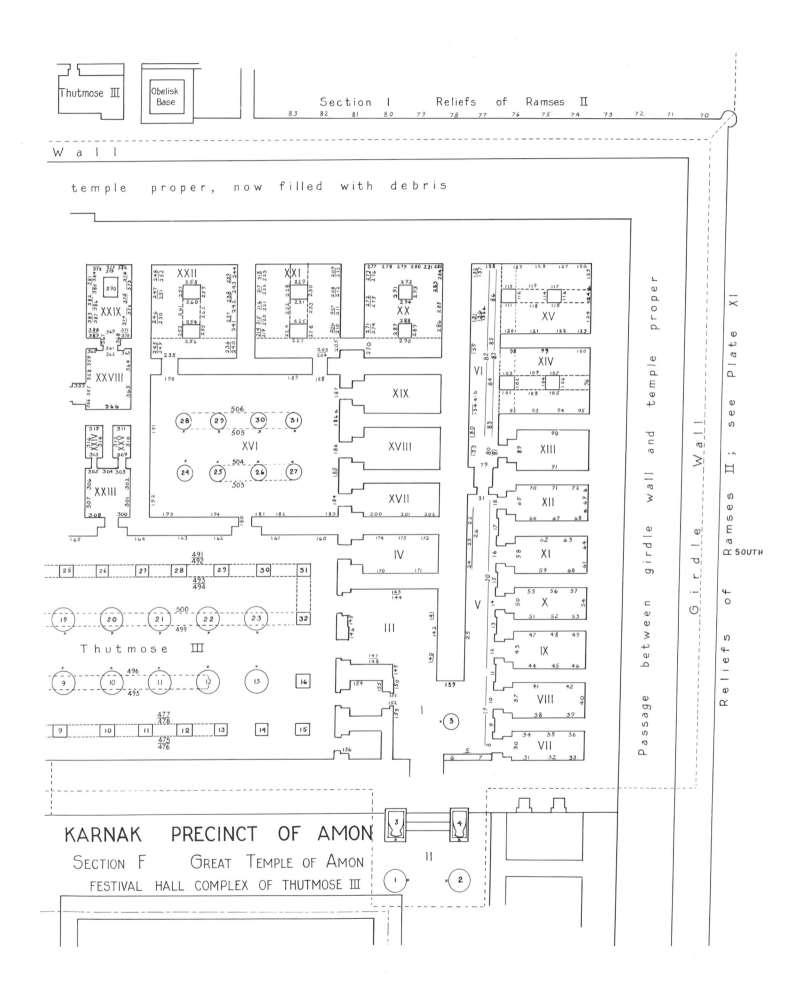

Thutmose III

Obelisk Base

Section I   Reliefs   of   Ramses II

83   82   81   80   79   78   77   76   75   74   73   72   71   70

Wall

temple   proper,   now   filled   with   debris

KARNAK   PRECINCT OF AMON

SECTION F   GREAT TEMPLE OF AMON

FESTIVAL HALL COMPLEX OF THUTMOSE III

Thutmose III

Girdle Wall

Passage between girdle wall and temple proper

Reliefs of Ramses II ; see Plate XI

SOUTH

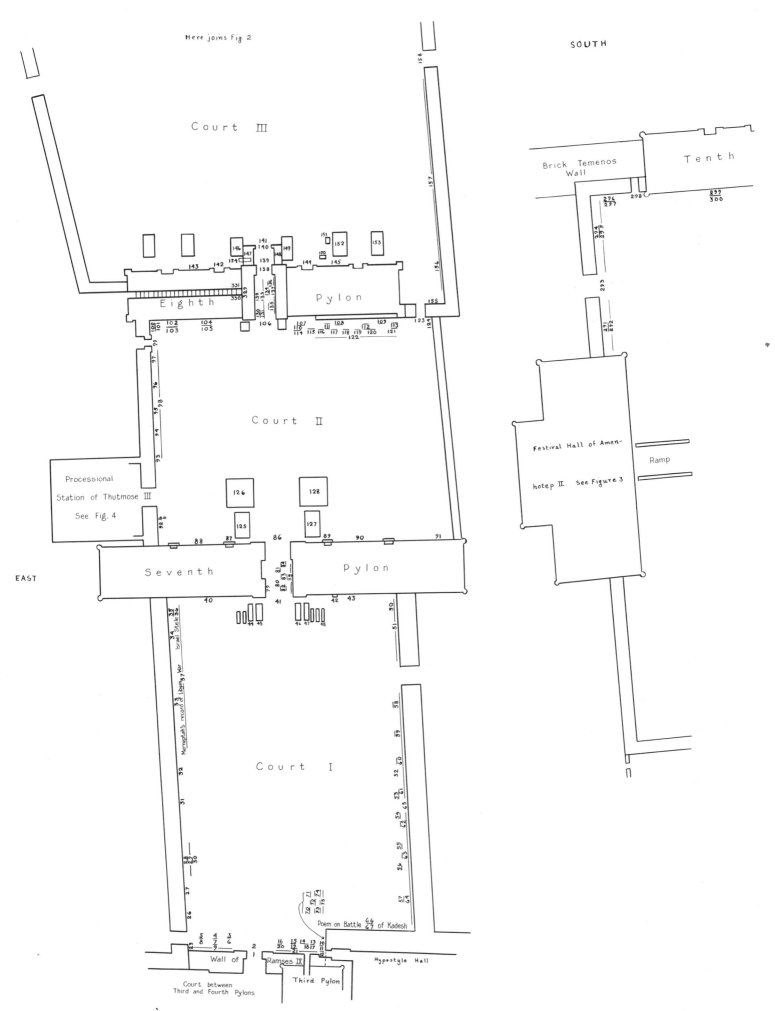

Figure 1. NORTH HALF

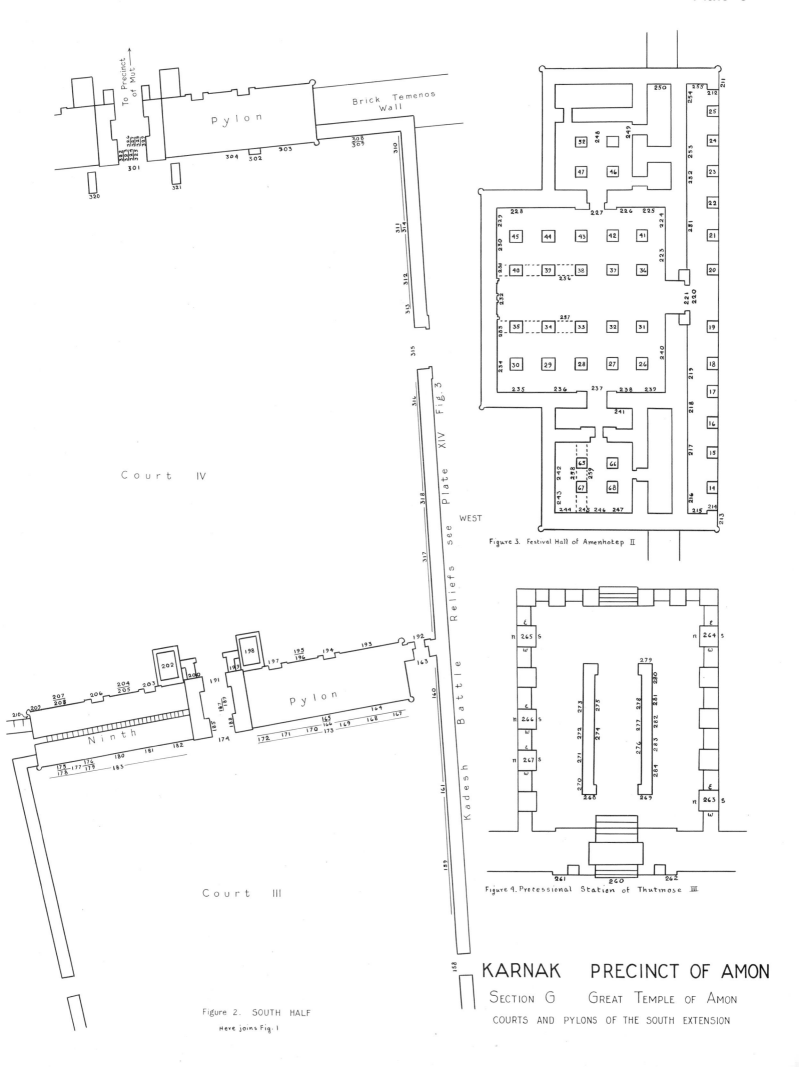

Plate 8

Figure 2. SOUTH HALF

Here joins Fig. 1

Figure 3. Festival Hall of Amenhotep II

Figure 4. Processional Station of Thutmose III

KARNAK PRECINCT OF AMON

SECTION G GREAT TEMPLE OF AMON

COURTS AND PYLONS OF THE SOUTH EXTENSION

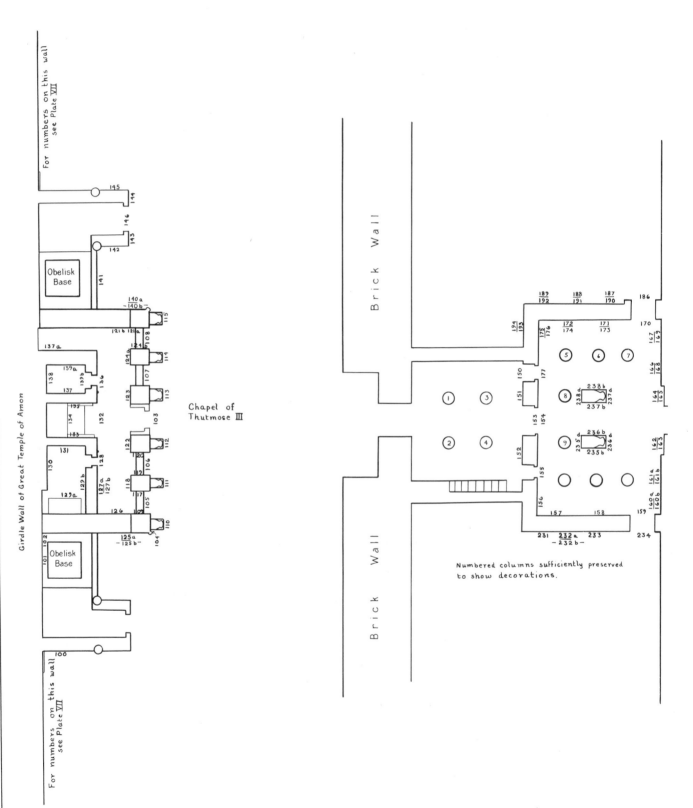

WEST

Girdle Wall of Great Temple of Amon

For numbers on this wall
see Plate VII

Obelisk
Base

Obelisk
Base

For numbers on this wall
see Plate VII

Chapel of
Thutmose III

Brick Wall

Brick Wall

Numbered columns sufficiently preserved
to show decorations.

Plate 9

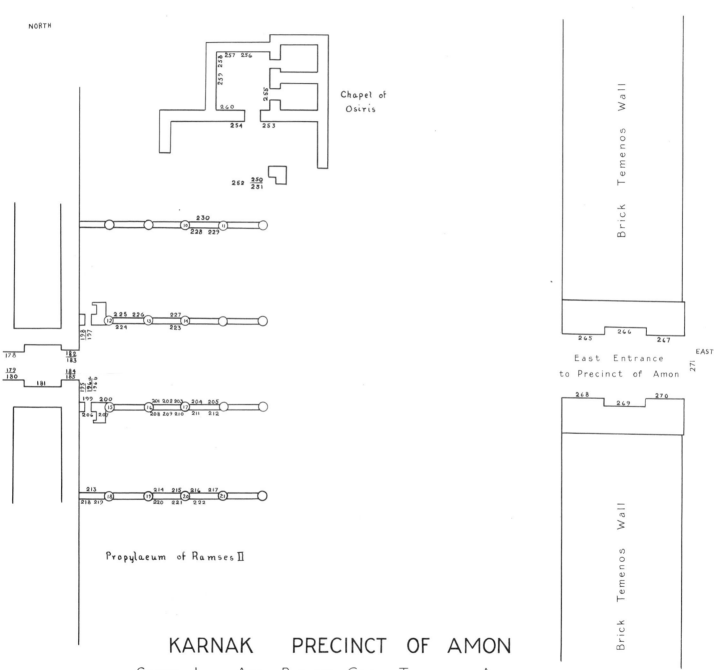

KARNAK PRECINCT OF AMON

SECTION 1   AREA BETWEEN GREAT TEMPLE OF AMON AND EAST BRICK TEMENOS WALL

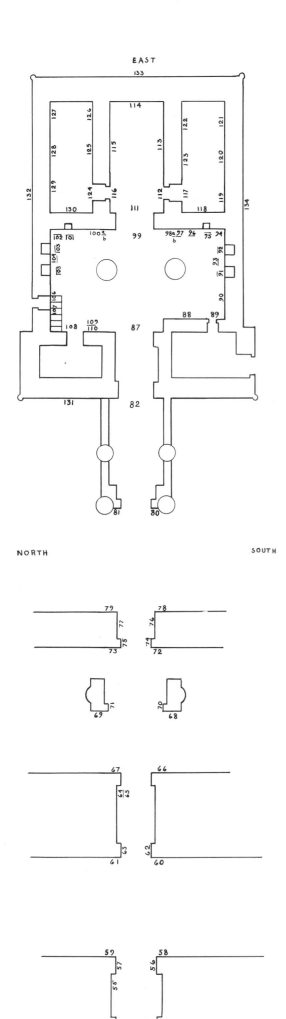

Temple of Ptah
Figure 1

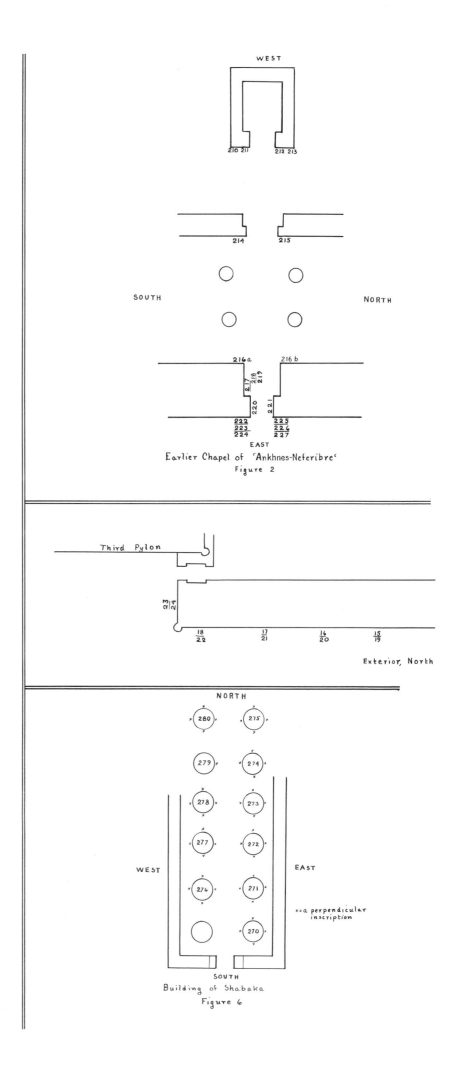

Earlier Chapel of 'Ankhnes-Neferibre'
Figure 2

Third Pylon

Exterior, North

x = a perpendicular
inscription

Building of Shabaka
Figure 6

Plate 10

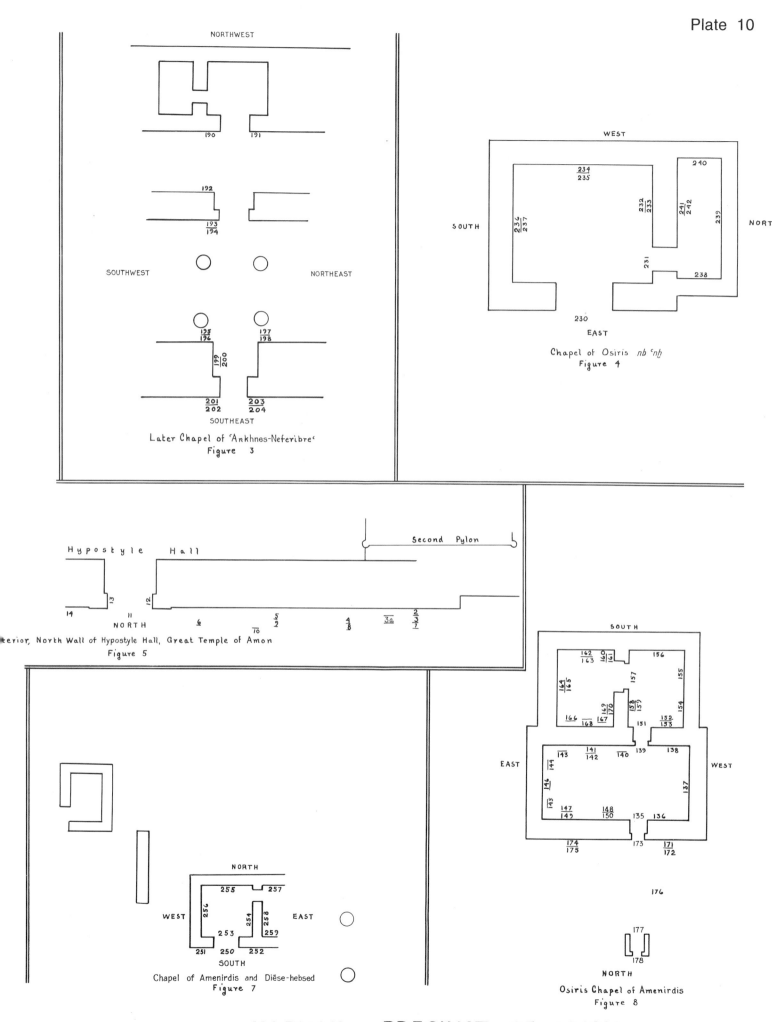

NORTHWEST

190 191

192

193
194

SOUTHWEST ○ ○ NORTHEAST

○ ○

195 197
196 198

199 201
200 202

201 203
202 204

SOUTHEAST

Later Chapel of 'Ankhnes-Neferibre'
Figure 3

WEST

234
235 240

232 241
233 242 239

236 231
237 238

230

EAST

Chapel of Osiris *nb ʿnḫ*
Figure 4

Hypostyle Hall Second Pylon

13 12 14 11

NORTH 6 5 4 3a 2
10 2 8 1

Interior, North Wall of Hypostyle Hall, Great Temple of Amon
Figure 5

SOUTH

162 160 156
163 161

164 157 155
165

169 158
166 170 159
168 167 152 154
151 153

143 141 140 139 138
144

146 137
145

147 148 135 136
149 150

174 173 171
175 172

176

EAST WEST

177
178

NORTH

255 257

WEST 256 254 258 EAST
253 259

251 250 252

SOUTH

Chapel of Amenirdis and Diēse-hebsed
Figure 7

○

○

Osiris Chapel of Amenirdis
Figure 8

KARNAK   PRECINCT OF AMON

Section H   Minor Buildings North of Great Temple of Amon

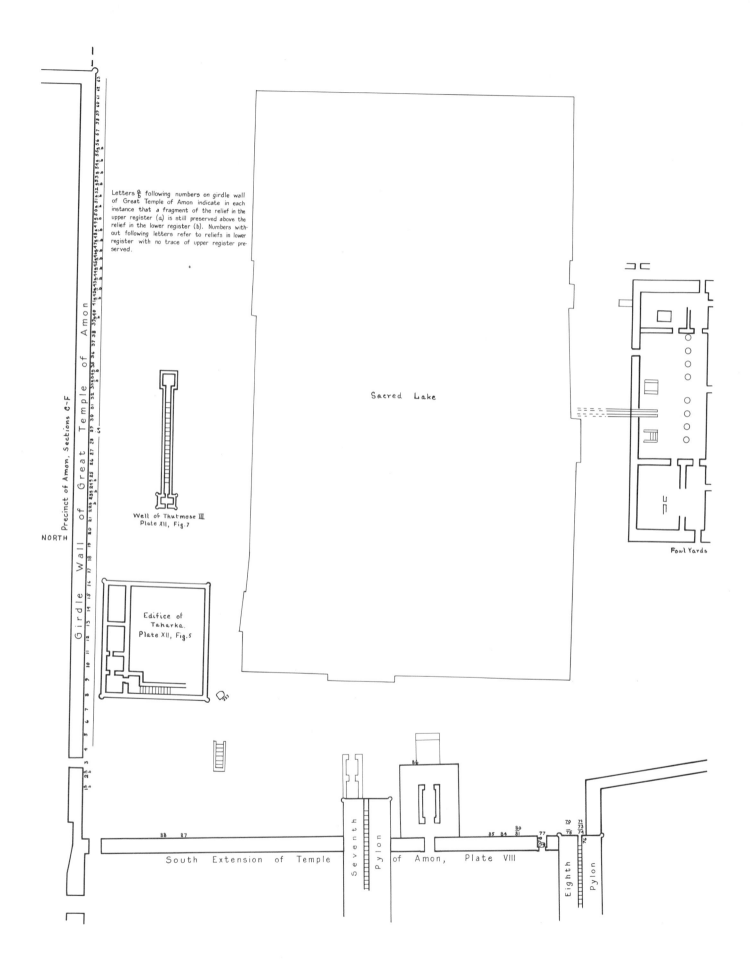

NORTH

Precinct of Amon, Sections C-F

Girdle Wall of Great Temple of Amon

Letters $\frac{a}{b}$ following numbers on girdle wall of Great Temple of Amon indicate in each instance that a fragment of the relief in the upper register (a) is still preserved above the relief in the lower register (b). Numbers without following letters refer to reliefs in lower register with no trace of upper register preserved.

Sacred Lake

Well of Thutmose III
Plate XII, Fig.7

Edifice of
Taharka.
Plate XII, Fig.5

Fowl Yards

South Extension of Temple

Seventh Pylon

of Amon, Plate VIII

Eighth Pylon

Plate 11

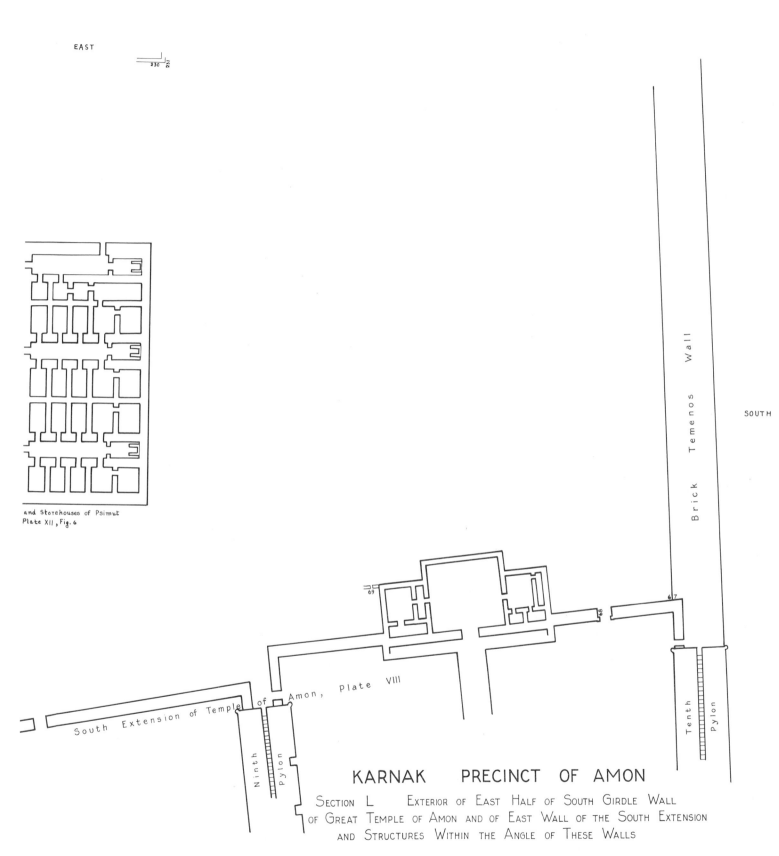

EAST

SOUTH

WEST

and Storehouses of Psimut
Plate XII, Fig. 6

Brick Temenos Wall

South Extension of Temple of Amon, Plate VIII

Ninth Pylon

Tenth Pylon

KARNAK PRECINCT OF AMON

SECTION L   EXTERIOR OF EAST HALF OF SOUTH GIRDLE WALL
OF GREAT TEMPLE OF AMON AND OF EAST WALL OF THE SOUTH EXTENSION
AND STRUCTURES WITHIN THE ANGLE OF THESE WALLS

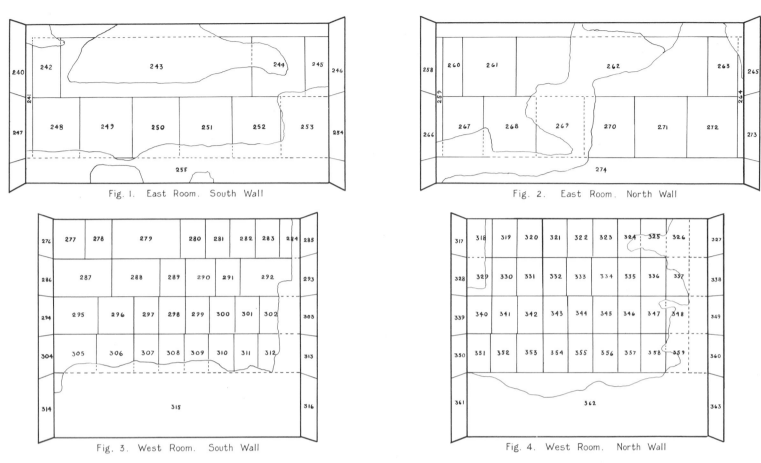

Fig. I. East Room. South Wall

Fig. 2. East Room. North Wall

Fig. 3. West Room. South Wall

Fig. 4. West Room. North Wall

Interior of Granite Sanctuary of Philip Arrhidaeus in Section D

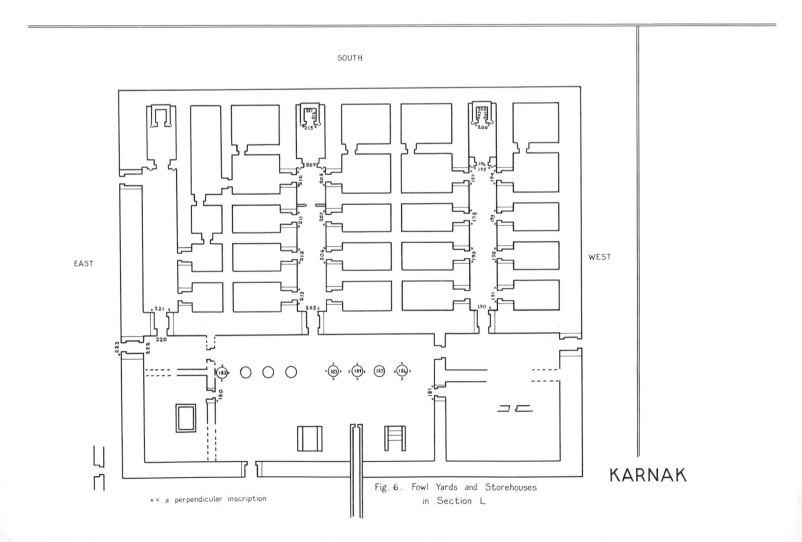

SOUTH

EAST

WEST

x = a perpendicular inscription

Fig. 6. Fowl Yards and Storehouses
in Section L

KARNAK

Plate 12

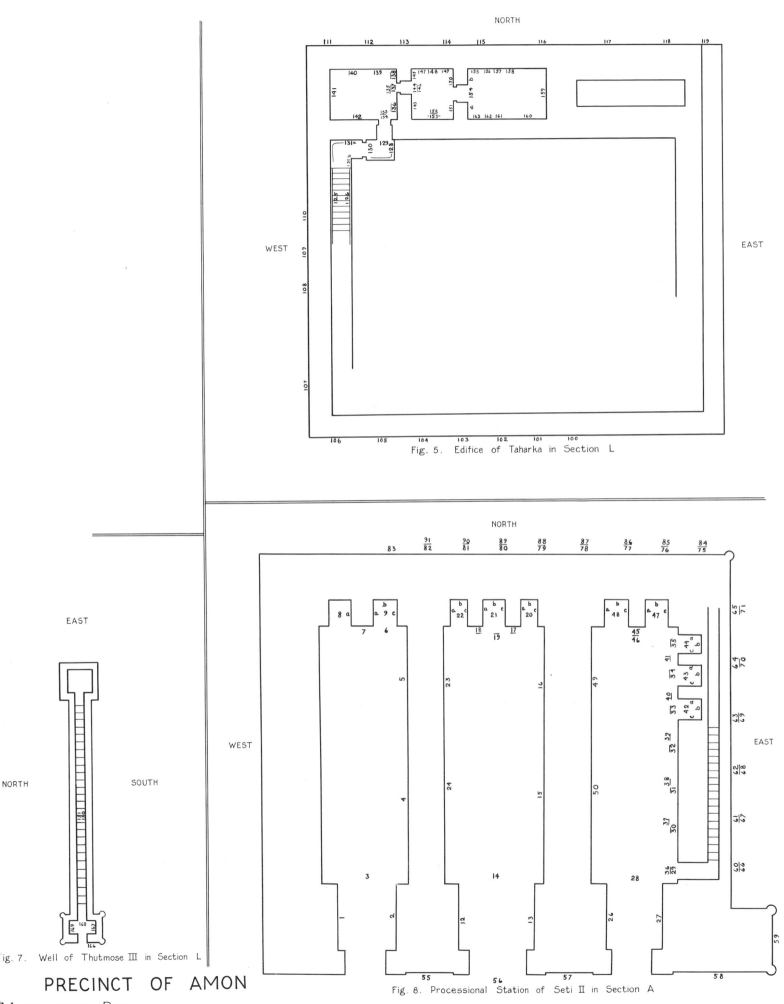

Fig. 5. Edifice of Taharka in Section L

Fig. 7. Well of Thutmose III in Section L

Fig. 8. Processional Station of Seti II in Section A

PRECINCT OF AMON

MISCELLANEOUS DETAILS

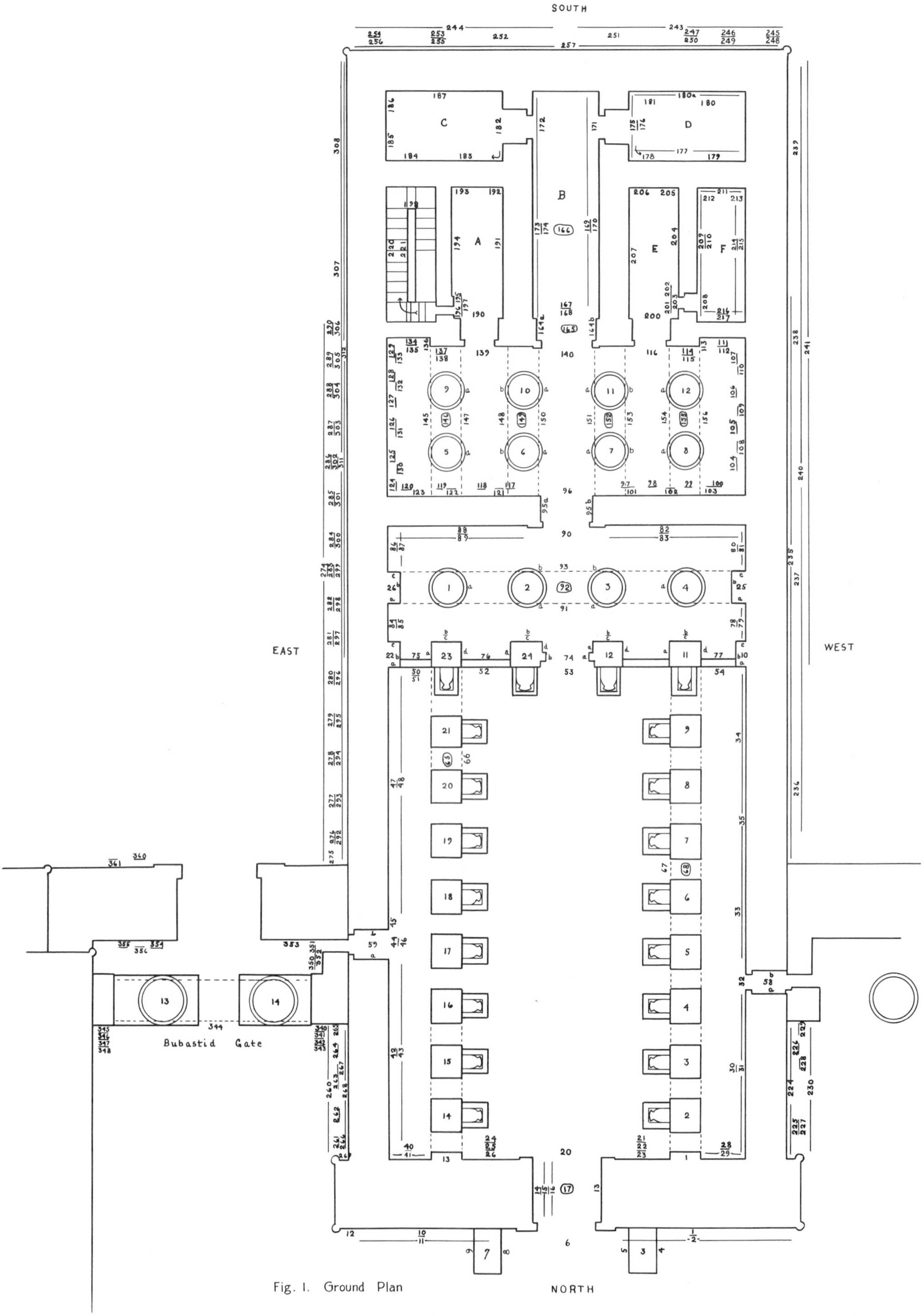

Fig. 1. Ground Plan

Plate 13

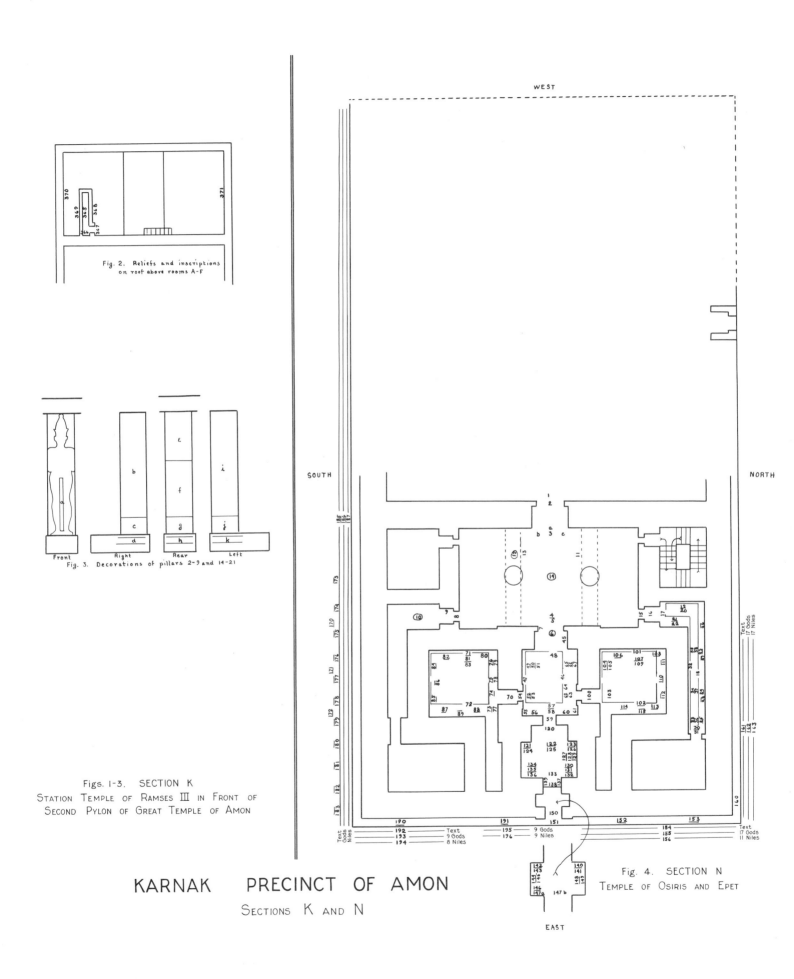

Fig. 2. Reliefs and inscriptions
on roof above rooms A-F

Fig. 3. Decorations of pillars 2-9 and 14-21

Front   Right   Rear   Left

Figs. 1-3. SECTION K
STATION TEMPLE OF RAMSES III IN FRONT OF
SECOND PYLON OF GREAT TEMPLE OF AMON

Fig. 4. SECTION N
TEMPLE OF OSIRIS AND EPET

WEST

SOUTH

NORTH

EAST

KARNAK   PRECINCT OF AMON
SECTIONS K AND N

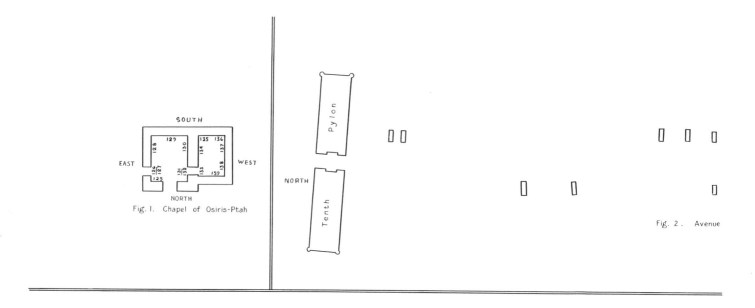

SOUTH

EAST   WEST

NORTH

Fig. 1. Chapel of Osiris-Ptah

Fig. 2. Avenue

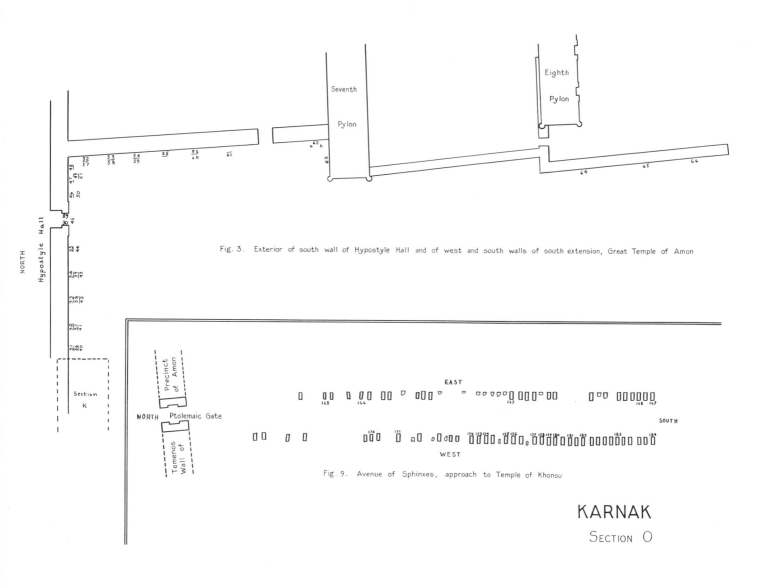

Fig. 3. Exterior of south wall of Hypostyle Hall and of west and south walls of south extension, Great Temple of Amon

NORTH   Hypostyle Hall

Section K

Precinct of Amon

NORTH   Ptolemaic Gate

Temenos Wall of

EAST

SOUTH

WEST

Fig. 9. Avenue of Sphinxes, approach to Temple of Khonsu

KARNAK

Section O

Plate 14

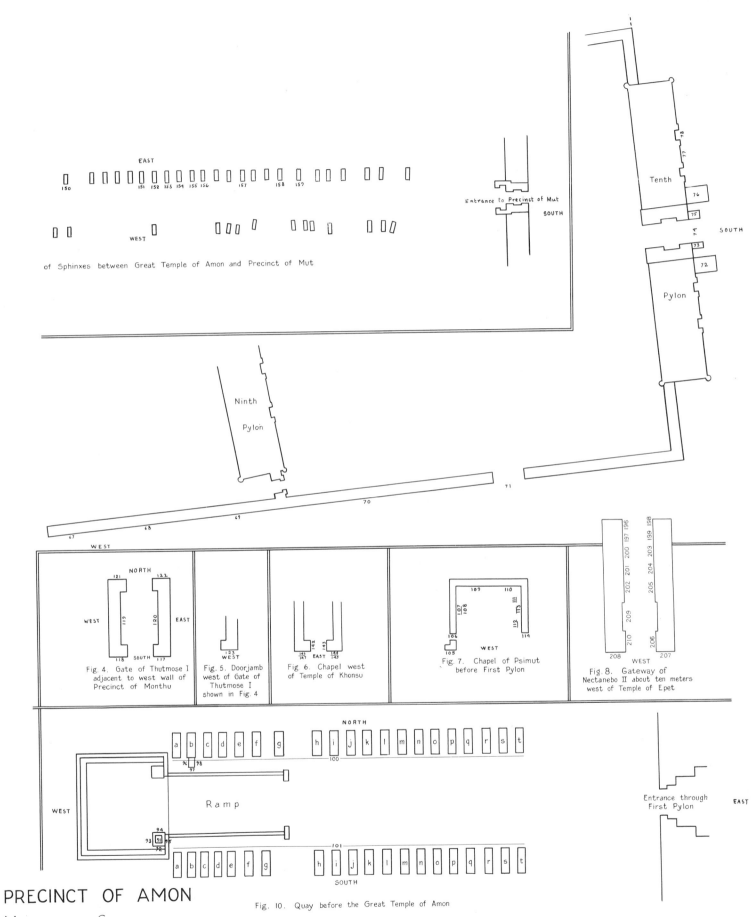

EAST

150 151 152 153 154 155 156 157 158 159

WEST

of Sphinxes between Great Temple of Amon and Precinct of Mut

Entrance to Precinct of Mut

SOUTH

Tenth

78

77

76

75

74 SOUTH

73

72

Pylon

Ninth

Pylon

71

70

69

68

67

WEST

NORTH

121 122

WEST 119 120 EAST

118 SOUTH 117

Fig. 4. Gate of Thutmose I adjacent to west wall of Precinct of Monthu

123 WEST

Fig. 5. Doorjamb west of Gate of Thutmose I shown in Fig. 4

141 142 144
147 143

WEST EAST

Fig 6. Chapel west of Temple of Khonsu

109 110
107 111
108

112

106
105 WEST 114

Fig. 7. Chapel of Psimut before First Pylon

195 196
197
198

202 201 200 199
203

205 204

210 209 206 207

208 WEST

Fig. 8. Gateway of Nectanebo II about ten meters west of Temple of Epet

NORTH

a b c d e f g h i j k l m n o p q r s t

96 98
97 100

Ramp

94
93 91 95
92 101

a b c d e f g h i j k l m n o p q r s t

SOUTH

WEST

Entrance through First Pylon EAST

PRECINCT OF AMON

MISCELLANEOUS STRUCTURES

Fig. 10. Quay before the Great Temple of Amon

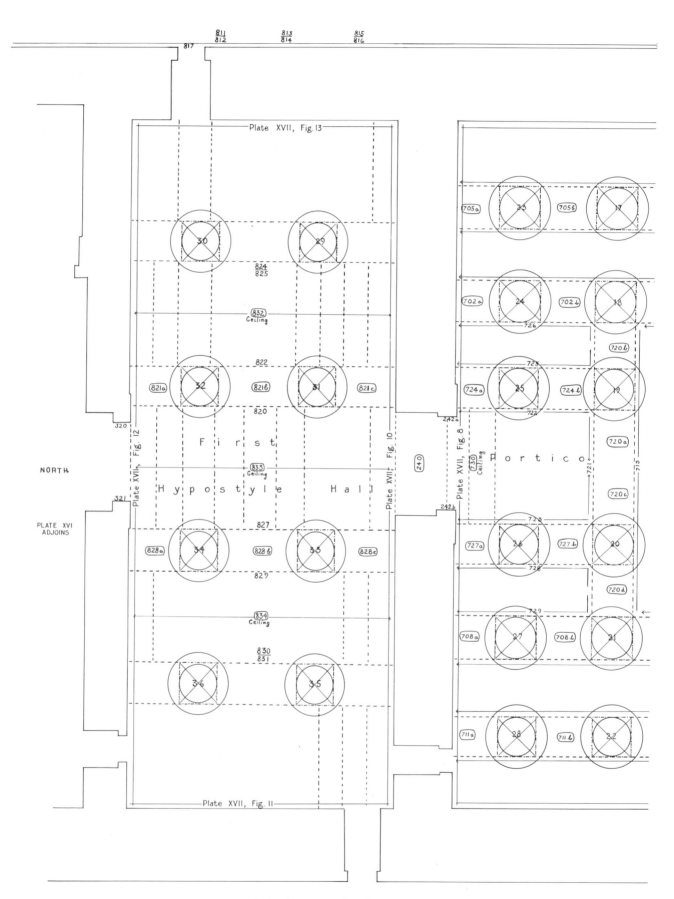

811
812   813   815
        814   816

817

Plate XVII, Fig. 13

705a 23 705b 17

702a 24 702b 18
          726

720b

824
825

832
Ceiling

728 723
724a 25 724b 19
          722

720a

821a 32 821b 31 821c
          820

822

320

321

NORTH

PLATE XVI
ADONS

First

Hypostyle   Hall

833
Ceiling

242a

240

730
Ceiling

Portico

721a

727a 26 727b 20
          728

720c

827

828a 34 828b 33 828c
          829

834
Ceiling

242b

729
708a 27 708b 21

830
831

36   35

711a 28 711b 22

Plate XVII, Fig. 11

For decorations on outer face of pylon and
on walls of court and hall see Plate XVII.

Plate 15

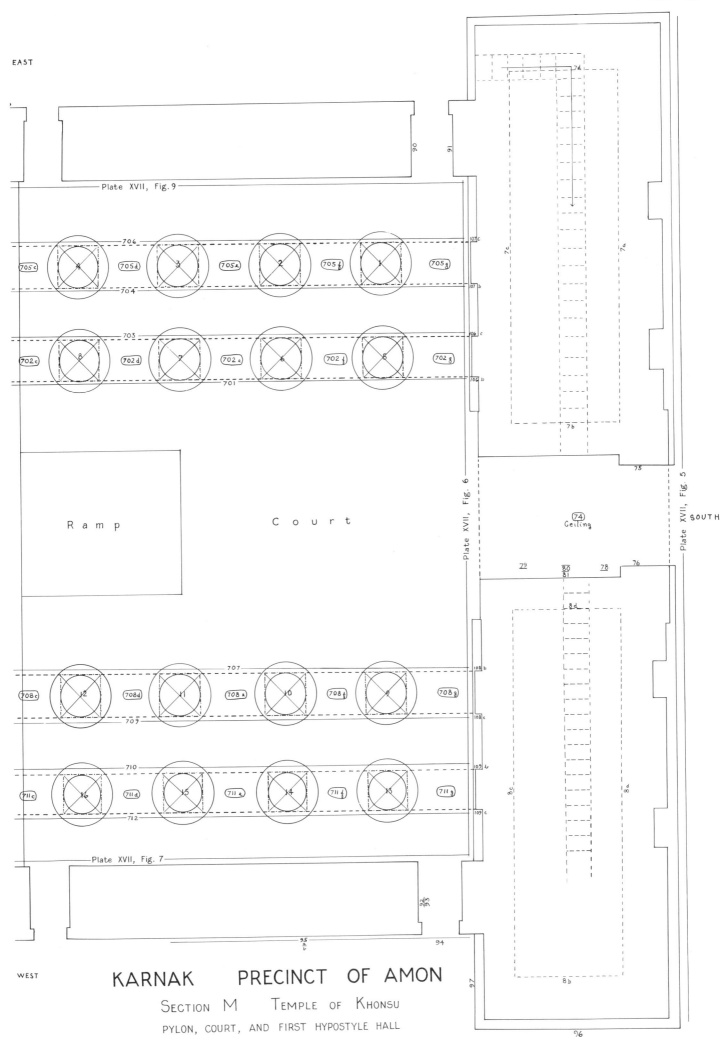

KARNAK   PRECINCT OF AMON
Section M   Temple of Khonsu
PYLON, COURT, AND FIRST HYPOSTYLE HALL

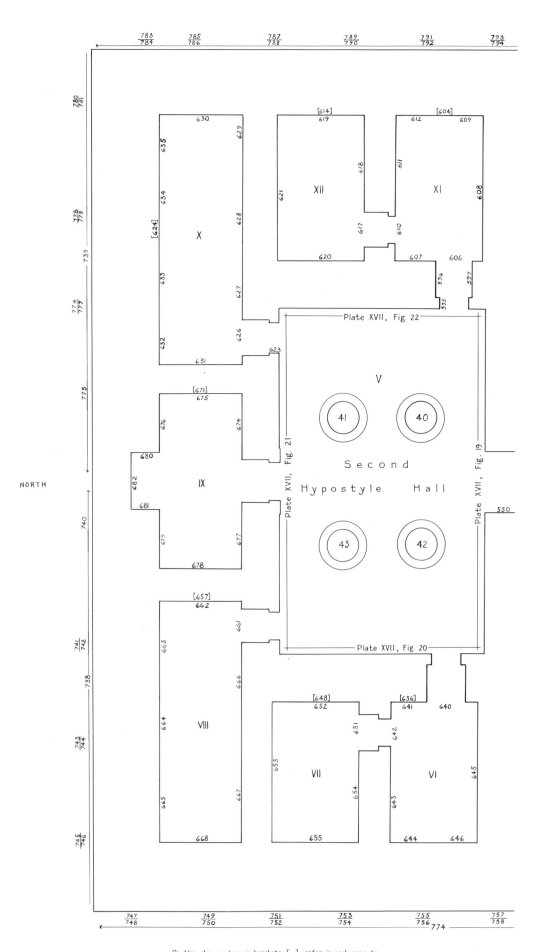

NORTH

Plate XVII, Fig. 22

Plate XVII, Fig. 21

Plate XVII, Fig. 19

Plate XVII, Fig 20

V

Second

Hypostyle   Hall

41 40

43 42

550

X

IX

VIII

XII

XI

VII

VI

On this plan numbers in brackets [ ] refer in each case to
frieze extending around room above reliefs. Room numbers
follow Porter-Moss.

Plate 16

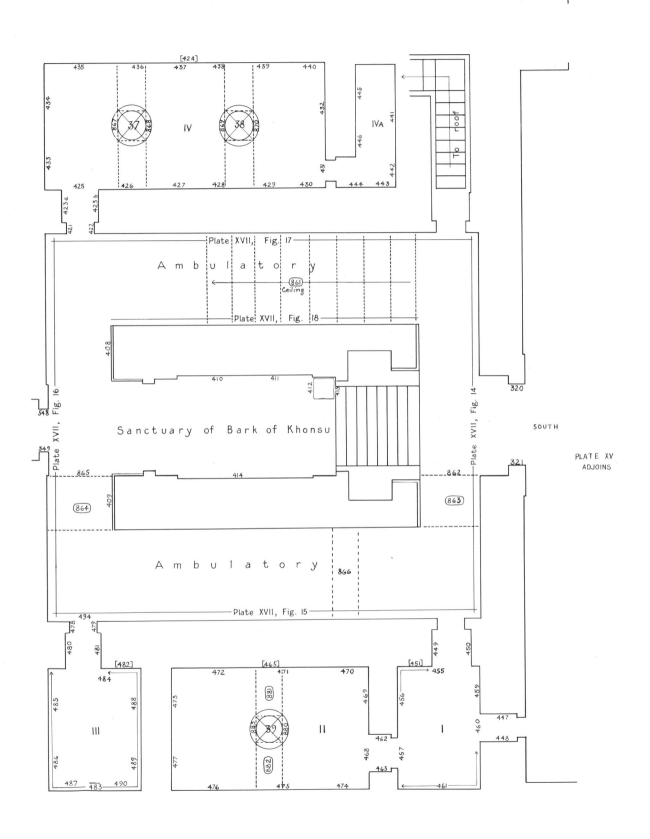

KARNAK PRECINCT OF AMON

SECTION M TEMPLE OF KHONSU

REAR HALLS AND ROOMS

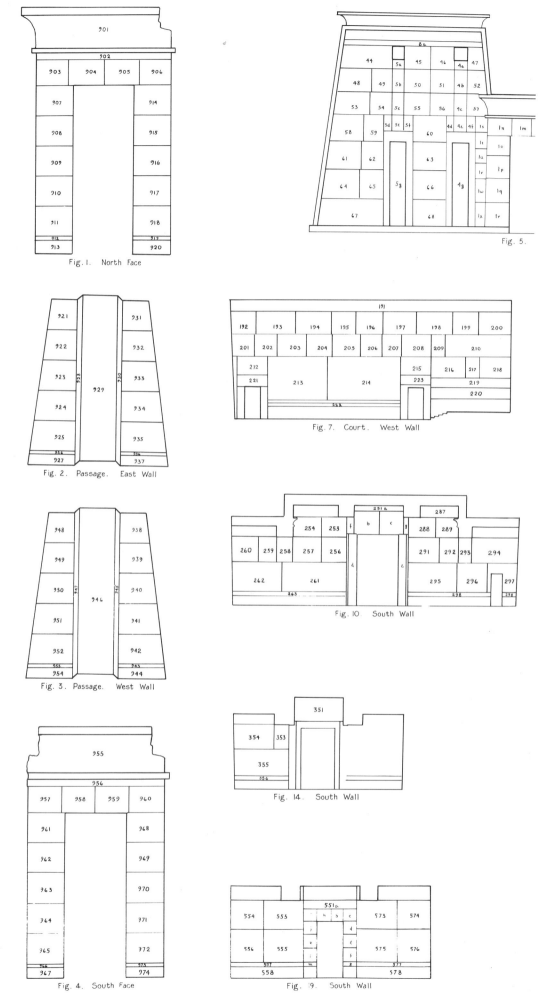

Fig. 1. North Face

Fig. 2. Passage. East Wall

Fig. 3. Passage. West Wall

Fig. 4. South Face

PTOLEMAIC GATEWAY

Fig. 5.

Fig. 7. Court. West Wall

Fig. 10. South Wall

Fig. 14. South Wall

Fig. 19. South Wall

SECOND

Plate 17

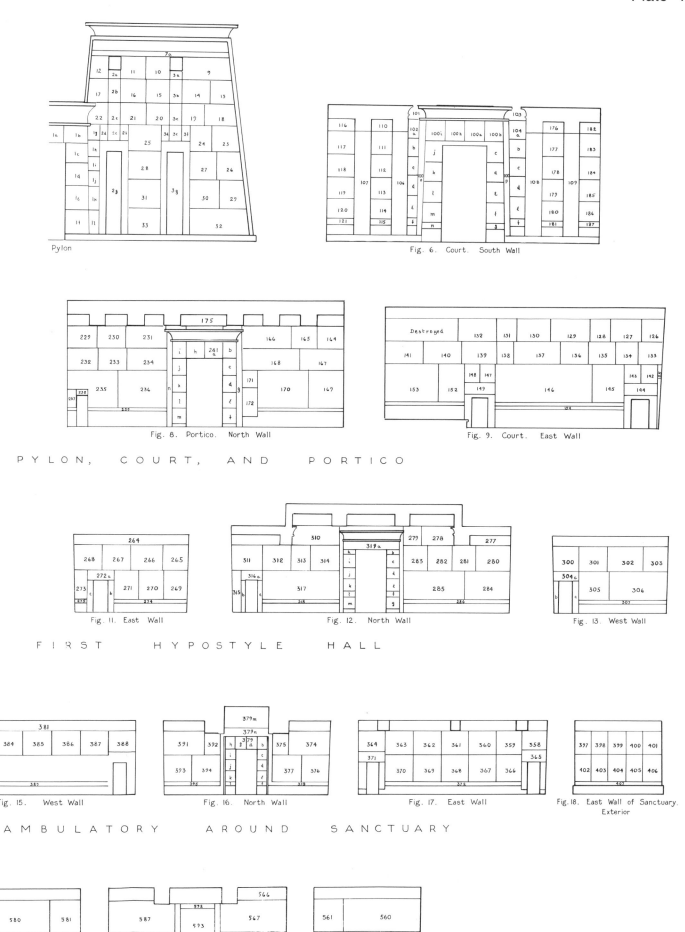

Pylon

Fig. 6. Court. South Wall

PYLON, COURT, AND PORTICO

Fig. 8. Portico. North Wall

Fig. 9. Court. East Wall

Fig. 11. East Wall

Fig. 12. North Wall

Fig. 13. West Wall

FIRST HYPOSTYLE HALL

Fig. 15. West Wall

Fig. 16. North Wall

Fig. 17. East Wall

Fig. 18. East Wall of Sanctuary. Exterior

AMBULATORY AROUND SANCTUARY

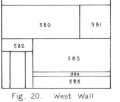

Fig. 20. West Wall

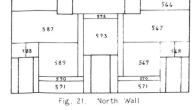

Fig. 21. North Wall

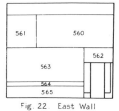

Fig. 22. East Wall

HYPOSTYLE HALL

KARNAK PRECINCT OF AMON

SECTION M TEMPLE OF KHONSU

PTOLEMAIC GATEWAY, FRONT OF PYLON, AND WALLS OF COURT AND HALLS

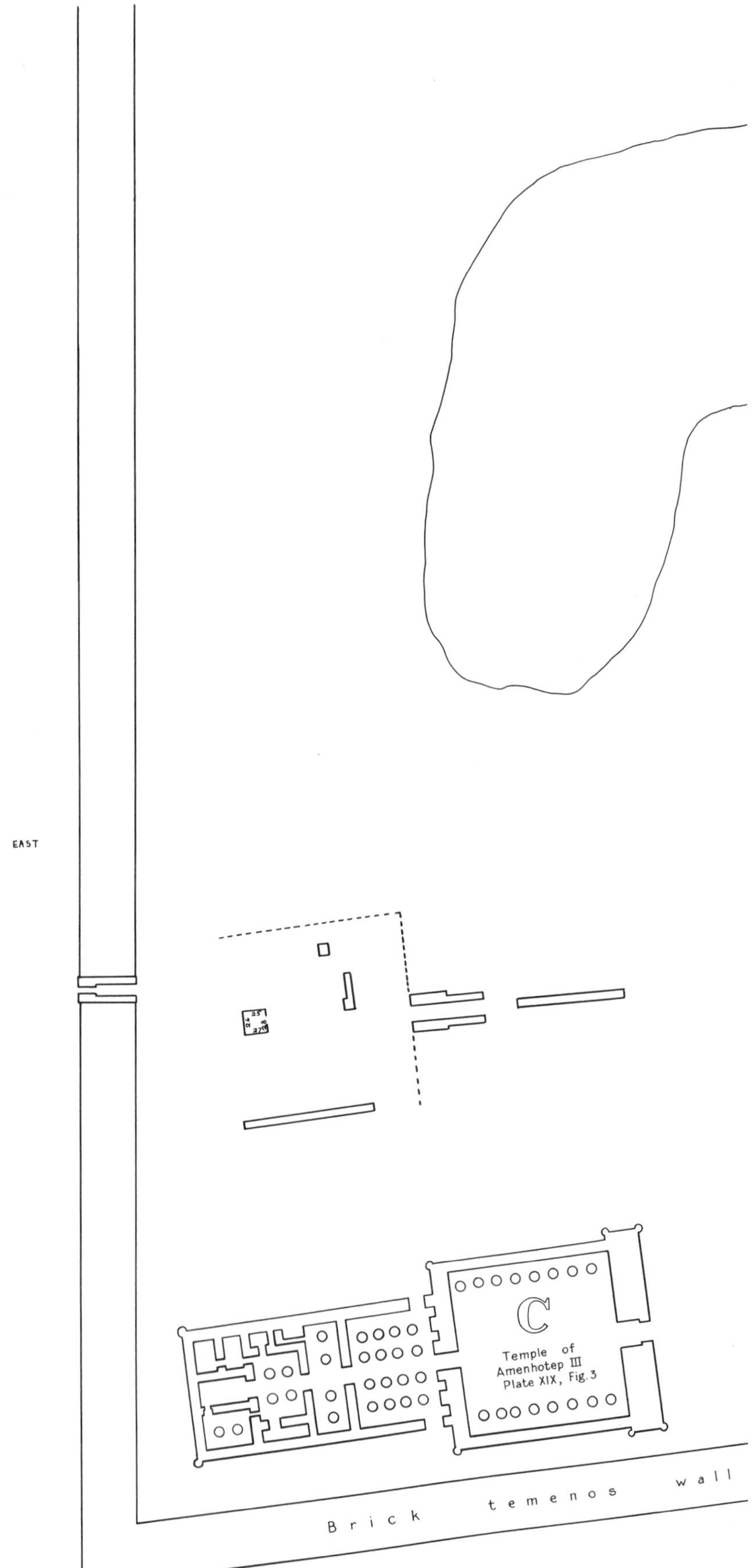

EAST

C

Temple of
Amenhotep III
Plate XIX, Fig.3

Brick   temenos   wall

Plate 18

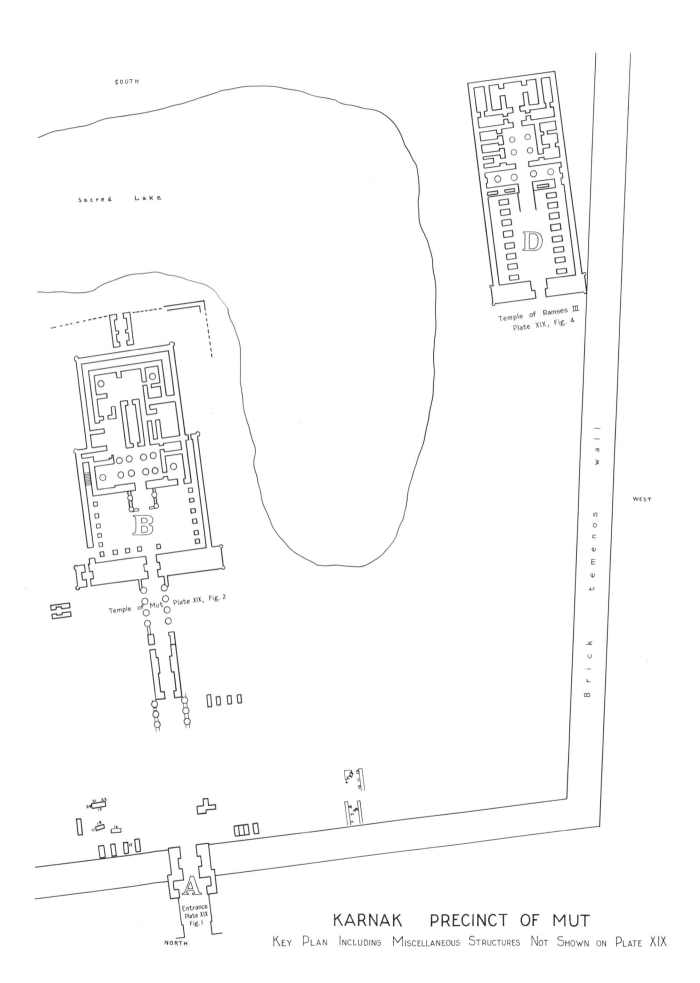

SOUTH

Sacred Lake

Temple of Ramses III
Plate XIX, Fig. 4

B r i c k   t e m e n o s   w a l l

WEST

B

Temple of Mut Plate XIX, Fig. 2

A

Entrance
Plate XIX
Fig. I

NORTH

KARNAK   PRECINCT OF MUT

KEY PLAN INCLUDING MISCELLANEOUS STRUCTURES NOT SHOWN ON PLATE XIX

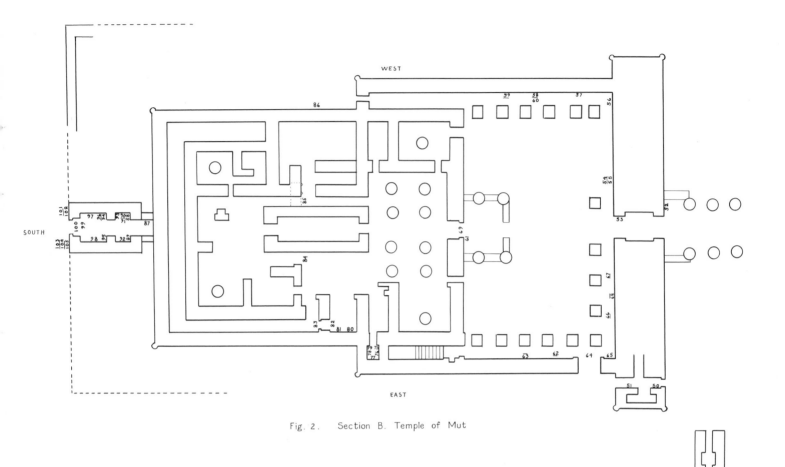

Fig. 2. Section B. Temple of Mut

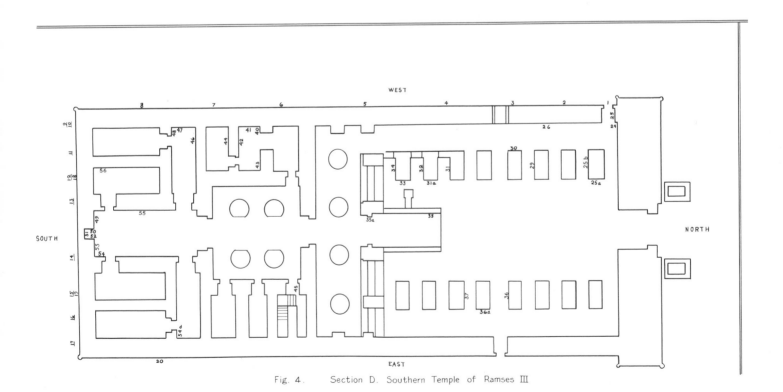

Fig. 4. Section D. Southern Temple of Ramses III

Plate 19

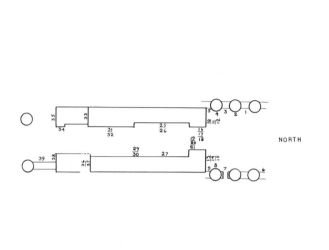

NORTH

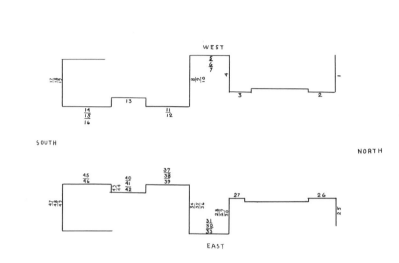

WEST

SOUTH

NORTH

EAST

Fig. 1.   Section A. Ptolemaic Gateway through Temenos Wall

KARNAK   PRECINCT OF MUT

Sections A-D   The Ptolemaic Gateway
and the Temples of Mut, Amenhotep III, and Ramses III

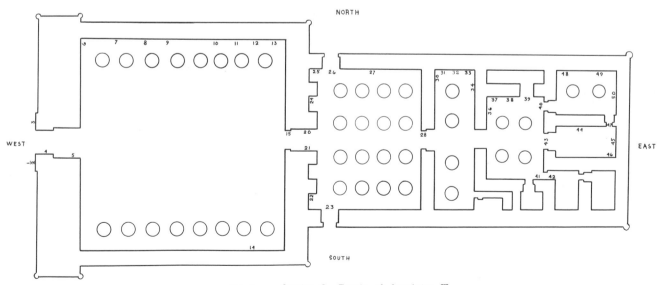

NORTH

WEST

EAST

SOUTH

Fig. 3.   Section C. Temple of Amenhotep III

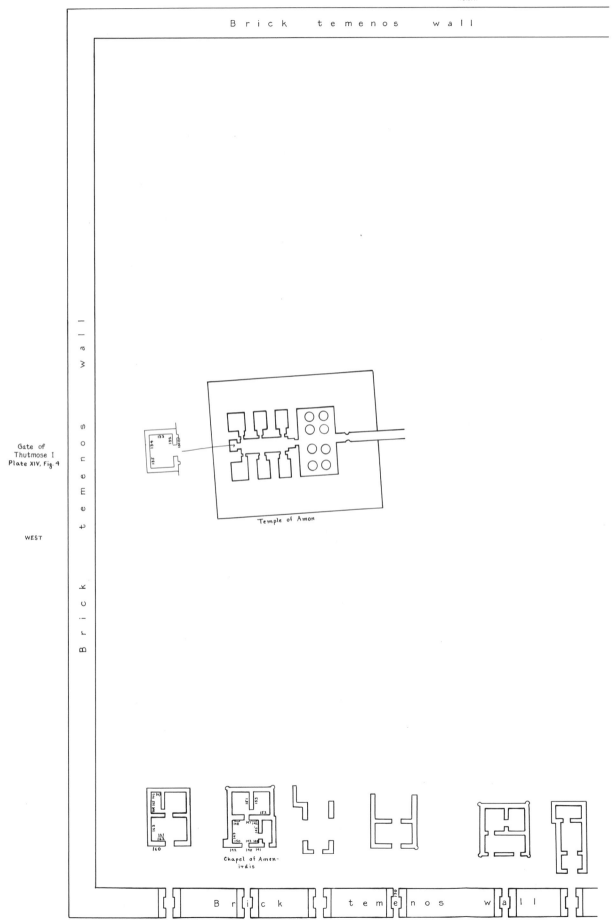

NORTH

Brick temenos wall

Gate of
Thutmose I
Plate XIV, Fig. 4

WEST

Temple of Amon

Chapel of Amen-
irdis

Brick temenos wall

SOUTH

Plate 20

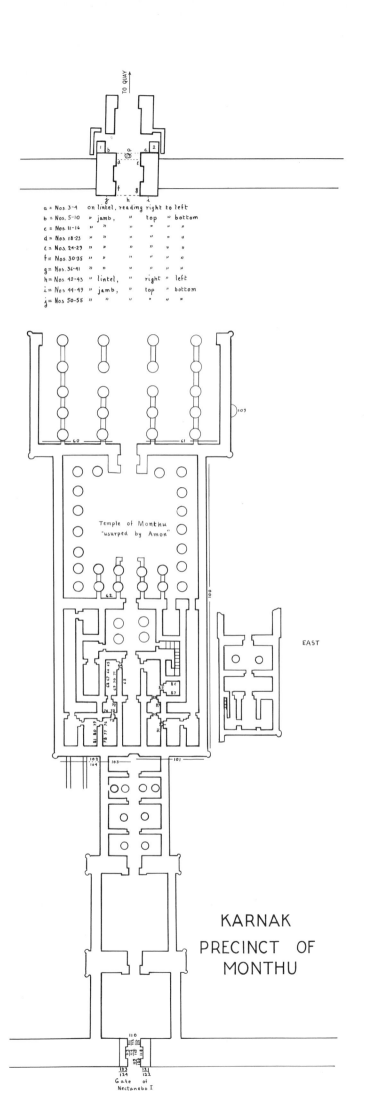

a = Nos. 3-4   on lintel, reading right to left
b = Nos. 5-10   "   jamb,   "   top   "   bottom
c = Nos. 11-16   "   "   "   "   "
d = Nos. 18-23   "   "   "   "   "
e = Nos. 24-29   "   "   "   "   "
f = Nos. 30-35   "   "   "   "   "
g = Nos. 36-41   "   "   "   "   "
h = Nos. 42-43   " lintel,   "   right   "   left
i = Nos. 44-49   "   jamb,   "   top   "   bottom
j = Nos. 50-55   "   "   "   "   "

Temple of Monthu
"usurped by Amon"

EAST

KARNAK
PRECINCT OF
MONTHU

Gate of
Nectanebo I

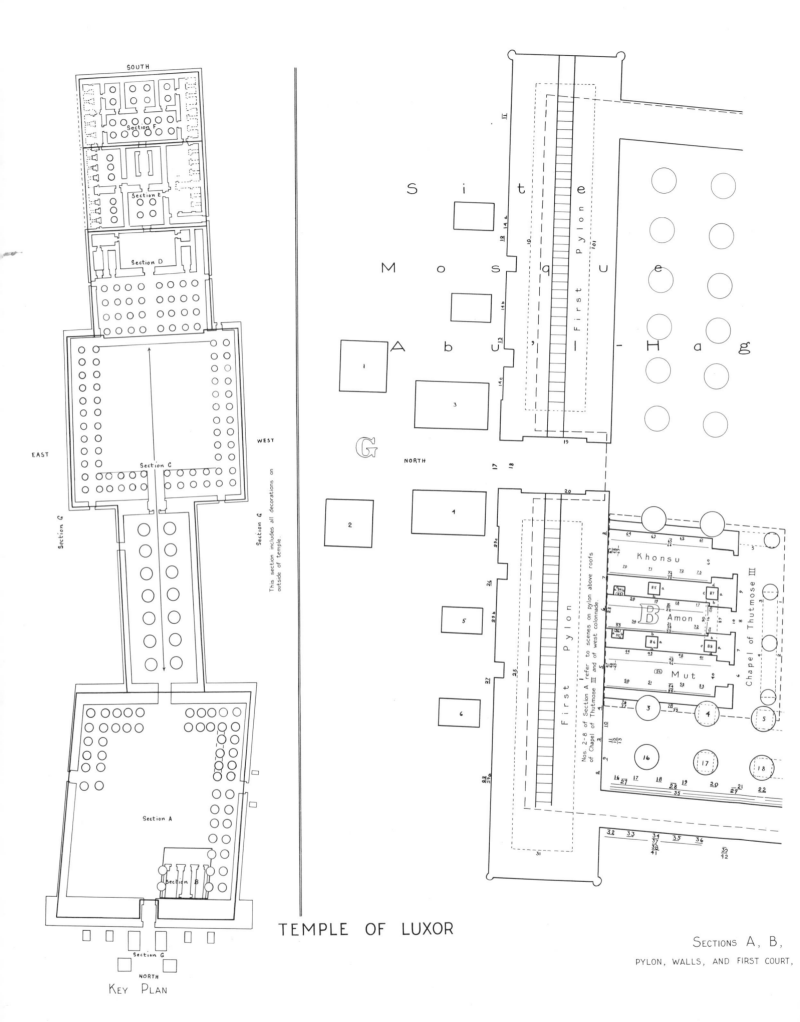

TEMPLE OF LUXOR

Key Plan

SOUTH

Section F

Section E

Section D

Section C

EAST

WEST

Section G

Section G

This section includes all decorations on outside of temple.

Section A

Section B

Section G

NORTH

Site Mosque Abu'l-Hag

S i t e   M o s q u e   A b u ' l - H a g

NORTH

First Pylon

First Pylon

Nos. 2–8 of Section A refer to scenes on pylon above roofs of Chapel of Thutmose III and of west colonnade.

Khonsu

Amon

Mut

Chapel of Thutmose III

SECTIONS A, B,

PYLON, WALLS, AND FIRST COURT,

Plate 21

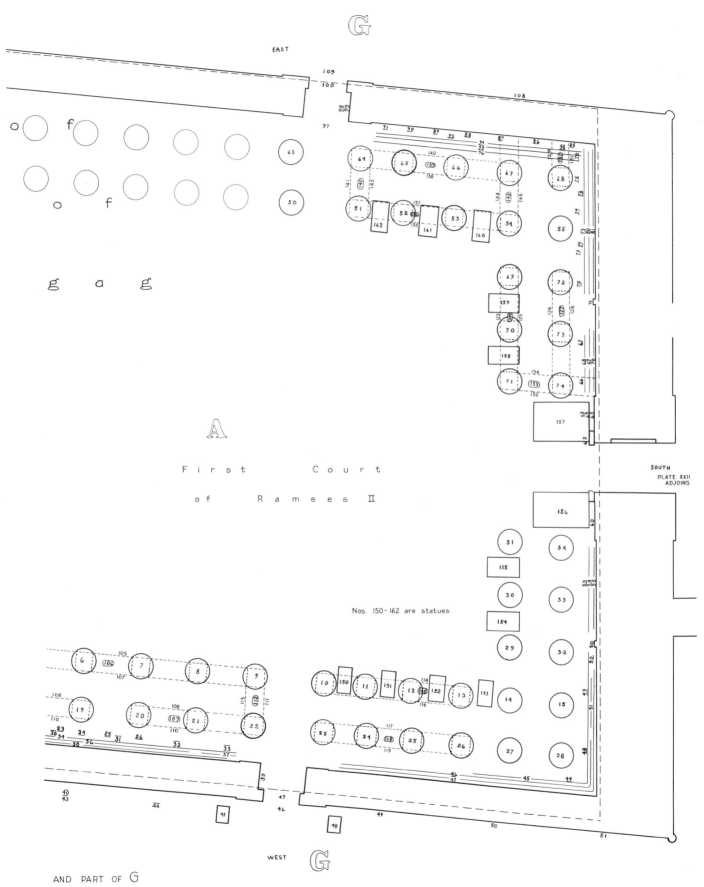

G

EAST

o f o f

g a g

A

First Court

of Ramses II

Nos. 150-162 are statues

SOUTH
PLATE XXII
ADJOINS

WEST G

AND PART OF G

INCLUDING CHAPEL OF THUTMOSE III

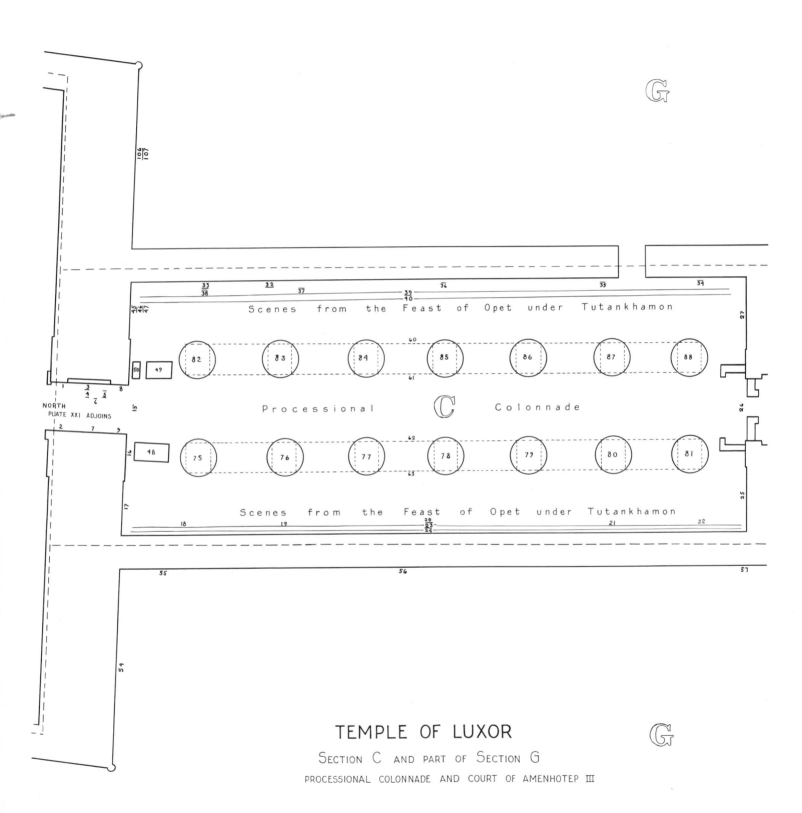

Scenes from the Feast of Opet under Tutankhamon

Processional C Colonnade

Scenes from the Feast of Opet under Tutankhamon

NORTH
PLATE XXI ADJOINS

TEMPLE OF LUXOR

SECTION C AND PART OF SECTION G

PROCESSIONAL COLONNADE AND COURT OF AMENHOTEP III

G

Plate 22

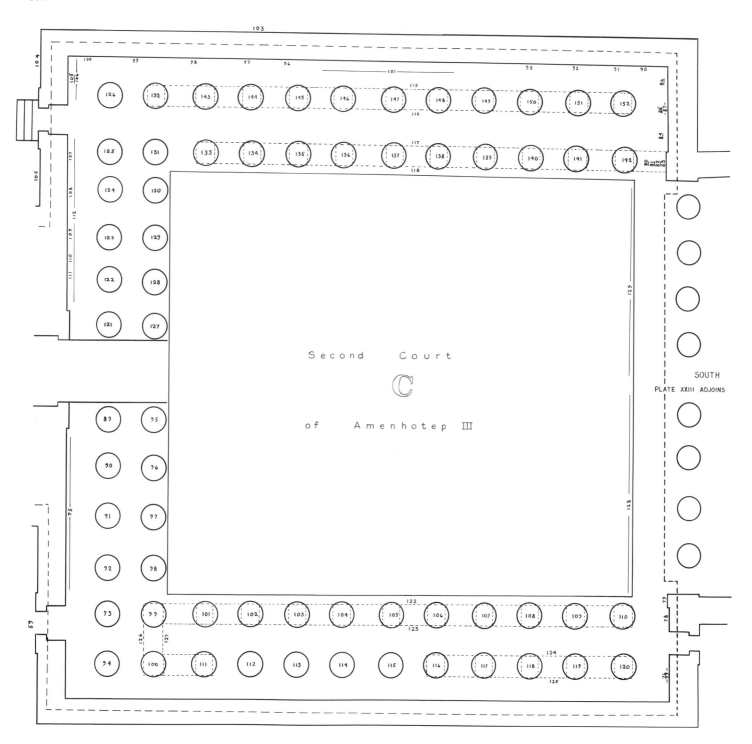

EAST

WEST

Second Court

of Amenhotep III

SOUTH
PLATE XXIII ADJOINS

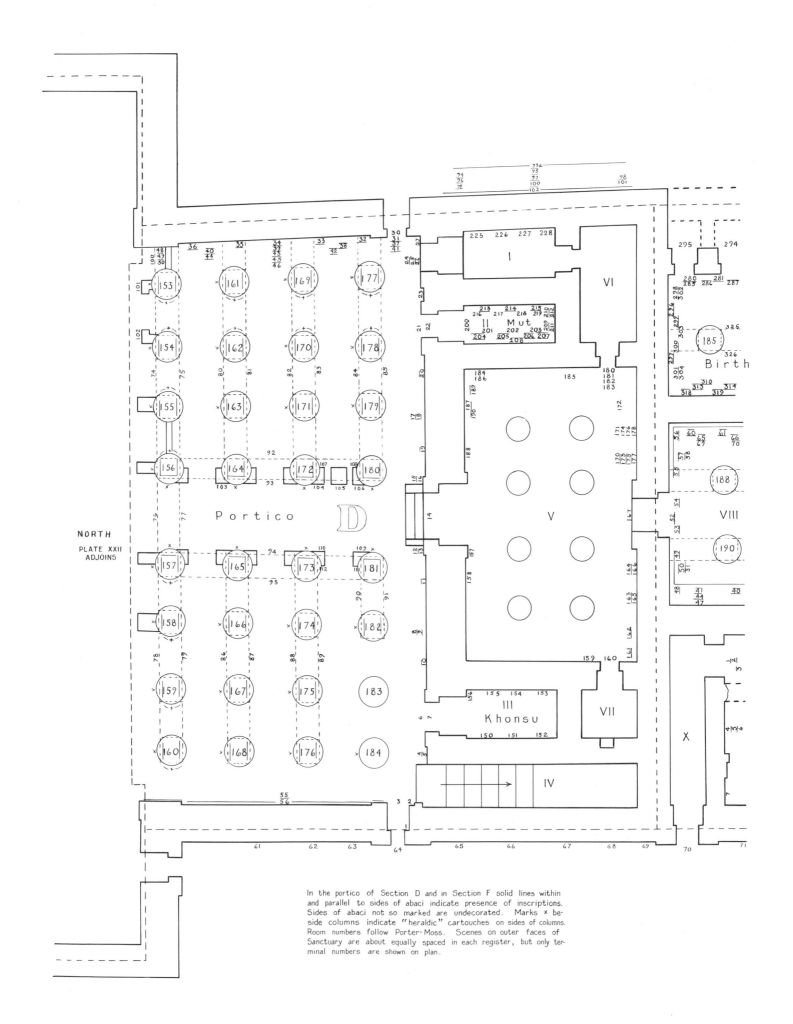

NORTH

PLATE XXII
ADJOINS

Portico **D**

I

II Mut

III Khonsu

IV

V

VI

VII

VIII

X

Birth

In the portico of Section D and in Section F solid lines within
and parallel to sides of abaci indicate presence of inscriptions.
Sides of abaci not so marked are undecorated. Marks ✗ beside columns indicate "heraldic" cartouches on sides of columns.
Room numbers follow Porter-Moss. Scenes on outer faces of
Sanctuary are about equally spaced in each register, but only ter-
minal numbers are shown on plan.

Plate 23

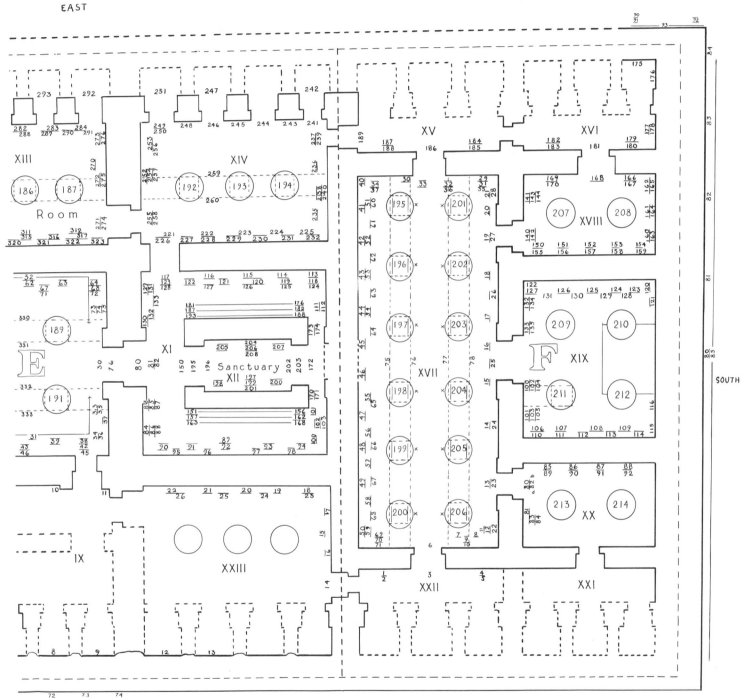

TEMPLE OF LUXOR
Sections D, E, F, and part of G
PORTICO AND REAR HALLS AND ROOMS

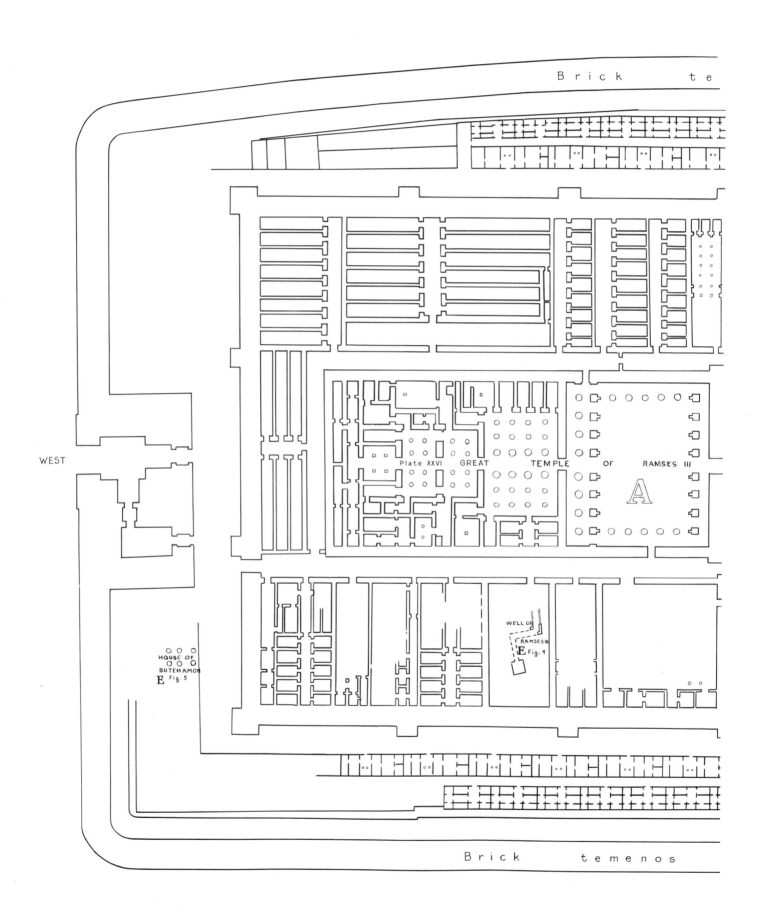

Brick te

WEST

Plate XXVI GREAT TEMPLE OF RAMSES III

A

WELL OF
RAMSES III
E Fig. 4

HOUSE OF
BUTEHAMON
E Fig. 5

Brick temenos

Plate 24

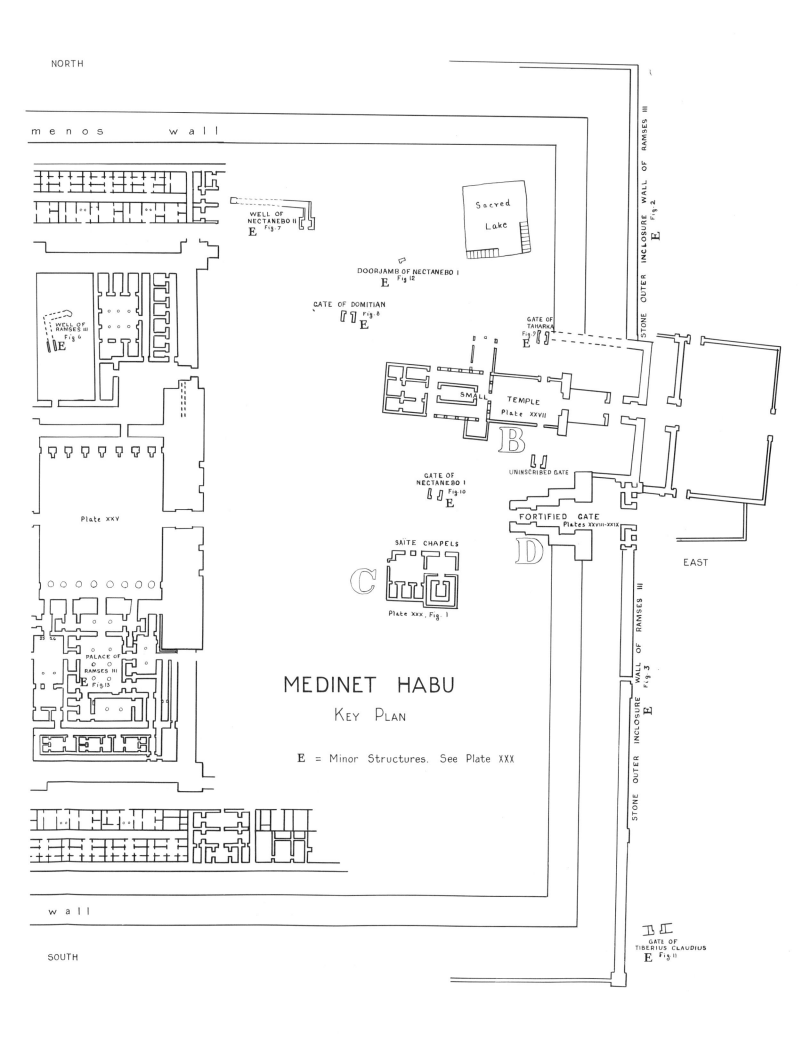

NORTH

m e n o s   w a l l

WELL OF
NECTANEBO II
E   Fig.7

Sacred
Lake

DOORJAMB OF NECTANEBO I
E   Fig 12

WELL OF
RAMSES III
Fig 6
E

GATE OF DOMITIAN
E   Fig.8

GATE OF
TAHARKA
Fig.9
E

SMALL   TEMPLE
Plate XXVII

B

STONE OUTER INCLOSURE WALL OF RAMSES III
E   Fig.2

Plate XXV

UNINSCRIBED GATE

GATE OF
NECTANEBO I
E   Fig.10

FORTIFIED GATE
Plates XXVIII-XXIX

D

EAST

25 26

PALACE OF
RAMSES III
E   Fig.13

SAÏTE CHAPELS

C

Plate XXX, Fig.1

MEDINET HABU

KEY PLAN

E = Minor Structures. See Plate XXX

STONE OUTER INCLOSURE WALL OF RAMSES III
E   Fig.3

w a l l

SOUTH

GATE OF
TIBERIUS CLAUDIUS
E   Fig.11

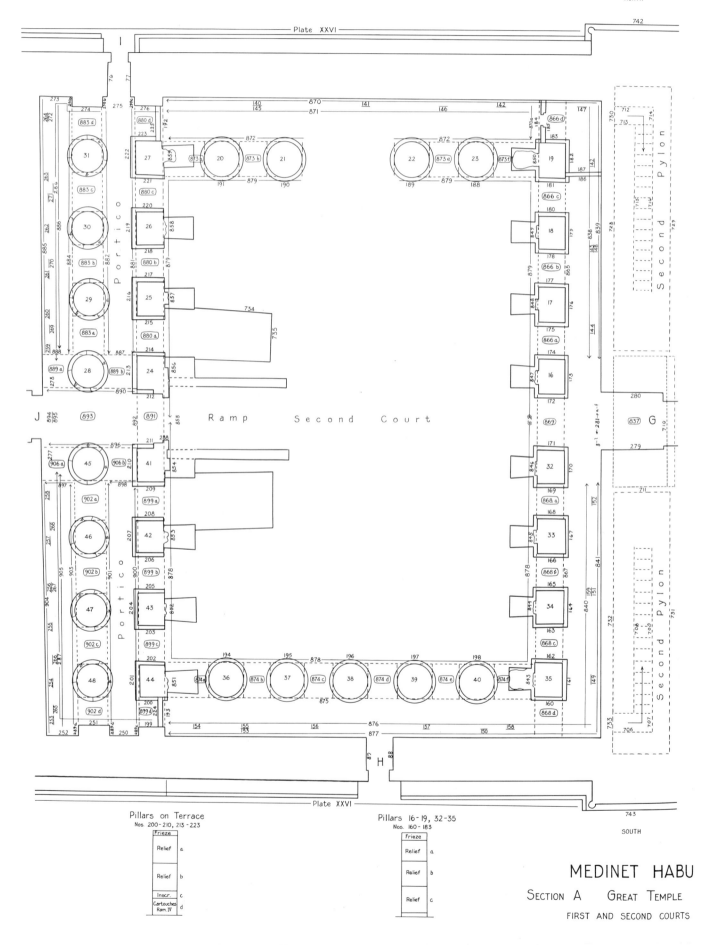

NORTH

Plate XXVI

Portico

J

Ramp　　Second　Court

Portico

Second Pylon

Second Pylon

G

H

Plate XXVI

SOUTH

Pillars on Terrace
Nos. 200-210, 213-223

Frieze	
Relief	a
Relief	b
Inscr.	c
Cartouches Ram.IV	d

Pillars 16-19, 32-35
Nos. 160-183

Frieze	
Relief	a
Relief	b
Relief	c

MEDINET HABU

Section A　Great Temple

FIRST AND SECOND COURTS

Plate 25

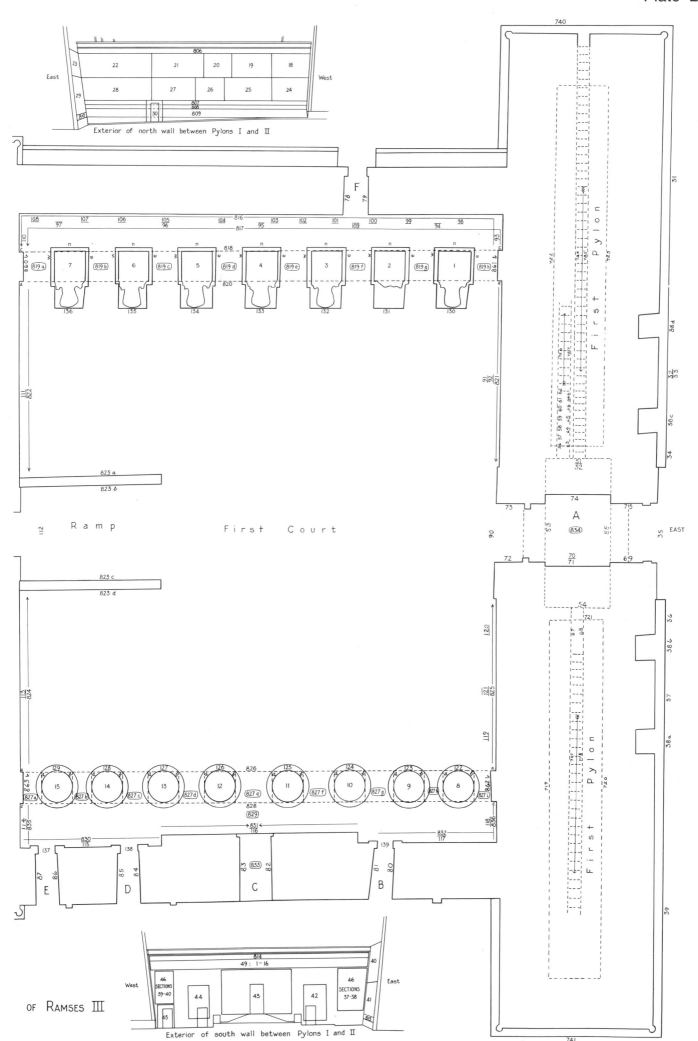

Exterior of north wall between Pylons I and II

Ramp

First Court

First Pylon

First Pylon

A

EAST

Exterior of south wall between Pylons I and II

OF RAMSES III

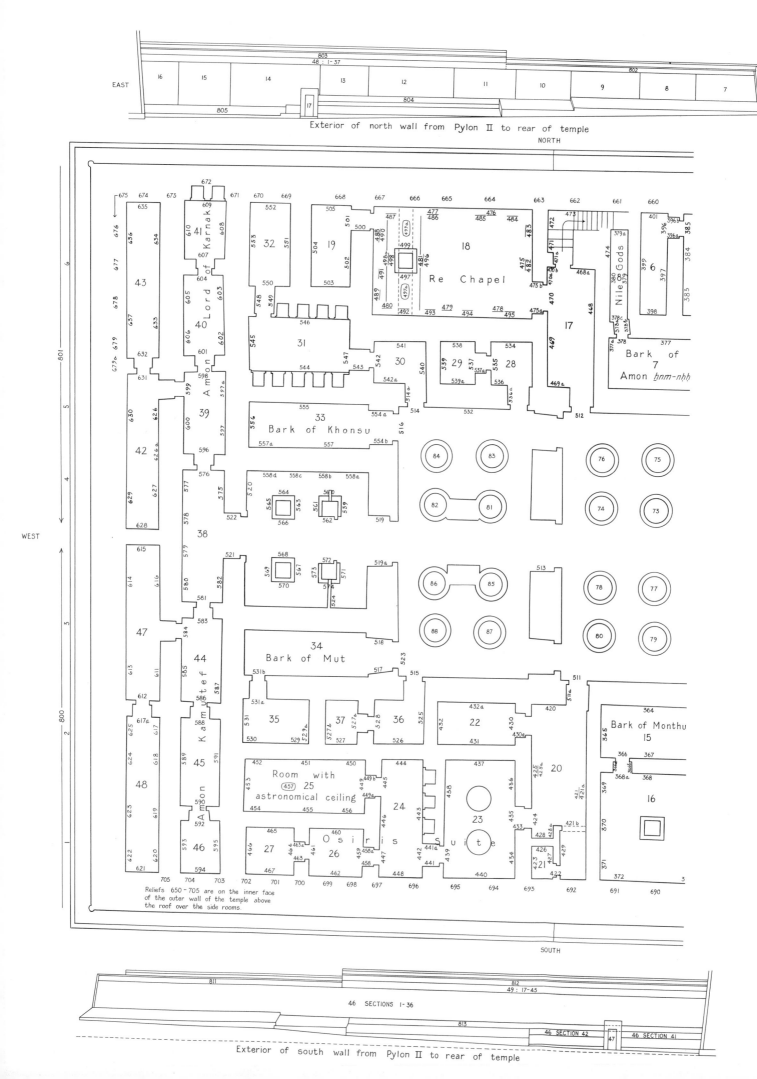

Exterior of north wall from Pylon II to rear of temple

Exterior of south wall from Pylon II to rear of temple

Plate 26

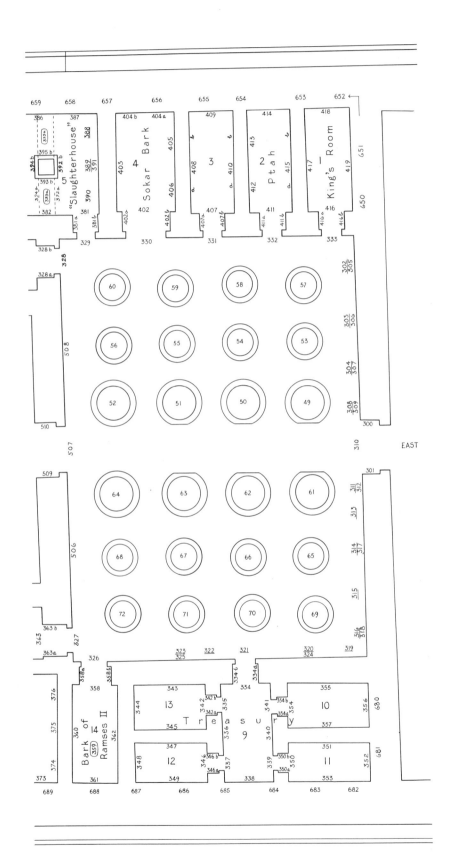

MEDINET HABU

Section A   Great Temple of Ramses III

Rear Halls and Rooms

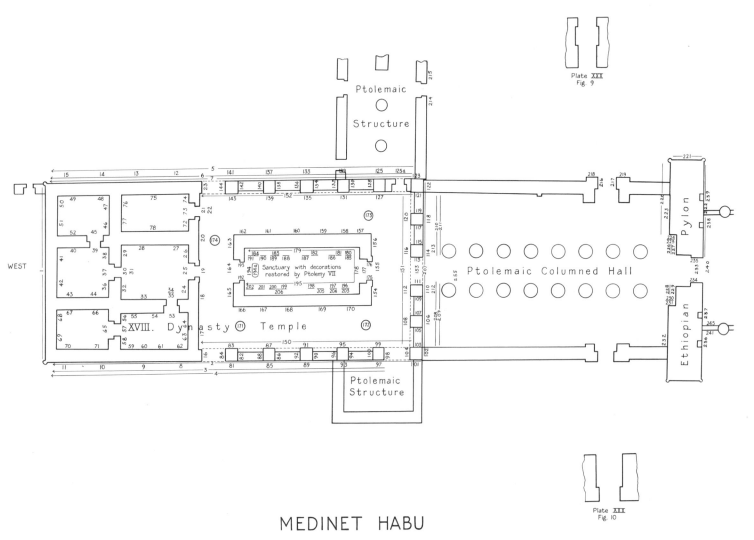

NORTH

Plate XXX
Fig. 9

WEST

Ptolemaic

Structure

Ptolemaic Columned Hall

Pylon

Ethiopian

Sanctuary with decorations
restored by Ptolemy VII

XVIII. Dynasty Temple

Ptolemaic
Structure

Plate XXX
Fig. 10

MEDINET HABU

SECTION B   SMALL TEMPLE BEGUN BY THE XVIII. DYNASTY

SOUTH

Plate 27

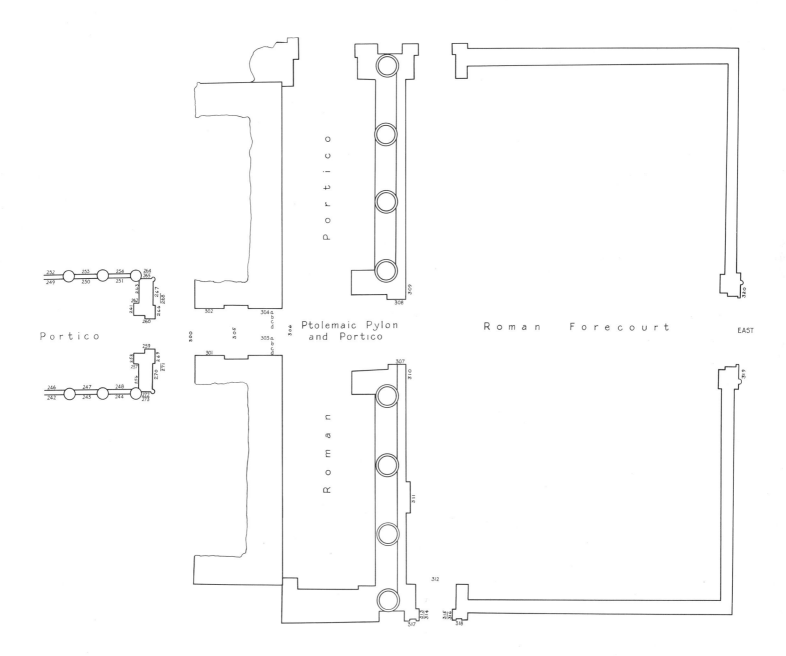

Portico

Portico

Ptolemaic Pylon
and Portico

Roman

Roman Forecourt

EAST

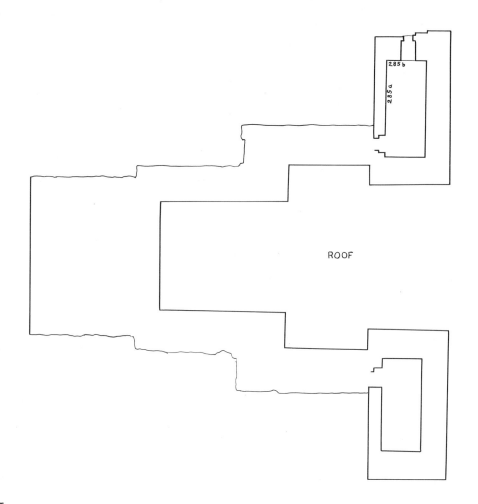

ROOF

WEST

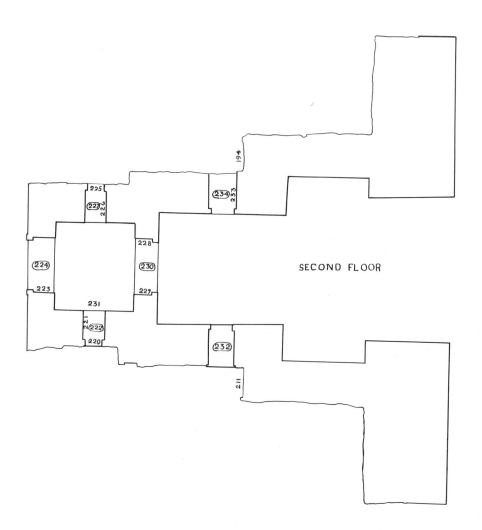

SECOND FLOOR

285 b

285 a

225

227

226

234

233

194

224

228

230

223

229

231

221

222

220

232

211

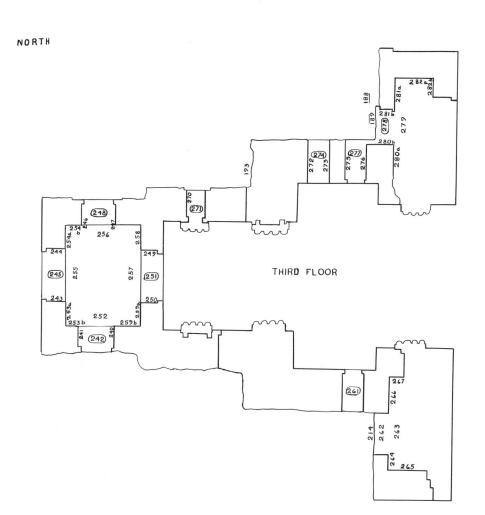

Plate 28

NORTH

THIRD FLOOR

EAST

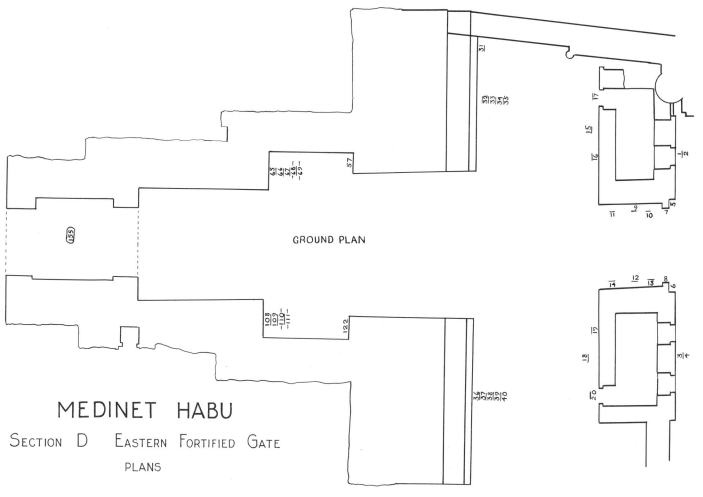

GROUND PLAN

MEDINET HABU

SECTION D EASTERN FORTIFIED GATE

PLANS

SOUTH

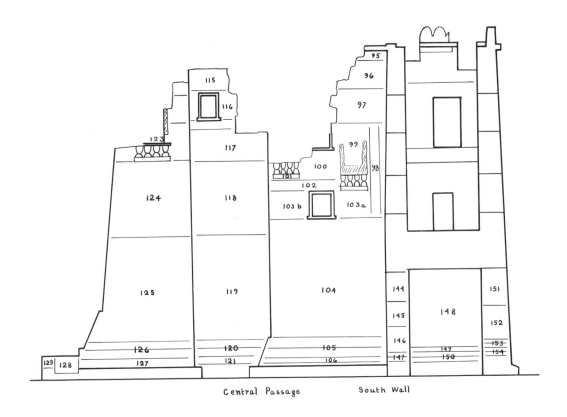

Central Passage   South Wall

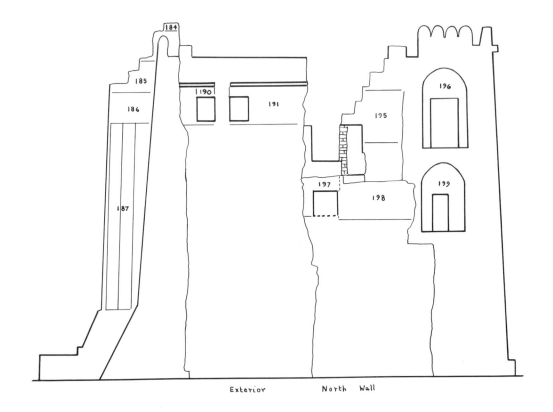

Exterior   North Wall

Plate 29

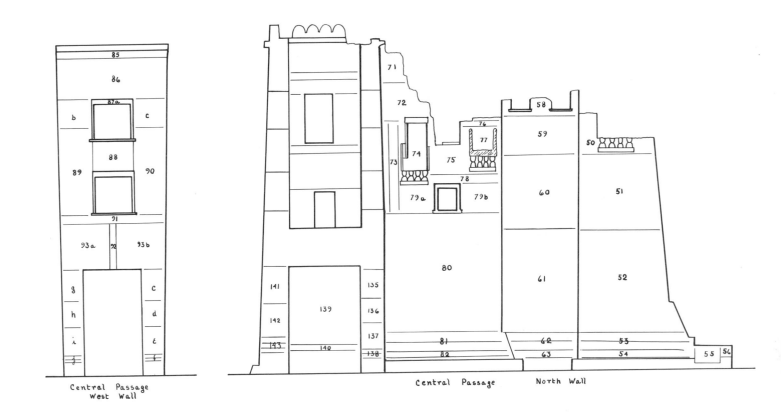

Central Passage
West Wall

Central Passage   North Wall

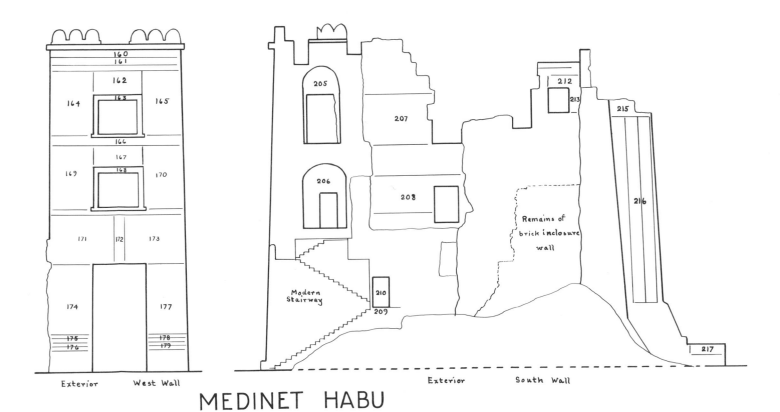

Exterior   West Wall

Exterior   South Wall

MEDINET HABU

SECTION D   EASTERN FORTIFIED GATE

ELEVATIONS

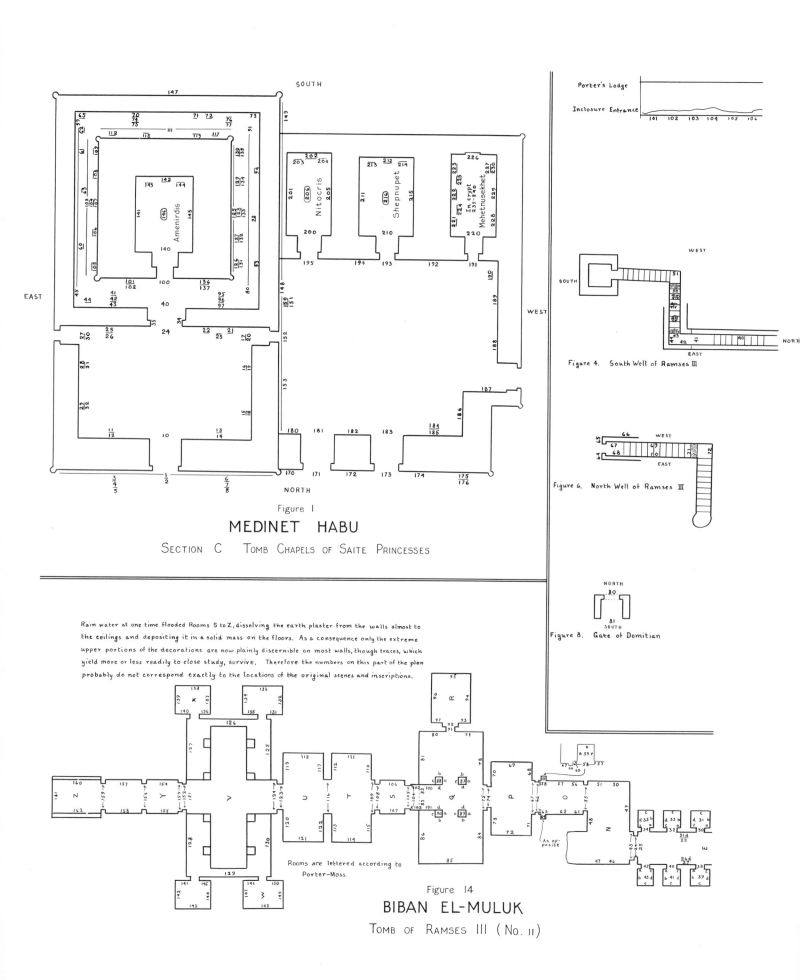

Figure 1

MEDINET HABU

SECTION C   TOMB CHAPELS OF SAITE PRINCESSES

Figure 4.   South Well of Ramses III

Figure 6.   North Well of Ramses III

Figure 8.   Gate of Domitian

Rain water at one time flooded Rooms S to Z, dissolving the earth plaster from the walls almost to the ceilings and depositing it in a solid mass on the floors. As a consequence only the extreme upper portions of the decorations are now plainly discernible on most walls, though traces, which yield more or less readily to close study, survive. Therefore the numbers on this part of the plan probably do not correspond exactly to the locations of the original scenes and inscriptions.

Rooms are lettered according to Porter-Moss.

Figure 14

BIBAN EL-MULUK

TOMB OF RAMSES III (No. 11)

Plate 30

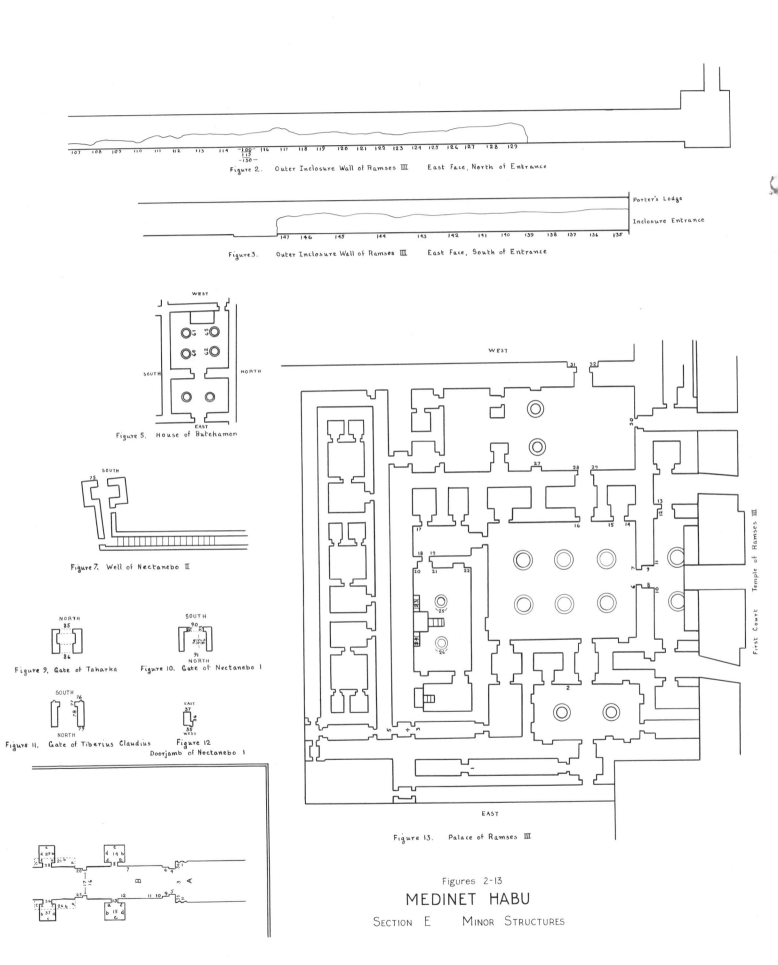

Figure 2. Outer Inclosure Wall of Ramses III   East Face, North of Entrance

Figure 3. Outer Inclosure Wall of Ramses III   East Face, South of Entrance

Figure 5. House of Butehamon

Figure 7. Well of Nectanebo II

Figure 9. Gate of Taharka   Figure 10. Gate of Nectanebo I

Figure 11. Gate of Tiberius Claudius   Figure 12. Doorjamb of Nectanebo I

Figure 13. Palace of Ramses III

Figures 2-13

MEDINET HABU

SECTION E   MINOR STRUCTURES

WEST

Plate 31

NORTH

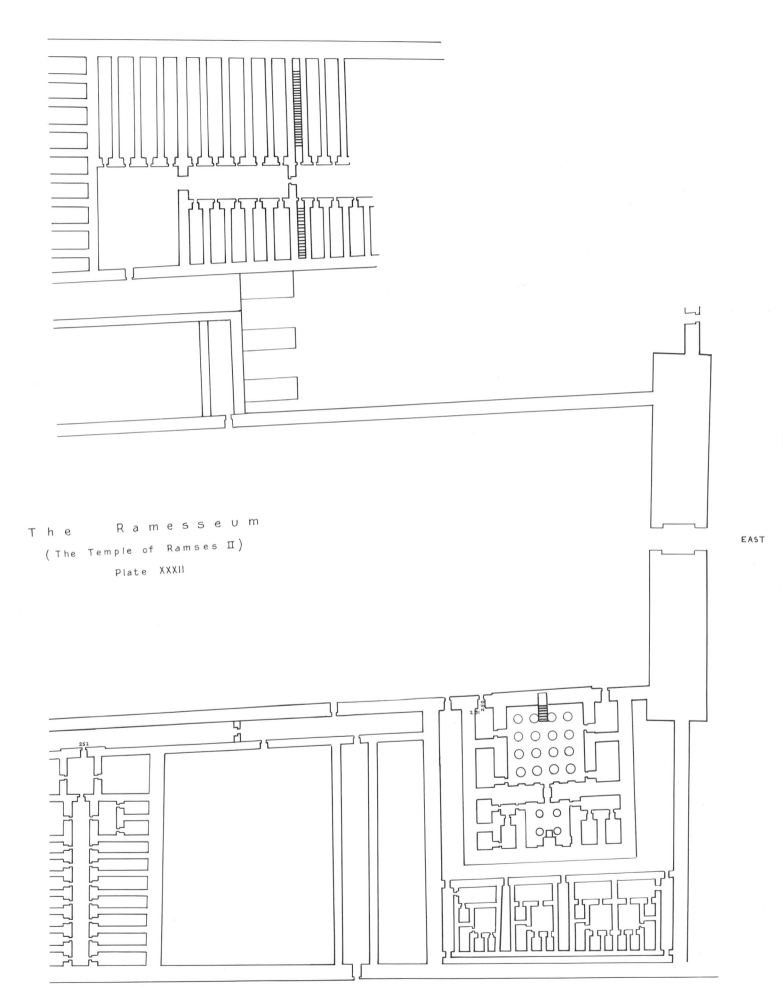

The Ramesseum
(The Temple of Ramses II)
Plate XXXII

EAST

SOUTH

THE RAMESSEUM PRECINCT

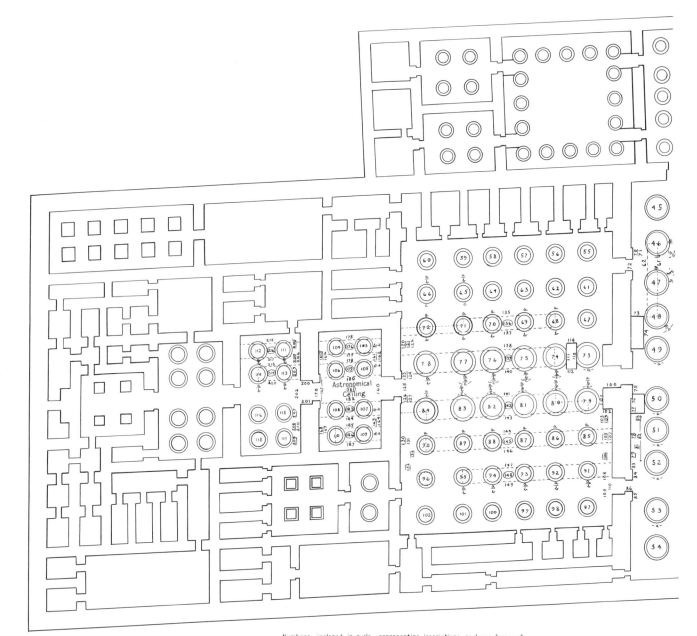

WEST

Numbers inclosed in ovals, representing inscriptions on lower faces of
architraves, apply in each case to full length of lower face. Pillars
are numbered in separate series from columns. Letters with curved
lines on either side (e.g. ⌒a⌒) refer to inscriptions around bases of columns.

Plate 32

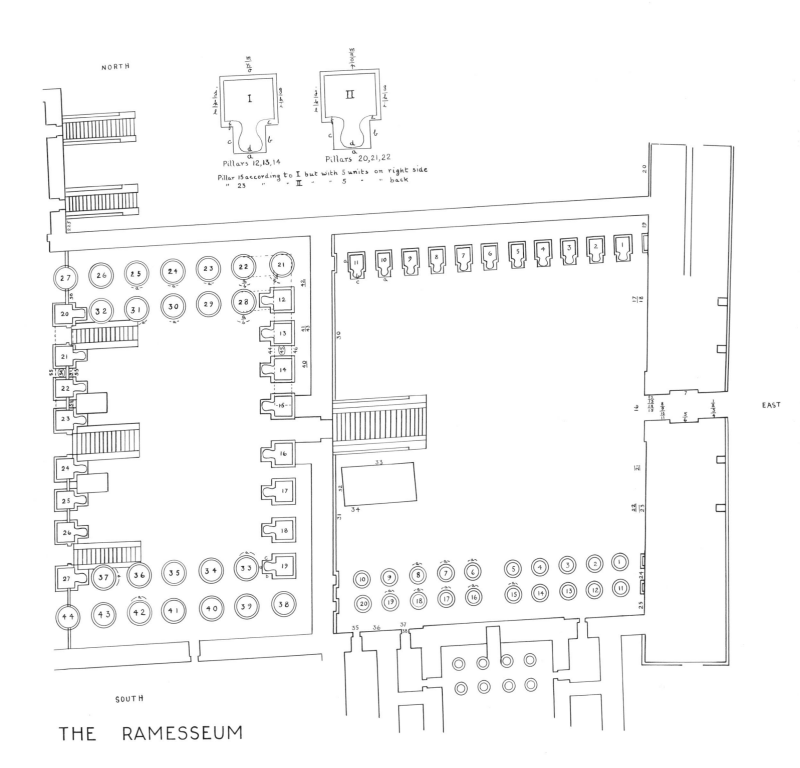

THE RAMESSEUM

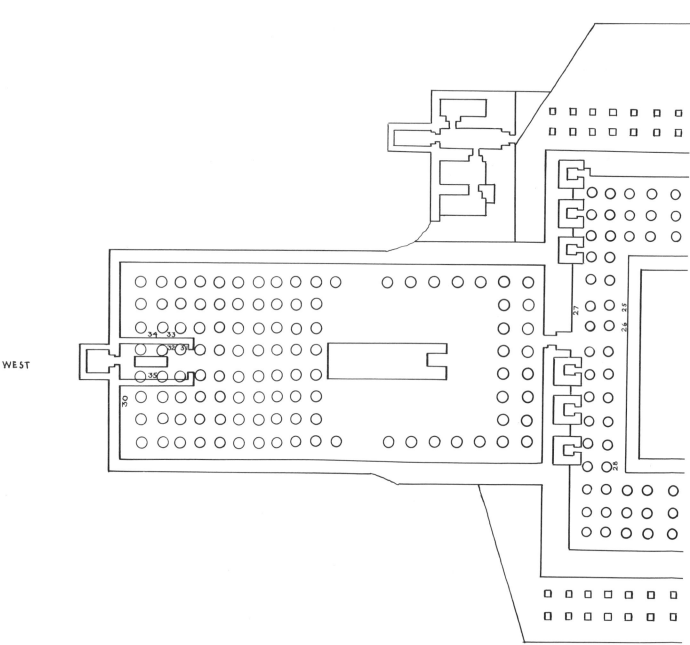

WEST

Plate 33

NORTH

EAST

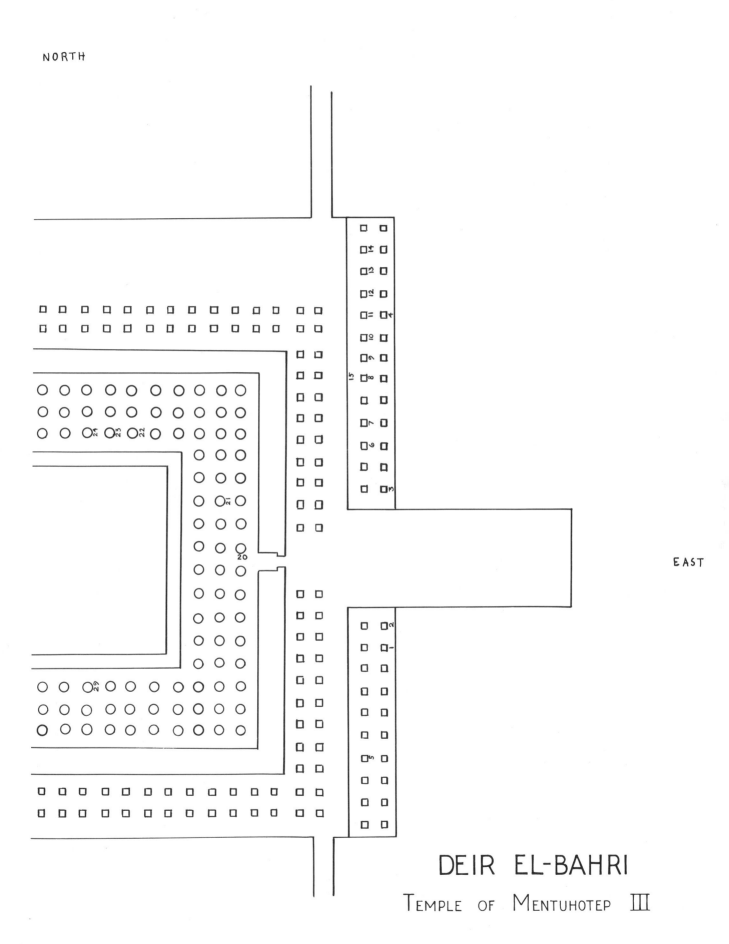

SOUTH

DEIR EL-BAHRI

TEMPLE OF MENTUHOTEP III

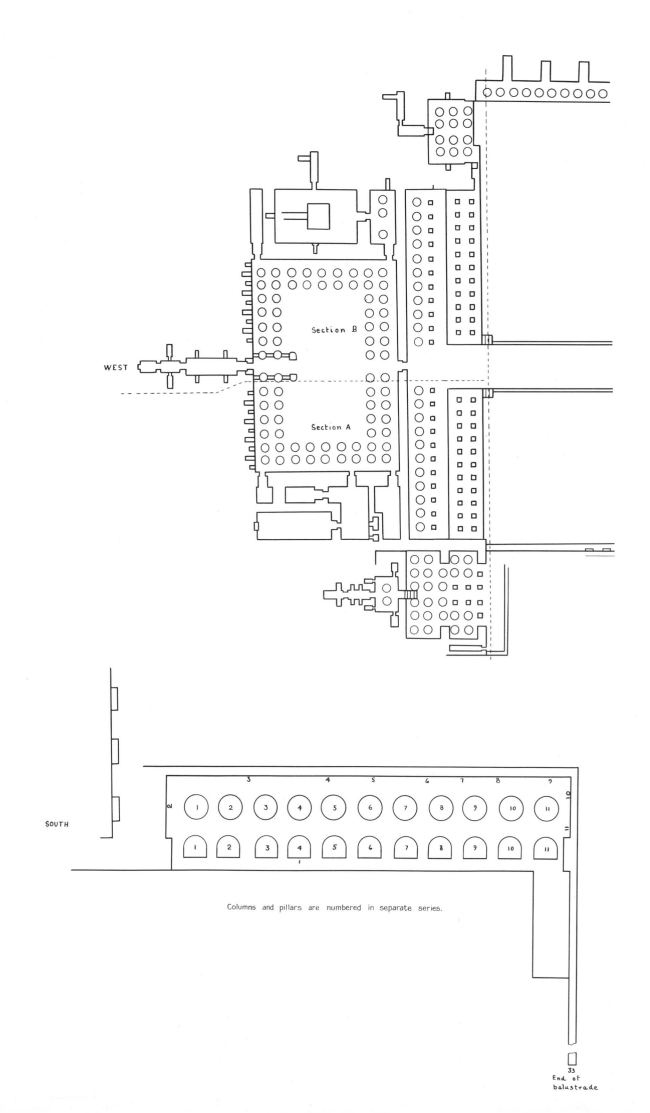

WEST

Section B

Section A

SOUTH

Columns and pillars are numbered in separate series.

33
End of
balustrade

Plate 34

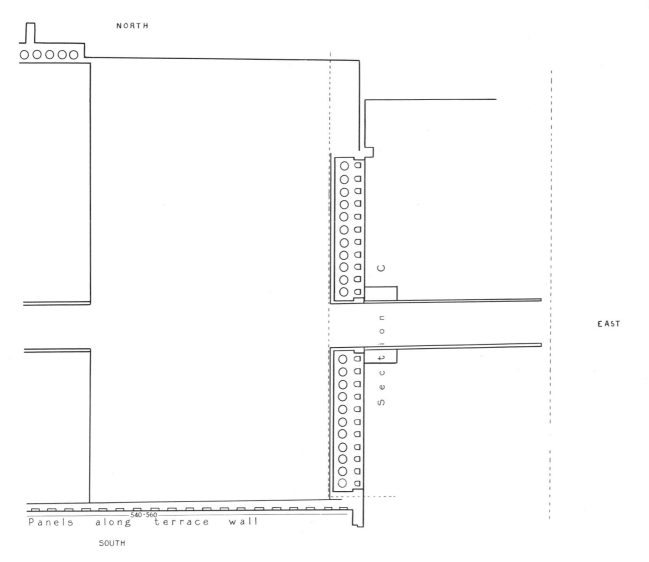

NORTH

EAST

SOUTH

540-560

Panels along terrace wall

Figure 1. Key Plan

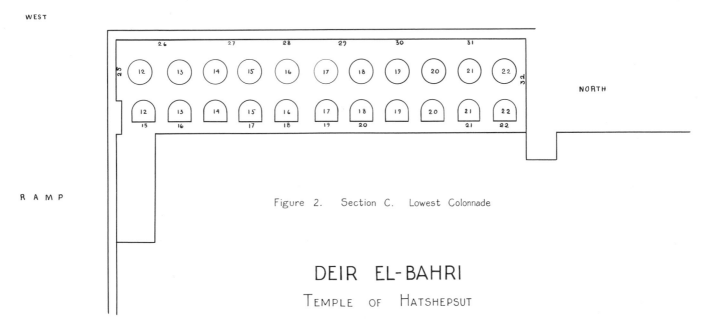

WEST

NORTH

RAMP

EAST

Figure 2. Section C. Lowest Colonnade

DEIR EL-BAHRI
TEMPLE OF HATSHEPSUT

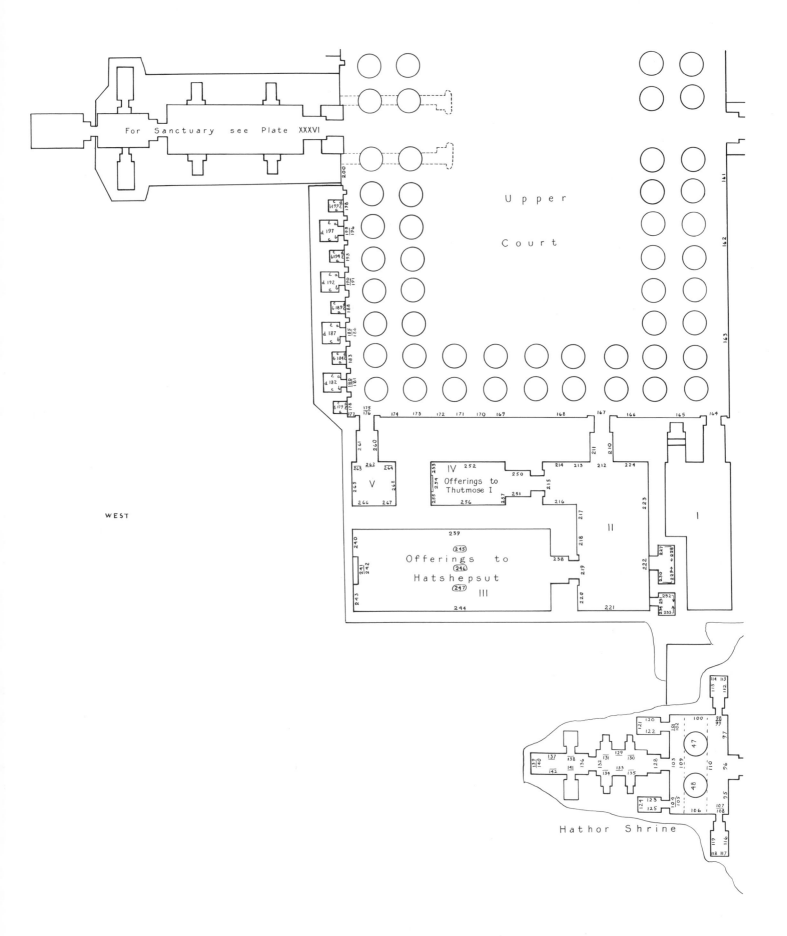

For Sanctuary see Plate XXXVI

Upper

Court

WEST

IV 252
Offerings to
Thutmose I

V

Offerings to
Hatshepsut
III

II

I

Hathor Shrine

Plate 35

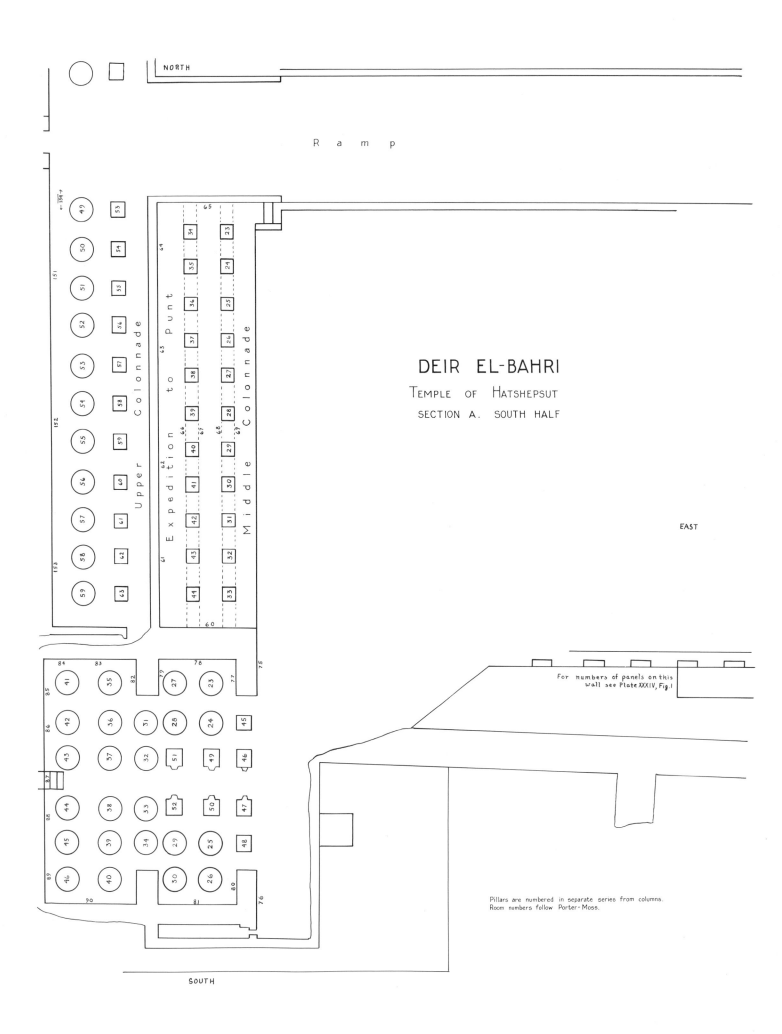

NORTH

R a m p

← 154 →

47

53

50

54

65

34

23

51

35

24

64

36

25

52

56

55

37

26

Punt

53

57

38

27

to

54

58

39

28

Upper Colonnade

151

Middle Colonnade

152

55

59

66

67

68

69

40

29

Expedition

56

60

41

30

41

57

42

31

153

62

DEIR EL-BAHRI

TEMPLE OF HATSHEPSUT

SECTION A. SOUTH HALF

58

42

43

32

61

63

43

44

33

EAST

59

44

33

60

84

83

78

85

41

35

82

79

27

23

77

75

86

42

36

31

28

24

45

For numbers of panels on this
wall see Plate XXXIV, Fig. I

43

57

32

51

49

46

87

88

44

38

33

52

50

47

45

39

34

29

25

48

89

46

40

30

26

80

90

81

76

Pillars are numbered in separate series from columns.
Room numbers follow Porter-Moss.

SOUTH

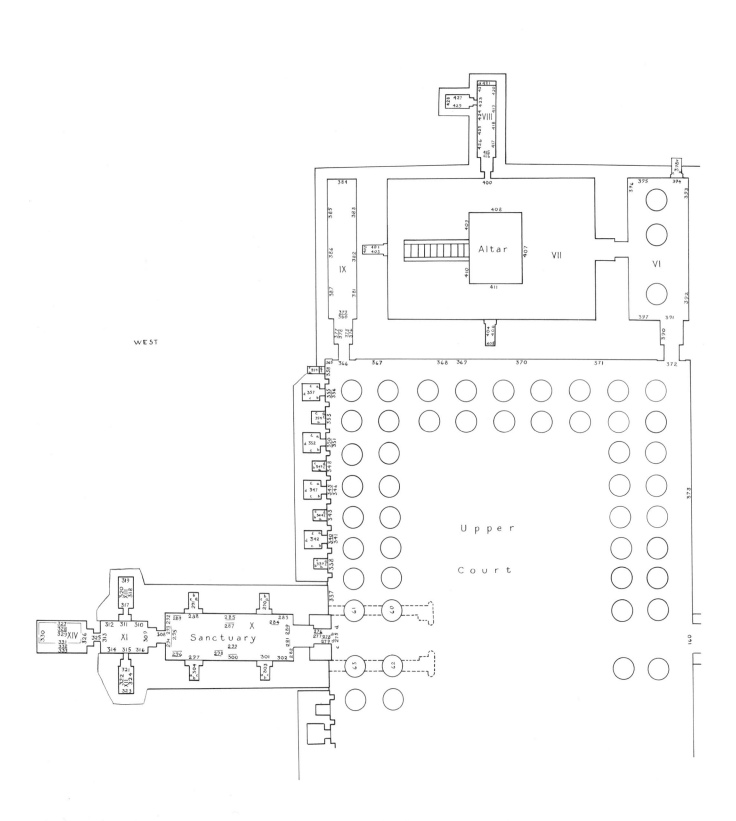

WEST

Plate 36

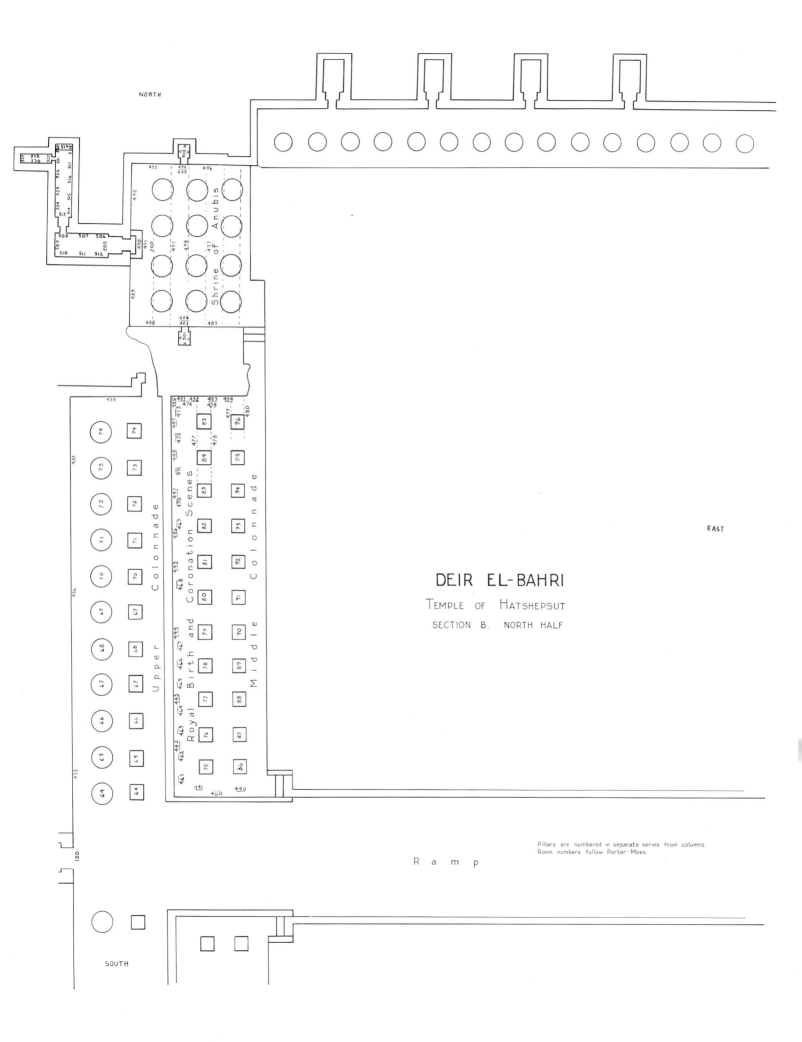

NORTH

EAST

Shrine of Anubis

Upper Colonnade

Royal Birth and Coronation Scenes

Middle Colonnade

DEIR EL-BAHRI

TEMPLE OF HATSHEPSUT

SECTION B. NORTH HALF

Pillars are numbered in separate series from columns.
Room numbers follow Porter-Moss.

R a m p

SOUTH

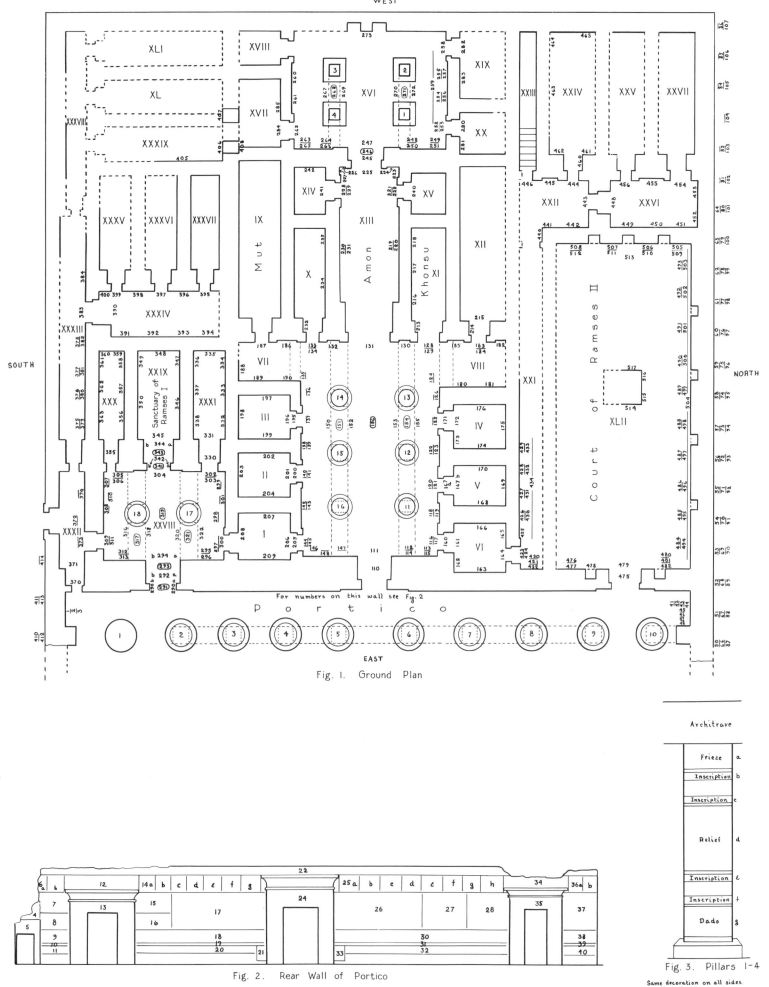

WEST

Fig. 1. Ground Plan

EAST

SOUTH

NORTH

For numbers on this wall see Fig. 2

P o r t i c o

Fig. 2. Rear Wall of Portico

Architrave

Frieze	a
Inscription	b
Inscription	c
Relief	d
Inscription	e
Inscription	f
Dado	g

Fig. 3. Pillars 1-4

Same decoration on all sides.

Figures 1-3

KURNAH TEMPLE OF SETI I

Plate 37

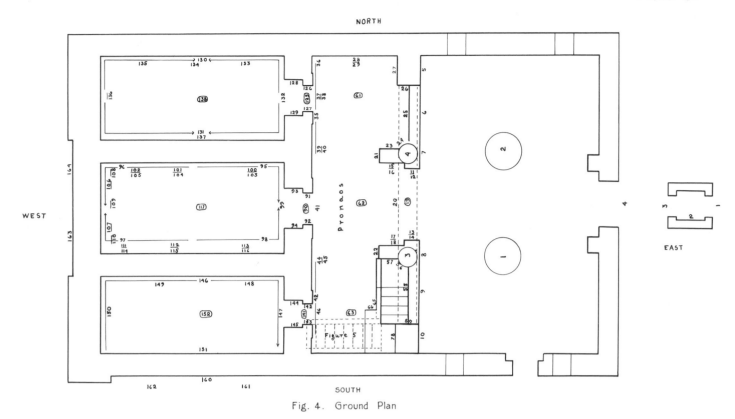

NORTH

WEST

Pronaos

EAST

SOUTH

Fig. 4. Ground Plan

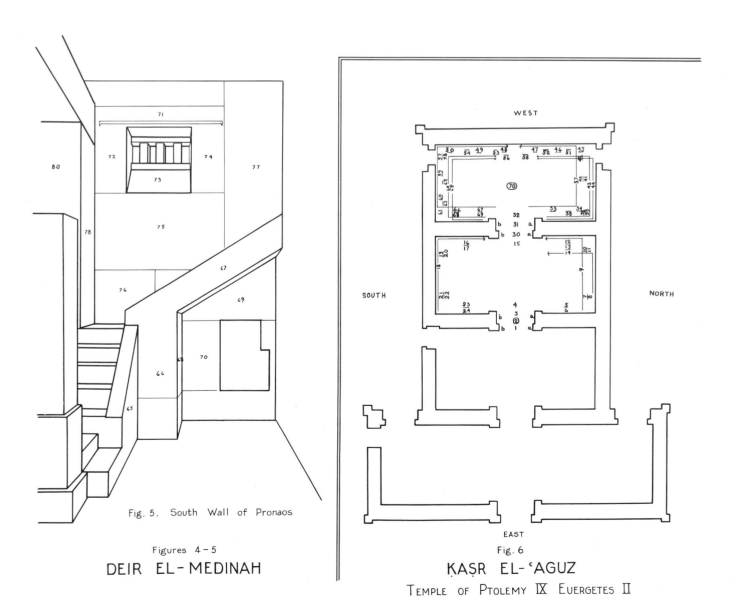

Fig. 5. South Wall of Pronaos

WEST

SOUTH

NORTH

EAST

Figures 4 – 5

Fig. 6

DEIR EL-MEDINAH

ḲAṢR EL-'AGUZ

Temple of Ptolemy IX Euergetes II

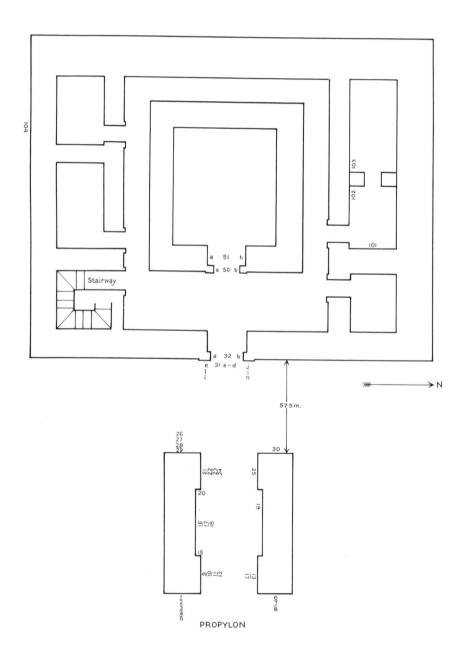

104

Stairway

a 51 b
a 50 b

103
102
101

a 32 b
e 31 a-d j
i n

57.5 m.

N

26
27
28
29
24
23
22
21

20

16
17
18

15

9
10
11
12

1 2 3 4 5 6 7

30

25

19

13
17

6 7 8

PROPYLON

Plate 38

FACADE OF SANCTUARY

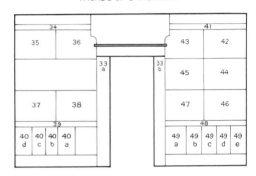

34			41	
35	36		43	42
		33 a	33 b	
			45	44
37	38		47	46
39			48	
40 d	40 c	40 b	40 a		49 a	49 b	49 c	49 d	49 e

SANCTUARY

E.WALL

93 c	92 c
52	53
54	55
56	57
95 c	94 c
58 a	58 b	59 a	59 b

N.WALL

93 b			
63	62	61	60
67	66	65	64
71	70	69	68
95 b			
72a	b	c	d	e	f	g	h	i

S.WALL

92 b			
73	74	75	76
77	78	79	80
81	82	83	84
94 b			
i	h	g	f	e	d	c	b	85a

W. WALL

	92 a	93 a	
86	88	89	87
	90	91	
	94 a	95 a	
d	c	b	96a	97a	b	c	d

DEIR SHELWIT